Contemporary Australia

Explorations in Economy, Society and Geography

SECOND EDITION

D. J. WALMSLEY

A. D. SORENSEN

Longman Cheshire

Longman Cheshire Pty Limited
Longman House
Kings Gardens
95 Coventry Street
Melbourne 3205 Australia

Offices in Sydney, Brisbane, Adelaide and Perth. Associated companies, branches and representatives throughout the world.

First published 1988
Second edition 1993

Edited by Debbi Barnes
Designed by Lauren Statham
Set in Plantin
Produced by Longman Cheshire Pty Ltd
Printed in Australia
by The Book Printer Pty Ltd

National Library of Australia
Cataloguing-in-Publication data

Walmsley, D.J. (Dennis James).
Contemporary Australia : explorations in economy, society and geography.

2nd edn
Bibliography.
Includes index.
ISBN 0 582 87501 3.

1. Human geography - Australia. 2. Australia - Economic conditions. 3. Australia - Social conditions. I. Sorensen, A.D. (Anthony D.). II. Title.

304.20994

Contents

List of Figures

List of Tables

List of Abbreviations

Proper names

ABARE	Australian Bureau of Agicultural and Resource Economics
ABS	Australian Bureau of Statistics
ACT	Australian Capital Territory
AGPS	Australian Government Publishing Service
AIUS	Australian Institute of Urban Studies
ALP	Australian Labor Party
ANU(P)	Australian National University (Press)
APEC	Asia-Pacific Economic Co-operation
ASEAN	Association of South East Asian Nations
ASIC	Australian Standard Industrial Classification
BAE	Bureau of Agricultural Economics
BHP	Broken Hill Proprietary Co. Ltd.
CBD	Central Business District
CEDA	Committee for the Economic Development of Australia
CER	Closer Economic Relations (with New Zealand)
CIS	Commonwealth of Independent States
COMECON	Council for Mutual Economic Assistance (Warsaw Pact Countries)
CSIRO	Commonwealth Scientific and Industrial Research Organisation
EC	Economic Community
EPAC	Economic Planning and Advisory Council
GATT	General Agreement on Tariffs and Trade
GDP	Gross Domestic Product
GNP	Gross National Product
IAC	Industries Assistance Commission
IAESR	Institute for Applied Economic and Social Research
IC	Industry Commission
JIT	Just in Time
LEI	Local Employment Initiative

MIA	Murrumbidgee Irrigation Area
MNC	Multinational Corporation
NAFTA	North American Free Trade Area
NATO	North Atlantic Treaty Organisation
NICs	Newly Industrialising Countries
NIDL	New International Division of Labour
NSW	New South Wales
NT	Northern Territory
NZ	New Zealand
OECD	Organisation for Economic Co-operation and Development
OPEC	Organisation of Petroleum Exporting Countries
OUP	Oxford University Press
QLD	Queensland
R & D	Research and Development
SA	South Australia
SRDs	Statutory Reserve Deposits
Stat. Div.	Statistical Division
TAS	Tasmania
TCF	Textile Clothing and Footwear (industries)
TNC	Transnational Corporation
TQC	Total Quality Control
UK	United Kingdom
UNE	University of New England
UNSW	University of New South Wales
US(A)	United States (of America)
USSR	Union of Soviet Socialist Republics
VIC	Victoria
WA	Western Australia

Other

BP	Before Present
FOB	Free on Board
GL	1000 million litres
Ha	hectares
kg	kilograms
kt	1000 tonnes
m	million
mL	million litres
n.a.	not available
n.e.i.	not elsewhere included
n.e.s.	not elsewhere specified

Preface to Second Edition

THIS book is aimed at all Australians. It attempts to provide an understanding of why the contemporary economic and social condition of Australia is as it is. In order to achieve this goal, the book provides a great deal of information about both living conditions and the economic, social, and political processes that influence those living conditions. In addition to this concern for understanding the present, the book tries to suggest what living conditions in Australia might be like in the future. Indeed, in some senses the book is a journey from the past to the future. It begins with the peopling of the continent, and ends with speculation as to how future generations might develop the country. The message throughout is that *geography matters*. By this we mean to imply there are significant variations from place to place in both living conditions and levels of economic development.

The origins of the book lie in joint teaching commitments in the Department of Geography and Planning at the University of New England. In a very fundamental sense, then, we owe a debt of gratitude to those students who, over the years, have taken courses in which we have questioned why Australia is like it is and where it might be heading in the future. Their constant questioning helped us to sort out our ideas. Likewise we have been privileged to work in a convivial environment and among colleagues who are always ready to discuss ideas in an informed (and invariably humorous) way. Many of them have contributed more to our thinking than they might realise.

This volume represents a revised edition of a book first published in 1988. Much has happened in the world generally and in Australia specifically since the first edition. We have attempted to take stock of these changes and to explore the implications for the future. As with the first edition, we have been extremely fortunate to have excellent support during the time that this book was being written: Megan Wheeler, Bev Waters and Judi Winwood-Smith provided secretarial support second to none while Grahame Fry added to the maps and diagrams already drawn for the first edition by Steve Clarke and Mick Roach. We are very grateful to all of them. Above all, though, we would like to express thanks to our families for their support and patience during what seemed, at times, to be a never ending project.

D. J. Walmsley
A.D. Sorensen
Armidale
March 1992

INTRODUCTION

THE image that Australians have of their nation, and which the nation projects to the rest of the world, has changed markedly over the years. In the late eighteenth century, for example, Australia was generally regarded by the British as an extremely remote cesspool of depravity that was suited mainly to being a repository for the criminal classes. This negative view did not however endure for very long, particularly in a Europe interested in empire building. By the middle of the nineteenth century Australia, along with much of the rest of the 'New World', was viewed from Europe in a generally positive light. In particular, rural Australia at this time was envisaged as a land of plenty, an attractive and bountiful landscape ready to be peopled by patriotic, industrious, virtuous and independent individuals who would make small-scale farming their way of life (Powell, 1978).

This highly romantic vision of the colonization process was, of course, one that conveniently overlooked the hardships encountered in the Australian environment and the very significant differences that existed between the new landscape faced by European colonists and the one to which they had previously been accustomed. It was also a view that conveniently ignored a very extensive Aboriginal presence. Nevertheless, the image was consciously promoted in Britain and the rest of Europe in order to stimulate emigration. Often such promotions rested on both skimpy knowledge and atypical observations. For example, a short, sixteen day survey of the Swan River area of Western Australia in 1827, undertaken under extremely favourable environmental conditions, did much to conjure up an image of a vast, latter-day 'Garden of Eden' that turned out to be quite out of proportion to reality (Cameron, 1974). Elsewhere colonial administrators sought to encourage settlement by equally positive views of the carrying capacity of the land and by equally romantic imagery.

The romanticism of early images of the 'bush' was perhaps important in that it may have assisted early European settlers in Australia to adjust to, and ultimately to accept, the strange environment with which they were confronted (Powell, 1978). Romanticism may also have contributed to the emergence of the 'bush ethos' and to the 'mateship' that is frequently deemed to be a characteristic of European settlement in Australia (see Ward, 1958). Images must, however, ultimately be congruent with reality if they are to be sustained. In this context, the notion of Australia as a continent suited to the 'yeoman farmer' crumbled in the face of expediency as early settlers began to encounter some of the vagaries of the Australian climate and environment. It was soon realised, for example, that much of the continent was effectively a 'wilderness' that was alien, hostile, and often threatening (see Powell, 1978). Despite this, and very much in the spirit of the times, attempts were made to 'tame' the wilderness. Land clearance was in vogue in the later part of the nineteenth century and cultivation was pushed into areas that were marginal at best. A widely held view was that 'rain followed the plough'. In reality, of course, this observation only held true for those areas where early European settlers were favoured by good seasons. Eventually the marginal nature of much crop production became apparent, as in the case of grain growing north of 'Goyder's Line' in South Australia (Meinig, 1970).

In addition to its potential as an agricultural producer, Australia in the nineteenth century also projected the image of being a healthy place to live, particularly when compared to the industrialised and urbanised parts of Western Europe. In the eyes of some, Australia offered an earthly 'Elysium', a state of ideal happiness (Powell, 1978). The Australian climate was seen as an effective cure for tuberculosis, which was rife in the damp, overcrowded conditions found in the cities of the northern hemisphere. It is not surprising, then, that the emigration of 'consumptives' to Australia was actively encouraged in Europe. Of course, the promoters of those emigration schemes that extolled the virtues of the Australian climate only heard the message that they wanted to hear. No stock was taken of the fact that hot summers, and rapid diurnal temperature variations in all seasons, could actually accelerate the deterioration of health (Powell, 1978). The same 'selective perception' also characterized the promoters of utopian settlement schemes in Australia. Although such schemes were very much less common in Australia than in the 'new lands' of North America, such schemes nevertheless existed in the early days of European colonization when various new models of society based around the co-operative ideal were promulgated (see Powell, 1978).

To a very large extent, all the nineteenth century images of Australia held by Europeans were myths, albeit very powerful ones. The notions of Australia as 'Arcady', as 'Elysium', as a wilderness, and as a testing ground for new models of societal organisation, all stemmed from the interplay of three factors: the basic geographical characteristics of the continent as perceived by the early settlers; the nature of the observer (and, in particular, the vested interests that the observer had in pushing a point of view); and the media through which information was communicated to those commentators who were responsible for helping to build the images (Heathcote, 1972).

In the absence of extensive first-hand experience of the Australian environment, many images were built up on the basis of second hand descriptions, often based on transcribed records of early contacts with the Aboriginal population. The dangers of misinterpretation and of over-generalisation were therefore acute. As a result it is not surprising that many of the early images did not square with reality. After all, these images of Australia reflected not only the local conditions as experienced, but also the interplay between a European heritage, individual and group aspirations, and an emerging Australian nationalism (Powell, 1976). Early settlers not only saw what they wanted to see; they also saw what they had been told to expect. It was therefore only as knowledge of the continent of Australia was accumulated during the nineteenth century that the myths held by early European settlers were exploded. Only with the emergence of a national consciousness could the cultural blinkers of Western Europe be slowly removed. Indeed, it was not until well into the second half of the twentieth century that any serious attempt was made to acknowledge the Aboriginal presence in Australia and to appreciate the bonding that exists between the Aboriginal people and the environment in which they live.

National consciousness in Australia obviously received a major fillip with Federation in 1901. Indeed, one of the principal reasons advanced for the formation of the Australian federal system of government was the need to foster a national point of view in a changing world. Despite this, Australia throughout the first half of the twentieth century remained very closely tied to Britain (see Blainey, 1982). Australia might have come of age as a nation at Gallipoli, it might have begun to appreciate its own place in the world economic order during the depression of the 1930s, and it might have had its geopolitical position brought home to it most forcefully during the Second World War (especially with the bombing of Darwin), but it was nevertheless effectively an outpost of empire for the best part of fifty years. Only after 1945, with the influx of large numbers of people from sources other than the United Kingdom and Eire, did attitudes begin to change quickly. To a large extent the import of these changes was not appreciated at the time. It is, after all, very difficult for a contemporary commentator to differentiate between significant events and background 'noise' in order to identify the direction in which a particular society is moving. As a result it is perhaps not surprising that the first real attempts to take stock of the rapidly changing nature of Australia's economy, society, and politics emerged only in the 1960s.

The prevailing view of Australia in the 1960s was captured very well by Horne (1964) when he coined the expression 'the lucky country'. Certainly Australia's abundant natural resources, relative to the size of its population, seemed to ensure the indefinite continuation of high levels of material well-being. Horne's book was not however a eulogy. In fact it was very critical of Australia's ruling elites. Horne (1964; p. 20) observed that Australians in the 1960s could get what they wanted: 'a house, a car, oysters, suntans, cans of asparagus, lobsters, seaside holidays, golf, tennis, surfing, fishing, gardening'. Life on the surface was therefore very pleasant. Horne also observed, however, that Australia was a country without great political dialogue, with little political ideology, and a place where politics was usually considered to be somebody else's business, and a dirty business at that. It was therefore a country where little attention was paid to questions of resource allocation and to differences in well-being between different sectors of the community. Likewise little attention was paid to the question of where the country might be heading. In fact a lack of concern with the future seemed to characterise the ruling elite. This led Horne to a fundamental question: Have the conditions that led to so much material success in the past also weakened adaptability and slowed down the reflexes necessary for survival?

Horne's view was that the key to success in the future lies with clever, educated people and with innovation and originality. He saw Australia as a nation that belittles intellectual affairs. Indeed, Horne cruelly labelled Australia 'a nation without a mind'. In his view, Australia has not been a country marked by great innovation. Rather, it has prospered by exploiting the innovation and originality of others. As a transplanted society itself, Australia had enough working similarities with the nations from which innovations came to be able to implement these ideas with only a minimum of inefficiency. Horne's fear, in other words, was that the good life had corrupted the ability of Australia's ruling elite to adapt to a changing world. With mindlessness seen as a virtue, with self interest pressure groups paramount in the political arena, and with cleverness being something to be disguised, Australia's ruling elites had lost both the ability to understand the changing world and the ability to respond to changes. Horne's strident criticism (1964; p. 239) can be summed up succinctly: 'Australia is a lucky country run mainly by second-rate people who share its luck. It lives on other people's ideas, and, although its ordinary people are adaptable, most of its leaders (in all fields) so lack curiosity about the events that surround them that they are often taken by surprise'. It is not difficult to understand therefore, in Horne's view, why Australians often subscribe to simplistic solutions to complex problems. For example, when most Australians think of economic growth, they commonly argue that growth can be achieved if people work harder. They thereby overlook the possibility that growth in the future might be contingent on people being 'cleverer' rather than working 'harder'.

Horne was among the first of many commentators on the changing nature of Australian society. He himself followed his early initiative with other books. Some of these tried to take stock of the changes that occurred in the 1960s in order to guess where Australia might be heading (Horne, 1970). Others reflected on the influence of economic values in shaping Australian society and contemplated the changes that took place in the 1970s. Indeed, Horne (1976) saw the 1970s as something of a watershed between the nation's imperial legacy and a new era that would require redefinition of Australia's place in the world. Inevitably, in Horne's view, such a redefinition would entail a re-examination of the centrality of economic and material values in Australian society, particularly at a time when economic growth could no longer be assumed to be 'normal' and predictable.

Other writers were less obsessed with the values of the elite and instead sought to understand the changing nature of Australian society (and perhaps the unchanging nature of the character of the average Australian) by delving into the national psyche (Conway, 1971). Above all, though, economic commentators probably had the greatest impact in focussing attention on the way in which Australia would have to face up to a changing world. And very often these writings were triggered by a realisation of the significance of the changes that overtook Australia in the 1970s. In the words of Walsh (1979; p. 1), 'Australia entered the 1970s with all the adolescent optimism of a young nation that had been endowed with an apparently limitless legacy of natural wealth. Prosperity was assured, domestic tranquillity guaranteed and seemingly it was pre-ordained that economic success would bring with it a measure of international regard and influence'.

By the end of the decade all that had changed and the mood in Australia was one of bewilderment and uncertainty. The events that brought abut this change of mood came, in Walsh's view, from both external impulses (such as changes in the price of oil and fluctuations in commodity prices) and through abysmally poor domestic economic management. In total these events led to a questioning of whether Australia had the inner resources and resolve to fully realise its heritage. Once again the question was asked as to whether or not Australia's 'lucky' endowment had in some way inhibited the nation's ability to be flexible and to adapt in the face of changing circumstances. Walsh (1979; p. 1) himself suggested that, if anything, Australia's natural wealth might have 'served to limit the nation's horizons, to institutionalize paranoia, to nurture neuroticism and to enshrine mediocrity'. Australians, it seemed, had had it too easy for too long and therefore could not grasp the enormity of the problems that were emerging on the international economic scene in the 1970s. Nor could they realise that the structure of society, and its underlying values, were also changing.

Many of the writers who commented on the changing nature of Australia's economy, society, and politics in the 1970s cleverly captured the spirit of the times. For example, it was a period of optimism when almost anything seemed possible. Nationalism was strong as Australia chose a new anthem, toyed with the idea of a new flag, and first gave serious, albeit tentative, consideration to the possibility of the country ultimately becoming a republic. Such manifestations of nationalism were however almost exclusively symbolic and whatever enthusiasm there was for significant and substantial change was seriously dented by the economic difficulties that emerged as the decade progressed. Despite this there was a widespread feeling that the decade was in some way a pivotal epoch and that things would never be quite the same again. It is the curse of all contemporary commentators, of course, to see their times as pivotal epochs. Horne (1964, 1970), for instance, had talked of the 1960s as a time when Australia needed to make a fundamental change in direction. Nevertheless the 1970s did seem special. To a large number of commentators, they appeared to be a time of turmoil. The uncertainty of the period was probably well captured in two of its more prominent slogans: 'It's time' and 'Life wasn't meant to be easy'. The former was a carefully crafted slogan that served as a focus for the Australian Labor Party's (ALP) successful 1972 election campaign. It implied that change was inevitable without specifying the nature of, or rationale for, the change. It therefore left uncertain the form that change would take. The latter slogan was really no more than an off-the-cuff comment by Mr. Fraser at the time when he was a Liberal Party Prime Minister. It carries with it the implication that the world is an uncertain place, plagued by constant change, where good times must be weighed against bad. Politicians, it seems, recognised the changing order of things, especially in the late 1970s, but appeared to have no clear idea of how change could be harnessed to create a 'better' Australia.

The idea of the late 1970s as a pivotal epoch has probably been taken furthest by West (1984) who has argued that, in the realm of politics at least, changes have occurred that are so profound as to qualify for description as a 'revolution'. In particular West has suggested that the Hawke government in the 1980s achieved a revolution by using the rhetoric of national unity to impose consensus politics on the community. The consensus in question involves the collusion of government, big business, and the trade unions. On the face of it, this 'revolution' might seem to be a good thing: it carries with it the potential to lock the nation as a whole into unified and appropriate policies for the problems that confront it. In practice, however, this will only work if the leadership is creative and innovative and fully understands the nature of the problems involved. In West's (1984; p. 94) words, we must realise that 'we are now moving into a new era in Australian politics when creative ideas and rational policy-making will matter more than ever before' because our major national problem is no longer merely the political one of redistributing wealth so much as the economic one of creating wealth in the first place.

Despite West's comments, more attention has focussed on the division of the economic cake than on ways to increase the size of the whole cake. The question of 'who gets what?' has, for instance, been the focus of much debate, a great deal of which has focussed on the goals and achievements of the welfare state (Van Dugteren, 1976). Indeed, several attempts have been made to assess whether or not the welfare delivery system in Australia is achieving its goals. Henderson (1981), for one, has challenged the view of welfare as a way of redistributing wealth 'downwards' from a hard-working middle class to an improvident working class. He has pointed out that many of the most valuable fringe benefits provided in Australia (e.g. superannuation, free tertiary education) go to people already in well-paid jobs. Henderson has also attacked current welfare policy for being out of tune with the times. Unemployment benefits, for example, were originally envisaged as a way of tiding people over short periods out of work, not as a way of sustaining them for the long periods out of employment that have become depressingly common in the 1980s and 1990s. Similarly, official family policy is still overwhelmingly based on notions of female dependency despite the rapidly changing nature of household structures.

One of the reasons why attention has increasingly focussed on 'who gets what' is the evidence that the disparities between the 'winners' and the 'losers' are growing. In other words, despite its abundance of resources, Australia has failed to come to grips with welfare injustices, with inequality in educational provision, and with social polarization in much the same way as it has failed to come to terms with the need for new technology and for innovation (see O'Leary and Sharp, 1991). As a result there exists a social and economic crisis in Australia in the 1990s. According to one commentator, two of the most disturbing features of this crisis are the widespread sense of its inevitability and popular acceptance of the view that there are no viable solutions (Sheehan, 1980). Little consideration seems to be being given, for example, to trying to understand why contemporary Australia is like it is. More to the point, and as if to exemplify Horne's (1964) contention about the lack of sophisticated political debate, there seems, very often, to be little beyond the very vaguest discussion of what the future might hold. A case in point is the oft-cited notion that Australia might gradually become a Eurasian-type society. Despite the frequency with which it has been raised, the 'Asianization' of Australia is not, however, a possibility that has been examined closely. After all, Australia still behaves very much as a white enclave in south-east Asia and Oceania, as evidenced by extensive tariff protection against imports from that region. More to the point, Australia still thinks like a white enclave. For example, a study of the 'mental maps' of Australian university students showed a bias towards the countries of the British Commonwealth (Walmsley *et al.* 1990).

Perhaps the lack of debate about the future reflects a national insecurity. Having borrowed so much from overseas, Australians perhaps turn unduly to overseas experts for guidance as to what the future might hold. Certainly when fourteen large Australian corporations wanted to examine how Australia might develop for the rest of this century, they turned to an overseas 'think-tank' in the form of the Hudson Institute of New York (see Kahn and Pepper, 1980). This is not to say, of course, that meaningful debate about the future is completely lacking within Australia. A major contribution to any analysis of the changing nature of Australian society, economy, and politics has come from a former Minister in the Commonwealth government (Jones, 1982). Likewise a Commission for the Future was set up in the 1980s with a brief to stimulate discussion of Australia's future. The fact remains, however, that Jones' thinking about the future was never central to government policy (and in fact he lost his Ministerial position) and the Commission for the Future enjoyed less than fulsome support from across the political spectrum.

Any consideration of how Australia might confront its current problems must be based on a sound understanding of why contemporary Australia is as it is. We need to understand the present in order to be able to speculate about the future. This is the goal of the present book: to describe and explain why Australia is like it is. It is unashamedly written from the point of view of the geographer. All too often consideration of contemporary Australia has assumed that the nation is virtually a monolithic whole. For example, great attention is paid to national unemployment figures. Frequently these are deemed so important as to head news broadcasts. Yet, in a fundamental sense, saying that the average unemployment rate is 9% is not much more meaningful than saying that the national average temperature is 20 degrees Celsius. Both statistics mask very large variations in conditions from place to place. The unemployed in Australia are not randomly distributed. Nor are they uniformly distributed. Rather, they tend to be clustered in certain areas. Likewise, the overall chances of being a 'winner' or a 'loser' in Australian society depend very much on where an individual lives. It is appropriate, therefore, to highlight such geographical differences in any description of contemporary Australia.

This book has a simple structure. It begins with the past and the peopling of the continent, and ends with the future and speculation about the alternatives that face Australia. En route it examines the nature of the economy, living conditions, the role of government, and Australia's changing position in the world economy. *Contemporary Australia* does not push any of the popular political views of the 1990s: the so-called 'economic rationalism', state interventionism, corporatism, and socialism. Rather, the book advocates economic realism, that is to say, an appreciation of Australia's place in the world and of the implications of that place for the conduct of domestic affairs. Throughout, the emphasis is on examining such simple questions as: Why does the settlement pattern take the form that it does? Where have Australia's immigrants come from? What are the current trends in immigration? How important is immigration to population growth? What are the overall demographic trends in Australia? How much migration is there within the country? Which areas are growing in population? Which areas are declining? How healthy is the economy? Which sectors of the economy are performing best? Which regions are prospering? How do fluctuations in world commodity prices affect Australia? How evenly are income and wealth distributed? Does the welfare state cater effectively for the disadvantaged? Which are the most disadvantaged parts of the country? What is the government doing about the problems that face Australia? What can the government do? How extensive is government activity in Australia by international standards? What are the relative responsibilities of the Commonwealth, the States, and local government? How are governments elected? How can Australia best cope with the restructuring of the global economy? Which areas of Australia are likely to gain from such restructuring? How important are multinational corporations in the Australian economy? What is the future for Australian manufacturing industry? What will rural life be like in the future? And what changes can be expected in the structure and layout of cities? Obviously this book cannot hope to provide definitive answers to all these and other questions. However it will have achieved its goal if it provides the reader with a broad understanding of why contemporary Australia is as it is.

The Peopling of the Continent

THE date of the first human settlement of Australia is not known. However it seems likely that humans were here at least 40 000 years before the present (BP). Certainly there are signs of an Aboriginal presence at Lake Mungo (New South Wales) from 35 000 years BP to 26 000 years BP, including evidence of the ritualistic funeral of an Aboriginal girl about 30 000 years ago. Likewise, artefacts from Mt Mulligan in north Queensland have been dated to 37 000 years BP and similar dates have been obtained for the Upper Swan in Western Australia and for Malakunanja in the Northern Territory. Indeed, settlement seems to have been well established throughout the continent by 25 000 years BP (Commonwealth of Australia, 1981). It is now known, for example, that even in the somewhat bleak climate of southern Tasmania, Aborigines camped in limestone caves near the Franklin River at various times between 20 000 and 5 000 years ago (Blainey, 1982). At that stage, in a global sense, this quite possibly represented the extreme of human settlement.

The most likely source of the early inhabitants of Australia is south-east Asia. Over 40 000 years BP land bridges existed between mainland Australia and both the island of New Guinea and the island of Tasmania. Thus colonization would have been very much easier. Nevertheless, the process of colonization from south-east Asia, via New Guinea, cannot have been simple. It would have necessitated at least one sea crossing of over 60 kilometres, as well as several shorter sea voyages (Commonwealth of Australia, 1981).

Because the original colonization occurred so long ago, there is no trace of it, and because there are no traces of colonization, speculation abounds as to its precise nature. Ward (1982), for example, has suggested that Aborigines might have arrived in Australia as long ago as 120 000 years BP. The reasoning behind this suggestion draws on the fact that sites as varied as Lake George (New South Wales), Kangaroo Island (South Australia) and Lynch's Crater (Queensland) all show an increase in the quantity of carbon in the soil, and an expansion of eucalypt woodland, at about that date, perhaps signifying the arrival of human beings with fire-sticks. This anthropomorphic interpretation of environmental change has not, as yet, received much support and few prehistorians place the date of first settlement much before 50 000 years BP (White and O'Connell, 1982). Indeed, speculation on the first peopling of the continent has focussed not so much on the timing of the first arrival as on whether there was one or several waves of settlement.

Birdsell (1975) has suggested that Australia was peopled in three waves. First came 'oceanic negritos', representatives of whom are to be found among the New Guinean population and the Aboriginal population of Tasmania. Then came 'murrayans' who colonized much of the south and east of Australia, so-called because evidence of their settlement is to be found along the River Murray. Finally, there came the 'carpentarians', a group that settled mainly in the north, hence their name. Clearly, this tripartite interpretation of the peopling of the continent rests very largely on physical anthropology and, in particular, on observation of present-day Aborigines and on the European documentation of Aboriginal life over the last two hundred years. As such it has come in for stern criticism, not least because some of the measures used as a basis for classification may be highly 'plastic' in particular environments (White and O'Connell, 1982).

Apparent differences between Aboriginal groups may, in other words, result simply from differing degrees of environmental adaptation and from different cultural practices rather than from fundamental differences in physical anthropology. Head binding, for example, can lead to markedly different skull shapes. Despite this sort of criticism, the notion that Australia was peopled in waves has proved popular (Mulvaney, 1969). Ward (1982), for instance, talks of 'australoids' settling on the continent before about 12 000 years BP with subsequent 'mongoloid' settlement, possibly from southern China. Irrespective of whether or not this classification is accurate, there does seem to be a good deal of evidence that two reasonably distinct types of Aborigine co-existed in mainland Australia for a time (Thorne, 1971). These are sometimes referred to as the 'gracile' and the 'robust' varieties. Whether these groups co-existed peacefully, or whether one group 'outcompeted' the other, is not known. Indeed the whole of the pre-European settlement history of Australia is presently a very exciting field of discovery and speculation.

Not all authorities accept that Australia was settled in waves. For instance, White and O'Connell (1982) argue that the limit of intentional sea voyages among the sort of people who first settled Australia was about 10 kilometres. Given that this was considerably less than the distance necessary to make landfall on the continent of Australia, even at a time of low sea levels, White and O'Connell argue that the first settlement was quite probably largely accidental, perhaps caused by boats being blown off-course in a storm. In short, White and O'Connell postulate that the presence of at least one substantial sea voyage between south-east Asia and Australia implies that settlement was accidental which, in turn, implies that there was little supplementation by later voyages. According to this view, it is possible that Australia was originally settled by a single population rather than by several waves of colonization.

Given the fragmentary nature of our present understanding of pre-European settlement in Australia, there is no way of telling which of the speculative explanations of original settlement is correct. All that can be said for certain is that, by the time of European settlement, Aborigines were present over the entire continent. Estimates vary as to the number of Aborigines in Australia in the later part of the eighteenth century but the most commonly cited figure is in the range 250 000–300 000 although some estimates put the number as high as 750 000 (Mulvaney and White, 1987).

The popular image of this population is that it lived in harmony with nature, achieving a maximum exploitation of local resources within the limits of technology (Commonwealth of Australia, 1981; p. 1). In practice, of course, there was a great diversity in the Aboriginal way of life and diet: the basic resources of the deserts of Western Australia, the swamps of Arnhem Land, the Darling Downs, and the New South Wales north coast were not the same (Blainey, 1982). Nevertheless, the pre-European Aboriginal population did share a common technological tradition. This has been labelled the 'Australian core-tool and scraper tradition' because it involved the use of one tool to make other tools such as wooden spears, digging sticks, and scrapers. Broad stylistic differences in tools from region to region implied the maintenance of subpopulations living in regional groups and transmitting their cultural idiosyncracies over millenia (Burnley, 1976). Indeed, at the time of European settlement there were probably 500–600 tribes in Australia. According to Ward (1982; p. 17) each of these had its own kinship system, its own distinctive ceremonial life, and its own language. In some cases elements of the cultural system of neighbouring tribes may have been very similar. This was particularly the case with language. Although the average size of tribes was about 500, actual numbers varied from one hundred to two thousand, depending on the extent of tribal territory and the resources it contained. Within tribal groupings there existed extended family groups or 'clans', numbering twenty, thirty, or more people (Ward, 1982). Daily life centred on these clans which tended to move around together in search of food, occasionally meeting with other clans for ceremonial events such as initiations.

Before the arrival of Europeans, Aborigines had almost no contact with groups other than neighbouring tribes. The only exceptions were to be found in Arnhem Land where it seems likely that there was at least some spasmodic contact with south-east Asia. In 1803, for example, Flinders came across vessels off Arnhem Land that had sailed two months earlier from the harbour of Macassar in the southern Celebes in order to collect trepang (sea-cucumber). These 'trepangers' travelled to northern Australia from island south-east Asia in 10–15 days using the north-west monsoon (Mulvaney, 1969). These 'trepangers' brought with them the tamarind tree, so they left behind biological markers of the location of their camps. Despite this, it is impossible to estimate the extent of contact with local Aborigines or the period of time over which such voyages had been conducted. Likewise, although it has often been suggested that Chinese explorers of the Ming Dynasty (1405–1433AD) discovered Australia, the evidence is less than clear-cut (Mulvaney, 1969). The same applies to claims that the Arabs visited Australia. Thus, it was not until the arrival of Europeans that the traditional Aboriginal way of life was disrupted to a significant degree.

The advent of Europeans

Several claims have been made in relation to the first European discovery of Australia. Some of these have more credence than others. Although references to a 'terra australis' are to be found in the works of writers in the early centuries after Christ, and evidence appears in maps and manuscripts from the Middle Ages onwards, there is no established and definite link between this supposed land mass and the known continent of Australia (Commonwealth of Australia, 1986; p. 1). Thus, the first substantial claims to the European discovery of Australia arise from the activities of Portuguese mariners in the early sixteenth century.

It now seems likely that Portuguese sailors under Mendonca visited the east coast of Australia between 1521 and 1523 (Collingbridge, 1982). The evidence for this rests partly on the 'Dieppe Maps', a series of world maps copied by French cartographers between 1536 and 1567 from originals that have long since been lost. One of these maps was the 'Dauphin Map' of 1536. When corrected in such a way as to take stock of the manner in which Portuguese sailors of the time calculated longitude, it provides a reasonably accurate portrayal of the Australian east coast (McKiggan, 1977) (Fig. 1.1). It can be safely concluded, therefore, that the existence of Australia was known to European explorers by the middle of the sixteenth century. Certainly, the position of the east and west coasts, and the outline of the Gulf of Carpentaria, appeared on Wytfliet's global map of 1597. It is not surpris-

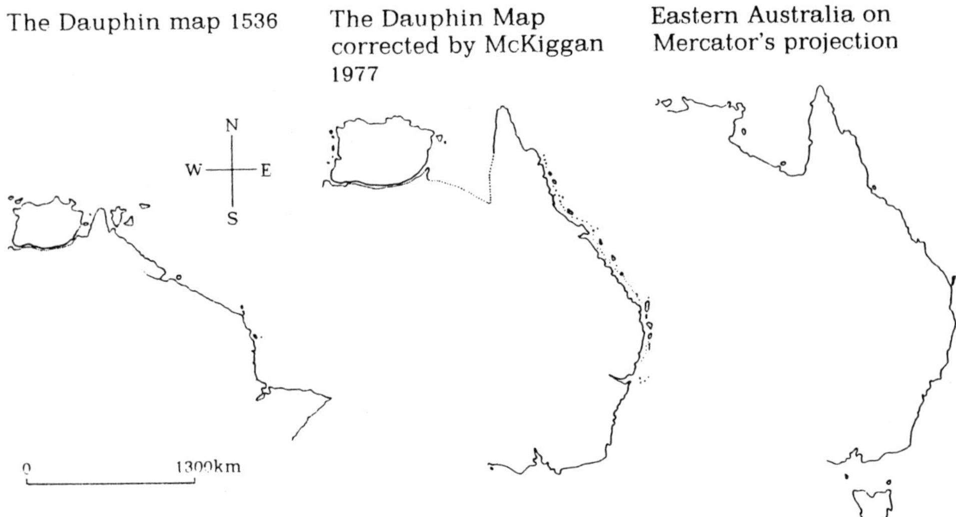

Fig. 1.1 McKiggan's correction of the 1536 Dauphin map
Source: McKiggan (1977); Ward (1982)

ing, therefore, that the seventeenth century saw a flurry of activity in the European exploration of the Australian seaboard.

Curiously, there is no evidence that the Portuguese followed up their early discoveries. Possibly the area was deemed worthless or too isolated. Possibly the discovery was kept a trade secret. Instead, Spanish and Dutch explorers undertook the next major European incursions into Australian waters. In 1606 Quiros led a Spanish expedition which landed in the New Hebrides, thinking that it had discovered the 'great south land'. As the main expedition sailed away eastward, one of its party — Torres — sailed westward, through the strait that now bears his name. Although he made no mention of it in his records, he probably caught sight of the Australian mainland.

In the same year, the Dutchman Jansz took his vessel *Duyfken* along the west coast of Cape York, providing the first thoroughly authenticated European discovery of the continent. A decade later in 1616 Hartog in the *Eendracht* explored the west coast of the continent. Thereafter there was a steady stream of Dutch mariners: in 1618 the *Zeewolf* and the *Mauritius* visited; in 1622 the *Leeuwin*, in 1623 the Cartensz expedition discovered that part of northern Australia known as Arnhem Land, in 1627 Thijssen explored the Great Australian Bight, in 1628 de Witt discovered land in the area of Northeast Cape, and in 1629 the *Batavia* was wrecked off the Australian west coast. Dutch influence culminated in 1642 and 1644 with the voyages of Tasman, during which he named Van Diemen's Land and visited the northern coast of Australia (Commonwealth of Australia, 1978; p. 2). In short, in less than forty years the Dutch had explored much of the Australian coastline. It is small wonder that the Western part of the continent was then known as 'New Holland'.

The British ventured into Australian waters in 1688 when Dampier arrived aboard the *Cygnet*. He returned in 1699 on the *Roebuck*. However, the most significant British visit came over seventy years later when Cook, commanding the *Endeavour*, landed at Botany Bay on 29 April 1770. On 22 August in that year, Cook formally took possession of the whole eastern coast, from latitude 38°S to latitude $10\frac{1}{2}$°S in the name of King George III. By the time that Phillip arrived on 26 January 1788 the area of the British possession had been defined rather more precisely to include the area from 10°37'S to 43°39'S and inland to 135°E. The area was then known as New South Wales.

New South Wales was first established as a penal colony. The transportation of convicts appealed to the British government for a number of reasons: it appeared to be a cheap way of dealing with criminals; it seemed to offer a deterrent to would-be offenders; it provided a means of removing from British society those who could not be deterred from crime; it opened up a possibility for the reform of criminals by putting them in a new situation and a new environment; and it provided, through free or cheap labour, an impetus to the development of the colonies (Shaw, 1966). It is not surprising, therefore, that the First Fleet consisted very largely of convicted criminals: the 1030 people who landed comprised the Governor and his staff of nine; the Surveyor-General, the Surgeon, and four assistants; the Chaplain, his wife, and two servants; 211 marines together with 27 wives and 19 children of marines; and 736 convicts plus 17 children of convicts (Department of Immigration and Ethnic Affairs, 1978).

In practice, transportation proved not to be a successful deterrent to crime. Additionally, it was not as cheap for the British government as had originally been expected. Indeed, as the cost of maintaining a penal colony at the other end of the world became apparent, the British government did all it could to transfer the burden to the Colonial Treasuries (Walmsley, 1988b). Nevertheless, transportation of convicts persisted as an official policy for 80 years from 1788. The numbers arriving in any one year varied markedly. In 1794, for example, only 84 convicts landed in New South Wales and, in 1795, only one convict arrived. So too did the destination vary. New South Wales and Van Dieman's Land were the main recipient areas, with lesser numbers being sent to Norfolk Island, Port Phillip, Moreton Bay, and Western Australia (Table 1.1). The peak year for convict transportation to New South Wales was 1833, when 4115 convicts arrived from Britain. In the same year Van Dieman's Land received 2665 British convicts. Transportation to New South Wales ceased in 1840 whereupon transportation to Van Dieman's Land increased, reaching its maximum extent in 1842 when 5342 convicts arrived from Britain. Van Dieman's Land itself ceased to receive convicts in 1853. Thereafter Western Australia received 7065 convicts before transportation was finally abandoned in 1868 (Shaw, 1966).

Table 1.1 The arrival of convicts in Australia from Britain

	Males	*Females*	*Total*[1]
New South Wales	66 414	12 083	78 497
Van Diemen's Land	52 503	12 595	65 098
Norfolk Island	3 668	0	3 668
Port Phillip	1 727	0	1 727
Moreton Bay	517	0	517
Western Australia	na	na	9 635

1 In addition New South Wales and Van Diemen's Land received 1321 convicts from colonies outside Britain, making a grand total of 160 463 convicts transported to Australia

Source: Commonwealth of Australia (1986)

In all, then, over 160 000 convicts from Britain arrived on Australia's shores. The overwhelming majority of these convicts were male, 84.6 per cent in the case of New South Wales and 80.7 per cent in the case of Van Dieman's Land. Although the policy of transportation had been motivated to a significant degree by a desire to rid Britain of its 'criminal classes', not all convicts fell into this category and the practice of transportation was used at various times by the Westminster government to exile individuals whose views and opinions may be seen, with the benefit of hindsight, to have been ahead of their time. Among such groups were Scottish advocates of fiscal and electoral reform, Irish 'rebels', and proponents of trade unionism.

The first convict settlement obviously focussed on Sydney Cove. Before the first year was out, however, moves had been made inland as far as Rose Hill (later named Parramatta). Subsequently, exploration and settlement proceeded along the Nepean and Hawkesbury Rivers west and north of Sydney, and along the coast north and south of Sydney Harbour. The Blue Mountains were thought to have formed a major barrier to penetration inland until 1813 when Blaxland, Lawson and Wentworth found a route through, thereby opening up the inland to subsequent explorers. This view may however be something of a myth because there seems little doubt that an ex-convict called Wilson crossed the mountains in 1798 (and possibly as early as 1792), a feat repeated by the explorer Barrallier in 1802 (Cunningham, 1992).

European exploration and settlement

The exploration of Australia was stimulated, in the main, by three factors: first, the desire to unravel the 'riddle of the rivers', that is to say a desire to identify the main waterways, to discover where they flowed, and to ascertain whether or not there existed an inland sea; second, the quest for new grazing land, particularly land suitable for sheep; and third, the search for minerals, and, especially, the lure of gold. The first explorers not unnaturally followed the river systems. For example Sturt explored much of the Murray River area between 1828 and 1833 and Mitchell travelled through the Hunter, Darling, Lachlan and Murray valleys between 1831 and 1836. Further north and west exploration took place somewhat later as settlement slowly pushed out into these frontier regions. Knowledge of the area between the Darling Downs and the Gulf of Carpentaria owes much to the efforts of Leichhardt in 1844–45. Likewise, the exploration of Western Australia was limited very much to the south-west corner until the expeditions of the Gregory brothers from the 1840s to the 1860s and the Forrest brothers in the 1860s and 1870s (Commonwealth of Australia, 1981). In large part these explorers were motivated by the desire to find new pastures. The same motivation had earlier taken Mitchell south into what became Victoria, and Cunningham north into the Darling Downs area of what became Queensland. Thus by the mid to late 1830s, all of south-eastern Australia as far north as the present Queensland border had been explored and was thinly settled. Likewise the south-east and south coast of the continent was reasonably well known and there existed cattle droving routes across to Adelaide. The movement of exploratory activity out from this core area is described in Figure 1.2.

There was of course a great gulf between the early activities of explorers in bringing back knowledge of an area and the subsequent settlement of that area. Figure 1.2 is, in other words, very far from being a settlement map. Among the first to move out into the newly discovered grazing lands were the 'squatters'. To a large extent these early squatters took up the land without official sanction. For example, the Port Phillip district of what became Victoria was settled without official blessing, principally by squatters from Van Diemen's Land (such as Henty and Batman) but also as a result of New South Welshmen travelling overland with their flocks. Understandably, such a situation was not to the liking of colonial administrators and in 1829 Darling attempted to put an end to the practice by establishing an approximately semi-circular limit about 400 kilometres from Sydney beyond which no-one was allowed to graze flocks or herds. Not surprisingly, this regulation, which could not be effectively policed, was flouted by squatters. The colonial administrators thus had no option but to legalise the situation by imposing leases and titles. Thus Bourke in 1836 allowed squatters to take up as much land as they pleased beyond Darling's 'limits of location' for a fee of ten pounds.

By 1840 squatters had moved extensively into what became Victoria and Queensland. The government of the day was therefore forced to recognise the inevitable and to declare the areas open for development: Victoria in 1836 and Queensland in 1842. This is not to say that colonization of the inland was an easy exercise. The work was hard, dangerous, and often lonely and, despite relatively better pay than was available in the cities, there existed a significant labour shortage. To a certain extent this was remedied, particularly after the

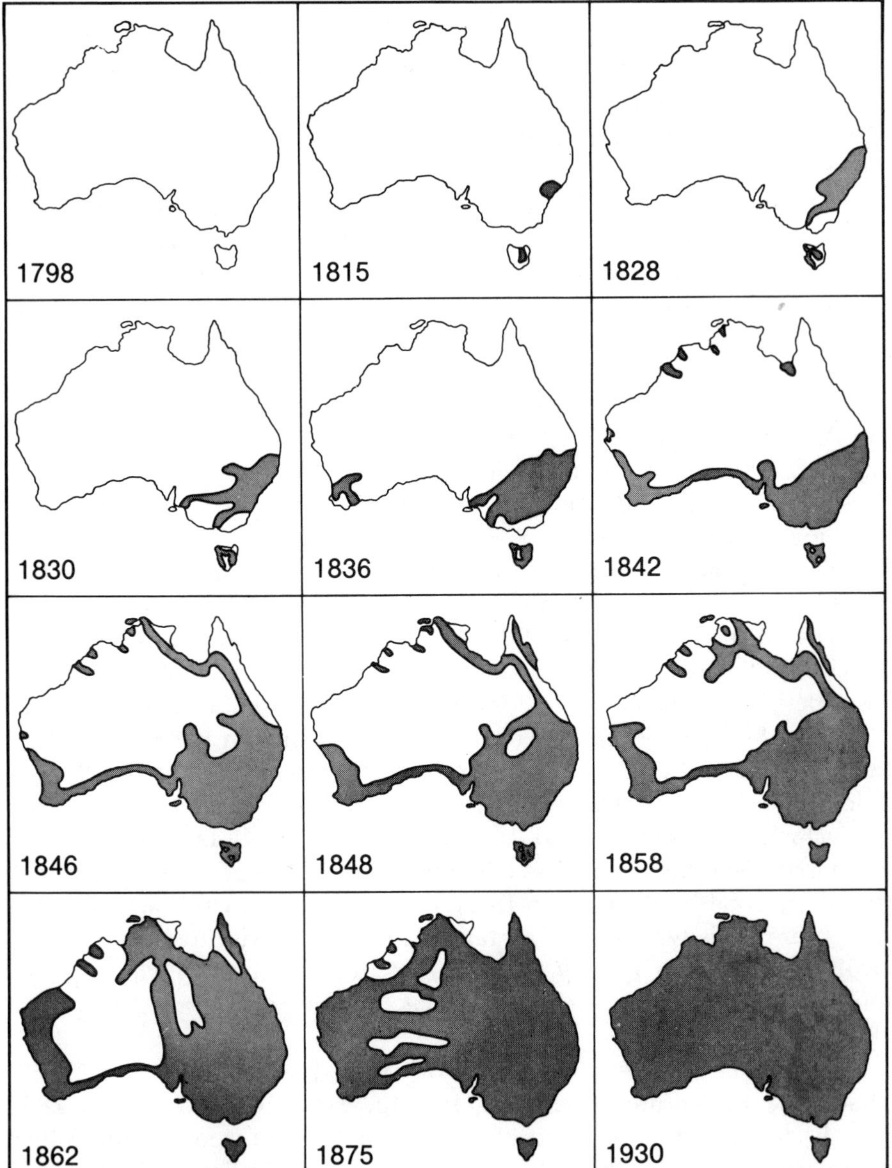

Fig. 1.2 European exploration of the Australian continent
Source: Commonwealth of Australia (1981)

1830s, through the practice of assigning convicts almost exclusively to up-country squatters. There thus arose a situation where the ratio of convicts, emancipists, and Australian-born to free overseas-born immigrants increased the further one went inland from Sydney (Ward, 1982; p. 88). The contribution of free settlers should not however be underplayed. Sydney saw its first free settlers as early as 1793 and those free settlers who came from the 1820s onwards brought livestock, a technology for livestock management, and labourers, thereby playing a significant role in the nation's economic development (Heathcote, 1977).

Free settlers were particularly important in the settlement of South Australia which progressed without the transportation of convict labour. Understandably, the appeal of Australia to free settlers was not great in the early days. After all, it was a land literally at the other end of the earth, a land from which the chance of return was low, and a land about which little was known, save that it offered hardships in an environment very different from that of Britain. It is not surprising, therefore, that of the 77 000 people who had arrived in Australia by 1830, only 18 per cent were free settlers. Obviously the offer of free passages alone was an insufficient inducement to long distance migration. The government therefore resorted to a 'bounty system'. This decision, like all policy decisions relating to migration prior to the establishment of responsible self-government in the colonies in the 1850s, was made in London.

Under the bounty system, private employers selected migrants in Britain and received a government bounty for each approved person landed in Australia. Approximately 40 000 'bounty migrants' came to Australia between 1835 and 1841. As a result, the proportion of all settlers who were free settlers increased markedly: for example, of the 116 000 arrivals between 1831 and 1840, 56 per cent were free settlers. Although the rate of immigration slowed in the 1840s (an economic recession, brought on partly by a fall in wool prices), the characteristics of free settlers began to alter as a result of developments that had taken place in the 1830s. Two features are particularly important. The first is the emergence of significant non-British migration, notably of Prussian Lutherans to South Australia. Second, a greater emphasis was placed on family migration, stimulated largely by Caroline Chisholm's Family Colonisation Loan Society which advanced money to enable families to migrate as units (Department of Immigration and Ethnic Affairs, 1978).

As settlement progressed, the economy of the grazing lands shifted from the subsistence production of mutton to the export of wool and by 1850 Australia accounted for 50 per cent of British imports of wool, a figure which climbed to 70 per cent by 1900 (Heathcote, 1977). Despite this emerging export orientation, inland transport was painfully slow, relying in the main on bullock drays. Only in the 1850s, with the discovery of gold, did communications improve dramatically. In 1853 paddle steamers began to operate on the River Murray and in the same year coaches, notably those of Cobb & Co., transformed overland travel. These coaches could cover up to 130 kilometres a day and by 1870 coach companies were harnessing 6000 horses a day on their way to total weekly journeys of about 45 000 kilometres (Ward, 1982).

Australia's European population had reached about 405 000 by 1850. Thereafter the population figures changed dramatically. Gold was discovered in Summerhill Creek on the western slopes of the Blue Mountains in February 1851. Later that year even richer finds were made at Ballarat in the then newly established colony of Victoria (Ward, 1982). Immediately a gold rush began. By 1852 vast numbers of hopeful prospectors were flocking to Australia and, notably, to Melbourne. By 1860 the nation's population had increased to 1 145 600. Melbourne had changed from a small town of 23 000 in 1852 to a thriving city of 140 000 by the end of the decade. This, then, was the period when the movement of free settlers to Australia increased tremendously, not least because international passage at this time was not hampered by passport restrictions. The increased immigration intake also differed in two significant ways from earlier flows. First, there was a much more even sex ratio among the immigrants, setting the scene in the short-term for relatively high levels of natural increase in the population. Thus in the 1860s the rate of natural increase in the population averaged almost 2.5 per cent per annum and the average remained over 2 per cent per annum until 1890 (Table 1.2). There was, in other words, a marked shift in the relative importance of immigration and natural increase as constituents of population growth: between 1788 and 1861 immigration accounted for 75 per cent of overall population growth, whereas between 1861 and 1900 it accounted for only 28 per cent of overall growth (Burnley, 1976). Part of this decline stems, of

Table 1.2 Population growth

Period	*Population at end of end of period ('000)*	*Average annual rate of growth (%)* Natural increase	Net migration	Total
1851–1860	1 145.6			
1861–1870	1 647.8	2.47	1.23	3.70
1871–1880	2 231.5	2.07	1.01	3.08
1881–1890	3 151.4	2.05	1.46	3.51
1891–1900	3 765.3	1.73	0.07	1.80
1901–1910	4 425.1	1.53	0.10	1.63
1911–1920	5 411.3	1.60	0.43	2.03
1921–1930	6 500.8	1.32	0.53	1.85
1931–1940	7 077.6	0.79	0.06	0.85
1941–1950	8 307.5	1.14	0.47	1.62
1951–1955	9 311.8	1.38	0.93	2.31
1956–1960	10 391.9	1.40	0.82	2.22
1961–1965	11 505.4	1.27	0.71	1.98
1966–1970	12 663.5	1.11	0.82	1.94
1971–1975	13 968.9	1.07	0.49	1.56
1976–1980	14 807.4	0.81	0.45	1.17
1981–1985	15 788.3	0.84	0.59	1.45
1986–1989	16 806.7	0.78	0.78	1.58

Source: Commonwealth of Australia (1986; 1990)

course, from cut-backs in immigration brought about by the ending of the gold rush and by restrictions imposed upon migrants. These restrictions owe a great deal to the ethnic diversity of immigration in the 1850s.

Although Chinese labourers were brought to Australia on five-year contracts by squatters in 1848, it was the discovery of gold which attracted them in great numbers. In 1861 there were 40 000 Chinese in Australia, making them the third largest immigrant group after the British and the Germans. Indeed, it has been estimated that, at the time, one in nine adult men was Chinese (Blainey, 1982). Complaints about the Chinese soon emerged: they were seen as insanitary, heathen, opportunistic, drug addicts, and gamblers. None of these charges could be levelled exclusively at the Chinese. Rather they applied to a great proportion of the goldfields population. What made the Chinese vulnerable was that they were clearly identifiable on racial, linguistic, and cultural grounds. They were therefore ideally placed to become scapegoats for all the perceived ills of the time.

Opposition to the Chinese took many forms. In 1854, for instance, the Victorian government passed the *Chinese Restriction Act*, imposing limits and charges on Chinese entry at Victorian ports. This merely had the effect of causing Chinese immigrants to land elsewhere and travel overland to the diggings. In another notorious incident in 1861, diggers of European extraction physically attacked Chinese diggers at Lambing Flat near Young in New South Wales and burned their belongings. It is small wonder then that the Chinese were a very mobile group. When new gold strikes were made, the Chinese tended to move on. So it was that they came to dominate north Queensland at the time of the rush to the Palmer goldfield in the 1870s. Chinese, at the time, comprised half of all new settlers in the region and, in what was to become the Northern Territory, they outnumbered Europeans by seven to one (Blainey, 1982).

It was not simply opposition to Chinese that led to a re-evaluation of migration policy. The end of the gold rush meant a questioning of the colonies' capacity to absorb migrants. In the light of this situation, the New South Wales Legislative Assembly refused to allocate funds for immigration in 1867 and by the 1880s assisted migration, begun in earnest following the cessation of transportation in 1840, had virtually ended other than to Queensland and Western Australia (Department of Immigration and Ethnic Affairs, 1978). In other words, the fervour with which Australian governments pursued a policy of assisting immigration varied with the vicissitudes of the economy. Nevertheless, net migration continued to contribute an average of over 1 per cent per annum to national population growth until 1890. In fact it was not until 1891 that the Australian population comprised more people born within the country than born outside.

Of the migrants who entered the country following the start of the gold rush, a majority were 'lower middle-class' or 'upper working-class' people. According to Ward (1982), this paved the way for a movement to 'unlock' the land from the grasp of the squatters. In other words, the *Settlement Acts* passed in New South Wales from 1861 onwards were not so much a grass roots movement aimed at getting people on the land so much as a middle-class movement designed to break the power and privilege of the 'squattocracy'. According to these Acts, anyone could select blocks of crown land up to 320 acres (128 hectares) in extent for a payment of one pound per acre (two pounds ten shillings per hectare), the first five shillings being paid immediately and the balance within three years. Selectors were also required to live on the block for a year and to improve it to the value of at least one pound per acre before they could receive freehold title. Squatters were given pre-emptive rights to 4 per cent of their land prior to the Acts, plus any areas where they had made improvements. Even though the legislation was bold, its impact on settlement patterns was slight. Australia was already very much an urban nation by the later part of the nineteenth century and the *Settlement Acts* did little to upset that situation.

Although Victorian legislation in 1860, 1862 and 1865 put more genuine farmers on the land, and thereby improved agricultural productivity, and South Australian farmers did well because of technological inventiveness (including mechanical strippers, seed drills, and the stump-jump plough), Australian agriculture did not really become profitable, other than in wool production, until the advent of the railways in 1880–1900. Before that time transport costs had hampered development. Ward (1982), for example, claims that in 1861 it was much cheaper to transport a ton of wheat to Sydney from Valparaiso in Chile than to carry it 250 kilometres by bullock dray from Goulburn.

The last two decades of the nineteenth century were important for Australia for reasons other than the spread of railways and their impact of economic competitiveness. At this time the birth rate began to decline. The birth rate stood at around 35 per 1000 population in 1880 but dropped to about 25 per 1000 in 1900 (Figure 1.3) (Department of Immigration and Ethnic Affairs, 1984). The decline in the number of children per family began first in metropolitan areas about 1880, spread to other urban areas in the late 1880s, and to rural areas in the 1890s (Burnley,1976). This probably reflects changing attitudes to smaller families and, possibly, the diffusion of information about birth control. Certainly, the rate of natural increase in Australia's population never again reached the level of the 1880s. One reason which may have contributed to the low birth rates in the 1890s was the economic recession which characterized that decade and which led, among other things, to a massive cut-back in immigration (Table 1.2). In 1892–93, and again between 1898 and 1900, departures from Australia actually exceeded arrivals. For a time the Victorian and South Australian populations actually declined as many people went west to the gold rushes at Coolgardie and Kalgoorlie (1893) (Ward, 1982). The 1890s were, in other words, turbulent times on the Australian continent. Not least among the things that were changing was the system of government.

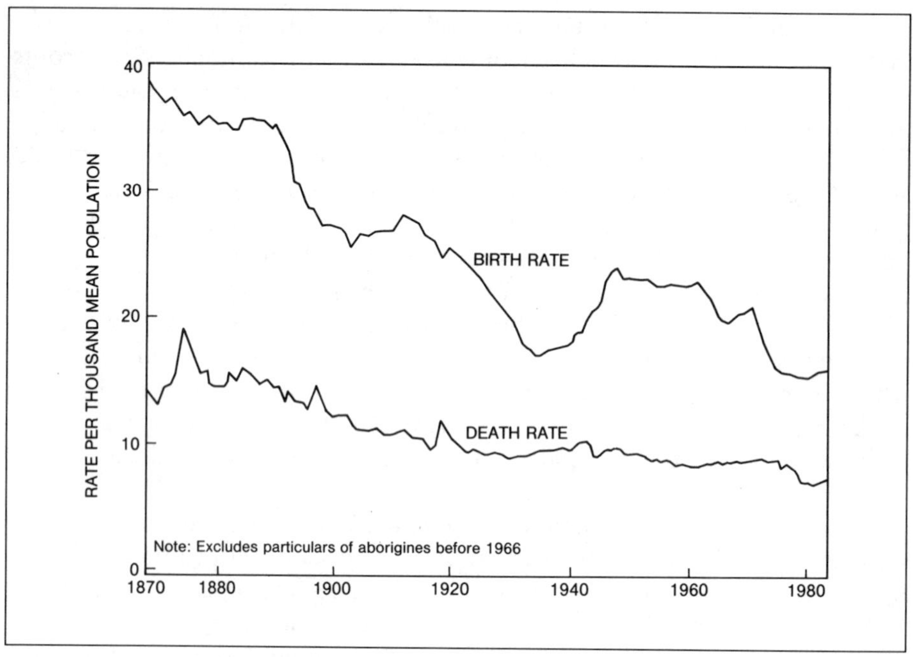

Fig. 1.3 Fluctuations in birth and death rates
Source: Department of Immigration and Ethnic Affairs (1984)

The beginnings of government

Government, in the modern sense, began in Australia with the arrival of Phillip in 1788. The British administrators sought to impose order on what was perceived to be, for convenience and in spite of evidence of an extensive Aboriginal presence, an empty continent. As if to emphasise the absence of any prior land use pattern, early colonial borders were drawn in terms of straight lines on a map, disregarding physical features in the landscape. Thus, New South Wales originally extended inland to 135°E (Figure 1.4). It soon became apparent of course that the sheer size of the continent, coupled with the sparseness of settlement, rendered the area too large to be controlled by a single colonial administration. There thus began a process of carving out new colonies again, with few exceptions, using lines of latitude and longitude as boundaries (Figure 1.4). The dates of first settlement of these Colonies are shown in Table 1.3 together with the date at which the Colony was formally established and the date at which responsible government was granted by the Colonial Office in London. Clearly, settlement spread quickly in the 1820s and 1830s and by 1860 all the Colonies, except Western Australia where population numbers were still very low, had self-government. This administrative framework remained substantially unchanged until Federation in 1901.

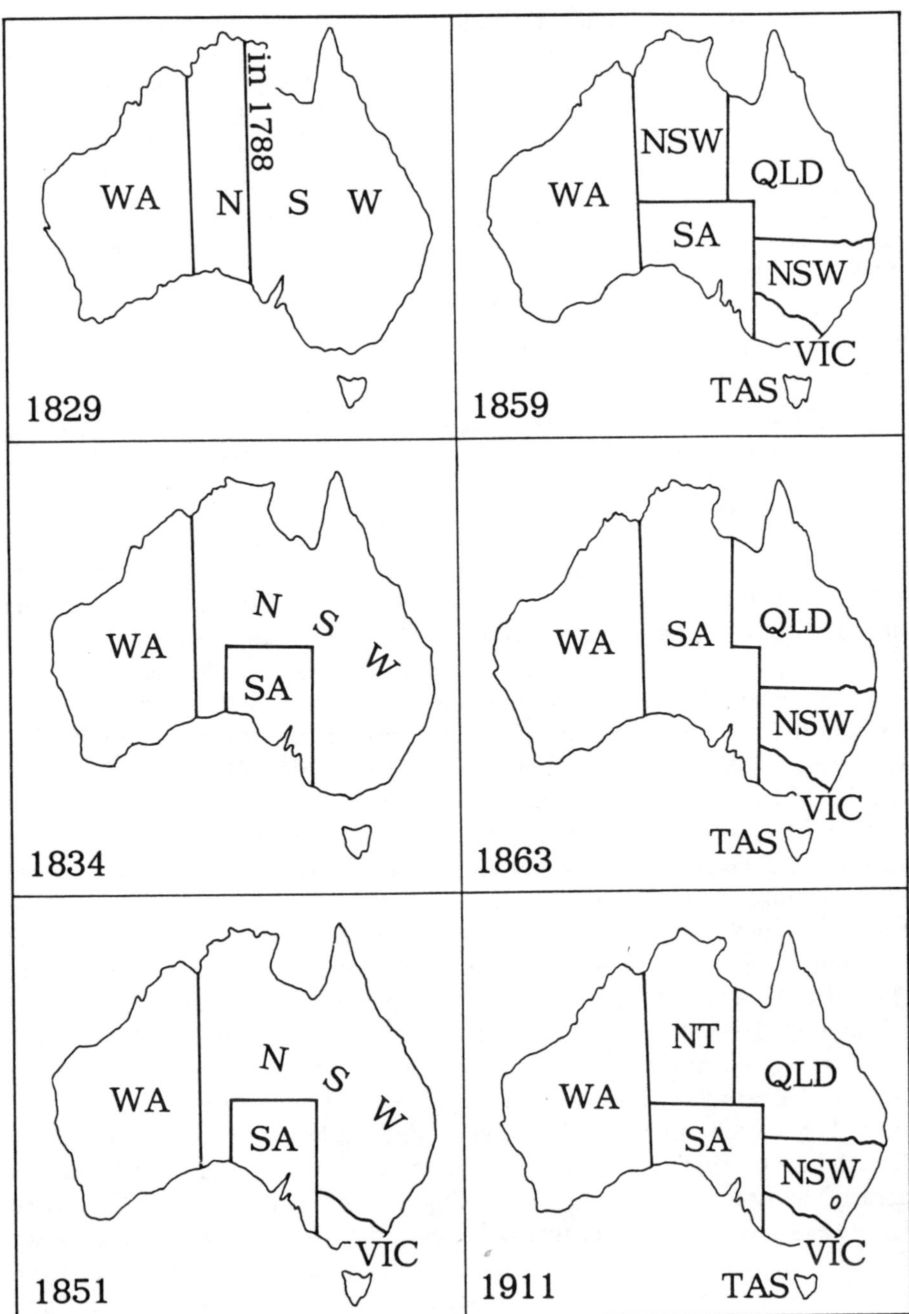

Fig. 1.4 Boundary changes in the Australian colonies

Table 1.3 The development of the Colonies

	First settlement	*Formation into separate Colony or Territory*	*Granting of responsible government*
New South Wales	1788	1786	1855
Victoria	1834	1851	1855
Queensland	1824	1859	1859
South Australia	1836	1834	1856
Western Australia	1829	1829	1890
Tasmania	1803	1825	1855
Northern Territory	—	1863[1]	1978
Australian Capital Territory	—	1911[1]	1989

1 The Northern Territory was under the jurisdiction of New South Wales until 1863. It was then under the jurisdiction of South Australia until 1911 when it, and the Australian Capital Territory, became a Commonwealth responsibility.

Source: Commonwealth of Australia (1986)

The case of local government is somewhat different. For the first fifty years after British settlement, local government issues came under the direct control of the Colonial Office in London. This proved to be a cumbersome and slow mode of administration as well as one that proved increasingly costly to Britain. It is not surprising, therefore, that pressure mounted for the initiation of some form of local government within the Colonies. After all such a move would, in the British government's eyes, provide a way of getting a local contribution to the running expenses of the Colonies, notably the cost of running police forces. Although such a move was opposed by pastoral interests, disenfranchised ex-convicts, and all those who thought that public services should be provided from consolidated revenue rather than from local taxation, the push towards local government led to initiatives being taken in the City of Adelaide in 1840 and in Sydney and Melbourne in 1842 (Walmsley, 1988b). These initiatives soon foundered because of confusion about the goals and role of local government and lack of support from the relevant Governors (Power *et al.*, 1981). Despite this, a form of local government began to be instituted just over a decade later, based loosely on the British idea of 'shires' in rural areas and 'municipalities' and 'cities' in urban areas. The precise form taken by local government varied from Colony to Colony (just as local government varies today from State to State — see Chapter 4). Fundamentally, there were two approaches used in the development of local government. The first, adopted in New South Wales and Queensland, imposed local government from above. In New South Wales, for example, early moves (from 1858) to encourage individuals to petition the Governor for the establishment of a local authority contained so few incentives that by 1875 only 25 per cent of the Colony's population was living in areas incorporated in local authorities. In Queensland the situation was much the same. As a result, the Colonial (and later State) governments moved to impose local authorities and boundaries, in Queensland in 1879 and in New South Wales in 1905. In contrast, in Victoria and South Australia local government developed very much as a response to a grass roots movement. In other words, the population of these Colonies showed no reluctance to petition for the establishment of local authorities. Victoria, possibly because of the gold rush and the rapid spread of settlement, had 85 per cent of its area incorporated into local authorities by 1864. As a result of voluntary formation, local authorities in Victoria and South Australia tended to have a greater degree of autonomy than authorities in New South Wales and Queensland. In Tasmania and Western Australia local government tended to develop as a blend of the 'voluntary' and 'imposed' systems.

But all local government remained relatively weak when compared to colonial administrations, and this position was exacerbated by the introduction of a federal system of government on 1 January 1901. Local government was not mentioned in the Constitution which enshrined the arrangements for Federation. Instead, local government remained a State responsibility, under separate pieces of State legislation, with significant interstate differences in powers and responsibilities (see Chapter 4). Federalism, in other words, enfeebled local government even further. Federalism itself did not arise in Australia from any groundswell of public support. Instead it arose because of the earnest endeavours of a few enthusiasts (Walmsley, 1988b). Australia did not feature any of the characteristics that had fostered federations elsewhere in the world. There were no major economic differences between the colonies. There were no significant and powerful minority groups within the population. Quite simply, the idea of federation was attractive because federalism, at the time, appeared to offer several advantages as a system of government: it offered multiple access points to power (Commonwealth, State, local) and therefore government close to the people; it offered flexibility in policy development in that it facilitated innovation and experimentation at a level (i.e. a State) which did not involve the whole nation; it promised public funding to the component regions; and it seemed to afford a way of promoting a national point of view in a changing world (Maddox, 1985).

The most significant effect of Federation was probably the fostering of nationalism. In particular the Commonwealth government took over responsibility for immigration policy. As a result, Commonwealth decisions started to have a major bearing on population levels. However, the main characteristics of the population *distribution* had been established prior to Federation and the nature of the settlement pattern has changed only slightly since that time. Table 1.4, for example, shows the percentage of Australia's population in each State in selected years since Federation. Only minor changes are apparent, notably the growing importance of Queensland and Western Australia as population centres. This lack of major change is because

Table 1.4 Australia's population by States

	National population (%)					
	1901	*1933*	*1947*	*1975*	*1984*	*1989 ('000s)*
New South Wales	35.9	39.2	39.4	36.2	34.3	5 761.9
Victoria	31.8	27.5	27.6	27.6	25.7	4 315.2
Queensland	13.2	14.3	14.6	14.2	16.8	2 830.2
South Australia	9.5	8.8	8.5	9.2	8.5	1 423.3
Western Australia	4.9	6.6	6.6	8.1	9.5	1 591.1
Tasmania	4.6	3.4	3.4	3.1	2.7	451.0
National population ('000s)	3773.8	6629.8	7579.4	13 067.3	16 806.7	

Source: Calculated from data in Commonwealth of Australia (1986; 1990)

the rudiments of Australia's settlement pattern are dictated in large measure by the twin concerns of climate and economy. Much of the continent is too dry to support significant settlement except in mining towns such as those in the Pilbara. Likewise much of tropical Australia has remained outside the realm of major European settlement. Indeed a map of population density shows that, except for a band along the Queensland coast, the areas of Australia where population density exceeds 2 persons per square kilometre are generally south of the Tropic of Capricorn and coastward of the 400 mm isohyet (Figure 1.5). In other words, in much of Australia densities are remarkably low. Indeed, instead of talking in terms of persons per square kilometre it is often more appropriate to speak of square kilometres per person. For example, much of inland Queensland, by no means the 'emptiest' part of the continent, has densities of 20–40 square kilometres per person and in the outback densities can fall as low as 130–400 square kilometres per person (Holmes, 1973).

Highest densities of population are clearly along the coast and, notably, around the mainland state capitals. Australia, with a land mass of approximately 7 682 300 square kilometres, is the sixth largest nation in the world (after the Russia,Canada, China, the USA, and Brazil). Yet in population terms, with approximately 17 000 000 people, it ranks as only the forty-seventh largest in the world. Moreover, an extremely high percentage of Australia's population live in cities. This has always been the case. For example, by 1891 two-thirds of Australia's population lived in cities and towns, a figure not reached by the USA until 1920 and Canada until 1950 (Holmes, 1977). Today, approximately 85 per cent of Australia's population lives in urban settlements of more than 1000 people. Similarly, 85 per cent lives within 80 kilometres of the coast (Holmes, 1977). Several reasons have been put forward to account for this remarkable concentration. The colonial

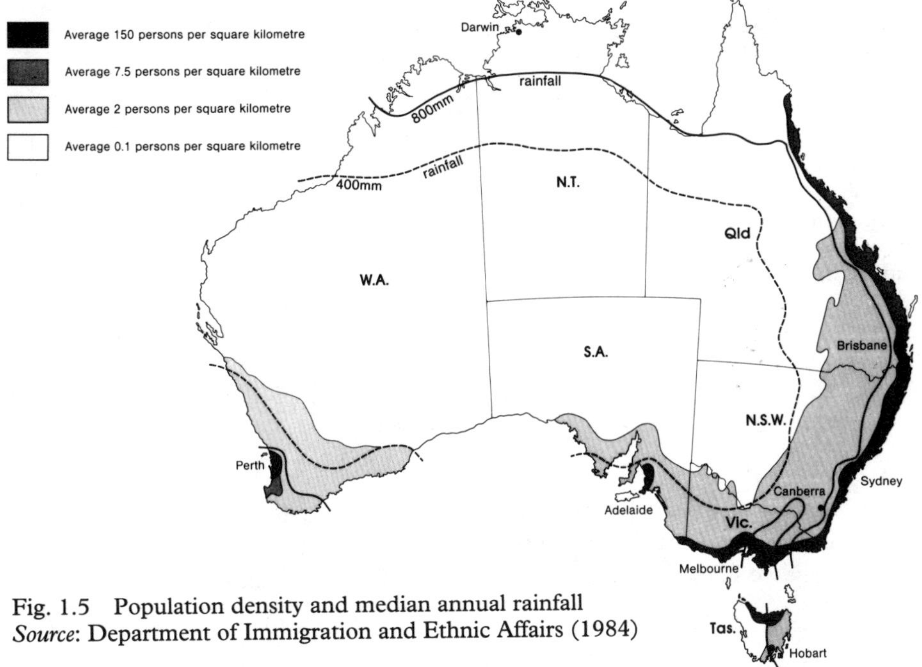

Fig. 1.5 Population density and median annual rainfall
Source: Department of Immigration and Ethnic Affairs (1984)

heritage is obviously important. In particular the administrative centralization fostered by colonial governments accounted for the growth of capital cities. The export orientation of the economy, especially in primary produce, also led to a focus on the main ports and capital cities. This focus encompassed both physical infrastructure (such as the radial rail networks) and a mental outlook that made people look to the major cities for leadership in sport, the arts, culture, and government. The growth of Australia's mainland capitals was also fostered by the lack of intensively settled inland farming areas (cf. the Corn Belt in the USA) and the absence of both inland industrial belts (cf. the Witwatersrand area of South Africa) and natural inland routeways that might have encouraged the growth of entrepots (Holmes, 1977). Moreover, the failure of closer settlement schemes, and in particular the soldier settler schemes developed after the two world wars (Powell, 1978; 1988), also contributed to the lack of alternative population concentrations. In short, in the absence of alternative locations, investment by both the public and the private sectors focussed on State capitals, setting in motion a multiplier effect that ensured future growth. In this way the metropolitan areas came to dominate first the Colonies, then the States. State capitals, in other words, can be thought of as primate cities in that they are, in most cases, very much larger than the next biggest cities. The percentage of each State's population resident in the respective capital cities at various dates since Federation is shown in Table 1.5 together with recent estimates of city size. Clearly, the degree of primacy has increased steadily over the last seventy years. It is very

Table 1.5 The dominance of cities in Australia's settlement pattern

	State population (%)				*Population estimate*
	1911	*1947*	*1981*	*1988*	*1988*
Sydney	42.1	55.1	62.5	63.1	3 596 000
Melbourne	45.1	59.7	71.1	70.4	3 002 300
Brisbane	23.3	37.4	44.8	45.2	1 240 300
Adelaide	45.0	59.2	72.5	72.7	1 023 700
Perth	38.0	54.2	70.6	72.4	1 118 800
Hobart	21.0	30.1	40.2	40.1	179 900
Australia	–	–	–	–	*16 538 153*

Source: Stimson (1982); Commonwealth of Australia (1986; 1990)

high in all areas except perhaps Queensland (where the State capital (Brisbane) is in an eccentric position) and Tasmania (which has always had a reasonably well developed system of towns of various sizes).

Population growth and immigration policies since Federation

Although the population distribution did not change significantly after Federation, the size and the nature of the population most certainly did. At Federation the population numbered 3 765 000. By the outbreak of the Second World War it was just over seven million. Today it is approximately seventeen million. In other words, at the time of the Bicentennial (1988) the population was over four and a quarter times as large as at Federation (1901). Interestingly, 50 per cent of the increase since Federation has occurred since 1951. Throughout the period since 1901 natural increase contributed significantly more to population growth than did net migration (Table 1.2). The first dozen or so years after Federation actually saw the rate of natural increase accelerate due to a rising birth rate and a falling death rate (Figure 1.3). Thereafter the birth rate fell sharply during the 1930s depression and the war years. In comparison the death rate fluctuated little but, overall, the annual rate of natural increase fell to an average of 1.60 per cent between 1911 and 1920.

The birth rate picked up after the Second World War, again with little change in the death rate, resulting in the so-called 'baby boom' of the 1950s when the rate of natural increase began to approach the levels experienced in the first two decades after Federation. Since that time the birth rate has dropped, particularly since the mid-1970s, so that the rate of natural increase of the population is averaging scarcely more than 0.8 per cent per annum

(Table 1.2). Nevertheless, natural increase in the 1980s still contributed about 61 per cent of total population growth. This is identical to the figure for the decades 1951–1960 and 1961–1970 but slightly lower than the 69 per cent recorded between 1971 and 1981 and substantially lower than 1901–1940 when natural increase accounted for about 82 per cent of total population growth.

Table 1.2 also suggests that immigration has accounted for somewhere between thirty and almost forty percent of Australia's population growth since 1950. Between Federation and the Second World War it accounted for only about 20 per cent of total growth. In other words, net migration to Australia since the Second World War has contributed between 0.5 per cent and 0.9 per cent per annum to population growth (Table 1.2). At Federation the Commonwealth government took over responsibility for immigration. It is therefore appropriate to look at the various ways in which this government has fostered immigration over the years. This is necessary background for an appreciation of the ethnic composition of the immigrant community.

Federation followed hard on the heels of the economic depression of the 1890s, during part of which Australia had seen a population movement where overseas departures exceeded arrivals. It was understandable, then, that the *Immigration Restriction Act* of 1901 sought to impose reasonably stringent controls on the entry of new settlers. After all, the last thing the new Commonwealth government wanted was an exacerbation of the unemployment of the depression years. However, the form taken by the legislation, and government policy generally, probably owed more to a long-standing fear of cheap, energetic Asian labour than to anything else. For example, the legislation included a provision whereby intending settlers could be given a dictation test in any European language as part of the assessment of their suitability for entry. This provision was not abolished until 1958. Overseas, the government's policy was perceived to be aimed at excluding non-European, and particularly Asian, migrants, not least because it followed reasonably closely on moves in Western Australia to ban Chinese from the gold diggings. Thus the government's stance on immigration became known overseas as the 'White Australian policy' although this expression was never formally used in Australia.

Shifts in government immigration policy from these first initiatives until the late 1970s have been set out very clearly by the Department of Immigration and Ethnic Affairs (1978). Immediately after the 1901 legislation Australia lapsed into another period (1902–1906) when departures exceeded arrivals. Despite this the tone of government policy remained unchanged and the *Naturalisation Act* of 1903 explicitly denied Australian nationality to natives of Asia, Africa, and the Pacific Islands (except New Zealand). It is not surprising, then, that immigrants who were of non-British and non-European origin comprised only 1.8 per cent of the total population in 1911. By 1921 this figure had fallen to 1.3 per cent. Immigration itself virtually stopped with the First World War. After the war, there was a widespread feeling that Australia's continued security and prosperity depended upon a significantly larger population than then existed. There were no really serious or official attempts to quantify what might be regarded as an optimum population but immigration was certainly encouraged as a way of boosting numbers. In consequence, 300 000 migrants arrived in the 1920s, two-thirds of them 'assisted' migrants who were given help with transport costs. Among these groups were significant numbers of Europeans. As a result, the number of Italian-born people in Australia rose from 8205 in 1921 to 26 756 in 1933 and the number of Greeks rose from 3686 to 8337 over the same period (Department of Immigration and Ethnic Affairs, 1978).

The economic depression of the 1930s ensured that there were virtually no assisted passages granted between 1931 and 1937. In fact between 1930 and 1932 Australia experienced another net outflow of people. The Second World War also put an end to large-scale immigration although Australia did take 7000 political refugees fleeing Nazism before hostilities began in 1939. After the War, Australian official thinking on immigration was again dominated by the view that the country needed a substantially increased population in order to defend itself effectively. A notional figure of 30 million people was often quoted. Large-scale immigration was again in vogue. Migrants were needed, in particular to rectify the economic dislocation caused by the war: thousands of houses had to be built, coal and steel production needed to be increased, and public transport systems were generally in need of improvement. Some figure obviously had to be set as an immigration target.

In order to arrive at such a figure, a rather curious argument was used. It was assumed, without necessarily a vast amount of evidence, that the maximum rate of population growth that a nation could sustain without overburdening services and infrastructure was about 2 per cent per annum. Given that the natural increase in the population seemed to be in the vicinity of 1 per cent per annum, it was argued that the migrant intake should be of such numbers as to generate a 1 per cent per annum increase in the total population. Given this guideline as to total numbers, a decision then had to be made about the source of migrants. In this regard, a pointer to government thinking had been given in 1944 when Australia had rejected a proposal by the Freeland League for Jewish Territorial Colonisation to set up a Jewish settlement in the Kimberleys. Rejection was on the grounds that the government did not want to encourage settlements by any one single type of migrant that were 'likely to develop into a new political entity' (Department of Immigration and Ethnic Affairs, 1978). Instead, the government believed that immigration policies should be conducted on a basis that allowed for settlers to be selected from several different sources and in such a way that they could reasonably expect to assimilate to the overall Australian way of life. The first initiatives, in 1946, sought British ex-servicemen and Dutch farmers. Despite this the years 1945–1947 saw departures exceed arrivals. At the time of the

1947 Census, 90 per cent of the population had been born in Australia, 7 per cent in the United Kingdom and 1.3 per cent elsewhere in Europe. That situation changed markedly with the arrival of 'displaced persons'.

In 1947 Australia undertook to accept individuals displaced as a result of the war in Europe and from 1948 such 'displaced persons' could nominate relatives and friends as migrants. Under the terms of their migration, 'displaced persons' were required to work for two years in a job allocated to them. Thereafter they were free to move to a job anywhere in the country. The program lasted until 1952 by which time 170 700 'displaced persons' had arrived, mainly from Eastern Europe (Poland 63 000; Yugoslavia 25 000; Latvia 19 000; Ukraine 14 000; Hungary 12 000). This influx led to a turn-around in Australia's net migration figures: in 1947–1948 arrivals exceeded departures for the first time since the war. At first the net gain was modest (29 000 in 1947/48) but it soon increased substantially (over 160 000 in 1949/50). With the demise of the 'displaced persons' program in 1952, Australia turned to assisted passage agreements with a variety of countries: the Netherlands and Italy from 1951, Austria, Belgium, Greece, Spain, and West Germany from 1952, the USA, Switzerland, Denmark, Norway, Sweden and Finland in 1954, and Turkey in 1967 (Department of Immigration and Ethnic Affairs, 1978). Assisted passages for British migrants of course continued throughout the period in question.

Despite the goal of attracting sufficient settlers to contribute 1 per cent to overall population growth, actual migrant intakes varied with the state of the economy. For example, a recession in 1952 led to a cut-back in immigration. The other thing that periodically upset immigration targets was the presence of political refugees. About 14 000 Hungarians came to Australia after the abortive 1956 uprising in their country and approximately 6000 Czechs came after the Warsaw Pact intervention in Czechoslovakia in 1968. Counting the 'displaced persons', a total of 300 000 refugees arrived in Australia in the period 1946–1968. At the same time there was a slow weakening of the 'White Australia policy' as Australians were allowed to introduce non-European spouses who would be eligible for citizenship. This was very much in line with another element of migration policy which was of emerging importance, namely an increasing emphasis on family reunion.

Immigration rose to a peak in 1969/70 with 185 000 arrivals. Most of these were from Europe. This was a time, after all, when Europe was very much 'closer' to Australia in the sense that it was separated by only a relatively short travelling time. In contrast to the First Fleet, which took over 240 days to sail to Australia, and the steamers which plied their trade in about 35 days at the beginning of the twentieth century, migrants travelling to Australia in the 1970s could reach their destination in a little over a day (Figure 1.6). Such were the numbers that arrived in the 1960s that the birthplace profile of Australia's population had changed substantially by 1971. At the Census in that year 80 per cent of the population had been born in Australia, 8 per cent

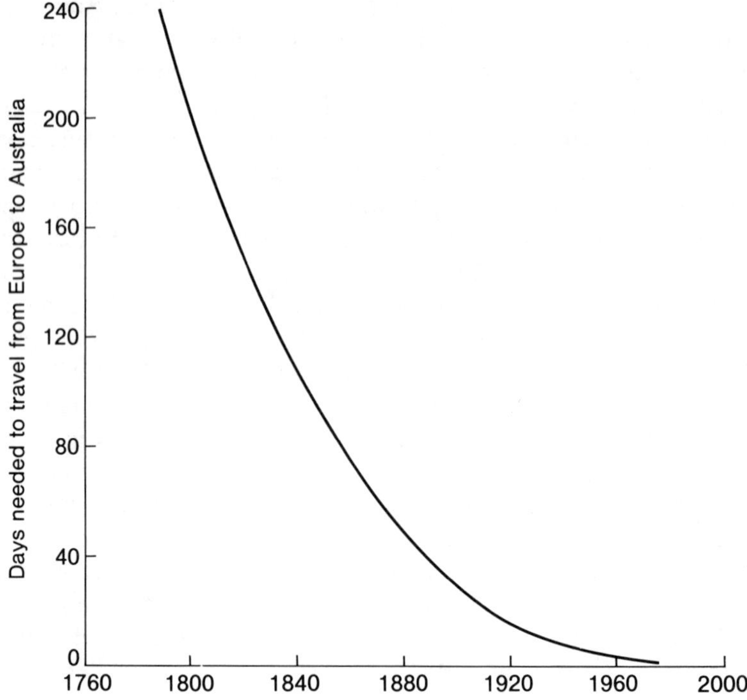

Fig. 1.6 Travel time between Europe and Australia

in Britain, and 12 per cent elsewhere. Almost 27 per cent of the workforce had been born overseas, indicating the importance of immigration to economic growth (Department of Immigration and Ethnic Affairs, 1978). The advent of a Labor government in 1972, after an absence of twenty-three years, saw the abandonment of the 1 per cent per annum philosophy as immigration targets were increasingly set in-line with labour market requirements (Shergold, 1984). What this meant, of course, was that economically hard times in 1975 led to a cut-back in immigration. Indeed, 1975 was the last year in which more people left Australia than arrived. The 1970s also saw the final disappearance of the last vestiges of the 'White Australia policy' and an increased willingness to accept Asian migrants. According to Blainey (1982), this attitude change reflected an awareness of Britain's demise as a world power and an appreciation of the economic power and trade significance of Australia's Asian neighbours. To begin with, political refugees from Indo-China figured prominently among the Asian migrant intake, but over time most Asian immigration was in the category of family reunion. The significance of assisted migration also lessened over time. Between 1966 and 1970, 67 per cent of all migrants were assisted by means of cheap fares and subsidised accommodation on arrival. By 1976–1980 this proportion had fallen to 27 per cent. By 1984 there were no assisted migrants as such (although political refugees in effect receive assistance).

Between 1945 and 1985 over 3 350 000 migrants came to Australia. The size of the main nationality groups born overseas is given in Table 1.6. Together these ten groups account for just over 2 300 000 out of a total overseas born population of a little over 3 million at the 1986 Census. Such figures of course underestimate the size of ethnic communities because they take no account of the Australian-born children of migrants, yet the 1986 Census showed that there were over 3 000 000 people born in Australia who had at least one parent born overseas. Many of these individuals identify with migrant communities. As a result, the size of such communities is often much greater than a simple head count of birthplace would suggest. Understandably, these migrant groups are not spread evenly throughout the Australian settlement pattern. Rather they tend to cluster in such a way as to reflect occupation, point of arrival, and the need to have close proximity to kinship, religious, and linguistic groups. Indeed, the distribution of ethnic groups is so varied as to warrant the publication of an *Atlas of the Australian People*, detailing the identity of the residents of each State (see Hugo, 1990a; 1990b).

The distribution of the ten major overseas groups by States and by major metropolitan areas is shown in Table 1.7. If 'concentrations' are defined for any one nationality group on the basis of presences at least 50 per cent greater than that nationality's share of Australia's total population, it can be seen, at the level of States, that certain States have 'concentrations' of certain ethnic groups: in New South Wales it is the Lebanese; in Victoria, Italians and Greeks; in Queensland, New Zealanders; in South Australia, the British; in

Table 1.6 Overseas-born groups in Australia, 1986

	Group	*Number*	*Australia's population (%)*
1	UK-Eire	1 127 196	7.2
2	Italy	261 878	1.7
3	New Zealand	211 670	1.4
4	Yugoslavia	150 040	1.0
5	Greece	137 637	0.9
6	Germany	114 810	0.7
7	Netherlands	95 095	0.6
8	Vietnam	83 044	0.5
9	Poland	67 676	0.4
10	Lebanon	56 341	0.4
Total overseas born		3 247 381	20.8
Total Australian population		15 602 156	–

Source: 1986 Census

Table 1.7 Nationality groups by States and by urban centres, 1986

		State population (%)							
		NSW	*Vic*	*Qld*	*SA*	*WA*	*Tas*	*NT*	*ACT*
1	UK-Eire	6.0	6.2	6.1	10.9	13.8	5.0	5.9	7.8
2	Italy	1.4	2.7	0.7	2.2	2.0	0.3	0.5	1.1
3	New Zealand	1.4	0.8	2.4	0.6	1.8	0.6	2.3	1.2
4	Yugoslavia	1.1	1.5	0.3	0.7	0.8	0.2	0.2	1.5
5	Greece	0.8	1.7	0.2	1.0	0.3	0.2	0.8	0.6
6	Germany	0.7	0.8	0.6	1.1	0.7	0.5	0.7	1.1
7	Netherlands	0.4	0.7	0.6	0.8	0.8	0.7	0.5	0.6
8	Vietnam	0.6	0.7	0.2	0.5	0.4	0.1	0.3	0.5
9	Poland	0.4	0.6	0.2	0.6	0.5	0.3	0.1	0.5
10	Lebanon	0.8	0.3	0.0	0.1	0.0	0.0	0.0	0.1
		Urban centre population (%)							
		S	*M*	*B*	*A*	*P*	*H*	*D*	*C*
1	UK-Eire	6.9	6.8	7.6	12.4	15.3	5.8	7.0	7.8
2	Italy	1.9	3.6	0.7	2.9	2.5	0.6	0.7	1.1
3	New Zealand	1.8	1.0	2.6	0.7	1.9	0.8	2.7	1.2
4	Yugoslavia	1.4	1.9	0.4	0.8	0.9	0.3	0.2	1.5
5	Greece	1.4	2.4	0.3	1.3	0.4	0.4	1.6	0.6
6	Germany	0.7	0.9	0.6	1.2	0.7	0.6	0.8	1.1
7	Netherlands	0.4	0.6	0.6	0.8	0.9	0.4	0.6	0.6
8	Vietnam	1.1	1.0	0.6	0.7	0.6	0.1	0.5	0.5
9	Poland	0.5	0.8	0.3	0.8	0.6	0.6	0.1	0.5
10	Lebanon	1.4	0.4	0.1	0.3	0.1	0.0	0.0	0.1

S Sydney, *M* Melbourne, *B* Brisbane, *A* Adelaide, *P* Perth, *H* Hobart, *D* Darwin, *C* Canberra

Source: 1986 Census

Western Australia, the British; and in the Northern Territory, New Zealanders.

A similar pattern emerges at the city scale: Sydney has a 'concentration' of Vietnamese and Lebanese; Melbourne: Greeks, Italians, Vietnamese, Polish, and Yugoslavs; Adelaide: British, Italians, Germans and Polish; Perth: British; Brisbane: New Zealanders; and Darwin: New Zealanders and Greeks. It should be remembered, of course, that these 'concentrations' are only relative and they describe no more than the presence of an above-average proportion of any particular group. These 'concentrations' are in no way socially undesirable. In fact they are entirely to be expected given the nature of the migration process and the characteristics of immigration policy. The process whereby concentrations emerge is perhaps best shown by studies of one of the major new migrant groups, the Vietnamese. Here the tendency has been for concentrations to emerge around former migrant hostels (e.g. at

Cabramatta in Sydney). Such concentrations foster a sense of identity and security. They also reflect migration constraints on a non-English speaking group at a time of economic recession (Burnley, 1989b; Wilson, 1990).

The other interesting thing revealed by Table 1.7 is the fact that overseas born groups are concentrated more in metropolitan areas than in the States as a whole. This metropolitan concentration is slightly less in Queensland and South Australia. This suggests a greater preponderance of overseas-born in the rural economy of these two States, perhaps exemplified by German involvement in vineyards in South Australia and Italian involvement in tobacco growing and sugar cane production in Queensland. The strong metropolitan concentration of the overseas-born population of New South Wales and Victoria reflects their relatively high involvement in city-based manufacturing, particularly in the case of migrants from non-English speaking countries. For example, in 1971 no less than 48 per cent of Yugoslav males worked in manufacturing (Storer, 1980) at a time when the overall national rate showed that only 21 per cent of all males in the labour force worked in manufacturing. Despite such statistics, it is remarkably difficult to generalize about the status of different ethnic groups in the labour force because the labour market is highly fragmented into different metropolitan labour markets (Morrison, 1990). Nevertheless, there is a good deal of evidence that Anglophones get the top jobs and non-Anglophones the unskilled (or at best semi-skilled) jobs (Bottomley, 1988).

The fact that large numbers of migrants have settled in Australia since the Second World War obviously reflects bipartisan support for the immigration program. It therefore suggests that, in the eyes of most Australians, there are net benefits to be gained from immigration. Most usually, when attention has focussed on 'the immigration debate', these net benefits have been perceived in *economic* rather than *social terms* (Norman and Miekle, 1985). Even here, however, opinion has been divided as to the true extent of the economic advantage flowing from a large-scale immigration program. Many commentators have stressed the economic disadvantages of large-scale immigration. The main economic arguments for and against have been summarized briefly in Table 1.8 (see Douglas, 1982; Birrell and Hill, 1979; Shergold, 1984 for more detailed discussion). Clearly, there are both very real advantages and very significant disadvantages to the sort of immigration program that Australia has pursued over the last four decades but it is impossible to quantify these precisely. Whether or not a particular effect of migration is perceived to be good or bad depends very much on the commentator's point of view. As a result it is difficult to say what the precise impact of immigration has been on the Australian economy.

Nevile (1990) has attempted to calculate the level of population growth which maximises living standards. In other words, Nevile looked at the argument that immigration reduces the rate of growth of output per capita

Table 1.8 Perceived advantages and disadvantages of immigration

Advantages	*Disadvantages*
1 Provides a skilled workforce without the costs of education and training	1 Belittles the importance of education and training by encouraging the attitude that skills can be imported
2 Overcomes bottlenecks in the labour market	2 Detracts from labour market planning by fostering the attitude that labour shortages can be solved on an *ad hoc* basis
3 Stimulates aggregate demand (for migrants tend to have a high rate of consumption in years after arrival), thereby encouraging economies of scale in production and increased competitiveness in industry	3 Depresses wage rates and increases unemployment, thereby creating hardship
4 Stimulates the housing and construction industry by increasing demand	4 Creates housing shortages, forcing up rentals
5 Facilitates change in industrial structures because migrants are more mobile geographically, industrially, and occupationally than Australian-born	5 Inhibits structural change because migrants tend to concentrate in inefficient, protected and declining industries (e.g. textiles, footwear, clothing)
6 Promotes inflow of capital, technology, and entrepreneurial spirit	6 Is irrelevant to the promotion of growth because technology tends to come either through direct import or internal company transfer, capital brought by migrants is insignificant compared to capital needs, and entrepreneurial skills are around anyway
7 Raises per capita income of population thereby increasing living standards of the nation	7 Places a heavy demand on public sector social services (e.g. health, education, water, sewerage) and is therefore a burden on the taxpayer
8 Increases population thereby fostering economic development	8 Increases population pressure thereby encouraging environmental degradation

(and hence living standards) by reducing the amount of capital available for the average worker to use. He balanced this against the argument that immigration means increased population growth, increased economic activity, and reduced unemployment. Overall, his view was that the rate of population growth that maximizes living standards is 1.36 per cent per annum (with the proviso that there is very little difference in the effect on living standards of growth rates between 1.1 and 1.6 per cent per annum). Others have been less sanguine and have questioned the wisdom of a large scale immigration policy on environmental grounds (see Day and Rowlands, 1988; Clarke *et al.*, 1990) and in terms of the costs which migrants impose on urban infrastructure (see Murphy *et al.*, 1990).

Given this diversity of opinion, when the politicians responsible for the immigration program have been asked to justify its existence, it is not surprising that they have usually resorted to vague and unobjectionable ideals. Mackellar (1979), for example, said that there were seven main reasons for the immigration program:

1 to supply the labour market with much needed skills;
2 to help growth in the domestic economy;
3 to help in the transference to Australia of new technology;
4 to maintain a youthful population despite a falling birthrate;
5 to promote the importation of new cultures so that Australians can understand themselves and others better (and thereby build more enduring relations with other countries);
6 to facilitate a humanitarian response to the problems faced by refugees; and
7 to help with family reunion.

The last three points suggest a *social* rationale for immigration, and raise the question of what happens to migrants once they arrive. Do they share justly in the resources of the Australian community? Do they have equal access with the Australian-born population to the services that are available? Are they accepted by the Australian-born population or is there a degree of resentment? These questions only recently became the subject of serious study. Before that, the immigration debate focussed overwhelmingly on selection procedures and criteria rather than on the question of integrating migrants once they arrived on Australia's shores. In hindsight this emphasis was both misplaced and unfortunate, particularly as many Australians are reasonably ignorant about the numbers of new settlers arriving in the country and exhibit a latent dislike or fear of immigrants (Buchanan, 1976). In the late 1970s, however, a number of reports focussed attention on the treatment of migrants in Australian society.

In 1977 the Australian Population and Immigration Council published a report which sought to stimulate debate about immigration by advocating a net intake of approximately 50 000 settlers a year. One of the first major responses to this document came from the Australian Ethnic Affairs Council (1978) which noted that such an intake would necessarily involve accepting migrants from a wide variety of cultural backgrounds, and it therefore sought to establish guidelines that would be appropriate in the development of a 'multicultural' Australia.

Unfortunately, the term 'multiculturalism' is bandied around a good deal without necessarily being clearly defined. For example, 'multiculturalism' is often used by politicians to mean little more than a tolerance of immigrants.

In order to progress beyond this sort of vague ideal, the Australian Ethnic Affairs Council re-focussed attention on some of the issues raised by the Australian Population and Immigration Council (1977). In particular, they emphasised three critical considerations for migrants to participate fully in a multicultural Australia.

1 The government should promote *social cohesion* by ensuring that society's resources are used for the well-being of the entire community rather than for the betterment of sectional groups.
2 There should be *equality of opportunity* so that individuals are neither advantaged nor disadvantaged in their access to resources by belonging to some particular category of the population.
3 All groups should have the right to maintain their *cultural identity* and in this way have the ability to develop a sense of belonging and attachment to a particular way of living.

Pursuit of these principles would, it was felt, lead to the emergence of a situation where society embraces groups of people with different cultural identities. In this way a truly multicultural Australia would be born. However, the Australian Ethnic Affairs Council warned that, in moving towards this goal, Australia must be careful to avoid both cultural stratification (where certain cultural groups are forced into inferior positions in society) and the differentiation of cultures by regions, because both of these states of affairs would rupture the harmony of Australian society.

The Australian Ethnic Affairs Council (1978) was at pains to point out that multiculturalism in Australia contains the seeds of many different kinds of future development. Multiculturalism can manifest itself in different ways: it can show up in folk dancing and folk costumes; it can show up in private lives (the tendency for members of some cultural groups to live close to each other and to inter-marry); or it can show up in 'structural pluralism', a tendency for different cultural groups to set up their own institutional structures and organizations, paralleling the organizations that exist in mainstream Australian society.

The desirability or otherwise of structural pluralism was explored in a joint publication from the Australian Population and Immigration Council and the Australian Ethnic Affairs Council (1979). Together these bodies stressed that ethnic cultures cannot exist apart from the groups that are the carriers of those cultures and that, in order to maintain a culture, a group will need formal and informal organizations. The report suggested that four options are open to the government in dealing with ethnic groups and in promoting the continuance of cultural identity:

1 to maintain existing institutions and organizations within society but encourage the advancement of minorities (e.g. the accelerated promotion of ethnic police or teachers);
2 to build into the public service a formal quota system in order to protect minorities by ensuring their employment and representation;

3 to encourage the creation of branches within existing organizations to cater specifically for migrants (e.g. ethnic boy scout troops); or
4 to encourage ethnic organizations that parallel, and perhaps therefore compete with, institutions already existing in Australia.

Generally speaking, Australian governments have not seriously considered any of these options. There has been a reluctance to countenance the fourth option for fear that the structural pluralism inherent in it would in some way encourage divisiveness in Australia. In fact, it was largely with this in mind that foreign language newspapers were regulated immediately after the Second World War. Similarly, non-English language broadcasting was not condoned until the 1970s. Indeed, in the early years of post-war immigration, the basic assumption of government policy was very much that migrants would be 'assimilated' into Australian society with a result that 'ethnicity would become a residual phenomenon manifested only in the costumes and dances of folk festivals' (Zubrzycki, 1977). When this clearly did not happen, official thinking drifted more to the goal of 'integration', the notion that migrants would become full members of Australian society while, at the same time, retaining some of their cultural identity. Of course, once the maintenance of cultural identity was encouraged, it became inevitable that Australia would sooner or later become recognised as a 'pluralistic' society, held together by a common bond but containing groups that differ in terms of ethnicity, culture, language, religion, lifestyle, and so on. A recognition of pluralism hastened discussion of multiculturalism.

Multiculturalism as a goal has had the support of all major political parties in Australia, as has the post-war immigration program. This reflects the prevailing Australian view that ethnicity is irrelevant to the political process because the units that are of political significance (e.g. parties, unions) cut across ethnic backgrounds. Conventional thinking seems to be that if ethnic minorities are to become involved in the political process in any way then it should be as pressure groups lobbying for support, rather than as formal political units (Australian Ethnic Affairs Council, 1978).

The selection and treatment of migrants was not an issue of major political controversy for the best part of four decades after the inception of the massive post-war immigration program. This changed in 1984 largely as a result of the questioning by Blainey (1984) of the level of Asian immigration. Australia has always had a proud record of taking in political refugees. This humanitarian response, possibly coupled with a sense of guilt over the Vietnam War, led to the Australian government, with the support of all major political parties and the trade union movement, accepting Indo-Chinese refugees after the fall of Saigon in 1975. The most vivid image of these refugees was of 'boat people' arriving on Australia's northern shores but in actual fact the overwhelming majority of the more than 90 000 Indo-Chinese refugees who arrived in the period 1976–1986 were from refugee camps in Malaysia and Thailand or directly from Vietnam as a result of family reunion schemes. Once in Australia these refugees tended to concentrate in certain areas, often around Commonwealth migrant hostels. For example about 30 per cent of the Indo-Chinese refugees in New South Wales live in the Sydney municipality of Fairfield (Shergold, 1984).

The arrival of Indo-Chinese refugees coincided with a period of economic recession when unemployment was reasonably high. The refugees fared poorly in this situation, given problems of language and training, and as a result suffered extremely high levels of unemployment. In 1984, for instance, when unemployment in the Australian-born workforce stood at about 8 per cent, 41 per cent of Vietnamese migrants were unemployed. Political refugees from the Middle East were only slightly better off, with 33 per cent of Lebanese refugees unemployed (Blainey, 1984). Clearly the refugees were not displacing large numbers of Australian-born workers. Nevertheless there was an element of resentment towards such groups, perhaps best exemplified by inner-city graffiti. This resentment found a focus when Blainey made a speech which, in passing, offered the observation that the level of Asian immigration might be proceeding at a level beyond that which public opinion supported. The result was instant furore as a great many commentators projected on to Blainey's words their own views, both for and against immigration.

In fact Asian immigration had begun to grow significantly before the advent of the first 'boat people'. Asians provided 14 per cent of permanent settlers in 1974, 25 per cent in 1975, and 33 per cent in 1976 (Blainey, 1984). The reasons for this change are to be found in the altered procedures by which Australia selects migrants. After the demise of the 'White Australia policy' and in order to promote a truly non-discriminatory immigration policy, Australia moved in 1979 to a Numerical Multifactor Assessment System (NUMAS) whereby intending migrants were allocated points to reflect such things as family ties, occupational skills, fluency in English, employment record, age, and education. Acceptance for the immigration program depended on individuals attaining a minimum points score. In short, neither ethnicity nor racial characteristics had any direct bearing on an individual's likelihood of being selected as a migrant, and even fluency in English was dropped for a while as a required characteristic.

Predictably, the settlers most anxious to take advantage of the government's policy of fostering family reunion were the most recent arrivals, Asian migrants. After all, among these were many who had had family ties ruptured by war in the relatively recent past. In the first eight months of 1982, in relation to every 1000 settlers already resident in Australia, the Vietnamese sponsored 50 relatives to join them, Filipinos 37 relatives, Hong Kong residents 31 relatives, and Malaysians 23 relatives. This contrasts with 4 relatives per 1000 British migrants and one per 1000 Greeks and Italians (Blainey, 1984). It is easy to understand, therefore, how Asian immigration came to account for almost 48 per cent of permanent settlers in 1984 (although it should be noted that, in these immigration statistics, 'Asia' refers to the lands east of the Mediterranean, an area much more extensive than popular Australian perceptions of 'Asia'). It is equally easy to understand why certain people began to talk about the 'Asianization' of Australia (see Introduction). Of course, another factor which contributed to the increasing relative importance of Asian immigration was the cut-back in the overall level of permanent new settlers and the decline in arrivals from 'traditional' sources in Europe.

The net effect of Blainey's remarks was to stimulate debate about immigration and about the policy of multiculturalism which underlies the treatment of migrants once they are in the country. The importance and urgency of this debate cannot be overstated. If immigration were to continue at the present rate, then Australia would gain an extra ten million people over the next forty years, 35 per cent of them settling in Sydney given that this is now the principal port of entry (Betts *et al.*, 1991). The planning problems arising from such growth are prodigious. Notwithstanding this, the debate about immigration and multiculturalism in the late 1980s was important in another sense: for the first time it forced many Australians to ask what was meant by 'multiculturalism'. Academics made a substantial contribution to this debate. Foster and Stockley (1988), for example, traced multiculturalism from the pre-Whitlam era to the time of Hawke and examined the threat to multiculturalism posed by the Hawke Government's economic rationalism and vision of the 'clever country'. They saw three possible roles for multiculturalism in the future:

1 as a simple slogan, devoid of much meaning;
2 as a means of politicising ethnic affairs and aiming at genuine institutional reform so as to cater better for ethnic minorities; and
3 as an ongoing critique of mainstream Australian culture.

To a certain extent, similar sentiments lay behind Jayasuriya's (1990) critique of multiculturalism. Jayasuriya argued that, as a social ideal and pragmatic response to mass immigration policy, Australian multiculturalism may have exhausted its utility with the result that we need to think again about what multiculturalism involves. In Jayasuriya's view, the conventional model of multiculturalism (highlighting ethnic identity and thereby focussing on 'life style' rather than 'life chances') is becoming increasingly irrelevant to the new wave of migrants from Asia who are confronted with a changing social reality and the consequences of global economic restructuring (see also Bullivant, 1989).

Multiculturalism might well have been a sound strategy for alleviating the stresses of migration and the attendant sensations of alienation and rejection felt by newcomers, but its time as a 'psychic shelter' has probably passed. Indeed, Jayasuriya drew a distinction between 'identity politics' (where the emphasis is on helping people because of their membership of a particular group) and 'rights politics' (where the emphasis is on equity in the distribution of society's resources).

> By resorting to 'identity politics', Australian multicultural policies have failed to address important issues such as labour market performance, gender inequalities, racism, discrimination, and full participation in the structures of society which lay more in the public than the private domain. (Jayasuriya 1990, p. 55)

The confusion that surrounds the term 'multiculturalism' was demonstrated very clearly in an Office of Multicultural Affairs survey of what the term meant to the electorate (Foster and Seitz 1990, Table 1.9). Clearly, there are widely held positive and negative views both about multiculturalism in general and about its impact on such things as cultural identity, social justice, and economic efficiency. This variety of opinion is important because it was against this background that the Committee to Advise on Australia's

Table 1.9 Public views on multiculturalism

	Multiculturalism in general	
Positive	*Negative*	*Neutral/Factual*
Helps tourism & trade	Deprives Australians of jobs	Basis of Australia's immigration policy
Provides greater variety of food, music, dance	Migrants get too much government help	
Promotes a fair go for all	Creates suburbs with high concentrations of ethnic groups	Is a fact of life in Australia
Necessary if people from different cultures are to live in harmony	Undermines loyalty to Australia	
	Specific components of multiculturalism	
	Positive	*Negative*
Cultural identity	Provides greater variety of food, music, dance	Creates suburbs with high concentrations of ethnic groups
	Necessary if people from different cultures are to live in harmony	Undermines loyalty to Australia
Social justice	Promotes a fair go for all	Migrants get too much government help
Economic efficiency	Helps tourism and trade	Deprives Australians of jobs

Source: Foster and Seitz (1990; p. 283)

Immigration Policies (popularly known as the FitzGerald Committee) reported in 1988 (Department of Immigration, Local Government and Ethnic Affairs, 1988). In simple terms, this Committee's brief was to address the relationship between immigration and economic, social, and cultural development. In its report, the Committee argued that times were tough and that, as a consequence, immigration policy should be tailored to the best interests of Australia.

> It is of critical importance to the consensus on immigration and to immigrants themselves that what we demand of the rest of the populace we demand also of immigrants. And in current economic strategy this means entrepreneurship, skills and multi-skills, and some self sacrifice. (Department of Immigration, Local Government and Ethnic Affairs, 1988; p. 15).

In short, the Committee advocated a focus on young, entrepreneurial and skilled migrants prepared to make a commitment to Australia, this commitment to be made evident through such things as taking out Australian citizenship. In other words, the Committee recommended that immigration policy be instrumental in developing an Australian identity and an Australian role in a changing world. In order to encourage the hitherto largely symbolic acquisition of citizenship, the Committee recommended linking welfare entitlements and privileges (including the right to sponsor family reunion migrants) to the possession of citizenship. In numerical terms, the FitzGerald Report suggested that 150 000 migrants be admitted in 1989 (likely to result in a net immigration rate of 125 000) with a slight decrease in family reunion migration and an increase in the 'open' category (to be decided on the basis of labour market skills, entrepreneurship and special talents, age, language capacity, kinship, links with Australia, and the attributes of spouses) (see Birrell and Betts, 1988).

Basically, then, the FitzGerald Committee came down in favour of a high level of immigration. It concluded that, given widespread misgivings about multiculturalism, community support for a high level of immigration could only be sustained if such immigration were obviously contributing to the well-being of Australia as a whole, hence the emphasis on entrepreneurial ability and citizenship. This recommendation implied something rather different from the bipartisan policy that had developed over four decades since the Second World War, and perhaps explains why the government has been slow to either implement or reject the recommendations.

The changing Aboriginal population

The hard times suffered by political refugees in the 1970s and 1980s should not obscure the fact that Aborigines are the ethnic minority who have suffered most in Australia. From the time of the first British settlement Aborigines were dispossessed, disregarded, discriminated against, and disadvantaged.

Early colonists had an 'unfaltering belief in the superiority of western culture and its right to usurp, convert and distort all 'lesser' cultures' (Gale, 1977; p. 362). In many areas, Aborigines had their traditional way of life shattered. They fell prey to previously unencountered European diseases. Some were deliberately killed. Many more died as a direct or indirect effect of starvation brought on by the loss of water holes and traditional food supplies. White Australian attitudes to indigenous people were partly based on the belief that Aborigines were an inferior race, 'fading away' in the face of western culture. Although the precise number of Aborigines in Australia in 1788 is not known, the Aboriginal population suffered so much at the hands of white settlers that it had fallen to, at most, one fifth of its former level at the time when the 1921 Census revealed an Aboriginal population of about 62 000. At this time only 6000 Aborigines remained in New South Wales and 15 500 in Queensland (Burnley, 1976).

The presumption that Aborigines were dying out encouraged a paternalistic attitude towards them on the part of white Australians. A system of missions and reserves was set up, partly to remove Aborigines from cattle killing and partly to enable an effort to be made to improve Aboriginal living conditions (Burnley, 1976). In practice, however, conditions on the reserves were often worse than outside. This was partly because the limited education and vocational training offered to reserve Aborigines, together with their complete absence from decision-making roles, resulted in a situation where all initiative was squashed. 'The years of seclusion spent on reserves armed many Aborigines with a deep sense of injustice' with a result that this may be virtually the only trait which the different groups of Aborigines of mixed descent have in common (Gale, 1977; p. 363). Even as late as the 1960s there were many laws in force, notably in Queensland, which restrained Aborigines' movement, controlled their places of residence, and put constraints on their civil rights (Rowley, 1972 and see Chapter 3). The prevailing attitude, until the relatively recent political awakening of Aboriginal consciousness, was that Aborigines should be led into more effective imitation of 'white Australia' in order that they might advance into the white community (Rowley, 1972).

Section 127 of the *Australian Constitution* decreed that 'Aboriginal natives shall not be counted' in censuses. As a result it is extremely difficult to assess the number of Aborigines in Australia prior to the deletion of Section 127 in 1967. Whatever estimates are available tend to come from government departments responsible for Aboriginal welfare. Even after 1967, data can be confusing. Table 1.10, for example, shows the number of Aborigines enumerated at Censuses in 1971, 1976, 1981 and 1986. The massive increase in numbers between 1971 and 1976 and the subsequent decline in 1981 owe more to the phrasing of Census questions concerning Aboriginal affiliation than they do to demographic changes. The increase in 1986 represents both population growth and a greater willingness on the part of individuals to identify themselves as Aborigines. Despite the fluctuations from census to

Table 1.10 Australia's Aboriginal population

	1971		*1976*		*1981*		*1986*	
	No.	*Total pop. (%)*	*No.*	*Total pop. (%)*	*No.*	*Total pop. (%)*	*No.*	*Total pop. (%)*
New South Wales	23 873	0.5	40 450	0.8	35 367	0.7	59 011	1.1
Victoria	6 371	0.2	14 760	0.4	6 057	0.2	12 611	0.3
Queensland	31 922	1.7	41 345	2.0	44 698	1.9	61 268	2.4
South Australia	7 299	0.6	10 174	0.9	9 825	0.8	14 291	1.1
Western Australia	22 181	2.2	26 126	2.3	31 351	2.5	37 789	2.7
Tasmania	671	0.2	2 942	0.7	2 688	0.6	6 716	1.5
NT	23 381	27.0	23 751	24.5	29 088	23.6	34 739	22.4
ACT	255	0.2	827	0.4	823	0.4	1 220	0.5
Australia	115 953	0.9	160 915	1.2	159 897	1.1	227 645	1.5

census, it is probably accurate to say that 1.0–1.5 per cent of Australia's population is Aboriginal. The actual number of Aborigines and their proportion of the total population are expected to increase reasonably quickly in the future for two reasons: first, the birth rate is high and very much higher than for white Australians, and secondly, there is a high proportion of females of child-bearing age within the overall Aboriginal population (Figure 1.7).

One statistic often used in projecting natural increases in populations is the Net Reproduction Rate (NRR). At any one time the NRR is a measure, relative to the total population, of how many girls are born who survive to reproductive age. The statistic is computed so that a NRR of 1.0 indicates a population that will exactly reproduce itself. It is difficult to estimate the net reproduction rate for Aborigines because of the dearth of reliable information on both fertility and mortality, especially in isolated parts of the continent. Despite this, the National Population Inquiry (1975b) suggested that the NRR for Aborigines in the early 1970s was approximately 2.18. At that time the birth rate for Aborigines was about 35 per 1000 and the death rate about 16 per 1000 (although there was considerable variability from region to region). Given these figures, the Aboriginal population would increase very rapidly. The National Population Inquiry suggested, however, that both the birth rate and the death rate would fall as a result of better health care programs and the wider acceptance of birth control techniques. Indeed their prediction was that the NRR for Aborigines would reach 1.00 by 2001. If this prediction is accurate, the National Population Inquiry predicted that the Aboriginal population at the turn-of-the-century will be approximately 230 000 of whom 30 per cent will be under 15 years of age. If the net reproduction rate of the early 1970s were to continue unchanged, the Aboriginal population in 2001 would be about 285 000 of whom 45 per cent would be under 15 years of age. (These figures are at odds with those shown

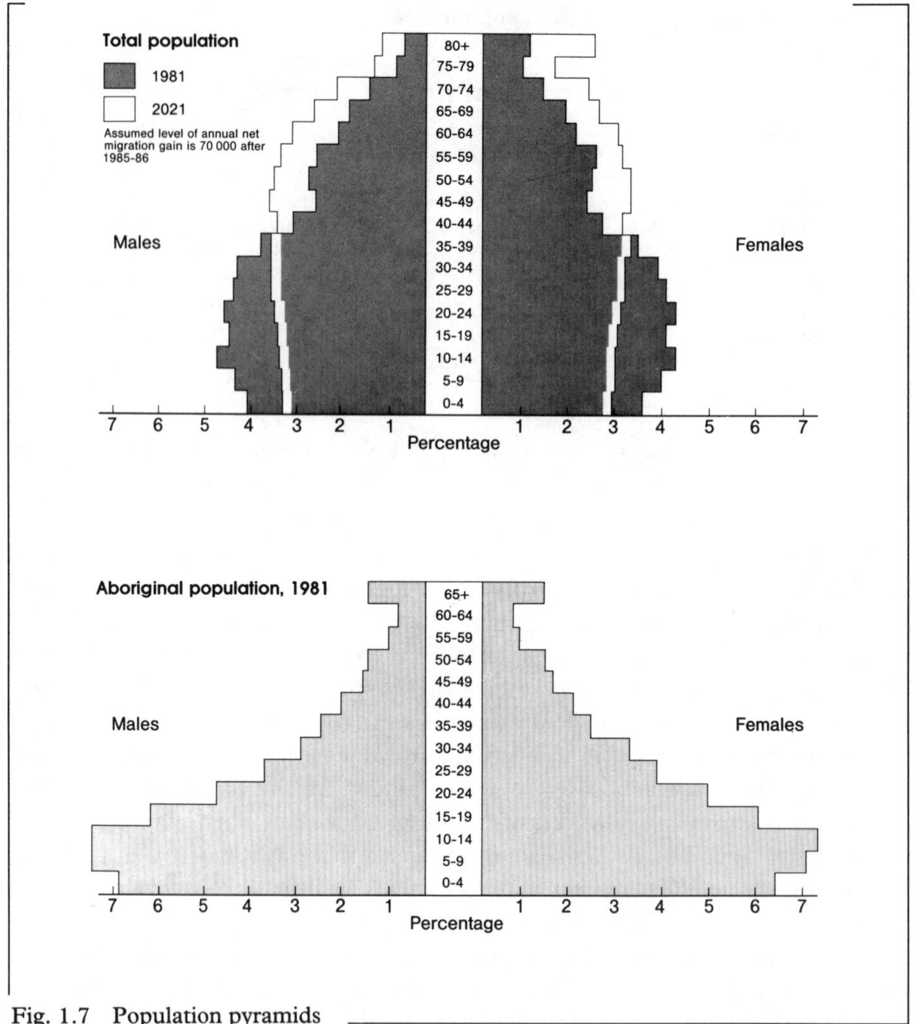

Fig. 1.7 Population pyramids
Source: Census of Australia 1981

for the 1986 Census in Table 1.10 because the National Population Inquiry figures do not take stock of the growing tendency for individuals to identify themselves as Aborigines.) So the number of Aboriginal children attending school will rise by between 50 and 100 per cent between 1975 and 2001. This is obviously going to place demands on the education system. Moreover, these demands, like those for housing, health care, and community infrastructure, will be geographically selective because the Aboriginal population is very rapidly becoming a metropolitan population.

Table 1.11 shows the percentage of Aborigines living in rural areas, in towns with populations of between 1000 and 99 999, and in cities with more

Table 1.11 The urbanisation of Aborigines (%)

	NSW	*Vic*	*Qld*	*SA*	*WA*	*Tas*	*NT*	*ACT*	*Aust.*
1961									
Cities (> 100 000)	9.5	21.8	4.4	10.5	4.2	18.4	–	2.2	5.0
Towns (1000–99 999)	30.1	26.8	21.9	13.8	9.8	34.2	9.5	–	17.4
Rural areas	60.4	51.4	73.7	75.7	86.0	47.4	90.5	97.8	77.6
1971									
Cities (> 100 000)	27.3	54.8	9.1	25.0	10.4	29.5	–	34.9	14.9
Towns (1000–99 999)	39.4	30.2	32.1	21.1	29.7	43.2	17.5	–	29.4
Rural areas	33.3	15.0	58.8	53.9	59.9	27.3	82.5	65.1	55.7
1981									
Cities (> 100 000)	31.8	47.0	14.6	32.7	20.7	22.7	–	78.7	19.7
Towns (1000–99 999)	45.6	39.8	41.0	31.2	35.9	48.3	32.0	–	38.7
Rural areas	22.6	13.2	44.4	36.1	43.4	29.0	68.0	21.3	41.6

Source: National Population Inquiry (1975b); 1981 Census

than 100 000 population in 1961, 1971, and 1981. The change is striking. Overall, the big city population has grown from 5 per cent of the total to almost 20 per cent. Conversely, the proportion of Aborigines in rural areas has fallen from about 78 per cent to about 42 per cent. However, as with all migratory patterns, the trends in Aboriginal migration are complex. Some of this complexity is described in Taylor's (1989a) account of Aboriginal employment in the construction of the new RAAF Tindal airbase in the Northern Territory. In this case, government attempts to foster Aboriginal employment had the effect of stimulating long-distance migration rather than helping local communities.

National demographic trends

The most far-reaching analysis of Australia's current demographic trends appeared in the National Population Inquiry (1975a). This report traced the growth of the nation's population. It also pointed out that in 1971 life expectancy was 68 years for males and 74 years for females. By the mid-1980s these figures had increased to 71 and 78 years respectively. In addition the report showed how the average number of children born to each marriage fell from about 6.0 at Federation, to 5.0 in 1911, to 4.0 in 1921, to 3.0 in 1941, to somewhere between 2.4 and 2.9 in the 1970s. Of more significance, however, were the Inquiry's conclusions in relation to population projections for the future. In order to make such projections, the Inquiry calculated the Net Reproduction Rate (NRR). This was found to have fluctuated considerably in the fifty years prior to the National Population Inquiry. In 1920 the rate stood at 1.4 before falling to about 1.1 in 1930 (and below 1.0 for a time in the 1930s). In 1940 the NRR stood at almost exactly 1.0. It increased to 1.4 in 1950 and 1.6 in 1960 but by 1970 it was down to about 1.1 and still falling. In 1991 the NRR stood at about 0.9. The National Population Inquiry concluded that population growth was likely to be considerably less than was at that time popularly imagined. So instead of a turn of the century population of between 20 and 25 million, as some projections had suggested (Australian Institute of Urban Studies, 1971), the National Population Inquiry indicated that, unless there was a major upsurge in the NRR, the population in 2001 might be as low as 15 900 000 plus whatever net immigration occurred. For example, a net immigration rate of 50 000 a year would lead to an Australian population of 17.6 million in 2001.

Such projections are fraught with danger. Birth rates, and hence NRRs, can change quickly, as is amply demonstrated in Figure 1.3. Currently the birth rate is about 15–16 per 1000 population which, when compared with a death rate of 7–8 persons per 1000 population, yields a natural increase of about 8 persons per 1000 population. Given the historical record as set out in Figure 1.3, little change can be expected in the death rate. The birth rate is however likely to fluctuate and, as a result, a substantial growth in the rate of natural increase is quite possible. Similarly, migrant intake can be adjusted to suit both the whim of the government at a particular time and perceptions of what would be appropriate given the state of the economy (Table 1.2). Nevertheless, in the absence of a 'baby boom', population growth will be only modest.

'Booms' are of course entirely possible and two have occurred in post-Federation Australia. The first was between 1920 and 1922 and can be largely explained as a 'catching up' of births postponed at the time of the First World War. The second 'baby boom' began in 1948. In some senses this, too, entailed a 'catching up' of postponed births. However more was involved. There was, for example, a simultaneous 'marriage boom', particularly between 1947 and 1954, with more women marrying and marrying earlier. Additionally, between 1954 and 1961 there was an increase in the number of children born to each marriage. After 1961 this fertility level declined, particularly in the 1970s, as more and more women entered the paid work-force (Department of Immigration and Ethnic Affairs, 1984). The other factor besides 'baby booms' that can affect population projections is a change in the rate at which migrants return to their country of origin. Over the period 1947–1973, 21 per cent of British and Irish migrants returned home, 31 per cent of Germans, 25 per cent of Dutch, and 23 per cent of Italians. In contrast, only 7 per cent of refugees leave Australia. Given the relatively high refugee intake in recent years, there may well be less loss of migrants than has been the case in the 1960s and 1970s. This, in turn, may mean net immigration in the order of 70 000 a year and a turn-of-the-century population of 18.9 million.

The changes outlined by the National Population Inquiry (1975a) and subsequently examined by the Department of Immigration and Ethnic Affairs (1984) have very important implications. To begin with, they give a reasonably accurate estimate of the number of people for whom the Australian government will be catering in the future. Such projections are set out in Table 1.12. Of course, the population will not only grow; it will also change its age profile. Accordingly, Table 1.13 describes the likely age structure in the years 2001 and 2021. Quite obviously, unless there is a change in the birth rate and or the level of immigration, Australia will have an increasingly elderly population and, moreover, a population growing at a steadily slower rate. (It should be noted, of course, that Table 1.12 shows only the relative size of age cohorts. The apparent decline in the number of children aged 0–14 is therefore perhaps a little misleading because the *actual number* of children in Australia will increase until 2021, as a result of overall population growth. In short, the percentage shares set out in Table 1.13 are shares of an increasing total.)

Nevertheless, the rate of increase of the 65+ age group has two fundamental implications:

Table 1.12 Population projections for Australia

Year	*Projected population*	*Annual growth (%)*	*Median age*
1991	17 060 900	1.17	32
2001	18 912 400	0.92	35
2011	20 490 400	0.74	37
2021	21 918 100	0.61	39

Source: Department of Immigration and Ethnic Affairs (1984)

Table 1.13 The future age distribution of Australia's population (%)

	Age groups		
Year	*0–14*	*15–64*	*65+*
1983	24.4	65.6	10.0
2001	21.2	67.0	11.8
2021	18.8	65.3	15.9

Source: Department of Immigration and Ethnic Affairs (1984)

1 Because the rate of increase of this age cohort is faster than that of the working age population (even assuming no change in the age of retirement), there will be a shift in the ratio of supporters to supported within the welfare system with relatively fewer taxpayers having to support relatively more pensioners. Put another way, there will be 0.24 persons aged 65+ for each person aged 15–64 in 2021, as opposed to 0.15 in 1983. This shift comes out clearly in the age pyramids contained in Figure 1.7 which show, among other things, an increasing ratio of females to males among the over-sixties.

2 The second implication is that the most rapidly growing age cohort is going to be the very one which places the highest demands on the welfare system, notably for health care. Hugo (1986) has dramatically illustrated this shift by comparing 1981 sickness levels for the 65+ age group with projections for the year 2001. He estimates that the number with chronic diseases will increase from 1 132 900 to 1 774 900, the number confined to the home will increase from 207 400 to 370 300, and the number with some sort of handicap will grow from 450 900 to 783 100. Clearly the cost of catering for these groups is going to be substantial. It is not surprising, therefore, that some people have argued for an increased level of immigration to combat ageing. C. Young (1988; 1990) has demonstrated, however, that such a policy would be ineffective in that Australia's aged population will stabilise in the middle of next century at 20–22 percent of the total, irrespective of whether immigration runs at 50 000 or 150 000 a year. If ageing needs to be combatted, pro-natalist policies might be the answer (e.g. encouraging the community as a whole to bear the cost of children).

Internal migration

A high proportion of Australia's population changes its place of residence in a year (Hugo, 1988). This is important because, in the absence of significant inter-regional variations in fertility (Wilson, 1990), it is internal migration (coupled with overseas immigration) which serves to redistribute Australia's population. Data on internal migration can be obtained from the five-yearly censuses and from an annual survey of about two-thirds of 1 per cent of the population conducted for most of the 1980s (see Australian Bureau of Statistics, 1987). These sources reveal that, in a twelve month period, about 16 per cent of people change their place of residence. Of these, about 19 per cent migrate interstate while 81 per cent move within their State of residence. Males are slightly more mobile than females overall, with 102 males changing residence to every 100 females. The most mobile age group comprises individuals aged 20–29. According to the Australian Bureau of Statistics, about 36 per cent of Australians aged 20–24 changed their place of residence in the year to 30 June 1986. The figure for individuals aged 25–29 was 31 per cent (Commonwealth of Australia, 1986). The actual level of mobility varies from State to State. For each 1000 population, the number of 'movers' in the various States in the year ended 30 June 1986 were as follows: New South Wales 146; Victoria 136; Queensland 191; South Australia 154; Western Australia 200; Tasmania 167; Northern Territory 236; and Australian Capital Territory 169 (Australian Bureau of Statistics, 1987). Mobility is clearly greatest in the northern and western parts of the continent, perhaps reflecting resource development and the pioneer status of some of those areas.

Predictably, the majority of moves are over only a relatively short distance. After all, moves within familiar territory involve no major upheaval to social life, feelings of belonging, and day-to-day activity. The types of migratory moves made by Australians in the year ended 30 June 1986 are given in Figure 1.8. This shows that the most common type of move was one which

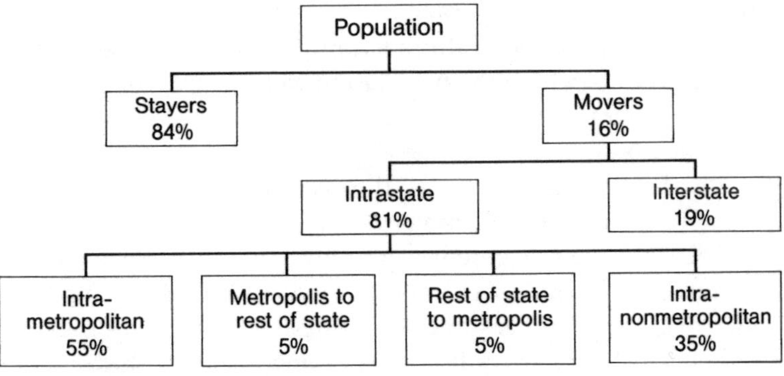

Fig. 1.8 Types of migratory moves within Australia, 1986
Source: Calculated from Australian Bureau of Statistics (1987)

Table 1.14 The number of migratory moves made in 1985–86

	Number of moves ('000s)							
	NSW	*Vic*	*Qld*	*SA*	*WA*	*Tas*	*NT*	*ACT*
Into the State or Territory	56.9	41.4	66.3	23.7	26.1	9.8	12.7	15.4
Out of the State or Territory	78.2	48.8	48.6	20.3	15.6	12.7	12.0	16.2
Within the State or Territory	722.3	509.7	412.7	182.8	248.5	63.1	20.6	26.9

Source: Australian Bureau of Statistics (1987)

occurred within a metropolitan area. Second most common were moves within the non-metropolitan parts of the States, again very many of them short-distance moves. The numbers of moves taking place in each State, as revealed by the Australian Bureau of Statistics' 1986 survey, are presented in Table 1.14.

Aside from the high level of intrastate migration in relation to interstate migration, this Table shows that in 1985/86 some States were net losers of people whereas other States were net gainers: New South Wales, Victoria, Tasmania and the ACT lost population while Queensland, South Australia, Western Australia, and the Northern Territory had net gains in population through interstate migration. It would be unwise, of course, to place too much reliance on figures for net migration in a single year, particularly when those figures are based on only a small sample survey. A far more authoritative picture can be gained from looking at Census returns. Table 1.15 shows the net changes to the population of each State and Territory over the period 1966–1986.

Queensland and Western Australia have obviously been the big winners and New South Wales, Victoria, and Tasmania the losers. The net loss for the Northern Territory between 1971 and 1976 is accounted for by the massive evacuation following Cyclone Tracy in 1974, and the more recent reversal stems from cuts in Commonwealth spending programs (Taylor, 1989b). A more precise picture of where the population gains come from is presented in Figure 1.9 which demonstrates quite dramatically the northward and westward drift of the population.

The westward shift is in response to the economic development of Western Australia generally, as reflected in economic growth in the Perth region. It does not reflect massive movement to mining areas because such areas tend to have capital intensive rather than labour intensive undertakings.

The move to Queensland is somewhat different. It predates the movement to the west (Queensland's net inflows beginning just after the Second World War, in contrast to Western Australia's net inflows from the early 1960s

Table 1.15 Population change resulting from internal migration

	1966–71	*1971–76*	*1976–81*	*1981–86*
New South Wales	- 20 069	- 74 010	- 24 470	- 68 900
Victoria	- 26 848	- 38 736	- 55 420	- 41 800
Queensland	+ 15 388	+ 65 438	+ 83 558	+ 95 700
South Australia	- 16 865	+ 6 247	- 14 809	- 8 300
Western Australia	+ 22 564	+ 19 625	+ 10 597	+ 17 200
Tasmania	- 6 810	- 4 044	- 4 515	- 1 800
Northern Territory	+ 8 816	- 875	+ 4 458	+ 3 400
Australian Capital Territory	+ 23 824	+ 26 357	+ 601	+ 4 700

Source: Australian Bureau of Statistics (1984a); Commonwealth of Australia (1990)

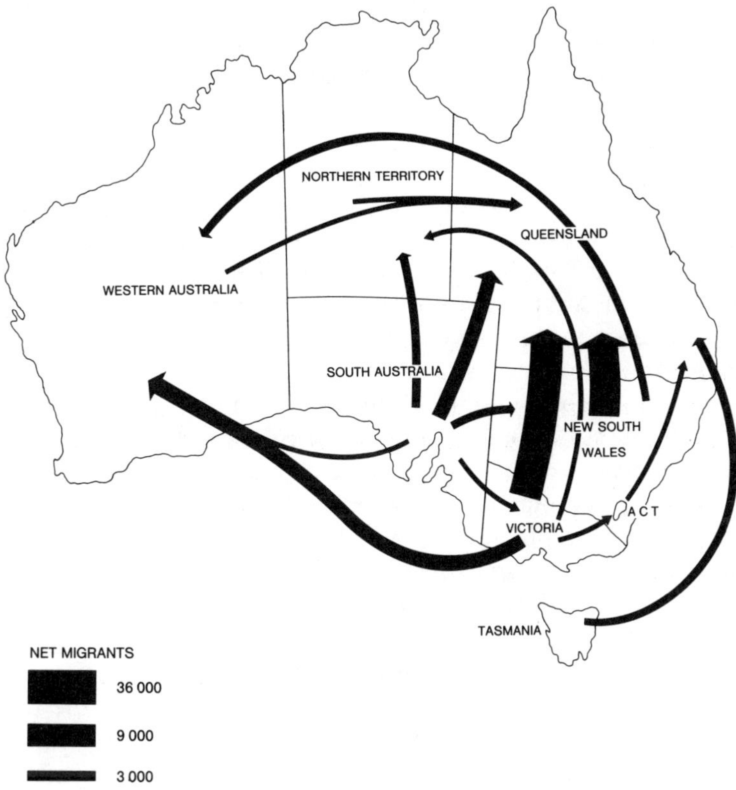

Fig. 1.9 Interstate migration

onwards) and it probably reflects both the economic development of that State (mining, tourism, farming) as well as climatic attractiveness. In recent years, too, Queensland has had a State government that has attempted to foster in-migration by putting economic development above most other considerations and by abolishing death duties, thereby enhancing the attractiveness of the area to retired people (a move subsequently copied in the other States).

Although the level of interstate migration is low relative to the level of intrastate migration, the trend in recent years has been for increasing numbers of Australians to migrate to other States. Moreover the rate of such migration is itself increasing. For example, in the period 1966–1971, 461 000 people migrated across State borders, a figure which represented a migration rate of 40 per 1000 resident population. By 1971–1976 there were 569 500 interstate migrants (equivalent to a rate of 46 per 1000 population) and in 1976–1981 651 200 interstate migrants (a rate of 49 per 1000 population). Compared to intrastate migration, movement to other States was a slightly more male dominated activity (with 107 male migrants to every 100 female migrants). Interestingly, the interstate migration of retirement age groups started to become numerically significant in the 1970s, manifesting itself very much in a movement northward along the eastern seaboard (Australian Bureau of Statistics, 1984a).

The reasons behind migration are many and varied. Generally speaking, in advanced western countries such as Australia, approximately 15 per cent of all changes of residence may be thought of as 'forced', the remainder being 'voluntary' moves (Walmsley and Lewis, 1984). Moves brought on by eviction, demolition of dwellings, retirement, ill-health, and divorce figure prominently in the motivation of 'forced' migrants. For the most part the migratory response to this sort of stress involves only a short-distance move. 'Voluntary' moves, in contrast, can be over much greater distances. Indeed the motivation behind 'voluntary' moves seems to vary with the distance involved. Thus a survey by the Australian Bureau of Statistics (1987) has shown that the main reasons for intrastate migration were to do with housing needs (31 per cent of migrants), location (especially the desire to be closer to friends, relatives, workplace, or school — 19 per cent), and employment (10 per cent). In contrast, employment loomed much larger in the reasons for interstate migration (41 per cent of cases), and housing was very much less important (4 per cent).

Itemising reasons makes the decision to migrate seem simple and rational. Despite this, the pattern that emerges in the mapping of the totality of individual migration decisions may be complex. Even when consideration is restricted to net flows (i.e. arrivals less departures), the overall pattern may seem confused, particularly for intrastate migration.

In contrast to maps of net interstate migration, which show clear general trends (Figure 1.9), maps of intrastate movement, such as the example of New South Wales portrayed in Figure 1.10, reveal countervailing flows despite a general drift towards the coast and towards the north of the state. This coastward and northerly movement is in itself interesting because it reflects on the reasons listed above as being important in migration decisions. Moves from Sydney to the north coast, the predominant migration path in

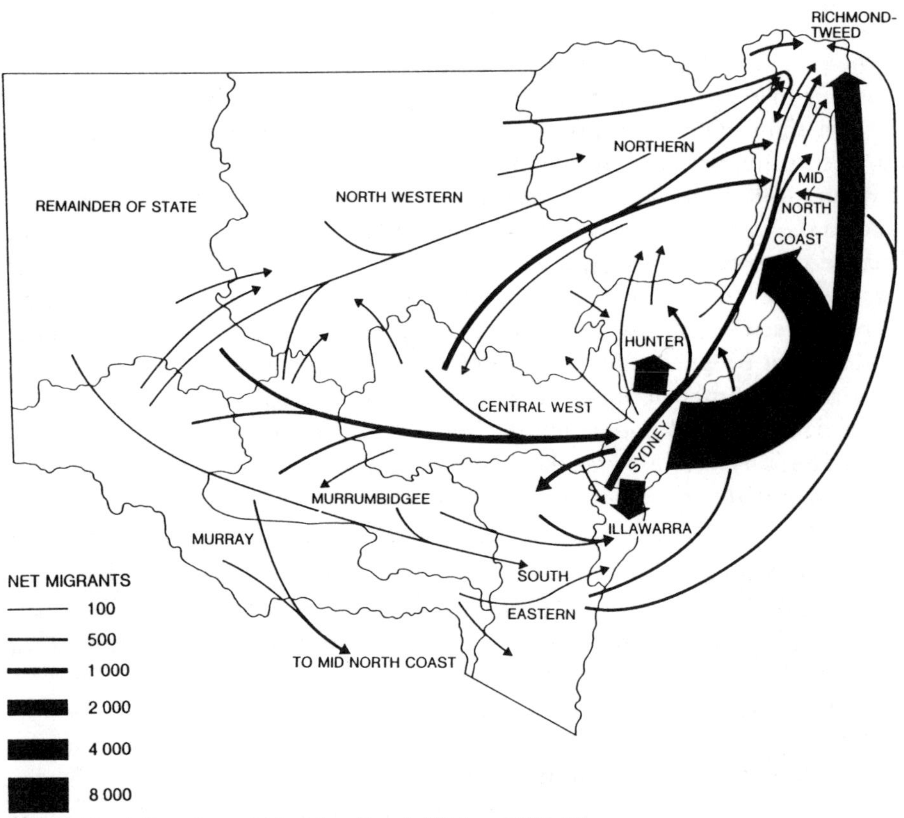

Fig. 1.10 Migration within New South Wales, 1976–81
Source: Department of Environment and Planning (1985)

New South Wales, probably have little to do with either employment or housing. Instead they are probably motivated by 'life style' considerations (e.g. leisure time pursuits, access to beaches, climate) and a desire to escape the stresses of metropolitan living (e.g. long commuting time, pollution). Movement to the north coast, in other words, probably reflects a perception that the 'pull' factors associated with the towns in the area, plus the 'push' factors involved in wanting to leave Sydney, are sufficient to overcome the inertia that would otherwise convince people to stay where they are, and sufficient also to justify the cost of moving, both social and economic. Moves to the NSW north coast probably also reflect retirement migration, again prompted by environmental amenity and lifestyle preferences. Satisfaction with such migratory moves is often high, as demonstrated by Murphy and Zehner's (1988) study of in-migrants in Port Macquarie.

Of course the numbers involved in such net flows are not great when considered in relation to the present population distribution. The net five-yearly outmigration from Sydney shown in Figure 1.10 is equivalent, for example, to not much more than 1 per cent of that city's population at the end of the period (1981). Many commentators have stressed that internal migration within Australia is more concerned with maintaining the settlement pattern than with changing it. In fact, not since the gold rushes of the nineteenth century has internal migration led to significant population shifts. Rowland (1979), for instance, has shown that, historically, the drift from the land to the 'big smoke' has not had a major impact on metropolitan growth. Instead the sprawl of Australia's capital cities has been fuelled by overseas immigration. Indeed rural depopulation tends to have been combatted by increasing settlement along the coast, the popularity of 'hobby farms', and the tendency for people to move off the land but still stay in country towns, with the result that metropolitan areas have not necessarily been the main net beneficiaries of rural population decline. In fact, in Rowland's view, internal migration in Australia is unlikely to promote rapid change in the contemporary population distribution for several reasons:

1 metropolitan dominance is so firmly entrenched that the role of capital cities in both government and economy is unlikely to change very quickly;
2 there are no large labour surpluses in declining industrial areas from which economically growing areas could attract migrants (a situation that contrasts markedly with historical trends in parts of Western Europe);
3 there is likely to continue to be a reliance on international migration to meet the demands for labour in economically expansive regions, thereby obviating the need for internal migration;
4 farming areas, which cover much of the country, will change only slowly, with a result that they will neither create nor attract large pools of migratory labour;
5 much of the migration involved in resource development is transient, as evidenced by the appearance of 'ghost towns' when mineral exploitation ceases;
6 the cost of promoting 'decentralised' development in inland areas is enormous and generally prohibitive, especially at a time of economic recession; and
7 most social and technological changes affecting society (e.g. increasing employment in service industries, increased female participation in the paid labour force, shorter working weeks, the advent of computers) can be accommodated in the existing settlement pattern rather than through regional population redistribution.

Despite Rowland's views, some commentators have talked about a 'population turn-around' and have sought to identify in Australia the type of 'counterurbanization' that has been prominent in both Europe and North America. The evidence for such counterurbanization is however somewhat underwhelming. Unlike Europe and North America where there is undoubtedly evidence of people leaving the cities for the perceived advantages of small town and village living, migration from Australia's metropolitan areas has focussed overwhelmingly on the coast (Burnley, 1988). As such, it tends to have been age-specific. Those most likely to move have been those with the greatest leisure time and thus the greatest potential for gaining lifestyle advantages, notably the retired, especially the 'young old'.

The failure of internal migration to create significant population redistribution means that Australia's large cities will continue to dominate the settlement pattern in the foreseeable future. Large cities are not, however, monolithic. Nor are they unchanging. Figure 1.8 shows, for example, that there is a great deal of residential mobility within cities as people move from one area to another. On top of this cities attract reasonable numbers of in-migrants and lose reasonable numbers of out-migrants. Figure 1.8 shows these two flows to be balanced for Australia's metropolitan areas taken as a whole. In practice, of course, some cities are net losers, as was shown for Sydney in Figure 1.10.

Migratory moves into and within cities are not random. People sort themselves out (if they are purchasers or owner-occupiers who can choose their place of residence), or are sorted out (if they rely on rented accommodation and are therefore subject to assessment by either public housing authorities or private landlords and their agents), in such a way as to reflect income, ethnicity, age, stage in life cycle, and life style. One of the most far-reaching examinations of residential mobility in Australian cities was undertaken by Maher (1984), analysing the period 1971–1976.

Although the details may have changed in the intervening years, the overall picture Maher presented throws a good deal of light on the actual process of intra-urban migration. He showed, for example, that between 1971 and 1976 the proportion of the population aged five or more which had moved was 30 per cent in Sydney, 31 per cent in Melbourne, 26 per cent in Brisbane, 27 per cent in Adelaide, 30 per cent in Perth, 26 per cent in Hobart, 24 per cent in both Newcastle and Wollongong, 23 per cent in Geelong, and 21 per cent in Canberra. The higher figures for the largest cities reflects the fact that they have more complex structures and therefore both more opportunities for movement and greater incentives to move when the stresses of urban living render a particular residential location unsatisfactory. A change of job, for instance, may not necessitate a change of house in a small city where commuting may be relatively easy, but it may necessitate a move in a big city if the new journey-to-work is longer than can be tolerated.

Not all groups of city residents are, however, prone to intra-urban migration. Most mobile are those aged 20–24 . Maher (1984) showed that 45 per cent of this group moved in the five years under study as opposed to only 20 per cent of those aged 45 and over. Young families are also more mobile than older ones, the respective rates of movement being 60 per cent for families whose head was aged under 30 and 19 per cent for families whose head was aged over 45. Clearly, this reflects changing housing needs as families grow in size. It perhaps also reflects changing housing tenure as accrued savings, plus mortgages, allow individuals to move from being tenants to being owner-purchasers.

The purchase of a dwelling can, of course, act as a brake on mobility in so far as it represents fixed capital assets. It is not surprising, therefore, to find that the mobility rate for owner–purchasers (25 per cent in Sydney and 28 per cent in Melbourne over the period 1971–1976) is very much less than the mobility rate for individuals who are tenants of private landlords (51 per cent in Sydney and 53 per cent in Melbourne) (Maher, 1984). High income groups are more mobile than low income groups. After all, high income means a greater degree of choice and hence a greater number of opportunities. In short, different groups have differential rates of movement. The net effect of these movements is invariably the continuing suburbanization of big cities. Again, this can be illustrated by reference to Sydney. Figure 1.11 shows the net movement between the regions of Sydney between 1976 and 1981. The pattern that emerges is indicative of declining inner city populations and suburban sprawl at the metropolitan periphery. What fails to show up on this map of net transfers is the fact that there has been a movement back to the inner city. Relatively affluent middle class groups have, for example, been active in 'doing up' traditional working class inner suburbs, thereby providing residential locations within easy access of the social and cultural amenities of the city centre. This 'gentrification' process is discussed further in Chapter 3.

One of the most notable manifestations of the residential sorting that goes on in Australian cities is the emergence of neighbourhoods and even suburbs that have a strong presence of particular ethnic groups.

The degree to which different groups congregate together varies according to the length of time they have been in the country, their internal coherence, and their degree of affiliation with institutions like churches. An index of dissimilarity is commonly used to measure the residential segregation of minorities from the host population. This index is calculated in such a way that a score of 0 indicates a population distribution the same as the population as a whole whereas a score of 100 indicates complete separation. In terms of the index as applied to local government authorities within cities, the Vietnamese appear to be the most clustered group (scoring 62.0), followed by Greeks (48.5), Yugoslavs (40.6), and Italians (40.2). In contrast, both New Zealanders (26.5) and British and Irish migrants (19.0) have low indices (Hugo, 1986). These indices are significant because most post-war overseas immigrants have tended to settle in cities. They have done this for a number of reasons: the frontier of rural settlement was no longer expanding at the time of their arrival and therefore offered few opportunities for rural living; most migrants lacked sufficient capital for pastoralism; cities offered a greater range of employment opportunities; and, above all, cities with their established ethnic minorities offered a form of community solidarity which was particularly important to individuals from non-English speaking backgrounds (Burnley, 1977).

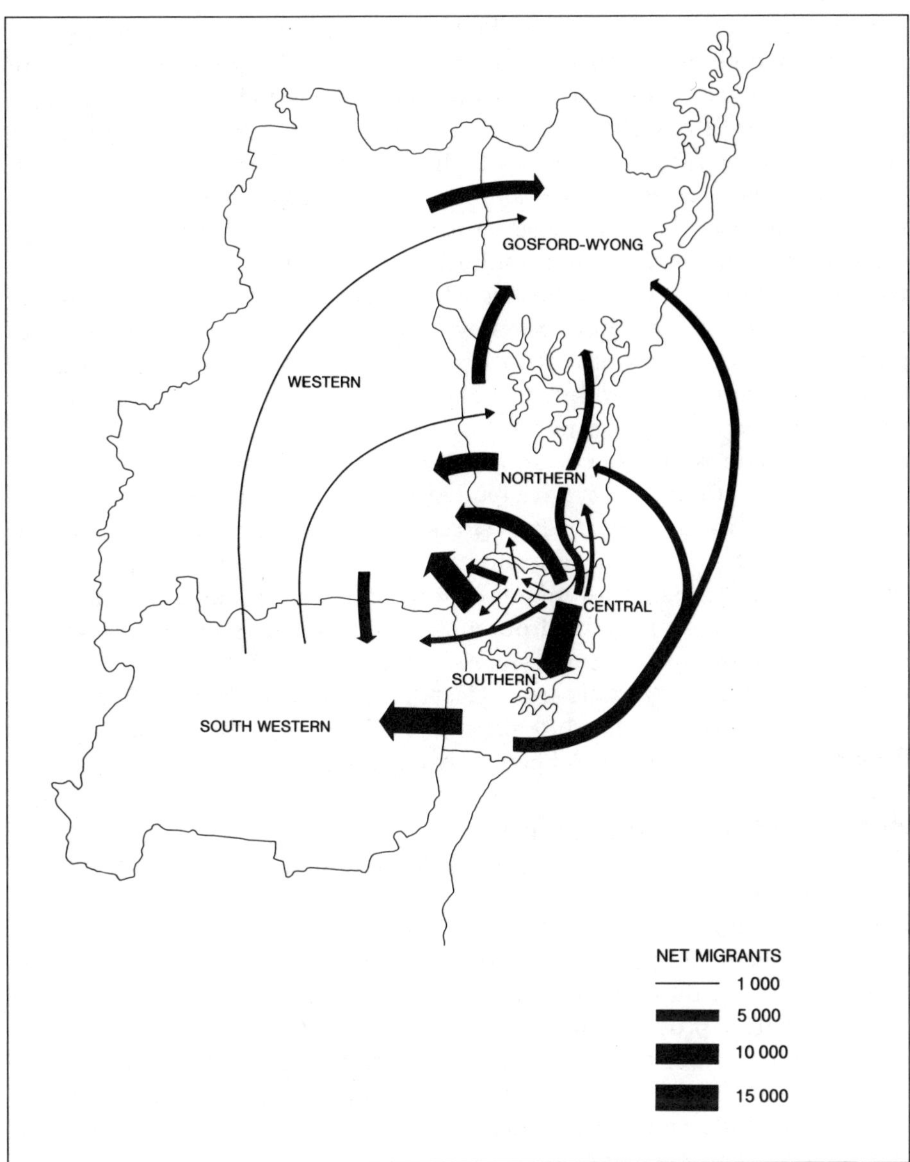

Fig. 1.11 Inter-regional migration within Sydney, 1976–81
Source: Department of Environment and Planning (1985)

In short, overseas migrants tended to settle in the capital cities which were their ports of entry. The exceptions to this were few and concerned mainly inter-city migration (as with the British moving from Sydney and Melbourne to Brisbane and Perth, Germans moving to Adelaide, and Poles to Melbourne and Geelong) or movement into specific rural areas (as with Greek movement to Renmark (SA) and Italian movement to Griffith (NSW), Shepparton (Vic) and Myrtleford (Vic)) (Burnley, 1977).

Burnley (1976; 1977) has described the movement of overseas immigrants in Australian cities in considerable detail. Generally speaking, immigrant settlement tended to follow a 'population succession model' whereby the host population tends to move out of an area (e.g. an inner city suburb) to be succeeded by a migrant group which, in turn and in time, moves out, ultimately being replaced by yet another immigrant group. Obviously, this is too simple a picture to bear close scrutiny. After all many immigrant groups did not move initially to the inner suburbs but rather tended to cluster around the Commonwealth migrant hostels where they were first housed on arrival in Australia (Whitelaw and Humphreys, 1980). Nevertheless the model does point out some truisms of Australia's migration history. To begin with, it suggests that levels of concentration of immigrant groups tend to decline over time. Moreover it highlights the fact that some groups tend to move to secondary centres of concentration after first establishing themselves elsewhere: Italians, for instance, have tended to move to Fivedock, Lilyfield, and Drummoyne in Sydney and to Preston, Coburg, and Northcote in Melbourne. This process of concentration is of course helped by chain migration, that is the tendency for migrants from certain source areas to follow the paths taken by earlier migrants from those very areas and establish themselves in the same host area. Examples are to be seen in both the Italian and the Greek communities (settlers from Castellorizo and Kythera to Redfern in Sydney, Calabrians to Penrith, Fairfield, and Holroyd in Sydney and settlers from Florina to Richmond and Collingwood in Melbourne) (Burnley, 1977).

Trends in internal migration, such as those outlined above, have brought about changes in the social geography of Australian cities in the last two or three decades. However, in recent years other changes have occurred in Australian society that are potentially of equal importance. These changes relate to the significance of family life. For a long time, Australia's immigration program and its welfare state has placed great emphasis on families. At the same time the construction industry catered for the family home and the tax structure provided financial assistance to families. It is interesting to note, therefore, that the conventional family appears to be of decreasing importance. Table 1.16 presents the marital status of Australia's population in 1971 and 1986 and shows that a lower proportion of people are married and more are separated or divorced at the later date. The changes are small, but significant. Moreover, alternatives to the nuclear family seem to be emerging. In 1971 about 9 per cent of births occurred outside marriage; by 1982 this figure had risen to approximately 14 per cent. Over the same period the marriage rate fell by 14 per cent and the divorce rate increased by 190 per cent (Department of Immigration and Ethnic Affairs, 1984). This has led to a situation where, at the 1981 Census, there were over 217 000 'families' comprising a single adult female plus dependents (Edwards *et al.*, 1985). Because of the mode of operation of the housing market, such single parent families tend to be concentrated in certain parts of the city. Burnley (1989a),

Table 1.16 The marital status of Australians (%)

	Australians aged 15+	
	1971	*1986*
Married	64.4	57.8
Never married	25.0	28.4
Separated but not divorced	2.0	2.6
Divorced	1.5	4.7
Widowed	7.1	6.5

Source: 1971 and 1986 censuses

for instance, has shown how the proportion of single parent families exceeds 20 per cent in Randwick, 26 per cent in Leichhardt, and 25 per cent in North Sydney. These figures compare markedly with the low figures for some of Sydney's northern suburbs: Baulkham Hills 8 per cent; Kuring-gai 9 per cent. This is not to say that Australian society is changing simply in a way which will lead to the increasing fragmentation of families. Remarriage is very popular. For example, the percentage of marriages in which at least one partner was remarrying increased from 14 per cent in 1971 to 32 per cent in 1981 (Department of Immigration and Ethnic Affairs, 1984). There has therefore been a rise in 'blended' families. At the same time society has seen the emergence of young, upwardly mobile, professional people and households comprising a dual income and no kids. Clearly, the lifestyle of such households is likely to be very different from that of nuclear families. In short, the nature of Australian society is changing. These changes are inextricabIy linked with the changing nature of economic activity. They result in changes to the quality of life of the population involved. The next two Chapters will examine the nature of the economy and the quality of life in considerable detail.

The Nature of the Economy

A NUMBER of fundamental questions must be posed in any consideration of the nature of the Australian economy: What is produced where? Why is that so? What are the consequences for the prosperity of the places in question? This chapter seeks answers to these questions for several sectors of the economy including farming, mining, manufacturing, transportation, commerce, and recreation and tourism. Each sector is treated in turn, placing particular emphasis on major component industries as measured in output terms or on those industries where rapid change is taking place. As a prelude we present a brief overview of the recent evolution and contemporary form of the Australian economy, to place the individual sectors in an overall context and draw attention to both common trends and mutual interdependencies. Many of the key factors which influence the structure and location of production in Australia are identified. These are fashioned into a descriptive model which is then used to give a common form to the discussion of each industry sector.

An overview of the economy

Australia is one of the world's wealthiest countries and also has, despite its small population, one of the world's largest economies. Table 2.1 ranks Australia's 1988 per capita income of US$12 340 as eighteenth among those

Table 2.1 World rankings, Gross National Product per capita

Rank	*Country*	*GNP per capita 1988 US$*	*Population (millions)*
1	Switzerland	27 500	6.6
2	Japan	21 020	122.6
3	Norway	19 990	4.2
4	USA	19 840	246.3
5	Sweden	19 300	8.4
6	Finland	18 590	5.0
7	Germany, F.R.	18 480	61.3
8	Denmark	18 450	5.1
9	Canada	16 960	26.0
10	France	16 090	55.9
11	UAE	15 770	1.5
12	Austria	15 470	7.6
13	Netherlands	14 520	14.8
14	Belgium	14 490	9.9
15	Kuwait	13 400	2.0
16	Italy	13 330	57.4
17	UK	12 810	57.1
18	Australia	12 340	16.5

Source: Compiled from The World Bank, World Development Report, 1990.

countries whose populations exceed 1 million inhabitants. Australia's 1987 total gross domestic product (GDP) of US$176.3 billion was fifteenth. However, over the years Australia has steadily been slipping down these rankings due to low rates of real (constant price) GDP growth. For example, Table 2.2 shows that, although GDP grew at a compound rate of 3.8 per cent over the 24 years to 1988/89, Australia's comparatively rapid population growth (for an industrialized nation) reduced the per capita rate to only 2.0 per cent. This rate is comparable to that for the United States, but below the OECD average (excluding the USA) and the strongly performing Pacific Basin NICs. The growth rate is also highly variable. Two peaks are evident in Table 2.2: one associated with the mining boom of the late 1960s and another following the end of the major 1980s drought in 1983. That drought severely depressed national growth performance.

The image of Australia as a great trading nation on account of its large natural resources and weak industrial sector is popular, but scarcely supported by the available statistics. Exports and imports averaged 16.1 per cent and 17.1 per cent of GDP respectively over the period 1974–81, well below the corresponding OECD figures 18.5 per cent and 18.8 per cent (Dornbusch and Fisher, 1984) and, in the case of exports alone, the levels recorded in 1982 by countries such as Canada (23.8 per cent) and Sweden (27.1 per cent) with which Australia is often compared (Krause, 1984). By 1989 Canada's exports had risen to 25 per cent of GDP while Australia's still

Table 2.2 Australia: gross domestic product at current and constant prices

	GDP at current prices	*GDP at constant (av 1979-80) prices*	*Av. annual % change over prev. 3 years (constant prices)*	*Estimated resident population (31 Dec) '000*	*GDP per capita at constant (Av. 1979-80) prices $*	*Av. annual % change in GDP per capita over previous 3 years (constant prices)*		*Av. annual % change in real GDP per capita over previous year — selected countries*			
								Australia	*USA*	*OECD (excl. USA)*	*Pacific Basin NICS*
1964–65	19 601	66 782		11 680	5 980		1961–68	3.0	3.2	4.4	n.a.
1967–68	24 068	75 021	4.1	11 904	6 302	1.8					
1970–71	34 897	91 236	7.2	12 639	7 219	4.9	1969–73	3.5	2.2	4.6	6.3
1973–74	53 426	104 543	4.9	13 614	7 679	2.1					
1976–77	87 118	112 535	2.5	14 110	7 976	1.3	1974–79	1.3	1.6	2.0	5.3
1979–80	121 349	121 349	2.6	14 603	8 310	1.4					
1982–83	170 263	126 209	1.3	15 277	8 261	–0.2	1980–82	0.1	–0.9	0.7	3.3
1985–86	238 390	145 280	5.0	15 859	9 160	3.6					
1988–89	337 599	162 261	3.9	16 960	9 567	1.5					
	Compound annual rate of change 1964/65–1985/86		3.8	Compound annual rate of change 1964/65–1985/86		2.0					

Source: ABS Australian Demographic Statistic cat. no. 3101.0: Australian Economic Indicators, cat. no. 1350.0; Quarterly Estimates of National Income and Expenditure: Year Books Australia; Economic Planning and Advisory Council (1986b);

languished at 17 per cent. Only in 1991 did the exports-to-GDP ratio soar to the Canadian level as Australia finally joined the world economy and ran a large trade surplus. The poor trade performance over most of the post-war period partly reflects the strategy pursued by all Australian post-war governments until the 1970s of developing manufacturing industries behind high protective barriers in the form of tariffs (taxes on imported goods), quotas (quantity restrictions on imports) and bounties (subsidies to local producers). Also known as import substitution, this strategy reduced the demand for imported goods. Simultaneously, the unit prices received for Australian raw materials have tended to decline, although this has been counter-balanced to a large extent by increased export volumes.

There is another aspect to Australia's poor trade performance: Australia traditionally runs a current account deficit on international trade. Imports of goods usually exceed exports, and there are heavy bills for interest paid on overseas loans, shipping charges, insurance, financial services, royalty payments and so on. This deficit has usually amounted to between 1 per cent and 4 per cent of GDP, with occasional surpluses interposed. Recent years have seen the deficit widen to about 6 per cent as a consequence of Australia's declining terms of trade and heavy interest payments due on overseas borrowings (recorded in the 'invisibles' category) (Table 2.3 and Figure 2.1). The decline in terms of trade means that import prices for mainly manufactured goods have risen more than those for exported raw materials, the latter being in considerable over-supply.

In order for the Australian dollar to retain its parity with other currencies there has to be a compensating inflow of overseas capital. This takes two forms: foreign investment in enterprises and financial deposits with private or public institutions in this country (Table 2.3). The former often accounts for between 12 per cent and 20 per cent of domestic investment according to Krause (1984). Where the current account balance deteriorates without compensating capital flows, currency markets engineer a devaluation of the currency concerned. This happened to the Australian dollar in 1985 and 1986 when, as Table 2.3 shows, export receipts worsened and invisible payments rose sharply. The same thing occurred at the end of 1991 and into early 1992. Such a devaluation boosts the earnings of exporters and effectively increases the competitiveness of manufacturers in both domestic and export markets. Conversely, an over-valued currency, which Australia had in the 1970s and early 1980s, enables import penetration at the expense of local producers. Thus imported goods rose from 8 per cent of sales in 1972/73 to nearly 13 per cent in 1984/85 (Indecs, 1986).

Table 2.4 encapsulates the structure of Australia's trade. Export destinations are more diversified than import sources. Japan, the EEC and the United States, which together comprise the major industrialized nations, take a little over half of Australia's exports but supplied about 63 per cent of its imports in 1990/91. However, their dominance as a source of imports

Table 2.3 The main components of Australia's balance of payments

	1981/82	*1983/84*	*1985/86*	*1987/88*	*1989/90*
Current account					
Exports FOB	19 083	23 719	32 235	40 541	47 671
Imports FOB	–22 376	–23 497	–35 618	–40 386	–50 991
Trade balance	–3 293	222	–3 383	155	–3320
Net invisibles	–5 699	–7 570	–10 439	–11 236	–17 833
Current account balance	–8 992	–7 348	–13 822	–11 081	–21 153
Capital account					
Net foreign investment	8 510	6 735			
in enterprises			12 033	8 824	13 095
Other capital	1 836	2 463			
Capital account balance	10 346	9 198	12 033	8 824	13 095
Net monetary movement	1 354	1 850	–1 789	–2 257	–8 058
Current account deficit as percentage of GDP	6.0	4.9	5.8	3.7	5.7

Source: ABS Balance of Payments Australia, Quarterly cat. no. 5302.0; Australian Economic Indicators cat. no. 1350.0

declined markedly over the previous five years. The next most important group of trading partners, with whom trade is somewhat in Australia's favour, lie in the Asia-Pacific region. This includes New Zealand, the ASEAN countries, Taiwan, China and South Korea. There is a trade surplus with the most important trading partner, Japan, but a substantial deficit with other advanced economies, a situation that reflects the pattern of commodities traded (bottom half of Table 2.4). Australia's main exports are raw materials — traditionally up to 70 per cent of the total, whereas imports tend to be high value-added manufactured items — between 70 and 80 per cent of the total. Indeed, 'other machinery and equipment' and 'transport equipment' accounted for nearly half of all imports in 1990/91 (Table 2.4).

This pattern of trade has altered markedly over the last forty years or so. In the early 1950s wool alone accounted for 50 per cent of the value of exports, but this dwindled to less than 10 per cent by the early 1980s and less than 5 per cent a decade later. Coal, on the other hand, increased its share from 0.1 per cent in the 1950s to over 12 per cent in 1990/91. The rise to prominence of other metals and minerals has been less dramatic, growing from about 7.4 per cent to nearly 25 per cent over the same period. Since about 1960 manufacturing's share of exports remained a fairly constant 20 per cent until a surge in the late 1980s took its share past that for farm produce for the first time ever in 1991. Over the twenty years to 1973/74 the rate of growth in the value

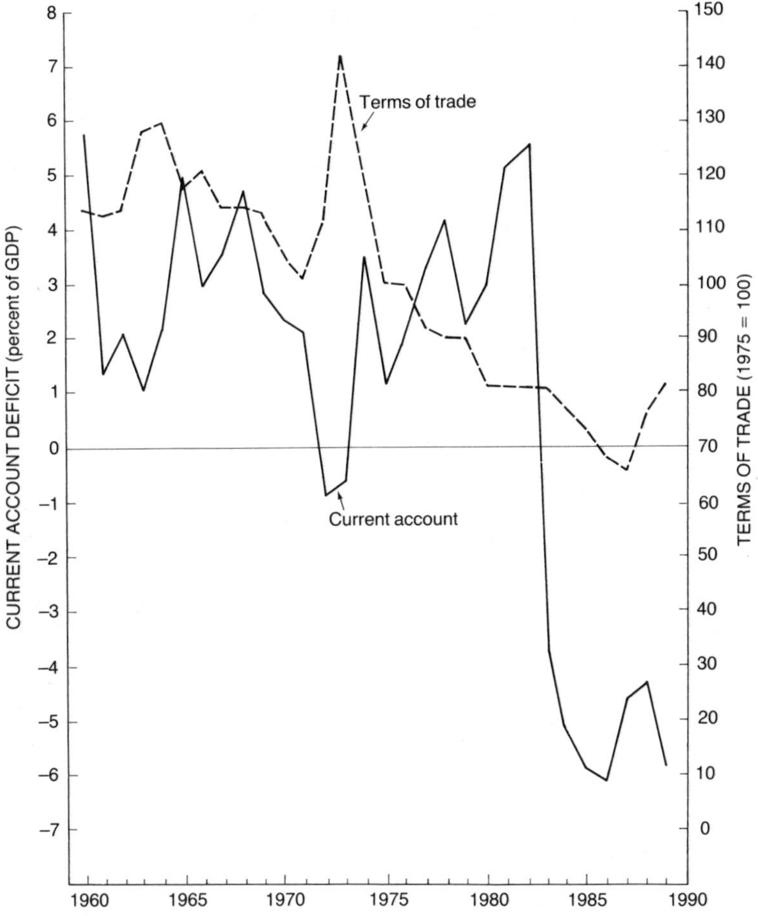

Fig. 2.1 The current account and terms of trade, 1960–89

of manufacturing exports matched global levels, but fell a long way behind during the next decade due mainly to a lag in export volumes. During the latter period both agriculture and mining export volumes also performed poorly (EPAC, 1986e). The direction of trade has also changed substantially for both imports and exports, as Table 2.5 demonstrates. Trade with the UK has slumped over the past forty years as ties with the 'mother country' have loosened culturally, socially, economically and politically.

Japan has replaced the UK as Australia's major trading partner and is easily the most important export destination with over one quarter of the total trade. To some extent this ties Australia's economic performance to Japan's which is fine as long as the latter enjoys prosperity, but potentially dangerous otherwise. The remainder of the UK's declining share of imports into this country has been acquired largely by the United States and the EC, but Australia's exports to both have performed poorly, especially to the latter.

Table 2.4 The distribution of exports and imports by major country groups and commodities, 1990-91

	Exports to		*Imports from*	
	$m	*%*	*$m*	*%*
Japan	14 455	27.5	8 854	18.1
EC	6 353	12.1	10 678	21.8
ASEAN	6 309	12.0	3 461	7.1
USA	5 806	11.1	11 475	23.5
NZ	2 584	4.9	2 150	4.4
Taiwan	1 965	3.7	1 752	3.6
Others	15 020	28.6	10 547	21.6
Total	52 492		48 917	

Exports	*$m*	*%*	*Imports*	*$m*	*%*
Metalliferous ores and scrap metal	7 787	14.8	Other machinery and equipment	15 951	32.6
Coal, coke and briquettes	6 440	12.3	Transport equipment	8 017	16.4
Non-ferrous metals and manufactures of metal	4 217	8.0	Chemicals, petroleum and coal products	6 332	12.9
Textile fibres and their wastes	3 665	7.0	Manufactures of metal	3 400	7.0
Petroleum, petroleum products etc.	3 221	6.1	Miscellaneous manufactured articles	3 130	6.4
Meat and meat preparations	3 206	6.1	Textile yarn, fabrics, etc	2 128	4.4
Machinery, vehicles and transport equipment	3 094	5.9	Food etc.	2 081	4.3
Cereals and cereal preparations	2 542	4.8			
Other	18 275	34.8	Other	7 870	16.1
Total	52 447	99.8	Total	48 912	100.1

Source: ABS: Exports and Imports, Australia; ABS Foreign Trade Merchandise Exports, cat. no. 5424.0 ABS F.T. Merchandise Imports cat. no. 5426.0

There are many competing sources of raw materials for industrial nations to draw upon, but far fewer of high quality or high technology manufacture from which Australia can buy. Australia's trade with her neighbouring region is less than might be expected, given its large population and rapid economic development, but it seems to have been growing in recent years, especially for exports. South-east Asia alone now takes nearly 20 per cent of these.

Australia's share of world trade has been declining steadily over the last forty years. It halved between 1955 and 1975 from 2.2 per cent to about 1.2 per cent at a time when great international prosperity, coupled with a growth of free trade sentiments on the part of governments (formalized through the

Table 2.5 The direction of Australia's exports and imports

Country	*1949/50 to 1953/54*	*1959/60 to 1963/64*	*1969/70 to 1973/74*	*1979/80 to 1983/84*	*1989/90*
Exports					
UK	35.9	21.3	9.7	4.5	3.5
EC	21.7	16.2	9.9	8.8	10.4
Japan	6.7	16.4	28.5	27.0	26.1
S & SE Asia[1,2]	8.7	9.0	12.9	14.5	18.7[1]
USA	9.6	9.6	12.2	10.8	10.9
Imports					
UK	46.9	31.1	19.3	7.3	6.5
EC	8.8	11.2	13.4	13.3	15.5
Japan	1.9	5.8	15.5	19.5	19.2
S & SE Asia[1,2]	13.2	9.7	7.0	12.5	12.1[1]
USA	11.1	20.0	23.0	22.1	24.1

1 Defined as Bangladesh, Brunei, Burma, Hong Kong, India, Indonesia, Kampuchea, Laos, Macao, Malaysia, Maldive Is., Pakistan, Philippines, Singapore, Sri Lanka, Taiwan, Thailand and Vietnam.

2 After 1969/70, the countries of S Asia and the former Indo-China are deleted and Papua New Guinea is added, except for 1989/90.

Source: Krause (1984); Economic Planning and Advisory Council (1986e); ABS Australian Economic Indicators cat. no. 1350.0

General Agreement on Tariffs and Trade, GATT), led to a massive increase in world trade. To some extent these contrary trade events are causally connected, but, as noted earlier, Australian governments pursued, during this period, a conscious policy of trade reduction by encouraging the development of import substituting industries.

The apportionment of GDP among the various sectors of the economy is shown in Table 2.6. In 1988/89 the services sector accounted for 41 per cent of GDP, more than twice as much as either of the next two largest sectors —

Table 2.6 Industries as a proportion of GDP

Industry	*1962-63*[1]	*1972-73*[1]	*1980-81*[1]	*1984-85*[2]		*1988-89*[2]	
Agriculture	8.5	5.5	5.6	4.6	(5.2)	4.1	(4.6)
Construction	8.3	8.4	7.3	6.0	(6.7)	7.1	(7.8)
Manufacturing	25.7	25.4	22.7	17.8	(20.0)	16.6	(18.3)
Mining	1.6	3.6	3.5	6.4	(7.2)	4.1	(4.5)
Other services[3]	33.5	35.4	38.6	37.9	(42.6)	40.8	(44.9)
Ownership of dwellings	5.4	6.2	7.0	11.0		9.2	
Wholesale and retail trade	17.0	15.5	15.3	16.3	(18.3)	18.1	(19.9)

1 *Source*: Caves and Krause (1984). Adjusted to 1974/75 prices

2 *Source*: ABS *Australian National Accounts*. Unadjusted. Figures in brackets are adjusted for omission of ownership of dwellings

3 Includes finance and business services, community services, public administration, entertainment and recreation, communications and utilities.

manufacturing and distribution (wholesale and retail trade). Agriculture and mining, the traditional mainstays of export income, shared only 8 per cent between them, less than the imputed rental income from the national housing stock. This structure of output incorporates three major changes that have occurred since the early 1960s. Manufacturing industry's apparent share has contracted sharply. In part this may reflect an increased tendency for that sector to contract in specialist services from outside. Agriculture's share of output has reduced even more rapidly, whereas mining has perhaps tripled its own, reflecting the cumulative effects of two mining booms. The 'other services' sector, which is often seen as the power-house of post-industrial society, has recorded unspectacular growth in its share of GDP over the twenty-two year period.

Turning now to employment structures by industry (Table 2.7), there are some interesting contrasts. Manufacturing's share of employment has shrunk even faster than its output. This suggests, incidentally, substantial productivity gains. This picture is the reverse of that for agriculture, where output share has fallen faster than that for employment. In this case we cannot infer that productivity gains in agriculture have lagged behind other sectors. More likely, some combination of adverse climatic conditions and depressed prices have reduced the value of output. Mining's share of the workforce has remained relatively static for many years at a time of dramatically increased output. Its productivity is far higher than that of any other sector, and nearly five times the average for all producing sectors. In contrast, the share of employment attributable to 'other services' rose by over one third in the 25 years to 1990, much faster than output. If the relatively efficient communications and utilities sectors were removed, the discrepancy would be even greater, thereby illustrating the labour absorbing and low capital intensity of much of the services sector. This was illustrated dramatically in the 1991 recession when both governments and private companies alike shed labour rapidly in a belated attempt to improve cost efficiency in service delivery.

Table 2.7 Employment by industry

	Labour force (%)				
Industry	*1967*[1]	*1972*[1]	*1981*[1]	*1982*[2]	*1990*[2]
Agriculture	8.7	7.9	6.5	6.2	5.4
Construction	8.1	8.3	7.4	7.1	7.5
Manufacturing	25.6	23.7	19.4	16.7	15.3
Mining	1.3	1.4	1.5	1.5	1.2
Other services	36.0	37.8	45.2	48.7	50.0
Wholesale and retail trade	20.4	20.7	19.9	19.8	20.6

1 *Source*: Caves and Krause (1984)
2 *Source*: ABS Labour Statistics, Australia cat. no. 6101.0

Table 2.8 demonstrates which occupational categories have been the winners and losers in recent years. White-collar occupations have mostly increased their share, though none so spectacularly as professional and technical workers. This occupational category nearly doubled its share of the labour force over the 24 years to 1985. Allowing for a change in ABS occupational classification in 1986, this growth pattern showed little subsequent change. Since the workforce increased over 50 per cent in size during the same period, the total number of professional and technical employees tripled. The two categories registering the greatest fall in proportion of the workforce were, not surprisingly, tradesmen and farm workers. Their performance parallels that for manufacturing and agriculture. These trends appear to have continued between 1986 and 1990, despite the radical changes in occupational classification introduced by the ABS.

Table 2.8 Employment by occupation

	Labour force %						
Occupation	*1961*[1]	*1971*[2]	*1981*[2]	*1985*[3]	*1986*[5]	*1990*[5]	*ABS new occupation categories from 1986*
Professional, technical	8.6	10.9	14.8	15.8	12.0	13.0	Professionals
Administrative	7.3	6.3	6.2	6.8	5.9	6.0	Para-Professionals
Clerical	13.3	16.5	17.4	18.2	11.0	11.0	Managers/Administrators
Sales	7.8	8.4	8.8	9.1	17.3	17.0	Clerks
Farm	11.4	8.1	7.1	6.9	13.8	14.9	Sales/Personnel/Service
Mining	0.8	0.7	0.6	—[4]	7.9	7.4	Plant/Machine Operators
Transport	6.6	6.1	5.3	5.0	16.8	15.5	Trades-persons
Tradesmen, etc.	37.2	34.6	30.4	28.5	15.4	15.2	Labourers
Service, etc.	7.2	8.5	9.4	9.7			
Total employed (millions)	4.1	5.5	6.4	6.6	6.9	7.8	

1 *Source*: Adapted from Kasper *et al.* (1980). Not strictly comparable with sources 2 and 3 below.
2 *Source*: ABS *The Labour Force, Australia* cat. no. 6203.0
3 *Source*: ABS *Labour Statistics, Australia* cat. no. 6101.0
4 Included in Tradesmen, etc. category
5 Occupational classifications were changed in 1986; farmers and miners are no longer separate categories. The two classifications are not readily compared.

To some extent the structure of output between various producing sectors in Australia is artificial, in the sense that it has been distorted by a variety of government industry protection policies. These apply mainly to agriculture and manufacturing and are designed to raise the level of domestic output at the expense of imports. In general, the higher the level of protection assistance, the greater the degree of distortion in the sector concerned. For example, the clothing and footwear industry shelters behind an enormous effective rate of assistance of 170 per cent, though that is down from its early 1980s peak of 220 per cent (Table 2.9).

A combination of tariffs (taxes on imports) and quotas (restrictions on the volume of imports) greatly increases the price of imported goods to the consumer and allows higher cost local producers to compete in the market-place. Without such assistance the domestic industry would contract significantly. Australia and New Zealand have easily the highest rates of protection among OECD countries, although governments in both countries

Table 2.9 Effective rates of assistance for groups of agricultural activities and manufacturing industries (per cent)[3]

Activity/Industry	*1971–72*	*1977–78*	*1982–83*	*1988–89*
Horticulture	29[1]	23[1]	32	17
Extensive cropping	25	5	8	1
Irrigation/High rainfall crops	20	–2	16	14
Extensive grazing	13	12	8	5
Intensive livestock	65[2]	36[2]	53	29
Total agriculture	21	13	16	9

ASIC code		*1971–72*	*1977–78*	*1982–83*	*1988–89*	*Mid–90s estimate*
21	Food, drink and tobacco	19	10	9	3	2
23	Textiles	45	47	54	79	63
24	Clothing and footwear	86	141	220	170	112
25	Wood, wood products and furniture	23	18	13	17	10
26	Paper, paper products, printing, publishing	52	24	24	12	7
27	Chemical, petroleum and coal products	32	19	14	12	11
28	Non-metallic mineral products	14	5	4	3	2
29	Basic metal products	29	10	11	9	7
31	Fabricated metal	58	30	27	20	14
32	Transport equipment	50	48	72	39	29
33	Other machinery and equipment	44	20	18	19	12
34	Miscellaneous manufacturing	32	30	25	20	18
	Total manufacturing	35	23	25	17	12

1 Excludes bananas
2 Excludes bee-keeping
3 The effective rate of assistance is the net assistance provided to an activity, industry etc., after making allowance for the effects of tariffs and other forms of protection which increase the cost of the activities concerned.

Sources: Economic Planning and Advisory Council (1986d), Industry Commission (1990)

are now consciously trying to reduce the prevailing rates. This is indicated by the projected assistance rates for the mid-1990s shown in the final column of Table 2.9.

As shown in Table 2.9, agricultural production is on average much less protected than manufacturing, and its protection level is also falling slightly faster. Average figures are misleading, however, as they conceal major differences between sectors. At least two rural industries, horticulture and intensive livestock (including dairying), have high protection even by the standards of manufacturing. Conversely, extensive cropping (mainly cereal production) enjoys very little assistance. This must be galling to cereal producers as they face a great financial crisis. In manufacturing, too, there is a great variation in the protection provided by government. Two of the sectors, food and non-metallic mineral products (construction and building materials), have low assistance, partly one suspects because they are protected by the 'tyranny of distance' stemming from Australia's geographical isolation. Apart from clothing and footwear, both textile and transport equipment (including automobiles) producers need considerable protection if they are not to be bankrupted by a flood of cheap imports. Indeed these three sectors are so weak that they ran counter to the long-term trend of declining protection recorded by all other sectors in the early 1980s — before the Hawke government introduced its industry restructuring programs. Table 2.10 demonstrates that protection helps some states more than others. Not surprisingly, the industrial states (NSW, Victoria, and South Australia) gain manufacturing subsidies at a higher per capita rate than the remainder. Victoria is especially advantaged, and Queensland the least advantaged. Perhaps, therefore, there is some justice in Queensland having the highest per capita agricultural subsidies and NSW the lowest. However, levels of agricultural subsidies are substantially below those in manufacturing, and interstate deviation is much higher for the latter. Victoria is easily the biggest winner from the whole protection game.

Table 2.10 Real net subsidy equivalents per capita for agriculture and manufacturing by States in constant 1982/83 dollars

State	*Manufacturing 1982/83*	*Agriculture 1983/84*
New South Wales	387	37.1
Victoria	619	53.1
Queensland	224	56.1
Western Australia	227	44.1
South Australia	413	51.9
Tasmania	241	51.7

Source: Adapted from Economic Planning and Advisory Council (1986d)

In 1990 Australia's working population stood at 7.8 million (Figure 2.2). Of these, 79 per cent worked full-time, and 59 per cent were male. Both these figures declined marginally over the late 1980s. Females dominate the part-time and males the full-time workforce. Between 1966 and 1990 employment grew about 64 per cent, but that trend masks major shifts in the structure of the workforce. Figure 2.2 reveals that part-time employment grew at six times the full-time rate. Moreover, female employment grew much more rapidly than the male rate. This stems both from a growing workforce in absolute numbers and from a steadily increasing female participation rate as married

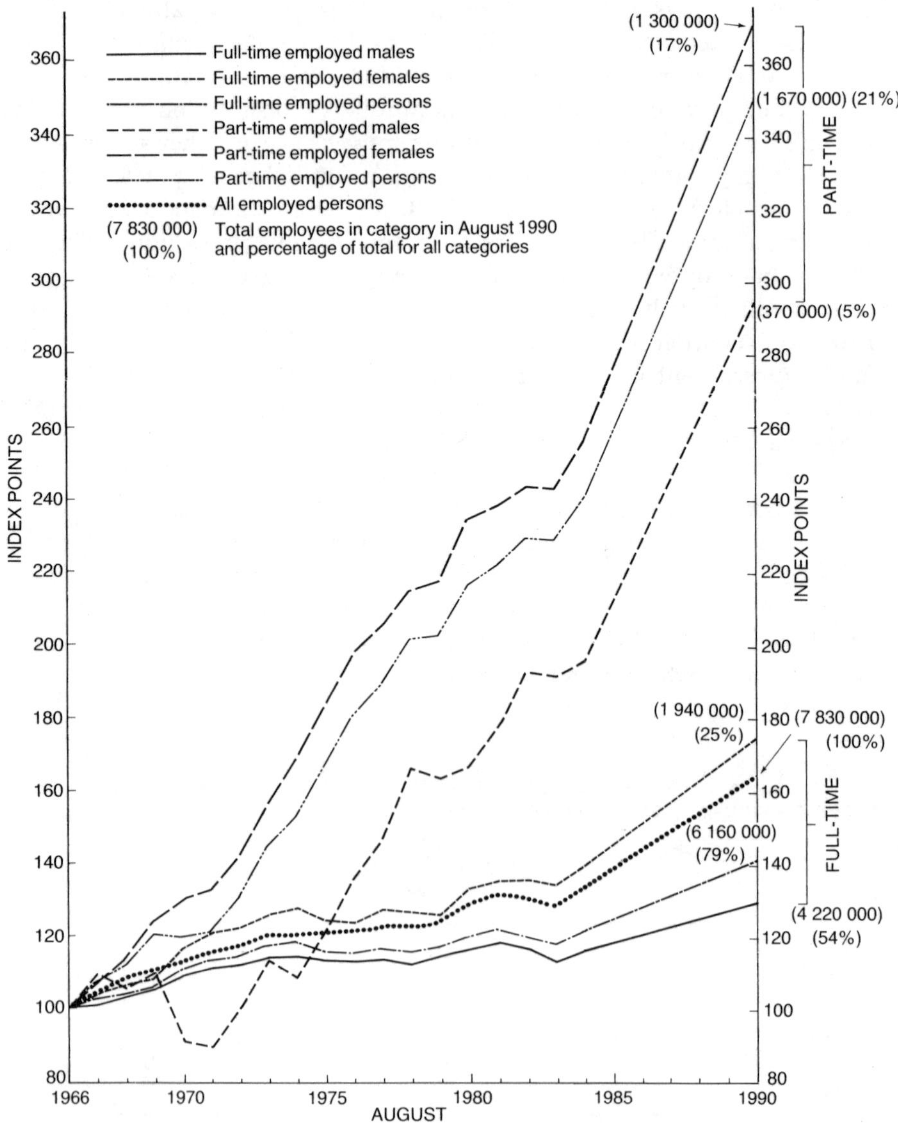

Fig. 2.2 Full-time and part-time employment trends, 1966–90

women entered employment (Figure 2.3). Their participation rate rose from about 30 per cent to 53 per cent in 1966–1991. At the same time, the male participation rate declined from 84 per cent to 75 per cent. As a result of these contrary movements, the overall participation rate of Australians older than 15 years in paid employment has remained remarkably constant over many years. Only during the boom conditions of the late 1980s did the participation rate rise significantly above the long-term trend, only to fall back in the 1991 recession.

The reduction in the male participation rate reflects three concurrent events: earlier retirement, the growing length of formal education and the withdrawal of 'discouraged' workers from the workforce as a result of their being unable to find employment. In particular, each recession creates a pool of unemployed who, through no fault of their own, lack the skills required during the subsequent up-swing. This problem was much less evident during the 1950s and 1960s when the low unemployment rate of less than 2 per cent generally prevailed.

Australians tend to perceive themselves as an advanced industrial nation. This view is certainly true in terms of material possessions, overall quality of life, and the range of possible lifestyles available. In matters such as environmental management, working conditions, quality of medical services, and equality of income (all touchstones of western civilization), Australia has traditionally ranked highly. Yet beneath this veneer, the economy is remarkably immature and quite at variance with mainstream OECD nations. To some extent it is colonial or third-world in nature. We have already seen, for

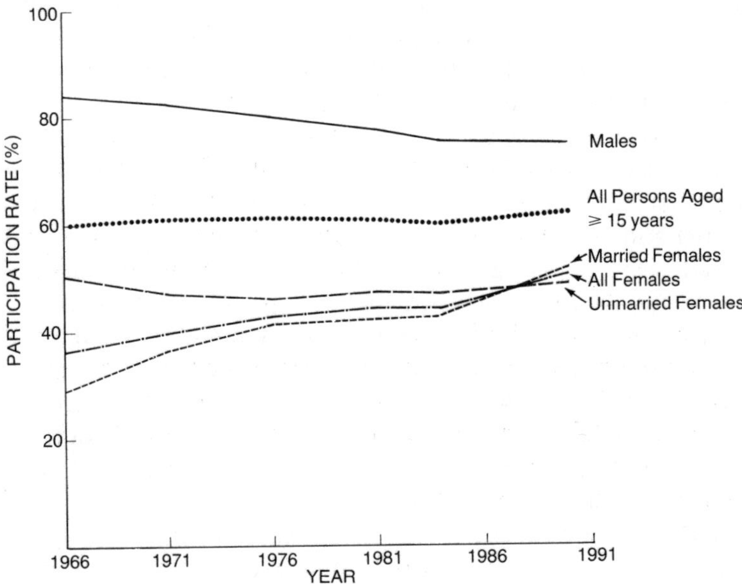

Fig. 2.3 Male and female participation rates, 1966–90

example, the domination of exports by raw materials and the import-substitution character of some manufacturing industry. This analogy can be taken much further.

As Crough and Wheelwright (1982) point out, many major sectors, whether in manufacturing, mining or services, are dominated by foreign owned companies. The production of aluminium, automobiles, chemicals and pharmaceuticals, electrical and electronic goods, foodstuffs, oil and gas, iron ore, and cotton is associated with high levels of overseas control. So, too, is advertising among the service industries. Krause (1984) suggests that about 40 per cent of the total equity in Australian manufacturing and 50 per cent of that in mining industry is foreign *owned*. The rate of foreign *control* is higher still, since control of a company can be exercised with much less than 100 per cent of its equity. Over many years foreign direct investment in Australia has averaged 15 per cent or so of domestic investment.

At the end of 1991 Australia's net foreign debt was about A$140 billion, a sum of Latin American proportions. It grew at nearly 35 per cent per annum compound throughout the 1980s, partly because local capital markets were too small to provide all the monies needed for the mining, housing and tourism booms, the construction of associated public infrastructure, the financing of the corporate takeovers thought necessary to create Australian companies of global stature, and to support the national debt binge consequent on financial deregulation. The size of the debt has also been magnified by the large devaluation of the Australian dollar, whose trade weighted index slipped by one quarter over the period 1980–1989.

Perhaps because of high levels of foreign ownership which encourage the importation of second-hand technology, or because domestic industries have been protected by a cocoon of trade barriers and have not been forced to innovate to survive so much as their overseas competitors, Australia's record of research and development (R & D) expenditure is dismal. In 1981/82 it mounted to about 1 per cent of GDP compared with 2.5 per cent in high-flying nations such as Japan and West Germany. Worse still, an unusually high proportion of the funds available came from government sources (nearly 50 per cent) and comprised basic or applied research rather than product development. Only agriculture, with 4 per cent of its gross product spent on R & D, experienced a large research effort, nearly all government funded (all these figures come from EPAC, 1986a). Subsequent events have changed little. It is not surprising therefore that Australia's manufacturing productivity growth has lagged behind most advanced nations. Productivity growth is also a function of capital investment and that, too, has performed poorly. In 1985 capital per worker was only 96 per cent of the 1970 figure, after discounting trends in productivity (EPAC, 1986b).

Australia's economy, then, is one of paradox and duality. High material standards of living and an employment structure reminiscent of post-industrial society (e.g. an internationalized and thriving finance sector) exist alongside an almost third-world economic base comprising raw materials exports and protected import-substituting manufacturing industries. Yet many of the primary export sectors are both highly efficient, exploiting Australia's natural comparative advantage, and globally significant. This contrasts with the small-scale, parochial and almost colonial status of much manufacturing whose very existence is a contrivance of government. These broad stereotypes mask, however, some notable exceptions: world leadership in some high technology manufacturing industries and relatively inefficient primary industries. Other dualities transect these. Prosperous industries co-exist with those experiencing financial crisis, though which is which may not reflect the intrinsic efficiency of the activities concerned. Both wheat and wool production are efficient in global terms, yet both suffered large-scale hardship at the start of the 1990s. Some industries are stagnant in employment and output; some are dynamic and growing rapidly. Still others suffer great variations in income and profitability.

Factors influencing the geographical location of economic activity

Figure 2.4 presents a model of the major factors influencing the geographical location of economic activity — 'space economy' for short. The decision to undertake a productive activity at a particular place can be seen as a two-stage process: first comes a commitment to produce, followed by a choice of site. Production decisions themselves result from the interplay of two circuits, one international and the other domestic. Their relative importance varies according to both government policy and private assessment of the investment climate. Governments can virtually isolate their economies from the rest of the world, as China did in the 1950s and 1960s, or there may be virtually no constraints on trade or investment. Australia has a relatively open economy. Where few constraints exist, the level and form of private investment in particular countries tends to depend on the rate of return such investment can earn relative to other places and its security. Nations with poor investment climates effectively isolate themselves from international movements of private capital, except perhaps for debilitating capital flight.

In both the domestic and the international circuits, investment arises from the interplay of three sets of factors: various tiers of government policy, decreasing in importance from the national level; the stock of physical capital and human resources; and business behaviour. Governments develop, regulate and control resources just as they do capital. Business is also involved in resource development and, in a kind of feedback loop, seeks to influence both public opinion and policy-makers.

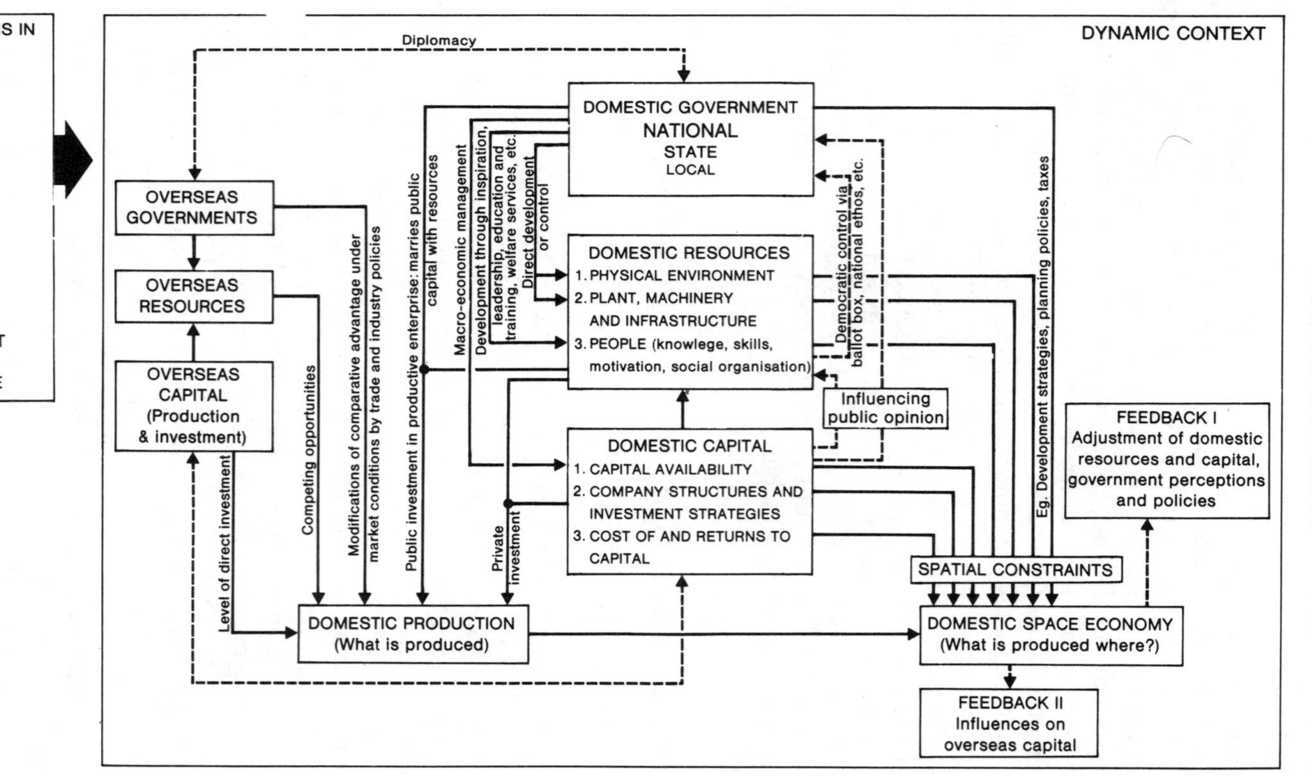

Fig. 2.4 A model of the factors influencing the location of economic activity

The location of production is also a function of public policy, resource availability and business behaviour. Governments have a portfolio of spatial development strategies and environmental planning policies designed to further their perceived public interests. Companies, on the other hand, view locational decisions mainly in the context of their private imperatives: profitability, acquisition of market share, production and distribution linkages. Both are constrained by the potentialities of the physical environment, human abilities, and the considerable weight of existing development. Locations, once selected, slightly alter the subsequent decision-making calculus, as indicated by the feed-back loops to both domestic and international circuits. This calculus is also constantly shifting as a consequence of changes in technology, information and attitude.

The relative importance of the various components in this model is not fixed. It varies with industry, ideology, time, place, technology, human skills and perceptions, the state of international relations and a host of other factors.

Rural primary production

Spatial patterns of land use

The geographical distribution of rural commodity production across Australia and the intensity of output are constrained primarily by the availability of water, although other factors such as topography, length of growing season, and temperature are also vital. Water is available from three main sources: rainfall, stored catchment run-off, and sub-surface bores (much of it artesian water). Only the first two contribute to cropping since artesian water tends to be too saline for irrigation purposes. Figures 2.5 and 2.6 reveal that south of the Tropic of Capricorn cropping is restricted to areas with annual rainfall exceeding between about 500 and 550 mm. In tropical areas the extreme seasonality of rainfall and high evaporation rates restrict most cropping to well-watered coastal districts. Since most water storage dams are located in the well-watered highland zone of southeast Australia, irrigation farming is largely restricted to the adjacent inland plains (Figure 2.5).

Greater water availability permits a more intense volume and value of output per hectare, and thus smaller sizes of viable farm holding. This view is confirmed in Figure 2.7 which shows the small size of holdings associated with some of the irrigation zones, thereby reflecting the intensity of horticultural production. Horticultural activities also surround the state capitals. Properties also tend to be small in the sugar-growing districts of coastal Queensland.

The distribution of livestock is less climatically restricted than cropping (Figures 2.5 and 2.8). Nevertheless, production is much more intensive in well-watered areas. Indeed dairying, which requires good year-round pastures to sustain yields, is restricted mainly to coastal locations. Dairy properties

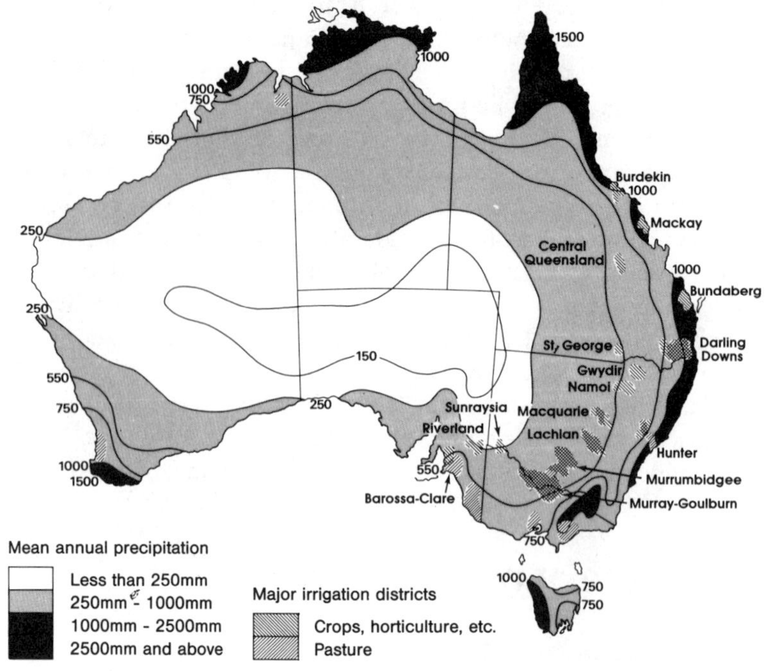

Fig. 2.5 Rainfall and irrigation

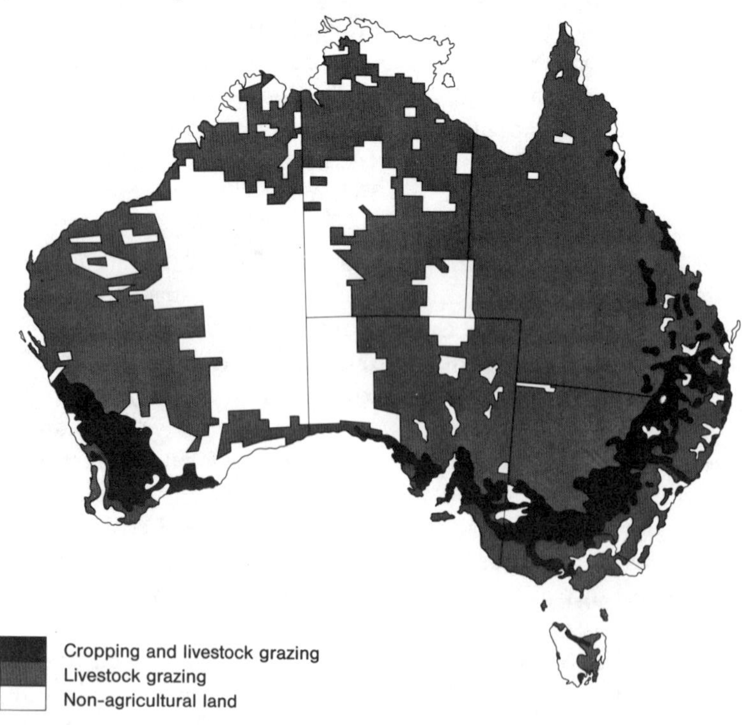

Fig. 2.6 Agricultural land use
Source: Adapted from the *Atlas of Australian Resources, Third Series, Volume 3,* and Hanley and Cooper (1982)

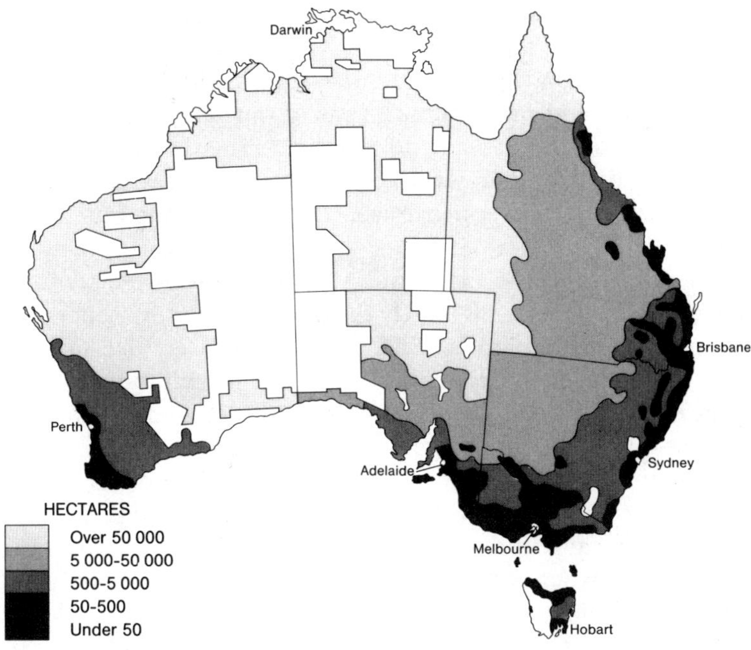

Fig. 2.7 The scale of operations in Australian rural production

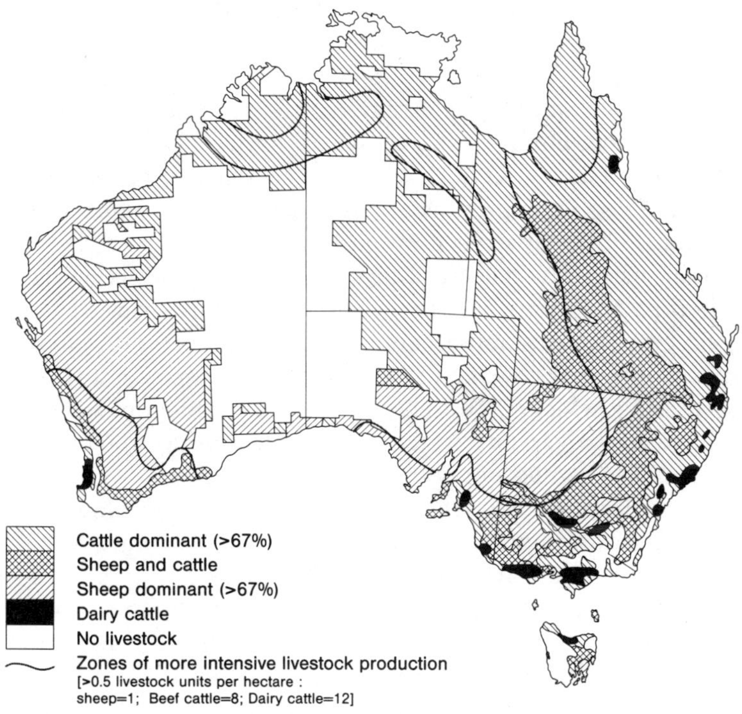

Fig. 2.8 Livestock production zones
Source: Adapted from the *Atlas of Australian Resources, Third Series, Volume 3,* and Hanley and Cooper (1982)

average about 150 ha (BAE, 1987a). In contrast, beef properties average over 400 000 ha in the Northern Territory and exceed 50 000 ha over much of the inland.

Cattle are more climatically tolerant than sheep, and dominate pastoralism in the hotter, drier and more humid areas of northern, central and coastal Australia. Sheep, on the other hand, dominate the drier parts of southern Australia. Their distributions overlap in parts of the eastern highlands, in some of the principal cropping areas, and throughout much of central Queensland.

Figure 2.9 illustrates the distribution of major crops. Apart from water availability, their distribution is largely restricted to flat or undulating country inland from coastal highlands. This permits the easy use of large-scale machinery at all stages in production from soil preparation to harvesting. Geographically, wheat is the most widespread crop. Taken together, the other dryland crops — barley, oats, sorghum and oil seeds in order of importance — mirror the distribution of wheat. Sorghum and oil seeds are grown in the warmer districts of northern NSW and southern Queensland. Sugar production requires high rainfall and warmth, which ties it to coastal districts in Queensland and northern NSW. Two other specialist crops, cotton and rice, are grown in Australia under irrigation. Cotton growing has developed in the Namoi and Gwydir Valleys of NSW, while rice is grown with water from the Murrumbidgee and Murray rivers (see Figure 2.5).

Where crops are grown is primarily determined by physical conditions. Within that broad area, the specific locations of crops depend on infrastructure investment. The production of wheat, for instance, often closely follows the grain silo and railway facilities used to market the crop. Likewise, certain location economies spring up where farmers can share machinery, contractors, maintenance services, seed and chemical supplies and research or advisory services. Sugar production, as one example, is highly restricted by cane crushing facilities at sugar mills and bulk terminal ports for shipment. The sugar industry revolves around some 30 or so mills and six ports. Industrial crops such as oilseeds and cotton have also tended to generate downstream processing establishments: crushing plants for oil extraction and cotton gins. Both sugar cane and raw cotton suffer considerable weight loss during processing, which, if carried out near to production, saves transport costs. In the case of sugar, one hectare commonly produces 80 tonnes of stalk from which only 11 tonnes of raw sugar are extracted.

Horticultural output covers small areas in widely scattered locations. Table 2.11 sets out the most important producing areas. Three regions stand out in particular: the irrigation districts of the Murray and Murrumbidgee river systems; a belt of southern Victoria from Ballarat in the west to Sale in the east; and southeast Queensland including part of the Darling Downs. The Adelaide region also has a large horticultural area, but it is almost exclusively given over to grape production and is not broadly based in its production emphasis.

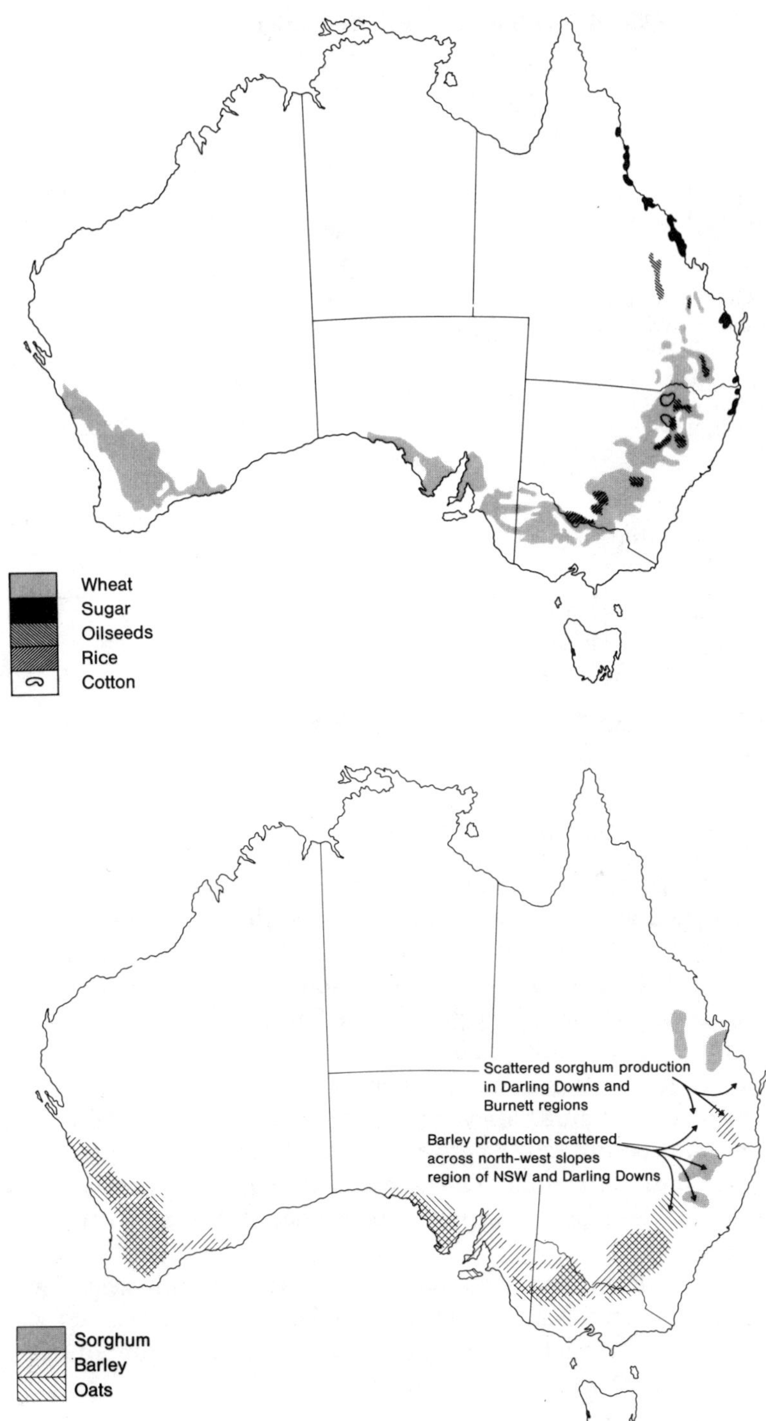

Fig. 2.9 The distribution of major crops
Source: Adapted from the *Atlas of Australian Resources, Third Series, Volume 3*

Table 2.11 The location of horticultural production

	1	*2*	*3*	*4*	*5*	*6*	*7*	*8*
Sydney region/Hunter (NSW)	••				•	•		
Melbourne region/Gippsland(Vic)		••	•			••	••	
Adelaide region		•			••			
South-east Qld/Toowoomba				••		••	••	
Riverland (SA)	••		••		••			
Sunraysia (Vic)	••				••			
Murray-Goulburn (Vic)		••	••		•			
Murrumbidgee Irr. Area	••		••		••	•		
Northern Tasmania						••	••	
Central/Southern Tablelands (NSW)		••	••			••	•	
Green Triangle (SA)						••		
Stanthorpe (Qld)		••	•					
Perth (WA)	•				•			
Bunbury (WA)		••					•	
North-east Victoria								••
Atherton Tablelands (Qld)								••
Burdekin (Qld)						••		

1 Citrus 2 Pome fruit 3 Stone fruit 4 Tropical fruit

5 Grapes 6 Vegtables 7 Potatoes 8 Tobacco

•• Major production • Minor production

Source: Adapted from *Atlas of Australian Resources (Third Series), Volume 3, Agriculture*, 1982

The structure of farm output

The Bureau of Agricultural Economics (BAE) estimated the 1990/91 value of rural production at $21.1 billion, of which just three commodities — wool, beef and wheat — accounted for almost half (Table 2.12). These industries have long headed the list of rural output, though their order varies from time to time depending on prevailing prices. The fourth-ranking rural industry was dairying, with manufacturing milk (for cheese, butter, etc.) and market (fresh) milk together accounting for about 9 per cent of rural output. A further group of commodities including barley, sugar, vegetables, cotton, poultry, pigs and sheep-meats, accounting for between 2 and 4 per cent each, added up to another one-fifth of the total. Thus, despite an enormous variety of commodities produced, Australian farming depends heavily on the fortunes of a few major items.

To some extent this pattern of output is stable. Certainly wheat, wool and beef have long been the mainstays of rural Australia, but a casual glance at Table 2.12 suggests that the share of total output contributed by various commodities has changed substantially during the 1980s, both in terms of gross value and gross volume of production. Movements in these measures need not be synchronized due to sharp changes in unit prices.

Some industries performed poorly in the early years of the decade: especially rice, sugar and sheep-meats. In each case their output value declined by around 40 per cent during the five years to 1985/86 (or about 60 per cent in real inflation adjusted terms). Most of the fall reflects a slump in unit prices received, although in the case of rice and sheep-meats the volume of output also contracted. Domestic and export sheep-meats markets were weak, but output was also depressed by the relative profitability of wool production and the need to rebuild flock strength after the severe drought of the early 1980s. The 1980s drought also helps explain the reduced volume of beef production. In this case, much stronger meat prices — a 25 per cent increase in unit values — compensated partially for lower production, and beef's share of the gross value of farm output declined only marginally.

By 1991 the mantle of depression had fallen on wool and wheat. At one stage wheat growers were receiving less than A$120 per tonne, compared with a rough break-even price of A$150. And wool-growers found that their industry was heading towards bankruptcy as their grossly inflated floor price of over 880¢ per kilo cleaned wool led to the normal market response of reduced consumer purchases and expanding production. Wool stockpiles therefore sky-rocketed. Not only did these require expensive storage, but the value of the stockpile declined way below purchase price. In fact when the floor price was eventually scrapped, and the auction price plummeted to just above 400¢ a kilo. Prices received recovered to about 580¢ in late 1991, though the ABARE forecast lower prices for most of 1992. Many wool growers were not only operating at a loss on current production but were being levied to cover the stockpile's losses.

Barley, oats and cotton recorded large increases in output volumes despite substantial unit price reductions. This appears to fly in the face of economic theory which predicts a positive correlation between prices received and output. In farming, however, there are many unpredictable factors at work. 1980/81 may have witnessed exceptionally low output or high prices, or the situation could have been reversed in 1985/86. And, at least in the case of cotton, additional water supplies from the Copeton Dam enabled long-term industry expansion in the Gwydir valley.

The economic causes of structural change

The previous discussion identified several reasons why an industry's output, as measured by gross value of production, might change. Volume and unit price are at least partially related. Volume is susceptible to one-off events such as drought, ideal climatic conditions, excessive rainfall at critical moments in the production cycle, herd rebuilding, clearing new land, and additional supplies of irrigation water. In the long run, however, farming is an economic activity and its survival at a particular location, and the mix of commodities produced there, will reflect the relative profitability of various possibilities.

Table 2.12 The gross value of rural production at current prices

	1980/81		1985/86		1990/91[1]		Change 1980/81 to 1990/91 in		1990/91 Index of average unit values (current prices)
							Value	Volume	
	$m	%	*$m*	%	*$m*	%	%	%	*1980/81 = 100*
Cereals for grain	2524		4061		3459				
Wheat	1684	15	2694	17	1961	9	16.4	41.9	82
Barley	381	3	587	4	546	3	43.3	55.1	92
Sorghum	152	1	181	1	119	1	(21.7)	(26.7)	107
Oats	140	1	138	1	164	1	17.1	39.5	85
Rice	138	1	81	1	124	1	(10.1)	8.1	83
Fruit	570		910		1154				
Apples	119	1	189	1	212	1	78.2	(4.9)	188
Citrus	116	1	179	1	213	1	83.6	7.6	58
Wine &table grapes[2]	101	1	149	1	206	1	104.0	7.1	170
Dried vine fruits[2]	70	1	140	1	157	1	124.3	33.6[3]	156
Bananas	60	1	102	1	190	1	216.7	37.1	234
Other crops	2205		2457		4361				
Sugar cane	800	7	494	3	752	4	(6.0)	6.2[4]	91
Other vegetables	339	3	508	3	890	4	162.5	54.6	n.a.
Cotton	147	1	330	2	783	4	432.7	362.2[5]	130
Potatoes	162	1	206	1	284	1	75.3	29.6	128
Other crops	576	5	895	6	1569	7	172.4		

Livestock slaughterings	3488		3904		5482				
Cattle	2057	18	2367	15	3565	17	73.3	(2.5)	154
Poultry	361	3	559	4	809	4	124.1	47.5	146
Pigs	660	3	438	3	660	3	95.3	33.0	137
Sheep (domestic)[2]	565	5	371	2	382	2	(32.4)	9.3	94/10[6]
Sheep (live exports)[2]	167	1	109	1	66	*	(60.5)	(42.8)	n.a.
Livestock products[2]	2754		4203		6653				
Wool	1670	14	2693	17	4607	22	175.9	55.3	180
Manufactured milk[2]	380	3	648	4	994	5	161.6	26.0	165
Market milk[2]	297	3	533	3	710	4	139.1	12.6	174
Gross value of rural production—all commodities	11541		15535		21109		82.9		125
							Index of prices paid (1980/81 = 100)		208

1 Preliminary
2 BAE estimates
3 Fresh weight
4 Sugar (94 nt)
5 Cotton lint
6 Lamb/mutton
* <0.5%
Figures in brackets are negative
Sources: Bureau of Agricultural Economics (1986a, 1987a); Australian Bureau of Agricultural and Resource Economics (1990, 1991a).

Profits are the difference between revenues and costs. This section examines the complicated sets of factors which determine farmers' revenues and costs and how they are currently working to change the structure and location of production.

One general observation is worth making. Table 2.12 shows that unit values increased on average during the decade to 1990/91 by 25 per cent, whereas input prices paid grew by 108 per cent. In practice this large adverse movement in farmers' terms of trade represents an acceleration of a long-term trend. In the 30 years to 1980/81 the terms of trade halved. In the next two five-year periods they declined a further one quarter and 17 per cent respectively. This does not mean that farming is about to become bankrupt, although individual farmers will do so because of incompetence or bad luck.

Farming has compensated by becoming more efficient, so that a unit of cost produces much more value of output than before. This is achieved in numerous ways: new crop varieties which yield more and grow faster; leaner and faster growing cattle; bigger, more powerful machines; better chemicals and improved methods of application; more widespread irrigation; new tillage and soil conservation systems; better response to drought; improved marketing and commodity handling techniques; better financial management; and farm amalgamation yielding economies of scale. All farm sectors have gained in efficiency by these means, with both general and particular spatial consequences.

Technological change has served to amalgamate holdings and reduce the demand for on-farm labour. The consequent rural depopulation is balanced in part by the expansion of maintenance, research, advisory, retail and contract services in nearby towns. The family farm is yielding ground to the corporate farm, which has greater access to necessary capital, and at cheaper rates of interest, and whose diversity of interests may cushion it better against cyclical financial hardship.

New production techniques also favour some locations rather than others. For instance, the development of irrigation in the Murrumbidgee Irrigation Area (MIA) and elsewhere has served to concentrate fruit production. Increased scale economies in dairy and egg production have served to concentrate those industries.

Australian farms are subject to two different price regimes: the international circuit, for commodities which are primarily exported, and the domestic circuit, for locally consumed production. Exporters take whatever prices are offered on world markets, and these are basically set by the interplay of current production and accumulated stocks against demand. The prices can be volatile.

In the year to May 1987 the Australian Wool Corporation's market indicator rose 37 per cent to 741¢/ kg, whereas in 1991 the price halved in the space of a few months. The wool price index shown in Table 2.12 was close to 180 in 1990/91 (1980/81 = 100), reflecting temporarily the artificially high floor price.

Over the same period cotton prices rose 30 per cent in current price terms after more than doubling from US 30¢/ kg to US 68¢/kg in the first half of the 1980s.

Wheat, in contrast, experienced a sudden 17 per cent fall in its Australian dollar value during the September quarter of 1986, so that by December of that year the index of unit value reached 94 compared with 113 for the previous financial year.

Finally, world sugar prices in December 1988 were US 10¢ per pound. Eighteen months later they reached 15¢ before falling to 8¢ in June 1991. This volatility is both exacerbated and ameliorated by unstable exchange rate parities between the Australian dollars and other major currencies.

Export prices are increasingly being distorted by government intervention in some countries, particularly in Europe, Japan and the USA. Australia and New Zealand, in contrast, offer their farmers low protection. The aims of the interventionists are varied:

- to increase self-sufficiency;
- to protect local producers against cheaper imports;
- to promote regional development by increasing rural incomes;
- to prevent people moving to already overcrowded cities;
- to preserve rural lifestyles;
- to clear stockpiles, and so on.

These goals can be achieved by placing quotas or tariffs on imports, regulating domestic prices, buying up local produce at a predetermined price, paying bounties, or subsidizing input costs. The inevitable consequence is to raise global production levels, which, in the absence of a corresponding growth in demand, will tend to depress export prices. Worse still, governments may be tempted to dump surplus production on world markets at give-away prices, leading to further price deterioration.

Just about all Australian exporters have experienced the consequences of these policies in recent years. Australia cannot subsidize its producers to any large extent to protect them from the trade policies of competing nations: rural exports are too prominent in the economy. To some extent currency devaluation increases the returns to exporters, but it is a blunt instrument and benefits already prosperous industries as well as the weak.

Farms producing commodities for local consumption — especially in the horticultural, dairy and poultry industries — have more stable returns. Their unit prices received have also out-performed much of the export-oriented sector (Table 2.12). They are subject to a battery of government regulatory policies — rationalisation schemes, quotas, licensing, price controls, market zones — which serve to raise producer returns at the expense of consumers. This protection is substantial, as indicated by Table 2.9.

One crop, sugar, is exposed to both regimes simultaneously. Local prices are controlled and only occasionally approximate export returns. Figures for 1985/86 gave an average price to mill from domestic sales of $341.50 per tonne against the export equivalent of $190.10. Five years before, export prices of $330 per tonne greatly exceeded the then domestic price of $251.67. To some extent this arrangement can be justified if it imparts a degree of stability to the industry. About 60 per cent of sugar production is exported (Table 2.13) and that output rode the roller-coaster to financial disaster in the early 1980s. In 1980/81 sugar accounted for over 14 per cent of rural exports; the next year, 10 per cent; and by 1985/86, 5 per cent before recovering slightly to 7 per cent at the end of the decade. Export prices declined 20 per cent over the same period. Without domestic price support the regional economies of parts of the north Queensland coast could have faced ruin.

Table 2.13 identifies the major export commodities and therefore some of those industries most at risk from uncontrolled price fluctuations. Various small volume industries not listed may face a similar risk if export oriented. Of the major commodities wool, wheat, sugar, and cotton have the greatest exposure to international markets. Only in the case of wool, where Australia is the dominant market trader, did the industry feel it had some small leverage over prices through a stockpile system and promotional activities. This impression proved false when the Wool Corporation tried to defy economic gravity and the scheme collapsed under the weight of greed and managerial incompetence. Unfortunately for Australia, 53 per cent of total export income in the farm sector is from wool, wheat, and beef/veal. Clearly, it would be disastrous for the Australian economy if all three simultaneously experienced depressed conditions. By a stroke of luck the 1986 wheat price slump was counterbalanced by a wool boom and the rather more severe 1991/92 recession in the wool and wheat industries have been offset by reasonable trading conditions for beef.

The profitability of an industry sector also reflects its cost structure. Here, too, both international and domestic circuits operate, though it is more difficult to disentangle their respective influences. For example, the Commonwealth government faced a balance of payments crisis in the mid-1980s, largely created by a collapse of rural and mineral commodity prices. The government adopted, for political reasons, a combination of two policies to combat that crisis: currency devaluation and interest rate management. Their relative weighting had a large effect on the economies of farm production, though individual sectors were affected differently.

Currency devaluations are, as noted above, a blunt instrument. They are also inflationary. A high interest rate strategy reduces the magnitude of devaluation and consequently helps control inflation. High interest rates also reduce the level of economic activity and the inflationary effects of excess demand for labour, materials and goods. Consider the position of a wheat farmer with a $100 000 debt. The farmer would gain enormously from a large currency devaluation and low interest rates. The higher prices received would offset considerably the extra input cost of imported machinery caused by the lower value of the dollar. Of course farmers would, like the rest of the community, pay more for imported consumer goods. This would not bother them much, unlike most others, since personal consumption comes a poor second to business survival.

In contrast there is reason why farmers have complained bitterly about high interest rates. In 1985/86 all broadacre industries experienced an average business debt at 14 per cent of farm capital (BAE, 1987b) which declined to 10 per cent by the end of the decade (Peterson *et al.*, 1991). The corresponding figures for wheat and other crops farms, the sector that was the most indebted, were 18 and 15 per cent, though plunging farm values in the 1991 rural recession may once more raise the debt to equity figure. These figures are not high by most business standards, but the ability to sustain debt depends on the level of income the business receives. If we examine the debt servicing ratio (the ratio of interest payments to gross cash surplus) we find that the figure rose to over 35 per cent in both the rural recessions of 1986 and 1991, compared with only 10 per cent a decade earlier. Grain producers, who tend to experience higher debt levels than other producers, are therefore poorly placed to withstand high interest rates. However, during the 1991 recession the hardest hit farmers were the wool producers, despite their lower average debt levels. This is because the decline in wool income was so severe that many could not cover their costs and pay the interest due. Other sectors with high average farm debts include horticulture and irrigation cropping (especially rice and cotton growers) — both of which are more capital intensive than livestock farming.

Of course, there are major inter-farm and geographical differences in the incidence of debt in all sectors. Thus in 1988/89 the average debt of wheat and other crops properties was about $129 000. Yet a quarter of properties had zero or trivial debts of less than $3 000, while another quarter had outstanding loans of greater than $156 000 (Peterson, 1991). In 1985/86 the average debt of a NSW grain farm was twice the national figure; Western Australia's about 50 per cent higher. The BAE (1987b) calculated that in 1985/86 approximately one-fifth of wheat and crops producers were 'at risk' nationally. Farms are defined as being 'at risk' if they satisfy two conditions:

1 negative cash margins after allowing for off-farm income and
2 equity less than 70 per cent of capital value. Because of their greater debt burden, NSW and WA farmers experienced 'at risk' rates of 53 per cent and 27 per cent respectively. Only a small proportion of 'at risk' farmers will ultimately fail, but those surviving will experience considerable poverty and mental anguish. This picture is replicated in a less dramatic way for most farm sectors.

The particularly perilous financial circumstances of NSW wheat and crops farmers stem largely from the trend to 'get big or get out' in the early 1980s. Production extended territorially and farms were often consolidated using borrowed capital. The demand for cropping land pushed its price rapidly

Table 2.13 The export performance of rural commodities

	Value (current prices)		Percentage change	Volume		Percentage change	1990/91 Index of av. unit value (current prices)	Proportion of output exported in 1990/91	Proportion of all exports accounted for by major items 1990/91
	1980/81 $m	*1990/91 $m[1]*	*1980/81– 1990/91*	*1980/81 kt*	*1990/91 kt[1]*	*to 1990/91*	*1980/81 = 100*	*by volume (%)*	*by value (%)*
Selected crops									
Wheat (incl.flour)	1 753	1 748	(0.3)	10 648	12 191	14.5	112.1	179	13
Sugar	1 146	872	(23.9)	2 558	2 612	2.1	51.7	61	7
Raw cotton	92	716	678.3	59	314	432.2	101.7	74	5
Barley (incl.malt)	341	492	44.3	2 076	284	36.8	82.9	7	4
Rice	100	184	84	276	434	57.2	101.2	55	1
Sorghum	58	25	(56.9)	463	166	64.1	115.1	19	*
Selected livestock products									
Wool—greasy	1 462	1 915	31.0	532	416	(21.8)	136.4	55	15
other	473	798	68.7	189	181	(4.2)	138.7		6
Beef and veal	1 037	2 529	143.9	498	733	47.2	133.4	43	19
Live sheep	167	55	(67.1)	5 771	3 300	(42.8)	93.1	100	*
Mutton	227	259	14.1	187	181	(3.2)	113.9	47	2
Lamb	71	124	74.6	41	42	2.4	106.1	14	1
Cheese	104	206	98.1	54	63	16.7	129.8	36	2

Table 2.13 continued

Wholemilk powder	71	101	42.3	44	39	(11.4)	120.1	65	1
Butter	30	114	280.0	16	60	275.0	84.9	57	1
Total of commodities listed	7 132	10 138	42.1						
All rural exports	8 030	13 101	63.2				116.0		
Major items as per cent of all farm exports	88.8	77.4							
Total prices paid in production (1980/81) = 100)	100	208	108						

1 Provisional * < 0.5
Source: Compiled from statistics provided by the Bueau of Agricultural Economics (1986a, 1987a); Australian Bureau of Agriculture and Resource Economics (1991a).

higher. The debt burden is thus pronounced in more marginal areas further inland where much of the expansion of cropping occurred. Unfortunately these localities also suffer higher costs, particularly for transport, and, for climatic reasons, lower and less stable yields. Farm failures, further farm consolidation and consequent rural depopulation are likely to be greater, therefore, in marginal areas. Moreover, these localities may see an early switch to other kinds of output, leaving cropping activities to more favoured locations. Many farmers indeed moved into wool production in the late 1980s, only to be hit by a second recession more severe than the first.

The experiences of wheat producers mirror closely those of rice and sugar farmers in recent years. Unlike wheat, these industries are spatially concentrated and their financial problems have had more noticeable adverse regional effects in towns such as Griffith and Mackay. For broadacre farmers the range of substitution possibilities is limited: subject to capital availability, wheat can sometimes be replaced readily by other crops (according to environmental circumstances) and by livestock. Farmers in coastal or irrigation zones, in contrast, have a wider range of options in place of sugar or rice: temperate and tropical fruits, vegetables, nuts, flowers, and even 'sea-foods' in the form of fish and crustaceans.

While the interest on farm debt is possibly the most serious adverse cost movement experienced by farmers in recent years, significant rises in other costs may be important for particular industries or locations. Rises in the cost of irrigation water levied by the NSW Water Resources Commission, an attempt to recoup a more realistic proportion of its own outlays, were most ill-timed from the point of view of rice farmers experiencing depressed prices. The federal government's import parity pricing policy for fuels has likewise worked to the disadvantage of fuel-hungry grain farmers.

In conclusion, it is somewhat ironic that the farm sectors which have experienced the greatest reductions in output prices in recent times have also tended to experience the greatest input price rises. This cost–price squeeze may, however, be a temporary phenomenon. A major crop failure in the wheat-lands of Russia and the Ukraine or North America could greatly reduce stocks and sharply raise prices. Whatever the case, we can be assured of one thing: most farm sectors will continue to experience fluctuating economic fortunes. Place prosperity is consequently also volatile.

Forestry and fishing

Forestry and logging (the husbandry and extraction of timber resources) is a relatively minor component of Australian primary production, notwithstanding Mercer's (1991) claims that it rivals the wool industry in importance. Its 1978/79 output of $276 million was roughly similar to the fishing industry and pig production and about 1.6 per cent of primary production. About

17 600 workers were employed in the industry at the time (3.9 per cent of the primary production workforce), but that number represented a 40 per cent drop over the previous twenty years. Output declined by 30 per cent over the same period in constant (real) price terms. The industry therefore experienced a considerable contraction in the 1960s and 1970s. In part this reflected the exhaustion of more valuable timbers and the extension of national park boundaries. The latter factor should not be over-stated, however, because the vast majority of Australia's 42.7 million hectares of forest are still 'available' for exploitation (although admittedly many national parks lock away some of the better timbers). Part of the contraction in output also reflects a tendency towards greater conservation of the resource. While the workforce continued to contract to about 11 000 in 1990/91, production stabilised in the latter part of the 1980s at about 17 million cubic metres.

The distribution of commercial forests is most uneven (Figure 2.10). There are the jarrah and karri forests of Western Australia and the pine plantations of South Australia; much of Tasmania is forested; so too are the highlands of Victoria and NSW; the coastal areas of eastern Victoria and NSW have a heavy covering of timber; Queensland's resources are scattered throughout the State's southeast and, in the form of rainforest, along the

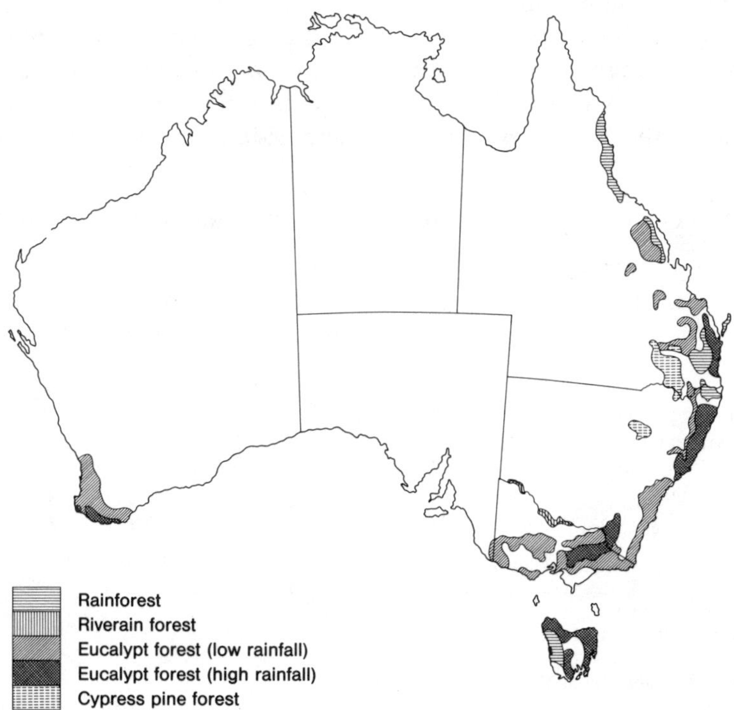

Fig. 2.10 Principal commercial forest regions
Source: Adapted from the *Atlas of Australian Resources, Second Series*, and Smith (1981)

north tropical coast. Away from the coast there are extensive cypress pine forests on the Darling Downs and in the pilliga scrub. The three mainland eastern states have about 80 per cent of the forested area, but only 65 per cent of the workforce (Table 2.14). This is a consequence of the rather greater intensity of forest operations in Tasmania, South Australia and Western Australia as shown by the final column of Table 2.14. According to Chisholm and Anderson (1991) about 85 per cent of the forest comprises native eucalypt and paperbark species.

In the case of South Australia, the State's only significant forest resources are the man-made *Pinus radiata* plantations in the southeast. Thus the entire resource is tended permanently for the purpose of commercial timber production (and the index measure in Table 2.14 is correspondingly high). Exotic pine species are found in all other States and the ACT, but especially in western Victoria adjacent to the South Australian border, in the Latrobe Valley, the southwest slopes of NSW near Tumut, near Oberon and north of Perth. Although they constitute only 2 per cent of Australia's forested area, their economic importance is considerable to the regions concerned and much greater than the percentage suggests. In 1981, for example, it was estimated that coniferous plantations would supply 38 per cent of the national volume of saw- and pulp-logs by 1985 and that this share would rise to 63 per cent by 2020 (South, 1981).

Apart from the south-west corner of the continent and all regions of Tasmania, the main areas of forestry based on native vegetation include the Ballarat, Latrobe Valley and Gippsland regions of Victoria, the far south, mid north and north coastal regions of NSW, and widely separated parts of coastal

Table 2.14 Forestry and logging: magnitude of the industry by state, 1978/79

	1	*2*	*3*	*4*	*5*	*6*	*7*
New South Wales	15.5	19.3	99	94	4.8	27	0.7
Queensland	11.8	6.8	99	88	4.1	23	0.8
Victoria	6.0	26.2	97	98	2.6	15	1.1
Northern Territory	3.3	2.4	100	90	0.2	1	0.1
Western Australia	3.1	1.2	97	97	2.0	11	1.5
Tasmania	2.9	42.3	98	96	3.1	17	2.5
South Australia	0.1	0.1	0	100	0.8	4	17.1
ACT	0.1	27.0	78	100	0.2	1	4.3
Australia	42.7	5.6	98	93	17.6	99	1.0

1 Forested area (M ha)
2 Proportion of state's area (%)
3 Proportion native forest (%)
4 Proportion available for timber production (%)
5 Employment ('000)
6 Proportion of Aust. forestry and logging workforce (%)
7 Index of intensity of use of forest resources

Source: Bureau of Agricultural Economics (1982)

Queensland. With the exception of wood-chips, very little of the output is exported (the amount being only 4 million cubic metres of the total domestic production of 15 million cubic metres in 1977/78 (Gunnerson, 1981)). In fact, over one quarter of local timber requirements are imported, mainly for construction and paper uses.

With the exception of woodchips, the scale and form of the industry is primarily determined by the domestic circuit of factors described in Figure 2.4. But unlike farming, forestry is dominated by the public sector which accounts directly for about three-quarters of output, and heavily regulates private activity. Woodchipping, which is environmentally sensitive, is only permitted under licence for export. And tax concessions have long been available for persons investing in plantations.

The industry remains economically buoyant. The export side, mainly in the form of wood-chips, enjoyed a 1986 index price of 165 (1980 = 100). Compare this with price indices in Tables 2.12 and 2.13. In the domestic area, consumption of paper and paperboard has grown steadily, and, given the strong competitive positions of local producers *vis-à-vis* imports, demand for wood-pulp has remained strong. Although demand for sawn timber fluctuates according to the health of the construction industry, prices have generally increased faster than the rate of inflation. The 1980s currency devaluations helped to protect local producers by greatly increasing the prices of competing imports and boosting export earnings. Exports expanded steadily in the 1980s to nearly $600 million per annum, two-thirds in the form of woodchips.

One final element in the industry's stability is the relatively fixed geographical distribution of forest resources, especially under conditions of careful management where timber is renewed at its rate of extraction. Where extraction exceeds renewal, as long occurred on the NSW north coast, the industry must decline as resources become scarcer. The reverse can occur, as for example near Walcha on the Northern Tablelands of NSW where extensive softwood plantations are being developed and employment is increasing. Unlike farming, these changes occur only slowly and over a long time. Only where licences are suspended, or national parks and wilderness areas are proclaimed, is the industry stopped dead in its tracks.

The location of Australia's major fisheries are shown in Figure 2.11, and the structure of output is given in Table 2.15. Export markets dominate most items, except for fresh and frozen fish. The value of production has long been dominated by crustaceans and shell-fish. A long and appropriately configured coast-line offers ample breeding grounds for these two items, and output is generally of high quality. Strong overseas demand and a shortfall in supplies of all items except oysters have combined to keep prices high and sustain a rise in the value of output despite recent volume decline. In the case of prawns, abalone, and scallops quotas have been placed on catches to conserve resources and prevent declining yields through over-exploitation. Oysters

Fig. 2.11 Principal commercial fisheries
Source: Adapted from the *Atlas of Australian Resources, Second Series*, and Smith (1981)

have been 'farmed' in artificial beds for many years, but the idea is being extended to prawns and other crustaceans. A prawn farm has been located adjacent to Townsville's airport to permit ready despatch to southern and overseas markets. Black Marlin are being raised in artificial dams on a property in Western Australia.

Despite this optimistic picture for crustaceans and shellfish, events have conspired to make Australian waters a relatively poor prospect for fishing in general, due to a narrow continental shelf and nutrient poor waters resulting from low continental run-off and warm waters, especially to the east and north. Consequently, imports still exceed exports despite a sharp rise in fish exports over the five years to 1990/91 — due, in part, to strong prices. Alas, current fishing levels and therefore exports are thought to be unsustainable. Influences at work here include good Japanese demand for bluefin tuna for the sashimi market and higher world prices caused by over-fishing in the northern hemisphere. Fish, too, can be farmed to increase the quality and security of output. Atlantic salmon which are prized by the gourmet market are, for example, tended in sea-water pens south of Hobart in the D'Entrecasteaux Channel.

Table 2.15 The gross value of fisheries production at current prices

	Production		*Per cent change*	*Value of exports*[2]		*Value of imports*
	1985/86	*1990/91*[1, 4]	*1985/86–1990/91*	*1985/86*	*1990/91*	*1990/91*
	$m	*$m*		*$m*	*$m*	*$m*
Prawns	195	261	33.8	205	185	
Rock lobster	166	289	74.1	146	250	
Abalone	60	81	35.0	86	113	159 (Prawns to Oysters)
Scallops	24	34	41.7	19	31	
Oysters	29	35	20.7	n.a.	n.a.	
Fresh & frozen fish	102	300	194.1	9	105	
(excluding tuna)						255 (Fresh & frozen fish and Tuna)
Tuna	17	30	76.5	7	6	
Major items	593	1030	73.7			

Share of:	Qld	WA	NSW	SA	Vic	Tas	NT	
Gross value of production (%)	24	23	19	13	8[3]	8	6	(1980/81)
Licensed fishermen (%)	21	19	23	15	8	8	8	(1978/79)

1 Provisional
2 May include some processing, withdrawal from stocks, or re-exports
3 Rough estimate
4 Including $34 million mariculture

Source: Bureau of Agricultural Economics (1987a); ABS Fisheries, Australia (1984/85); Senate Standing Committee on Trade and Commerce, (1982)

Some communities depend heavily on the health of the fishing industry. These include Eden, Ulladulla, Lakes Entrance, Maclean, the D'Entrecasteaux Channel, Port Lincoln, Albany, Jurien Bay, Geraldton, Denham and Karumba (see Figure 2.11). Several have canneries which process part of the catch. There are, however, many other small communities whose livelihood is tied to the sea's resources (see *Atlas of Australian Resources*, 2nd Series, Fish and Fisheries). Employment is often seasonal, itinerant or on a part-time basis so it is difficult to enumerate the workforce. Figures can be based on licences issued, although individual fishermen may hold them simultaneously in several States. The Senate Standing Committee on Trade and Commerce (1982) identified 20 000 commercial fishermen in 1978/79 located mainly in NSW, Queensland, WA, and SA. The distribution accords approximately with the value of production, although output per head is highest in Queensland and WA, which have a disproportionate share of output in high value crustaceans and shell-fish.

More even than farming, Australian fishing operations are conducted on a small scale and through unincorporated entities owned by individual fishermen and their families. Many businesses are operated spasmodically and are often not tied to a particular area. Equally, many are highly profitable — for example abalone diving — and there is little incentive to diversify or expand operations. The Senate Standing Committee also discovered that the more marginal fishermen did not have access to adequate capital to expand operations and that few were prepared to endure the discomforts of remaining at sea for lengthy periods to exploit more remote resources.

The industry is therefore likely to remain small-scale, fragmented and geographically parochial, largely for behavioural reasons. The precise form and scale of operations in particular areas will tend to depend on a mixture of resource availability, domestic government resource management policies, and prices largely set by the international circuit of capital.

Mining

The relationship between mining and the rest of the economy is frequently uncomfortable: it is never less than capricious but on other occasions it has benefitted the nation enormously. Yet the industry employs only 1.5 per cent of the workforce and accounts for a little over 6 per cent of GDP depending on commodity prices at the time (Tables 2.6 and 2.7). The industry clearly influences the country's economic health out of all proportion to its size. A few basic statistics help explain why.

Mining contributed one third per cent of Australia's export income in 1990/91 and about two-thirds of its output was exported. Its prosperity is therefore largely determined by the international circuit of forces identified earlier over which the Australian public and government have little control. In no individual commodity does this country control a sufficient volume of production to permit market rigging. Nor is the establishment of producer cartels possible on a long-term basis to regulate and stabilize prices (even the well-respected tin agreement to which Australia was party broke down in the mid-1980s). There are three reasons why attempts to sustain artificially high commodity prices tend to fail: many commodities can be substituted by other cheaper alternatives; high prices stimulate exploration and uncover new competing resources; and there is a propensity for cartel producers to cheat by raising production or lowering prices in order to expand market share. Miners and mining companies are therefore price takers, not price setters. The greatest testimony to this fact is the failure of the Organisation of Petroleum Exporting Countries (OPEC) to sustain high oil prices over the long term despite attempts in 1973 and 1979 to do just that. Nor did the 1991 Gulf War do more than raise prices for more than a few months. Real oil prices are now similar to their levels twenty years ago.

This would not matter were the prices received not fairly unstable in the short-term and generally adverse in the long-term. This is clearly demonstrated in Fig. 2.12. The prices of Australia's principal metal exports (copper,

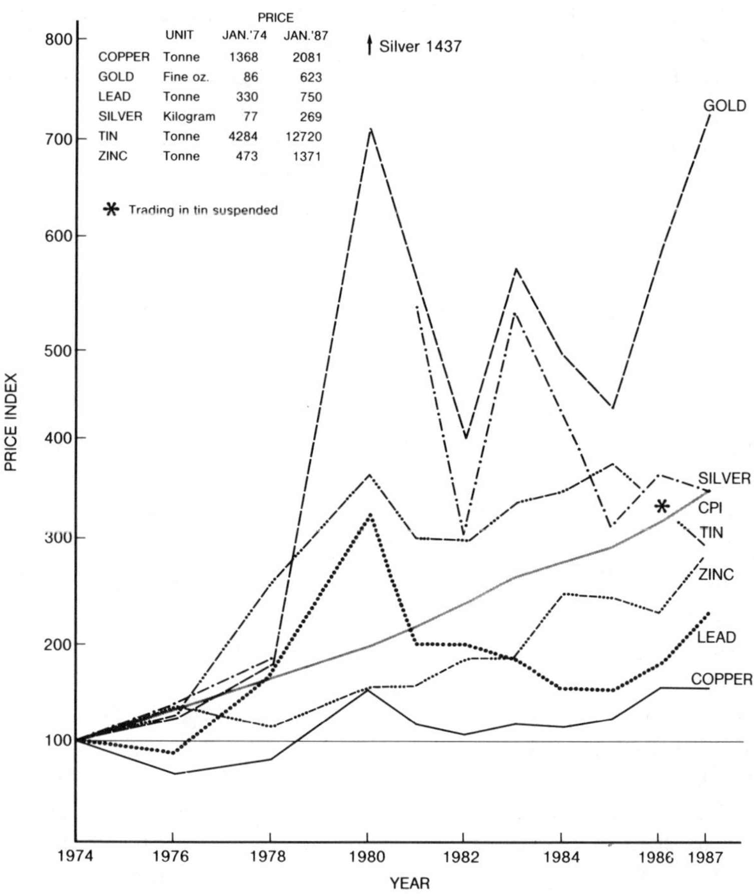

Fig. 2.12 The price indices for major metals (Australian dollars)
Source: Department of Mineral Resources

lead, zinc and tin) failed to keep pace with inflation over the thirteen years to 1987. Silver, after some wild gyrations, only just managed to keep pace with cost increases. If the demand for and supply of a mineral is roughly in balance, as occurs most of the time, sudden changes in supply or demand can radically and quickly affect prices. These are *spot prices* set by speculators and traders on the floor of institutions such as the London Metal Exchange (LME), not long-term bilateral contract prices under which most of Australia's minerals are produced. However, the latter are negotiated bearing in mind spot prices and anticipated market trends. Mine disasters, strikes, wars, social unrest, political coups, closures of unprofitable mines, or the artificial restriction of output can all restrict supplies and raise prices. Few of these problems afflict Australia, but they are endemic in many key producing nations: the Middle East (oil), South Africa (precious metals, gemstones, coal etc.), and Chile (copper), for example. Naturally, anything which increases supply, including solution of the above problems, lowers prices.

Demand can be quite unstable, too, but rarely in connection with real end-usage. During the second oil-shock of 1979, such large oil users as electricity utilities decided to switch to coal to drive their generators. This substitution put strong upward pressure on coal prices. More often the demand for metal gyrates for speculative reasons. Sometimes individuals or organisations (governments) try to corner a market (for example, the Hunt family in 1980 in silver and the Malaysians in tin in 1986, as shown in Fig. 2.12). At other times mineral commodities are seen as stores of wealth much like Rembrandts or Ming vases. This is particularly true at times of civil strife, currency devaluation, monetary inflation or other economic uncertainty: gold, silver, diamonds, platinum and other not-so-rare items can be transported readily and are proof against inflation in particular. This situation occurred in 1980 (Fig. 2.12).

Commodity prices reflect the interaction of supply and demand, but because of the ever-present element of speculation and the time lags involved in matching supply and demand, price movements are often exaggerated. If the problem is a real or perceived shortage, prices often skyrocket before settling back more slowly. With excesses, the reverse occurs. A spectacular example is the price of gold in 1980. It started the year on US$599.00 per ounce and reached US$765.00 by 16 January. On 21 January it peaked at US$843.00, before falling back to a low of US$474.00 by mid-March. The collapse of spot oil prices in 1985/86 from over US$30 per barrel to as little as US$7 for Saudi light crude and their subsequent recovery to US$18 is another example. The gold price movement was spurred by economic recession and high inflation in industrialised nations, partly as a consequence of massive oil price increases the previous year. The oil price collapse was engineered by one OPEC cartel member, Saudi Arabia, in order to stop member nations from cheating on above-quota sales at her expense. This was achieved by swamping the market with excess production.

Such events can have a major impact on the Australian economy in all kinds of interrelated ways: on the value of mineral exports, the value of the Australian dollar, the domestic rate of inflation, the level of mineral exploration and production, and rates of capital inflow. For example it was estimated in 1986 that the value of Australia's coal and iron ore exports would decline by 1 billion dollars in 1987 as a consequence of global oversupply of those commodities, fierce competition between producing nations, reduced Japanese steel production, the low price of oil (a coal substitute), and the sheer economic power of the Japanese which enables them to force lower prices. In the absence of countervailing price movements in other agricultural or mineral exports, such a drop in export income would increase the trade deficit, depress the value of the dollar, unleash inflationary forces and make life difficult for the government of the day. Unlike many real banana republics, Australia's primary production is broadly based and the price movements of some commodities are counter-cyclical. Depressed 1987 coal and iron ore prices were fortunately balanced by soaring gold, wool and cotton prices.

Historical development

The pivotal role of mineral production in the economy has been intermittent: periodic booms have been followed by low activity rates. The first great boom of the 1850s and 1860s corresponded with gold discoveries in NSW and Victoria, and was attended by drastic economic, social and political change (Doran, 1984). From 1851 to 1865 the average capital inflow from Britain was six times previous levels. In the ten years to 1860 Victoria's population more than quintupled and that of the six colonies tripled (see Chapter 1). There was a great expansion of railways and other infrastructure. Import replacing industries grew and even pastoralism flourished. Ultimately these gold discoveries provided the basis for democratic government, social security programs and nationhood.

For most of the twentieth century mining was of low or declining importance to the economy. Mineral production as a percentage of GDP bottomed in 1962/63 at about 1.5 per cent compared with about 16 per cent in 1860 (Porter, 1984), and the Vernon Committee of Enquiry reported in 1965 that the mining industry was 'not a major sector of the economy'.

Thereupon the industry went through two successive boom periods which re-established its preeminence in the economy, and wrought havoc. The first boom, in the late 1960s and early 1970s, was the more important. It contained a string of great mineral discoveries which coincided with a burst of rising prices, and the opening up of a giant new market in Japan. These three factors constituted fortuitous, somewhat related, events. The minerals concerned were iron ore, bauxite, nickel, and petroleum, but this era also saw the discovery of major reserves of uranium, manganese, coal, tin, tungsten, beach sands (titanium) and copper (Porter, 1984). Mining's share of export revenue tripled to 39 per cent in the eleven years to 1974/75.

The boom was a mixed blessing. On the surface it ushered in an age of prosperity, much like the gold rushes a century or so previously. Immigration boomed, the currency strengthened on the basis of increased export income and capital inflow, and many sectors of manufacturing industry benefitted from high consumer expenditure and capital works. The adverse consequences took longer to emerge, but there was a sudden collapse in 1974 as a consequence of the 1973 oil shock. This collapse triggered widespread recession in the industrialized OECD nations and major falls in commodity prices. Two particular adverse outcomes have been detected: a shrinking of the traditional rural export sector; and an increased quantity of imports and thus reduction in the size of the import-competing sector (Gregory, 1984).

Gregory sees these outcomes as the logical concomitant of a massive new source of export income, but Porter (1984) and Cook and Sieper (1984) are not so sure.

But it is not possible to lay the blame for the structural changes of the 1970s entirely on the mining industry. Several farm sectors were depressed in the early 1970s and manufacturing industry shed labour throughout the decade. Wool, for example, had a marketing problem in the face of growing competition from synthetic fibres, and Australia's 'import-replacement' type industries were technologically outmoded and hopelessly fragmented geographically. Almost certainly the mining boom accelerated and exacerbated looming problems in these other producing sectors, but it was not their direct cause. As Gregory claims, a higher valued currency riding on the back of mineral exports would depress the income of farm exporters and open domestic manufacturing to import competition. But numerous, probably more significant factors were at work, too, as we shall see in the next section.

The brief mining boom of the early 1980s paradoxically occurred for the same reason that the previous one failed: a large oil price rise engineered by the OPEC producer cartel. This time world financial markets were better prepared to re-cycle petro-dollars (the huge financial assets accumulated by oil-producing nations). There was no immediate recession in western countries and the response was instead a search for alternative cheap energy sources, notably coal. Australia has a lot of coal — 35 billion tonnes of demonstrated recoverable economic reserves in 1984 and an additional 300 billion tonnes of inferred recoverable reserves. Furthermore, Australian resources are frequently amenable to low-cost strip-mining and are price-competitive in export markets. Consequently the export value of coal and coal-related products increased 68 per cent between 1979 and 1984 at constant, inflation-adjusted, prices; production rose 49 per cent and exports 76 per cent over the same period.

This 'resources boom' also encompassed aluminium smelting. Aluminium (otherwise known as congealed electricity) is produced with very large amounts of energy and it therefore makes some sense to locate smelters close to cheap energy sources and to major ports such as Gladstone, Newcastle and (more questionably) Portland. Because it focussed primarily on coal as an energy resource, the 1980s resource boom, unlike its predecessor, was restricted mainly to the coalfields and industrial cities of eastern Australia rather than far-flung outback sites (see Fig. 2.14). Like the 1970s boom, however, it stumbled on international recession and a collapse in commodity prices, especially the value of the substitute rival, oil.

This brief historical survey has served to demonstrate the instability of the mining sector in terms of the value and volume of output, some of the economic consequences of its development, and the extent to which events are influenced by overseas factors. We now consider the industry's present economic and geographical structure.

Industry structure

Table 2.16 identifies the major minerals produced in Australia in 1989/90, excluding construction materials. Petroleum products appear to be the largest valued item but the figure quoted includes a range of heavy duties, royalties and other charges. Next most valuable are black coal, alumina and aluminium, and gold bullion. Then comes a group of metals of roughly similar value: copper, nickel, and zinc. A third tier of output by value comprises diamonds, manganese, lead, uranium, zircon and tin. After 1984 gold's rank rose sharply as production increased to about 100 tonnes in 1987 and 214 tonnes in 1989/90. At about A$525 per fine ounce, this represents an income of approximately $3.5 billion (about eight times the 1984 level). The increase was partly a response to the announced taxation of gold mining starting in 1991 and the producers' consequent attempts to maximise short-run output.

Australia is self-sufficient in nearly all the major commodities listed and in a position to export a high proportion of its output. This is particularly true for items such as rutile, tungsten, uranium and zircon where there is little or no local processing. In the case of bauxite, copper, lead, nickel, tin and zinc, considerable local processing occurs, with between about a half and three-quarters of the refined metal being exported. The only commodities which are not the source of considerable export income are industrial and construction minerals including clays, limestone, silica, crushed rock and so on. These have a low value in relation to bulk and are abundant world-wide. Most iron ore produced is also exported, but the deposits are high grade and require only preliminary concentration prior to shipment.

In 1988/89 the total value of the minerals produced, excluding processed metals, was A$21.0 billion of which just over A$15.9 billion worth (or 76 per cent) was exported. In contrast, imports totalled only A$3 billion of which crude oil accounted for 70 per cent. Phosphate rock, diamonds, and sulphur were also major imports. The renaissance of the mining sector after 1965 was closely bound to the rise of the Japanese economy so that ten years later Japan took over half of Australia's mineral exports. This is a risky position since it ties the industry effectively to the fortunes of one country. This risk dissipated a little during the 1980s when Japan's share of the export market declined to below 40 per cent. Other Asian destinations including the Republic of Korea, Hong Kong and Taiwan have taken up most of the slack. Asia, apart from Japan, accounted for almost 30 per cent of exports in 1988/89.

The mining and mineral industry is also closely tied to the foreign circuit of capital through investment in exploration and production facilities. The total investment in new fixed capital expenditure in mining, smelting and refining in 1988/89 was over $4.2 billion, or 16.6 per cent of the total for all industries. Exploration accounted for $1.3 billion more. At the height of the mining boom in 1981, mining's share of total investment approached 26 per cent. Local capital markets have traditionally been unable to supply capital on

Table 2.16 The production and export of major minerals, 1989/90

	Unit of quantity[1]	*Quantity*	*Estimated value (A$mill.)*	*Australia's share of world production by volume (%)*[2]	*Share of production exported by volume (%)*
Bauxite	kt	39 900	n.a.	35.9	n.a.
alumina	kt	11 041	3 618	25.5	76.7
aluminium	kt	1 235	2 813	4.8	75.5
Coal					
black (saleable)	kt	160 400	8 929	4.0	65.0
brown	kt	46 300	n.a.	3.2	nil
Construction materials[3]	kt	139 686 [4]	n.a.	n.a.	nil
Copper					
blister	kt	310	n.a.	2.2	n.a.
refined	kt	245	852	2.0	58.4
Diamonds	'000 carats	32 155	391	n.a.	99.5
Gold bullion	kg	214 400	3 573	3.4	81.9
Iron ore/concentrate	kt	109 900	2 427	11.7	90.9
Lead					
ore/concentrate	kt	522	n.a.	12.1	n.a.
refined	kt	197	197	4.1	75.6
Manganese ore	kt	2 281	351	8.0	67.8
Nickel (refined)	t	66 000	634	5.2	n.a.
Petroleum products					
crude oil/condensate	GL	32	3 792	n.a.	31.3
petroleum products	ML	39 300	13 788	n.a.	7.1
natural gas	GL	20 264	2 752	n.a.	12.9
LPG (natural)	ML	3 785	n.a.	n.a.	55.9
Silver (refined)	kg	404 000	91	7.8	n.a.
Tin					
concentrate	t	8 199	n.a.	4.8	95.8
refined	t	381	39	1.8	n.a.
Titanium					
Rutile	kt	235	164	45.7	n.a.
Ilmenite	kt	1 652	122	430 [5]	n.a.
Tungsten					
Scheelite/Wolframite	t	2 070	n.a.	4.2	n.a.
Uranium oxide	t	4 089	302	11.1	100.0
Zinc					
concentrate	kt	866	n.a.	9.2	128.6
refined	kt	295	587	4.7	76.3
Zircon	kt	481	318	n.a.	n.a.

1 kt= 1 000 tonnes; ML= million litres; GL= 1000 million litres;
2 1984 data
3 includes clays, limestone, silica, crushed rock
4 excluding WA output for some items
5 excluding CIS(ex USSR) output
n.a. not available

Source: Bureau of Mineral Resources (1984); Australian Bureau of Agriculture and Resource Economics (1991a).

that scale, and foreign companies have been prepared to supply the necessary finance. Of the total foreign investment in all industries of $281 billion in 1991, $29.8 billion (10.3 per cent) was in mining though this was sharply down from 23 per cent in 1984 (Bureau of Mineral Resources, 1987; ABS, 1992). Foreign penetration was greatest in energy production (72 per cent) and metallic minerals (55 per cent) as measured by share of value added according to Hartley (1984). The pattern is similar for exploration expenditure. Hartley also notes that Australian ownership and control are more concentrated in the smaller firms in each industry.

The merits of this reliance on foreign capital inflow have been hotly debated (Hartley, 1984; McColl,1984; Wheelwright, 1984), especially as the level of foreign control has come to exceed greatly the level of foreign ownership. The overall level of control in mining is much greater than for any other sector of the economy (Wheelwright, 1984). On balance the role of foreign capital can be defended readily. Benefits include: accelerated national development; higher per capita incomes; the sharing of low-cost resources with the rest of humankind; the spreading of the risk more broadly in what is a high-risk industry; the stimulus for exploration research and development; and innovation in mining and its support industries. The one major defect is not loss of Australian sovereignty over resources, but the volatility of capital flows in an economy which is heavily dependent on capital inflows as a balancing item in the trade account, as noted earlier (Table 2.3). This can make government economic management difficult. Early in a mining boom equity or loan capital flows in, but later on profits, interest, royalties, and repayment of principal (loans) often lead to substantial capital outflows. Thus, in 1976/77 after the end of the 1960s–1970s resources boom, mining registered a net capital outflow of $17 million (McColl, 1984). Seven years later, after the boom, there was another net outflow of $314 million compared with the previous year's net inflow of nearly $2.6 billion.

In general, production and investment proceed when a particular deposit is profitable. Exploration is sometimes a chance activity so that new deposits can be found at any time, as Lang Hancock claimed to have done with iron ore in the Hammersley Ranges in 1952. He had to keep the discovery to himself for several years as the West Australian government refused to issue prospecting licences for the search for iron ore. Where exploration is capital intensive, it tends to rise and fall according to the industry's profitability. This is true of subsurface deposits where drilling is required to prove their existence. Thus during periods of high oil prices (the early 1980s), nickel prices (the early 1970s) or gold prices (1985–87), frenetic exploration occurred in those respective minerals.

Profitability is a function of both costs and revenues. So far this section has concentrated almost exclusively on revenue. That is because, in the main, the volatility of prices determines whether or not a venture is opened up or kept in production. Costs can nevertheless be important in determining the existence of a producing rather than a mothballed mine. Two different circumstances can be identified: a decline in ore grades or sudden changes in input prices, with the former occurring more frequently.

Once a discovery is made and exploited, miners naturally work the richest and therefore most profitable deposits first. There is a consequent tendency for the grade of deposit being mined at a particular location to decline over time. Costs subsequently rise simply because more rock must be mined and crushed to yield the same output as before. More overburden must be stripped, or deeper shafts or wells constructed, or a greater effort put into pumping. Occasionally the discovery of richer new seams or the advent of new technology can reduce costs and extend the life of a mine. Much effort has been put, for example, into improving oil recovery rates by pumping brine solutions into deposits to increase the underground pressure — forcing oil out of the porous rock which contains it. The advent of the cyanide and K-Process treatment systems for gold deposits has similarly enabled the profitable reworking of old deposits.

Input prices, including freight charges, tend to change slowly in response to events such as increased award wages, currency movements (which affect machinery prices), legislation regulating mine working conditions, improved transport technology or mining machinery and equipment, and government infrastructure pricing policies.

Many coal-mining companies complain bitterly about high freight charges imposed by the Queensland and NSW governments on their operations, which are then used to subsidize other loss-making rail services. These charges operate effectively as a tax on coal production (Forsyth, 1984).

Taxes have the same effect on the viability of mine operations as other input costs. Sudden changes in tax regime can affect mine profitability much more rapidly than other input price changes. For example, the introduction of a Resource Rent Tax (or the Crude Oil Levy before it) on oil production could accelerate the closure of marginal fields. We have noted that the introduction of the gold tax altered producer behaviour significantly in the short term. However the tax regime is probably not a major contributing factor to the industry's buoyancy, and is critical for only the most marginal producers.

Unlike farming, a mining company faced with unprofitable operations has no substitution option. In the case where a mine produces several commodities, as frequently occurs with lead, silver, copper and zinc, profitable commodities may be able to carry unprofitable ones. Unprofitable mines often simply close down until they can be reactivated as an economically viable proposition. This is more likely to occur with small single-commodity mines owned by individuals or small companies. In the New England region of NSW, for instance, there are several examples of marginal operations which used to open and close periodically: the Woodsreef asbestos mine; the Hillgrove antimony mine; and tin workings at Tingha and Emmaville. Figure 2.13 illustrates this process for a hypothetical mining venture.

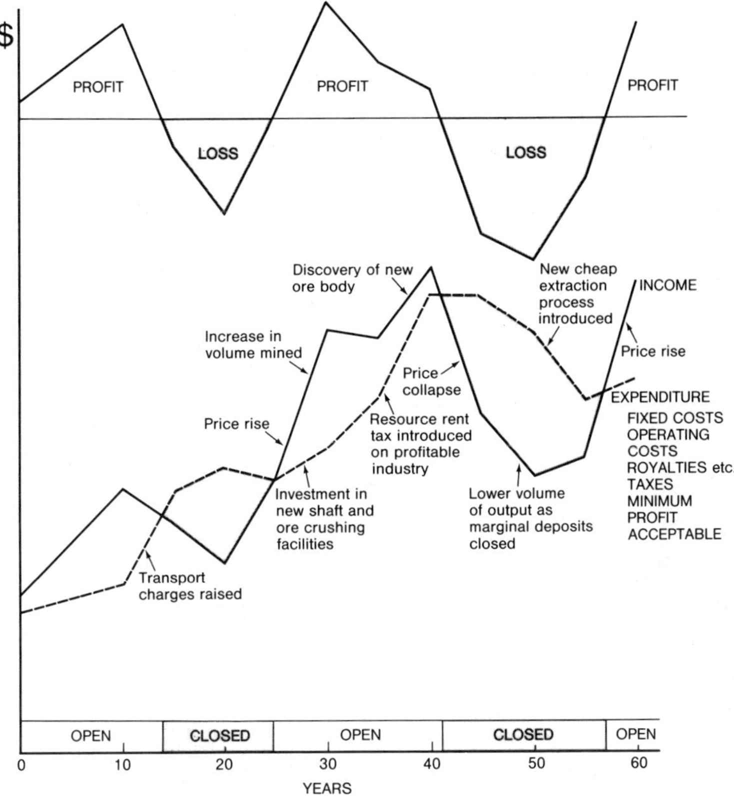

Fig. 2.13 The financial circumstances of a hypothetical mine

Also unlike farming, when the resource gives out, that is the end of the mine and often the settlement which goes with it. There is little left of Hill End, Sofala, Hillgrove and other places associated with nineteenth century gold rushes. And the settlement of Mary Kathleen was eradicated at auction in the early 1980s after the uranium mine there was finally worked out.

Geographical distribution of production

Figure 2.14 shows distribution of mining activity for selected major commodities. It specifically excludes prospective mines and those in care-and-maintenance. Obviously the distribution of mines corresponds to the occurrence of ore-bodies and many of these are located in inhospitable parts of the continent. Indeed, it has been the lure of easy wealth from minerals that has served as much as anything to develop the outback. Nowadays, though, the individual prospector working a small lease has been largely superseded by the corporate world of giant equipment, instant air-conditioned towns, bulk

Fig. 2.14 The location of mineral production
Source: Compiled from the Bureau of Mineral Resources (1987) and Hore-Lacey (1982)

handling facilities and ready communications with the outside world. Road, railways, airports, ports, and the facilities of modern metropolitan suburbs have all been constructed in most unlikely places: the Pilbara or Central Queensland, for example. Three of the largest inland cities, Kalgoorlie, Mount Isa, and Broken Hill, owe their origin and current existence in large measure to rich mineral resources.

Minerals are not scattered randomly about the continent. Rather, they tend to occur in mineral provinces. Figure 2.15 outlines the principal metalliferous provinces yielding iron ore, copper, lead, zinc and precious metals. Energy resources, on the other hand, are restricted to sedimentary basins along the eastern seaboard, to parts of central Australia and to coastal districts of Western Australia, but more especially in the region of the Northwest Shelf. Two other highly prospective areas are the Otway Basin in Victoria and the Timor Gap to the northwest of Darwin. This broad pattern is still being sketched in more detail and major metalliferous provinces may yet be found beneath surface sedimentary structures. The discovery of the deep-seated copper-uranium ore-body at Roxby Downs using inferential geology and remote sensing techniques is one such example.

Figure 2.14 shows that many metalliferous regions, including Mount Isa, Broken Hill, the Cobar district, and western Tasmania, produce a variety of

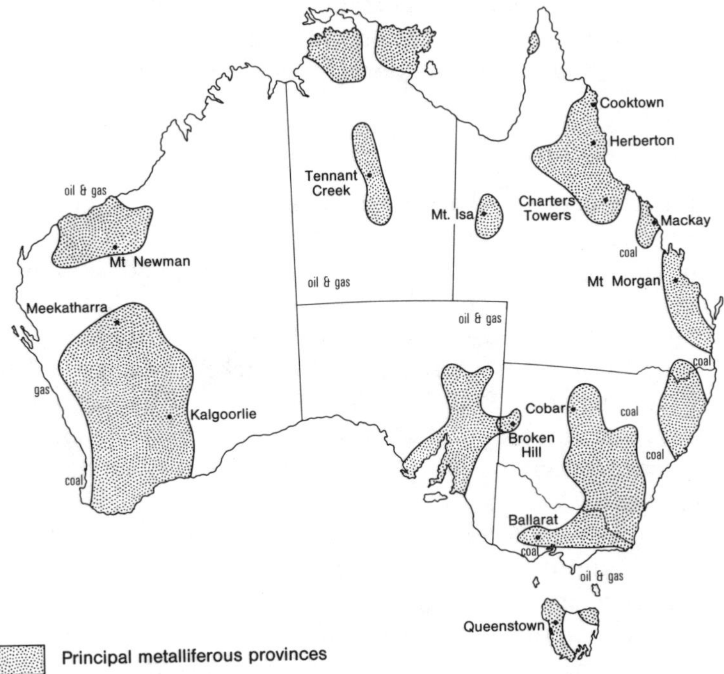

Fig. 2.15 Principal metalliferous provinces

commodities involving some mixture of copper, gold, lead, zinc, silver, and manganese. This broad-based output offers the regions concerned some protection against strong peaks and troughs of well-being brought about by fluctuating commodity prices because the price movements of different commodities are rarely synchronized. Thus between 1974 and 1987 lead and zinc prices ran counter to each other (Fig. 2.12).

In contrast to the long-established mining centres just described, the major developments of the last twenty years have tended to involve single low value and high bulk minerals which are mined on a large scale: coal, gas and petroleum, iron ore and bauxite. Often, too, these minerals occur in remote locations, but their scale of operations is sufficient to make it worthwhile for the large corporations involved to construct complete private towns and such infrastructure items as railways and ports to service the mines. Gove, Weipa, Mt. Tom Price, Paraburdoo, Mt. Newman, Shay Gap, Dysart, Moranbah and Roxby Downs are typical settlements of the era. In more settled regions such as the Hunter Valley and Gippsland, the development of large-scale coal mines faced a different set of problems, mainly in environmental planning. One issue concerned management of existing settlements like Singleton and Muswellbrook, to ensure adequate serviced residential lots (at a reasonable price) and adequate community facilities. The rapid population growth of such places often proved traumatic. Other issues concerned the preservation of prime agricultural land, restoration of the landscape, and augmentation of water supplies. Of course, not all recent mine developments have been on a large scale. Many operations connected with uranium, nickel, gold and tin are small and isolated and living conditions are not attractive.

Mineral processing

Numerous settlements owe their existence and prosperity, either wholly or in part, to their role in processing minerals. Processing can be pursued to various degrees from concentration and washing to smelting and refining, or even electricity generation in the case of coal. Some of the better known processing centres shown in Figure 2.14 include Port Pirie (lead, zinc), Risdon (zinc), Mt. Isa (copper), Yabulu (nickel), Kalgoorlie (nickel), Gladstone, Kuri Kuri, Point Henry, Portland, Bell Bay, Kwinana and Pinjarra (alumina or aluminium), and Dampier and Port Latta (iron ore pellets). Two areas contain major concentrations of coal-based electricity generating capacity: the Latrobe and Hunter Valleys.

The well-being of all these areas is heavily tied to the continued production of their mineral inputs. Even interruptions in mineral supplies through industrial disputes can cause hardship. A strike in the mines at Broken Hill in 1986 caused the temporary shut-down of the lead smelter at Port Pirie, for example. And like many mining settlements, many of the places concerned with mineral processing have a male-dominated working-class society which offers few female employment opportunities (Sorensen and Weinand, 1985).

Manufacturing

Geographical distribution

Manufacturing employment and output is overwhelmingly concentrated in state capital cities and a few smaller industrial cities such as Newcastle, Wollongong and Geelong. These locations, shown in Figure 2.16, accounted for nearly 83 per cent of the manufacturing workforce, but only 66 per cent of the nation's population in the mid-1980s (Table 2.17). The pattern has not changed markedly since then. In practice, manufacturing is even more concentrated than these figures suggest. Just three cities, Sydney, Melbourne, and Adelaide, had 46 per cent of the population but nearly two-thirds of the industrial jobs. And of these, Melbourne has a strong claim to being the industrial heartland of Australia. Its industrial employment exceeds Sydney's, despite having a smaller population.

These aggregate figures conceal considerable variation in the geographical distribution of various industry sectors. Table 2.17 shows, for example, that

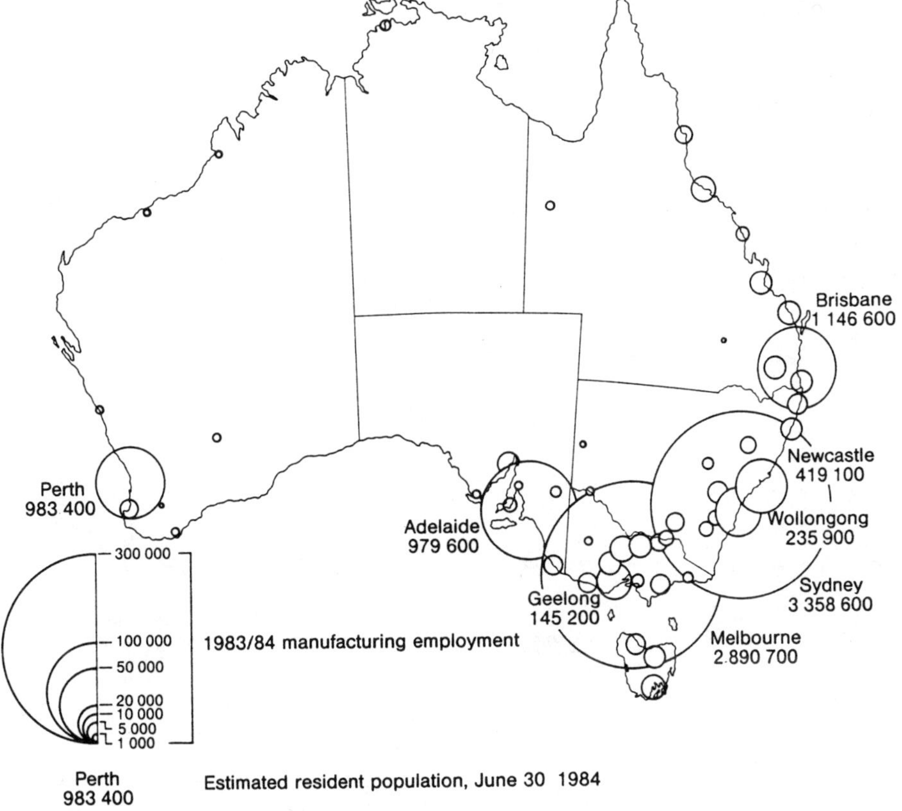

Fig. 2.16 The location of manufacturing employment, 1983–84
Source: After Rich (1987)

Table 2.17 The geographical distribution of manufacturing employment by industry sub-division, June 1985[1]

ASIC[3] code	*21*	*23*	*24*	*25*	*26*	*27*	*28*	*29*	*31*	*32*	*33*	*34*	*Total manufacturing*	*Population[2]*	*Share of manufacturing/share of population (Industry Concentration Index)*
New South Wales	30.9	28.6	28.9	32.0	35.4	47.0	33.9	51.6	38.3	27.1	43.0	36.5	35.8	34.8	1.02
Sydney Stat.Div.	20.8	21.1	23.0	21.7	30.4	44.5	22.2	13.3	30.4	22.6	37.4	34.0	26.7	21.5	1.24
Hunter Stat.Div.	2.3	3.1	1.6	1.7	1.2	1.6	2.5	15.9	3.1	2.0	2.5	0.7	3.1		
Illawarra Stat.Div.	0.8	0.3	2.2	n.p.	n.p.	0.3	4.0	22.3	1.2	0.3	1.0	0.3	2.6	13.3	0.68
Rest of State	7.0	4.1	2.1	9.6	3.8	0.6	5.2	0.1	3.6	2.2	3.1	1.5	3.4		
Victoria	29.6	54.2	57.6	26.5	33.5	35.7	26.5	16.6	32.0	45.5	33.7	39.2	35.0	26.2	1.34
Melbourne Stat.Div	19.4	40.1	47.5	19.2	29.2	32.2	19.1	12.0	28.0	38.9	31.0	36.8	28.7	18.6	1.54
Barwon State Div.	0.9	5.0	2.8	1.0	0.5	2.9	2.9	3.2	0.8	4.2	0.5	0.3	1.8	7.6	0.96
Rest of State	9.3	9.1	7.3	6.3	3.9	0.6	4.5	1.4	3.2	2.4	2.2	2.1	5.5		
Queensland	18.8	2.8	5.4	15.0	10.2	5.7	15.9	8.7	12.8	9.2	6.9	8.2	10.8	16.1	0.67
Brisbane Stat.Div.	8.4	1.8	4.1	9.0	7.5	4.8	9.9	2.5	9.9	6.1	4.6	6.9	6.5	7.4	0.88
Rest of State	10.4	1.0	1.3	6.0	2.7	0.9	6.0	6.2	2.9	3.1	2.3	1.3	4.3	8.7	0.49
South Australia	9.1	8.3	5.8	10.3	7.2	4.5	8.4	9.5	7.5	13.5	9.9	10.9	9.1	8.7	1.05
Adelaide Stat.Div.	5.4	6.9	5.5	6.9	5.8	4.1	7.5	3.0	6.9	12.8	9.2	10.8	7.2	6.3	1.14
Rest of State	3.7	1.4	0.3	3.4	1.4	0.4	0.9	6.5	0.6	0.7	0.7	0.1	1.9	2.4	0.79
Western Australia	7.1	3.0	2.0	10.8	7.0	5.5	11.5	7.9	7.2	4.0	5.6	4.4	6.3	8.9	0.71
Perth Stat.Div.	n.a.	n.a.	n.a.	n.a.	n.a.	n.a.	n.a.	n.a.	n.a.	n.a.	n.a.	n.a.	5.1	6.3	0.81
Rest of State	n.a.	n.a.	n.a.	n.a.	n.a.	n.a.	n.a.	n.a.	n.a.	n.a.	n.a.	n.a.	1.2	2.6	0.46
Tasmania	3.4	n.p.	1.2	4.7	5.6	n.p.	2.2	4.6	1.6	0.5	0.6	0.6	2.4	2.8	0.86
Hobart Stat.Div.	1.2		n.a.	n.a.	n.a.		n.a.	n.a.	n.a.	n.a.	n.a.	n.a.	0.9	1.1	0.82
Rest of State	2.2	3.1	n.a.	n.a.	n.a.	1.6	n.a.	n.a.	n.a.	n.a.	n.a.	n.a.	1.5	1.7	0.88
Territories	1.1		0.0	0.7	1.0		1.6	1.1	0.4	0.2	0.3	0.2	0.6	2.6	0.23
Australia	100.0	100.0	100.0	100.0	100.0	100.0	100.0	100.0	100.0	100.0	100.0	100.0	100.0	100.0	
Total by industry ('000)	167.8	33.0	74.3	72.7	101.8	55.1	38.7	76.9	92.9	119.8	127.0	58.7	1018.7		
% share of manufacturing workforce	16.5	3.2	7.3	7.1	10.0	5.4	3.8	7.5	9.1	11.8	12.5	5.8	100.0		

1 Excludes single establishment enterprises employing fewer than four persons
2 June 1984 estimates
3 See Table 2.9 for a description of ASIC codes
n.p.—not published
Source: ABS *Census of Manufacturing Establishments* cat. nos 82010, 82040 (1986)

two sectors — food, beverages and tobacco (ASIC 21) and wood, wood products and furniture (ASIC 25) — are disproportionately concentrated in rural areas, the source of their raw materials. Even so, metropolitan centres have managed to capture successfully a large share of both industries. Furthermore, non-metropolitan employment is often concentrated in low-level processing or refining activities — for example, sugar refining, oil seed crushing, or livestock slaughtering — while more elaborate processing and packaging of items for final consumption is located in capital cities.

Textiles (ASIC 23) and clothing and footwear (ASIC 24) together make up the so-called 'TCF' industries. These are heavily concentrated in both metropolitan and country districts of Victoria, with Melbourne itself accounting for nearly half of Australia's clothing and footwear workers. The chemical industry (ASIC 27) is dominated by Sydney and Melbourne, especially Sydney. Together they share nearly two-thirds of the chemical industry's workforce, reflecting the concentration of oil-refining capacity that is also the principal source of chemical industry feedstocks.

Basic metal industries (ASIC 29) are of two main types: metal refining or manufacture and downstream processing activities. Refining includes smelting of lead, copper, zinc, bauxite and other non-ferrous ores and manufacture of iron and steel. Most of these activities are located at the ore-body or in non-metropolitan industrial cities. In part this reflects economic considerations such as good access (usually by sea or rail) to necessary raw materials — including the ores themselves, coal, limestone and so on. In addition, these industries are a major source of environmental pollution and are best located away from large centres of population. The iron and steel industry, which is not so environmentally hazardous as some of the other smelting activities, owes its location at Newcastle and Wollongong primarily to coking coal resources, and at Whyalla to both iron ore deposits in the Middleback Range and to the economies offered by back-hauling coal from the east coast. Traditionally, therefore, ASIC 29 industries have been much more locationally constrained than most others. To some extent this is breaking down for technological reasons. Mini steel mills, for example, have become a viable proposition when based on abundant scrap steel found in large cities. Smorgon Consolidated Industries has opened a mini steel mill in Melbourne, and there are others in Sydney and Brisbane.

The downstream semi-processing basic metal industries produce castings, forgings, extrusions, pipes and tubes, sheet metal, coils and so on. They tend to be located in close proximity to the source of their input materials. For example, part of the output of BHP's Port Kembla steelworks is processed locally by John Lysaght Australia into flat steel or stainless steel products or by Tubemakers of Australia into pipes. Whyalla's output is further processed at that location to become universal sections, structural steel or rails. As a consequence of these strong linkages, employment in ASIC 29 is spatially concentrated. NSW accounts for half of the jobs, most of which are found in Newcastle and Wollongong. Non-metropolitan South Australia also records a high concentration of workers in the industry based on BHP's Whyalla operations and Broken Hill Associated Smelter's lead–zinc refinery at Port Pirie.

The more elaborate manufacture of metal products (ASIC 31) is, somewhat paradoxically, mainly concentrated in capital cities. Sydney, Melbourne, Brisbane and Adelaide account for three-quarters of the sector's employment which produces items such as metal furniture; cutlery; hand tools; nuts, bolts and screws; steam, gas and water fittings; and metal blinds and awnings. But these are relatively small-scale and clean industries compared with the large-scale *smokestack* industries which dominate cities like Newcastle and Wollongong.

The same four capital cities also share over 80 per cent of the workforce involved in producing transport equipment (ASIC 32). However, the industry looms largest in Melbourne's and Adelaide's economies because they are home to the major car assembly plants of all four main domestic producers: Holden, Ford, Toyota and Mitsubishi. Vehicle building is also a significant part of Geelong's economy due to plant owned by the Ford Motor Company and a few component suppliers. Sydney's transport sector is more diversified, with considerable employment in the fabrication of railway locomotives and rolling stock.

The remaining industry sectors (ASIC 33 and 34) comprise various kinds of light industry: scientific instruments, electronic goods, household appliances, cable and wire, industrial machinery and equipment, rubber and plastic goods, sporting equipment, packaging, jewellery and so on. Between them these sectors contain a significant proportion of high-technology industries which are likely to provide the basis of future growth in both the employment and output of secondary industry. Since just three cities — Sydney, Melbourne, and Adelaide — account for over 80 per cent of the employment in both sectors, it is not surprising that they have an important lead over other cities in the industrial renaissance that began to occur towards the end of the 1980s. In contrast, non-metropolitan localities are poorly provided with jobs in these kinds of industries.

The spatial imbalance of secondary industry is best summed up by reference to the industry concentration index in Table 2.17. Not only is Melbourne the pre-eminent industrial city, but the whole state of Victoria has a greater relative concentration of manufacturing jobs than either Sydney or Adelaide. Nevertheless, both the latter have, relatively speaking, much more significant manufacturing economies than the remaining state capitals. Rural Queensland and Western Australia, together with the Territories, have very little manufacturing industry, and what there is tends to be resource-based.

Post-war industrial development

The broad patterns we have described reflect the interplay of numerous domestic and international forces over the last fifty years. Several authors, including Wadley and Rich (1983), Rich (1987), Linge (1987) and Fagan (1987), have analysed this period in some detail, and are more or less agreed that three distinct development phases can be identified during which different sets of causal factors were dominant and particular spatial consequences emerged: growth, transition and restructuring.

The *growth phase* lasted from the late 1930s until the start of the 1960s. Recovery from the great depression, the wartime stimulus for self-sufficiency, and post-war reconstruction were the immediate stimuli for a doubling of the manufacturing workforce in this period. By 1960/61 there were over 1.1 million manufacturing jobs, and these as a share of total employment amounted to 28–29 per cent, close to the all-time peak. The prime mover in these events was undoubtedly the federal government, under both Chifley and Menzies, whose diverse policy strands proved for a while remarkably serendipitous. These included high levels of immigration, the imposition of import restrictions in 1952 necessitated by a shortage of foreign exchange (itself caused in part by a collapse in commodity prices after the Korean War), import replacement policies aided by protection measures for infant industries, and the wooing of foreign investment. The relationship between immigration and the growth of manufacturing industry was particularly symbiotic. Migrants helped create a rapidly expanding market for consumer goods and also supplied the labour to make them. Fagan (1987) notes that of the 228 000 new manufacturing jobs created between 1947 and 1961, 70 per cent were filled by migrants.

International events also helped encourage and cocoon Australia's nascent industries. For some years after the Second World War there was a global shortage of manufactured goods that protected local producers. Later the rapid growth of transnational corporations (TNCs), especially of United States origin, saw inter-firm rivalry focus on the maintenance of global market share through setting up branch plants overseas. Australia received much of this type of investment. For example, Ford and Chrysler followed General Motors in setting up car assembly plants.

Not surprisingly most of this growth was tied to the existing industrial cities and to the State capitals. Capital cities were the entry points for migrants, who tended to gravitate towards their own ethnic districts rather than adventure into the interior. Large cities offered an ideal location for manufacturers of materials, access to capital, a wide variety of labour skills and supplementary services, and access to markets. Also, overseas capital naturally tended to favour cores rather than peripheries (especially Sydney and Melbourne) although in varying degree each of the other state capitals constituted a core within its respective state (Fagan, 1987).

During this era, two other major factors were at work. Each State government saw itself in competition with the others in the development stakes, and sought 'a more fully rounded portfolio of manufacturing activities' (Linge, 1987). Inducements were offered to would-be investors in the form of long-term leases over mineral or other resources, cheap land, improvements to transport and other infrastructure facilities, electricity at concessional rates, government contracts, provision of housing and so on. More generally, all governments attempted to create business environments conducive to investment. Sir Thomas Playford, a long-serving Premier of South Australia, was particularly successful. Similar manoeuvres occurred in Western Australia and Queensland: in 1960 BHP agreed to construct a blast furnace at Kwinana in order to retain control over high-grade iron-ore leases at Koolyanobbing, while in 1957 Comalco was permitted to mine bauxite at Weipa on condition that an alumina plant was built in Queensland (eventually at Gladstone).

Finally, much of the industrial development in the immediate post-war years was on a large scale; car plants, steel works, oil refineries, chemical works, whitegoods production (washing machines, refrigerators etc.), and electrical goods. Many of these industries require deep-water port facilities and, more importantly, the large labour reserves offered by major cities.

All these forces contributed to the rapid expansion of manufacturing employment and output up to 1960, but at a high price in terms of efficiency. Australian industrial establishments tended to be small-scale and under-utilized by world standards. These, and small production runs, raised unit costs which were unfortunately easy to pass on to consumers in the form of higher prices. Manufacturers were protected from their inefficiency by import quotas and a battery of high tariffs. One absurd pattern of production quoted by Linge (1987) saw sixteen refrigerator manufacturers operating at twenty locations producing for a local market of 350 000 units in 1960. At that time a minimum output of 500 000 units per plant was regarded as efficient.

Another important defect in Australia's industrial structure was its use of low-level second-hand product and production technology often imported from United Kingdom or United States parent companies. There was little indigenous research and development effort aimed at producing high quality goods able to penetrate export markets. High local production costs also made exporting a difficult task anyway. Consequently, Australian manufacturing became inward looking and divorced from global commercial pressures.

The *transition phase* lasted from about 1960 until 1973/74. During this period manufacturing employment grew much more slowly to 1.3 million, and real value added peaked simultaneously. However, due to faster growth in other sectors of the economy — especially services and minerals — manufacturing's share of employment and output was already declining. In Fagan's view a principal feature of the period was not so much change to the spatial pattern of production created during the growth phase as the reorganisation of ownership and control. For example, starting in the early 1960s, TNCs such as Unilever, Amatil (formerly British-American Tobacco) and George Westons began a spate of takeovers in the food industry to create diversified corporations. This in turn stimulated a series of defensive takeovers by locally based companies — the Petersville Group, Allied Mills and Arnotts — in order to remain competitive (Fagan, 1987). Fagan notes that such takeovers served to increase the control exerted by Sydney and Melbourne over the manufacturing sector.

On the surface, manufacturing industry remained prosperous throughout the golden age of the 1960s and early 1970s. In Australia the mining boom and the surge of immigration which accompanied it created a buoyant market for local producers. Other industrialized nations were also enjoying rapid economic growth, thereby helping to maintain the value of Australia's raw material exports.

In practice, the foundations on which the manufacturing sector had developed were being undermined. Six mechanisms were at work:

1 Many industry sectors grew progressively less competitive in global markets since the plethora of small-scale fragmented operations could not take advantage of increasing production scale economies.
2 Wage increases tended to run ahead of productivity growth without any compensating currency devaluation. This also tended to make local producers less competitive against foreign competition.
3 The volume of foreign competition was also growing rapidly. Newly industrializing countries (NICs) in south-east and east Asia developed TCF, metal fabricating (ASIC 31) and consumer goods (ASTC 33 and 34) industries which, due to low wage rates, experienced much lower costs than Australian producers. Fagan (1987) sees this as part of a New International Division of Labour (NIDL) created by TNCs as they seek out low cost production opportunities and by endogenous growth forces in the countries concerned which created favourable business environments. These endogenous growth forces included stable governments, docile and hard-working labour, favourable tax regimes, undervalued currencies and little administrative red tape.
4 As a semi-peripheral economy with a low research and development effort and poor innovation record, Australia was missing out on investment in newer industries in the field of electronic equipment, machine tools, scientific instruments, chemicals and pharmaceuticals, and plastics. In short, new manufacturing jobs were not being created fast enough to replace those in declining old-style low value-added smokestack industries.
5 Ripped-off consumers and industry groups whose cost structures were adversely affected by the inefficient edifice of industry protection began to argue the case for freer trade. They were supported by the economic arguments of what is now the Industry Commission.

6 In 1973 came the *coup de grace*. The dollar underwent, belatedly, successive revaluations to reflect the consequences of the 1960s mining boom — the capital inflow and increased mineral exports. Two further domestic measures and one international event sealed the fate of Australian manufacturing. There was a 25 per cent across the board tariff reduction and equal pay legislation for women. The OPEC engineered oil price rise forced many nations to become aggressive exporters to pay the higher fuel bills and accelerated the quest for low cost production locations. These trends reinforced the NIDL.

Two concluding remarks are in order in this account of the 'transition period' in Australian manufacturing development. First, the spatial pattern of industry set up in the *growth phase* reflected primarily the interplay of domestic government policy and the Australian environment, with foreign and domestic capital playing a fairly passive role. The passage of time reversed this position, and foreign capital especially came to dominate the structure and organisation of Australian manufacturing. Local capital's role was increasingly one of emulation (e.g. transferring production to cheaper locations offshore, or industry consolidation through takeover). In terms of Figure 2.4, therefore, the international circuit of factors came to over-shadow the domestic circuit.

Secondly (with the unfair benefit of hindsight) Australia's post-war industrialisation can be seen to have pursued a disastrous strategy of import replacement. Countries which have pursued this path, including also New Zealand, Argentina, South Africa and many black African and Latin American nations, have experienced low economic growth compared with those adopting an export strategy. It is now recognized that, within the NIDL, high wage countries must develop high value added (often high technology) industries. The small size of Australia's economy need not be a problem in this regard, providing appropriate market niches are discovered and exploited. Such activity necessitates, however, an export orientation.

The third phase of Australia's post-war manufacturing development was one of major *restructuring* on account of the forces outlined above. The most significant feature was the loss of almost one quarter of the workforce in the 15 years to 1988/89 (Table 2.18). No industry sector was immune, except for paper and printing. The 'TCF' group, 'basic metals' and the 'other machinery' sectors fared worst, losing about one-third of their workers. During this period manufacturing's share of an expanding workforce declined precipitously from about 25 per cent to 15 per cent. The loss of jobs occurred in two bursts with a plateau between. Almost two hundred thousand jobs disappeared in the four years to 1977 and a further one hundred and fifty thousand were lost in 1982 and 1983. After its late 1980s revival, manufacturing again lost numerous jobs in the 1991/92 recession. These losses correspond to periods of national and international recession. To some extent local and international events are connected, but on all these occasions local

Table 2.18 Changing employment in industry subdivisions, 1973/74–1988/89

					Percentage change			
	Employment[1]				1973/4	1978/9	1973/4	1973/4
ASIC					to	to	to	to
code	1973/74[2]	1978/79[3]	1984/85	1988/89	1978/9	1984/5	1984/5	1988/9
21	204 172	189 655	167 000	176 400	−7.1	−11.1	−18.2	−13.6
23	54 619	36 528	33 500	32 100	−33.1	−8.3	−38.7	−41.2
24	109 968	80 880	74 500	73 300	−26.5	−7.9	−32.3	−33.3
25	85 677	74 458	72 700	84 400	−13.1	−2.4	−15.1	−1.5
26	108 034	98 042	102 100	112 100	−9.2	+4.1	−5.5	+3.8
27	67 107	61 779	55 100	53 400	−7.9	−10.8	−17.9	−20.4
28	55 456	44 987	38 600	42 300	−18.9	−14.2	−30.4	−23.7
29	98 149	90 001	76 700	70 700	−8.3	−14.8	−21.9	−28.0
31	119 040	105 852	93 200	108 000	−11.1	−12.0	−21.7	−9.3
32	158 880	136 797	119 600	116 300	−13.9	−12.6	−24.7	−26.8
33	198 971	160 406	126 700	137 400	−19.4	−21.0	−36.3	−30.9
34	78 371	64 508	58 700	66 100	−17.7	−9.0	−25.1	−15.7
Total	1 338 379	1 143 891	1 018 400	1 072 500	−14.5	−11.0	−23.9	−19.9

1 Averaged over whole years and including working proprietors
2 Includes employment in establishments with less than four employees—excluded after 1974/5
3 ASIC revised slightly in 1978

Source: ABS *Manufacturing Industry: Summary of Operations, Australia* cat. no. 82020

events exacerbated Australia's problems: government mismanagement, wages explosions, the curtailment of mining booms and, in 1982 and 1991, severe droughts.

In the case of 'TCF' and 'other machinery' industries the cause of job losses appears to be a rapid growth in import penetration of the local market, coupled with an extremely poor export performance. However, all sectors except food, drink and tobacco experienced considerably greater competition from imports whose share of the market rose from 18 per cent in 1968/69 to 26 per cent in 1981/82. TCF establishments also shed their labour early on. Most of the losses had occurred by 1978 as the 25 per cent tariff cut and equal pay legislation bit deeply. In the basic metal products sector, labour shedding and plant closure came later on as cheap steel from NICs entered the market place and the second resources boom collapsed. Those sectors which performed best included those primarily involved in processing local resources. Star performer, if one can call it that, was the paper, printing and publishing sector which benefitted from its close association with the packaging and information processing industries (see also Tables 2.6 and 2.7).

To some extent these figures overstate the decline of manufacturing industry because productivity gains enabled fewer workers to sustain output at the existing level. Value added per employee increased at over 3 per cent annually in the five years in 1984/85 in real terms, and total real value added consequently remained static. But the pattern of job losses is important because it affects the welfare of the communities unfortunate enough to have declining industries. Thus Victoria's economy with its heavy concentration of TCF workers was badly hit in the mid-1970s. On the other hand, NSW (and especially Newcastle and Wollongong) bore the brunt of restructuring in ASIC 29 and 33 in the early 1980s.

The figures in Table 2.18 also conceal intra-sectoral variations in employment opportunity. At the same time as steel production declined from 7.8 million tonnes in 1980/81 to 5.3 million tonnes two years later and employment dropped by one-third, employment and production in the aluminium industry were increasing (see Rich, 1986). Because the steel industry is concentrated geographically and dominates its host communities, its economic plight in 1982 and 1983 created large-scale under-employment in Newcastle and Wollongong and necessitated federal government intervention in the form of the 1984–88 Steel Industry Plan.

The spatial adjustment problems of many industries have been severe (Rich, 1987, Linge, 1987). For example, the number of establishments making tyres declined from 12 in 1966 to 5 in 1980, with the industry being consolidated in Melbourne. The number of whitegoods firms declined from 27 in 1972/73 to 7 in 1986, of which four (Email/Simpson, Philips, Hoover and Rheem/Vulcan) accounted for nearly the entire output. And the number of whitegoods factories fell from 34 to 12, with Adelaide and Orange faring the best. Total employment in the industry also fell by at least 60 per cent. The motor vehicle industry lost about one-third of its work-force in the decade to 1983/84 and real value added fell by one-quarter. Brisbane and Sydney experienced several major plant closures as the industry tended to concentrate in Melbourne and Adelaide.

Such are the serious regional consequences of industry restructuring, that governments have frequently intervened in an attempt to direct events. The Steel Industry Plan has already been mentioned, but other current schemes are operating for TCF industries and car assembly. The latter aims to abolish quota protection by 1992 while ensuring industry viability by reducing the number of manufacturers and models to as few as three and six respectively. In doing so the ultimate aim is to protect over the long term the jobs of car workers principally located in Melbourne and Adelaide.

In the mid-1980s there was accumulating evidence of a major reversal in the fortunes of manufacturing industry brought about by successive devaluations of the Australian dollar. These have served to reduce labour costs relative to competing nations and make Australian exports price competitive in world markets. Declining commodity prices have brought home to industry and political leaders the considerable risks involved in having exports dominated by raw materials with volatile prices. Consequently encouragement is being given to manufacturing industry development once again. This time around the emphasis is on the export of manufactured goods rather than import replacement, and on industries which can compete globally with minimal artificial support. Thus policies are aimed at improving research and development performance, reducing expensive restrictive work practices, better labour training, export promotion and other matters concerning efficiency in production and distribution. Since many other nations can produce goods for mass markets more efficiently than Australia, any industrial renaissance will need to be based on serving specialist market niches, advanced technology, high quality, or integration with large-scale global production systems. The last of these includes such things as the production of automobile components (e.g. engines from Holden's Fishermen's Bend plant in Melbourne) or offset arrangements to supply parts of military and civilian aircraft. Developments of this nature stand to rewrite Australia's industrial geography at least as thoroughly as the initial post-war boom. This time, however, the distorting influence of government may be less evident. Consequently the new era could see an increased concentration of manufacturing industry in its original heartland: Sydney and Melbourne.

There is some evidence in Table 2.18 of the reversal of manufacturing's fortunes. Fabricated metal products, wood products, miscellaneous manufacturing, and non-metallic mineral products all saw their employment rebound strongly after 1985, though the trend is likely to have been halted by the last recession.

Service industries

It was noted earlier that the service sector accounts for a large share of national employment and output. In 1988/89 approximately 70 per cent of the workforce was in service industries which contributed over 65 per cent of GDP, excluding ownership of dwellings (Tables 2.6 and 2.7). White collar occupations, which dominate the services, also account for about 62 per cent of the workforce (Table 2.8). As of mid-1991, about one-fifth of NSW employees were in each of the distributive trades (wholesaling and retailing), community services (including education and health) and 'other industries' (which includes public administration, communications, and personal services) (see Table 2.19B). Another 13 per cent were in finance and business services and perhaps 6 per cent in transport and storage.

Several of these sectors, including distribution, transport, 'other industries' and community services have a geographical distribution of employment which tends to match the overall spatial pattern of the workforce, as illustrated in Table 2.19C. This is hardly surprising as most service industries directly serve, and therefore have to be accessible to, the general public. Furthermore, those sectors have, with the notable exception of community services, generally increased their employment in line with population and workforce growth over the last fifteen years (Table 2.19A, B). Community services have grown a little more rapidly than the service sector as a whole.

Table 2.19 Changing employment structure of service industries, New South Wales, 1976–1991

Date	Industry sector						
	Wholesale, retail	*Tansport, storage*	*Finance etc.*	*Community services*	*Other[1] industries*	*Other primary–secondary*	*Total*
A Numbers employed ('000)							
Nov. 1976	416.5	119.6	177.0	293.3	333.0	728.4	2 069.4
Feb. 1980	441.9	121.6	192.9	309.5	349.9	753.2	2 170.7
Feb. 1987	466.7	137.9	280.6	396.9	386.4	697.4	2 364.0
Aug. 1991	520.6	145.3	343.9	488.0	590.9	493.4	2 582.1
B Percentages							
Nov. 1976	20.1	5.8	8.6	14.2	16.1	35.2	100.0
Feb. 1980	20.4	5.6	8.9	14.3	16.1	34.7	100.0
Feb. 1987	19.7	5.8	11.9	16.8	16.3	29.5	100.0
Aug. 1991	20.2	5.6	13.3	18.9	22.9	19.1	100.0
C 1987 employment by region ('000 with percentages in brackets)							
Central Sydney, Inner Western and Southern Sydney	107.5 (23.0)	38.7 (28.1)	85.5 (30.5)	103.7 (26.1)	91.8 (23.8)	158.2 (22.7)	585.4 (24.8)
Western and South-western Sydney	103.7 (22.2)	29.3 (21.2)	54.7 (19.5)	77.6 (19.6)	76.1 (19.7)	177.5 (25.5)	518.9 (22.0)
Northern Sydney and Gosford-Wyong	107.4 (23.0)	23.8 (17.3)	85.5 (30.5)	75.9 (19.2)	70.2 (18.2)	77.6 (11.2)	440.4 (18.6)
Remainder of coastal NSW	96.0 (20.6)	26.8 (19.4)	36.2 (12.8)	88.7 (22.3)	105.3 (27.3)	174.8 (25.2)	527.8 (22.3)
Inland NSW	52.1 (11.2)	19.3 (14.0)	18.7 (6.7)	51.0 (12.8)	43.0 (11.0)	107.4 (15.4)	291.5 (12.3)
Totals	466.7 (100.0)	137.9 (100.0)	280.6 (100.0)	396.9 (100.0)	386.4 (100.0)	695.5 (100.0)	2 364.0 (100.0)

[1] Includes mining, utilities, communications, public administration and defence, personal and other services.
Source: ABS *The Labour Force*, Australia cat. no. 62030

Office activities

The major exception to this general pattern has been the finance and business services sector, whose total employment grew about 150 000 (78 per cent) in the decade to 1991 in NSW. This rapid growth also occurred nationally, though the rate in NSW exceeds that elsewhere. Furthermore, Table 2.19C demonstrates that the intra-state distribution of finance and business services is anything but uniform. Country districts are much under-represented; so, to a lesser extent, are Sydney's western suburbs. In contrast Sydney's north shore and central regions have a great concentration of financial and business employment. This sector covers the law, banking, accounting, real estate, share and commodity trading, advertising and promotions, life and property insurance. Of course, many of these services are used by the general public and to a certain extent reflect the geographical distribution of the population. Many suburban commercial centres, for instance, have branches of the major trading banks or building societies, a solicitor and an accountant, and perhaps a couple of real estate agents. Nevertheless, the concentration is remarkable.

The rapid growth of this sector's employment has been stimulated by five main factors:

1 Spates of corporate takeovers have occurred in the last twenty years or so, prompted by the need for manufacturing industry rationalisation, for access to scale economies, to combat large overseas companies, to penetrate overseas markets, and to control the firms' operating environments more effectively. No segment of business has been exempt from the rush to form larger companies. Takeover battles during the 1980s saw industry concentration in the media (especially the rise to dominance of Murdoch's News Ltd. over the printed word); retailing (the formation of the Coles-Myer group accounting for about one-fifth of Australia's retail sales); brewing (involving initially the Bond Corporation until its interests were devolved to Lion Nathan of New Zealand; and Elders-IXL Ltd. in which Asahi Brewing of Japan now has an interest); and banking (the formation of the Westpac and National Australia Banks). At the same time several giant conglomerate business empires rose and usually fell, each headed by a noted entrepreneur: the Bell Group (Holmes a Court); Adelaide Steamship (Spalvins); IEL Ltd (Brierley); Elders-IXL (Elliot); Bond Corporation (Bond), and Quintex (Skase).

   Takeovers themselves are important to the growth of office employment because they require a bevy of lawyers and accountants and access to a fistful of dollars thoughtfully supplied by an array of financial institutions including merchant banks. Once up and running the large corporation employs its own, or contracts in, legal, accounting, real-estate, advertising, currency trading and insurance services of a highly specialist kind. The net effect is therefore to create more office jobs.

2 The spectacular development of financial markets has arisen partly through the need to finance takeovers. Other contributing factors include the substantial degree of deregulation of the Australian dollar and banking industries which occurred under the Hawke government. This has permitted a whole new activity to arise, involving little else than around-the-clock buying and selling of major currencies. Banking has grown partly in response to corporate inability to finance expansion from retained earnings or equity raising through the stock exchange, and partly through the massive increase in financial transactions of all kinds occurring in metropolitan central business districts (CBDs). Such increased transactions include: buying and selling real estate; share and commodity trading; and life assurance or superannuation. Again, the net effect of this growth of financial markets has been to greatly increase employment in the service sector of the economy.
3 Hand in hand with takeover activity and financial deregulation there has been a transformation of share and commodity trading. A large array of futures markets has arisen, in which participants can speculate on the future price of shares and such commodities as gold, other metals, cattle or grains. In addition, the Perth stock exchange pioneered a second board listing of small, often rather speculative companies, to enable them to seek funds to expand production and engage in research and development. And on the main boards a combination of takeovers, new listings, institutions awash with money, and a bull run that survived until October 1987 ensured a large increase in the volume of business in the middle years of the decade. This business, in turn, generated service employment.
4 Institutions — mainly assurance companies and superannuation funds — have a large and rapidly increasing volume of money at their disposal to invest, with shares and property being the main destinations. This simply reflects the growing popularity of life assurance and superannuation among the public at large — encouraged by the federal government in order to wean the public off State pensions. Both were, and still are, a popular fringe benefit among executives and the self-employed small business-person. Since many fringe benefits were taxed after mid-1987, superannuation has been described as a last great tax shelter, partly because a substantial portion can be taken in lump-sum form at a low taxation rate. It is not surprising therefore that Trade Unions elected to campaign in 1985/86 for a 3 per cent superannuation benefit for all workers. The government subsequently conceded a 12 per cent claim. Insofar as unions run their own funds, they will join the ranks of the capitalists on the floors of Australian stock exchanges. The continued growth in the size of investment institutions is, in other words, more or less assured.
5 The fifth factor encouraging growth of service employment is computer technology, and improved communications (optical fibres, microwaves,

satellites etc.). Computer technology enables the large-scale storage, retrieval and analysis of information and the communications improvements permit rapid geographical dissemination of the information throughout the world. Financial assets can also be moved from one place to another with amazing rapidity. These developments have aided the development of large corporations by enabling adequate control over geographically widely-dispersed operations. It matters little whether the company is national or international in character. Developments have also permitted the creation of international markets for finance or tangible commodities. Both developments have either created jobs in new industries and new occupations or expanded the art of paper-shuffling.

There is a considerable degree of interdependence between the various finance and business service activities, at the heart of which lie a group of financial institutions. Their interdependence is both functional, and geographical. All the high level business activities we have discussed tend to congregate together in the CBDs and ancillary centres of capital cities such as Sydney and Melbourne. This is a matter of practical convenience, since the participants in takeovers and other corporate battles, or in trading and investment, have traditionally valued face-to-face contact in their dealings. Modern communications which appear to offer great opportunity for geographically decentralised negotiations have actually done little to offset the perceived advantages of immediate inter-personal contact.

So great have been the centripetal tendencies of office-based activities and the increase in the number of office workers to be accommodated that the last twenty years have seen an almost frenzied burst of CBD property development which has transformed the physical appearance of the larger cities. Office buildings and, to some extent, hotels, CBD residential apartments and retail facilities have shared a massive level of investment (Daly, 1982b; Adrian, 1984a). To some extent, the centralisation of activity has been facilitated by developments in office building technology which have permitted the construction of ever-taller buildings. On the other hand, the demand for central city accommodation has raised the rental rate of such property (and thus the price of land) to levels which provide economic justification for tall buildings.

The commercial dominance of Sydney and Melbourne

Although Australian capital cities dominate the commercial life of their respective states, only two cities dominate the national economy: Sydney and Melbourne. This is true not just of the finance and business services sector, but also of private commerce in general. Tables 2.20 and 2.21 illustrate their control of the financial arena, except for 'retail' finance institutions such as building societies and credit unions. Head offices of development banks, overseas banks, merchant banks, major finance companies, life assurance

Table 2.20 The head office location of major financial institutions, 1983

Type of institution	*Sydney*	*Melbourne*	*Sydney–Melbourne*	*Other*
Reserve Bank	1	–	–	–
Trading Banks	3	2	1	2
Development banks	2	1	–	–
Representative offices of overseas banks	73	6	15	–
Merchant banks	41	14	–	1
Major finance companies	16	4	–	4
Authorised money market dealers	5	4	–	–
Ten largest life assurance companies	7	2	–	1
Twenty largest general insurance companies	13	7	–	–
Building societies	33	36	–	40
Credit unions	285	186	–	149
Australian companies: top 200 by profitability	100	70	–	30

Source: Daly (1987)

Table 2.21 All trading banks: share of deposits and advances by State and Territory, December quarter 1988

	NSW	*Vic*	*Qld*	*SA*	*WA*	*Tas*	*NT*	*ACT*	
Deposits	43.2	24.7	13.5	6.5	9.3	1.0	0.5	1.2	99.9
Loans etc.	45.1	25.6	10.0	7.9	8.4	1.2	0.5	1.2	99.9
Population *31 Dec. 1988*	*34.1*	*25.6*	*17.0*	*8.4*	*9.6*	*2.7*	*0.9*	*1.7*	*100.0*

Source: ABS *Banking, Australia* cat. no. 56050 (1988); ABS *Australian Demographic Statistics* (December 1988)

companies and general insurance companies are almost exclusively located in Sydney and Melbourne. NSW, for which read Sydney, is also the locus of a disproportionately large volume of trading bank deposits and advances. Queensland's share of financial flows seems to be particularly over-shadowed by its southern neighbour. Table 2.22 shows that Sydney and Melbourne are the headquarters of most of Australia's top 100 companies as measured by shareholders' funds and market capitalisation, a pattern which has existed for many years.

It is also clear from these figures that Sydney is now the pre-eminent commercial centre of Australia and that this pre-eminence has been growing in recent years. It has the headquarters of many more financial institutions than Melbourne (Table 2.20), and this pattern was reinforced by the allocation of the 16 new banking licences under deregulation policies in the early 1980s. Its share of the value of trading bank transactions is nearly double Melbourne's (Table 2.21). It has overtaken Melbourne's share of the top 100 companies and rapidly increased its share of corporate profits. Table 2.22C

Table 2.22 The changing economic strength of Sydney and Melbourne

A Location of the top 100 company headquarters[1]

	1953	*1963*	*1973*	*1983*
Melbourne	50	47	39	36
Sydney	37	44	50	50
Other locations	13	9	11	14

B Location of the profits of the top 100 companies (%)

	1953	*1963*	*1973*	*1983*
Melbourne	60.0	53.1	59.3	45.8
Sydney	27.7	40.0	33.7	45.9
Others	12.3	6.9	7.0	8.3

C Changes in the top 100 company list 1978–83

	Number of companies which:			
	Improved in ranking within top 100	*Declined in ranking within top 100*	*Entered top 100*	*Exited from top 100*
Melbourne	12	16	7	9
Sydney	21	14	12	13
Others	5	2	6	4

1 Shareholders' funds and market capitalisation

Source: O'Connor and Edgington (1984)

also shows that Sydney-based firms have also improved their asset rankings to a greater extent than their Melbourne counterparts.

In Fagan's (1987) view, Melbourne's earlier pre-eminence in financial matters reflected a development phase dominated by British financial links. Sydney's subsequent rise is connected in part with a reorientation of financial ties towards the USA and other Pacific Rim nations. In this connection Sydney's industrial base was perhaps stronger than Melbourne's in the sense that it faced less structural adjustment pressures. Moreover, its financial markets, which played a major part in capital raising for the 1960s mining boom and various corporate takeovers, were more innovative. In short, Sydney dominates, with Melbourne being the only other really significant finance centre. O'Connor and Edgington (1984) in fact see the two capitals as 'gateway cities' — a term which means that they serve as the principal channels for the finance, people, goods, and information which link the domestic circuit of capital with the outside world. They note, however, that this gateway role is tilting in Sydney's favour as it has become the principal point of entry to Australia in the age of air travel. Just as significant in explaining Sydney's emerging dominance may be the fact that it contained the headquarters of the former Overseas Telecommunications Commission

(OTC — now merged with Telecom to form The Australian and Overseas Telecommunications Corporation — AOTC) and the Reserve Bank, two critical organisations for the financial world. Also operating in Sydney's favour during the last twenty years has been the success of companies headquartered there in takeover battles (Fagan, 1987). Its broader industrial base with smaller more aggressive domestic-based companies must also have helped.

It is difficult to see other capital city locations around Australia making much dent into the commercial dominance of Sydney and Melbourne. Indeed, the continued integration of the Australian and global economies is likely to reinforce the situation. As Fagan notes, TNCs prefer core locations for their activities. Nowhere is this clearer than in foreign property investment in this country. Table 2.23 gives the value and destination of major real estate investments by overseas organisations for two financial years: 1982/83 and 1988/89. In 1982/83 about 84 per cent was targeted on capital cities and 57 per cent on NSW. One can readily infer that Sydney was the principal destination for investment. By 1988/89, at the height of the real estate boom, the incoming flow reached nearly $10.5 billion, an eleven-fold increase on seven years earlier. The NSW share fell to only 38 per cent (slightly ahead of its population share) and a massive 41 per cent went to Queensland — two and a half times its population share. The remaining states picked up a few

Table 2.23 The value and destination, by State, of major overseas investments in Australian real estate, 1982/83 and 1989/90

Destination	*NSW*	*Vic*	*Qld*	*SA*	*WA*	*Tas*	*ACT*	*Australia wide*	*Total*
Value (1982/83 ($million)	534.6	143.3	90.3	6.5	96.1	3.0	12.9	45.9	931.9
Percentage	57.4	15.4	9.7	0.7	10.3	0.3	1.4	4.9	100.0

	NSW	*Vic*	*Qld*	*WA*	*Other*[1]	*Total*
Value (1989/90) ($ billion)						
Commercial for development	2.10	0.57	0.97	0.20	0.65	4.49
Developed commercial	0.83	0.11	0.43	0.09	0.06	1.53
Residential for development	0.97	0.06	2.81	0.31	0.14	4.30
Developed residential	0.06	0.03	0.04	0.01	0.01	0.15

Destination 1982/83	*CBD*	*Captial city non-CBD*	*Both*	*Provincial city*	*Capital and Provincial city*	*Total*
Percentage	58.2	20.3	5.5	11.8	4.2	100.0

1 other states and multi-state investment

Source: After Adrian (1984b)—compiled from Foreign Investment Review Board data; *Foreign Investment Review Board* (1990).

crumbs. Note that a large part of Queensland's receipts went to newly developed residential property and that NSW was still the preferred destination for commercial development.

Table 2.24 sets these overseas property investment trends in a wider context. Real estate takes some 40 per cent or so of overseas investment — or 60 per cent if tourist ventures are included. Only about one quarter (or nearly half if tourist ventures are included) went into productive sectors that might increase exports and foreign earnings, reduce imports and improve the national balance of payments. Even then, a large part of the money bought existing assets rather than expanding the stock of assets. The table also indicates that Japan, Britain, and the USA were the main sources of capital in line with established patterns. When we consider all investment together, and make a notional distribution among the states of the 'other' column, the main beneficiaries were NSW, Queensland and Western Australia in that order. Victoria was a distant fourth. A similar pattern exists for tourist investment, but with NSW in a far more dominant position.

Two distinct economic cleavages seem to be emerging. The first distinguishes between the financial cores of inner Sydney and Melbourne (together with their outliers North Sydney and St. Kilda Road) and the rest of Australia. The former controls Australia as a whole: core against periphery.

Table 2.24 Foreign investment in Australia 1989/90

Sector	*$ billion*[1]	*Per cent*	*Source*	*$ billion*	*(%)*
Manufacturing	2.1	13.5	Japan	8.4	34.9
Mining	2.0	12.8	Australia[2]	4.4	18.3
Finance and Insurance	–	–	UK	2.6	10.8
			USA	1.8	7.5
Services (excl. tourism)	1.4	9.0	New Zealand	1.8	7.5
Tourism	3.1	19.9	Hong Kong	1.0	4.1
Real Estate	6.5	41.7	Singapore	0.3	1.2
Other	0.5	3.2	Other	3.8	15.8
Total	15.6	100.11	Total	24.1	100.1

Destination (all investment)

State	NSW	Vic	Qld	WA	SA	Tas	ACT	NT	Other[3]	Total
$ billion	7.1	1.3	6.3	2.6	0.1	0.0	0.1	0.2	6.4	24.1
Percentage	29.5	5.4	26.1	10.8	0.4	0.0	0.4	0.8	26.6	100.0

Destination (tourist investment)

State	NSW	Qld	WA	Other[3]	Total
$ million	1 928	1 042	338	584	3 892
Percentage	49.5	26.8	8.7	15.0	100.0

1 investments larger than $50 million only
2 investments by overseas subsidiaries of Australian companies; migrants
3 includes multi-state development

Source: Foreign Investment Review Board (1990)

The periphery, according to Fagan, has the characteristics of a branch(-plant) economy: lower decision-making levels, a reduced diversity of quaternary (decision-making) occupations, limited research and development, standardized capital intensive production technology and perhaps poor local linkages. Adelaide and Tasmania are classic examples.

In contrast, the cores are not only the locus of economic control, but mediate between the periphery and the outside world. Furthermore some parts, especially commodity and currency speculation activities, are effectively components of the world economy and have little relationship to events in the rest of Australia. To a small extent they are located in Australia because Sydney's time zone conveniently fills in a gap in the 24-hour operations of commodity and currency markets. More significantly, the Australian dollar is one of the world's most heavily traded currencies. In the language of Figure 2.4 (p. 80), the functional characteristics of the core are substantially, if not totally, determined by the international circuit of factors.

The second cleavage has to do with current patterns of foreign investment and the foreign ownership of Australian assets. The current game is overwhelmingly focused on NSW, Queensland and Western Australia. This is where most resource and tourist development is taking place, profits can be made, and there are capital gains prospects. In other words, the foreign investors' mental maps of Australia are sketchy about Victoria and barely recognise South Australia, Tasmania, and the Territories. These places have a major development problem given the importance of foreign capital relative to the total of new Australian investment.

Tourism

Tourism, whether involving Australian residents or overseas visitors, is a major activity of rapidly growing importance. Together with related activities it accounts for about 5 per cent of GDP and some 40 000 jobs are directly or indirectly involved. This is more than the TCF and motor vehicle industries combined. Overseas visitors contributed $2.5 billion to the Australian economy in 1984/85, 40 per cent of which was on airfares. The remaining $1.5 billion is equivalent to export income, which puts tourism in the same league as iron ore, meat, petroleum products, aluminium oxide and wool. And while Australia's rank as an exporter slid from twelfth to twenty-third place in the decade to 1983, its ranking in the tourist industry improved (although, admittedly, the country is still only a small player on the international stage, accounting for only 0.3 per cent of international travel movements and 1 per cent of receipts).

The rapid rate of growth in the number of overseas visitors in recent years is shown in Figure 2.17. As of 1990, Japan, New Zealand, the UK and the USA provided about 65 per cent of the foreign visitors. Successive dollar

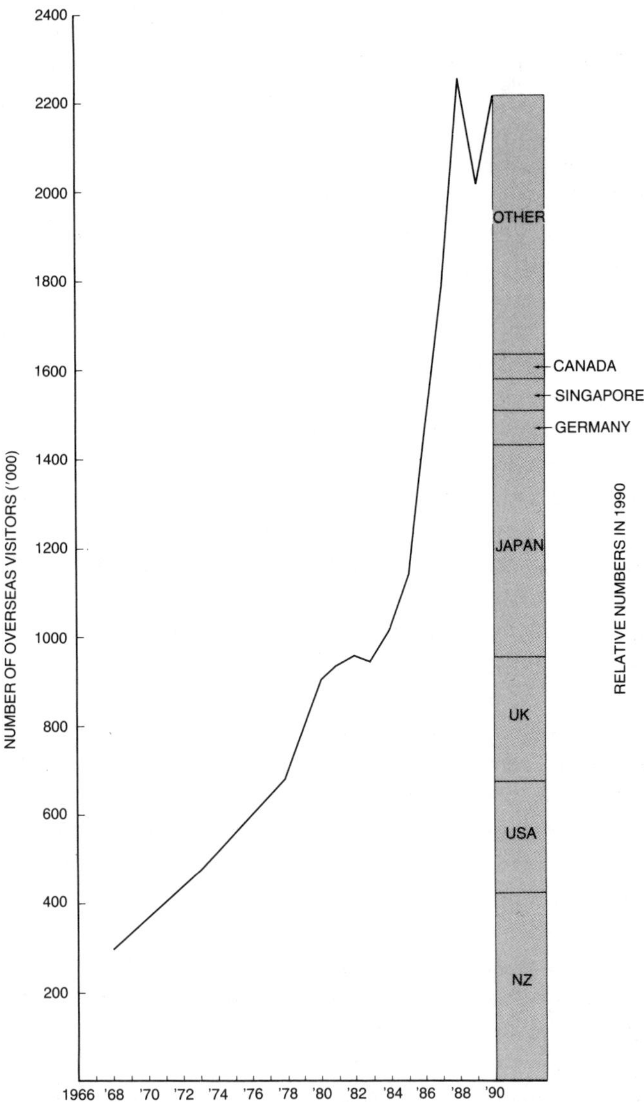

Fig. 2.17 Overseas visitors: origins and numbers, 1968–90

devaluations and effective tourist promotions through the likes of Paul Hogan, *Crocodile Dundee*, koalas, frilled-necked lizards, the America's Cup and the bicentennial have raised this country's profile as an interesting, even exciting, safe and inexpensive tourist destination. Consequently, the number of overseas visitors accelerated towards the two-million mark as the bicentennial approached, with Japan and the USA being the two most rapidly expanding markets. Recent figures suggest that the 1991/92 total is likely to approach 2.4 million visitors. Australia, which has traditionally had a large deficit on international tourist trade, is thus approaching a balance, thereby adding valuable national income at a time of low export returns. All of this is a far cry from the start of the 1970s when the country attracted less than 400 000 overseas visitors.

There are many advantages inherent in the growth of the tourist industry. It is geographically widespread and offers work in many places with otherwise limited employment prospects. It is labour intensive: 26 average overseas visitors or 250 domestic tourists create one job. And three-quarters of the jobs are directly concerned with the tourists' immediate well-being, often being of a semi-skilled or unskilled nature. Potentially, therefore, the industry is a useful antidote to unemployment, although employment is often part-time or seasonal. Environmentally, tourism sells the same resource over and over again and tends to conserve rather than destroy assets. It is, for example, hardly in the operator's interest to reduce the attractions which people appreciate: views, historical associations, wildlife, recreational opportunity and so on. Finally, in a macro-economic sense, the industry suffers few of the ills which bedevil world trade. It does not face weak commodity markets, protectionism, dumping or oligopolistic control.

Everything considered, tourism has a lot going for it, but in Australia more than most other places. To date the country has been a long-haul special interest destination for overseas visitors: it has taken a lot of time and money to experience the country's attractions. Both these barriers are being reduced as available leisure time increases among the growing ranks of the world's wealthy citizens and the cost of air travel diminishes. Moreover the local industry has barely tapped the global market. For example, in two major markets for the industry, Japan and the USA, Australia recently attracted only a tiny fraction of potential visitors: 4 per cent of Japanese tourists (1985) and 2 per cent of US tourists (1984).

Although overseas visitors constitute the major growth segment of the tourist market, domestic trips probably account for 325 000 of the industry's 400 000 jobs (or about 80 per cent of the total), and a much higher proportion of trip numbers. Domestic trips can be split into two kinds: day trips and over-night trips, involving at least one night's stay away from home. Day trips include visiting friends and relatives, sightseeing, picnicking, playing or watching sport, and visiting museums, animal parks or historical monuments. They show little regional variation in intensity either in the popularity of the different categories or in their total frequency of occurrence (see Bureau of Industry Economics, 1984 for further details). Day trips are therefore geographically neutral: their incidence reflects the spatial distribution of population.

The destinations of visits involving an overnight stay are much less spatially neutral. Some places clearly benefit more than others. This applies both between and within states. Inter-state variations are shown in Table 2.25. In terms of total trips (row 6) the States' shares roughly match their population

Table 2.25 Domestic expenditure on trips involving an overnight stay, by State and destination ($A million)

Origin	*NSW*	*Vic*	*Qld*	*SA*	*WA*	*Tas*	*Total*
1 From other States	1627	527	1870	347	490	172	5279
(%)	30.8	10.0	35.4	6.6	9.3	3.3	
2 Within State	2742	1427	2230	614	1172	150	8231
(%)	33.3	17.3	27.1	7.5	14.2	1.8	
3 Total	4369	1954	4100	961	1662	322	13 510
4 Expenditure in home State by outbound interstate travellers	723	536	732	216	130	92	2763
5 Total	5092	2790	4832	1177	1792	414	16 273
(%)	31.3	17.1	29.7	7.2	11.0	2.5	
6 Expected total expenditure[1]	5549	4166	2766	1364	1562	439	
7 Surplus or deficit on expenditure	–457	–1376	2066	–187	230	–25	
8 Percent of surplus or deficit	–9.0	–49.3	+42.8	–15.9	+12.8	–6.0	

1 assuming State's share matches share of population
2 including ACT/NT
Source: Haigh and Rieder (1989)

share: NSW, Victoria and Western Australia have a slight deficit and the others a surplus. When it comes to expenditure, the picture changes markedly. Victoria's share of the tourist dollar drops sharply. Perhaps due to its compactness, the State's residents tend to take fewer overnight stays intra-state, but mainly Victoria is not a favoured destination of inter-state visitors. Overall Victorians spent $1376 million more outside their State than inter-state visitors spent in Victoria (row 7). NSW also records a slight deficit on expenditure, but Western Australia, due mainly to its vast size which leads to longer trips, tends towards a large surplus on expenditure. Paradoxically, South Australia is also a large state with a highly nucleated population distribution, but trippers within or to that State are not big spenders.

Queensland, and to a lesser extent Tasmania, are the major gainers from longer duration trips, especially those of inter-state origin. Queensland has the largest surplus expenditure on inter-state travel, but Tasmania's surplus looms larger relative to the size of its economy. Of course, within each State the geographical distribution of expenditure on trips involving an overnight stay is also uneven. Taking NSW as an example, the greatest beneficiaries are:

- the coast fringe, but more especially the north coast with its excellent climate

- nodal attractions including cities: Sydney and Canberra; natural environments: the Blue Mountains or Snowy Mountains, rainforests or wilderness areas; other human-made features: Hunter Valley vineyards, dams (fishing and other water sports), historical villages, or the Western Plains Zoo, for example.
- routeways which benefit from passing traffic such as the Hume and New England highways.

Table 2.26 shows that the spatial incidence of overseas visitors is most uneven. Two-thirds visit Sydney, one-third Melbourne or Queensland and one in seven gets to Adelaide or Perth. Sydney is therefore easily the most important destination. In almost all cases the State capital is the stepping stone to other intra-state destinations, except for Queensland and the Northern Territory. Approximately 12 per cent of Queensland's visitors do not get to see Brisbane, mainly because Cairns and Townsville have their own international airports. Two of the Northern Territory's most popular tourist attractions — Ayers Rock and Alice Springs — can be accessed directly from other state capitals without going through Darwin. Since the Territory only contains about 1 per cent of Australians and is expensive to reach, it is doing very well to attract over 6 per cent of overseas visitors. In fact, Tasmania is the only State which does not appear to attract its share of overseas visitors.

Sydney's dominance of the international segment of the tourist industry in part reflects its role as financial capital of Australia. Many foreigners arrive in Australia for primarily business purposes. Of course Sydney is also Australia's largest city, which makes it the logical destination of many incoming flights and consequently an easy place to reach. Finally, in a continent where tourist attractions are scattered widely and are often difficult to get to, Sydney has the greatest concentration of things the visitor can do.

Numerous industries benefit from tourism. The major ones are shown in Table 2.27. Both domestic and overseas travellers spend almost half their money on travel, although the mode of transport is distinctly different between the two groups. Overseas travellers, who are often pressed for time,

Table 2.26 Inter-state distribution of overseas visitors, 1988/89[1]

	NSW	*Vic*	*Qld*	*SA*	*WA*	*Tas*
Percentage of visitor nights	33.0	21.00	28.00	6.00	8.00	2.00
Total expenditure $ million	1252	797	1063	228	304	76
Percentage of arrivals in each State	55.1	17.0	17.4	1.4	7.9	0.3

1 excluding ACT and NT

Source: Haigh and Rieder (1989)

Table 2.27 Where the tourist dollars go, 1988/89

	Domestic		*International*		*Total*	
	($mill.)	*(%)*	*($mill.)*	*(%)*	*($mill.)*	*(%)*
Food and beverages	1306	8.0	528	8.9	1835	8.2
Petroleum	3315	20.3	166	2.8	3481	15.6
Road transport	735	4.5	291	4.9	1026	4.6
Air transport	1894	11.6	2671	45.0	4565	20.5
Other transport	392	2.4	18	0.3	410	1.8
Entertainment	555	3.4	119	2.0	674	3.0
Restaurants, hotels, clubs	4425	27.1	1128	19.0	5553	24.9
Other	3707	22.7	1015	17.1	4722	21.2
Total	16 330		5935		22 265	

Source: Haigh & Rieder (1989)

Expenditure is actual trip expenditure *adjusted* for transfers and additions, ie: **Plus** additional domestic expenditure (e.g. motor vehicle non-petrol costs, camping equipment) **Minus** domestic transfer expenditure (i.e. expenditure which would have occurred regardless of the decision to travel). **Plus** fares paid to QANTAS by overseas visitors. **Plus** expenditure in Australia by international airlines attributable to the carriage of overseas visitors.

prefer air travel, whereas domestic tourists prefer to travel by road. If we assume that new breeds of overseas visitors (such as Japanese honeymooners) maintain existing expenditure patterns, the major beneficiary of the current large rise in foreign tourists will be the aviation industry, together with manufacturers of souvenirs and the hospitality industry. In terms of employment created by both domestic and foreign tourists together, hotel and restaurant jobs are the most numerous (39 per cent), followed by those in wholesale and retail trade (18 per cent), transport (16.5 per cent), and manufacturing (11 per cent), according to the Bureau of Industry Economics (1984).

It is therefore incontestable that the growth of tourism is desirable not just from the point of view of a few fortunate locations but because of the wider multiplier effects it has throughout the economy. It is already a major economic sector, but has the chance to become even more significant in future years.

The tourist industry is ultimately located according to the spatial distribution of attractions and the access routes to them. To a considerable extent this pattern is determined by Australia's environment, although governments and developers have some control over events. They can create attractions: Jupiter's casino, the Sydney Opera House, Seaworld or the Western Plains Zoo, for instance. They can build infrastructure, particularly in the form of accommodation and transport — the Yulara resort at Ayers Rock, the Iwasaki resort near Yeppoon, and international airports at Cairns and Townsville spring to mind. And they can promote tourist attractions in various markets.

Governments react mainly to domestic events, although the international factors which brought about the 1985/86 devaluation of the dollar created an opportunity to promote Australia overseas which was enthusiastically grasped at all tiers of administration. The extent to which the private sector is influenced by international or domestic factors in its investment decisions depends largely on the market served. Investment to serve primarily overseas visitors is particularly sensitive to any factors which might choke off or stimulate the stream of tourists, notably currency changes, competing opportunities in other countries, visitor tastes and preferences, political and industrial stability, and the quality of Australian service. Domestic-oriented investments are much more conditioned by the local business climate and the prospect of receiving a satisfactory return on capital. There is not much overlap between the two segments.

Concluding remarks

Several key sectors of the Australian economy have been examined in this chapter in terms of their spatial organisation, their recent development and the factors or processes which underlie our observations. The pattern of economic activity in Australia is rapidly changing, events in one sector of production have important implications for the well-being and organisation of other sectors. It is worth emphasizing how much everything is interrelated.

Secondly, geographical patterns are mostly the product of a myriad of chance government and business decisions. Where geography is important it tends to act as a passive backdrop of environment and resources, a kind of stage on which the drama of business and government is acted out. Frequently the spatial consequences of particular decisions are not considered at all, or if they are, the outcomes are unintended.

Finally, Australia's economy is becoming more open and increasingly integrated with the world economy. Consequently the locus of the stream of decisions which shape the location of economic activity is increasingly shifting off-shore and in particular to the cores of global markets such as London, New York, Tokyo, Washington. We might, interestingly, add Beijing and Moscow to the list. Even ostensibly domestic decisions by the federal government are frequently taken with one eye on international reactions. This trend is set to continue and it almost certainly means that geographical considerations in development and welfare will diminish in importance relative to aggregate macro-economic targets. In short, overall national economic well-being is the issue which will increasingly attract policy-makers' attentions, not the well-being of particular areas — except, perhaps, in the case of regional economic disaster where lobby groups can be effectively organised (the steel and sugar industries are recent examples where this occurred in the middle and late 1980s).

THE QUALITY OF LIFE

BY world standards, Australia is a relatively affluent and harmonious country. It does not have the widespread poverty and malnutrition that bedevil much of the Third World and it is mercifully free from the sort of civil strife that characterises the Middle East, Northern Ireland, Sri Lanka, South Africa and a host of other countries. By international standards, then, Australia is probably widely perceived as having a reasonably good 'quality of life'. However, the notion of 'quality of life' cannot be measured easily: it is extremely difficult to define what contributes to the 'quality of life' in a given area.

If a person is thought to have a good 'quality of life' then that person might be expected to have good housing, good health, a good education, and a good job. Additionally the person might well have abundant leisure time and good opportunities for recreation. This does not mean, however, that a person's 'quality of life' can be assessed simply by measuring his or her accessibility to housing, to health care facilities, to schools and universities, to employment opportunities, and to recreational facilities. For one thing, other issues may be every bit as important. It may be, for example, that there are factors which cannot be readily assessed but which are central to a feeling of well-being and thus to a good 'quality of life'. The person may for instance feel respected by the community in which he or she lives. Without such respect, fine housing and a good job may count for little. For another thing, what it is that is deemed truly important is likely to vary from one person to another. One person might, for instance, lay great emphasis on education as a major contributing factor to an overall good 'quality of life' whereas another person might consider housing or employment to be all-important. In short, there does not exist a definitive list of concerns that people take account of when assessing their quality of life. Whether or not people rate their 'quality of life' as good depends, in other words, on their aspirations — which in turn reflect their value systems. It is not unknown, for example, for old age pensioners, in poor health, with only fair housing, and with limited finances, to rate their quality of life more highly than young, relatively well-paid professional people who have a great many of the materialistic trappings usually thought of as indicators of the 'good life' (Abrams, 1973). The reason for this apparent anomaly is of course that the old age pensioners had lower aspirations and expected less from life than the younger professionals, who were preoccupied with the cost of mortgages, family life, and promotion prospects. The uncertainty and thwarted ambition that characterised the younger group was reflected in poor self-assessments. This suggests, in turn, that a person's 'quality of life' may vary in accordance with the stage that that person has reached in his or her life cycle. When an individual first leaves home and establishes a separate household, the child-rearing years, and retirement are all stages in the life cycle when changed financial circumstances can influence both a person's 'quality of life' and that person's perception of their circumstances.

Different people place different emphases on housing, health, employment and other aspects of human existence. It is very difficult therefore to make accurate statements about the 'quality of life' in particular geographical areas. For example, it is impossible to state categorically that the 'quality of life' on Sydney's North Shore is greater than the 'quality of life' in the inner suburbs because there is no way of knowing how the respective residents of the two areas rate their lives. On paper, as revealed in the census, the North Shore might have lesser degrees of crowding, more high income earners, fewer unemployed, more owner occupied housing, and more motor vehicles but this does not of itself prove that the 'quality of life' is greater because such measures reveal nothing about whether or not residents are happy and satisfied with their lives. 'Quality of life' is, after all, an intensely subjective concept that can only really be examined through direct survey techniques.

The costs involved in surveys concerning subjectively perceived 'quality of life' have severely limited their use on other than a very localised scale. As a result, social scientists interested in how living conditions vary from one place to another have searched around for surrogate variables that, in providing a substitute for surveys, throw some light on overall 'quality of life'. One commonly used surrogate is *gross domestic product (GDP) per capita*. In many ways this economic statistic provides a measure of the wealth of a nation. Its significance as far as Australia is concerned lies in the fact that Australia's position in the international league table of nations ranked according to GDP per capita has changed markedly since Federation in 1901. As is often pointed out, Australia in 1900 probably had the highest GDP per capita in the world. By 1980 it ranked sixteenth, having been overtaken by, in turn, Kuwait, the United Arab Emirates, Qatar, Switzerland, Sweden, the USA, Canada,

Denmark, Norway, West Germany, Belgium, France, Luxembourg, Libya and the Netherlands. This decline in Australia's international ranking is often interpreted as an indication that the country is falling behind in the march of progress and must therefore lift its game in order to maintain its international competitiveness. There is, however, a danger in laying too much store by this sort of sporting analogy. Unlike sporting league tables, figures for GDP per capita are rather unsatisfactory measures of performance. To begin with, the data on which the rankings are based are not always thoroughly reliable. Secondly, international comparisons prior to the 1940s are fraught with danger because it was really only since that time that international organisations began to monitor the world order in any truly systematic way. This means that Australia's claim to being a world leader in 1900 may be less secure than is usually acknowledged. And finally, the GDP per capita ranking at any point in time is very heavily dependent on current commodity prices. Thus the collapse of oil prices in the mid-1980s may well have advanced Australia's ranking by adversely affecting the ranking of Kuwait, the United Arab Emirates, Qatar, and Libya.

The apparent slippage in Australia's international ranking over the last eighty years has come about largely as a result of other countries catching up rather than as a result of Australia suffering a fall in real 'quality of life'. Indeed, there is a good deal of evidence that, in many senses, 'quality of life' in Australia has improved. Such basic statistics as life expectancy and maternal mortality show, for example, significant improvements. Moreover, Australia is still one of the most egalitarian countries in the world and, of the countries above Australia in the 'league table', only the Netherlands has a more even distribution of income over the population. In short, what Australia lacks in relation to its position in the international league table, it perhaps makes up for in the evenness with which economic benefits are distributed. The degree of egalitarianism in Australia should not be overstated however. Income and wealth are both concentrated even if the degree of concentration is relatively low by international standards. Moreover, there are undoubtedly barriers which will slow any future move towards greater equality in income distribution in Australia, notably the existence of privilege (as reflected in the inheritance of wealth), the persistence of inequalities in the education system (manifested in low retention rates among senior students in schools in disadvantaged areas), and the inequality of citizens before the law (sometimes reflected in the positive correlation between wealth and the quality of legal representation) (Mendelsohn, 1979; pp. 60–5). In addition, 'Australia's long neglect of education and training, its excessive economic protectionism, its small internal market in an increasingly fenced-in world, and the manifest conservatism and reluctance of management and unions to modernise and make short-term sacrifices for long-term gains' have all played a part in Australia's fall down the international league and will continue to affect the country's international standing in the future (Mendelsohn, 1979;

p. 60). Despite this, the distribution of income and wealth has become more even and a complex welfare state has been built up to prevent any member of society suffering undue hardship. It is appropriate therefore to look at the distribution of income and wealth and at the growth and development of Australia's welfare state, not least because 'the welfare state' becomes very important in times of recession such as those experienced in the early 1990s.

The distribution of income and wealth

A person's income has a big bearing on that person's quality of life in so far as income influences, to a large extent, the command that the person has over goods and services. In a capitalist nation like Australia, a high income enables an individual to buy good quality housing in pleasant surroundings, high quality health care (often in private hospitals) and a good quality education. A substantial disposable income also gives a person a significant degree of choice in the selection of recreation and leisure time activities. Thus, although the quality of life cannot be reduced simply to economic criteria, the significance of income is such that it cannot be dismissed as a major determinant of living conditions. Much the same can be said about *wealth*. Basically wealth refers to the dwellings, durable goods, pension fund reserves, equities, and other financial assets owned by individuals. Thus an individual's wealth can, in principle, be measured by calculating the value of all his or her assets and then subtracting from that figure the value of the individual's liabilities (such as debts and outstanding mortgages).

By and large governments in Australia have chosen not to try and measure wealth. There are several reasons for this. First, data on wealth are often unreliable. For example, people often fail to disclose fully their assets for fear that these might subsequently become a target for taxation. It is therefore very difficult to assess whether the data obtained in wealth surveys are true and accurate records of the real state of affairs. Secondly, national surveys of wealth would be costly. Finally, governments have often been loath to examine the distribution of wealth in any detail for fear that the results of such a survey would reveal a degree of concentration that might be politically embarrassing.

A belief in egalitarianism is a strong force in Australian politics even if the egalitarian nature of society is more apparent than real and, as a result, governments have generally fought shy, until relatively recently, of any moves that might explode the myth of egalitarianism. As a result it is not surprising that the last *official* national wealth survey was conducted as long ago as 1915. This showed that the top 1 per cent of the population owned over 39 per cent of the wealth that was in private hands. The top 5 per cent owned over 60 per cent and the top 20 per cent held over 89 per cent. This very high level concentration was reflected in a high value Gini coefficient. This statistic measures the unevenness of a distribution and is calculated in such a way that a value of 0.0 would indicate a situation where all people had the same level of provision of whatever it is that is under consideration (in this case, net assets or wealth) while a value of 1.0 would indicate a situation where all resources are held by a single unit (in this case a single person). The Gini coefficient derived from the 1915 wealth data was 0.861 (Podder and Kakwani, 1976).

No official national surveys monitored changes to the 1915 distribution of wealth. As a result it was left to academic researchers doing smaller scale surveys to see whether the level of concentration of wealth was changing over time. One of the most important of these studies was undertaken by Podder and Kakwani using data on consumer finances over the period 1966–1968. Their results are shown in Table 3.1. Clearly the level of inequality in the distribution of wealth evident in 1915 had decreased markedly in the ensuing fifty years. By the late 1960s, the top 1 per cent of the population owned only 9 per cent of privately held assets, the top 5 per cent owned 24 per cent, and the top 20 per cent owned 53 per cent. The spreading of wealth was reflected in the fact that the Gini coefficient stood at only 0.52. It is also interesting to note that the distribution of income was very much more even than the distribution of wealth (reflected in a Gini coefficient of only 0.305 for income). In part this reflects the impact of Australia's progressive income tax structure whereby the tax rate is increased as the level of earnings goes up.

In addition to surveys of consumer finances, researchers have often used estate duty data and probate returns to examine the distribution of wealth in Australia. Raskall (1977), for example, looked at the period 1966–1972 and suggested that the distribution was such that the top 1 per cent owned 22 per cent of total wealth, the top 5 per cent owned 45 per cent, and the top 20 per cent owned 72 per cent. Although these figures are for very much the same period as the information used by Podder and Kakwani (1976), the results are strikingly different and indicate a very much higher concentration in the

Table 3.1 The distribution of income and wealth (per cent)

	1915	*1966–68*	
	Wealth	*Disposable income*	*Net worth*
Bottom 20 per cent	0.03	6.77	0.91
Bottom 40 per cent	0.46	20.84	8.71
Top 20 per cent	89.71	37.68	53.51
Top 5 per cent	66.22	13.99	24.57
Top 1 per cent	39.46	4.60	9.26
Gini coefficient	0.861	0.305	0.520

Source: Extracted from Podder and Kakwani (1976)

ownership of wealth. This, then, suggests that the data used can have a big influence on the results obtained in any study of the distribution of wealth in Australia. In particular, the use of probate returns seems to produce figures that suggest greater concentration than does the use of data on consumer finances. Nevile and Warren (1984), for example, corroborated the finding that the top 5 per cent of adult individuals own 40–50 per cent of the wealth in Australia, again using probate data. Piggott (1984), too, has claimed that the top 1 per cent own about 25 per cent of total private wealth and the top 5 per cent about 50 per cent of total private wealth. These figures are generally in agreement with more recent ones from Dilnot (1990) who argued that the top 1 per cent own 19.7 per cent, the top 10 per cent own 55 per cent and the top 20 per cent 72 per cent of all wealth. On this basis the concentration of wealth appeared to be slightly greater than in the USA but very much less than in the UK.

Of course, the abolition of death duties in all States over the period 1977–1984 has meant that probate data are no longer available as a basis for analysing the distribution of wealth. As a result, recent research has tended to look instead to other sources and to focus on how the distribution of wealth may be changing. In this context Helliwell and Boxall (1978) have shown that private wealth for the nation as a whole grew faster than the population over the period 1958–1975, thereby indicating that *on average* people were becoming better off. In a similar vein, Williams (1983) looked at the market value of dwellings owned by individuals (such dwellings accounting for about 60 per cent of all privately owned wealth) and showed that the real per capita wealth of the nation increased significantly over time: expressed in 1980/1981 dollars, per capita wealth rose from $14 580 in 1966, to $17 840 in 1970, $21 120 in 1975, and $22 480 in 1980. In other words, people were becoming better off in real terms. Their assets were increasing in value at a rate which outstripped the rate of inflation. The other interesting point to emerge from Williams' study was that the ratio between net wealth and income remained fairly constant throughout the 1960s and 1970s at about 3.6:1. In other words, people tended on average to have net wealth equivalent to between three and four times their annual income. A more recent study by Raskall (1986) has also traced the increase in the net wealth of the nation (assets less liabilities) and showed how this increased from $52 700 million in 1966 to $501 600 million in 1984 (at current prices), indicating a per capita average net wealth of approximately $30 000 at the later date. Raskall raised a cautionary note, however, in questioning whether average per capita figures were really very meaningful given that the richest 200 000 Australians have as much wealth as the poorest 2 500 000.

At the same time that information about wealth has become more difficult to obtain as a result of the abolition of death duties, and thus the cessation of probate returns, information on *income* distribution has become more available. The Australian Bureau of Statistics has conducted a number of income surveys. The results of the 1986 survey, together with comparable 1979 data, are shown in Table 3.2. The Table appears to show a very slight increase in inequality in income distribution in so far as high income earners had a marginally greater share of total earnings in 1986 than in 1979 (notably the top 40 per cent). It must be remembered however that the figures in the Table are somewhat biassed in favour of the 'top end' of the income profile because the income surveys included individuals in receipt not only of wages and salaries but also in receipt of cash benefits, pensions, superannuation, bank interest, rent, and dividends. Given this scope, there are likely to be a great many 'income earners' who receive very little by way of income. In short, the Table is not restricted to income earners in the workforce but rather encompasses all manner of income earners. Nevertheless, it is safe to conclude that there exists a fair degree on inequality in income distribution with the top 20 per cent of income earners receiving almost a half of total earnings.

Table 3.2 Income distribution in 1979 and 1986 (per cent)

	1979	*1986*
Top 10 per cent	27.8	28.1
Top 20 per cent	45.5	45.3
Top 40 per cent	60.0	69.7
Top 50 per cent	82.0	78.4

Source: Commonwealth of Australia (1986; 1990)

The figures contained in Table 3.2 raise an interesting question: is the income distribution pattern in Australia more or less unequal than in overseas countries? A partial answer to this question has been provided by Podder (1972) using the Gini coefficient. He found that Australia's Gini coefficient of 0.317 showed a more even distribution than existed in the UK, the USA, and Canada (all of which had coefficients of 0.39). Australia's income distribution was very much more even than that of Italy which had a Gini coefficient of 0.41. The substance of these findings was confirmed by Roberti (1974). Podder also examined the share of national income going to the top and bottom 20 per cent of income earners and found that, by international standards, Australia had a low proportion going to the top quintile and a high proportion going to the bottom quintile. Australia, in other words, has a more egalitarian distribution of income than most other advanced western nations. This equality comes about partly because of the wage fixing and arbitration system ensuring adoption of adequate pay scales and partly because of the progressive nature of income taxation.

It would be wrong, however, to assume that the rich in Australia necessarily pay more tax than the poor and that the tax system is always effectively as well as nominally progressive (Mathews, 1980). The scope for tax minimisation on the part of the rich is very substantial, enabling them to avoid and sometimes evade the contributions that they might otherwise be expected to make. Indeed, in terms of taxation, the notable recent trends have been the increasing reliance of government on the contributions of Pay-As-You-Earn (PAYE) taxpayers and the tendency for inflation to push wages and salaries into higher and higher tax brackets. Chapter 4 examines the relative contributions to income tax revenue made by PAYE taxpayers and the self-employed.

Lee (1978) showed how inflation in the first half of the 1970s led to taxpayers paying more: for example, single taxpayers on average annual earnings experienced increases in their average and marginal tax rates from 19.2 per cent and 32.9 per cent respectively in 1969/1970 to 24.4 per cent and 44.0 per cent in 1974/1975, despite the tax scale having been changed four times during the period in question. Equally dramatic is the fact that the top (60 per cent) tax rate at the end of 1984 started at a taxable income which was equivalent to 1.7 times the average weekly earnings of adult males (not counting overtime); but the 60 per cent rate in 1967/68 did not start until taxable income reached a figure 6 times greater than the average weekly earnings of an adult male. In other words, through wage fixing based on the consumer price index, inflation led to higher incomes which in turn attracted higher tax rates. In 1955/56 someone on average earnings paid only just over 10 per cent of their income in tax; by 1975/76 the same average earner paid almost 23 per cent of their income in tax (Lee, 1978). Since then, taxation rates have gone up and then down with a result that, by 1990, the figure again stood at about 23 per cent. Much of this increased taxation revenue went, of course, towards expenditure on 'the welfare state'.

The rise of the welfare state

Since the Second World War all advanced western countries have introduced legislation to provide income security, health care, education, housing, and a good many other social services for their citizens. This body of legislation, together with the bureaucracy and personnel needed to apply it, is now such an important part of government activity that the term 'welfare state' is commonly used to describe the system under which such services are provided. The rationale behind the welfare state is well established (see Marshall, 1963; Titmuss, 1968). In brief, social policy in the welfare state is aimed at the elimination of poverty, the maximization of well-being, and the pursuit of equality (Graycar, 1983).

In many places, including Australia, the welfare state has grown in an *ad hoc* fashion as policies have been devised to attack the social problems of the day. Moreover, the growth of the welfare state has usually rested on certain unchallenged assumptions which have been at the heart of social policy since

1945. It has been taken for granted, for example, that education improves life chances, that health care spending improves the health of the populace, and that improved housing changes people's behaviour for the better (Jones, 1980). Only recently have these assumptions seriously been questioned as governments have been called upon to justify the huge amounts that are currently spent on welfare policy.

The origins of welfare policy in Australia lie in the nineteenth century, in a time when prevailing attitudes, current problems, and overall social philosophies were very different from the ones that prevail today. In the first half of the nineteenth century, and indeed until the Second World War, welfare policy was very highly selective. Stringent tests were used to decide who were the 'deserving poor'. Welfare policy involved either the institutionalization of the 'recipients' (e.g. orphanages, asylums) or government financial support for public bodies engaged in 'good works'. Benevolent societies were thus prominent in the care of the disadvantaged, leading examples being The Benevolent Society of New South Wales (founded in 1813) and the Melbourne Ladies' Benevolent Society (founded in 1846) (Mendelsohn, 1979). In essence, then, social and welfare services were seen as 'charity', bestowed upon the deserving by the well-to-do, and thus reflecting an authoritarian social structure (Dickey, 1980). The conservative social values that prevailed at the time stressed 'self help' in times of difficulty and laid great store by the work ethic and the notion that industriousness, enterprise, thrift and effort could overcome most social problems (Jones, 1980). Rugged individualism was the order of the day.

With Federation the tenor of social welfare policy changed a little. The period 1901–1914 was one of optimism and advance that saw the introduction of age and invalid pensions (Mendelsohn, 1979). In this sense, the early years of Federation perhaps marked a time when capitalism and individualism came under challenge as the dominant ideology of Australian society. The principal alternative put forward in this challenge to a reliance on self-help was the radical liberal doctrine of *universal rights* (Dickey, 1980; p. xvi).

Pensions for the old and for invalids can be seen in this light as both initiatives implied that a benefit from the State should be universally available to those in need. Likewise, the emergence of the notion of a 'basic wage' as a result of the 'Harvester case' of 1906 is further evidence that the thinking of the time favoured basic rights that applied uniformly throughout the country. The notion of universalism should not be interpreted too literally, of course. Much social policy remained very highly selective and, in particular, subject to a means test that prevented all but the very poor from becoming beneficiaries of whatever funds or services were available. Moreover, social welfare policy in general remained a relatively minor concern of government. Most governments had balanced budgets at this time and thus had little left over for welfare spending. The role of the State, as far as it was articulated, was simply to provide the social infrastructure (e.g. education systems, relief works) necessary to maintain the existing social structure and mode of production of goods and services and keep the population reasonably contented (Jones, 1980).

Social welfare policy was not uniform across the various States of Australia. Under s.51 of the Constitution social policy is very much a States-rights issue, and it is therefore not surprising to find that significant variations existed in both the scope and nature of the policies that were adopted. For example, at Federation all States had made provision for the welfare of mothers and children but only New South Wales and Victoria had made provision for old age pensioners. The tendency at the time was to blame the victim for poverty in Australia and to give welfare policy as low a profile as possible. Inter-state differences in welfare provision have been described at length by Mendelsohn (1979) who pointed out, for example, that Queensland kept its benevolent asylum, its lazaret, and its inebriate institute on relatively isolated islands far from public view. Queensland also exemplified the selectivity and stringency with which charity was dispensed in its distribution of rations to the unemployed: these rations were given out by the police every eight days subject to the constraint that no man could receive them at the same place twice! This enforced a type of ritualized nomadism on work-seekers (Mendelsohn, 1979; p. 96). South Australia was perhaps the most 'progressive' State in recognising a formal responsibility for relief in that it set up a Destitute Board but, even here, help was refused to the able-bodied unemployed so as to keep the focus of attention on the aged and the unprotected (principally children). The prevailing view seemed to be that poor relief should not be so generous as to foster dependence (Mendelsohn, 1979).

Attitudes changed with the major economic recession of the 1930s. By 1932 30 per cent of the workforce was unemployed. Given this state of affairs, the unemployed could no longer be dismissed as unenterprising, probably lazy, and work-shy (Mendelsohn, 1979). By the 1930s, a system of labour exchanges had been set up and during the Depression these were used to ration relief work and to distribute relief payments. However, the help provided to the unemployed was miserly. The main burden fell on the State governments (because the Commonwealth did not assume responsibility for unemployment benefits until after the Second World War, see Chapter 4) but even the levy, in some States, of special taxation to relieve unemployment did little to remedy a general lack of funds. Generally speaking, relief to the unemployed necessitated participation in a public works program. Indeed it was only in the 1930s that New South Wales led the way in introducing dole payments without relief work.

A realisation during the 1930s that hardship could befall individuals through no fault of their own encouraged a further shift towards universalism in social welfare thinking. So long as unemployment was seen as something that could strike more or less anyone anywhere, it followed that relief should be available everywhere and to everybody, not just to those who could make a good case to benevolent societies. The organisation best equipped to cope with such universal benefits was, of course, the government. 'Minimum rights for the many', the principle underlying universalism, became the guiding notion of much social welfare policy in the period after the Second World War. There thus arose a piecemeal extension of the benefits administered by the government (Dickey, 1980).

A list of major welfare benefits, together with their date of introduction, is presented in Table 3.3. This Table restricts attention to basic pensions and benefits. It does not take stock of government assistance provided through other welfare organizations (e.g. in care of the aged). Likewise it does not cover health care spending or education outlays (e.g. AUSTUDY). This Table also restricts attention to Commonwealth benefits because these are the ones available nationwide. Indeed, as explained in Chapter 4, the Commonwealth since the Second World War has assumed constitutional responsibility for the payment of *cash* pensions and benefits. The States, however, retain responsibility for social welfare policies involving actual services (e.g. schools, hospitals, prisons, etc.)

Clearly, Table 3.3 indicates that the period during and immediately after the Second World War witnessed a flurry of activity the like of which was not to be seen again until the mid-1970s. The extension of government services accorded very well, of course, with the prevailing orthodoxy of Keynesian economics. Social welfare spending was seen as a good thing in that it helped

Table 3.3 Commonwealth welfare benefits and recipients

		1989	
Benefit	*Date of introduction*	*Number of individual recipients*	*Amount paid ($ million)*
Age pension	1909	1 328 814	6 973
Invalid pension	1910	307 795	2 416
Family allowance	1941	1 927 015[1]	1 315
Widow's pension	1942	83 642	535
Unemployment benefit	1945	429 350	
Sickness benefit	1945	76 759	3 867
Special benefit	1945	23 929	
Sheltered employment	1967	10 120	73
Supporting parent benefit	1973	239 469	2 132
Handicapped children allowance	1974	36 777	51
Family income supplement	1983	164 746[1]	400
Carer's pension	1985	94 321	–[2]

1 families
2 included in invalid pension

Source: Commonwealth of Australia (1990)

maintain, if not increase, consumer demand. Filling the gaps in the Australian welfare system was therefore easily legitimised. Welfare problems came to be viewed as structural rather than individual failings: their causes were seen to lie in society's mode of operation, not in individual weaknesses. Despite this, the Australian welfare delivery system really set out to do little more than provide a 'safety net' for those who fell upon hard times (Jones, 1980).

In summary, then, the history of social welfare in Australia until 1970 sees the emphasis of policy shift from a highly selective, charity-based distribution of relief to the 'deserving' poor to a system with a wider range of universally available benefits, albeit many of them subject to a means test that restricted access to low income earners. In social welfare terms, Australia in 1970 ranked as a conservative country where there was little forward planning, relatively little social research, and very little humane commitment to breaking down the stigma that went with being a welfare recipient (Graycar, 1978; p. 8).

This situation changed with the advent of a Labor government in 1972 after twenty-three years of conservative rule. The Labor government, pledged to reform, introduced a new series of Commonwealth benefits (see Table 3.3). More important, however, was the vast increase in Commonwealth spending on existing social policies such as those relating to health, education, and social security and welfare payments (principally cash benefits and pensions). Some increased spending is, of course, inevitable at a time of inflation and population growth. What happened in the early 1970s was however quite remarkable. *After* allowing for both inflation and population growth, Commonwealth spending (both current and capital) on social welfare issues increased by massive amounts each year in real terms. Between 1972/73 and 1975/76 health and education spending increased, for example, by 48 per cent and 57 per cent per annum in real per capita terms (Table 3.4).

Cut-backs by the Liberal–National Country Party government when it came to power in 1975 led to spending on health and education being reduced in real terms. In contrast, social security spending continued to increase because of increased unemployment. Even under the Hawke Labor

Table 3.4 Increases in Commonwealth spending on social issues

	Mean annual real per capita increase (%)			
	1972/3–1975/6	*1976/7–1982/3*	*1983/4–1989/90*	*1972/3–1989/90*
Health	+ 47.8	– 5.0	+ 10.3	+ 8.5
Education	+ 57.3	– 1.8	– 0.7	+ 8.2
Social security and welfare	+ 18.4	+ 2.8	– 0.9	+ 6.1
General public service	+ 7.3	+ 0.9	– 1.2	+ 0.9

Source: Calculated from Commonwealth Yearbooks

government, cut-backs continued as the overall size of government was reduced. For example, on average, overall expenditure on general public services diminished by 1 per cent per annum in real per capita terms. This reflects a commitment in all major parties to reduce the size of Commonwealth government. Nevertheless, over a 20 year period, real increases in expenditure of 6–8 per cent per annum are not uncommon.

Similar increases occurred in State spending, partly as a result of the Commonwealth passing on specific purpose grants for spending on social areas and partly because the Commonwealth to States transfer of funds changed in the 1970s in such a way as to give the States the capacity to increase their expenditure in real terms each year (see Chapter 4). Given the overall real per capita increase in spending on social welfare issues over the period 1972/73–1989/90 (Table 3.4), it is not surprising that the stage has been reached where a large proportion of the population are in receipt of some sort of Commonwealth government benefit. In 1969, for example, 96 out of every 1000 people comprised Commonwealth pensioners or beneficiaries or the dependent spouses and dependent children of such pensioners and beneficiaries; by 1983 the ratio was 265 out of every 1000 (Australian Bureau of Statistics, 1984b). Even more startling perhaps is the fact that in 1971 there were 213 pensioners and beneficiaries for every 1000 persons in the labour force but by 1981 this had risen to 401 (Graycar, 1983; p. 6).

In addition to increasing spending on social welfare issues, the Labor government of 1972–1975 tried to nudge social policy thinking in a relatively new direction. The underlying philosophy of social policy, as far as there was one, shifted from 'minimum rights for the many' to 'distributional justice for all' (Dickey, 1980). In fact, the Labor government followed overseas examples where the basis for social policy had moved 'from charity to justice' (Romanyshyn, 1971). This shift entailed a move from viewing social welfare organizations as things that came into play only when other units (such as the family) had failed, to a position that social welfare planning is one of the major tasks of industrial society (Wilensky and Lebeaux, 1965; Graycar, 1979). From this perspective, social welfare is no longer a 'residual' exercise concerned with mopping up the residue of cases that cannot cope with hardship through 'normal' activities like self help, but an 'institutional' exercise. Large institutions (notably government bureaucracies) are set up specifically to plan for the well-being of the entire population, thereby doing away with the notions of stigma, crisis, and personal inadequacy that have traditionally attached to welfare recipients. Under the new outlook of the 1970s, social policy was to become concerned with the just allocation of goods and services.

The Labor government experiment with social policy in the 1970s was shortlived. Grand ideas of social planning emphasising 'justice for all' were abandoned. One of the side effects of the Labor initiative was however that it encouraged close scrutiny of the aims and objectives of social welfare policy.

In other words, it brought on to the political agenda the controversy about 'whether the role of the welfare state is to build a protective set of institutions to encourage stability and coherence, social development and self-fulfilment, or whether its role is to pick up the pieces, with maximum skill and efficiency, after people have crumbled' (Graycar, 1979; p. 1). Investigation of this controversy brought evidence that the middle class has become the dominant consumer as well as the major provider, through taxes, of welfare (Jamrozik, 1983). The middle class has always been important in Australian politics, because of its voting power, because it provides a large proportion of income tax revenue, and because it can be used by politicians to help pass judgement on the legitimacy or otherwise of claims for welfare benefits (Graycar, 1979). However, the fact that the middle classes were also the main beneficiaries alarmed many people and led to left-wing attacks on the welfare state. The same left-wing groups also accused the welfare state of having done nothing to redress inequality and of being nothing more than a mechanism of social control in which the working classes are kept only sufficiently healthy and literate as to ensure the continuation of capitalism (Graycar, 1983). In addition, some commentators deplored the 'deception' of a society which set up welfare structures whose real purpose is to make government transfers to small, politically influential groups like farmers, public servants, and people who want to send their children to college and university, while purporting to do something else (Tullock, 1981; p. 15). There has arisen, in other words, an attack on the welfare state from all quarters.

Right-wing politicians, in particular, have criticised the welfare state for being overly bureaucratic, wasteful, inefficient, big spending, and reliant for its funds on high levels of taxation (Graycar, 1979). Furthermore, according to this point of view, the welfare state stifles initiative and fosters dependency. In some respects, the 'New Right' has hijacked the welfare debate and has set the agenda for discussion (O'Connor, 1990), despite the fact that the views of this group probably underestimate the popular support for the welfare state (see Papadakis, 1990).

Given this widespread attack, it is perhaps not surprising that Australia has witnessed 'a retreat from the welfare state' in recent years. Increasingly an attempt is being made to question the legitimacy of welfare claims against the state and to steer those in need of welfare assistance in the direction of the family, employers, and the local community (Graycar, 1983; p. 2). Increasingly, therefore, welfare demands will be met by voluntary organizations of one sort or another. After all, the formal, government-based welfare system in Australia has always been better at providing income (in the form of cash benefits) than at providing services (such as counselling). The assumption always seems to have been that, given income, people will be able to purchase the services they require (Graycar, 1983; p. 5). Because these services are not available to the extent that they are required, the voluntary sector of Australia's welfare delivery system has grown to the size it has.

The voluntary sector of the welfare delivery system comprises all non-government organizations concerned with welfare delivery. Very little was known about such organizations until a survey conducted by the Social Welfare Research Centre at the University of New South Wales and the Australian Council of Social Service in 1982 (see Yates and Graycar, 1983). This revealed that there were at least 37 000 non-government welfare organizations operating in Australia, many of them being local branches of larger organizational networks. About 27 per cent of them had a significant religious input. The scope of their activities was very varied. They operate in such diverse fields as the provision of housing for the aged and disabled, the provision of assistance to handicapped persons, and the delivery of meals on wheels. Some organizations provide services to individuals, others provide material aid; some provide back-up support to state-run services, others see themselves as an alternative to the State. They provide welfare delivery units that are far less rigid and bureaucratic than state-run enterprises, and as a result they are flexible in catering for changing demands; they provide more scope for innovation and experimentation than large government organizations; because of their small scale they probably know their clients rather better than government departments; and, above all, they provide a cheap way of catering for welfare demand. It is far less costly to provide subsidies to non-government welfare organizations than it is to increase the size of the public service.

Not all units in the voluntary sector receive government support however. Of the organizations studied by Yates and Graycar, 40 per cent received no government funding. In contrast, 25 per cent of organizations were reliant on government for three-quarters of their funding. Non-government welfare organizations are not always an unqualified success, either — at times they can provide only fragmentary services. Nevertheless, Australia's welfare delivery system could not survive without them. If nothing else, they harness a vast army of unpaid labour that it would be beyond the means of government to pay without substantially increasing the budget deficit or taxation rates. Yates and Graycar (1983) estimated that there were 1.5 million people providing voluntary help to non-government welfare organizations. If these workers average four hours a week, their contribution is the same as 160 000 full-time jobs (equivalent to an annual wage and salary bill of over $2 000 million).

Non-government welfare organizations are a vitally important part of Australia's welfare delivery system. Strictly speaking, it is wrong to speak of a welfare delivery 'system' because that implies an integrated coherence and co-ordination among the services provided. In practice this is not the case. Welfare services in Australia developed in a piecemeal fashion in response to what were perceived to be social problems. Welfare services would therefore be more aptly described as a 'patchwork' rather than a 'system'. Nevertheless massive amounts of money are spent each year on what might be generally termed welfare issues and a great number of people are involved in providing social welfare services, both in a paid and in a voluntary capacity. It is appropriate to ask, therefore, who are the winners and losers in the welfare state and whether the rise of the welfare state has enhanced the well-being of the population to a significant degree.

Harding (1984) set out to determine who benefits from the Australian welfare state. Any answer hinges on precisely what is included in the welfare state. Generally speaking, the welfare state can be taken to include three bundles of policies:

- those related to taxation, particularly progressive taxation where the rich pay more than the poor;
- those related to cash transfers from the government to individuals and families (e.g. pensions and benefits); and
- those related to the provision of services (e.g. education, health care).

In relation to taxation, Harding argued that the redistributive effect of income tax (i.e. its attempt to take more from the wealthy in order to fund services for the disadvantaged) was negligible because the progressive effect of income tax was reduced by the regressive nature of indirect taxes (i.e. the tendency for the poor to pay a greater share of their income in tax). For example, local government rates (a form of taxation) give no attention to the use made of facilities or to the ability of individuals to pay; similarly, a sales tax on goods imposes a bigger relative burden on the poor than on the rich. In short, the poor do not seem to benefit to any really significant degree from the taxation component of the welfare state. Nor do they benefit spectacularly from cash transfers and the provision of services. Cash payments such as unemployment benefits and old age pensions have never been large enough to enable recipients to follow anything other than a frugal existence and the main beneficiaries of service provision (education, health, etc.) seem to have been the middle classes. After all, government expenditure on education, health and housing in Australia has been fairly evenly distributed among all households, rather than being pro-poor (Harding, 1984; p. 100). It may well be, then, that the welfare state has served to improve the well-being of the population as a whole rather than the condition of the poor. This raises the question of how well-being can be measured.

The well-being of the population

A great deal has been written about the well-being of Australia's population. Some writers have taken a rather jaundiced view and argued that the country is being

> increasingly polarized into a threefold society: a group of brassy multimillionaires, home-grown and foreign, profiting from the resources boom; a prosperous middle group of business and professional people, white and blue-collar workers, who

> successfully ride the inflationary wave; and an enlarged group of losers, who fail in the economic struggle and receive only a dusty redress — blame and stigma for their failure, and inadequate care for their needs (Mendelsohn, 1982, pp. vii–viii).

It is very difficult to test whether this sort of proposition is true. By some European standards Australia is certainly a low tax, low social welfare expenditure country. However, there has been something of a backlash against increased welfare spending in Australia since the late 1970s. Indeed, in Australia the prevailing view seems to be of welfare as a 'safety net' for the disadvantaged and, in this context, any further expansion in the welfare arena is likely to be dependent on economic growth making more funds available, rather than funds being diverted from other purposes. This is creating problems in the early 1990s for governments anxious to project an image of financial probity but committed, for political reasons, to job creation schemes designed to reduce record levels of unemployment, especially among teenagers.

There is always a temptation for commentators at any one point in time to exaggerate the importance of contemporary developments and to fail to appreciate the historical context in which change takes place. Thus there is a danger that, in highlighting the plight of growing numbers of disadvantaged people in the late1980s and early 1990s, commentators will fail to appreciate the very significant transformation that has taken place in Australian society since the early days of the twentieth century. The overall quality of life, as measured by GDP per capita, has improved markedly. Allowing for inflation and calculating figures to enable direct comparison between different years, Butlin (1977) has shown that, in constant dollar terms based on 1966/67, GDP per capita in 1900/01 stood at $840 and rose to $1060 in 1910/11 before falling to $880 in the Depression (1930/31). Since that time there has been significant growth with GDP per capita in constant dollar terms climbing from $1390 in 1950/51 to $2730 in 1980/81. Paralleling this improvement in the quality of life, there have been increases in life expectancy, decreases in family size, increased participation of women in the paid workforce, the spread of owner-occupied housing, and decreases in the length of the working week. In short, society is in a state of flux.

Social scientists have been anxious for a long time to monitor the ways in which societies change. There has been a widespread feeling that, if social scientists could measure societal change quantitatively (in much the same way that econometricians measure the state of the economy), then social science could make a big impact in the realm of policy formation. This challenge is urgent because unfortunately at present 'for many of the important topics on which social critics blithely pass judgement, and on which policies are made, there are no yardsticks by which to know if things are getting better or worse' (Bauer, 1966; p. 20).

One of the first government attempts to monitor societal change was initiated in the USA in the 1920s by President Hoover. His idea was that statistics should be gathered to trace the transformation of the USA into a 'great society'. Poor Hoover was unluckier than most politicians: Wall Street crashed and the greatest economic depression of modern times ensued. Nothing more was heard of 'social indicators', as statistics on societal change came to be known, until 1962 when NASA gave the American Academy of Arts and Sciences the brief of enquiring into the spin-off benefits to American society of the space race. This move was undoubtedly politically motivated and had a great deal to do with attempts to legitimize huge expenditure on the space race at a time when there were perceived to be pressing social problems, not least in black, inner city ghettos. In any event the move put social indicators back on the political and research agenda and it was not long before the United States Federal Department of Health, Education and Welfare began publishing statistics on the nature of American society. Other countries followed. The Australian Bureau of Statistics, for example, now publishes *Social Indicators, Australia*.

Ideally a 'social indicator' should be a statistic that shows whether the condition of society is getting better or worse. In this sense 'GDP per capita' could be interpreted as a social indicator in that a real increase in its value should indicate that society is better off (subject to the proviso that the increasing wealth has been spread over the entire population and not concentrated to the advantage of one small group). Unfortunately, however, such data are hard to come by. It is particularly difficult to get social indicators that enable conclusions to be drawn as to the success or otherwise of specific government policies. As a result, most so-called 'social indicators' amount to little more than census figures that show such features as the percentage of the population in owner-occupied housing, the percentage who migrated within the past year, the percentage divorced or separated, and so on. Although interesting in their own right and in providing a 'social profile', these data are in no sense indicators of whether society is getting better or worse.

One of the major problems involved in attempting to use social indicators is that of deciding just what it is that should be measured. It is rather vague to talk of 'societal change'. Decisions have to be made as to what aspects of change are worth monitoring. One attempt to identify 'fundamental social concerns' for which governments need to collect data was made by the Organization for Economic Co-operation and Development (OECD) in 1973. The conclusions of this study are presented in Table 3.5. This table contains all the idealism (and jargon) that one would expect from an international organization trying to define concerns common to all advanced, industrial societies. It therefore provides an excellent check-list of what should be considered in any examination of the quality of life in a given area. However there is no way in which social indicators are likely to be developed for each of these concerns. As a result there is no way in which the listing can be used to assess the overall well-being of the population.

An alternative approach to the study of well-being is to look at whether society caters at all well for basic human needs. If a society caters for human

Table 3.5 Fundamental social concerns

Health

A1 The probability of a healthy life through all stages of the life cycle.

A2 The impact of health impairments on individuals.

Individual development through learning

B1 The acquisition by children of the basic knowledge, skills and values necessary for their individual development and their successful functioning as citizens in their society.

B2 The availability of opportunities for continuing self-development and the propensity of individuals to use them.

B3 The maintenance and development by individuals of the knowledge, skills and flexibility required to fulfil their economic potential and to enable them to integrate themselves in the economic process if they wish to do so.

B4 The individual's satisfaction with the process of individual development through learning, while in the process.

B5 The maintenance and development of the cultural heritage relative to its positive contribution to the well-being of the members of various social groups.

Employment and the quality of the working life

C1 The availability of gainful employment for those who desire it.

C2 The quality of working life.

C3 Individual satisfaction with the experience of working life.

Time and leisure

D1 The availability of effective choices for the use of time.

Command over goods and services

E1 The personal command over goods and services.

E2 The number of individuals experiencing material deprivation.

E3 The extent of equity in the distribution of command over goods and services.

E4 The quality, range of choice and accessibility of private and public goods and services.

E5 The protection of individuals and families against economic hazards.

Physical environment

F1 Housing conditions.

F2 Population exposure to harmful and/or unpleasant pollutants.

F3 The benefits derived by the population from the use and management of the environment.

Personal safety and the administration of justice

G1 Violence, victimisation and harassment suffered by individuals.

G2 Fairness and humanity of the administration of justice.

G3 The extent of confidence in the administration of justice.

Social opportunity and participation

H1 The degree of social inequality

H2 The extent of opportunity for participation in community life, institutions and decision-making.

Source: OECD (1973)

needs effectively then that society might be deemed to have a high level of well-being. One of the first attempts to define basic human needs, and still one of the most widely used, was developed by Maslow (1954). He proposed the hierarchy of needs that is set out in Table 3.6. The most basic human needs are physiological (e.g. food and shelter). Thereafter human needs become more and more abstract until at the 'top' of the hierarchy is the need for intellectual and aesthetic stimulation. Again, however, this listing provides an insight into the factors to be considered in any study of well-being but not a basis for data collection. Many of the issues listed by Maslow are not amenable to study through widely available social statistics. It might be possible, for instance, to estimate the extent to which housing needs are met by using census data but there is no possibility of assessing whether or not higher order needs are met without actually going out and asking people. Such subjective surveys are prohibitively expensive. Moreover such surveys beg the question of what is meant by need. There are in fact at least four ways of defining need, none of which is entirely satisfactory:

- 'normative' need refers to the shortfall that exists between existing provision and a desirable standard set down by experts;
- 'felt' is that shown in surveys when individuals are asked directly if they feel a need for a certain facility;
- 'expressed need' is revealed in actual usage patterns (or in waiting lists); and
- 'comparative' need is that which can be detected when one group of people has a lower provision of a particular good or service than another group (Bradshaw, 1972; Clayton, 1983).

In view of these problems it is perhaps best to focus on how well Australian society 'performs' in terms of the individual social concerns that contribute to overall well-being. Obviously it is not possible to deal with all of the twenty-four issues listed in Table 3.5. Instead attention will focus very briefly on health, on housing, and on the interrelated issues of employment, unemployment, and poverty. In this way a general picture will be provided of the well-being of Australian society.

Table 3.6 Maslow's hierarchy of human needs

1. Physiological needs such as the need for food and shelter in the form of housing.
2. The need for safety and security, exemplified by the need to be protected from danger and the need to have privacy.
3. The need for affiliation, particularly the need to feel a sense of belonging to the community in which one lives.
4. The need for esteem, notably the need to be recognised as worthy by those with whom one interacts.
5. The need for self-actualisation (in the sense of fulfilling one's potential).
6. The need for aesthetic, cognitive and aesthetic stimulation.

Source: Adapted from Maslow (1954)

Health

Generally speaking Australians are healthy. Life expectancy is high and has increased significantly since the Second World War. For example, males born in 1989 could expect to live 73.3 years and females born in the same year could expect to live 79.6 years. These figures compare favourably with life expectancies of 66.5 years for males and 71.7 years for females in 1950. They also compare well with the overseas experience in 1988 because at that time life expectancies for males were 71.6 in the United States, 72.5 in the United Kingdom, and 71.1 in New Zealand. The figures for women in the same year were 78.6 in the United States, 78.2 in the United Kingdom, and 77.5 in New Zealand (OECD, 1986; Commonwealth of Australia, 1991b). Over the period 1950 to 1989, Australia also witnessed a fall in perinatal mortality from 36 deaths per 1000 live births to 8 deaths per 1000 births, a figure comparable with many other advanced countries despite the geographical and medical isolation of part of the Australian population.

Better diet and better hygiene probably account, in part, for these falling death rates. Although it is unlikely that the quantity of food per head consumed in Australia has changed much over the years, improved dietary knowledge may have resulted in the better utilization of available supplies and a greater use of vegetables and fruit. In the long term, this may have contributed, as Mendelsohn (1979) points out, to both greater longevity and increased physical stature. Certainly Mendelsohn produces interesting data to show that both the height and weight of children has increased: children aged 15 in the New South Wales school system, for example, measured on average 158.7 cm (boys) and 156.7 cm (girls) in 1913–15 but 169.1 cm (boys) and 160.3 cm (girls) in 1970. Over the same period average weights for boys increased from 47.0 kg to 58.1 kg and average weights for girls from 47.4 kg to 53.4 kg.

Table 3.7 Average number of disability days, July 1977–June 1978

Age	*Females*	*Males*	*Total*
Under 15	14	13	14
15-24	18	13	15
25-44	22	16	19
45-64	24	27	25
Over 64	37	34	35
Overall average	21	18	20
Canada 1978–79	19	13	16
Sweden 1977	25	25	25
UK 1980	27	21	24
USA 1980	21	17	19

Source: OECD (1986)

Both physical stature and death rates are poor indicators of health status. It is far better to look at sickness, usually called *morbidity*. Table 3.7 shows, from survey data, the average number of days in 1977/78 when members of various age groups had to restrict their usual activities because of injury or illness. Clearly, the morbidity rate increases with age. It is also clear that Australia compares well with overseas countries. Such positive findings should not however obscure the fact that many Australians suffer from mental and physical disorders. Survey data for 1981 in fact reveal that 12.6 per cent of males and 11.5 per cent of females suffer from physical disabilities (including sight loss, hearing loss, musculoskeletal disease) and 2.4 per cent of males and 3.1 per cent of females have a mental disorder. The problems

Table 3.8 Average weekly household expenditure, 1984

Item	*$*	*%*
Food and alcoholic beverages	71.22	19.68
Transport	59.00	16.31
Housing	46.46	12.84
Recreation	43.13	11.92
Household furnishings and equipment	27.69	7.65
Miscellaneous commodities/services	25.93	7.17
Clothing and footwear	23.46	6.48
Household services	15.70	4.34
Medicine and health care	14.07	3.89
Alcoholic beverages	12.30	3.40
Fuel and power	10.56	2.92
Personal care	6.60	1.83
Tobacco	5.73	1.58
Total	361.84	100.00

Source: Commonwealth of Australia (1986)

are most intense in those over 75, where more than half of the population have disorders (Australian Bureau of Statistics, 1984b). Over and above these disabilities, a good deal of use is made of the medical system by otherwise healthy people.

A survey in 1989 and 1990 showed, for instance, that 20 per cent of the population had consulted a doctor and 5.3 per cent a dentist in the two weeks prior to the interview. Almost 7 per cent had taken time off school or work and a staggering 64.2 per cent had taken some sort of medication (ABS, 1991). Given this it is rather surprising that health care costs are such a minor component of average weekly household spending patterns, as revealed in the last survey conducted in 1984 (Table 3.8). The results of a follow-up health care survey conducted by the Australian Bureau of Statistics in 1990 should provide a chance to monitor change in health status over time.

Housing

Housing is the biggest investment that most people make during their lifetime. The home and its environs are also the focus of upwards of two-thirds of all human activity (Walmsley and Lewis, 1984). It is not surprising, therefore, that governments of all political persuasions in Australia have paid special attention to housing policy since 1945. Generally speaking, such policy has been two-pronged: it aimed to encourage the owner-occupation of dwellings, and it sought to provide public housing for those who, for one reason or another, were unable to become owner-occupiers (the public housing in question being built by State authorities, largely with money derived from Canberra through various Commonwealth–State housing agreements).

The types of dwellings occupied in Australia at the 1986 census, and the type of tenancy in 1988, are shown in Table 3.9. Quite obviously, owner-purchasing is dominant, as is the separate dwelling. Overwhelmingly,

Table 3.9 Housing in Australia

	Ownership and tenancy 1988			
	Owner-occupied	*Public tenancy*	*Private tenancy*	*Others*
NSW	68.4	5.1	21.9	4.6
Vic	74.6	3.2	17.8	4.4
Qld	65.8	2.9	24.8	6.5
SA	69.3	10.8	14.9	5.0
WA	68.4	6.3	18.0	7.3
Tas	71.6	9.1	15.1	4.2
NT	34.3	18.1	16.0	31.6
ACT	59.2	13.1	21.1	6.6
Australia	69.3	5.2	20.1	5.4

	Dwelling type 1986						
	Separate house	*Semi-detached house*	*Terraced house*	*Other medium density*	*Flat 3+ storeys*	*Caravans in parks*	*Other, not stated*
NSW	73.8	2.1	1.5	15.4	3.2	1.2	2.8
Vic	79.7	2.1	1.2	12.2	1.5	0.7	2.6
Qld	81.0	0.7	0.2	10.9	1.5	3.2	2.5
SA	77.2	6.9	0.7	12.1	0.4	0.7	2.0
WA	78.3	2.1	0.6	13.1	1.5	2.3	2.1
Tas	85.2	1.4	0.6	9.2	0.5	0.4	2.7
NT	61.9	1.1	1.1	16.6	1.2	8.1	10.0
ACT	82.0	2.5	0.7	12.1	1.0	0.5	1.2
Australia	77.5	2.3	1.0	13.1	2.0	1.5	2.6

Source: 1986 Census; Commonwealth of Australia (1990)

dwellings are single-storey cottages and since 1970, 80 per cent of completed dwellings have been of brick (Paris, 1985). There are nonetheless substantial differences between the States. Overall, owner-occupation (including purchasing) dropped from 71.1 per cent of the housing stock in 1981 to 69.3 per cent in 1988. Public tenancy is generally limited with the exception of South Australia, the ACT, and the Northern Territory. This means the supply of public housing is relatively inelastic. Thus 5.2 per cent of housing stock was owned by the government in 1988 compared with 5.3 per cent in 1981. An increase in private tenancy from 17.6 per cent in 1981 to 20 per cent in 1988 reflects decreasing house affordability. The type of dwelling also varies between the States. Overall, low density living prevails. Only in NSW do forms of medium density living (terraces, units, flats) reach 20 per cent of housing stock. Interestingly, substantial numbers of people live in caravan parks in the Northern Territory, Queensland, and Western Australia.

Post-war public housing was planned to serve two functions (see Paris, 1985):

- to house the working class who could not, or chose not to, become owner-purchasers, and
- to house incoming migrants.

Although public housing accounted for 10 per cent of post-war housing construction, it presently comprises only just over 5 per cent of total housing stock. This is because approximately half of the public housing built since the Second World War has been sold to sitting tenants. Although public housing is ostensibly aimed at needy groups (and is allocated by State housing authorities subject to means and eligibility tests), only 26 per cent of families in poverty are actually in public housing (Commission of Inquiry into Poverty, 1975). This is partly because there exist long waiting lists for public housing and it is therefore not easy for public housing authorities to cater quickly for families who, perhaps through unemployment, find themselves in poverty. Predictably, waiting lists grow in times of economic recession: for example just over 54 000 households were admitted to public housing waiting lists in 1979 but by 1981, when the economic downturn was more marked, this figure had risen to almost 72 000 (Paris *et al.*, 1985). In an attempt to eliminate the tendency for households to remain in public housing when their financial circumstances have improved significantly, there has been a move towards charging market rather than subsidized rents (subject to the proviso that poor families pay no more than one quarter of their income in rent). Even this strategy, however, is unlikely to go very far towards meeting the rising demand for public housing.

One reason why the demand for public housing is increasing is to be found in the escalation in the price of private land and houses for sale. At a time of economic recession, this escalation puts the Australian dream of home ownership out of the reach of many. Although mortgage finance is still available, there is simply not enough available to bridge the gap between selling prices and deposits. It is likely, therefore, that the level of owner-purchasing and owner-occupying in Australia will drop. This may be no bad thing, according to critics of Australia's housing policies. In the eyes of these people, Australia has viewed housing as a private service distributed by market forces and has therefore tended to overlook the possibility of using the provision of housing as a vehicle for the redistribution of wealth (through subsidizing the housing costs of poor people) (Neutze, 1981). To peg mortgage interest rates, to help first home buyers, and to provide tax relief on mortgage interest and rates — as happened on and off over the last thirty years — produces incentives that can only really be taken up by the middle classes.

Another criticism commonly made of Australia's emphasis on owner-occupation is that it has tied up vast financial reserves in housing at a time when those reserves could have been better used in productive resource exploitation, a field in which there has arisen an intrusive level of foreign ownership (Kemeny, 1983, see also Chapter 2). Coping with mortgage repayments has placed a major financial burden on some households. Australia's obsession with privately owned detached housing has also fuelled suburban sprawl as extensive areas have been subdivided for residential development. Not only is this an inefficient land use, particularly when it leads to poor utilization of public transport, but also it imposes considerable strains on women.

Australian cities are essentially man-made in that they were designed and created in accordance with a set of ideas about how society works, about who does what, and about who goes where (Walmsley, 1988a). Indeed, the housing market tends to be founded on the twin notions that patriarchal households are the norm and that home ownership is rational and in some way natural (Watson, 1988). Women simply do not figure in such a view. Specifically, many suburban areas were planned on the basis of sexist assumptions about family life and about the role of women. A woman's place was, quite simply, in the home. Women who have tried to adopt an alternative lifestyle and enter the workforce have often found their employment opportunities restricted to a narrow range of places that can be easily accessed by public transport. Even those who have more or less accepted the stereotyped role of mother and minder have often suffered the anguish of loneliness and paid the cost for low density development where shops, doctors, libraries and even friends may be considerable distances away.

Although the plight of some suburban women may be severe, the group which faces the most critical housing problems in Australia is probably the group which is forced to rely on renting accommodation from private landlords. By and large private renting has been ignored by policy makers in Australia as attention has focussed overwhelmingly on either owner-purchasing or State housing authorities. Little is known about private rental markets, and it is unwise to generalise about the private rental market given that there are several different types of landlords (individual investors, corporate investors, employers, institutions) and different sorts of tenants (mobile households, temporary renters who will ultimately move on to owner-purchasing, and households unable to afford to buy) (Paris, 1984). Nevertheless, it is probably true that private renters are financially disadvantaged. There is no constraint on the proportion of their income that they pay in rent (as there is in public housing) and no equity in the dwelling (as is the case with owner-purchasing). The position is particularly acute in inner city areas where much of the privately rented accommodation is located. Figures for Sydney in 1981 showed, for example, that residents renting private dwellings in the inner city suburbs of Woolloomooloo, Surry Hills, and Marrickville commonly paid rents equivalent to 50–60 per cent of their incomes (Sandercock and Berry, 1983). The reasons for this lie in the investment market. In the early 1970s high inflation, low real interest rates, good prospects for capital gains, and rising rents all made investment in private rental housing appealing. In the 1980s, in contrast, interest rates were high and other charges tended to increase more quickly than rents, thereby making investment in private rental housing unattractive (Paris, 1985). As a result, the stock of such housing has dwindled at the very time when, because of economic recession and high house prices, the demand for private renting is high. The result is high rents and a burden on these households reliant on this form of accommodation.

Employment, unemployment, and poverty

Employment makes a very important contribution to a person's overall well-being. Not only does it provide the money with which to buy goods and services but it also helps define a person's social standing and provides a role without which many people would be lost. Conditions of employment are therefore something that should be taken into account in any examination of well-being. Basically, legislation concerned with conditions of employment has focussed on two issues: actual operating conditions within the workplace, and the fixing of wages and salaries. Most of the rudiments of the existing system of control over conditions of employment were laid down in the period between 1890 and the First World War. They have been described in detail by Mendelsohn (1979).

Working conditions began to be regulated about 1890 when first Colonial and then State legislation set down minimum conditions for lighting, ventilation, safety, and the employment of children. These minimum conditions have been periodically upgraded as changing technology and changed operating methods have presented new problems. Of rather more interest, however, is the growth and development of the conciliation and arbitration system, not least because this has some claims to being pioneering by world standards.

> A concept of social justice concerning the rights of working men to a fair share of the products of their labour, and widespread emotions of disgust at the industrial turmoil of the 1890s, were motivating forces leading to Australia's highly characteristic system of wage fixation (Mendelsohn, 1979, p. 140).

Basically a system was set up wherein wages boards fixed the pay levels in particular industries, and arbitration commissions sought to settle conflicts operating across a wide variety of industries. Over time the system evolved such that the Arbitration Commission arbitrates on disputes and the Commonwealth Industrial Court enforces decisions. The landmark event in the evolution of the system was the so-called 'Harvester case' of 1906 which introduced the idea of a basic wage. For a man with a wife and three children this was set at 42 shillings per week. The idea was that no employee with a family to support should receive less than this amount. In practice, of course, the Arbitration Commission has always been under pressure to take stock of the capacity of employers' ability to pay. Thus when, during the 1930s Depression, the Industrial Court *decreased* all award payments by 10 per cent, a precedent was set that wages should be such as the economy can sustain. Of course, the arbitration system is by no means as simple as this brief outline implies. Commonwealth bodies tend, for instance, to be duplicated by State bodies, sometimes leading to squabbles as to which award unions wish to be registered under.

Nevertheless, the arbitration system has been effective in mediating between the interests of labour and capital. It has, for example, overseen the reduction in the length of the working week. The eight-hour day was in at the time of Federation. By 1914 the working week was approximately 49 hours. This was reduced to 44 hours in the mid-1920s and to 40 hours in 1948. In the 1980s some industries saw the introduction of the 36 hour week. This does not mean, of course, that all workers labour for a shorter time. The effect of shorter-hours legislation has very often been to increase labour costs by allowing a greater part of the working week to be claimed at overtime rate. In 1989, for example, full-time male workers averaged 44.8 hours per week (Commonwealth of Australia, 1990).

Almost 90 per cent of all Australian wage and salary earners have legal minimum rates of pay set down by either Commonwealth or State industrial tribunals: 42 per cent of males and 24 per cent of females are covered by federal awards, and 41 per cent of males and 65 per cent of females are covered by State awards (Commonwealth of Australia, 1986). Details on earnings in various industries are published regularly by the Australian Bureau of Statistics based on surveys of employees. In November 1989 average weekly earnings for males, including overtime, were $540. In addition to wages, many workers get non-wage benefits. For example by 1986 78 per cent got sick leave, 79 per cent got annual leave, 64 per cent got long service leave, 47 per cent got superannuation, 8 per cent got telephone, and 17 per cent got transport allowances. Many of these arrangements are formally written into industrial awards. It is therefore in the interests of trade unions to be registered with, and recognized by, the various arbitration tribunals. This is why the threat of deregistration is often used against unions in industrial disputes. As of 1989 there were 299 unions in Australia; 62 per cent of male employees and 44 per cent of female employees belonged to a union. These figures may of course change in the 1990s with new industrial relations legislation in New South Wales reducing the pressure on workers to join trade unions. In fact, some authorities have argued that moves towards labour market flexibility at the enterprise level will lead to a reduction in the size of the labour force and an increasing polarisation between those with increased wages and profits and those experiencing an acute decline in living standards (Gill, 1989).

Despite the gains made by workers through the arbitration system, one group lagged behind, in terms of their employment conditions, until relatively recently: women. In 1901, at the time that the arbitration system was being set up, women were socially and economically substantially defenceless. They were vulnerable when deserted or ill-treated and they could draw on only very poor maternal and child welfare services. Where women were in employment, they received low wages. This reflected a deliberate view of their position in society, the fact that they were given the worst jobs, and their generally inferior education (Mendelsohn, 1979). Today the position is much different. Women have much higher levels of workforce participation, suffer much less economic inferiority, and have their positions protected by anti-discrimination and equal opportunity legislation. The breakthrough in the fight for equality really came during the Second World War when the range of war-time jobs done by women exploded the myth of their employment inferiority. However even in 1948 the basic wage for females was only 75 per cent of the male rate and equal pay in the Commonwealth Public Service was not finally achieved until 1972.

Until 1966 there were still restrictions on females becoming permanent employees in the public service (Mendelsohn, 1979). In short, then, the employment conditions of women have improved, reflecting their changing status in society as a whole. However the ideal and the reality of women's employment experience continue to diverge, as shown in the fact that women are still under-represented in the ranks of the professionals (Broom, 1984). More to the point, the average annual income of female employees as recently as 1981/82 was only 48 per cent of the average annual income for male employees (admittedly up from 35 per cent in 1968/69), a situation that comes about because 'traditional' female jobs tend to have lower wage rates and because women are over-represented in the ranks of part-time workers (Cass, 1985). By 1990, the average weekly earnings of females employed full-time were about 83 per cent of those of males employed full-time.

In August 1989 the labour force comprised 4 571 900 males and 3 155 700 females. This meant that 74.9 per cent of all males aged 15 and over were in the labour force as opposed to 50.8 per cent of all females aged 15 and over.

Table 3.10 Labour force participation rates, 1989

Age group	Percentage in labour force		
	Males	*Married females*	*Unmarried females*
15–19	59.6	56.6	57.1
20–24	89.2	65.3	83.3
25–34	94.4	60.2	78.1
35–44	93.3	69.6	70.7
45–54	88.7	58.5	62.6
55–59	74.9	30.7	36.6
60–64	49.8	13.8	13.3
65+	8.5	3.1	1.6
Overall	84.2	57.2	65.1

Source: Commonwealth of Australia, (1990)

This figure for females is a dramatic increase on the figure of 7 per cent in 1911 (Wajcman and Rosewarne, 1986). Overall, 62.7 per cent of Australians aged 15 and over were in the labour force. The term 'labour force' is a little misleading in this context because it includes both those in employment and those unemployed but looking for work. The 1989 labour force figure of approximately 7.75 million is significantly greater than the 6.7 million who were in the labour force at the start of the decade and very much greater than the 4.8 million that comprised the Australian labour force in the mid-1960s. Clearly, the labour force has grown substantially, although the numbers in employment have grown less quickly, leaving a large number unemployed.

The proportion of different age groups in the labour force is given in Table 3.10. The highest participation rates occur in the 25–34 age group for males, the 35–44 age group for married females, and the 20–24 age group for unmarried females. There is very little difference, other than between 20 and 34, in the overall participation rate between married and unmarried females. The figures in Table 3.10 take stock of both part-time and full-time employment, as well as taking into account those unemployed but seeking work. Part-time employment is very much a female phenomenon: by 1990 only 7.8 per cent of males in employment worked part-time compared to 40.0 per cent

Table 3.11 The percentage growth in the labour force, 1971–81

Area	*Males*	*Females*
Metropolitan areas	12	38
Major urban areas	24	64
Other urban areas	13	59
Rural areas	13	106

Source: Weinand (1985)

of females. Part-time working is however becoming much more the order of the day for the entire workforce. No less than 60 per cent of new female jobs and 43 per cent of new male jobs created between 1973 and 1985 were part-time (Wajcman and Rosewarne, 1986). This fact goes some way to explaining the very rapid rate of growth of the labour force outside metropolitan areas. Table 3.11 shows, for instance, that the female labour force grew by an astounding 106 per cent in rural areas over the decade 1971–1981. Much of this growth was, of course, in part-time employment. Moreover, much of it was occasioned by women taking off-farm employment in order to supplement family income at a time of rural crisis. The high percentage figures also owe something to the relatively low base at the start of the period. Nevertheless, the tendency for women to enter the paid labour force clearly accelerated in the 1970s, thereby accounting for the participation rates shown in Table 3.10.

Statistics on the growth of the labour force mask the fact that one of the most prominent trends in the Australian workplace over the period since the early 1970s has been the growth of unemployment. Throughout the 1960s commonly less than 2 per cent of the labour force were out of work. The unemployment rate began to rise in the 1970s. By 1980 it stood at 5 per cent for males and 8 per cent for females. Thereafter it peaked in 1983 at 9.9 per cent for males and 10.5 per cent for females before falling back a little in the later 1980s (5.2 per cent for males in 1989 and 6.9 per cent for females). However, by the beginning of the 1990s, unemployment was rising again. At the beginning of 1992 unemployment again was over 10 per cent. As the figures show, females bear more of the unemployment burden than males, possibly because the part-time employment in which they are characteristically heavily involved offers little job security. Unemployment rates should, of course, be taken as no more than crude indicators and it may well be that *real* unemployment rates are very much higher than official figures suggest (Crough *et al.*, 1980). Nevertheless, official figures are useful in providing a picture of how unemployment is hitting the country and, in this context, it is evident that the main burden falls upon the latest arrivals in the job market, namely school leavers and recent migrants (Sloan and Kriegler, 1984).

Approximately 23 per cent of 15–19 year olds were unemployed at the peak of the 1980s unemployment crisis. Leaving school early, or failing to gain a subsequent qualification, lessens considerably the chances of getting a job. As a result the experience of recent school leavers affords a stark contrast with that of workers with a degree (where unemployment in 1984 was 2.8 per cent for males and 4.7 per cent for females) and workers with a trade certificate (1984 unemployment rates of 5.2 per cent for males and 6.7 per cent for females). Even in the relatively 'good' times of 1989, the pattern was the same: unemployment among the 15–19 year olds was 13.7 per cent compared to 3.6 per cent among 35–44 year olds (Commonwealth of Australia, 1991b).

Table 3.12 Migrant unemployment rates, 1987

	Percentage of migrant labour force unemployed	
	Males	*Females*
Arrived 1961–70	6.9	6.7
Arrived 1971–80	8.7	9.8
Arrived after 1980	16.1	22.6

Source: Commonwealth of Australia (1991a)

The statistics for recent migrants are equally depressing, as revealed in Table 3.12. Migrants who have been in Australia for a long time have roughly the same chance of unemployment as the Australian-born workforce (see Marshall, 1991). However recent arrivals fare very much worse. Unemployment among the Vietnamese stood at 24.3 per cent in 1987 and at 27.6 per cent among the Lebanese (Cass, 1988). Some ethnic groups attempt to cope with this situation by developing small businesses based on extremely long hours, child labour, and poor working conditions (see Tait *et al.*, 1989).

A further depressing aspect of Australia's current unemployment problem is the length of time many people have been unemployed. At the peak of unemployment in the mid-1980s, for example, out of those unemployed and looking for either full or part-time work, 32 per cent had been unemployed for more than a year, and 50 per cent had been unemployed for more than 6 months (Commonwealth of Australia, 1986). At the end of the decade (1989), with unemployment much lower, the pattern was the same: 23 per cent had been unemployed for more than a year and 41 per cent had been unemployed for more than six months (Commonwealth of Australia, 1991b). Unfortunately there is evidence that this sort of long-term unemployment is more prevalent in Australia than overseas because in 1980 56 per cent of Australia's unemployed had been out of work for over 14 weeks compared to 24 per cent in the United Kingdom, 34 per cent in Sweden, and 35 per cent in Canada (OECD, 1986).

The consequences of such long-term inactivity are profound, and Windschuttle (1979) has cited unemployment as a major cause of domestic violence, vandalism, drug abuse, and other escapist behaviour. The long-term unemployed may also be subject to high rates of stress-induced health problems. Certainly, many of the individuals involved become 'discouraged workers'. They do not show up in official statistics because they do not register as unemployed because they believe that there are no jobs available or that they are too old or unqualified (Carson *et al.*, 1989).

There are no easy solutions to the unemployment problem because it is complex in its origins, reflecting changes in the structure of the international economy, changes in Australia's industrial structure, and the advent of new technology (Stilwell, 1981, and see Chapter 2). It seems unlikely that increased technology will provide the volume of jobs necessary to reduce unemployment very much. Nor is a substantial revival of manufacturing industry likely in the short term. As a result, job growth will probably occur at the unskilled end of the labour market. Certainly this has been the recent experience: between 1971 and 1981 the major growth areas for males were as junior labourers (up 54 per cent), as storemen (up 44 per cent), and in fast food outlets (up 278 per cent). For females the growing opportunities were as waitresses and barmaids (up 77 per cent), as cashiers (up 59 per cent), and as shop assistants (up 50 per cent) (Windschuttle, 1984). When the results of the 1991 Census are published, they are likely to show a continuation of these trends.

The unemployment situation poses a problem for Australia's welfare policy makers. The unemployment benefit system, a central feature of welfare policy, was meant to tide people over brief periods without work during times of full employment (Henderson, 1981). Changes in 1991 whereby unemployment benefits were renamed 'Job Search' and benefits to the long-term unemployed were labelled 'New Start' were merely cosmetic. Any attempt to get the unemployed to retrain or to show a commitment to seeking out work opportunities is unlikely to meet with great success at a time of recession when some regions experience high levels of unemployment (especially youth) and little sign of growth in the labour market. In short, Australia's unemployment benefit system is ill-equipped to cope with long-term endemic unemployment. Nor are there any policies to cope with the poverty that may be caused by long-term unemployment.

Poverty

There are many causes of poverty. In some instances it may result from factors internal to the people affected, such as inherent weaknesses in personality leading to fecklessness and idleness. In such cases the appropriate policy response might be to motivate people to do better and improve themselves. In many cases, however, poverty is caused by factors external to the victims, over which the victims have no control. Examples are poverty caused by unemployment, racial discrimination and educational disadvantage. In such cases the appropriate policy response requires that something be done about the problems in the fabric of society that create hardship. Before any policy initiative can be undertaken it is necessary to know something about the incidence of poverty.

Very little was known about poverty in Australia until the 1970s when a Commission of Inquiry into Poverty undertook a major national survey. This Commission came to the conclusion that, in terms of income, about 10 per cent of the population was 'very poor'. After allowing for the fact that some people were able to make do on small incomes because they did not pay very much for housing on account either of living in subsidized public housing or being owner-occupiers with few or no mortgage commitments, 7 per cent of the population was found to be 'very poor' (Commission of Inquiry into Poverty, 1975). The major disadvantaged groups were fatherless families (30 per cent very poor), the unemployed, sick and invalid (18 per cent very poor), and aged males (13 per cent poor).

The way in which the Commission operated was to focus on 'income units' — groups of individuals supported by a single income. A poverty line was then set for what was called a 'standard unit' (worker, dependent spouse, and two dependent children). This poverty line was calculated to be equivalent to 56.5 per cent of average weekly earnings (based on earlier research in Melbourne in the 1960s). The poverty line for larger and smaller units (e.g. families with more than two children, people living alone) was calculated by multiplying the standard poverty line by a value that reflected the costs of different sized households. Unfortunately Australian data were not available on the relative costs incurred by different sized households and, as a result, the Commission used New York data for 1954. Because of this the Commission has attracted stern criticism. After all, relativities from a different country twenty years earlier might not have borne much resemblance to the costs incurred by Australian households in the 1970s. Nevertheless, armed with a range of poverty lines for different sized income units, the Commission undertook a Survey of 22 000 households to discover, by examining their income, how many fell into poverty. If a unit had an income below the poverty line, it was described as being 'very poor'; if it had an income up to 20 per cent above the poverty line, it was described as being 'rather poor'.

The method of measuring poverty adopted by the Commission is obviously open to question. Some authorities argue that poverty cannot be reduced to monetary terms because it involves a host of other attributes such as low self-esteem and negative outlook. Others argue that monetary poverty lines are better set by specifying the goods and services needed for a subsistence standard of living (see Social Welfare Policy Secretariat, 1981). Since 1945 the Morgan Gallup Poll has asked the question 'What is the smallest amount a family of 2 adults and 2 children need a week to keep in health and to live decently, the smallest amount for all expenses including rent?' Although it does not mention poverty explicitly, this question could be taken as seeking a popular definition of 'the poverty line'. Interestingly, responses to the question indicate a minimum level well in excess of that resulting from the method adopted by the Commission of Inquiry into Poverty, often over 30 per cent higher (Saunders and Bradbury, 1989). Whatever the merits of these arguments about measurement, and whatever the shortcomings of the Commission of Inquiry, the fact remains that its report provided some sort of datum against which changes in the incidence of poverty after 1975 can be assessed. And there have certainly been changes. Increases in pensions have done much to reduce the number of aged poor. However increasing numbers of younger people have found themselves in poverty. It has been estimated that, largely as a result of unemployment, 21 per cent of single people aged 15–24 living alone were 'very poor' by the early 1980s. At the same time the plight of single parents had worsened, with 40 per cent being 'very poor'. Single parents living in privately rented accommodation were particularly badly hit, especially in Sydney where a chronic shortage of private rental dwellings forced up rents in the 1980s. In consequence, no less than 54 per cent of single parents with one child and 77 per cent of single parents with 2 children were in poverty if they lived in privately rented accommodation in Sydney in the early 1980s (Henderson and Hough, 1984). Overall, poverty levels (defined on the basis established by the Commission of Inquiry) had probably risen by the mid-1980s to the point where 11 per cent of families were 'very poor' (Vipond, 1986).

Geographical variations in well-being

This Chapter so far has shown that the well-being of the Australian population is far from uniform. Some groups are 'winners' in the sense of having high levels of well-being while other groups are 'losers' in that they have low levels of well-being (see Walmsley, 1990). Prominent among the 'losers' are unemployed school leavers, those on low incomes but in costly privately rented accommodation, and those in poverty generally. These variations in well-being often find geographical expression: the 'winners' tend to cluster in certain areas and the 'losers' in other areas, so that it is entirely possible to talk about the geography of inequality (see Coates *et al.*, 1977). A simple example of the sort of geographical variation in well-being that occurs in Australia is shown in Table 3.13 which details the level of poverty in each State and in

Table 3.13 Geographical variations in poverty

	Income units in poverty after housing costs taken into consideration (%)
New South Wales	8.3
Victoria	6.9
Queensland	10.9
South Australia	6.8
Western Australia	9.1
Tasmania	8.4
Sydney	7.1
Melbourne	5.4
Other metropolitan areas	6.3
Towns and cities over 25 000 population	6.1
Towns less than 25 000 population	7.9

Source: Commission of Inquiry into Poverty (1975)

certain sizes of cities, as determined by the Commission of Inquiry into Poverty. In the 1970s Queensland obviously had the worst incidence of poverty. Similarly, Sydney has a much higher level of poverty than both Melbourne and other metropolitan areas.

Unfortunately the analysis contained in Table 3.13 cannot be pressed too far. Not only are the findings rather dated but the Commission of Inquiry into Poverty sampled only 22 000 households over the entire country and, as a result, the sample size in some areas was too small for meaningful conclusions to be drawn. It is not possible to say, therefore, exactly how poverty varies from place to place within the city. All that can be said is that no part of Australian cities is without its poor but nowhere is the percentage of poor households greater than 15 per cent of the total population (Manning, 1976). Nevertheless, the example of poverty does show the importance of looking carefully at geographical variations in well-being. It therefore makes a prima facie case for the use of what have become known as *territorial social indicators*. These are simply statistics, available for small geographical areas, that describe the well-being of the population (Walmsley, 1980a; Stimson, 1982).

Basically there are two approaches to the use of territorial social indicators. The first, or *univariate*, approach plots one indicator at a time.

Figure 3.1a) plots unemployment rates and Fig 3.1b) crime rates for local government areas in Sydney (*see* pp.176–77). In both cases the north shore comes out well and the inner suburbs and the far west come out badly. This sort of situation, where the geographical patterns of different social problems are very similar, has led to calls for the *multivariate* approach to the use of social indicators. Under the multivariate approach a range of indicators is collected for all the different areas under study (i.e. 'multiple variables') and then statistically reduced to just one or two variables that summarize the original data, thereby taking account of the similarity in the geographical patterns for the individual variables.

Logan *et al.* (1975), for example, used 22 variables from the 1971 Census to measure the 'standard of living' in all rural local government areas (LGAs) in Australia. They then condensed these variables to a single measure labelled 'social deprivation'. Figure 3.2 plots the most 'socially deprived' 20 per cent of rural LGAs and in doing so shows that the outback and the north fare worst. Logan *et al.* (1975) also used 22 variables (but not the same ones) to examine variations in socio-economic status within cities. The resultant patterns are again interesting. Far from being confined to certain sectors and zones the best and worst status areas are quite scattered (exemplified by Sydney and Melbourne in Fig. 3.3, *see* pp. 179–80). In short, then, the analyses by Logan *et al.* show that both city and country areas contain significant place-to-place variations in well-being. More recently, Sorensen and Weinand (1991) used 22 variables to group all Commonwealth electorates, ranking the electorates from 1 to 148 in terms of overall social stress, family stress, and housing stress (Table 3.14, p. 178).

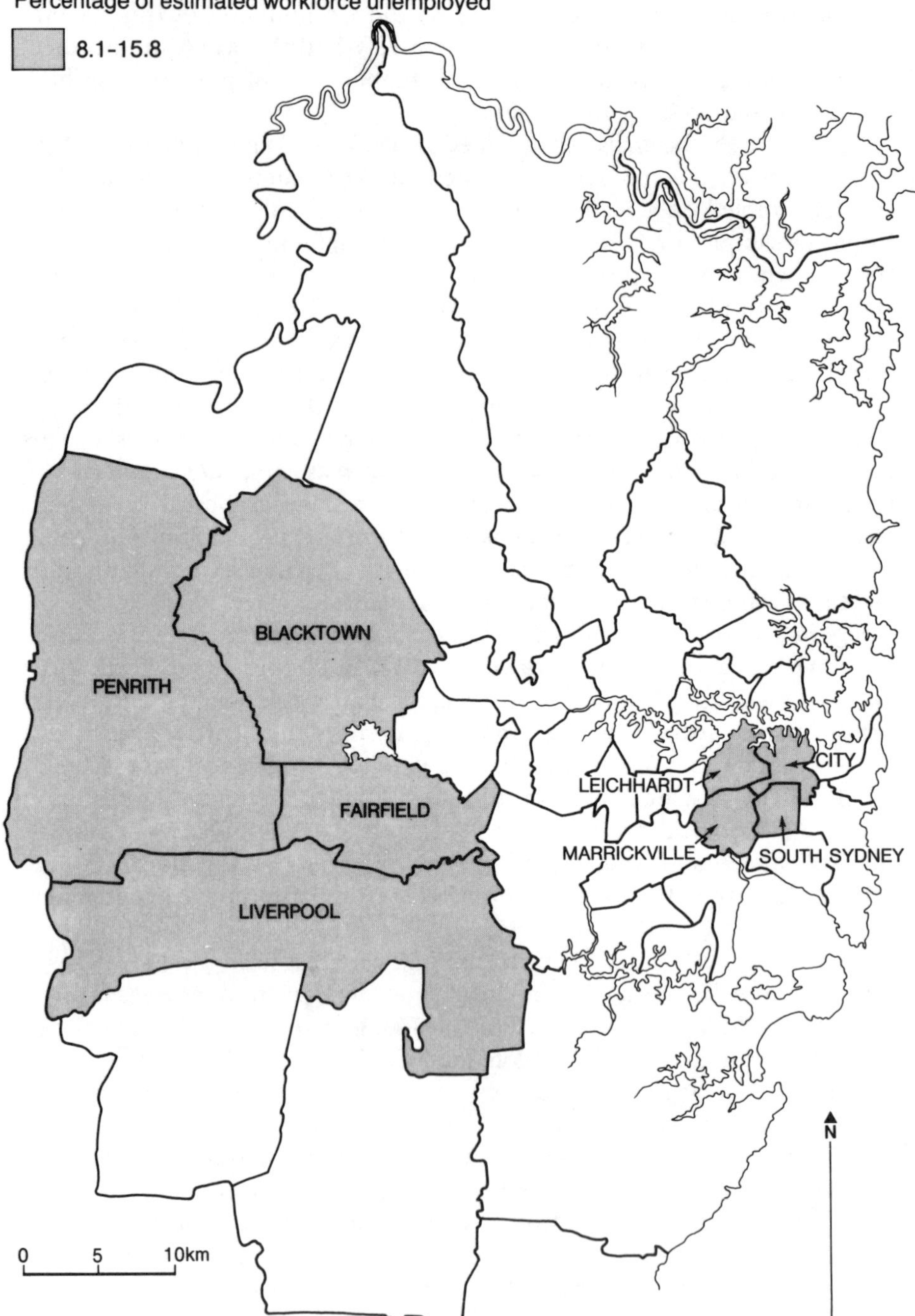

Fig. 3.1 The distribution of a) unemployment and b) crime in Sydney in the 1970s
Source: Planning and Environment Commission (1978)

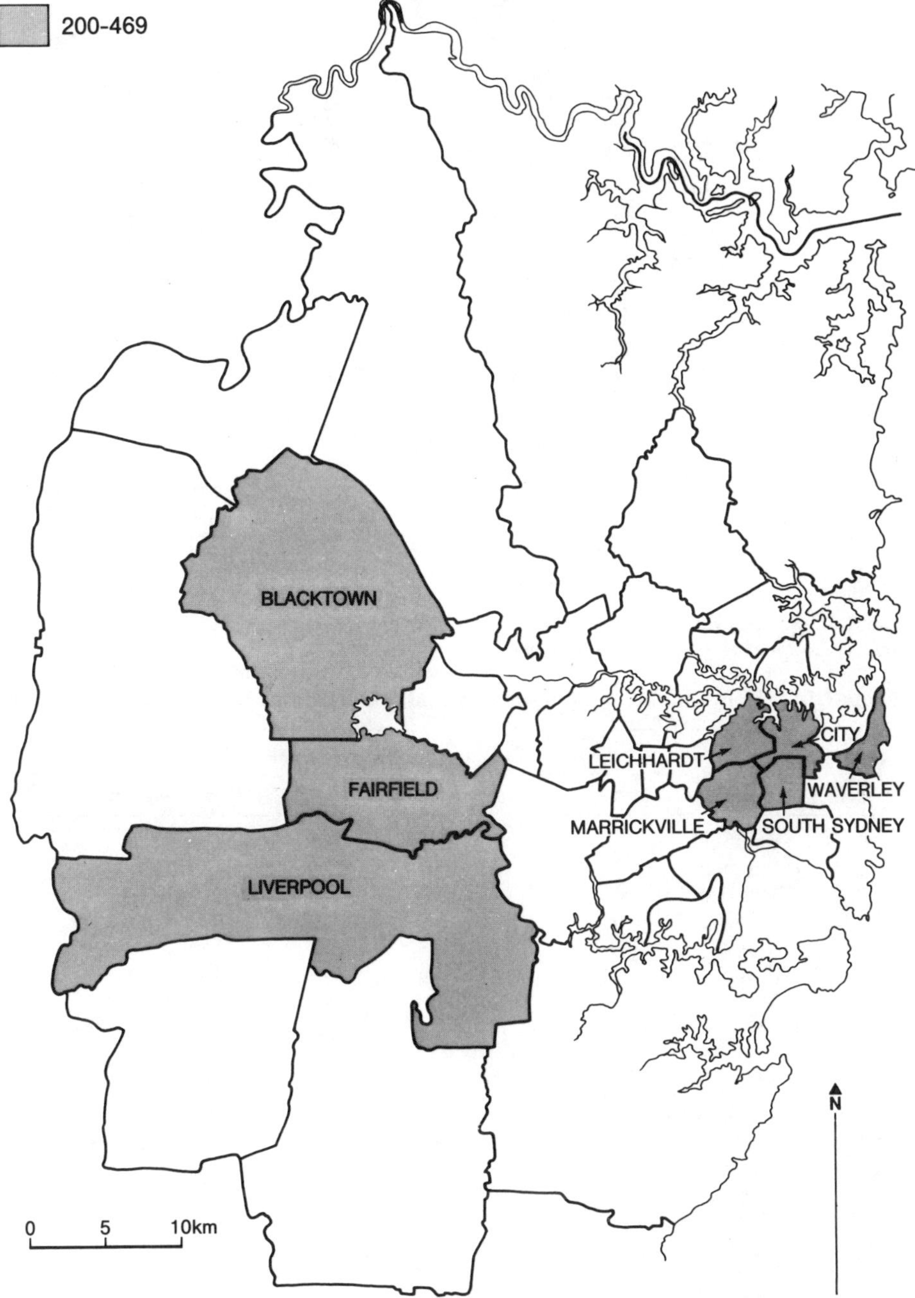
Appearances in Petty Sessions:
Rate per 10 000 males 18 years and over: worse areas
200-469
BLACKTOWN
FAIRFIELD
LIVERPOOL
LEICHHARDT
MARRICKVILLE
CITY
WAVERLEY
SOUTH SYDNEY
N
0
5
10km

Fig. 3.2 Socially deprived rural areas
Source: Adapted from Logan *et al.* (1975)

Table 3.14 A classification of Commonwealth electorates in terms of well-being

	Hightest and lowest status electorates[a]		
	Overall social stress	*Family stress*	*Housing stress*
1	Bradfield	Bradfield	Grey
2	Mitchell	Menzies	Franklin
3	Menzies	Ryan	Northern Territory
4	Berowra	Tangney	Bonython
5	Casey	Fraser	Fraser
6	Bruce	Mitchell	McMillan
7	McEwan	Makin	Denison
8	Aston	Canberra	Braddon
9	Deakin	Bruce	Lyons
10	Lalor	Kingston	Kalgoorlie
139	McPherson	Fowler	Warringah
140	Page	Gellibrand	North Sydney
141	Bonython	Rankin	Wentworth
142	Richmond	Wills	Menzies
143	Melbourne	St. George	Moncrieff
144	Swan	Maranoa	MacKellar
145	Griffith	Blaxland	Fairfax
146	Fairfax	Kennedy	Bradfield
147	Port Adelaide	Reid	Mitchell
148	Cowper	Grayndler	McPherson

a A ranking of 1 indicates the highest level of well being, 148 the lowest.
Source: Sorensen and Weinand (1991)

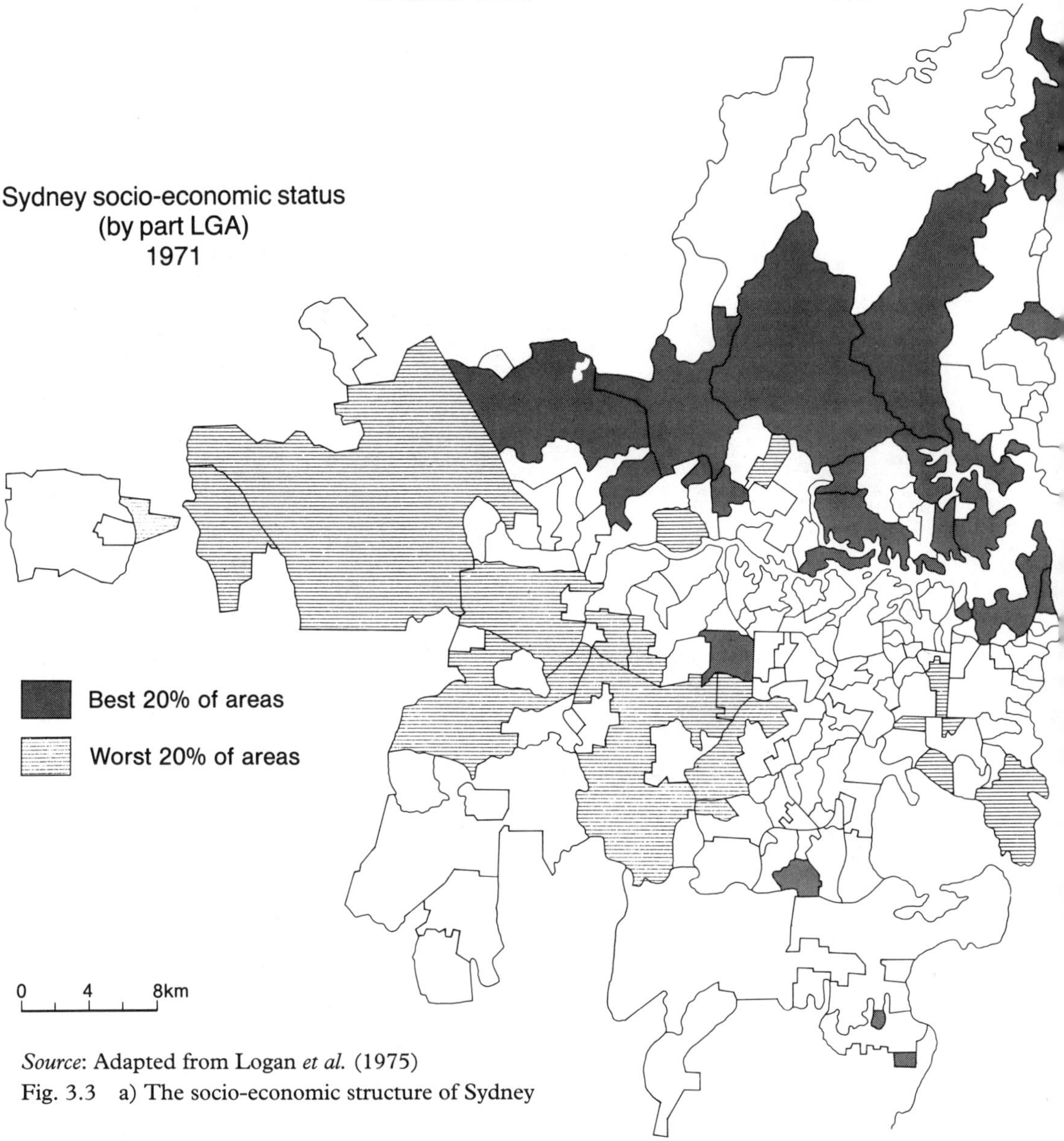

Sydney socio-economic status
(by part LGA)
1971

Best 20% of areas

Worst 20% of areas

0 4 8km

Source: Adapted from Logan *et al.* (1975)

Fig. 3.3 a) The socio-economic structure of Sydney

Well-being within the city

Australia is an urban nation. At the 1986 Census approximately 85 per cent of the population lived in towns or cities (defined as settlements with at least 1000 people). Indeed, in many respects Australia is a metropolitan nation in that most of its inhabitants live in big cities (see Table 1.5, p. 30). In 1981,

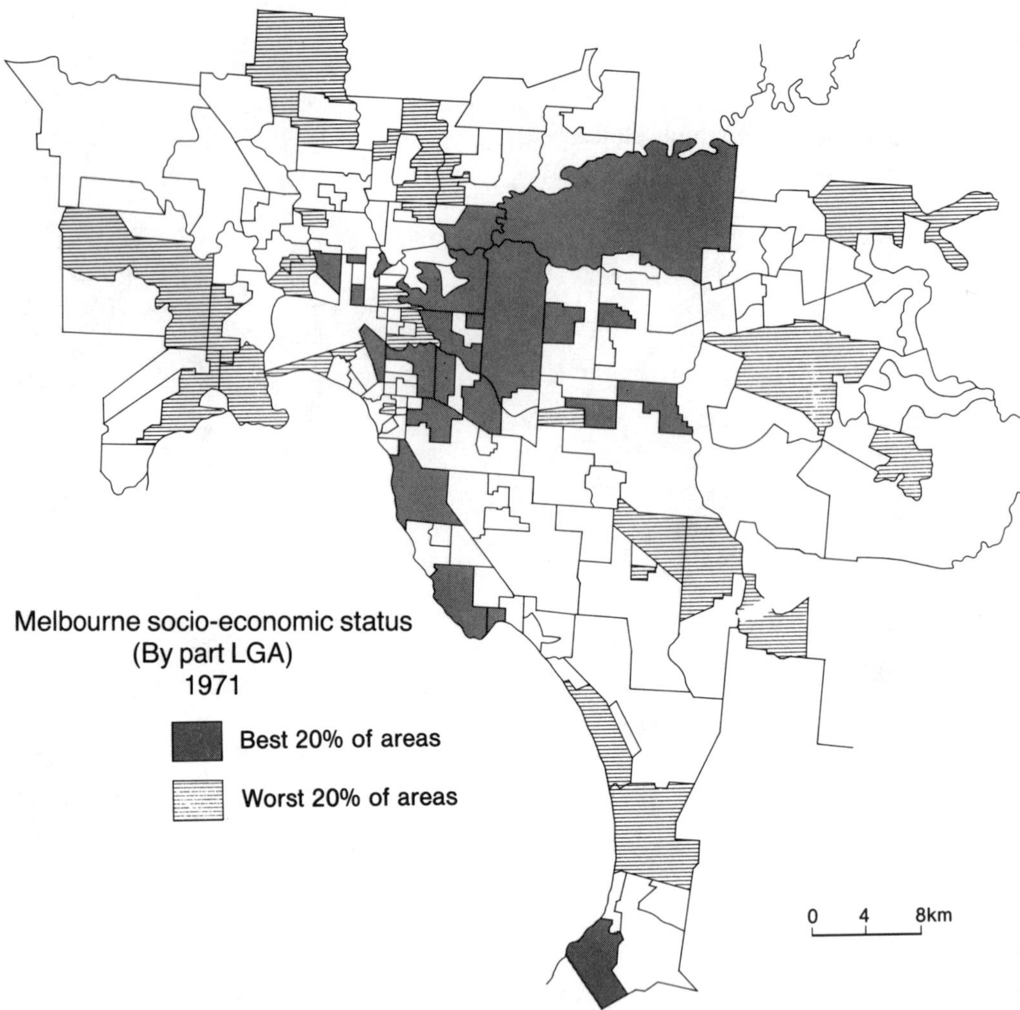

Fig. 3.3b The socio-economic structure of Melbourne

for example, 37.4 per cent of Australians lived in cities with greater than one million population, 55.5 per cent in cities with greater than half a million population, and 63.1 per cent in cities with populations greater than 100 000 (Maher, 1985). The rate of growth of big cities has been substantial over the last twenty years (Table 3.15 and see Daly, 1988). Although Perth, Brisbane, and Canberra have grown most quickly, all the capitals have grown significantly (despite the fact that some metropolitan growth rates have tended to fall behind overall national growth rates in recent years). After a slow down in the 1970s, metropolitan growth rates seem to be increasing again. Of course, Australia's cities are changing as well as growing. For example, Melbourne, in common with a number of cities, is experiencing changes in the nature and location of economic enterprise, the structure and composition of the population, and the general competitive strength of its region (Maher, 1988). Many cities are also witnessing a suburbanization of activities formerly provided in their central business districts (see Walmsley and Weinand, 1991).

Table 3.15 Population growth rates in cities

	Mean annual percentage growth				
Statistical division	*1966–71*	*1971–76*	*1976–81*	*1981–86*	*1986–88*
Sydney	2.1	0.6	0.9	1.2	1.8
Melbourne	2.3	0.8	0.6	0.9	1.2
Brisbane	3.7	2.0	1.9	1.8	1.9
Adelaide	3.0	1.3	0.7	1.0	1.0
Perth	5.9	2.8	2.1	2.8	3.3
Hobart	1.6	1.1	0.8	0.9	0.3
Canberra	8.9	6.6	1.8	2.8	2.9
Australia	2.2	1.4	1.3	1.5	1.6

Source: Maher (1985); Australian Bureau of Statistics, *Australian Demographic Statistics Quarterly* cat. no. 3101.0; Commonwealth of Australia (1990).

The preponderance of urban settlement in Australia might suggest that urban policy would have been a major concern of government in the years since Federation. This is far from the case. In fact it was not until the election of the Labor Government in 1972 that urban affairs figured prominently at the Commonwealth level. In campaigning for office Whitlam (1972) made what now seems to be a self evident (and perhaps sexist) point but what at the time was taken as something of a revelation:

> Increasingly, a citizen's real standard of living, the health of himself and his family, his children's opportunities for education and self-improvement, his access to employment opportunities, his ability to enjoy the nation's resources for recreation and culture, his ability to participate in the decisions and actions of the community, are determined not by his income, not by the hours he works, but by where he lives.

This statement, when applied to cities, did much to put urban issues on the political agenda. The resultant urban policy, like earlier initiatives by the States, had many strands. Part of it was concerned with making cities efficient (e.g. providing efficient transport systems and avoiding overconcentration) so as to help the overall growth of the economy; part of it was concerned with the promotion of health and a good quality of life (e.g. through the imposition of minimum standards on development); part of it was concerned with social welfare (notably the provision of public housing); and part of it was concerned with making cities beautiful through clever architecture and environmental design. Despite this very wide range of government activity, cities remained very much the creation of private enterprise with governments providing at best a supplementary role (Neutze, 1978; p. 20).

Town planning was relatively weak, as it always had been, largely because planning departments never had enough power at either State or Commonwealth levels to challenge successfully the traditional centres of administrative and bureaucratic power, notably treasury departments. As a result planning has all too often been seen as somehow separate from all other forms of social, political, and economic activity (Troy, 1981). Its potential in redressing the inequalities in society and in providing for the overall well-being of the population has therefore usually been overlooked. Cities have developed very unevenly, with some suburbs often housing many more resources than other suburbs (see Pinch, 1991). Cities are often unfairly structured in so far as the distribution of 'good things' (e.g. education and health care facilities) and 'bad things' (e.g. congestion, pollution) reflects factors other than need, demand, and the effort of residents in attempting to obtain facilities (Badcock, 1984). However, it would be wrong to talk simply of some places suffering 'locational disadvantage' because such descriptions tend to group together dissimilar places and thus gloss over the way in which the interaction of class, gender, ethnicity and race tends to work itself out at the local level in distinctive patterns of inequality and inequity (Fincher, 1991).

It may be that a great many public policies concerned with urban planning and the urban environment have inegalitarian effects (Stilwell, 1974), possibly because the promotion of economic growth has traditionally been seen as far more important than the remedying of social ills — with the result that the social implications of some planning initiatives have scarcely been considered. In fact, in the eyes of some commentators, the entire exercise of urban policy-making tends to centre around the devising of land use plans that disadvantage the poor but profit the rich (Sandercock, 1975). *Land use zoners* are often seen as the major villains in this exercise. Town planners have, of course, always placed great faith in *zoning*. Separating residences from workplaces enables families to live away from the dirt and noise of factories and away from the traffic of shopping areas. It also enables city dwellers to have the privacy of their own house and garden (Neutze, 1978; p. 13). In this sense it has much to recommend it.

However, zoning is an activity that involves winners and losers. In fact, land use zoning can, in many senses, be regarded as a welfare policy. The welfare and quality of life of an individual is very much influenced by that individual's command over goods and resources which, in turn, is very much a function of how accessible the individual is to such things as employment opportunities, schools, beaches, and social services (Sandercock, 1975; p. 2). Land use zoning decides who will be near to such facilities and who will be distant. Heavy industry is far from a commonly applicable (yet interesting) example because of the decline in factory employment that has occurred in recent years (see Chapter 2): in many ways it makes sense to keep noxious industry out of major residential areas in order to prevent pollution, noise and dirt from spoiling the environmental quality of residential neighbourhoods. Such exclusionary zoning may, however, have the side-effect of pushing up land and house prices in the neighbourhood to the point where they are beyond the means of many of the workers employed in the offensive industries. As a result these workers may be forced to reside in less than salubrious surroundings in areas near to factories or, alternatively, they may be forced to distant residential areas where land and houses are cheap but where commuting costs are high. In effect, then, one of the by-products of zoning can be the encouragement of social and economic segregation in the housing market. In some respects this may not be a bad thing because it may make easier the provision by government of the facilities a neighbourhood wants, and it may lead to fewer local tensions, more self-help, and closer friendship bonds (Neutze, 1978). It does however sometimes lead to a situation where family 'running costs' are so high as to impose a major financial burden.

Despite these shortcomings, planning has proved to be immensely popular. It is something that all States felt they had to get involved with. In consequence, plans have been devised for all of Australia's major cities (see Alexander, 1981). Sydney led the way with the County of Cumberland Plan, approved in 1951. This plan stressed the social benefits of decentralising industrial and retail activity and the need to provide a range of facilities and amenities in suburban areas. Despite this it allowed for a 10 per cent increase in downtown office employment, plus the establishment of radial freeways, thereby facilitating the continued administrative and financial dominance of the rest of the city by the central business district (CBD). Melbourne's Metropolitan Planning Scheme of 1954 placed even more emphasis on facilitating central city growth. Its emphasis was firmly on economic efficiency rather than social equity. Perth's first major city plan of 1955, too, was dominated by thoughts of economic growth and in fact it was not until the Adelaide Development Plan, approved in 1967, that considerations of dispersal from the CBD, first mooted in the County of Cumberland Plan, again came to prominence (Alexander, 1981). Generally speaking, metropolitan plans such as these were more successful in decentralising manufacturing jobs than in decentralising office employment (and even here the success was minor because of the general decline in manufacturing described in Chapter 2). The CBD continued to be the focus of most office jobs, and where dispersal occurred it tended to be highly selective in that it focussed on only a few suburban centres (such as Chatswood, Crows Nest, Hurstville, and Parramatta in Sydney, and Preston, Footscray, Box Hill, Moorabbin, and Dandenong in Melbourne). A realisation that both residential growth at the urban fringe, and dispersal of activity to the suburbs, were likely to be highly selective lay behind most of the second generation metropolitan plans to be developed. Both the Perth Corridor Plan of 1970 and the Sydney Region

Outline Plan of 1968, for example, specified the directions which such growth would take.

The continued growth of Australian capital cities (Table 3.15) has been fuelled to a great extent by large numbers of overseas immigrants settling in such areas. Growth itself has been incremental in that new housing tends to have been tacked on to the metropolitan fringe with very little infilling or redesign of basic city structure. In any one year new houses add, on average, only 2–3 per cent to the existing housing stock of cities (Neutze, 1977) but such has been the persistence of growth, and so widely accepted has been the idea of low density development, that the geographical scale of cities has increased enormously. Sydney's built up area, for instance, increased from 400 km^2 in 1945 to 1200 km^2 in 1981 (Rich *et al.*, 1982). Since that time, it has grown even further. In this context, any plan which specifies growth corridors is almost bound to encourage speculation: it removes any uncertainty in the speculators' minds as to which areas will be developed. This certainly proved to be the case in Sydney where the years 1958 to 1974 saw a quite remarkable boom in land and real estate. The nature of this boom and the reasons behind it have been analysed in detail by Daly (1982a; 1982b). In the period 1950–1966 land and housing prices increased by 7.3 and 2.7 times respectively; over the much shorter period 1966–1974 they increased 4.2 and 2.5 times respectively. This boom in prices was brought about partly by population growth putting a strain on existing resources (i.e. demand outstripping supply). In large measure, however, the boom came about as a result of changes in both the world, and Australia's, financial market (see Chapter 2). The mining boom of the 1960s had led to Australia becoming more prominent in the international financial arena at a time when European banks, particularly those based in London, were awash with dollars largely as a result of the USA funding the Vietnam War by means of deficits. This so-called 'Eurodollar market' provided a ready source of funds for Australia's resource developments. In the five years to 1971/72 Australia experienced a massive inflow of funds equivalent to $1500 million. Two-thirds of this went into mining development and significantly one-third went into banking, finance, and property development — much of it focussing on Sydney, which had become a major international financial centre for the Pacific Basin. To begin with there was a boom in office development.

When there arose a surplus of office space, investment moved into retail developments. The growth in retail space in Sydney in the early 1970s was in fact four times as large as the growth in population (Daly, 1982b). At the same time, real wage increases in Australia (i.e. increases faster than the rate of inflation) led to there being plentiful domestic funds available for investment. These funds were mopped up quickly by permanent building societies and finance companies (offering high interest rates to attract deposits) and re-invested in real estate. This ready availability of funds helped push up prices. The boom reached its peak in early 1973. In April of that year land prices rose by 5.5 per cent, in May 3.3 per cent (Daly, 1982a: 13). The bust came with the tighter money policies that the Labor government introduced in the 1970s in order to control inflation. This had the effect of making Australia less attractive to overseas funds. Some property companies which had borrowed heavily found themselves in difficulties. Needing a cash flow to maintain profitability, they were faced with a situation where there was less liquidity around. Some spectacular company crashes ensued. By 1977 when Parkes Developments crashed, the rate of increase of Sydney land and house prices had fallen back considerably.

Of course, the bust of the mid-1970s was followed by a new boom. Indeed the Australian housing market has been characterised by booms and busts, the intensity of these perhaps being magnified by financial deregulation in the 1980s (Badcock, 1991). A measure of how housing costs in Australia generally have increased relative to other items of household expenditure is shown in Table 3.16. The costs of housing and transport have clearly gone up

Table 3.16 The movement of the price index for household expenditure[1]

	Price Index					
Year	*Food*	*Clothing*	*Housing*	*Household equipment*	*Transport*	*All goods*
1974–75	164.0	173.0	187.4	153.8	173.0	171.1
1979–80	283.6	295.1	314.3	244.2	296.5	287.2
1984–85	420.5	406.3	488.7	376.7	465.6	431.1
1988–89	563.5	556.6	684.2	493.4	628.6	590.6

1 All figures are relative to a datum of 100.0 for 1966–67
Source: Commonwealth Yearbooks

Table 3.17 The cost of a typical Sydney inner suburban cottage

	Land	*Land plus cottage*
1968	9 000	18 000
1970	12 000	23 000
1972	18 500	32 000
1974	26 000	48 000
1976	27 500	50 000
1978	35 000	65 000
1980	62 500	110 000
1982	90 000	150 000
1984	120 000	175 000
1988	215 000*	325 000*
1990	211 000*	309 000*

*Average of representative sites and cottages in selected suburbs
Source: Valuer-General's Department (1985; 1990)

much more quickly than other items. As has been seen, the price rise was most dramatic in Sydney. Estimates of the cost of 'a typical inner suburban cottage' are given in Table 3.17. The slowdown in price rises after the bust of the mid-1970s obviously did not last long and rapidly escalating prices have since been re-established as the norm, albeit with a downturn in 1990. Between 1968 and 1990, when the consumer price index increased approximately sixfold, inner suburban land values increased over twenty times and inner-suburban house and land packages about seventeen times. Between 1987 and 1990 alone, despite a downturn in 1990, the price of cottages in the inner suburbs of Sydney (0–6 km from the city centre) increased by 82 per cent. Over the same period similar sorts of dwellings in middle distance suburbs (6–25 km from the city centre) increased by 80 per cent and those in the outer Sydney suburbs (beyond 25 km from the city centre) increased by 72 per cent. To some extent, the rate of increase was accelerated by a flight of investors from the stock market to real estate after the stock market crash of October 1988 (Wettenhall, 1989). Notable variations were evident within each zone: in the inner suburbs in 1990 'representative' cottages sold for $750 000 in Bellevue Hill but only $155 000 in Erskineville; in middle suburbs the range was from $620 000 in Gordon to $135 000 at Chester Hill and in outer suburbs from $285 000 at Cronulla to $110 000 at Penrith (Valuer-General's Department, NSW, 1990). The price rises in Melbourne and other cities have been less spectacular but everywhere the impact of such rises has been the same: the areas in which average and low income households can afford to buy have been very much reduced in number. In Melbourne in 1967, for example, a single income family on average weekly earnings ($66), with bank interest at 5.7 per cent, could afford to buy an average house in 46 of Melbourne's 55 local government areas (LGAs). By 1977, however, with average weekly earnings at $200 and bank interest at 10.5 per cent, the family in question could afford to buy in only one of Melbourne's 55 LGAs (Sandercock and Berry, 1983).

One effect of surging house and land prices was to encourage sprawl at the metropolitan fringes because there the cheapest land was to be found. Public housing authorities were often as guilty of encouraging such sprawl as private developers. In the 1960s the New South Wales Housing Commission built massively in the Mt Druitt area 40 km west of Sydney's city centre. Likewise in Green Valley, 36 km southwest of Sydney's city centre, the Housing Commission settled 25 000 people in the space of four years. This sort of development of 'green fields' sites offered economies of scale and thus proved attractive to a public authority under great pressure to build the maximum number of houses with its available funds, thereby reducing the waiting lists for public rented accommodation. Low density cottage development also seemed to be in tune with the prevailing views on housing standards in Australia and avoided the pitfalls commonly associated with high rise inner city flat development. In practice, of course, the peripheral housing estates were far from ideal and the problems associated with them have been documented both in Sydney (Brennan, 1973) and Melbourne (Bryson and Thompson, 1972).

Early settlers in new, peripheral housing estates lack social, commercial, welfare, educational, and child-minding facilities. This is because commercial facilities obviously do not set up in business until demand reaches a threshold at which a service can be provided profitably, and public sector activity tends to be poorly provided because of a lack of co-ordination between housing authorities and other arms of government. Non-government welfare organizations tend also to be lacking in the initial period. The population of such estates tends to be biassed through an over-representation of young children, young mothers, large families and unskilled workers (precisely the groups who might be expected to make large demands on government services). Often the resident population is much greater than anticipated. In Green Valley, for example, the total number of persons per household at the time of settlement was 33 per cent greater than at the time of allocation because families grew during the time they were on the waiting list (Brennan, 1973). Newness and unfamiliarity also present problems.

Above all, though, the lack of local job opportunities means long, expensive commuting that disrupts family life both socially and financially. Because of this many households find it hard to make friends and few have the time or the training to become community leaders. Particularly badly hit among those facing problems are women and unemployed school leavers. A survey of women on a peripheral public housing estate in Sydney showed, for example, that 47 per cent admitted to feeling 'lonely' and 30 per cent had no friends within walking distance (Sarkissian and Doherty, 1984).

The problems of unemployed school leavers may be even worse. The disadvantage and boredom that comes with unemployment has frequently been seen as a cause of vandalism and anti-social behaviour generally (Windschuttle, 1979). There is however an unfortunate tendency for the media to exaggerate social unrest and to equate disadvantage and deprivation with depravity. A case in point was media treatment of a so-called 'riot' at Bidwell in the west of Sydney in 1981 (Mowbray, 1985). This 'riot' amounted to a fight between two 13 year old girls, watched by an audience of peers. After the British city riots the media were probably in the right frame of mind for a story on unrest. In the event they arrived in helicopters. The police, too, had an interest in seeing good coverage of the 'riot' because it would help their argument for a greater number of officers to be posted to the western suburbs. It is not surprising, then, that the *Daily Telegraph* the following day had a headline that read: 'Savage night of violence: 1000 kids in wild rampage'. Such exaggerations create a myth which sticks and areas which attract a poor reputation tend to find it difficult to change that reputation both in the eyes of their residents and in the eyes of the outside world (Brennan, 1978). This can lead in some instances to the children of such disadvantaged areas having feelings of loneliness, rejection, and social alienation (Homel and Burns, 1985).

Given the problems of isolation at the metropolitan fringe, it is not surprising to find that there has been something of a reappraisal of the advantages of inner city living. Until recently the stereotyped image of inner suburbs probably focussed on congestion, noise, crowding, and pollution, with the suburbs in question being reception areas for migrants. Traditionally inner city areas have been working class domains where residents gained cheap housing and accessibility to the city centre at the expense of poor living conditions. In recent years, however, different groups have come to place a high premium upon accessibility to the cultural, recreational, social and employment opportunities of the city centre.

Basically these groups are middle class, often professional people, sometimes labelled 'trendies' in comparison to the traditional working class (Day and Walmsley, 1978). Because they are middle class, and are a modern day equivalent of the 'gentry', the process by which they buy and renovate characteristically working class inner suburban dwellings has become known as 'gentrification' (Kendig, 1979). The influx of the middle classes has done much to push up the cost of inner suburban housing and the cost of inner suburban rented accommodation. Not all inner city areas have been affected by gentrification and even in the 'trendy' areas the proportion of inhabitants who are middle-class immigrants is often quite small. Nevertheless, it seems that the lifestyle and ready access to the central business district make inner suburbs attractive to gentrifiers (Day and Walmsley, 1981). Additionally, of course, the prospect of capital gains through 'doing up' cheap housing provided an important incentive (Williams, 1984). The changes brought about by gentrification are quite striking in some areas.

However, as a housing process, gentrification has little or no impact on the twin problems of continuing metropolitan sprawl and decreasing house affordability. In order to tackle these problems, the authorities responsible for metropolitan areas (notably the NSW government) are trying to foster urban consolidation whereby a greater number of people will be housed in the already built up areas (see Collie, 1990). Changes have been made to the planning of Sydney to facilitate multiple dwellings on a single parcel of land. Attempts are also being made to introduce innovative housing styles (e.g. cluster housing) with a markedly higher density than standard suburban sprawl (see Department of Industry, Technology and Commerce, 1990; Commonwealth of Australia, 1989).

Underlying the attractiveness of the inner suburbs, and disenchantment with the metropolitan fringe, is the issue of access to resources. The resources that matter to city dwellers are not uniformly distributed. Rather they are concentrated in and around the central business district and often at selected suburban nuclei. This is true of jobs, hospitals, doctors, government offices, welfare organizations, shops, and recreation and leisure time facilities. Thus

Table 3.18 The length of the journey to work, 1974 (per cent)

	Travelling less than:		*Public transport*[1]	*Private car driver/passenger*[1]
	30 mins	*60 mins*		
Sydney	49.9	83.1	29.7	61.8
Melbourne	56.0	89.5	24.4	65.7
Brisbane	60.8	92.4	20.8	69.1
Adelaide	69.6	96.6	16.9	72.6
Perth	68.0	96.0	15.1	75.3
Hobart	82.0	97.7	19.5	71.2
Canberra	81.1	98.3	9.3	82.6

1 These figures do not sum to 100 per cent because some people walked, cycled, or jogged.
Source: Department of Home Affairs and Environment (1983)

people wanting to use these resources have to travel considerable distances. And the larger the city, the greater the distances that sometimes have to be covered. Figures on commuting, although dated, illustrate this very well (Table 3.18). In 1974 almost 17 per cent of Sydney's workforce took more than an hour to get to their place of employment (compared to only about 3–4 per cent in Adelaide and Perth) and over half of all employees in Sydney took more than 30 minutes to get to work.

The problems of accessibility to facilities within the city can be overcome, albeit at a cost, by those with private transport. Those reliant on public transport are less fortunate. Public transport systems tend to be better developed and better used in big cities (Table 3.18). This means that the residents of smaller cities often have rather less choice as to their mode of travel and are forced to rely on private cars. This is not to say that residents of big cities have good transport systems. Sydney's transport system, for example, is characterized by

1 a lack of consumer choice,
2 a low rate of innovation in services,
3 a suboptimal taxi industry,
4 social and geographical inequities in the pattern of subsidies,
5 poor pricing strategies, and
6 an irregular spatial form where the CBD is in an eccentric location (Sorensen, 1990b).

In addition, there are certain groups that are disadvantaged, in transport terms, irrespective of the size of the city they live in. These are primarily the young, the old, the poor, homemakers, and the disabled (Table 3.19).

The nature of the disability varies but its effect is usually to restrict travel to public transport or to negate travel entirely. It is important to realise then that there are two sorts of public transport user: users by choice (e.g. commuters who find that the services available are well suited to their needs and provide a more attractive proposition than travel along congested roads by

Table 3.19 Transport disadvantaged groups

Transport disadvantaged group	*Nature of disadvantage*
Young	
1 Preschool children	Unable to travel alone.
2 School children	Unlicensed, and dependent on parents, older friends or public transport for motorised mobility.
3 Working or unemployed youths without a car (working or living in outer suburbs)	Difficulty of reaching employment (actual or potential) via public transport, especially in outer areas.
Old	
4 Aged/frail	May never have learnt to drive. Failing physical faculties reduce ability to drive, and/or to use other means of transport (including walking).
Poor	
5 Resource-poor	Lack of money to own and run a car and/or to afford cost of public transport.
6 Information-poor (e.g. migrants, new residents)	Lack of knowledge of available services
Homeworkers	
7 Homemakers	Household car may not be available during the day. Sometimes unable to drive (unlicensed). Also tied to children (time constraints, prams and associated paraphernalia).
Disabled	
8 Handicapped	Difficulty in driving and/or in using conventional forms of public transport. Availability of parking spaces close to destination is critical.
9 Physically ill	

Source: Morris (1981)

private car to locations at which parking is difficult) and captive users (notably the one in six, mainly low income, urban households that neither own a car nor have access to a company car) (Morris, 1981). The problems of the transport disadvantaged are most acute in the outer suburbs where public transport networks are invariably poor and where the costs of running a private car are very high because of the distances that have to be covered:

> families migrating to new residential estates on the metropolitan fringe discover that the benefits of the modern dwelling they acquire are offset by the longer distances they have to travel to jobs, schools, shops, health facilities and social-kinship links (Faulkner, 1981).

The friction of distance can in fact prevent workers in some areas from participating fully in the labour market (i.e. restrict them entirely or limit the number of locations at which they can take up a job). It can thereby contribute to unemployment. In Sydney in 1981, for example, the inner ring of suburbs had 20 per cent of the population, 22 per cent of the workforce but 41 per cent of the jobs; in contrast, the middle ring had 30 per cent of population, workforce, and jobs and the outer ring had 50 per cent of the population, 48 per cent of the workforce, but only 29 per cent of the jobs (Vipond, 1985). Clearly, workers in the outer suburbs are disadvantaged in relation to others in the provision of local jobs. They are also disadvantaged because commuting is difficult and costly.

What can be done to rectify these geographical variations in well-being within the city? One possibility is to make the population in disadvantaged areas more mobile by either

- introducing demand sensitive public transport systems (e.g. dial-a-bus) on routes that are presently uneconomic, or by
- altering the fare structure of public transport so as to make its use less burdensome.

In this context it is worth noting that Australia-wide experience seems to suggest that a 10 per cent increase in fares leads to a fall in patronage of about 5 per cent in the short run. Curiously, though, a 10 per cent increase in petrol prices leads to only a 0.2–0.7 per cent reduction in consumption (Morris, 1981). The alternative to making people more mobile is to locate services so as to cater better for need. This should theoretically be possible with government services which are relatively free from commercial cost-accounting. An intriguing question, therefore, is why it has not happened in the past. Why has public sector spending been such as to allow inequalities to develop in the provision of services? A partial answer to this question is to be found in the interesting example of fire brigade provision in Sydney. Adrian (1984c) has shown, for example, that in order to understand why some areas are poorly served with fire services, it is essential to look at the way institutions in question actually operate. Thus attempts to please the insurance industry (which contributes to fire services through a levy) meant that contributions were kept low, resulting in little funding being available for new fire stations. At the same time union intransigence led to bans on reductions in staffing levels at certain stations, thus making it impossible to redeploy labour as the geographical pattern of demand shifted.

Although fire fighting is important, it is perhaps not as prominent in the public mind as other services which impinge upon well-being, notably the provision of health care services and education facilities. Although Australia is a world leader in several areas of medical research and has a generally sound health care delivery system, there exist striking inequalities in service provision; to take but one example, in the mid-1970s the average provision of one general practitioner (GP) per 1325 people in Adelaide masked a range from 1: 448 in the high status suburb of Burnside through to 1:5678 in the peripheral Munno Para area (Stimson, 1982). The distribution of doctors tends to reflect the distribution of affluence and the social structure of the city generally. This comes about because ' GPs tend to locate their facilities in order to achieve the goals of income maximization, family orientation, social prestige and professional interaction' (Stimson, 1982; p. 23). The Australian health care delivery system relies overwhelming on GPs in private practice as the first point of contact between patients and medical professionals. Approximately three-quarters of all doctors are in private practice (Donald, 1981). Figure 3.4 illustrates the distribution of GPs in Sydney in 1979 and demonstrates quite vividly their concentration on the central city, inner suburbs, and north shore. The information on which Fig. 3.4 is based is of course dated. Nevertheless the pattern revealed in the figure remains substantially unchanged. Worst served are newly developing areas and low socio-economic status areas away from the inner suburbs. Many doctors practise in the inner suburbs because this is the location of the major hospitals that provide ancillary and back-up facilities to GPs.

Over 80 per cent of New South Wales patients are treated in public hospitals (Donald, 1981) and the distribution of hospital beds focusses on the city centre for two reasons: these locations were very close to the geographical centre of the metropolitan area when the hospitals were established (often in the nineteenth century); and such locations were close to the point of maximum access given the radial nature of the transport networks. Moves are

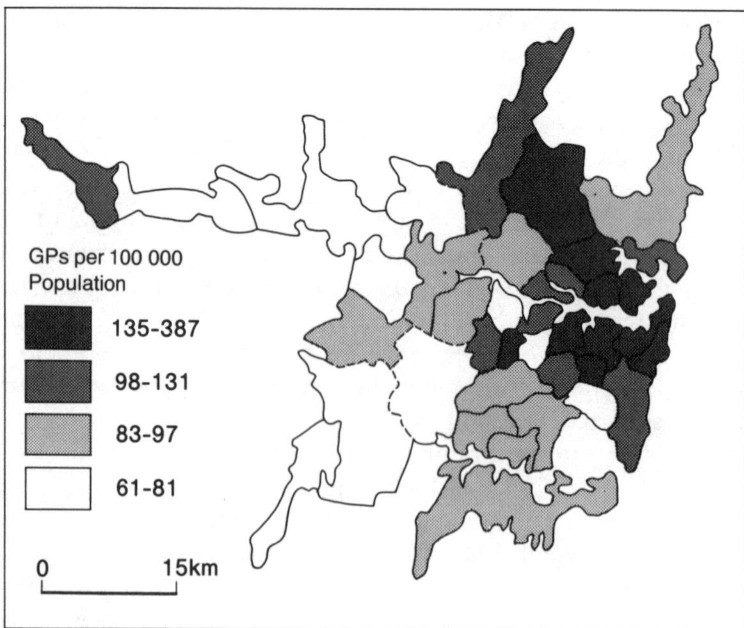

Fig. 3.4 Doctor: patient ratios, Sydney 1979
Source: Donald (1981)

being made to decentralise health care facilities to places like Sydney's Western suburbs, but even such apparently rational action is meeting with strong opposition from vested interest groups based around existing hospitals.

The relative over-provision of medical services in inner and affluent areas is paralleled, to some degree, in the provision of educational facilities. It is risky to generalise nationally about educational services, because these are provided by the States, and there are marked inter-state differences in educational provision. For example there were pronounced variations in the percentage of 17–19 year olds who were participating in post-secondary education in 1977. The highest figures were 36 per cent in South Australia, 33 per cent in Western Australia, and 27 per cent in New South Wales and the lowest figures 21 per cent in Victoria, 19 per cent in Tasmania, and 16 per cent in Queensland (Stimson, 1982; p. 258). Just why these differences came about is unclear. It is clear, however, that the main beneficiaries from the education system are the middle classes:

> going to a state school, or belonging to a low-income family, or living in a rural area or a low-income inner city area, reduces the educational opportunities of the young in Australia (Stimson, 1982; p. 255).

This was vividly demonstrated by Badcock (1977) who showed, for Sydney, that secondary students in 'better' areas (where there was a high proportion of the population

1 with tertiary qualifications,
2 in professional, executive, and managerial occupations, and
3 on high income)

tended to perform 'better' (in the sense of having higher IQ scores) and also tended to stay on at school longer.

A similar tendency for high school retention rates to be highest in areas of high social status has been noted in Melbourne (Teese, 1987). In order to redress these sorts of inequalities, governments over the last two decades have identified certain schools as disadvantaged and therefore deserving of increased funding, notably in inner city and low status outer metropolitan suburbs. Educational disadvantage can however start even before children enter school, as pre-school and child care facilities are often unfairly distributed. In the early 1970s the whole of Sydney was under-served with child care facilities (less than 20 per cent of children under five were within walking distance of a child care centre), but the western suburbs were especially under-endowed. In the city centre there were 267 child care places for every 1000 children aged 0–4; in Fairfield in the western suburbs there were only 16 places for every 1000. Predictably, profit-making child care centres reflected the income distribution. Curiously, though, non-profit centres also tended to be concentrated in affluent suburbs, perhaps suggesting that the middle class are very effective in doing whatever lobbying is necessary to attract resources (Freestone, 1977) as evidenced, in another context, by the tendency for community health projects funded by the government to go (in Melbourne at least) to the most articulate and best organized rather than the most needy (Jackson, 1985).

Well-being in country areas

Country areas exhibit the same geographical variations in well-being as city areas. However in country areas it is not simply a matter of poor or newly established areas missing out (although affluence and inertia are again very important influences on the location of facilities *within country towns*). There is also the problem of *isolation*, a problem that affects almost all country dwellers irrespective of their social status. Politicians regularly pay lip service to this issue. The Hawke Labor Government, for example, pledged itself to a 'fairer Australia' (Commonwealth of Australia, 1988a) and to improving the living standards of all Australians irrespective of where they live (Hawke, 1989). Such views are, of course, unobjectionable. Although the bulk of Australia's population lives in cities, there are substantial numbers of people in non-metropolitan areas. These non-metropolitan dwellers make a substantial contribution to the well-being of the nation, through the primary sector of the economy. What happens in country areas is therefore of importance to the nation as a whole, and many country towns are currently facing hard economic times and declining populations. Service towns in grazing areas are particularly affected (Holmes, 1988), but the problems are more widespread. Sorensen (1990a), for example, has pointed out that many country towns are trapped in a vicious cycle of decline from which there seems to be very little prospect of escape. In his view, there is a Darwinian element to Australia's rural settlement pattern in that only the 'fittest' places will survive. In Sorensen's view, the fulcrum between a 'vicious cycle of decline' and a 'virtuous cycle of growth' varies with the type of environment, possibly being as low as 5000 people on the plains of western NSW and as high as 15 000 in coastal areas.

To some extent, the decline of country towns can be attributed to falling commodity prices. On top of this, however, is decline brought about by neglect. Humphreys (1988), for instance, has pointed out that government inaction can have the effect of allocating resources disproportionately to areas characterized by economic viability rather than social vitality. Investment channelled into areas thought to have the best economic prospects can mean abandonment of other areas. Other writers are less pessimistic and see both lifestyle advantages in country town living (Hudson, 1989) and the scope for local development through concerted local initiatives (see Wildman *et al.*, 1990). Sadly, however, regional policy in Australia has been dormant since the time of Whitlam (Murphy and Roman, 1989) and there is little by way of a concerted governmental attempt to ameliorate living conditions in isolated areas. Such problems are clearly seen in relation to health care delivery.

As discussed earlier, Australia has a generally sound health care delivery system. Nationally, in 1981 Australia had approximately one doctor for every 521 people, and may have 1:405 by 2001 because of both increased output from medical schools and the immigration of overseas-born doctors. In principle, a greater number of doctors should mean a lessening in geographical differences in health care provision as GPs are forced into areas that presently have poor doctor:patient ratios. In practice, of course, many doctors will be reluctant to move and will maintain incomes in a diminishing market by servicing their existing patients rather more (e.g. encouraging regular check-ups). This may be a good thing, particularly if it puts the emphasis on preventative rather than curative medicine, but it will do little to help rural dwellers who presently lack adequate access to medical facilities.

Accessibility is a very slippery term. It encompasses considerations of physical access (can patients reach a facility when it is needed?), social access (is there any discrimination which prevents certain sections of the community from using the facilities that are available?), and economic access (are the facilities affordable by everyone?) (Moseley, 1979). In practice these three considerations are inter-related. As a result, whether or not patients use health care facilities is influenced by

1 factors intrinsic to the patient (e.g. the nature of the illness, education and awareness of health threatening situations),

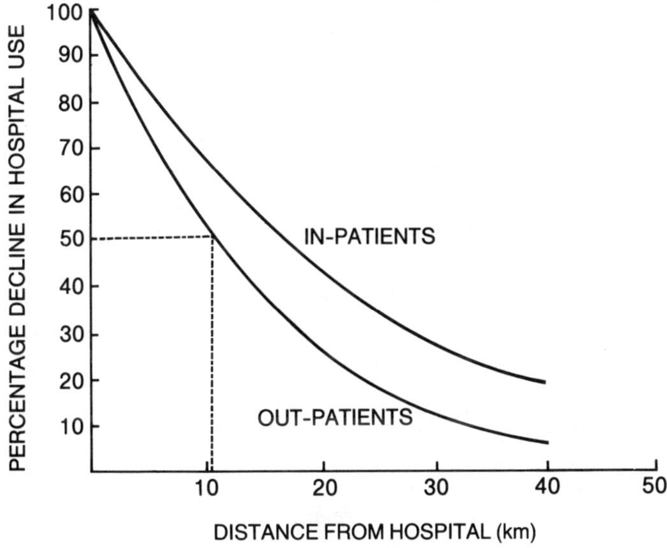

Fig. 3.5 The distance decay effect in hospital-usage patterns
Source: Walmsley (1978)

2 factors associated with the socio-economic environment (e.g. the dissemination of information about services), and
3 factors related to the health care facility as they reflect availability and accessibility (Walmsley, 1978).

Accessibility is very important in country areas. Figure 3.5, for example, shows the decline in usage made of the Coffs Harbour Hospital the further patients live from the hospital. At approximately 10 km usage has fallen away by half. Unfortunately, it is not known whether this decreased usage affects the health of patients adversely or whether close proximity to a facility encourages the abuse of resources and overuse without concomitant improvements in health. Rural residents, when asked about service provision generally, rate access to medical services as extremely important (Humphreys and Weinand, 1991).

The coastal strip around towns like Coffs Harbour is relatively densely settled compared to the inland where population densities may be less than one person per square kilometre (see Chapter 1). In such sparsely settled cases the health care delivery system is very different. Figure 3.6 shows, for example, that vast areas of western Queensland had no resident doctor in 1979. Likewise, in these areas hospitals are few and far between, so that many people are much further from health care facilities than those whose behaviour is summarized in Fig. 3.5. In some senses, then, people in areas such as the Queensland outback could be thought to have an unfairly low share of the nation's health care resources, despite the outstanding performance of the Royal Flying Doctor Service (Fig. 3.7). Of course, whether or not their share is unfair depends on what is deemed to be the appropriate basis for resource allocation. At least four alternatives present themselves:

- the egalitarian principle which seeks to make everyone's health status the same by focussing resources on the needy;
- the equal access principle which states that facilities should be equally available everywhere irrespective of need;
- the libertarian principle which argues that resource allocations should be left to market forces and doctors should be allowed to set up practice wherever they want; and
- the efficiency principle which offers the fewest number of service points so as to achieve the maximum economies of scale in the operation of the facilities at each point (Humphreys, 1985).

In Queensland the tendency of government has been to focus on cost-effectiveness rather than health effectiveness in allocating resources such as hospitals. In the words of Humphreys:

> Economic considerations such as threshold requirements, economies of scale, demand, and so on, are foremost in this allocation and distribution, but one cannot neglect the considerable importance attached to such factors as historical inertia, vested interests, local sentiments, the distribution of wealth, political pressure in terms of access to power and ability to influence decisions, and political vulnerability. (Humphreys 1985, p. 223)

Whether or not an area has a hospital depends, in part, on the political clout of its residents. Given a State government that emphasises economic development and is unwilling to regulate the locations of doctors, it is not surprising, according to Humphreys, to find an inequitable distribution of health care facilities.

In some respects the situation in relation to health care for rural residents might get worse. Humphreys (1990), for example, has pointed out that rural Australia is characterized by

1 a diminishing number of persons available within households as 'invisible carers' (because of women entering the paid workforce or taking on unpaid farm tasks),
2 a tendency for the informal neighbourhood economy (i.e. mutual help) to be replaced by contractual and/or paid relationships, and
3 a situation where voluntary charitable organizations (e.g. meals-on-wheels) are under pressure as the demand for services increases and the supply of volunteers decreases.

In this situation, rural residents are turning increasingly to formal welfare agencies. In the case of health care, this tends to mean the facilities provided by the State, largely because of the difficulty of attracting private medical practitioners to sparsely populated areas where the aggregate demand (and therefore cash flow) is limited. It is interesting, and somewhat alarming, to note therefore that some of the policies being applied by Australian governments to wind back the size of government might exacerbate the problems faced by rural Australians. In particular, some of the moves being made to allocate resources on an 'economically rational' basis might detrimentally affect country residents. For instance, the 'regionalization' and 'centralization' of health care facilities in major country towns imposes very long journeys on many individuals seeking help, the privatization of services and advocacy of the 'user-pays' principle can pose difficulties at a time of rural recession, and the tendency for medicine to become specialised means that many types of care are only available at widely separated locations (Humphreys, 1990).

Predictably, not all authorities agree that country dwellers like those of outback Queensland are under-served by health care and other facilities in a manner that is unfair. Holmes (1987), for example, is of the opinion that outback servicing is possibly no less than can be expected given logistical problems and higher delivery costs. It may even be that outback populations have lower health needs than normal in that only the fit and youthful choose to go there. In fact Holmes suggests that, on a per capita needs basis, outback populations might do rather well in terms of hospitals even if they are rather far apart. Similarly, Australia Post charges the same for its services in the outback as in the city even though the delivery costs per item in remote areas can be up to 40 times the national average, and the Queensland government supplies electricity to all consumers at an equalised charge rate regardless of supply cost. Queensland, in other words, may be a State where the interests

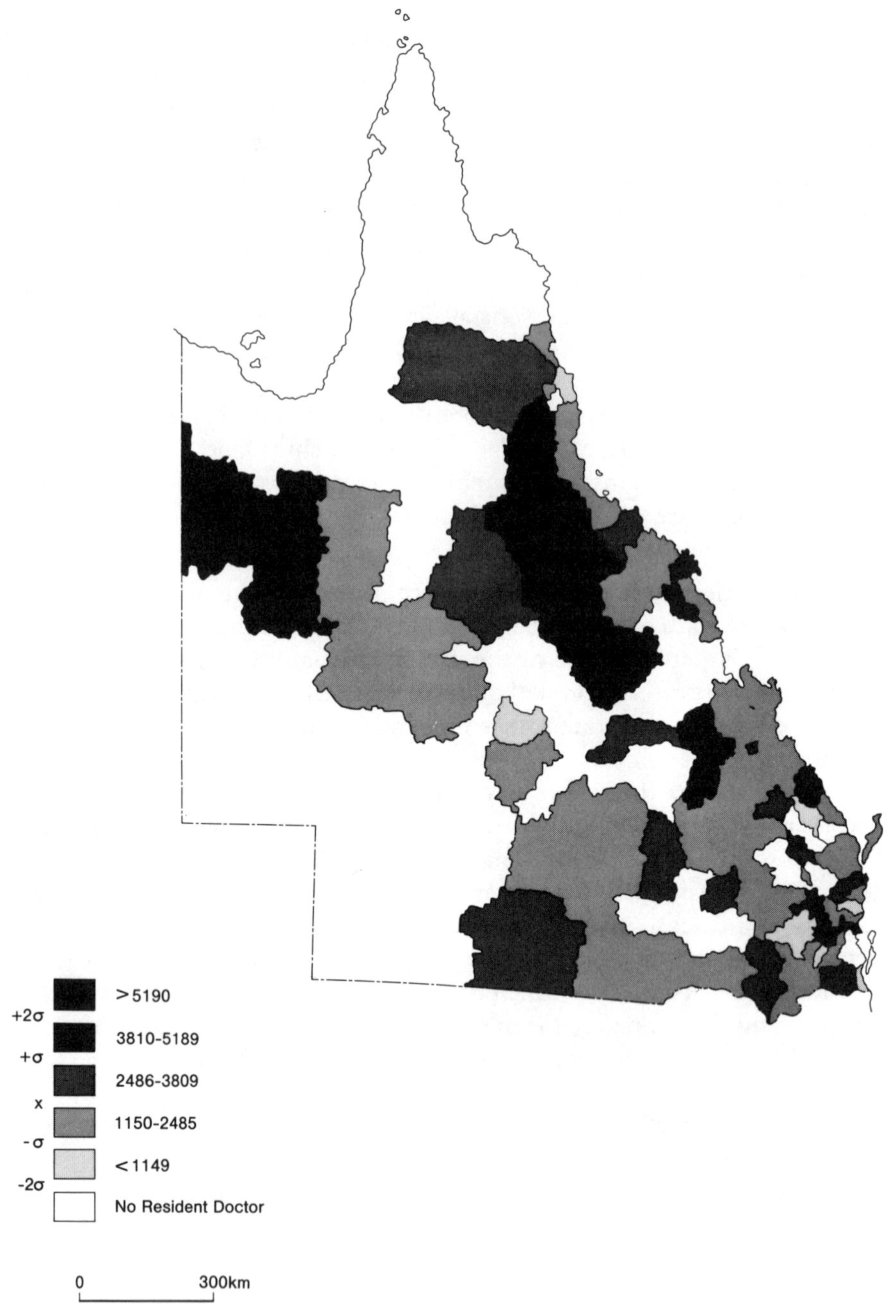

Fig. 3.6 Doctor:patient ratios in rural Queensland, 1979
Source: Humphreys (1985)

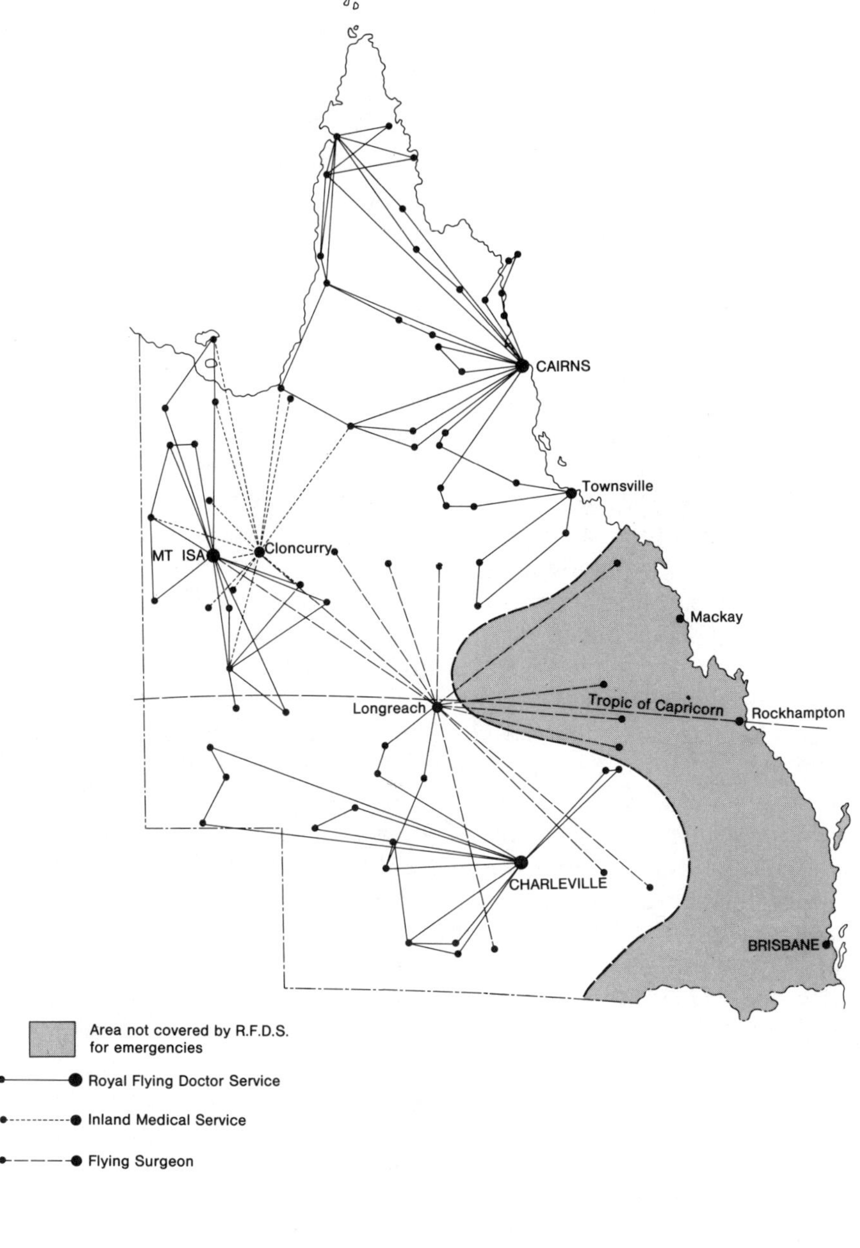

Fig. 3.7 Mobile health services in Queensland, 1980
Source: Humphreys (1985)

of remote dwellers are well looked after, possibly because malapportionment in the political system until the 1990s has given residents of the remote west and north a far greater say in parliament than their numbers alone would warrant (see Chapter 4).

Even if Queensland does not have inequity in its distribution of health care services, New South Wales most certainly did in the recent past and this fact was recognised by the State government when it moved in 1976 to change the method of allocation of hospital grants (see Eyles, 1985). Prior to that time funding had been on an incrementalist basis whereby existing hospitals tended to get a little more each year. In 1976/77 a formula was devised to take stock of both population figures in each of the State's health regions and the differential propensity of various age and sex groups to use hospitals. The following year, allowance was also made for dispersed populations and for the existence of private hospital facilities on a large scale in areas such as Sydney.

In 1979/80 the State government also 'rationalised' the distribution of hospital beds, mainly by closing hospitals in inner city areas. The net effect of all these changes was to reduce the amount of hospital funding that went to the inner city area from 37 per cent of total funds in 1975/76 to 31 per cent in 1983/84. The main beneficiary of the redistribution was not the country, however, but rather the western suburbs which saw their share of funds increase from 13.7 per cent to 20 per cent. Over the same time the funds going to non-metropolitan regions declined marginally from 36 per cent of the total budget to 35.4 per cent of the total budget (Eyles, 1985) . In other words, rural areas were called upon to make a small contribution to righting the inequities suffered by residents of one part of the metropolitan fringe.

The story of hospital funding in New South Wales suggests that the inequality in resource allocation suffered by country people may not be as great as that suffered in some areas of the city. This may be true but it is important to remember that there is one group in rural Australia that is severely disadvantaged on almost all indicators, no matter where they live. That group is the Aboriginal population. Social indicators are not available for rural as opposed to urban Aborigines but the overall figures paint a bleak picture of the state of Aboriginal well-being in 1981: life expectancy at birth was 55 (compared to 75 for all Australians); infant mortality was 26 deaths per 1000 live births (cf. 10 per 1000 for all Australians); average family income was $6000 (cf. $12 000 for all Australians); the unemployment rate was 25 per cent (cf. 6 per cent for all Australians); the proportion in education after the age of 15 was 4 per cent (cf. 24 per cent for all Australians); and the prison population was 775 per 100 000 population (cf. 67 per 100 000 for all Australians). In addition there was a high incidence of leprosy and tuberculosis among Aborigines, a major trachoma problem among communities living in desert climates, and massive abuse of alcohol. Approximately 11 per cent of Aborigines had never attended school (cf. 1 per cent of all Australians). In 1984 the retention rate of Aborigines through to Year 12 of schooling was only 13.2 per cent (admittedly up from 7.7 per cent in 1980). The percentage of Aborigines employed in the Commonwealth public service was only 0.6 per cent nationwide, well below their level of representation in the population as a whole (Department of Aboriginal Affairs, 1986) .

Even these awful statistics do not tell the whole story. They fail to capture the sense of isolation and rejection felt by many Aborigines.

In an attempt to counter this rejection, and in order to help foster a sense of identity especially among rural Aborigines, a great deal of attention has focussed in recent years on the issue of *land rights*. The argument in favour of granting land rights to Aborigines is both complex and powerful. It takes stock of the bonding that ties Aborigines to their land as well as going some way to compensating Aborigines for the dispossession they have suffered over the last 200 years (Kirk, 1986).

First moves towards land rights came with the Woodward Royal Commission in 1974. This Commission recommended the granting of land rights. Legislation followed in the Northern Territory in 1976. Under this legislation Aborigines were granted, subject to establishing their links with the land, inalienable freehold title to crown land not needed for any other purposes, plus the right of veto over mining on the land in question. Titles were to be held by Land Councils comprised of elected Aborigines. Originally, the Labor Government under Hawke pledged itself to uniform legislation along the lines of the Northern Territory model in all States. However, the government backed away from this pledge under pressure from the States and the mining industry. The States wanted to introduce their own legislation while the mining industry wanted to avoid the Aboriginal right to veto mining schemes. Indeed, some States have shown a certain reluctance when it comes to land rights legislation. The Queensland *Aboriginal Land Act 1991*, for instance, does not mention land 'rights' but rather speaks of converting existing reserves and unneeded crown land to inalienable freehold title (Preston, 1991).

Likewise, the mining industry has often claimed that Aboriginal land rights would 'paralyze' exploration, a claim which seems exaggerated despite the fact that the need to negotiate with Aboriginal groups can slow the pace of some mineral exploration (O'Faircheallaigh, 1988). The current state of play is therefore that legislation is being left to the States. As a result the amount granted varies enormously, as is shown in Fig 3.8 (Department of Aboriginal Affairs, 1986). The most progressive State seems to be South Australia which actually *negotiated* an agreement with the Pitjantjatjara people for the transfer of ownership of what had formerly been the NW Aboriginal Reserve. Under this agreement one-third of any mining royalties would go the Pitjantjatjara, one-third to the Minister for Aboriginal Affairs to be spent on South Australian Aborigines, and one-third to the State Treasury. New South Wales has also introduced pioneering legislation.

In principle, such negotiations would seem to indicate acceptance of the force of the Aboriginal claim to land. In practice, however, the approach

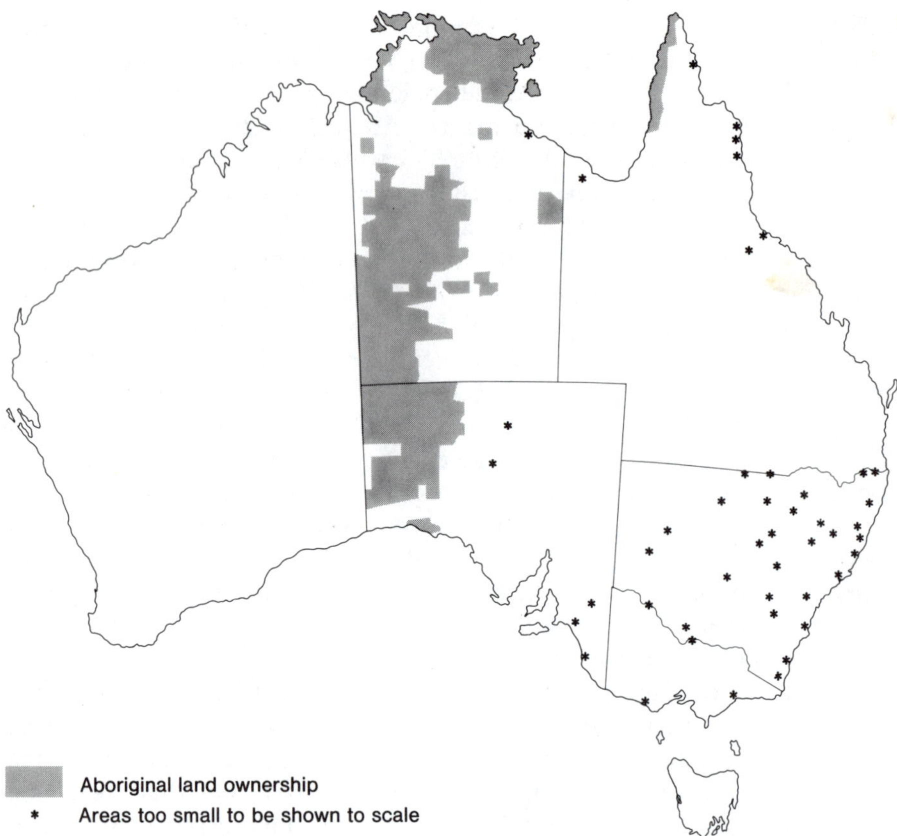

Fig. 3.8 Land owned by Aboriginal groups, under land rights legislation, 1990

adopted even in South Australia may be less than satisfactory because it tends to focus on the demonstration of *traditional* ties to land, as evidenced in sacred sites, ritual, and language. It thereby adopts an interpretation of 'Aboriginality' that does little to help those Aborigines who live outside their traditional territory and who participate extensively in the mainstream community. In other words, there is an element of inequity and competition in the way in which different Aboriginal groups are given access to land (Jacobs, 1988). This anomaly is increasingly recognised. For example, in arguing that rural land is of little value to increasing numbers of urbanized Aborigines, the New South Wales government set aside 7 per cent of the revenue from land tax for 15 years to enable Aboriginal Land Councils to buy urban land on the open market. In addition, Aborigines in that State can claim title to land that they consider to have been traditionally theirs, subject to the areas comprising vacant Crown land not needed for any other purpose. These land rights include the right to minerals (except gold, silver, coal, and petroleum) and the right of veto over prospecting and mining subject to local and regional land council decisions being ratified by the State Aboriginal Land Council (Kirk, 1986). Royalties are to be divided up such that 30 per cent goes to the local land council, 30 per cent is invested, and 40 per cent is divided between regional land councils on the basis of population. On top of this there are national moves to develop some sort of 'treaty' or 'compact' with Aborigines, moves which seem to be making slow, if any, progress (Edmunds, 1988).

The granting of land rights will go some way towards the re-establishment of an Aboriginal sense of identity. It will not, of itself, do much in a direct sense to improve the low quality of life experienced by Aborigines. This problem may be addressed by giving Aborigines more responsibility for their own affairs. In this context, it is interesting to note the commencement of the Aboriginal and Torres Strait Islander Commission in 1991, and the reformulation of elected Aboriginal representation on this Commission. Under this Commission will be 60 elected regional councils, grouped into 17 zones, each zone being represented on the Commission (the other three members of the Commission being appointed by the Federal Government: Rowse, 1990).

The other way of helping Aborigines is, of course, to develop employment initiatives because the record of Aboriginal participation in the labour market has been a poor one, especially in rural areas. Although there is potential for tourism to be harnessed to the benefit of Aboriginal communities (see Altman, 1988), the pattern of economic development in Australia has usually been one in which Aborigines have been marginalised. Where they have gained pastoral leases, external pressures have often forced Aborigines to follow the conventional development path through the establishment of commercial enterprises. These ventures have often failed because of physical isolation, lack of management skills, and the demands for reciprocity that are common in Aboriginal society (Young, 1988). Where there has been mineral development, Aborigines tend to have been ignored and neglected. Howitt summed this up well in his description of the Pilbara.

> The booming regional economy produced local extremes of wealth and poverty, characterised by overt consumerism in the new towns and dire poverty in the Aboriginal population. These patterns were reinforced rather than redressed by various state and federal government policies. Programs ostensibly aimed at meeting basic Aboriginal needs were typically restricted to symptomatic rather than structural issues, addressing delinquency rather than powerlessness; housing rather than dispossession; literacy rather than alienation; alcoholism rather than dependency (Howitt 1989, p. 167).

Where there have been employment schemes, these tend to have been starved of funds (Sanders, 1988). All this suggests that levels of well-being can only really be improved by action on the part of government, positive discrimination that gives a disproportionately large share of society's resources to the needy. It is important to understand, therefore, the scope of government power in Australia and, in particular, the jurisdiction of the various tiers of government (see Chapter 4).

The Role of the Government

AUSTRALIA is part of a 'turbulent' world. Change is the norm in most walks of life. Uncertainty is an everyday occurrence. From Australia's point of view, the changes with which the nation has to cope are both exogenous and endogenous. That is to say, some of them have their origins in events and happenings overseas, whereas others arise from forces that are operating within the country. Among the endogenous (i.e. domestic) changes that confront Australia, one of the most prominent is the trend towards an increasingly aged population. This trend is such that, by 2021, about 16 per cent of the population will be aged 65 or more, assuming no significant changes to the birth rate, the death rate, and the rate of immigration. This obviously has implications for the costing of welfare, pension and superannuation programs (see Chapter 3). Another change which faces Australia centres on the increasingly multicultural nature of the population. This trend is likely to continue despite the misgivings of Blainey (1984) and others about the rate of Asian immigration reached by the mid-1980s.

Family structures also are changing with over a quarter of a million single parent families presently existing. Of course, these endogenous changes are not immutable. The birth rate could rise, the migrant intake could be altered by the government of the day, and the nuclear family might experience a resurgence in popularity. Nevertheless, the fact remains that the trends that are presently in evidence look like continuing and ensuring that Australia at the turn of the 21st century will be a different place from what it is today. Such endogenous changes, although important, may however be dwarfed in the extent and nature of their impact by exogenous changes that stem from events and personalities overseas and therefore beyond the control of Australia's business and political leaders. Examples of changes which have occurred in the recent past, and which have led to a degree of 'turbulence' for Australia, are easy to find. Perhaps the most often cited was the quadrupling of oil prices of OPEC in the period 1973/74. In Australia (and elsewhere) this triggered inflation, contributed to a wages explosion (because of centralized wage fixing pegged to the consumer price index), and stifled whatever incentive there was for innovation and structural adjustment, notably in manufacturing industry. At the same time, of course, it stimulated interest in alternative energy sources, notably coal. On the face of it, this worked to Australia's advantage. Unfortunately, however, domestic capital for such resource exploitation was often not available in the amounts and at the price required with a result that many companies looked for investment funds overseas. This has contributed to a situation where Australia's net foreign debt increased from a figure equal to 8 per cent GDP in 1979/80 to a figure equal to about 33 per cent in the early 1990s (Foster and Stewart, 1991). Another factor to impact significantly on Australia's economy and society is, of course, technological change. Australia is very much a 'technological colony', in that it relies very heavily on imports for technological innovation (Hill and Johnston, 1983). This means that the activities of overseas firms and research organizations will have a big influence in forcing Australians to develop new attitudes to work (e.g. job sharing, early retirement) in order to cope with the diminishing aggregate demand for labour that will almost inevitably follow the introduction of hi-tech (Jones, 1982). Further examples of exogenous changes creating a 'turbulent' environment for Australia are easy to find (Walmsley, 1990). The collapse of communism in Eastern Europe and the demise of the Soviet Union are glaring examples with important ramifications in terms of trade. The continued rise to economic prominence of the so-called East Asian 'tigers' is another example. However, instead of looking for further examples of change, it is important to look at the implications of these changes.

The main implication from the 'turbulence' created by endogenous and exogenous changes is a heightened degree of uncertainty surrounding the appropriateness of both government policy and business strategy (Walmsley, 1990). This uncertainty manifests itself in many ways (see Emery and Trist, 1973 for a full discussion of 'turbulence'). For instance, the unplanned consequences of action may be far-reaching and yet almost entirely unseen. By way of example, advocacy of family reunion as a basis for immigration led, eventually, to the mid-1980s backlash against Asian immigration. Likewise, the 'fast-tracking' of development projects in order to ensure completion dates that meet with political approval can lead to situations where there is a divergence between private benefits and public costs, with 'the government' often being called upon to remedy the resultant problems (see Mercer, 1991).

At the same time, 'turbulence' can lead to a deepening interdependence between economic and non-economic aspects of life. Nowhere is this better seen than in the way in which the rural recession of the late 1980s and 1990s, although primarily economic in origin, had profound effects on social relationships in rural areas. Finally, and perhaps most importantly, 'turbulence' encourages the growth of large organizations, both in the public and the private sectors. After all, an organization needs to be big in order to monitor a complex situation effectively. And bigness also enables the risk inherent in coping with uncertainty to be spread, either by internalising many of the services needed within the organisation in question (thereby obviating the need to rely on other firms) or by spreading interests and investments over a wide portfolio.

Ultimately governments, like other organizations, have to respond to 'turbulence'. Generally, they do this by increasing the scope of government activity. It is very common, in the face of 'turbulence', for people from all sorts of walks of life to urge governments to 'do something' in order to reduce the uncertainty which confronts decision makers. Thus we find that manufacturers in Australia call upon governments to protect them from the uncertainties surrounding production by imposing tariffs and quotas. The 1990s recession in Victoria, for example, has seen pleas from the State government to the federal government to slow down the pace of tariff reduction so as to give Victoria a breathing space in which to restructure. In the rural arena, too, calls for government action are both common and effective. For example, governments have intervened in the past to facilitate international trading (e.g. Wheat Board, Grain Handling Authorities), to reduce uncertainty for primary producers (e.g. the activities of the Wool Commission in setting floor prices throughout the 1970s and 1980s) and in maintaining environmental quality (e.g. Prickly Pear Destruction Board, Tick Boards).

This is not to say, however, that government activity is always appropriate. After all, floor prices for wool were abandoned in 1991. Sometimes the operation of government can be unwieldy. Government can in fact become too big for the small things in life (such as counselling and help to the needy) and yet too small for the big things in life (witness the Australian government's impotence in the face of commodity price collapses). At the same time government can become ineffective through being fragmented. Bureaucracies, for example, tend to focus on particular issues (such as the old, the young, the unemployed, the sick) without always effectively handling the interrelationships between the issues under attention (Walmsley, 1980b). This problem is particularly acute in a federal system such as Australia's where there is inevitably a compartmentalization of responsibility between the different tiers of government. Moreover, governments, often for reasons of political expediency, and with an eye on the next election, tend to gloss over problems and tend to look at symptoms rather than causes. It is very common, for instance, to hear politicians argue about the meaning of minor shifts in the overall level of unemployment but much less common to hear them say anything with any great insight about the true causes of unemployment. Likewise many politicians are happy to give lip-service to tariff protection without realising what such a policy might do to Australia's relationship with the rapidly developing nations of Asia. It is good and well to hope that such nations will import Australian primary production but such a policy might be short-sighted until such time as Australia is prepared to reciprocate by allowing greater access to our market for their manufactured items.

Despite the inappropriateness of much government action in the face of 'turbulence', it is nevertheless to governments that many people turn for assistance. The 'do something' mentality is very strong. Indeed, it is this mentality that very much lies behind the growth of government activity to the point where many advanced western nations can be characterised as having 'Big Government'. The question must be asked, therefore, as to whether or not Australia has yet reached the stage of having 'Big Government' and what, if anything, Australian governments can be expected to do to help the nation cope better with 'turbulence'. These are profound questions that will occupy the rest of this Chapter. Exactly how governments cope is, of course, influenced to some degree by which party is in power, given that Australian political parties differ, if only in a relatively minor way, in ideology and philosophy. Perhaps more important than party political influences on what governments do to cope with uncertainty is the very *structure* of government. This structure is important, above all, because it is far more enduring than party policy. The jurisdiction of the Commonwealth and State governments in Australia is, for example, set out in a Constitution that has proved very resilient to change, only 8 of 42 attempts to change the Constitution by referendum having been successful in a period of more than ninety years (Commonwealth of Australia, 1988b; 1991b). Over the same time political parties have come and gone. However, before embarking on a discussion of what governments can do in Australia, it is appropriate to set such comments in context by reflecting on the 'theory of the state' as it exists in contemporary political writings.

Theories of the State

The term 'State' encompasses the whole apparatus whereby a government exercises its power. It includes not only elected politicians (together with the parties into which they organised) but also the various arms of the bureaucracy, an army of public servants, and a whole battery of rules, regulations, laws, conventions and policies. Predictably, there have been a great many theories of the State proposed by researchers interested in the field of government and administration and only some of the more major ones will be discussed here (for a fuller discussion see Clark and Dear, 1984).

Although opinions vary, there are three generally accepted functions of 'the State':

- the promotion of macro-economic goals such as full employment and economic growth;
- the promotion of a just distribution of income, goods and services; and
- the provision of those services that are not supplied, or are supplied inefficiently, by 'the market' (Musgrave and Musgrave, 1980).

Of these, the first and the second functions are usually fulfilled by the central government while the third function is often the responsibility of local government (e.g. the provision of roads and parks).

Given this definition of the role of the State, it is perhaps not surprising that one of the most commonly cited theories of the State is the one that suggests that its role is to act as a supplier of 'public goods'. In this sense, a 'public good' is something consumed by all members of a society in such a way that its consumption by one person does not detract from its consumption by other people. Clean air and defence are two obvious examples of public goods. According to this theory, there are a great many goods and services that cannot be provided by the private sector (or are provided inefficiently and in such a manner that some sections of the community are not served) and it is therefore the role of the State to provide these goods and services. Examples are to be found in the provision of police forces, fire brigades, schools, hospitals, and national parks. In many cases some of these facilities are provided by the private sector, at least in part. In those cases the role of the State is to enter the field of service provision in order to ensure that a certain standard is maintained. In principle, this might be a rationale that can be advanced for the provision of public hospitals.

A second theory views the State as a regulator and facilitator. In other words, according to this view, it is the role of the State to ensure that there exists fair and open competition in the private sector. It does this by having anti-monopoly legislation and a battery of regulations relating to fair trading, advertising standards, minimum wages and working standards. In short, this theory sees the private sector as the principal vehicle whereby wealth and prosperity are created, and it is therefore the role of the State to ensure that the private sector functions properly and efficiently. Additionally, according to this theory, the government can introduce budget deficits in order to 'prime' the economy, thereby stimulating consumption, economic growth, employment, and the private sector generally. In short, although the market might be a very good mechanism for the allocation of resources, it might not necessarily be able to achieve optimal allocation or full employment and, as a result, it is necessary for the government to step in (Clark and Dear, 1984; p. 19).

A third theory of the State sees it as a 'social engineer'. This may seem a strange term. It represents an analogy with civil engineering. Just as a civil engineer designs and builds roads and bridges, so the State can be thought of, in a metaphorical sense at least, as an agency concerned with the design and building of society. The design comes through the visions of political leaders and the building comes through policy initiatives. The exemplar of the social engineering view of the State is probably to be found in the social democracies of Scandinavia where the State takes an active role in politics, economics, and society rather than merely facilitating growth. The usual role for the state in such circumstances is in the field of reducing socio-economic imbalances within society and in helping disadvantaged groups. The State, in other words, is interested in what society ought to be, not what it is (Clark and Dear, 1984; p. 20). The focus of attention, then, is not on the operation of market forces but on the *outcome* of such forces, assessed in terms of justice and fairness. This, of course, raises the question of what bases should be used for assessing 'fairness'. Should the State adopt an egalitarian principle that focuses on the needy and tries to bring them up to the same level of service provision or well-being as the rest of society? Or should the activities of the State promote equal access to facilities by having government services available everywhere irrespective of need? And should both these ideals be blended with considerations of efficiency and the minimization of costs (Humphreys, 1985)? Obviously the answers to these questions will vary enormously from case to case.

Yet another theory of the State sees it as an umpire or arbiter whose main rationale for existence is in the resolution of conflict. According to this view, the main role of the State is to defend the rights of individuals and of groups. It does this by appointing judges, by overseeing the legal system, by prosecuting cases in the public interest, by providing legal aid, by guaranteeing free speech, and by introducing equal opportunity and anti-discrimination legislation. In addition, of course, the State invariably sets up electoral procedures whereby the will of the people can be translated into a political force. In not all cases, however, is the State successful as an umpire. Legal systems, for example, can become so cumbersome and costly that the poor miss out and the electoral system can be less than effective if significant groups of people are disenfranchised or if there is gerrymandering or malapportionment.

To all these theories of the State, for the sake of completeness, should be added the Marxist or neo-Marxist view. According to this perspective, the main role of the State is to convince those ruled of the legitimacy of the rulers, thereby ensuring their continuance of power. Since the rulers are essentially the owners of capital, the State contrives to facilitate the continued accumulation of capital. It also seeks to perpetuate the class system and, in particular, the reproduction of the working class. It is therefore in the interests of both the State and capital to have an education system that leaves some people poorly trained and therefore forced to accept low paid jobs. Likewise, the provision of public housing helps facilitate the reproduction of the working class. Of course to talk about a Marxist theory of the state as if it were a single holistic body of reasoning is to do a great injustice to what is a very wide spectrum of opinion.

One failing of much Marxist writing on the theory of the State is that it says very little about the State as it exists at the level of local government. This level of State activity tends to be overlooked entirely or viewed simply as a microcosm of the State as a whole. Much the same is true of other theoretical writings on the theory of the State. The view of the State as a provider of public goods, for instance, very often fails to do justice to the fact that the function of the 'local State' is substantially different from the function of the central State. Something of an exception is, however, to be seen in the writings of Bennett (1980) who has argued that the needs, costs, and preferences for public goods, as well as the ability to pay for them, vary as a function of geographical location with a result that area-specific needs and preferences are perhaps best catered for by local authorities. Such local authorities promote a sense of community while at the same time encouraging both democracy and political stability. According to Bennett (1980; pp. 279–81), such positive features generally outweigh the inertia, parochialism, economic inefficiency, and inequity in service provision that can result from a large number of geographically fragmented local authorities. Several other writers have also stressed that the local State is not merely a scaled-down version of the nation State but rather has importance in its own right (Dear, 1981). Prominent among these is Cockburn (1977) who has drawn a distinction between the central State which contributes to capitalist *production* (by facilitating the accumulation of capital) and the local State which contributes to capitalist *reproduction* (by focussing on the provision of schools and housing estates which perpetuate the class system). According to this view, the class struggle in capitalism is not just at the point of production (e.g. factories); it is also evident at the point of reproduction (e.g. schools, housing estates) where individuals are conditioned to accept their role in the overall political economy. In this sense, then, the local State is part of 'the social factory' in that its service provision (e.g. housing, education, health, social policy) conditions people to think of themselves as *clients* of the State, thereby legitimizing and perpetuating the State (Walmsley, 1984b).

Cockburn's writing relates, of course, to Britain where the functions and powers of local government are very different from those that exist in Australia. This point therefore raises the question of how relevant the various theories of the State are in the Australian context. There can be no simple answer, because theories in social science are only tools designed to aid the understanding of problems under investigation. Theories in social science should not therefore be viewed as being right or wrong: rather they should be viewed as being more or less useful. And in this light, almost all of the theories discussed above offer some sort of insight into the role of the State in Australia. The State in Australia, for example, supplies public goods (e.g. defence), it acts as a regulator and facilitator (e.g. macro-economic policies designed to stimulate growth), it behaves as an umpire (e.g. ensuring that both business and unions abide by 'the laws of the game'), and it is something of a social engineer in that it seeks, in some senses, to bring about a just distribution of income, goods, and services. Therefore, instead of pursuing some overarching (and probably elusive) theory of the State that has relevance to Australia, it might be more instructive to look at just exactly what governments do in Australia. An appropriate point to begin such an inquiry is with the growth of 'Big Government'.

The emergence of 'Big Government' in Australia

Claims that government in Australia is 'too big' were heard throughout the 1980s. Indeed such claims have been part of the rhetoric of the so-called 'new right' for some years, both in Australia and overseas (Antcliff, 1988). Over time, however, the idea that government might be 'too big' gained wider acceptance and won converts among those with no sympathy for the 'new right' perspective, notably key figures in the Australian Labor Party (see Head, 1988). This is largely because the evidence of growth in the size of government is both easy to find and striking. For example, the combined current account and capital account expenditure of the Commonwealth government increased from a figure equal to 23 percent of GDP in 1972/73 to a figure equivalent to 31 per cent of GDP in 1984/85 (see Foster and Stewart, 1991).This is a sharp rise which occurred despite an ostensible brake on government expenditure during the Fraser administration (1975–1983). Part of the increase can be attributed to the payment of salaries to government employees who had increased greatly in number.

Over the twenty year period 1961–1981, for example, the number of public servants in Australia increased by 88 per cent at a time when the population itself grew by only 41 per cent (Walmsley, 1990). For the most part this increase occurred at the level of the States which are by far and away the major employers of public servants. For instance, of the country's 1 668 886 public servants revealed by the 1986 census, 30 per cent were employed by the Commonwealth government, 61 per cent by the State governments, and 9 per cent by local government authorities (Office of Local Government, 1984).

The Hawke administration, on coming to power in 1983, made three promises to the electorate:

- that there would be no increase in government expenditure as a percentage of GDP;

- that there would be no increase in the government's income tax take as a percentage of GDP; and
- that the budget deficit would be decreased.

The Hawke administration sought, in other words, to freeze the growth of government activity, albeit at a level that was historically high by Australian standards. This shows that the Hawke administration recognized as very real the concern in the electorate about the emergence of 'Big Government'. Interesting, too, is the fact that the Hawke administration converted this concern into action. Thanks mainly to the initiative of the Treasurer, Keating, Commonwealth budgets in the late 1980s recorded a surplus rather than a deficit. In short, the Commonwealth spent less than it received from revenue, a situation very much at odds with the big spending days of the 1970s. It is no surprise, then, that the number of government employees increased only slightly more quickly than the population as a whole over the census period 1981–1986 (8.8 per cent as opposed to 7.0 per cent). Nor is it surprising to find that Commonwealth spending as a proportion of GDP had fallen to below 24 per cent by 1990. In short, the Hawke administration prevented further increases in the size of government and even, for a time, engineered cutbacks in some areas.

The concern expressed both in the electorate and by the Hawke administration about the size of government and the success of the government in tackling the problem, raises a question as to why government activity had grown to the extent where it could be considered alarming. Three contributing reasons stand out:

1 As the world economic and political order has become more complex, so bigger government has become necessary in order to ensure accurate monitoring of world events. By way of a simple example, as Australia's trade has become more complex (in both composition and direction) so the bureaucracy concerned with trade has grown.
2 The nature of the demands placed on the government has changed over the years. In particular, people now expect the government to provide services that were not considered part of the government domain twenty years ago. Examples are to be seen in child care centres, equal opportunity legislation, environmental protection, national parks, help for single parent families, and special programs for the unemployed.
3 The growth of 'Big Government' has come about because of what can be termed 'disjointed incrementalism'.

This is a term coined by the American political scientist Lindblom (1968) to refer to the tendency for there to be an incremental creep in the scope of government activity in a political system centred around two competing parties. In highly simplified terms, the argument is as follows: if Party A is in office, Party B's best chance of winning an election is by being seen to offer the electorate something not presently offered by Party A. Very often that 'something' will be a new government service. Assume, therefore, that Party B wins office. Party A's best chance of returning to office is then to adopt the same tactic and to try to offer the electorate something not offered by Party B. If this tactic is successful, Party A will return to power. Party A is however unlikely to revoke the initiatives introduced by Party B for fear of alienating part of the electorate. Each election, in other words, is likely to result in an incremental creep in government activity. The fact that the increments are dictated by political expediency (i.e. what the electorate will tolerate or wants at a particular point in time), means that the creep in the scope of government activity will be disjointed rather than part of some overall plan. Lindblom's ideas are deceptively simple and yet widely appropriate in that they describe very well what has happened in countries where 'consensus' politics dominate (in other words, countries where the major political parties agree generally on the scope of government policy). However, even the so-called 'conviction' politicians of the 1970s and 1980s (e.g. Thatcher, Reagan, and Fraser), no matter how committed they might have been to the rhetoric of 'small government', were unable to break away from the tendency for incremental creeps in the extent of government activity. Indeed, it is interesting to note that it was Australia's main 'consensus' government (under Hawke) that cut back the size of government, not the conservative Fraser administration that was ostensibly committed to smaller government.

The emergence of 'Big Government' in Australia manifested itself in many ways. For example, the increasing demands made on governments in the 1970s for social policy led to major expansions of government expenditure. Spending on the six items of education, health, social security and welfare, housing and community amenities, recreation and related cultural activities, and law and order increased from the equivalent of 7.8 per cent of GDP in 1971 to the equivalent of 13.4 per cent of GDP in 1981 (Walmsley, 1984a). The 1970s were not however a time of uniform advance in the scope of government activity. The biggest 'leaps forward' came in the early part of the decade when the Australian Labor Party came to power after a period of 23 years in opposition. Table 3.4 shows the mean annual real per capita increase in spending on three 'social' issues for the Whitlam, Fraser, and Hawke years (in other words, the increase after allowing for both inflation and population growth). The growth rates in spending in the early 1970s under Whitlam were staggering. The rates of change in the early 1980s were very different, with growth being restricted to health care.

A second manifestation of growth of 'Big Government' in Australia was to be seen in the proliferation of government rules and regulations. There are now few areas of economic or social activity that are not highly constrained by government. Over the period 1959–79 the Commonwealth and State governments passed 16 631 Acts and no less than 32 351 Statutory Rules. More particularly, in the 1970s there were 40 per cent more laws and 62 per cent more rules passed than in the 1960s. The cost to the private sector of complying with business regulations was put at $4 billion dollars as long ago as 1978/79 (70 per cent of these regulations being imposed by State governments) (McLachlan, 1985). Of course, many of these regulations have overwhelming support in the community (e.g. environmental and consumer protection legislation). Their existence merely serves to establish the legitimacy of some elements of the trend to 'Big Government'. The fact remains however that, in spreading its tentacles, government inevitably increased in size.

A third and final manifestation of the rise of 'Big Government' was the tendency for commissions of inquiry to be set up whenever a contentious issue arises (Walmsley, 1980b). Although often a substitute for government action, such commissions nevertheless represent a further legitimization of the extending field of government influence. In the 1990s, government itself has become the focus of attention in such commissions of inquiry (notably in Victoria, Western Australia, and South Australia).

The growth of 'Big Government' in Australia has been closely associated with the emergence of what are known as QUANGOs. Originally this term was coined to describe quasi-non-government organizations but nowadays its meaning has been corrupted somewhat so that it is commonly used to denote government organizational arrangements other than ministerial departments (Wettenhall, 1983). The first QUANGOs were set up, both in Australia and overseas, in the hope that they could be administered more efficiently if free from political pressure. In the strict sense, then, QUANGOs were not set up by governments although they often got funding from that quarter and certainly performed a public duty. Examples of such true QUANGOs are to be found in organizations such as the Australian Institute of Urban Studies and the Handicapped Citizens Association ACT Inc (Wettenhall, 1983).

More recently, there have emerged administrative arrangements that might be more appropriately labelled QUAGOs in that they are simply quasi-government organizations that involve the statutory delegation of powers by the government or the parliament to appointed bodies not directly answerable through the electoral process. Examples are to be seen in QANTAS, Australian Airlines, and the Wheat Board (Wettenhall, 1983). For the Commonwealth government alone there were over 200 such statutory authorities in 1977/78, employing 271 000 people and having fixed assets of $2 225 million and an income of $6 474 million. Such authorities are, in other words, a significant economic force, directly or indirectly owned by the taxpayer, and yet outside the departmental structure of responsibility and accountability. Moreover, many QUANGOs and QUAGOs operate under monopolistic or oligopolistic conditions created for them by parliament (Wettenhall, 1983).

Despite the growth in government spending and the emergence of QUANGOs, and despite the seeming desire to cut back on the size of government in the late 1980s, government in Australia is perhaps not 'big' by international standards. Table 4.1, for example, shows government final consumption expenditure as a percentage of GDP for a group of advanced western nations together with Indonesia, Malaysia, and the Phillipines. Clearly, a concern for controlling the size of government seems widespread, as evidenced by the generally smaller size of government in 1988 as opposed to 1983. Clearly, too, the size of government in Australia, as measured by current expenditure, is less than in most comparable nations. Perhaps, therefore, concern over Big Government in Australia stems not so much from the amount that is spent as from the rate of growth in that spending in the 1970s and, moreover, from the source of the revenue used to pay for that spending.

Australia has become increasingly reliant on personal income tax as a source of government funds. In particular, the Commonwealth government has become increasingly reliant on Pay-As-You-Earn (PAYE) taxpayers (basically wage and salary earners). In 1972/73 this group contributed 37.4 percent of the Commonwealth's total taxation revenue; ten years later, in 1982/83, this figure had risen to 46.1 per cent (Fiedler, 1983). Overall, all forms of personal income tax, as a percentage of total taxation receipts, have risen from 48 per cent in 1972/73 to 55 per cent in 1989/90. As a result Australia possibly has a narrower tax base, and one reliant more on personal income tax, than is the case in most other OECD countries (Table 4.2). In part, this reflects Australia's lack of a broadly based consumption tax. Additionally, Australia has a relatively high level of taxation on corporate profits.

Table 4.1 An international comparison of the size of government activity

	Government final consumption expenditure as a percentage of GDP	
	1983	*1988*
Sweden	28.5	26.0
United Kingdom	22.0	19.9
Canada	21.0	18.8
West Germany	20.0	19.5
USA	19.3	18.3
Malaysia	17.9	14.3
Netherlands	17.7	15.7
New Zealand	17.0	17.1
Australia	16.7	16.8
France	16.4	18.6
Indonesia	10.9	9.1
Japan	10.2	9.4
Philippines	8.0	8.8

Source: Calculated from United Nations (1986; 1990)

Table 4.2 An international comparison of the sources of government revenue

	Tax revenue as percentage of GDP				
	Personal income	*Corporate profit*	*Property & wealth*	*Goods & services*	*Other indirect*
Australia	14	7	5	0	17
Canada	13	6	6	0	17
Japan	7	15	6	2	6
Indonesia	1	16	1	6	4
Malaysia	5	3	0	0	15
New Zealand	18	7	6	17	10
Singapore	5	0	4	0	13
UK	9	9	9	12	10
USA	10	5	6	0	10
West Germany	11	4	2	12	8

Source: Calculated from data in *Australian Financial Review*, 10 February 1992

The nature of government in Australia

The size of government activity in Australia is remarkable, given that government, in the western sense of that word, only began 200 years ago when Phillip took possession of Van Diemen's Land, and that part of the continent of Australia that was east of 135 degrees E, under the name New South Wales. Since that time there have emerged 15 houses of parliament (unicameral legislatures in Queensland (which abolished its upper house in 1922), the ACT, and the Northern Territory, and bicameral legislatures in the five other States and the Commonwealth — see Maddox, 1985). The date of the first settlement in each Colony is given in Table 1.3 together with the date at which the Colony was formally recognised for the first time and the date at which responsible government was granted. Clearly, responsible government did not reach the Australian Colonies until the 1850s, some 70 years after the first European settlement. Before that time, however, attempts had been made to foster local government.

Until the 1840s Australia was ruled more or less directly from the Colonial Office in London with executive powers being vested in appointed Governors. The cost of such a system of administration soon became a burden on the British exchequer, and consequently attempts were made to foster local government in an attempt to get a local financial contribution to the running costs of the Colonies (McPhail and Walmsley, 1975). In particular, it was hoped that local property taxes would pay for half the cost of the police force (Jones, 1981). The first local government initiatives occurred in Adelaide in 1840 and in Sydney and Melbourne in 1842. Inevitably these moves were doomed to failure, given that local government had no clear goals, had to rely on inexperienced participants, and lacked a secure financial footing.

Additionally, local government as a whole was opposed by pastoralists who saw their interests as being under threat, by disenfranchised former convicts, and by all those who thought that services should be provided from consolidated revenue rather than from local taxes (Power *et al.* 1981).

As a result local government grew but slowly and mainly as a result of a permissive system whereby local residents could petition the Governor for their area to be designated as a local government authority. The financial inducements to petitioning were, however, for the most part slight and it is not surprising that, by 1875, only 25 percent of New South Wales' population lived in incorporated areas. In Queensland by 1878, only 20 per cent of the population were in incorporated areas (Jones, 1981). In both these States, in consequence, local government was not established on any widespread scale until the respective State governments imposed incorporating legislation 'from above' some years after Federation.

Things were rather different in Victoria and South Australia. In both of these areas there was a much stronger groundswell of support of local government. Victoria, because of its smaller size, its denser settlement pattern, and its experiences during the 'gold rush era', had 85 per cent of its population incorporated as early as 1864 (Jones, 1981). In contrast, South Australia, because of the sparseness of its settlement, still has 85 per cent of its *area* unincorporated and administered by the Outback Areas Community Development Trust. In Western Australia local government, like settlement as a whole, tended to appear on the scene rather later than elsewhere. It also tended to blend the 'imposed' systems of New South Wales and Queensland with the 'grass roots' systems of Victoria and South Australia. Tasmania was different again, having a local government system that grew out of police districts imposed during the Colony's early convict history.

By the end of the nineteenth century it was already apparent that local government was going to be a relatively minor component of the overall system of government in Australia. This weakness was exacerbated with Federation. Local government was not involved formally in the Constitutional Conventions that led to the establishment of the Australian federal state, nor was it mentioned in the Constitution which laid down the structure of government within the country. Instead, local government was relegated to a relatively minor role and fragmented into well over 1000 authorities.

The blend of federalism adopted in Australia in 1901 was curious. Australia exhibited none of the usual bases for federalism: there was no heterogeneity among the population and there were no major economic differences between the units that became the States (Spann, 1979). Rather, federalism caught on in Australia because it provided a way of dividing a vast territory into administrative units close to the people while at the same time maintaining a national government (Maddox, 1982). These advantages were generally thought to outweigh the waste and duplication, not to mention the opportunity for buck-passing, that arises whenever different governments have jurisdiction at the same place or, in functional terms, over similar matters (see Painter, 1988).

Federalism was not adopted in Australia because of some groundswell of public opinion. Its emergence owed rather more to the endeavours of a few enthusiasts who were able to sell their ideas. The curious nature of Australian federalism springs mainly from its attempt to combine the political traditions of Westminster and Washington (Galligan, 1980). In particular, federalism combined the notion of *responsible government* (borrowed from Westminster and centred on the idea of one dominant chamber of parliament where Ministers are answerable for their departments) with the notion of a federal *bicameral legislature* (borrowed from Washington and centred on the idea of two chambers of approximately equal power). Clearly, this arrangement means that the machinery of government can be deadlocked whenever the Senate chooses to veto the actions of a government centred in the House of Representatives. Such deadlock can often only be resolved by a double dissolution of parliament.

The relative jurisdictions of the Commonwealth and State governments are laid down in the Constitution. Local government authorities get their power from separate pieces of State legislation and thus their jurisdiction varies from State to State. Some idea of how responsibility for different items of government expenditure is divided up between the three tiers of government in Australia can be obtained from Table 4.3. In essence, the Commonwealth government is responsible for defence and foreign policy, national economic policy, the cash payment of pensions and benefits, and those industrial and commercial affairs that affect more than one State. State governments, in contrast, are responsible for social services such as schools, hospitals, welfare services, the police and prisons, town planning, and housing. Local government is primarily concerned with physical infrastructure (e.g. kerbs and gutters, roads, sewerage) and with recreation facilities (notably parks and

Table 4.3 Public authority outlay, 1987–88

	Percentage spent by:		
Item	*Commonwealth government*	*State governments*	*Local governments*
Defence	100	0	0
Health	12	86	2
Education	5	95	0
Social security and welfare	52	38	10
Fuel and energy	4	83	13
Recreation and culture	28	38	34
Housing & community development	8	80	12

Source: Calculated from Australian Bureau of Statistics (1989; 1990)

playing fields). The actual emphasis given to social services by the States varies of course from one case to the next.

Table 4.4 reveals, for instance, that New South Wales spent a greater share of its total current and capital outlay on social services than did the other States in 1987/88. Queensland devoted the smallest share to social issues. It is unwise, of course, to read too much into the figures for any one year. Moreover, in the case of the States, the total outlay is dominated by current account expenditure. In 1987/88, for example, 72 per cent of the State's outlay (including items not shown in Table 4.4) was current expenditure and 28 per cent capital expenditure. In the case of the Commonwealth government, current expenditure was even more dominant: 92 per cent as opposed to 8 per cent. For local government, however, the pattern was different again, largely on account of local government's involvement in the provision of facilities such as roads, and capital expenditure amounted to 47 per cent of total local government outlay.

The relative jurisdictions of the Commonwealth and State governments as set out in the Constitution are very difficult to change. In fact the only way that the Constitution can be changed is by a referendum which must be passed by a majority of voters in a majority of States and by a majority overall (an arrangement devised to protect the interests of the States with a small population relative to the interests of New South Wales and Victoria). This reluctance to change the Constitution is one of the reasons why the recommendations of the Constitutional Commission, set up to review the 1901 document, met with such a cool reception. Although the centenary of Federation is approaching, there is little sign as yet of any concerted moves towards constitutional change. Likewise, the boundaries of the States as defined at Federation (on the basis on earlier Colonial boundaries) have proved resistant to change. 'New state movements' in Capricornia, the Riverina, and New England have come to nothing. This rigidity of federal constitutional structures is striking and contrasts very markedly with the flexibility that has characterised the Commonwealth–State financial relations.

Table 4.4 State spending on social policy, 1987–88

% current and capital spending devoted to:	*NSW*	*Vic*	*Qld*	*SA*	*WA*	*Tas*
General public service	7	7	7	6	8	9
Education	36	33	29	33	28	29
Health	29	23	18	24	22	23
Social security & welfare	3	2	2	3	3	1
Housing & community amenities	4	3	2	4	2	4
Environmental protection	4	3	0	1	2	0
Recreation	6	2	1	3	2	3

Source: Calculated from Australian Bureau of Statistics (1989)

Intergovernmental financial relations

At Federation the Commonwealth took over exclusive control of customs and excise duty which to that time had provided the former Colonies with about three-quarters of their revenue. From 1901 the Commonwealth undertook to hand back 75 per cent of this revenue to the States. In other words, at the very outset the Australian federal system was characterised by a state of *vertical financial imbalance*. That is to say, the Commonwealth government had more resources than commitments and the States, given their jurisdiction under the Constitution, more commitments than resources (largely because the States were responsible for labour-intensive fields like health and education). As a result, the only way in which the federal system could function was for the Commonwealth to pass on some of its surplus of resources over commitments to the States. In practice the lower tiers of government in Australia rely on a 'trickle down' of funds from higher levels of government. The precise method by which funds are allowed to trickle down is determined by the Commonwealth parliament under s.96 of the Constitution which says that 'the parliament may grant financial assistance to any State on such terms and conditions as the parliament thinks fit'. These 'terms and conditions' have varied enormously over the years. Indeed the arrangements for fiscal federalism in Australia have been very flexible and on many counts the country can claim to have been something of a pioneer even by world standards (Mathews and Jay, 1972; Prest and Mathews, 1980).

Very soon after Federation it became apparent that vertical financial imbalance was accompanied by *horizontal financial imbalance*. This condition describes the different propensities of the units (e.g. States) at any one level in a federal system to provide services at standards comparable to those of the other units if they also impose taxes and charges at comparable standards (Walmsley, 1984a; p. 95). In Australia's case, such horizontal imbalance can arise from two sources. First, the size and sparseness in population in some areas can make the provision of basic services such as health care and education very expensive. Secondly, some areas have less developed economies and hence fewer local revenue bases to provide the funding for service provision. The first State to plead financial hardship was Western Australia in 1910. Tasmania followed in 1911 and South Australia in 1928. The Commonwealth government of the day responded favourably to these pleas for help and came to arrangements whereby each of the States in question received extra funding to help it cope with the financial difficulties it was experiencing relative to the more affluent States. The principle that the Commonwealth followed in handing down this special assistance was not to bring the poorer States up to the standard of the richer States, but to bring them up to some *minimum standard*.

The situation of the poorer States became worse in the depression years following the Great Crash of 1929. Western Australia was especially badly hit and actually voted for secession, imagining that its interests would be better served if it were a separate nation. The British government (which had set up the Federation of Australia by an Act of its parliament) rejected this plea for secession on the grounds that such a move could only go ahead with the consent of Canberra. This consent was not forthcoming. The Commonwealth nevertheless had to formalise its treatment of poorer States, if only to contain domestic political turmoil. One of the strategies was the establishment of the Commonwealth Grants Commission. This was set up as a quasi-judicial authority. It conducts public hearings, takes evidence on oath, and has an expert secretariat to help it assess claims from States that believe they are disadvantaged relative to the States with the highest fiscal capacities (namely New South Wales and Victoria) (Else-Mitchell, 1980). In the 1930s the Grants Commission rejected inequalities between the citizens of the various States, the poverty of State resources, and the differential impact of federal policy as bases for grants. They adopted the principle of *fiscal need* whereby funding was given to help the poorer States perform at a minimum standard but not to the standard of the richest States (Walmsley, 1984a). The Commonwealth, in other words, took it upon itself to help prevent the emergence of significant inter-state differences in financial health.

Major changes in Commonwealth–State financial relations occurred in 1942 when the Commonwealth monopolised income tax raising powers as part of the war effort, thereby bringing under one umbrella what had previously been 26 different Commonwealth and State income taxes. The principal effect of this change was to entrench the financial ascendancy of the Commonwealth over the States. Vertical financial imbalance increased, so that by the 1970s and 1980s the Commonwealth really did control the purse strings for the nation. Table 4.5 shows the share of taxation receipts going to each tier of government in both 1971/72 and 1988/89, together with the proportion of total government current account expenditure emanating from each tier. Quite obviously, the States' share of expenditure increased in the 1970s and 1980s without a commensurate increase in their share of revenue.

It is much less easy to measure horizontal financial imbalance than it is to measure vertical financial imbalance, because of differences in service provision, differences in revenue raising capacity, and differences in the severity of taxation. These difficulties are perhaps exemplified in Table 4.6

Table 4.5 Vertical financial imbalance in Australia (per cent)

	Taxation receipts		*All government current expenditure*	
	1971/72	*1988/89*	*1971/72*	*1988/89*
Commonwealth	81	79	45	35
State government	14	17	51	59
Local government	5	4	5	6

Source: Calculated from Commonwealth of Australia (1983; 1991b)

Table 4.6 Per capita income from taxes, fees, and fines, 1980–81 and 1987–88[1]

	1980/81	*1987/88*
New South Wales	100	100
Victoria	97	93
Queensland	68	63
South Australia	70	68
Western Australia	80	84
Tasmania	67	69

1 All figures are relative to a base of 100 for New South Wales.

Source: Walmsley (1984a) and calculations based on Australian Bureau of Statistics (1989)

which shows the per capita income from taxes, fees, and fines for each State in 1980/81 and 1986/87 , relative to a score of 100 for New South Wales which was the most heavily taxed State. Clearly, there is very considerable variability between the States. Moreover, with the exception of Western Australia and Tasmania, the tax burden in all States decreased in the 1980s relative to the tax burden in New South Wales, thereby exacerbating an already significant level of inequality. The variations come about for several reasons. Some States for example are able to get away with low taxes because they are low spenders (Queensland being a notable case in the 1980s) whereas other States have perhaps been able to peg State taxation through getting generous grants from the Commonwealth (Tasmania, Western Australia, and South Australia being possible examples).

Despite the difficulties inherent in measuring horizontal financial imbalance, the Commonwealth has tried to take this imbalance into account, together with vertical financial imbalance, when it has passed 'transfer payments' to the States. Although the nature of these payments has changed over the years, three sorts of grants had become dominant by the early 1970s. Most important were *financial assistance grants*. These were untied grants allocated each year at an annual Premiers' Conference. The funding given to each State took account of that State's relative financial health. Table 4.7 shows the relativities in per capita grants in both 1971/72 and 1975/76 (the year in which, as we shall see, financial assistance grants were abandoned) and thereby illustrates the geographic variability that is inherent in the trickle down of Commonwealth funds to the States. Clearly, the relativities changed over time with the tendency for the poorer States to get a greater share. The Premiers' Conference provided an opportunity for political grandstanding on the part of Premiers able to make an especially persuasive case for their State (Sharman, 1977). On top of all this, each State saw its grant increase each year in such a way as to take stock of inflation and population growth in the previous twelve months. Additionally, each State's grant included a betterment factor (which stood at 3 per cent in 1975/76). That is to say, in any one

Table 4.7 The relativities in Financial Assistance Grants[1]

	1971/72	*1975/76*
Victoria	1.00	1.00
New South Wales	1.00	1.03
Queensland	1.24	1.39
South Australia	1.35	1.53
Western Australia	1.65	1.67
Tasmania	1.80	2.00

1 All figures are relative to a base of 100 for Victoria

Source: Calculated from data in Commonwealth of Australia (1973) and Commonwealth Grants Commission (1981)

year each State was given 3 per cent more than it had received in the previous year. It was largely this betterment factor that enabled State expenditure in the early 1970s to increase at a rate much faster than that of the Commonwealth government (Table 4.8).

The second type of grant to feature in Commonwealth–State transfers in the early 1970s was the *specific purpose grant.* These were grants earmarked for expenditure on specific items. In other words, all such grants had expenditure restrictions. Some also had revenue restrictions and were only allocated where there was a matching contribution from the recipient State. The first specific purpose grants occurred in 1923, with a Commonwealth grant to the States for road building (this remained the main specific purpose grant until the 1970s). Specific purpose grants expanded massively under the Whitlam Labor administration (1972–75) when they increased as a share of total Commonwealth–State transfers from 21 per cent to 44 per cent (Mathews, 1976). This increase came about for very political reasons. The Whitlam government was pledged to a series of reforms, particularly in the field of social policy, but found itself unable to act directly because jurisdiction for such policy was, under the Constitution, a State responsibility. It was able to circumvent this constraint however by using its financial dominance to

Table 4.8 Mean annual real per capita increases in Commonwealth, State, and local government spending (per cent)

	1973/74 to 1975/76		*1976/77 to 1980/81*	
	Current account	*Capital account*	*Current account*	*Capital account*
Commonwealth	6	8	1	–8
State	18	13	2	0
Local	14	14	5	–2

Source: Calculated from data in ABS *Year Book Australia* (1973/74 to 1980/81)

influence how the States spent the money passed down to them (i.e. imposing expenditure restrictions).

The third type of transfer payment used in the early 1970s was the *special grant*. This was the money allocated by the Commonwealth Grants Commission to top up the funding of the poorer States to some minimum standard. Over the 1970s this mode of operation changed.

First, instead of looking at actual State budgets in order to assess fiscal need, the Commission shifted to a system where it made a *direct assessment* of the needs of the poorer States by applying a standard revenue effort to the difference between a standard revenue base and the claimant State's revenue base, and expenditure needs were assessed by calculating the additional costs to the claimant State of providing a standard range and quality of services (Mathews, 1975). This meant that a State need not impose the same level of taxes, or indulge in the same level of expenditure, as other States in order to qualify for a grant. In fact, a State's actual budget had no bearing on whether or not it qualified for a grant.

The second major change in the operations of the Grants Commission was a shift from the principle of fiscal need to the principle of *fiscal equalization*. This meant that the Commission no longer sought to define minimum standards but rather tried to put all States on an equal financial footing.

In the mid-1970s dissatisfaction grew with this threefold system of grants. The States resented Commonwealth interference, through specific purpose grants, in matters that were rightly their responsibility. They felt that such grants imposed Commonwealth political priorities on them. This was especially irksome where matching grants were required (Wade, 1974). It is not surprising therefore that a new idea was born (or at least borrowed from overseas). That idea was New Federalism. It was introduced by the incoming Fraser Liberal–National Party Coalition from 1976/77. Under New Federalism, financial assistance grants and specific purpose grants were to be absorbed into a new system of payment whereby the States would be guaranteed a fixed share of the personal income tax receipts collected by the Commonwealth. In other words, the goal of New Federalism was to increase the budgetary independence, responsibility, and flexibility of the States (Walmsley, 1984a). The amount of funding given to the States in any one year under New Federalism was equivalent to 39.87 per cent of personal income tax receipts in the previous financial year (this curious figure being the equivalent of the amount disbursed under the previous system of financial assistance grants and specific purpose grants). From 1978 the States were also given the power to impose a 2 per cent income tax surcharge in order to top up their coffers. None did.

On the face of it, New Federalism offered a good deal to the States. In practice, it too proved unpopular. This was largely because the introduction of New Federalism was followed closely by tax reforms (mainly tax indexation and tax cuts) which had the effect of slowing very considerably the rate at which income tax receipts grew. In other words, the States quickly realised that they had been given a guaranteed share of a major revenue base but no control over the policy decisions that influenced the size of that base. This situation contrasted markedly with the heady days of the Whitlam administration in the early 1970s when the States had been able to rely on a betterment factor each year. Not surprisingly, without a betterment factor, State spending was curtailed in the late 1970s (see Table 4.8). Bickering began between the States as to who got what and it soon became apparent that New Federalism would only work if there was some sort of monitoring of the justification for the relative shares allocated to each State. Even a change in 1982/83 from 39.87 per cent of personal income tax receipts to 20.72 per cent of total tax receipts (a base less subject to political manipulation) did nothing to ease the States' discontent. The task of monitoring State relativities fell to the Commonwealth Grants Commission.

The Commonwealth Grants Commission (1981) undertook the most thorough-going analysis ever made of State entitlements to Commonwealth funding using, as its base, data on revenue and expenditure for the period 1977–1980. The force of the Commission's recommendations is presented in Table 4.9. Basically, the Commission felt that the poorer States of Tasmania, Western Australia, and South Australia had been given rather more Commonwealth funding than they really deserved. As a result, the richer States of New South Wales, Victoria, and Queensland had got rather less than was warranted. The Grants Commission therefore recommended a redistribution that favoured the 'richer' States. Predictably, this was unpopular with the 'poorer' States. As a result, the Grants Commission was sent away to do further calculations, this time including data for 1980/81. Again its recommendations were much the same (Table 4.9). This time the Commonwealth government had no real option but to accept the recommendations.

Table 4.9 The relativities in State entitlements to Commonwealth funding

	Percentage allocated to:					
	NSW	*Vic*	*Qld*	*SA*	*WA*	*Tas*
Actual allocation 1980/81	30.7	22.7	17.9	11.7	12.1	4.9
Grants Commission:						
recommendation 1981	33.4	23.7	18.9	10.1	10.1	3.8
recommendation 1982	32.2	23.3	19.5	10.6	10.6	3.8
Actual allocation 1984/85	29.9	22.1	21.4	10.8	11.3	4.5
Actual allocation 1985/86	31.4	23.1	18.5	11.2	11.4	4.4
Actual allocation 1987/88	33.0	24.1	17.5	10.3	11.3	3.8

Source: Calculated from data in ABS *Year Book Australia* (1980/81 to 1987/88)

However, in forcing them through, it did what had been standard practice in Commonwealth–State relations for some time, and introduced change subject to a guarantee that no State would be worse off under the new system than under the old (a similar guarantee having been given when New Federalism was first introduced). The States were actually guaranteed real increases for three years. This cushioned the blow for the poorer States. The new arrangement was however shortlived. By the mid-1980s taxation revenue had increased to the point where, had tax sharing under New Federalism been maintained, the States would have received increases of a sufficient size to threaten the Hawke government's reasonably tight monetary policy. As a result, tax-sharing was abandoned and Commonwealth–State transfer payments reverted, from 1985/86, to a system very similar to the old financial assistance grants (again the change being subject to a guarantee of real increases). Reference to Table 4.9 shows that this has enabled the Commonwealth to go some way towards meeting the Grants Commission recommendations. Above all, though, the change showed how intergovernmental financial relations in Australia can be altered at short notice in the face of political expediency. As a side effect, the changes have also put the Premiers' Conference in mid-year back on the political agenda as a venue for at times acrimonious exchange. By the late 1980s, New South Wales and Victoria were beginning to see their 'under-equalization' addressed, mainly at the expense of Queensland, South Australia and Tasmania.

It is important to remember, of course, that Commonwealth financial assistance to the States extends well beyond the formal transfer payments that occur under s.96 of the Constitution. The tariffs that are imposed to protect manufacturing industry serve, for instance, as a *de facto* subsidy to those States (such as Victoria, New South Wales and South Australia) where manufacturing is strong (see Chapter 2). Similarly, some areas may receive a substantial and automatic input of Commonwealth funds if they have a significant number of residents in receipt of pensions and benefits. Areas with high unemployment (like the North Coast of New South Wales) are a case in point. On the other side of the coin, there may be areas that will in the future receive diminishing Commonwealth funding because of their expanding revenue bases. This may possibly happen in Western Australia and Queensland where revenue bases may grow if there occurs a resources boom that brings in vastly increased mining royalties (West, 1983; Galligan, 1982). Some writers have suggested that this might create severe strains in the federal system in that there might be both a vertical shift of economic power away from Canberra and a horizontal shift of economic power from New South Wales and Victoria to Western Australia and Queensland (Head, 1984). However this 'national fragmentation thesis' overlooks the fact that much of the benefit from resource investment leaks back to the head offices of companies based in Sydney and Melbourne (or even overseas). Moreover royalty revenue might be offset by infrastructure costs.

Any suggestion of 'fragmentation' and of shifting economic power brings into focus the Constitution because, ultimately, this is the document that determines what the two major tiers of the Australian federal system can and cannot do. Conflicts between the Commonwealth and States over their relative jurisdictions can only be settled by recourse to the High Court. Many High Court judgements may have important geographical implications in the sense of favouring the development of one area at the expense of others. The most famous case to be decided in recent years was probably the so-called 'Dams Case' centred on a conflict between legislation passed by the Tasmanian government and legislation passed by the Commonwealth. In 1982 the Tasmanian government passed the *Gordon River Hydro-Electric Power Development Act* with a view to generating electricity in the south-west of the State. The Labor Party campaigned against such a move in the 1983 federal election and, on winning office, passed the *World Heritage Properties Conservation Act* to prevent the Tasmanian Hydro-Electric Commission from proceeding with its scheme. A situation therefore arose where Commonwealth legislation was at odds with State legislation. Under such circumstances, according to s.109 of the Constitution, the Commonwealth law shall prevail. Everything hinged therefore on whether the Commonwealth was acting within its area of responsibility when it passed its Heritage Act. This was the matter that went to the High Court. In a now famous decision the Court decided that s.51(xxix) of the Constitution empowers the Commonwealth to make laws relating to 'external affairs' and, because Australia is a signatory to the United Nations *Convention for the Protection of the World Cultural and Natural Heritage*, the Commonwealth therefore had the power to act in such a way as to protect areas on the 'world listing' (South West Tasmania having been given world listing by the previous Commonwealth and State governments).

There is still controversy over the implications of this decision. Some constitutional lawyers see it simply as the latest in a series of High Court decisions going back to at least 1919 that have in effect extended the Commonwealth's jurisdiction by invoking the 'external affairs' power (Howard, 1983). Others, particularly State leaders, have argued that the Dams Case was an unusual and perhaps even extraordinary judgement, prompted by and couched in an almost unique political context that is virtually incapable of duplication (Burke, 1984; p. 4). Whether this is true remains to be seen. Other conservation issues may prove to be equally emotive, notably at Coronation Hill in the Northern Territory where mining has been pre-empted by a Federal decision in 1991 to include the area in question in Stage III of the Kakadu National Park. Furthermore, Australia is a signatory to over 1500 international agreements, treaties, and conventions and so the scope for the Commonwealth to legislate under s.51(xxix) is enormous (Walmsley, 1985).

The position of local government

Local government owes its existence to separate pieces of State legislation. As a result there are marked differences from State to State in what local government is legally empowered to do. Basically, however, the functions of local government centre on three areas:

1 a mandatory duty to provide a service (such as the supervision of building, health, and planning regulations);
2 the power to provide a service should the local council so desire (for example, the provision of aged housing or child health centres); and
3 the power to subsidize a service provided by other organizations (for instance meals-on-wheels and child care facilities).

The scope for local government activity is, in other words, potentially great. In practice, of course, local government rarely takes up this potential. Instead, its activities are usually restricted to

- roads and bridges,
- drainage,
- recreation facilities,
- cemeteries, pounds, and aerodromes,
- sewerage and garbage,
- town planning, and
- gas, abattoirs, and saleyards (Power *et al.*, 1981).

In short, local government has been viewed in Australia largely as a mechanism for providing the infrastructure and amenities necessary for urban and rural life, rather than as a full partner in the federal system (Chapman and Wood, 1984).

The relatively feeble position of local government can be traced back to the nineteenth century. At that time the focus of Australian politics was very much on Colonial issues and on the move towards Federation. Jones (1981) has suggested, for instance, that an average of 30 governments at the Colonial level between the granting of responsible government and the turn of the century ensured that political attention focussed on the Colonial parliament rather than on the local council chambers. Additionally, of course, the primacy of the major cities meant that they dominated life in the country (see Chapter 1). It may also be pertinent to point out that Australia, being relatively recently settled, has none of the deep attachment to place on the part of the residents of an area that serves as a basis for local government in areas such as Europe. On top of this, of course, the State governments have done their best to keep local government weak so as to protect their own interests. The States have never pushed the policy of local government amalgamation with any force, partly for fear that sizeable and well organized local authorities could be troublesome. In fact the States have tended to prevent local government authorities becoming big and powerful by setting up single purpose authorities (called County Councils in many areas) to provide services such as electricity and water supply which might otherwise have gone to existing local government (i.e. multi-purpose) authorities (Halligan and Paris, 1984).

The number of local government authorities existing in each State at the time of the last published census (1986) is given in Table 4.10 together with the average size of the authorities in terms of both population and area. Quite obviously, many authorities have a small population but a large area. Wiluna in Western Australia, for instance, covers 300 000 square kilometres. Some measure of the reluctance of State governments to force amalgamation on local government can be seen in the fact that there were 1067 local authorities in 1910, 888 in 1971, and still 828 in 1986. Between that time and 1988 there was a reduction of one authority in New South Wales, two in Victoria and two in South Australia but an increase of one in Western Australia (Office of Local Government, 1989). Overall, within the Australian federal system, local government accounts for only about 6 per cent of total government spending (see Table 4.5), a fact which testifies to its relative weakness. The actual items on which this money is spent vary considerably from State to State. The approximate figures for local government spending are set out in Table 4.11.

Table 4.10 The size of local government in Australia, 1986

	Number of authorities	*Average population*	*Average size (km^2)*
New South Wales	176	29 000	4 900
Victoria	211	18 000	2 000
Queensland	134	17 000	18 200
South Australia	127	10 000	1 600
Western Australia	138	9 000	19 100
Tasmania	42	8 500	1 800

Source: From data in Commonwealth of Australia (1986)

Table 4.11 Local government revenue and spending patterns, 1987/88 (per cent)

	NSW	*Vic*	*Qld*	*SA*	*WA*	*Tas*
Revenue from:						
Rates/local taxes	52	61	48	68	57	50
State & Commonwealth	22	28	23	26	33	25
Net borrowing	2	3	15	3	0	5
Other	24	8	14	3	10	20
Expenditure on:						
General public service	14	23	9	18	15	18
Health	2	4	2	2	3	1
Social security & welfare	2	10	1	2	2	2
Housing/community amenities	15	12	31	20	14	24
Recreation & culture	15	19	16	20	25	20
Road transport	28	26	38	27	34	34

Source: Calculated from data in Australian Bureau of Statistics (1989)

The item 'housing and community amenities' includes sanitation and sewerage. Recreation, roads and sanitation are clearly the three most important items listed. Given that 'recreation' includes the provision of parks, it is worth noting that between a half and three quarters of all local government expenditures goes on physical infrastructure.

In terms of income, local government is very dependent on the 'trickle down' of funds from higher tiers of government. Table 4.12 reveals, for instance, that although the States in aggregate only pass on 3 per cent of their total available funds to local government, that amount equals about 21 per cent of the funds that local authorities have available to them. Predictably, the source of local government finance varies from State to State (Table 4.11). Reliance on rate income is highest in Victoria and South Australia. Local government in Queensland relies much less on rates but very much more heavily on borrowing. Overall, local government rates account for between half and two-thirds of local government income.

Table 4.12 Intergovernment transfer payments, 1981/82

	Total available funds ($ million)	*Amount passed down as % donor's funds*	*Amount passed down as % recipient's funds*
Commonwealth	79 020	27	n.a.
State	52 951	3	45
Local	6 464	n.a.	21

Source: Calculated from Commonwealth of Australia (1991b)

The enfeeblement of local government is unfortunate because, in theory, there are many advantages to be had in developing local authorities as a strong arm of government (Walmsley, 1984b):

1 Local government might be very much more in tune with local problems and with local opinion than is possible in the case of the State and Commonwealth governments.
2 Local government is for the most part free from direct party political influences and is therefore able to respond to issues as they arise without the interference of the party machines.
3 Local government can be flexible. It can experiment with new policies on a scale that does not involve the commitment of vast sums of money or the involvement of great numbers of people.
4 Local government can foster political responsibility because of the high degree of coincidence that exists between the benefits and costs of political decisions. (An unpopular decision will, for instance, often result in an elected councillor having to face critics in person rather than merely replying to irate letters in a rather impersonal way.)

Against these advantages, local government does have weaknesses. The weak financial position of local government authorities generally, and their reliance on State funding, has already been alluded to. As well, local government often lacks skilled personnel, especially in the social policy arena and especially in small rural shires distant from capital cities. Finally, local government tends very often to be plagued by a poor image. Its role is seen as negative rather than positive. That is to say, it tells people what they cannot do (as in the control of land use zoning) rather than encouraging activity. As a result, local government is often viewed as having a 'kerbs and gutters' mentality.

Despite the problems it faces, the position of local government does seem to be changing somewhat, particularly as regards geographical fragmentation, co-operation with other tiers of government and financial equity. In terms of geographical fragmentation, moves have been made in some States to reduce the number of local authorities. New South Wales, for example, had a Committee of Inquiry into Local Government Areas and Administration in 1973. This Committee recommended that the 223 local authorities that existed at that time be combined into 97 District Councils. Although this recommendation was rejected, amalgamation does seem to have gone further in New South Wales than in the other States (see Table 4.10). Likewise South Australia had a Royal Commission into Local Government Authorities in 1974. This recommended reducing the number of authorities from 137 to 74. Once more the overall recommendation was rejected but some element of amalgamation did ensue. Of course, in some instances opposition to amalgamation comes not from the State governments but from the threatened local authorities themselves, particularly in rural areas where closure of the local shire office could have a significant effect on local job opportunities.

In terms of increased co-operation with other tiers of government a similar pattern can be observed: government inquiries have explored the potential for co-operation, their recommendations have been overlooked, but some moves towards co-operation have eventuated. The first main inquiry into the possibility of increased intergovernmental co-operation looked specifically at co-operation within the fields of health and welfare (Task Force on Co-ordination in Welfare and Health, 1977). In large measure it was found that local government could contribute little to increased co-ordination in this field because of its very small overall involvement. Nevertheless, since that time the Commonwealth has used local government as a basis for such welfare oriented schemes as local job creation. Moreover, local government authorities have often been encouraged to take a greater role in social services. To make this possible, of course, changes have been necessary to both the amount and equity of local government funding.

A major change to local government finances occurred with the *Grants Commission Act 1973*. Prior to this the Commonwealth government had been prevented from giving funds to local government (except in very limited areas of Commonwealth jurisdiction such as roads and aboriginal affairs) on the grounds that local government is nowhere mentioned in the Constitution but rather gets its powers from separate pieces of State legislation. With the passage of the 1973 Act that situation changed, and the Commonwealth became empowered to give funds to Regional Organizations of Councils (ROCs). Each of these bodies represented all the local government authorities in its respective area (McPhail, 1978).

One of the principal functions of ROCs was to make applications to the Commonwealth Grants Commission for special assistance on behalf of local government. The funds derived from this source were not meant to replace State or local revenue. Rather they were seen as part of a 'topping up' process designed to facilitate the expansion of local government activity especially in the field of 'human services'. Although ROCs handled applications, funds were actually calculated and allocated on the basis of individual councils. The policy adopted in the distribution of funds by the Commonwealth Grants Commission was one of *fiscal equalization*. The aim, in other words, was to equalise the financial capacity of local government to perform its functions providing an equal effort was made to raise revenue. Assessment of how much funding each authority needed in order to bring about equalization obviously presented enormous problems, given that there were more than 800 authorities, and the Commission had not really solved this problem at the time when the system of ROC funding was terminated with the demise of the Whitlam Labor government.

The demise of ROCs says a great deal about government attitudes to regionalism in Australia. The attitudes of State governments towards regional growth have always been ambivalent. Although decentralisation policies have supposedly been adopted, and 'growth centres' promulgated, there has been little sustained effort to encourage non-metropolitan growth. The advantages of decentralisation are widely recognized. After all, it offers a way of relieving the economic, social and physical ills of the big cities, a way of diminishing inter-regional disparities in economic and social opportunities, a way of improving quality of life, and a way of accommodating future population growth.

Some of these perceived advantages may be illusory. Certainly some fundamental obstacles have stood in the way of successful decentralisation. Prominent among these have been the unwillingness of city dwellers to move, the high cost of decentralisation (especially in relation to the establishment of infrastructure), and the uncertainty that business encounters when it moves away from competitors, markets, and the economies of scale to be found in metropolitan centers (Burnley, 1980). As a result decentralisation and regionalism generally have been the focus of only scant political attention in Australia. Even the Grants Commission did not get to grips with regionalism in its treatment of ROC applications. Little or no attention was paid to regional patterns evident in the distribution of equalization monies (Walmsley, 1984b). In other words, the regionalism inherent in the workings of the Grants Commission was not a regionalism aimed at regional government. Rather it was a regionalism of convenience: decision-making power was centralised in Canberra and the role of the regions was simply to administer the allocation of funding (Harris, 1974).

The regionalism implicit in the *Grants Commission Act 1973* was, in fact, an excellent example of regionalism imposed from above (as against regionalism desired from below, based on voluntary amalgamations) and therefore exemplified its attendant problems of weakness and lack of commitment (Power and Wettenhall, 1976).

Although the ROC experiment can probably be considered a failure that contains a salutary warning about regional policy in Australia, it did have one important legacy in that it bound local government to some sort of Commonwealth 'top-up' funding. Thus it was that local government became involved in New Federalism. Under this arrangement, local government was granted a share of personal income tax (hence the term PITS money). The actual amount of 1.52 per cent in 1976/77 (the first year of New Federalism) was increased to 2 per cent from 1980. The aim of the Commonwealth in distributing PITS money as general purpose assistance was to strengthen local government by achieving greater equality between the financial capacities of local councils (National Inquiry into Local Government Finance, 1985). To this end New Federalism specified that a major part of the PITS money had to be given out on the basis of fiscal equalization. The ratio between equalization grants and capitation (i.e. per capita) grants varied from State to State. It was 70:30 in Queensland, South Australia, and Tasmania, 67:33 in New South Wales, 60:40 in Victoria, and 20:80 in Western Australia (Chapman and Wood, 1984).

The actual disbursement of funds in each State became the responsibility of State Grants Commissions. In New South Wales, for example, 30 per cent of the equalisation grant was allocated on the basis of revenue disparities and 70 per cent on the basis of expenditure needs. As with the case of Commonwealth–State transfer payments, the smaller States tended to be favoured under the PITS scheme (Table 4.13). In fact only New South Wales and Victoria got less than they might have expected on the basis of population. The PITS money represented only about 50–60 per cent of Commonwealth payments to local government (much of the remainder being for roads and passed on via the States rather than handed over directly). The PITS money was nevertheless very significant, particularly because it tended to grow at a faster rate than inflation in the late 1970s and early 1980s (National Inquiry into Local Government Finance, 1985). This facilitated the real growth in local government expenditure noted in Table 4.8. However local government faced the same problem as the States in 1985/86: income tax receipts grew so quickly that maintenance of a 2 per cent share would have given local authorities a massive influx of funds, a situation unacceptable to the Commonwealth. As a result, from that year onwards, local government was

Table 4.13 State entitlements to PITS money

	1984 Population (% national total)	*1984 PITS entitlement (% total allocation)*
New South Wales	35.60	29.75
Victoria	26.86	22.24
Queensland	16.60	20.87
Western Australia	9.16	11.54
South Australia	8.90	11.01
Tasmania	2.88	4.38

Source: National Inquiry into Local Government Finance (1985)

given a guaranteed real increase in funding without the actual amount being pegged to taxation receipts. Thus, by the early 1990s, the amount given to local government was determined by the government in the light of prevailing fiscal and monetary policy.

The aim of fiscal equalisation in local government finance is not to impose uniformity but to provide equal opportunity. The argument implicit in fiscal equalisation is that local political choices as to tax rates and service provision should be adjusted for circumstances beyond the control of councils so that, as far as practicable, all citizens should be able to make their choice on similar terms wherever they live (National Inquiry into Local Government Finance, 1985). Untied equalisation grants may not, of course, mean that equal services will actually be provided. What happens in any particular case obviously depends on the enterprise, initiative, and skills of the local council.

The electoral process

The composition of local government councils, like that of the State and Commonwealth governments, is determined by the electoral process. In this respect Australia has, by international standards, a proud record. Secret ballots were introduced as early as the 1850s, plural voting was outlawed in all States by 1907, and adult suffrage had been introduced everywhere by 1909 (Walmsley, 1988b). The date of introduction of adult suffrage in each State is given in Table 4.14, together with the dates on which both compulsory voting and preferential voting were introduced. Clearly, preferential voting, which is the system now used, has a long history. Australian electoral practices have however changed many times: New South Wales experimented with a 'second ballot' between 1910 and 1917 and used proportional representation between 1918 and 1925; Queensland used 'first-past-the-post' voting from 1942 to 1962; and Tasmania has long had multiple member constituencies with MPs elected by a single transferable vote, as is the case with the Commonwealth Senate today — the Hare-Clark System (Rydon,

Table 4.14 The emergence of Australia's electoral system

	Year of first introduction of:		
	Adult suffrage	*Compulsory voting*	*Preferential voting*
New South Wales	1902	1930	1926
Victoria	1909	1927	1911
Queensland	1905	1915	1892
South Australia	1894	1944	1929
Western Australia	1907	1939	1907
Tasmania	1903	1931	1907[1]
Commonwealth	1902	1925	1918

1 Proportional representation

Source: Walmsley (1988b)

1973). At the national level, the House of Representatives was elected on a first-past-the-post system until 1918 and the Senate on a similar basis until 1919 (Walmsley, 1988b).

The Commonwealth parliament is probably the one on which most attention focuses in any discussion of representative government and the electoral process in Australia, largely because of the Commonwealth's dominance within the federal system. This parliament is structured in such a way that the size of the House of Representatives should be as nearly as practicable twice the size of the Senate. The size of the Senate itself has grown as the national population (and therefore the number of people to be represented) has grown.

Until 1949 the Senate comprised 36 members (6 from each State). It was increased in size to 60 in 1983. Presently it has 76 members (12 from each State and 2 from each of the ACT and the Northern Territory). The Senate has used the Hare-Clark voting system since 1949 with each State serving as a single electorate from which all 12 members are returned. The size of the House of Representatives is 145. Elections for this House are held on the basis of single member constituencies.

In all States and at the Commonwealth level, electoral boundaries are drawn by independently appointed Electoral Commissioners, a situation that has existed since 1929. However, the legislation under which these Commissioners operate varies from State to State. At the Commonwealth level it is the duty of the Electoral Commissioner to decide, firstly, how the 145 seats in the House of Representatives are to be divided up between the States. This exercise is undertaken in the twelfth month of each parliament and calculations are based on the number of electors (cf. population) in each State. If a State's entitlement changes, a redistribution is mandatory.

For much of this century the tolerance allowed in the variability in the size of Commonwealth electorates was 20 per cent on either side of the average. That tolerance has now been reduced to plus or minus 10 per cent. Because entitlements are calculated on the basis of electors rather than population, two sorts of areas tend to be relatively disenfranchised (in other words, do not have as many elected representatives as might be expected on the basis of their population): inner city areas where there are large numbers of migrants not eligible to vote, and outer metropolitan suburbs where there are often large numbers of children not old enough to be on the electoral roll (Hughes, 1977). Other than that, Commonwealth electoral boundaries are remarkably fair and go a long way to meeting the requirement that all Australians have an equal say in choosing their government (although a delay in introducing a redistribution at a time of very rapid population growth in the mid-1960s led to an aberration whereby the ratio in size of the largest to the smallest Commonwealth electorate at the 1966 election reached an astounding 4:1).

Some of the States have much less of a proud record in upholding the principle of 'one vote–one value'. Although independently appointed Electoral Commissioners take stock of such factors as lines of communication, physical features in the landscape, communities of interest, population trends, and isolation, in drawing up constituency boundaries, they often work under legislation which inevitably leads to a situation of malapportionment. The term *malapportionment* refers to the state of affairs where electoral boundaries are drawn to give proportionately greater representation to some areas (and therefore some people) than others. It should be distinguished from a *gerrymander*, which is a situation where the boundaries of electorates are drawn in such a way (often in a peculiar shape) as to favour one party over another. Unfortunately the two terms are often used synonymously.

The worst example of malapportionment in Australia in recent times occurred in Queensland where the electoral laws divided the State into 'zones'. In 1983 the South Eastern Zone (including Brisbane) had an average of 21 005 voters per elected member. At the same time the Provincial City Zone had an average of 19 600, the Country Zone an average of 13 971, and the Western and Far Northern Zone an average of 10 248. This meant that, in terms of its power to elect a member of parliament, a vote in the Western and Far Northern Zone was worth more than twice as much as a vote in the South Eastern Zone. The significance of this lies in the fact that one particular party (the National Party) is more popular in the areas with small constituences (in population terms).

The malapportionment stemming from the Queensland system of electoral zones did much to entrench the National Party in power. Because of this, in the eyes of many, it tended to encourage the sort of corruption in politics unearthed by the Fitzgerald Inquiry in Queensland. In order to remedy this situation and following the recommendations of Fitzgerald, an Electoral and Administrative Review Commission has been set up. The electoral zones have also been changed but not removed entirely. Such is the sparseness of the population in the inland, and so great are the problems served by parliamentarians seeking to represent these people, that some 'weighting' is felt to be justified. It seems likely therefore that inland constituencies will continue to be somewhat smaller than their metropolitan and provincial counterparts.

Queensland is not, of course, the only State to use 'zones'. They have also been used in the past in New South Wales, Victoria and South Australia. In 1983 the position in Western Australia was almost as bad as that in Queensland: the State comprised just two 'zones'; Perth and the country. Electorates in Perth had roughly twice as many voters as electorates in the country.

In some respects, too, there is an element of malapportionment even at the Commonwealth level. Tasmania, like all States, is guaranteed in the Constitution a minimum of five members in the House of Representatives. Tasmania also has twelve senators, the same as all other States. This means that, in 1990, Tasmania had one Commonwealth politician for every 18 240 electors. This contrasts with one for every 57 632 electors in New South Wales. The overall number of elected politicians in each State at Commonwealth and State level is shown in Table 4.15. In essence these are full-time politicians. It is easy to see from this Table why Australia is sometimes thought to be over-governed: in Tasmania, for example, there is one elected full-time politician for every 4400 electors. The situation is even worse in the Northern Territory, with one Commonwealth or Territory politician for every 2800 electors. And, of course, on top of this there are almost 9000 elected local government politicans in Australia.

In addition to the electoral system itself, the other major influence on the electoral process in Australia is the party system. Despite the presence of minor parties, Australia has essentially a two-party system with the Australian Labor Party (ALP) vying against the combined forces of the Liberal Party and the National Party. Despite this, minority governments existed in all States except Queensland at the beginning of 1992, the balance of power being held by independent members of parliament, often of environmentalist persuasion. Generally speaking, the Liberal and National Parties tend to form coalition governments (L–NP) although in some States one or other of the parties might sometimes rule on its own (as the Nationals have done recently in

Table 4.15 The number of elected politicians in Australia, 1990

	Commonwealth politicians	*State politicians*	*Ratio of electors: politicians*
New South Wales	63	154	16 732:1
Victoria	50	132	15 283:1
Queensland[1]	34	89	14 676:1
South Australia	25	69	10 281:1
Western Australia	26	91	8 401:1
Tasmania	17	54	4 367:1
Northern Territory	3	25	2 821:1
ACT	4	17	8 200:1

1 No Upper House

Source: Calculated from Commonwealth of Australia data (1991b)

Queensland and the Liberals have done in the past in Victoria). There are several differences between Australia's two major political groupings, but they are not major in terms of the entire spectrum of possible political opinion. In philosophical terms, the ALP is centralist and the L–NP has a decentralist orientation (Mathews, 1977). In terms of social policy, the ALP favours active involvement of government institutions in social planning whereas the L–NP looks upon social policy largely as a safety net for those members of the community who suffer hardship (Graycar, 1979).

The origins of the ALP go back to the nineteenth century. It began for two reasons:

- to seek improvement in the lot of working people; and
- as part of an international thrust to involve working people everywhere in the political process (Maddox, 1985).

Its origins were closely tied with those of trade unionism. It first met with significant electoral success in 1891 when it had 35 members out of 141 in the New South Wales Legislative Assembly, enough to secure the balance of power. In Queensland the world's first Labor Ministry was set up in 1899 albeit only for a few days. The conservative parties in Australian politics are much more recent creations although they are undoubtedly heirs to a political tradition and ideology that dates back to the beginnings of European settlement.

The National Party began life as the Country Party. It emerged as a coherent political force about the time of the First World War, and quickly became significant in the various State parliaments: Western Australia 1914, Queensland 1915, Victoria 1917, South Australia 1918, and New South Wales 1921. At the national level, the party emerged as a force after the 1919 elections. Although its origins can be traced back to pastoralists organising themselves against the great union strikes of the late nineteenth century, the National Party probably sprang more directly from the sense of relative deprivation felt by rural people and from a feeling that city-based politicians lacked an understanding of rural affairs (Maddox, 1985).

The Liberal Party is much more recent, and was founded in 1944. It grew specifically out of the United Australia Party. Its most remarkable characteristic, for a party not much more than forty years old, is that it has taken upon itself the air of being the natural party of the government, having held the treasury benches at the Commonwealth level from 1949 to 1972 and from 1975 to 1983.

Any comparison of the Labor, Liberal and National Parties inevitably raises the question of whether their apparent differences are translated into different policies and different spending patterns once they are in power. This is a profound and complicated question. Table 4.16 compares the outlay of the Commonwealth and of the States and local government combined during the Whitlam (ALP) administration, the Fraser (L–NP) administration, and the first few years of the Hawke (ALP) administration. If attention is restricted to

Table 4.16 Party political influiences on government spending patterns (per cent)

	Mean annual rate per capita increase in outlay		
	1972/73–1975/76	*1976/77–1982/83*	*1983/84–1988/89*
Commonwealth government	+12.7	+1.3	–1.1
State and local governments	+11.1	+2.8	–0.8

Source: Calculated from data in Foster and Stewart (1991)

the early part of the period covered by Table 4.16, there is clearly a prima facie case that the ALP is a bigger spender than the L–NP. Too much reliance should not, however, be put on one time period because no government is free from the context in which it finds itself operating. The Whitlam administration, for example, came to power at a time when there had been a considerable build-up of pressure from a variety of groups for government action on a wide range of issues such as social policy, urban affairs, environmental protection, and welfare (Scott, 1980). Responding to this pressure inevitably meant increasing government expenditure. Conversely, the Fraser administration was troubled for at least part of its term by an international economic recession that dictated cautiousness in government spending policy. And, for reasons that have been outlined already, the Hawke administration cut back on the scale of Big Government. In short, there is no clear link between political parties and spending. The ALP was responsible for both massive increases in spending and for the most sustained pruning of government activity.

In summary, governments are not free agencies able to pursue ideological commitments. Rather, what they can and cannot do is often very highly constrained by the circumstances in which they find themselves operating. In this context government in Australia presents a number of paradoxes. It was, for example, imposed from above by a colonial power and yet it has proved immensely popular to the extent that the country has one of the highest ratios of politicians to population in the world. Likewise, the rigidity of the constitutional arrangements for boundaries and jurisdictions can be contrasted with the flexibility that has characterised Commonwealth–State financial relations. Similarly, signs of a strong democracy have existed alongside blatant malapportionment. Above all, though, Australians have a tendency to look upon governments as powerful and somehow independent from the rest of the economy. In truth, of course, how governments cope depends very much on the activities of the private sector (see Chapter 5).

Australia in the World Economy

> A country, industry or company that puts preservation of blue-collar jobs ahead of international competitiveness will soon have neither production nor jobs (Drucker 1986, p. 77)

It became clear in Chapter 2 that Australia's economic development is partially influenced by a variety of international forces. These include the macro-economic and foreign policy decisions of governments; the operations of global financial and commodity markets; and the activities of multinational corporations (MNCs). Naturally the form and extent of this influence varies with the good or service produced. In general, the sectors with greatest exposure in export markets (particularly agricultural and mining raw materials) and those most open to import competition (including many segments of manufacturing industry) are affected most directly by international events. However, even those activities which serve almost exclusively a domestic market are not immune from the indirect influences of Australia's relationship with the outside world.

Indeed, Drucker (1986) claims that economic dynamics have decisively shifted from the national to the world economy, a situation which was largely ignored by Australian policy-makers until the mid-1980s. Drucker warns that terms of trade have moved strongly against raw material producing nations such as Australia because output has risen faster than consumption for most items. This situation is not likely to be reversed in the short-term because technological developments are rapidly improving both efficiency in resource use and the volume of resource output. Moreover, the value of material used in production comprises an ever more marginal share of the value of total output.

This Chapter sets out to probe the extent to which the actions of present day business and government decision-makers in Australia are constrained by foreign influences and how the picture is changing. It explores the consequences of this situation for national welfare, and whether anything can or should be done to rectify the problems that may arise. En route it examines how far this country's economic sovereignty is declining as international markets and companies grow in strength and international agencies are set up to regulate them. It also considers the technologies and business imperatives which underlie the emergence of financial, production and marketing networks at a global or international scale. This leads to a discussion of the merits of various policy options which confront nations should they wish to reverse or modify the impact of such international mechanisms. In Australia's case, we will conclude that there seems to be considerable advantage from being swept along in the main current of international affairs, though it can also be shown that there is much the country can do of its own accord to harness global processes to its own benefit.

Many of the forces which shape international events also clearly operate within Australia to delineate a marked set of regional cores and peripheries. Thus, for example, developments in communications technology serve to increase the geographical span of corporate control and to centralise political and economic power in a few places. Such matters, too, will be the focus of attention, because they raise vital questions concerning the extent to which federal and state governments should try to counteract the centralising tendencies of the private sector — and indeed their own instrumentalities.

Why are these questions and issues important ? As will become clear in Chapter 6, the future well-being and spatial development of the nation depends significantly on how governments and individuals perceive their current condition and adapt to it. As always, more rational responses are likely on the basis of a clearer understanding of the processes involved and the options available. This Chapter may make a modest contribution in that direction, since the powerful emergent external forces which it considers could be the major determinant of Australia's future well-being.

Towards a global economy

Table 5.1 sets out some of the principal international forces which influence Australia's economic development and, for that matter, the evolution of our attitudes towards a host of social, cultural and lifestyle issues. They are divided into five, closely interrelated, classes concerned with private and government organisation and behaviour, community attitudes, technological innovation and the resource base. Community attitudes, if sufficiently homo-

Table 5.1 International forces affecting Australia's economy

A Private sector organisation and behaviour

1 Multinational corporations (their investment, production, pricing, marketing, research and development strategies). Such corporations may be domestic or overseas based.
2 Business attitudes to innovation, investment, product design, quality control, sales promotion, ethics, etc.
3 The modus operandi of financial and commodity markets

B Government sector organisation and behaviour

4 Foreign and trade policies of individual countries: for example, preferred trading partners, industry protection and export incentives
5 Macro-economic policies of individual countries: for example, fiscal and monetary (taxation and money supply), savings and investment, & research and development policy.
6 International agencies:
Regulation of trade (e.g. GATT)
Trading blocks (e.g. EC, NAFTA, CER, ASEAN, APEC (Asia Pacific Economic Co-operation)
Trade cartels (e.g. OPEC)
Finance (e.g. World Bank, European Bank, and International Monetary Fund)
Political forums (e.g. Organisation of African Unity)
Defence (e.g. NATO, ASEAN)
Culture (e.g. Commonwealth)
Environment (e.g. World Heritage and Antarctic Treaty Organisations)
Labour (International Labour Organisation)
Law (International Court of Justice)
7 International Agreements with respect to:
Weights and measures
Telecommunications and postal services
Transport (e.g. air traffic control, aircraft maintenance, sea-borne trade)

C Community attitudes in Australia relative to overseas countries concerning such matters as:

8 The work ethic and leisure
9 The need for material wealth
10 The desirability of innovation
11 The merits of environmental protection
12 The benefits of tourism and recreation
13 The quality, value for money and status of foreign goods
14 The status of other nationalities, languages and customs

D Technological changes—any developments which, for example:

15 Reduce raw material inputs in quantity or price
16 Enable the substitution of materials
17 Increase, or reduce, scale economies in production
18 Enhance labour productivity
19 Increase available information or reduce its cost
20 Reduce the friction of distance
21 Improve product quality
22 Generate new products

E	**Resource base**
23	The supply of, and demand for, raw materials
24	The relative costs of production in different locations
25	The attractiveness of the natural environment (i.e. environmental quality)
26	The extent and quality of infrastructure, plant and equipment (i.e. capital stock)
27	The stock of workforce skills (i.e. human capital)
28	The stability, flexibility and quality of public institutions

geneous across the citizens of a particular country, may be thought of as a national ethos. In a relatively open economy and society like Australia's (where there is a fairly free flow of goods, services, ideas and people between it and the outside world), the critical issue affecting the rate and form of economic development is how domestic conditions compare with the norm among peer group countries — in our case, the current and aspirant members of the OECD. As the magnitude and influence of each of these forces increases, the sovereign ability of an individual government and people to manage their own affairs inversely diminishes and the country's relative standing on each issue becomes more critical. In closed societies such comparisons are much less important, except that in the absence of performance yardsticks and competitive pressures, economic efficiency tends to lag badly.

Of the five sets of international forces identified in Table 5.1, two are particularly significant: corporate organisation and behaviour, and technological development. Their mutual links were first explored in a thorough way by Joseph Schumpeter (1954). He pointed out that a principal characteristic of market economies is 'a gale of creative destruction' in which the path to business growth, profitability and survival lies through invention and innovation. These can take the form of new techniques of production, new products or services, better design, or superior quality control. Innovation, though risky, creates a temporary monopoly for the firm which translates into higher profit. Conversely, firms which fail to innovate tend to lose market share.

This process tends to favour some countries or locations within them at the expense of others. Thus the last twenty years have seen economic decline and stagnation in some of the maladaptive parts of the industrialised world of Australasia, Europe and North America, but rapid economic growth in parts of Southeast and East Asia. Indeed, if Schumpeter is correct, stress and disorder are a normal and desirable attribute of a dynamic world economy rather than a general impediment of capitalism. Thus Thrift's (1986) view that the 1970s witnessed a period of prolonged economic crisis for the capitalist world economy may only be partly correct at best.

Although the development of new technology is intimately bound up with the needs of industry and commerce, it is also driven by human curiosity which seeks answers to perceived problems, by human fascination with new products and services, and by the dictates of fashion. The technological imperatives of commerce reflect these innate preferences of its customers. Thus business has an incentive to pretend to create new products or services which hardly differ from existing ones in order to expand market share — a kind of false technology. Taken to its extreme, it might be possible to package products which are scarcely needed, or may even be harmful, and sell them by vigorous marketing as innovative and new (Galbraith, 1967).

The link between organisation and technology is often recursive in the sense that the technologies invented then permit, and indeed require, new larger scale corporate forms. Thus such innovations as satellite telecommunications, the computer, and the development of mass production techniques involving standardised goods have facilitated the effective operation of MNCs or their large domestic counterparts. At the same time, it is the large company which tends to have sufficient finance and diversity of assets to sustain the risks involved in research and development for new products or ways of doing things. Occasionally governments intervene through the funding of basic and applied research connected with either civilian or defence projects. To some extent this can reduce the technological risk faced by small firms and enables them to survive better the rigours of competition, but much government-funded research is complex and large-scale, which encourages the growth of large corporations.

By its nature, technology operates almost exclusively as a global mechanism. It is a tradition of scientific endeavour that new knowledge is disseminated as widely as possible for critical appraisal. Occasionally attempts are made to restrict the circulation of military and defence secrets, but it has usually proved difficult to stem the flow of this knowledge in the medium-term, since most of it in the western world is conducted by private companies and individuals motivated by the lure of financial gain. Commercial knowledge is even less secure. Patent and copyright protection laws give only brief protection to inventors and innovators before pirated versions or clones of products emerge. Genetic materials are also easily transported. No country, including the totalitarian societies of the communist world, can engineer effective technological isolation.

Several other factors underlie the growth in numbers and size of MNCs:

- Production can be concentrated at low cost locations;
- economies of scale can be realised;
- technology can be recycled to less well off nations;
- market share can be increased;
- trade barriers can be circumvented;
- monopoly profits may be exacted from unsuspecting nations;
- taxation can be avoided;
- vertical integration of production is facilitated; and
- risks arising from uncertain materials supply, disruption of production, or fluctuations in market demand, can be spread (Rugman, 1982).

All these things serve to increase the firm's competitive edge and thereby corporate security. Moreover, if a firm's rivals secure these kinds of advantage, the powerful imperative of business survival demands that it follow suit. There appears to be little evidence to suggest therefore that technologically-driven corporate growth is about to run out of steam.

In the last forty years the development of MNCs engaged in the production of tangible goods and services has been paralleled by the rise of global institutions or businesses connected with financial and commodity markets (Figure 5.1). These have developed a large array of related strategies and techniques such as Euro-dollar and futures markets which serve to increase the velocity of the circulation of capital and direct it to the most profitable long- or short-term investments, or to minimise risk. As with industry in

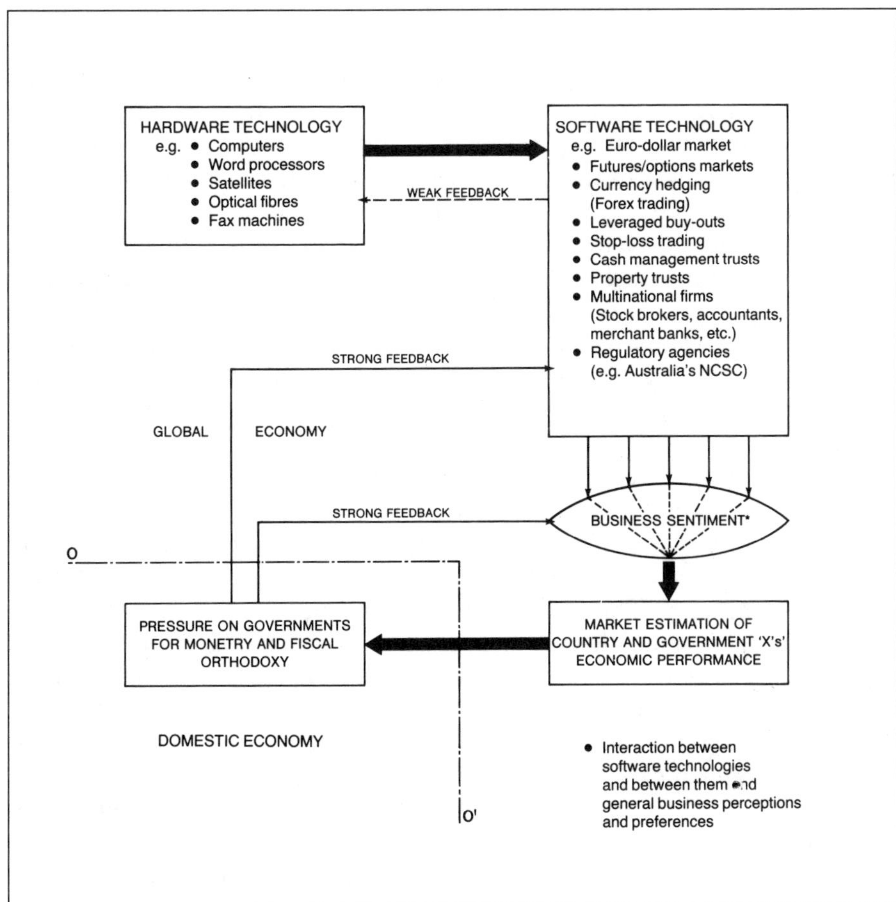

Fig. 5.1 The influence of global finance and commodity markets on national macro-economic management

general, the size and power of financial corporations or institutions is closely related to the development of appropriate technologies (Figure 5.1). These include not only financial devices or market mechanisms, but also innovations in information technology which permit the former to operate.

The stage has been reached where no open economy, and this includes all the member nations of the OECD, can insulate itself from the operations of financial and commodity markets. Nor can individual governments, even of the most powerful nations, exert much influence over their operations in the medium- to long-term. Short run manipulation may be possible on a small scale through such devices as monetary and interest rate policy, currency purchases and sales by the reserve bank, or international agreements to peg the relative values of currencies, but this is unlikely to have lasting effect. Commodity cartels like OPEC have also had great difficulty in making their arrangements stick for any lengthy period, and prices tend to reflect closely the balance of supply and demand. Moreover, markets adjust rapidly to changing conditions in line with business sentiment — itself largely an amalgam of estimates about profit and risk. It stands to reason, therefore, that government macro-economic policy cannot ignore market sentiment if it wishes to retain the level of business confidence necessary for economic development and well-being. Conversely, those governments whose policies do not measure up to the standard of their peers risk ostracism by investors. The whole process is reinforced by such specialist credit rating agencies as Moody's and Standard and Poor's whose adverse pronouncements on governments can cause currencies and stock markets to crumble, and whose positive comments can re-elect governments (*Australian Financial Review*, 12 February 1992). Since the strength of global financial markets is increasing, the pressure placed on individual governments to follow conservative economic strategies is also growing.

Many of the public sector forces listed in Table 5.1 are practical responses to problems resulting from the growth of global market relationships. Some, such as GATT, the IMF, and agreements over telecommunications or air traffic standards, are designed to increase flows of trade and information between countries. These generally involve multilateral agreements or conventions between nations. Others of a more unilateral kind are introduced by individual countries to regulate real or imaginary problems arising from the unrestrained operation of the private sector across international boundaries. Industry protection policies are of this kind. And a few represent attempts by select international cartels to corner the advantages of international trade or business for their own benefit. We may place OPEC and even the EC in this category. In contrast, inter-government dealings related to science, the environment, culture and national defence tend not to reflect the needs of the private sector. With the exception of defence, they often arise from a genuine mutual desire between countries to improve the condition of the human race.

In a competitive world community attitudes or national ethos are also becoming crucial factors in national well-being. For example, any nation which insists on working a leisurely 36-hour week when its competitors work flat out for 44 hours, which quarantines many of its resources in national parks, which values imported goods as status symbols irrespective of quality, or which indulges in crude cultural chauvinism is likely to lag in the economic growth stakes. Though we may lament it, there seems to be a considerable degree of homogeneity in the community attitudes of the most economically successful nations such as Japan, West Germany, Taiwan and South Korea: a preference for hard work, innovation, and education for example. Some outlooks, it seems, are preferable to others if economic growth is the goal. Berger (1986) notes, with approval, the 'Bourgeois Confucianism' (Robert Bellah's term) of East Asia with its capacity for delayed gratification and discipline, especially in the interest of family advancement. The region's other cultural underpinnings include pragmatism and practicality, an active rather than contemplative orientation to life, and an interest in material things. Contrast this with the kleptocratic tendencies of elites in many third-world countries which often appropiate resources to themselves much in the manner of a kleptomaniac.

The final element of Table 5.1, resources, is much broader than the conventional inventory of natural resources such as minerals, soil fertility or climatic and landscape quality. The list also includes a variety of humanly-made resources which are equally important for national welfare: social, urban and communications infrastructure; human knowledge and skills; and the range of public or private institutions erected to control the conduct of a nation's affairs. These institutions encompass the legal system, the apparatus of government, and institutions formed either to influence government or to promote social and cultural welfare. Olson (1982) argues that such institutional arrangements, and particularly the structure of government, are crucial to the economic and social welfare of nations. What matters especially is the degree to which government is able to respond rapidly, flexibly, imaginatively and accurately to the issues of the day. This in turn presupposes a dispassionate and well-informed bureaucracy, a legislature which is relatively free of short-term electoral and special interest group pressures, a clearly defined set of appropriate powers and duties, and an educated and informed public capable of taking part in rational debate.

It was once widely felt that the possession of natural resources was a primary determinant of national well-being. It is true that many of the oil-rich nations of the Middle East have high *per capita* incomes, but this example is counterbalanced by the case of Japan. Japan, with few natural resources, has accumulated great wealth largely on the basis of its human and institutional resources. Furthermore, the rapid development of the information society (Jones,1982) will tend to accentuate the importance of human over natural resources, since a growing proportion of the value added to goods and services will represent knowledge and organisational ability rather than raw materials. Thus those countries which nurture human skills and flexible social, economic or government institutions stand to develop more rapidly and at the expense of those which do not.

So, in the competitive world of national economic development, the options open to governments to manage their domestic affairs are becoming severely limited (Browett and Leaver, 1989). It is as if a policy strait-jacket is being imposed on nations, leaving them very little room for discretionary manoeuvres. This lack of room for independent action seems to stretch through all aspects of national life (economic, social and even cultural) and into the realm of foreign relations. This view tends to imply that society and culture may be dependent increasingly on economic events driven by the kinds of mechanism discussed previously. It may be that the years to come will see nations distinguished from each other only by a residue of historically or environmentally determined culture. The few differences in national outlook we may perceive could well mirror such aspects of the geographical environment as natural resource endowment, population density, and climate. It may be, for example, that the countries of the New World with their wide open spaces, relatively low population densities, and relatively abundant natural resources are likely to remain more individualistic and less regimented than those of the Old World.

This emergent global system does not yet meet the standard set out by Pronk (1983) for an integrated international economic order. He envisaged three major characteristics of such an order:

1 a set of more or less agreed values and principles among countries laid down in laws, constitutions and charters;
2 explicitly formulated and more or less coherent policies on investment, income distribution and market regulation; and
3 a set of institutions to oversee these policies, with guidelines for their operation.

We currently have a functioning global economy in which commercial interests are making the running while governments are slowly working towards the imposition of a standardised regulatory regime.

The internationalisation of Australia's economy and society, coupled with a widespread if somewhat erroneous perception of declining national well-being, has generated a furious debate over what constitutes the recipe for national success; that is, success in terms of a high per capita gross domestic product (GDP). The proponents fall into three main camps. There are those who see Australia's salvation lying in accelerated internationalisation through economic integration with the dynamic economies of north-east Asia (Garnaut, 1989) and of the ASEAN group of nations. From this perspective, the locomotive of economic growth is trade based on comparative advantage. The strategy involves the unilateral reduction of domestic industry protection coupled with the strong advocacy of international trade through such diplomatic channels as the Uruguay round of GATT. Though the ultimate goal would be the creation of an equitable economic enviroment, Australia would be content to see some trade preferences granted to weaker nations in the region. Australia's comparative advantage is seen to reside in 'niche' manufactures, raw materials and their early stages of processing, tourism and some services, notably education. The International Institute for Management Development (1991) placed this country in nineteenth place out of twenty-two countries surveyed in terms of outward orientation. Australia managed to export just 16 per cent of GDP in the late 1980s compared with 56 per cent for the Netherlands; 40 per cent for Austria; and 35 per cent for West Germany (Clark, 1991).

A second school, dominated by the thinking of Michael Porter (1990), accepts the benefits of trade based on national comparative advantage, but goes much further in its prescriptions — comparative advantage can be manipulated. The true path to national wealth is seen to lie in the promotion of competition among firms so that innovation occurs and resources are put to their most efficient use. EPAC (1991b) recommends this approach and quotes Porter with approval. This alone is not sufficient. Invention and innovation require flexible and educated workforces, good quality management that is able to perceive business opportunities and to offer the leadership necessary to pursue them, stable investment climates, a good supply of venture capital, and a focus on product quality (arising from good functional design, first rate materials, good workmanship and so on). Clark (1991) and the *Financial Review* (Anon 1991a, 1991b) discuss many of these inter-related requirements. Thus innovation itself is a spur to competition. This analysis poses problems for countries with small populations that cannot support many firms in each industry sector. Thus much Australian manufacturing is oligopolistic, by which we mean that output is concentrated in the hands of at most three or four producers who may find it comparatively easy to engage in anti-competitive strategies. If competition is a critical ingredient of economic success and is difficult to promote domestically, the government's fall-back strategy could be to reduce industry protection so that foreign firms act as surrogate competitors.

This brings us to the third school of thought. It accepts many of these ideas in principle, but wishes to retain a degree of national sovereignty over the course of events. Their arguments have two main strands. The first rests on the premise that market failure is significant and that governments can and should therefore play a major role in developing target industries (maybe in specific localities). Market failure is thought to occur when overseas producers dump their output in Australia or third world countries at below cost.

This is as true of the trade in farm products as it is in manufactures, as testified by the spectacular attempt by Saudi Arabia to sell wheat into New Zealand, one of Australia's traditional markets, at $25 less than the world price in late 1991. Given that the sale price was expected to be $125 a tonne and production costs were estimated at more than $750 a tonne, the subsidy was at least four times the sale price! The problem of dumping manufactured or rural produce into Australia itself would not be so severe if the dumping were long term. Australian consumers would simply benefit from cheaper goods subsidised by overseas consumers. However, the risk is that once local producers are driven out of business and the overseas supplier has captured local markets, prices will simply rise to previous levels or above. The outcome is lost jobs, for little or no demonstrable advantage.

Another dimension to market failure is that private calculus takes no account of strategic considerations: the need to retain broad-based domestic capacity to manufacture a range of defence related products. This case is recognised by current federal government off-set and corporate citizen policy aimed at retaining Australian plant and expertise in the armaments and electronics industries.

The third aspect of market failure relates interestingly to Porter's (1990) observation that industrial production and productivity is increased through the development of clusters of related industries. Sometimes market driven clusters appear autonomously, as in Silicon Valley located around San Jose at the southern end of the San Francisco Bay area, or along the M4 corridor westwards from London. Australia has nothing similar and it might be argued that the development of one or more integrated high technology nodes here requires kick-starting by government. That is one of the goals of the Multi-Function Polis (MFP) (Sorensen, 1991), though other mechanisms come to mind: targeted research through the CSIRO; tough government purchasing strategies; and tax breaks for, or government equity in, specific industries.

The second strand to the national sovereignty case holds that there is more to well-being than purely economic efficiency. Market forces, or Adam Smith's 'invisible hand', certainly ignore the spatial and social consequences of their behaviour, and the closure of industries, however desirable in efficiency terms, damages the well-being of some places much more than others (O'Neill, 1991; Winchester, 1991). Governments often feel, rightly, that they have a duty to assist localities whose inhabitants are economically disadvantaged and this has given rise to place-specific regeneration policies from time to time. The apparently successful steel industry plan of the mid-1980s is an excellent example. It focused primarily on updating BHP's steel operations at Newcastle and Wollongong so that they approached world levels of productivity and therefore guaranteed the industry's survival — together with the numerous downstream activities producing steel wires, bars, tubes and so on. In those localities where it is not possible to turn around a dominant industry in the longer term it could be argued that governments have a duty to at least slow down the pace of change, through carefully pitched but declining industry protection, to avoid social dislocation.

The third school is thus avowedly interventionist in flavour. In its more extreme forms it might be termed 'economic nationalist' and is somewhat conservative (Australian Manufacturing Council, 1990 — otherwise known as the 'Pappas Carter' report; Pusey, 1991; Carroll, 1991; and Manne 1991). The school, if it can be called that, brings together ideas from a wide variety of sources: sociologists, political conservatives in the Malcolm Fraser mould, political economists, and the representatives of sectoral interests adversely affected by economic change. It may become an important force in the 1990s much like free market economics (or libertarianism) was in the 1980s. To that end Donald Horne chaired a government funded 'Ideas for Australia' conference in February 1992.

Those advocating free trade and competitive environments tend to be called 'economic rationalists', as opposed to the economic nationalists who are somewhat protectionist and politically activist. In practice, such labels serve to obscure more than illuminate. The various sides might prefer to call themselves 'economic and social realists' who happen to harbour deep but genuine differences of opinion. Nor is the opinion within the camps necessarily monolithic. For example, there is ample discussion among the pro-competition school as to whether the Australian dollar or the level of overseas debt is too high (see the debate between Des Moore and John Pitchford in the 1989 Spring issue of Policy). The economic nationalists or conservatives may unite in their distrust of the market, but they also have a major difficulty in prescribing what might replace it in various problem situations, especially where pro-active strategies are mooted to accelerate a preferred industrial structure. Some would like governments to 'pick winners' among industries, even though governments almost everywhere have an awful record at trying to do so. Others would prefer a greater range of subsidies to training, research and development, and industrial infrastructure. Whatever path is selected is likely to have unforeseen consequences. Thus the creation of manufacturing jobs in Western Sydney, though admirable in its own right, might be at the expense of rural prosperity.

These matters have their counterpart in the geographical literature. Thus Fagan (1991) warns that:

> micro-economic policies ultimately driven by the narrow focus on debt and the balance of payments could lead to the further marginalisation of people and places which have already borne an unequal share of the costs of economic restructuring during the 1980s.

Interestingly, Fagan's treatment of the debt problem shares much in common with Pitchford's position, though the latter writes from quite different ideological territory. O'Neill (1991) also sounds a warning on spaceless economics and its adverse equity consequences for narrowly based economies in country towns, especially those dependent on the TCF industries. On the other hand, Linge (1991) stresses conventionally the importance of micro-economic reform to improved economic performance despite its tendency to marginalise parts of Australia. On the subject of labour market reform, Clark (1991) argues that while Australia's centralised labour market system is excessively inflexible and needs to be freed up, total deregulation is unlikely to work because there is

> just not enough geographical differentiation in the Australian economy ... few Australian regions and perhaps no large metropolitan areas have such distinct labour histories and institutions that a decentralised solution could be made a practical reality.

Consequences of the impending global economy

The time has now come to look in more detail at the possible consequences of these growing international forces from a mainly economic and Australian perspective. Some attempt will be made to evaluate the merits of the observed situation and trends, though this aim entails considerable risk since any interpretation naturally involves the authors' value systems. This section will also query how far the pattern of events might be subject to community control.

The Multinational Corporation

Of the forces we have identified, the single most important element of foreign control or influence imprinted on the public consciousness is the multinational corporation (MNC). Its actions, intentions and powers are frequently perceived as malevolent. Crough and Wheelwright's (1982) polemic is written in this vein. They advance a welter of statistics which purport to show that a considerable proportion of key economic sectors is under the *control* of foreign companies: three-fifths of mining; a half of minerals exploration, research and development, and advertising; and one-third of manufacturing, general insurance, and non-bank finance, for example. In practice, only Crough and Wheelwright's figures for mining relate to *control* and the rest involve *ownership*. However, the ownership of equity is often assumed to understate the level of control possible, since company policy can frequently be determined by parties owning as little as 30 per cent of the equity. Table 5.2 presents official figures for both ownership and control. Crough and Wheelwright's figures appear to be on the high side. It is also apparent that there is no simple relationship between control and ownership. For several sectors (life insurance, financial corporations, transport and especially banking) Australian control exceeds ownership. Moreover, there is no compelling evidence from the figures that foreign ownership is expanding

Table 5.2 Foreign ownership by industry sector

	Foreign ownership	*Australian ownership*	*Australian control*
Mining			
1972/73	49.5	50.5	
1982/83	50.4	49.6	
1984/85	44.7	55.3	48.5
Minerals processing			
1972/73	39.7	60.3	
1981/82	46.3	53.7	
Manufacturing			
1972/73	31.2	68.8	
1982/83	32.9	67.1	
1986/87	30.9	69.1	65.4
Life insurance			
1973	36.8	63.2	
1983/84	40.3	59.7	73.4
General insurance			
1972/73	45.4	54.6	
1983/84	34.1	65.9	64.1
Registered financial corporations			
1984	35.9	64.1	
1986	38.1	61.9	68.7
Agricultural land			
1983/84	5.9	94.1	
Transport			
1983/84	5.1	94.9	96.5
Banking			
1986	21.0	78.0	93.6

Source: Foreign Investment Review Board (1991)—based on various ABS Statistical Series; and *Yearbook Australia*, 1991.

significantly overall. Car assembly is totally foreign controlled, while oil refining, basic chemicals, brown coal and petroleum, silver, lead and zinc, black coal and iron ore range from 90 down to 47 per cent.

Crough and Wheelwright also claim that perhaps $36 or even more out of every $100 of after-tax company profits belong to foreigners. This appears to be contradicted by 1986 Foreign Investment Review Board (FIRB) figures which show that the proportion of after-tax company income payable overseas has remained a fairly constant 25 per cent over the previous ten years (FIRB, 1986b).

Australia has nevertheless a high level of technical dependency on foreign companies. In 1980 about 90 per cent of all patents lodged in this country were foreign, and a similar proportion of royalty payments went overseas. A major contributing factor to this dependency is the low proportion of GDP spent on research and development — 1.2 per cent in 1988/89 compared with at least twice that in the United States, France, Germany, Sweden and Switzerland (BIE, 1989). Worse still, from the perspective of developing an export oriented manufacturing sector, only 40 per cent of the $4.2 billion spent in 1989 was by the business sector. The remainder was government funded.

These figures seem impressive, but are selective. Many other producing sectors have low levels of foreign penetration — farming, transport, retail distribution, retail banking, and construction, for example. Consequently, the foreign-owned proportion of Australia's capital stock stood at 20.8 per cent in 1984 (A$ 36.5 billion out of $175.3 billion), up from 18.2 per cent in the early 1970s (see Table 5.3). Net income payable abroad stood at only 3.4 per cent of net domestic product in 1985/86 (FIRB, 1986b), though, more worryingly, income paid overseas as a proportion of the value of exports rose from 7.5 per cent in 1973/74 to 12.5 per cent in 1982/83 (FIRB,1985). However, this deterioration is not reflected in the ratio of Australia's investment overseas to foreign investment here. The ratio was 1:3 in 1980 and remained so a decade later (Table 5.4).

Table 5.3 The foreign-owned proportion of Australia's total capital stock

Five-year averages	*A Total capital $m*[1]	*B Estimate of stock foreign ownership of capital $m*[1]	*B/A (%)*
1970–74	37 632	6 834	18.2
1975–79	79 898	9 857	12.3
1980–84	147 428	24 472	16.6
1984	175 334	36 482	20.8

1 Estimates only

Source: Foreign Investment Review Board (1986a)

Table 5.4 Australia's international investment position ($ billion)

	Accumulated foreign investment at year end (a)	*Accumulated Australian overseas investment at year end (b)*	*Net international position*	*a/b (%)*
1986/87	177.3	62.0	115.2	35.0
1987/88	195.6	72.5	123.1	37.1
1988/89	229.3	84.0*	145.3	36.6

* United States $32.5bill.; UK $13.8bill.; Other OECD $13.0bill.; Papua New Guinea $8.9bill.

Source: Foreign Investment Review Board (1991)

One can continue to quote such figures *ad infinitum* but not come close to the key question which needs to be asked, namely: is the current level and pattern of foreign ownership and control in the private sector either undesirable or unavoidable? Table 5.5 tabulates the major potential costs and benefits of MNC investment (see also Wilson, 1986, pp. 131ff). It demonstrates that in best-case circumstances MNC investment is positively beneficial to national economic growth and efficiency but that, in others, considerable damage may be done to a country's well-being. This appears to be a prima facie case for Governments aiming to secure the benefits and obviate the costs. This strategy appears to be increasingly feasible for middle-ranking powers such as Australia as their policy-makers' regulatory armoury expands in a sensitive way to meet the challenge of the MNC.

Table 5.5 The potential benefits and costs of hosting multinational companies

Benefits	*Costs*
Increased employment	Exploitation of labour—low wages, long hours, poor conditions
Development of labour skills and management techniques	Little training; most key management decisions made overseas
Source of export revenue—part of world-wide production network	Import replacement strategies reduce exports
Access to new technologies; stimulus for R & D	Recycling old technology; payment of royalties overseas; inappropriate technology
Source of investment funds, and capital inflow	Profits repatriated
Greater tax base for the nation	Tax avoidance through transfer pricing and other mechanisms
Greater competition for domestic producers increases efficiency	Emergence of competing domestic enterprises thwarted; exploitation of local suppliers through monopoly power
Faster economic growth forces economic discipline on governments, and creates attractive business environment	Wrong kind of growth—often inappropriate goods; consumption encouraged rather than saving or infrastructure investment
	Domestic economic management made difficult by currency speculation, variable capital movements, etc.
	Environment despoiled; resources plundered
	Companies profit from community—provided infrastructure
	Collusive practices between MNCs raise prices or reduce quality of goods and services

For example, the Australian government is pursuing an active offset policy with foreign suppliers of such items as defence equipment, civilian aircraft and electronic goods to be consumed locally. In order to obtain contracts the companies involved have to agree to purchase Australian-made components. The beneficial consequences may include immediate local access to the most advanced technology, an expanded research and development effort, the growth of a pool of highly skilled labour, and increased exports of goods and services.

A development of the offset idea is the concept of the 'Corporate Citizen'. Offsets are negotiated on a deal-by-deal basis whereas corporate citizen companies gain a general 'pre-qualified offsets supplier status' (PQOS) which makes it easier for them to tender for large government business. To gain PQOS, Australian subsidiaries of MNCs have to commit themselves to spending 5 per cent of their annual turnover on research and development and lift their exports to equal 50 per cent of their imports in value added terms within seven years. In 1987 the government was negotiating PQOS with seven multinational computer companies including Wang, DEC and IBM. Since exports in the computer sector were running at $145 million in 1987 compared with imports of $3.5 billion, this arrangement also has the potential to bring about a large increase in high technology exports to balance a disconcerting trade imbalance in this sector. Rugman (1982) raises a warning about this strategy, if Canadian experience is any guide. Canadian science policy foundered on a lack of co-operation from MNCs, and Rugman advocates focusing policy on increasing the research and development effort of domestic firms only.

Many other programs may also attract high technology MNC investment with similar outcomes. Two examples are workforce training and fiscal incentives policies aimed at improving the nation's research and development performance and, secondly, macro-economic strategies designed to make Australian exports competitive in world markets. The former include the 150 per cent tax concession for research and development expenditure (BIE, 1989) and the 1 per cent training levy (since raised) which was imposed on all but the smallest businesses in 1990. Macro-economic strategies include the maintenance of a slightly undervalued currency, a low inflation and interest rate regime, and moderate corporate taxes. The numerous efficiencies that result from low inflation are set out clearly by EPAC (1991c), and include a better functioning of the price system, lower distortion in the tax system, and higher savings and investment.

Krause and Sekiguchi (1980) see the maintenance of an undervalued currency by Japan over much of the post-war period as an important element in that country's economic success. Japan also used mercantilist strategies to initial good effect. These effectively reduced the ability of overseas producers to export to Japan, and therefore encouraged a limited degree of MNC investment designed to overcome trade barriers. At the same time exports flourished and enabled the growth of Japan's own MNCs. The resulting trade surplus eventually had the effect of creating an over-valued currency which, indirectly, helped precipitate the global stock-market crash of October 1987. The lesson may be that a minor economic power such as Australia can get away to some extent with rigging the market place, but a major one cannot. The Japanese government also sought to nudge industrial investment towards certain products, though Garnaut (1989) warns against overstating its role in that direction.

OECD figures on the corporate tax burden in different countries suggest that Australian corporate taxes in the mid-1980s were indeed low by world standards once social security levies borne by employers are added in, despite the image created by the then 49 per cent tax rate (Cassie, 1987). At the start of the 1990s Australia's corporate taxes at 3.6 per cent of GDP were among the second lowest in the OECD, and compare with figures of 2.9, 5.0, and 7.9 per cent respectively in the USA, Britain and Japan. While it is difficult to ascertain the true value of a currency, the Trade Weighted Index (TWI) of the Australian dollar which stood at nearly 57 at the end of September 1987 was estimated as being 15 to 20 per cent undervalued using the Purchasing Power Parity theory of currency valuation (Clark, 1987). Things had probably changed little by the start of 1992 when the TWI stood at 56. This is at odds with the oft repeated claims of Australia's primary producers that the currency is over-valued.

Beneficial MNC investment, production and marketing strategies can also be fostered by ensuring an open competitive business environment which has low rates of industry protection and few artificial bars to entry. In theory at least, these conditions should provide the consumer with low cost and high quality goods and services. This is likely to be the practical outcome too. To see why, we have to ditch the tired clichés of dependency theory, with its notions of commercial exploitation of the impoverished periphery by the industrialized core (Higgott, 1984; Rimmer and Forbes, 1982), and substitute instead a more adequate understanding of how the commercial world really operates (see Tussie, 1983 and Alejandro, 1983 for a useful discussion of the issues involved). Their argument is that the path of development in Latin American countries is quite varied and not consistent with the simplicities of the Frank and Wallerstein core–periphery models.

When the USA dominated world industrial output as little as thirty years ago, and was home to most large, powerful and comparatively unrestrained MNCs, dependency notions made some sense. Now there are several industrial cores and more emerging, each of whose companies is locked in fierce competition for market share. The USA has been joined, for example, by a battery of competing European nations whose interests are far from mutual, by Japan, and by a constellation of other rapidly developing countries such as Hong Kong, South Korea, Taiwan, Mexico, and Brazil. The list of cores might even be expanded to include several republics of the Commonwealth of Independent States (the former Soviet Union) and such former Warsaw Pact countries as Poland, Czechoslovakia and Hungary (Ferrer, 1983). And even Frank (1967) acknowledged that economic crises in core countries serve to reduce their economic grip. Table 5.6 suggests that Australia is indeed slightly broadening its sources of MNC investment in line the with these observations, with less capital inflow from traditional countries. The 'other' category's contribution to foreign capital inflow rose from 20 to 30 per cent in just four years up to 1988/89.

In these circumstances it is perhaps more of a case of the periphery exploiting the core. In order to prosper in a highly competitive environment, MNCs compete not just in price and quality terms, but by effectively exporting jobs to subsidiary or joint venture companies located in lower cost countries towards the economic periphery. In fact, countries such as Japan, which are at the pinnacle of their economic success, are so desperate to unload their surplus income (to reduce appreciation pressures on their currencies and thereby maintain a degree of export competitiveness for their domestic industries) that a torrent of overseas investment has been unleashed. Much will be speculative and dissipated in the host countries, or ill-conceived and not earn a good return on capital, or, if invested wisely, will promote the development of the host more than the country of origin. In each case, MNC investment appears to be an advantage to the host country rather than the reverse. It follows, therefore, as Tussie (1983) has also argued, that lack of development may result from countries' failure to integrate sufficiently with the world economy rather than the reverse.

The recent performance of some Japanese capital in Australia seems to bear this out. Nissan decided in early 1992 to close its manufacturing operations in Melbourne after pumping about $1 billion over the previous five years into its facilities and products to keep them going. And the long-term wisdom

Table 5.6 The level of accumulated foreign investment in Australia, by country ($ billion)

Country	*1984/85*	*Rank*	*% of total*	*1988/89*	*Rank*	*% or total*
UK	26.1	2	23.5	47.2	1	20.6
USA	26.8	1	24.1	46.8	2	20.4
Japan	16.2	3	14.6	33.3	3	14.5
Germany (FR)	3.6	6	3.2	7.5	4	3.3
Switzerland	4.1	5	3.7	7.0	5	3.1
Hong Kong	3.4	7	3.1	6.8	6	3.0
Singapore	8.9	4	8.0	6.7	7	2.9
New Zealand	1.5	12	1.3	5.1	8	2.2
Others	20.7		18.6	68.9		30.0
Total	111.3		100.0	229.3		100.0

Source: Adapted from Foreign Investment Review Board (1991)

of many a Japanese property investment during the 1989 property boom is highly doubtful.

The Australian government has also devised policies which effectively encourage foreign MNCs producing in Australia to become major exporters of industrial goods. These have traditionally accounted for only one fifth of exports by value, but an argument can be made that Australia needs to develop rapidly its manufacturing sales abroad. This revolves around the view that increased export income from manufactures relative to other sectors would lessen Australia's exposure to the roller coaster of commodity prices, and help stabilise both export income and the value of the dollar. The value added by manufacture, or services for that matter, also tends to be higher than for the production of raw materials, on account of their large information and skill content. Thus the export of additional goods and services stands to improve living standards more than could be achieved by concentrating on raw material exports alone.

The single largest manufacturing exporter in Australia is the Holden Motor Company, mainly on account of its export of auto engines to assembly plants in the USA, Britain and Germany owned by the parent company, General Motors. It is most unlikely that an independent Australian owned company could have cracked that market. The engine plant was constructed to take advantage of a system of import credits devised by the federal government to help make the auto industry more efficient, while reserving 80 per cent of the market for small-scale and relatively high cost domestic producers. This scheme, parts of which were abandoned or watered down under the Button car industry plan, also allowed duty on low-cost imported components for the local assembly industry to be reduced by credits earned for the exports of other components such as engines. The main consequences are that producers, and ultimately the consumer, benefit from reaping scale economies not available to goods produced solely for the small Australian market, and that Australian exports of manufactured goods are increased. That the latter are to some extent balanced by additional imports of components does not matter much as there is considerable advantage in reducing national reliance on primary exports.

Well-managed off-set policies of the kind already mentioned also serve to increase the export volume of manufactures. Locally made parts of an FA-18 Hornet fighter aircraft or jumbo jet are not incorporated solely in the finished product purchased by this country, but in every aircraft produced wherever it is sold. In these cases, the nominally independent local producer effectively becomes tied in to the MNC's production network. If the government has a role in the negotiating a binding long-term contract, the producer is less vulnerable to commercial pressures to reduce prices or deliveries than where privately contracted to provide components for large companies.

MNC investment in productive facilities, whether from retained profits or through capital inflow, also has other advantages to the nation. Much fixed plant and equipment cannot be moved readily out of the country like finance capital placed in stocks or bonds, though it can be sold to local interests — perhaps at a discount for poorly conceived businesses — and the income repatriated. It depreciates, too, and continually has to be replenished in some way on a regular basis. Thus a significant MNC presence in a strong economy can lead to a persistent inflow of productive rather than speculative capital.

Australia's effort at promoting capital inflow from industrial MNCs (or, for that matter, their exports) pales into insignificance alongside some competing nations. The Republic of Korea, for example, has developed an impressive suite of trade and industry incentives over the last forty years (Department of Trade, 1986, p. 9) These include a variety of tax exemptions and credits, tariff exemptions on imported machinery and materials, export credits, export promotion and numerous subsidies to input costs. Thus, while Australia's exports grew 530 per cent by value in absolute terms during the period 1971 to 1984, Korea's increased almost 1450 per cent. Moreover, 83 per cent of Korea's exports were manufactured goods compared with 16 per cent for Australia.

Many of the disadvantages arising from the hosting of MNCs listed in Table 5.5 can be removed or ameliorated by the kinds of strategy just discussed. Others such as labour exploitation, tax avoidance, monopoly power and collusive practices, currency speculation and environmental despoilation can be negated by the development of suitable government legislation and regulatory institutions of both a public or private kind. This has occurred extensively in Australia. One case is the development of a powerful trade union movement and the creation, at its insistence, of an interlocking network of legislation to regulate labour conditions coupled with the mechanism of the Conciliation and Arbitration Commission to enforce it. Monopoly power can be reduced either by easing the establishment of competing firms or through aiding market penetration by imports. Currency manipulations by the Reserve Bank help reduce the dollar's short-term volatility, while sound macro-economic management in general serves the same end. Finally, environmental matters are now regulated by a sizeable body of legislation concerned with conservation or, in the case of mining, restoration issues. On the debit side, Rugman (1982) has concluded that foreign investment in the case of Canada, whose economy has similar structural characteristics to Australia, may exaggerate the rises and falls in the business cycle. There may be little a government can do about this in smaller, more vulnerable economies.

In conclusion, there seems to be little reason to worry about hosting MNCs even at the current and prospective levels of investment. All that matters is that governments succeed in getting their own act together by creating and enforcing the necessary regulatory environment while ensuring the profitability of investment through the development of a strong dynamic economy. This co-existent regime is required for both MNCs and large domestic companies alike. Moreover, it does not seem to make sense to shackle foreign MNCs at the very moment when many Australian companies are spreading their wings overseas. It is quite likely that the foreign assets of local firms will expand more rapidly than the Australian assets held by foreign companies. This view is based on the growing managerial and entrepreneurial expertise of the best run Australian (and New Zealand) companies as they have progressively lost their subservient or colonial mentality consequent upon financial deregulation and lower rates of industry protection. Such companies as News Ltd., National Australia Bank, Brambles, TNT, and Pacific Dunlop are now true MNCs with high profiles on foreign stock exchanges or in overseas markets. Some Australian subsidiaries of MNCs also perform a MNC role in their own right: CRA and BTR Nylex, for example. Note, too, that many leading Australian MNCs are in the growth sectors of transport, the media and banking.

Finance and commodity markets

A high proportion of Australia's exports are raw materials whose prices have long been determined by the interaction of global supply and demand on overseas commodity markets such as the London Metals Exchange. As indicated in Chapter 2, Australia has little influence over the fixing of commodity prices. In part this stems from the fact that local producers generally do not account for a sufficient share of the output of any commodity to be able to manipulate the market. Moreover, it is difficult to form producer cartels among nations with a great divergence of interests. The situation is not improved by the fact that most Australian commodities can be substituted readily by other materials if prices rise too high. Examples include silicon for copper, oil or uranium or solar power for coal, synthetic fibres or cotton for wool, artificial sweeteners for sugar, plastics for aluminium or steel, white meats for red meats and so on. Perhaps wool, with its stockpile and promotions schemes run by the Australian Wool Corporation, is the only major commodity whose market operations have been influenced to some extent by Australian producers, but only in the short run. Australia is certainly the largest producer of wool in the world by a long way, but despite that the stockpile scheme collapsed under the weight of its own mismanagement when prices were pegged at too high a level (Watson, 1990). Those prices brought forth the normal economic responses of increased production and reduced demand. The Wool Corporation's attempt to defy economic gravity almost bankrupted the wool industry and a large part of rural Australia.

Even where international trade in commodities is negotiated bilaterally between countries or private companies, the price agreed will tend to reflect expected market prices in the medium term, ignoring short run fluctuations. Sellers may accept a discount for the benefit of long-term fixed price contracts or demand premiums for reliable supply and exceptional quality. Purchasers may occasionally pay above ruling rates due to political pressures. In 1987, for instance, the trade imbalance between the USA and Japan in favour of Japan led to Japanese utilities purchasing American coal at prices higher than the comparable Australian product.

Producers of export commodities are for the most part, and traditionally always have been, price-takers rather than price-makers. Modern technology has influenced their finances in two related and beneficial ways. Markets are now able to anticipate incipient changes in supply or demand and therefore price more accurately on the basis of reasonably correct information. This is the consequence of continual monitoring of such things as climatic conditions, livestock numbers, consumption trends, strikes, civil disorder, resource discoveries, and areas planted to different crops in all producing and consuming nations. The development of satellite technology and remote sensing have proved a particularly valuable data source on production levels. Such information is useful to the producer in deciding how much to mine or grow and what to sell or stockpile. And, for those faced with the possibility of producing alternative commodities, it can assist in the choice of the optimum combination of outputs. Many farmers located within Australia's ecumene regularly confront this situation because to some extent various grains, oilseeds or livestock can be substituted at relatively short notice.

The second benefit arising from the operation of modern information-rich commodity markets is the possibility of trading in futures (Hughes, 1987). This option might be particularly attractive to grain or livestock farmers since they are small vulnerable price-takers. The farmer can contract to deliver any portion of the property's expected output of a given commodity to a purchaser at a fixed price and date. This price reflects current estimates by the futures markets of supply and demand conditions at that date. Effectively, the farmer covers the risk of prices falling over the period of the contract since in that event the purchaser must pay the current (higher) futures price, but foregoes any possible benefit arising from a price increase. Naturally the prospective purchaser's interests are diametrically opposed to the farmer, gaining when prices rise before the contract is realised but losing otherwise. This mechanism therefore enables the primary producer to insure against potentially disastrous price falls at the cost of losing the benefits of price rises.

Even where commodities are produced mainly for domestic consumption, as is the case in Australia with such items as dairy products, eggs and poultry, or fruit and vegetables, prices are still tied fairly closely to international trends. Import competition (whether in practice or threatened), product substitution, consumer knowledge, or producer competition help to keep local prices at or only marginally above ruling rates elsewhere and to promote efficiency. Commodity markets, we may conclude, are both unavoidable and beneficial. They induce competition between producers, but also provide them with vital information to enable optimum production decisions.

The rapid growth of international finance markets is a recent phenomenon (see Thrift, 1986). Some of the dimensions of this multi-faceted industry are outlined in Table 5.7. There is considerable money to be made in speculating on the movements in the value of convertible currencies, or from commissions received for raising optimum packages of investment capital which marry favourable interest payments and low exposure to risk arising from movements in currency value. Other investors in the financial game seek a home for their liquid assets which offers some combination of ready access, security and high interest. Yet others seek an acceptable package of capital appreciation and dividend return (in relation to risk involved) on the stock market. Some play commodity markets in a purely speculative way, never intending to take delivery of the physical commodity. Much trading in gold, silver or platinum tends to be of this kind. And an extensive network of advisory

Table 5.7 The finance sector: principal functions and institutions

Banking and finance
Central (reserve) bank
Trading banks
- corporate services, including capital raising
- 'retail' banking

Savings banks
Merchant banks
- services include capital raising, floating companies, advising on corporate takeovers, and cash management trusts

Fringe banking institutions such as credit unions and building societies
Finance companies—mainly small high risk loans at high interest rates
Venture capital raising enterprises—Management and Investment Companies (MICs)

Investment in
- equities (shares, debentures, etc. in private companies)
- government bonds
- trusts (dealing in equity portfolios [domestic or foreign], property, etc.)
- commodities (speculating or hedging in futures, options)
- property (both for capital appreciation and income)
- superannuation
  - Investment advisory services (run by specialist firms, stockbrokers, accountants, lawyers, bankers, etc.)
  - Investment institutions include stock exchanges, futures markets, banks, life assurance companies

Insurance industry
- insurance against all forms of risk

Regulatory agencies (for the protection of the public against individual or corporate fraud)
Reserve Bank
Company supervision (e.g. Australian Securities Commission)
Self-regulation by the finance sector (e.g. by the Stock Exchange or the Futures Exchange)

services has grown up alongside these activities to guide the uncertain investor or capital raiser down the correct path. These are provided by stock brokers, financial analysts, merchant and trading banks, insurance advisers, accountants and the like.

Few members of the general public realise how much they personally have at stake in the system. In theory, the whole interlocking financial edifice is a valuable, and indeed essential, component of the market economy. It constitutes the means whereby scarce financial resources can be directed towards the most profitable ends, and a verdict can be given on the economic performance of individual firms, complete industries, or entire nations. Thus it is instrumental in determining the level of national wealth and facilitating national economic growth. It may influence whether or not we are to find a job or the wages we might receive should we remain employed. And, through our contributions to superannuation funds, life insurance policies, or domestic savings, we are indirectly major players of the stock market with, for example, our retirement incomes hanging on the outcome.

The value of financial markets rests in practice on two issues: the quantity and quality of the information they receive and how accurately it is analysed; and the extent to which they can be manipulated by sectional interests. At the national level which primarily concerns us here, much of the information about the performance of market economies is provided by reasonably reliable statutory agencies such as the Australian Bureau of Statistics. Its information on trade and capital flows, foreign investment, balance of payments, the cost of living and other components of the National Accounts are highly regarded. Nor, at the national level, is it easy for private individuals or companies to manipulate such things as interest rates or the value of currencies. However, government instrumentalities such as the Reserve Bank can affect interest rates by altering the volume of money in circulation or the ability of financial institutions to lend it (by controlling the Statutory Reserve Deposits (SRDs) required of the trading banks). The level of interest rates set, together with the trading of Australian dollars for other currencies (leading to rises and falls in the country's foreign exchange holdings), can also affect the dollar's value to a small extent. But there is little a government can do to override significant bearish (unfavourable) or bullish (favourable) market sentiment about a freely traded (convertible) currency in the longer term.

When it came to power in March 1983, the Hawke government substantially freed financial markets from government control. The Australian dollar can be traded freely, there is more competition in the banking sector, a greater array of financial institutions have been permitted, there are no controls on capital repatriation by foreign companies or investment overseas by Australian investors, whether individuals or companies, and controls of overseas capital investment in this country have been relaxed. Initially the dollar floated freely, but thin trading facilitated strong fluctuations in its value and led to the Reserve Bank managing a 'dirty' or controlled float. Basically this involves the Bank in buying Australian dollars when traders are thought to have pushed the currency's value too low, and using them to purchase other currencies if its value appears to move too high.

These mechanisms have effectively provided overseas financial interests with an incentive and the means to pass judgement on the government's management of the national economy. A poor investment climate brought about by a combination of declining terms of trade, adverse budgetary and trade imbalances, and high inflation and interest rates will see little, if any, foreign capital inflow, the early repatriation of profits, and the flight of domestic capital in self-fulfilling anticipation of currency depreciation. Logically therefore, financial deregulation imposes on government an obligation to pursue such conservative economic strategies as balanced or low deficit budgets, the maintenance of a competitive exchange rate, and low growth in domestic demand in an attempt to stabilize the currency. This was precisely the path followed by the federal government in 1987 in response to the financial crisis of 1985/86 which was caused by Australia's declining terms of trade for raw materials. And in 1990/91 high interest rates were employed to restrict inflationary forces in a boom economy, again much to the approval of world currency markets who bid up the price of the dollar.

One might conclude that the policy of financial deregulation served the government well by forcing it to adopt rapidly the necessary remedial action to stave off economic crisis. However, its effects go far deeper. The perpetual scrutiny of the domestic economy by global financial interests will henceforth give the government little latitude in economic management. For example, to run budget deficits in the hope of encouraging economic growth or providing social welfare programs may be risky. As the global finance industry grows stronger and the competition for economic investment grows fiercer between nations, the pressures on government to follow orthodox policies could well mount.

Business behaviour

Whatever their size, product line, or corporate organisation, firms everywhere are increasingly locked in combat to maintain or increase their market share. Several probably irreversible factors underpin this situation. First, the barriers to international trade are being progressively reduced. These have been the target of successive rounds of international negotiation under the auspices of GATT with the object of securing the agreement of most industrial countries to reduce trade barriers in the form of tariffs, quotas and other artificial contrivances. So far, the general level of protection provided for manufacturing industry has been greatly reduced, even in nations with highly cocooned industrial sectors like Australia. The same cannot be said of trade in agricultural produce or services, both of which are surrounded by a web of artificial barriers and subsidies serving to distort world trade and to reduce the volume and value of Australian farm exports. Since this country has a comparative advantage in farm produce, it has attempted to organise a lobby group of similarly placed countries (including Canada, Argentina and Brazil) whose aim was to place agricultural trade on the agenda of international discussion and, in particular, on the agenda of the Uruguay round of GATT. A successful outcome could increase the prosperity of many of Australia's rural areas, but as of early 1992 that prospect was in doubt as the negotiations looked set to founder on the back of EC intransigence.

Secondly, the emergence of multi-nation trading blocks over the last thirty years has freed up trade on a more limited basis, that is between the signatory nations. The best known case is the European Community (EC), but there are many other examples. Australia and New Zealand negotiated the Closer Economic Relations (CER) agreement in 1983 to replace the New Zealand–Australia Free Trade Agreement dating from the mid-1960s. CER aims, among other things, to develop closer economic relations through an expansion of free trade between the countries by a gradual and progressive elimination of trade barriers under an agreed timetable (Department of Trade, 1983). There is also an emerging North American Free Trade Area that so far involves the United States, Canada and Mexico.

The development of large trading blocks poses dangers for international trade and for small economies like ours. Markets for our raw materials may be choked off, and demand for manufactured goods using these materials is unlikely to rise as fast as under free trade conditions. Bearing this in mind the Australian government launched the idea of the Asia Pacific Economic Cooperation (APEC) group in 1989 to head off moves to an Asian trading block modelled on European lines. APEC is a broadly based group that includes not just the ASEAN nations, Japan, Taiwan, South Korea, Australia and New Zealand but also such seemingly unlikely participants as The People's Republic of China, Hong Kong, the United States and Canada. The organisation aims principally at trade liberalisation rather than raising barriers against outsiders, which is what the Europeans have done. Ultimately the 15 member nations in 1991 may expand to include Mexico, Chile, Argentina, Ecuador, India, Russia and Papua New Guinea.

The loosening of trade barriers by whatever means serves to increase the number of competing firms in the market-place. The days of Imperial Preference and producer cartels have largely vanished. The kind of agreement negotiated in the 1920s by I. G. Farben of Germany, Du Pont of the USA, ICI, Solvay & Cie of Belgium and others to split the world chemical market into spheres of exclusive influence is unlikely to be repeated (Gart, 1986). Moreover, the growth of new industrial cores in India, South-east and East Asia and in Latin America could increase the number of competitors for American, European and Japanese producers in many markets.

There are three main business responses to an increasingly competitive and uncertain world. One is to improve business competitiveness, especially by raising business exposure to competition (EPAC, 1991b). Secondly, profitability can be increased by minimising tax liability. The other strategy is to try to regain some degree of market control. The latter is the impetus behind corporate mergers or inter-firm agreements to co-operate in various spheres of activity ranging from research and development, to product design, the joint production of components or co-ordinated marketing strategies. Inter-firm co-operation has been particularly noticeable in the automobile industry, where there are large scale economies in most aspects of production and the cost of tooling up for a new model is so high that product failure can place the firm's future in jeopardy. The Australian automobile industry is presently engaged in several such exercises: Ford's Laser is a clone of the Mazda 323 and Ford negotiated with Nissan at one stage for the latter to market its Falcon utility. Holden bought a Nissan engine for the Commodore, sold the Astra (a Nissan car with a Holden badge), and markets Daihatsus. Holden also has an agreement with Toyota to sell Toyota products with a Holden badge, while Toyota markets the Commodore as a Lexcen. Similar arrangements have been noted by Bloomfield (1981) in overseas automotive industries.

Intense competition has raised the pursuit of business efficiency to the status of a Holy Grail. Innovation is spurred by most firms' dread of being overtaken by their competitors in the race for sales and the subsequent threat to survival. It has led to companies seizing eagerly on each new management technique discovered in use among Japanese firms or invented by management gurus. Management by objectives, corporate planning, independent profit centres, quality circles, total quality control, and just-in-time stock control are a few of the approaches to have become fashionable over the years. By the same token any relevant communications, information, or product technology also tends to win rapid business acceptance. Academics pore over successful enterprises in the hope of detecting optimum combinations of management ingredients. Likewise geographers and planners study dynamic industrial regions such as Silicon Valley, Route 128 around Boston, or the M4 Corridor to the west of London in the hope of being able to replicate the necessary conditions for growth elsewhere (Hall and Markusen, 1985; Breheny and McQuaid, 1985).

On the tax front, Australian companies are faced with an apparently high domestic tax rate of 39 per cent. This is nominally higher than, or equal to, the rates prevailing in many developed economies, but in practice Australian corporate taxes are comparatively low among that group of countries once full imputation of dividends and the absence of social security imposts are taken into account. Nevertheless, Hong Kong, for example, has a corporate tax rate of about only 18 per cent and few financial restrictions (Byrnes, 1987). Some Australian multinationals (and New Zealand ones also) have floated separate companies on the Hong Kong stock exchange, with the legal argument that the new companies are separate entities from the parent and therefore not liable for Australian tax. It is not possible to avoid paying some tax in the home country by such means, but the overall bill is likely to be considerably less.

Thus nations such as Australia which maintain a relatively open economy — one in which there are few barriers to international trade or capital movements — force business to become efficient and sensitive to both domestic and export market demands, and to develop corporate structures designed to reduce tax liabilities. Consequently business becomes receptive to a continuous stream of overseas concepts and technologies. 'Innovate or perish' becomes the name of the game. This process places pressure in turn on community attitudes and institutions to adapt to the needs of business, especially in relation to work. The productivity, adaptability and flexibility of labour, its skills and remuneration, and its attitudes towards quality and product improvement will all have to reflect overseas conditions if local business is to survive. Perhaps the government also needs to look at company taxation, if only to put domestic companies on the same footing as Australian-based MNCs. Lower business taxes could be achieved by moving to a regime of higher indirect taxes, from greater horizontal fiscal equity (e.g. the government now taxes profits from previously exempt gold production), by reducing depreciation allowances, or through the removal of tax breaks for superannuation schemes. The Liberal Party's 'Fightback' package claims that the introduction of a Goods and Services Tax (or GST) would reduce producer costs through the elimination of payroll taxes and the refund of tax to exporters.

Some business tax concessions probably need to remain. One that seems to have stood the test of time is the 150 per cent tax deductability for research and development expenditure (BIE, 1989). One that failed is The Management and Investment Companies (MIC) Scheme that commenced in the 1983/84 financial year. This was designed to help raise venture capital for small innovative companies from individual or corporate investors by giving those investors a reduced tax liability to the extent of their contributions to an MIC. The MIC then took equity in qualifying companies, providing them with valuable working capital. One of the problems with Australia's capital markets has long been the shortage of venture capital (BIE, 1987), and the MIC scheme sought to plug this critical gap. Unfortunately, the MICs did not have a very successful investment record and cost the government too much lost revenue so the scheme was terminated in 1991.

Community control

In the light of the foregoing discussion, we can draw up a balance sheet of the apparent benefits and costs arising from the development of a global capitalist economic system. These are listed in Table 5.8. We can then investigate whether and how governments or independent community groups can attempt to capitalise on the benefits and ameliorate the costs.

Table 5.8 The benefits and costs of the global economy from an Australian perspective

Benefits/opportunities	*Costs/problems*
1 A more open, competitive economy leads to: • greater invention or access to advanced technology • faster rates of innovation and wider choice of product or service • cheaper, better, quality products and services • enhanced workforce skills • greater national self-discipline (affecting groups, individuals and governments) • interest groups less able to divert resources their way	1 Declining industries in some localities may create regional inequities in well-being 2 Declining occupations lead to an unemployment/retraining problem which may also have a regional identity 3 Pursuit of economic efficiency leads to homogeneity of social and cultural outlook between countries or regions 4 Devaluation of lifestyle, quality of life, and amenity issues 5 Decline in private and public morality. The pursuit of trade can corrupt a sense of right and wrong
2 Major force for equalisation of development between nations, provided participants play according to the rules preferred by the market order	6 National economic management made more difficult through market induced swings in terms of trade, currency, speculation etc.
3 Reduction in power of private cartels (though not necessarily those sponsored by governments)	7 Strongly disadvantages countries with corruption, weak rule of law, lax public administration, low labour skills and labour productivity, etc.

Chapter 5 has so far focussed almost exclusively on the benefits side of the equation, but, as Table 5.8 indicates, global economic forces are attended by some potential debits. Their impersonal dictates have the capacity to impose considerable costs on individuals or areas (items 1 and 2 under Costs). Declining industries or occupations are often concentrated geographically. In Australia this is especially so in the case of the TCF and automobile industries which are so significant in the Victorian economy. Unfortunately, the 'gale of creative destruction' tends to blow more furiously at a global level where entry into particular industries is largely unregulated and the potential cost competitiveness of new producers in NICs is great. Thus competition for established and somewhat sclerotic businesses in the developed nations can emerge rapidly in an open global economy, whereas such events would tend to proceed more slowly in the confines of a protected society. The resulting dislocation is serious for the communities affected, but we should remember that most citizens will benefit considerably from international competition through the outcomes listed under item 1 (Benefits) of Table 5.8.

The pursuit of an efficient industrial or service economy also has several side effects which some would consider undesirable (items 3 to 5, Costs, in Table 5.8). Most of the western industrialised countries now share remarkably similar lifestyles in terms of: occupational and family structures; the organisation of work; public institutions and systems of government; the range of social problems — and attempts to solve them; the array of sports, recreations and entertainments; and even legal systems. Put another way, geographical variations in society and culture seem to be diminishing in importance in the fabric of nations as they are swamped by the homogenising demands of an economic machine.

This machine also tends to value gross production more highly than either quality of life and amenity or private and public morality. The most obvious clash between economics and amenity occurs in Australia over environmental conservation issues (see Mercer (1991) and Brunton (1992) for contrasting and conflicting viewpoints on this subject). Should we log forests in Tasmania or around Eden on the far NSW South Coast for woodchips in order to provide export income and employment in locations where there is little alternative work? A similar question arises in North Queensland, where heritage listing of the Daintree rainforest will quarantine a potential economic resource. And is it worth proclaiming Stage III of the Kakadu National Park if it means losing export revenue from the minerals it contains? To what extent should Aborigines be able to protect their sacred sites and general way of life from mining companies and developers? These high profile issues are matched by numerous small scale examples in every-day life. How should, for example, mainstream society treat those who want to drop out and attempt to create self-sufficient communes which possibly constitute a drain on GDP?

The pursuit of financial reward also tends to override moral issues. Companies and governments are adept at condemning the mistreatment of other nations' citizens while simultaneously continuing to trade with them; or at selling arms to aggressors or to both sides in a conflict thereby prolonging it; or of trading in harmful substances. An argument often advanced to justify such trade is that if we don't do it, someone else will. Few companies relinquished their ties with South Africa, despite its system of Apartheid which amounted to racial exploitation. Nor is there any apparent reluctance on the part of business or governments to continue trading with various despotic regimes, military or religious, such as Li's China or, prior to the Gulf War, Hussein's Iraq. Trade embargoes on the former USSR for its invasion of Afghanistan also proved to be a nine-day wonder. The Australian Labor Party's anti-uranium policy folded in the face of a need to boost exports and the argument that, since other suppliers would fill the market, Australia might as well join in with a safeguards system aimed at trying to prevent the misuse of spent fuel for nuclear weapons. None of the trouble spots in the world seems to be short of weapons, partly financed in the case of the Lebanon by the narcotics trade.

Each of these possible costs is problematical. The assessment of their importance or validity varies from one person to another, depending on the individual's value system. In some circumstances a good case could be made that cultural diversity or exquisite natural environments should be compromised or sacrificed on the altar of economic development and prosperity. Few would wish to deny impoverished disease-ridden third world communities a better quality of life. In the industrialised countries, the trade-off between growth and culture or environment is complicated by a host of other issues. Economic development is not so highly prized relative to cultural or environmental conditions — indeed the distinction can blur as the latter gain economic value as tourist attractions; substantial conflicts may arise between local and national interests, between individuals and between social classes over their respective worth or merit; and the perceived needs of present and future generations may also be in conflict. However, given that cultures or environments which are destroyed cannot usually be restored and that the economic options which confront us are relatively numerous, thinking in western societies increasingly tends to favour conservation over development.

The morality of international trade is still more elusive. In general, private companies are not unduly concerned with whom they trade. In two examples, the Bond Corporation conducted business with Chile while singing the praises of Pinochet's dictatorship and Toshiba, the Japanese electronics firm, happily sold western military secrets to the Russians hoping not to be found out. If a general principle seems to apply from the corporate perspective, it is that they can do anything not forbidden by governments, who are the guardians of the national conscience. Governments, in turn, are not enthusiastic about using trade as a weapon of foreign policy to bring pressure to bear on other governments whose policies they wish to amend — because this strategy tends not to work. Jobs, exports and growth are often lost to the *moral* nation (i.e. the nation that acts according to high moral standards) and transferred to its competitors, while *target* governments (to whom the moral action and pressure is directed) rarely respond as desired. Indeed, trade sanctions may be counter-productive in that the *moral* nation loses diplomatic contact with, or engenders hostility in, the *target* country.

From another angle, there is debate about the propriety of trading particular products or materials with certain places — if at all. Military supplies and potentially harmful substances such as uranium come high on many people's list of goods whose trade should be restricted or halted. In most cases, any restrictions a nation imposes turn out to be fruitless gestures: the warm inner glow of righteousness pales beside *realpolitik*.

Uranium, therefore, presents a very real problem. An argument can be mounted that it provides a convenient means of providing electricity that is perhaps less damaging to the atmosphere than coal-fired power stations. In addition, there has been less loss of life in uranium mining than in coal mining. As against this, the consequences of a nuclear power station meltdown are horrendous, both in terms of environmental damage and loss of life. And, of course, uranium mining leads ultimately to the production of the plutonium used in highly destructive weapons. In short, the arguments for and against uranium mining are strong and it is therefore difficult to see how community agreement can be reached as to whether or not uranium mining should proceed.

The rise of global economic mechanisms, the growth of national interdependencies and the quickening pace of economic and social change will tend to increase the frequency and significance of all these dilemmas, and simultaneously make their resolution more difficult. Today, even the most powerful nations have insufficient economic or moral authority to steer the system towards particular ends, and their influence is being eroded by the addition of new concentrations of economic power. This situation, coupled with the difficulty of reaching any great degree of community consensus on many cultural, lifestyle or moral issues, suggests a growing dominance of economic influences on human welfare and of impassive market solutions to the problems confronting humankind.

In theory, the most effective path to public control of the global economy might be through the development of international agencies (see Table 5.1, item 6). However, most attempts so far do not inspire confidence in this strategy's effectiveness. The United Nations Organisation and its agencies exert little moral persuasion or effective power over their member nations, which are divided by economic interests, ideology, ethnic affiliation, regional outlook, and other factors. And overtly economic bodies such as the World Bank and the International Monetary Fund serve to reinforce the logic of market systems. Organisations like the EC, which are ostensibly created to ensure increased freedom of trade, end up as quasi-cartels distorting global patterns of trade in the short-term interests of their members. In brief, nations, like companies, have interests and rarely pursue altruistic goals on the world stage. Consequently, the global economy appears as a reincarnation of Adam Smith's 'invisible hand': a force organised largely on the basis of private or public self interest.

Items 6 and 7 in Table 5.8 remind us that market forces are a hard taskmaster. In a fiercely competitive international economic order, nations or states tend to be run like businesses (hence the terms Japan Inc., Malaysia Inc. or, closer to home, WA Inc.). Like successful businesses, successful nations are those which operate profitably on their trade account, innovate rapidly, invest wisely, pursue a common clearly defined goal, treat their workforces well, effectively develop labour skills, adapt their management structures to suit the prevailing conditions, seek good advice, and create channels by which the best leadership potential can be brought to the fore. Thus the kinds of problem listed under items 9 and 10 are, in some respects, not so much the consequences of the global economy as of national mismanagement. On the other hand it may be unfair to sheet home too much of the lack of economic development to particular governments or peoples. The cycle of disadvantage appears in part to be circular and cumulative: under-performance creates social and economic tensions which tend to preclude effective national development. This in turn leads to further division and conflict. Thus the comparative prosperity of some countries might create problems for others which are then reinforced by market processes. This view parallels to some extent, but at an international level, Myrdal's views on regional development, though the relative lack of development is seen more as a consequence of inadequate institutional, political and social structures or relationships than of purely economic forces (Myrdal, 1957).

It is doubtful, however, if the development of the international economy should be constrained to help the prospects of disorganised countries. Indeed, many of the sources of under-performance are amenable to domestic management under the slogan 'if you can't beat them, join them'. This appears to be Australia's response to the cathartic effect of collapsing commodity prices and the rapid loss of employment in inefficient manufacturing industries. The principal means used recently by the federal government for imposing discipline or changing outlook are listed in Table 5.9. They do not constitute an integrated long-term strategy, but arose as piecemeal responses to a variety of economic and social problems. Nevertheless, most items are consistent with the theme of promoting efficiency through greater use of market mechanisms. This package of measures is slim, though, compared with the measures introduced by Japan Inc. in the post-war years. Hosomi and Okumura (1982) chronicle a large range of measures designed to give industry a competitive edge. These include policies to permit a variety of cartels to promote exports, co-ordinate research, or rationalise plant; to raise the quality of exports and promote them; to detect and develop strategic industries; to encourage consensus; to modernise small business and so on.

In the development of the initiatives shown in Table 5.9 the Australian government was both responding to and leading public opinion. By the early 1980s an important coalition of interests in favour of a more open and out-ward looking market economy was emerging. It comprised government advisory bodies like the Industries Assistance Commission (now Industry Commission) and the Bureau of Agricultural Economics (now the Australian Bureau of Agriculture and Resource Economics), 'think tanks' such as the Centre for Independent Studies in Sydney, those entrepreneurial Australian companies which were beginning to tread the multinational path or operated in more efficient and less protected industries, various academic economists with pro-market leanings, and financial interests attuned to the opportunities opening up for Australia through the application of new communications technologies. These financial interests were clearly pin-pointed by the influential Campbell Committee set up by the Fraser government to advise

Table 5.9 Towards a more efficient Australian economy, 1983–87

Policy or strategy	*Consequence*	*Approx. date*
Financial deregulation	Fewer controls on currency capital flows, interest rates	1983 >
The Accord—various versions	Wage restraint; declining real value of wages	1983 >
Closer economic relations	Freer trans-Tasman trade—greater industry competition	1983 >
Improved educational or training programmes	Greater workforce skills 1% training levy	1983 > 1990 >
Management & Investment Companies Lic. Board	Increased supply of venture capital	1984–1990
Industry rationalisation plans	More internationally competitive industries e.g. auto, TCF, steel	various
Undervalued currency	Greater penetration of export markets; local industrial growth	1985–1989
Restrictions on domestic demand via interest rates	Diversion of output to exports	1985–1987, 1990–1992
Revision of tax system	Greater horizontal fiscal equity, lower marginal personal tax rates as workforce incentive	1985–1987
Campaign against fraud and corporate tax evasion		1985 >
Austrade	Overseas sales promotion upgrade	1985 >
150% R & D tax write-off	Promotion of R & D	1986 >
GATT initiative	Attempt to place agricultural trade on Uruguay round of GATT	1986 >
Privatisation on political agenda	Greater infrastructure efficiency	1986 >
Balanced budget	Lower cost of capital to business; lower national debt and interest payments; lower inflation	1987–1990
Revision of post-secondary education	Greater emphasis on supplying industry with necessary skills	1987 >
Corporate citizen and off-sets strategy	Greater R & D, production and export potential in high-tech industries	1987

on reform of the banking system and financial markets in general (Campbell, 1981).

It is ironic that this coalition's precepts were acted upon to a significant degree by an ALP federal government which has subsequently had sufficient political clout to sell the resulting measures to its traditional constituency. This includes a powerful trade union movement and the welfare lobby. The trade union movement's own youthful and entrepreneurial leadership could, fortunately for the government, sense which way the winds were blowing and adapt to them in their members' interests. Thus the Mark III version of the Accord negotiated in early 1987 provides for union members to gain a 4 per cent wage increase in return for genuine productivity gains arising from the abandonment of restrictive work practices. A start has also been made on trimming expensive welfare programs by reducing fraud and over-servicing, and by means-testing delivery. To neutralise objections by the strong welfare lobby to cuts in welfare programs the government has endeavoured to assist those in need at the expense of middle class welfare recipients.

The government's appreciation of Australia's current malaise, the remedies available and the preferred options among them are probably some way ahead of much of the electorate, by providing both need and scope for an unusual degree of political leadership. This quality of leadership and a surprising degree of maturity on the part of the Australian electorate may well be a fortunate alliance in overcoming two emerging problems at the interface between the global economy and democracy. The mechanisms, constraints and opportunities of the global economy are sufficiently complicated so that governments might prefer to avoid distraction by a largely uncomprehending electorate in formulating an adequate response. The rapid pace of change induced by world markets can also create headaches for democratic governments, in that swift and large changes in public policy may be needed to grapple with the problem. In this environment two strategies stand out: a longer electoral cycle and greater reliance on market mechanisms for the allocation of resources. Reliance on the marketplace helps take difficult decisions out of the government's hands, simplifies government options, serves to discipline fractious interest groups (including party factions), and provides a useful scapegoat. Thus the government's embrace of market forces is not just a response to particular difficult national circumstances brought about by the growing strength of the world economy, but a generally appropriate adaptation to that event from both economic and political stand-points. It is another of those choices which enable a nation to adapt to the world economy to reap its rewards.

Australia and the world economy

The foregoing discussion has tended towards one inescapable conclusion: that the structure, efficiency and prosperity of the Australian economy are inextricably bound up with the evolution of the global economic system and how government, business and society adapt to it. There appear to be numerous strategies by which the forces underpinning world markets can be harnessed to national advantage. In general, they are connected with efficiency and flexibility in resource use, with quality of output, with invention and meeting market demand, with sales effort, and with creating the appropriate environment for investment and encouraging the maximum use of workforce skills. This in turn involves a partnership between all sections of the community: government, investors, unions and private individuals. Of these, government may be the crucial element. It provides a stable operating environment via rigid and conservative control of the macro-economy, and also detects at an early date the changing political and economic relationships in and between countries. The latter may create both commercial opportunity or potential loss of trade and investment. The close link of foreign policy and trade was testified to by the third Hawke government's ministerial structure that put the two policy areas together — even though the Keating government subsequently split them apart. However the private sector, operating within the framework provided by government, is increasingly responsible for making investment decisions and allocating resources to their best use. There is now increasing evidence to refute Booker's (1978) claim that government and industry are dedicated to the mediocre.

Regional resource allocation

The issue of how Australia adapts to the changing global economy will have a big bearing on geographical patterns of social and economic development within the country. The way in which the nation conducts its affairs with the outside world is likely to be crucial in determining not just the pace and structure of economic development but also its spatial pattern, and, through that, the geographical arrangement of many other social, cultural and recreational features of the community. This is confirmed in Chapter 6.

Each economic activity tends to have a distinct set of locational requirements and preferences, as discussed in Chapter 2. Consequently any government policy or private investment strategy which directly or indirectly favours some activities over others, including the global forces discussed above, serves also to discriminate in favour of the places where those activities prefer to locate. Thus the path of technological research and development, the growth of new industries, adjustments to corporate organisation, changes in community lifestyle preferences, government fiscal and monetary policy and the pattern of resource discovery, exploitation or development, can all influence the economic attractiveness of different places and their rate of growth. Alternatively, any government policy which consciously favours (by means of taxes, subsidies or infrastructure investment) some places over others may alter the shape of the economy by encouraging the growth of industries favouring these target locations and, in a relative sense, penalising others. This may be termed *regional policy* to distinguish it from the great bulk of *sectoral policy* which has little or no deliberate regional content.

What, we may therefore ask, are the principal factors helping to shape Australian regional economic development in the last decade of the twentieth century? And what are the consequences? Let us start from the premise that the rise of the global economy and the federal government's response to it of creating a more open, market-oriented economy are the dominant factors at work. At least four important consequences can be identified:

1 Several regions will benefit directly from links with the global economy, especially Sydney, Melbourne and, increasingly, Brisbane. The first two act as the main interface between the domestic and international economic systems. Other regions to benefit are those whose products or services (including tourism and education) enjoy strong comparative advantage in world trade. Conversely, those locations with uncompetitive industries (i.e. those with low comparative advantage) stand to suffer economic decline.
2 *Regional policies* cannot reverse the thrust of *sectoral policies*, especially where the latter are consistent with the needs of international capital markets.
3 There is an on-going and subtle shift in the power of, and relations between, different tiers of government that is profoundly inimical to the regional development prospects of many areas.
4 The development of information technologies, and through them the rise of the large corporation, whether domestic or multinational, have effectively increased the colonial status of rural Australia *vis-à-vis* metropolitan cores. Furthermore, they have generated large spread and backwash effects within rural areas by helping to promote the competitive power of regional centres.

Several of the consequences of these processes are summarised in Figure 5.2. The dominant metropolitan cores (i.e. Sydney and Melbourne), and to a lesser extent subsidiary ones, are the headquarters of major international, national and local corporations. Regional cores tend to host branches of metropolitan businesses and the headquarters of local concerns, while the dominant business form of the periphery is the small independent firm. This pattern is not inconsistent with Taylor and Thrift's (1984) maps of the spatial distribution of three different segments of Australian business: global and

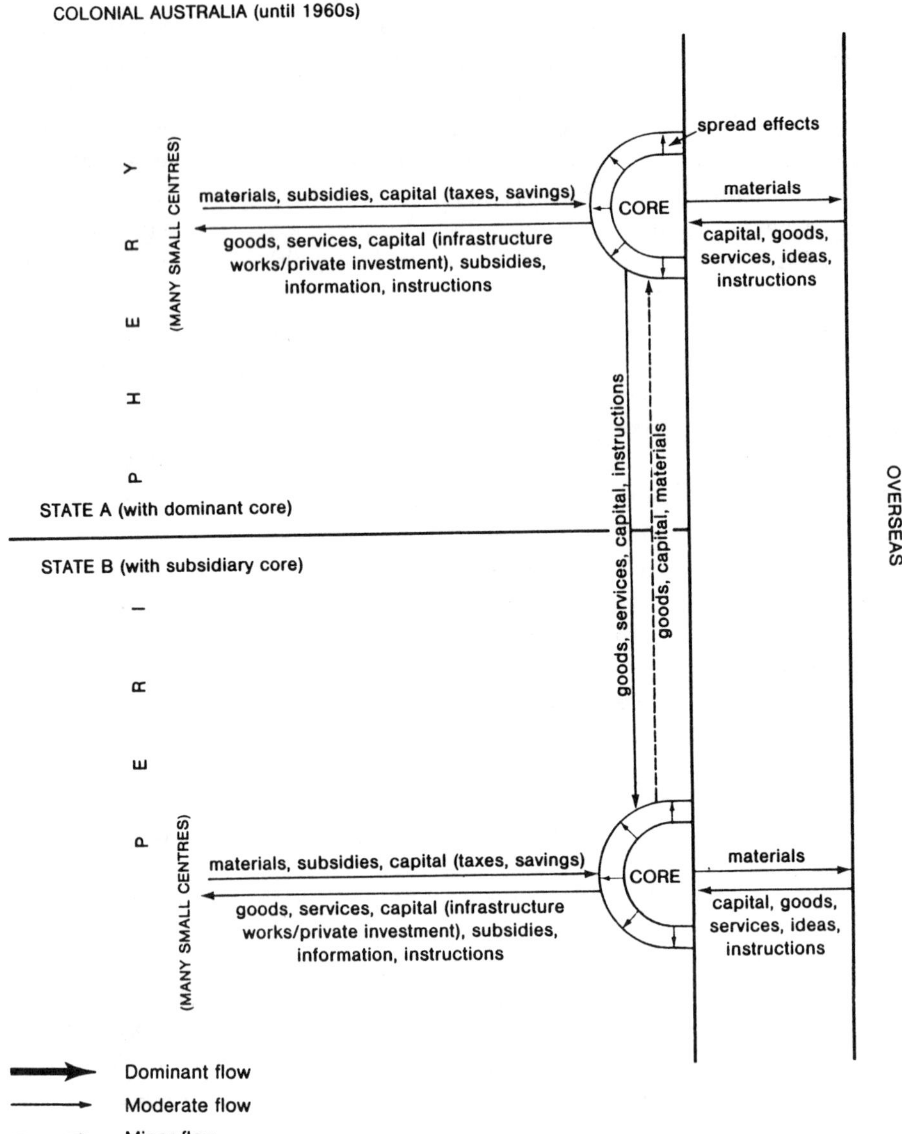

Fig. 5.2 Inter-regional economic relationships a) Colonial Australia (until 1960s) b) Deregulated Australia (1980s)

multi-divisional corporations; domestic, satellite and 'loyal opposition' firms; and small business.

Financial and commodity markets are the heart of the global economy. Their function is to circulate the capital and materials required by industry in

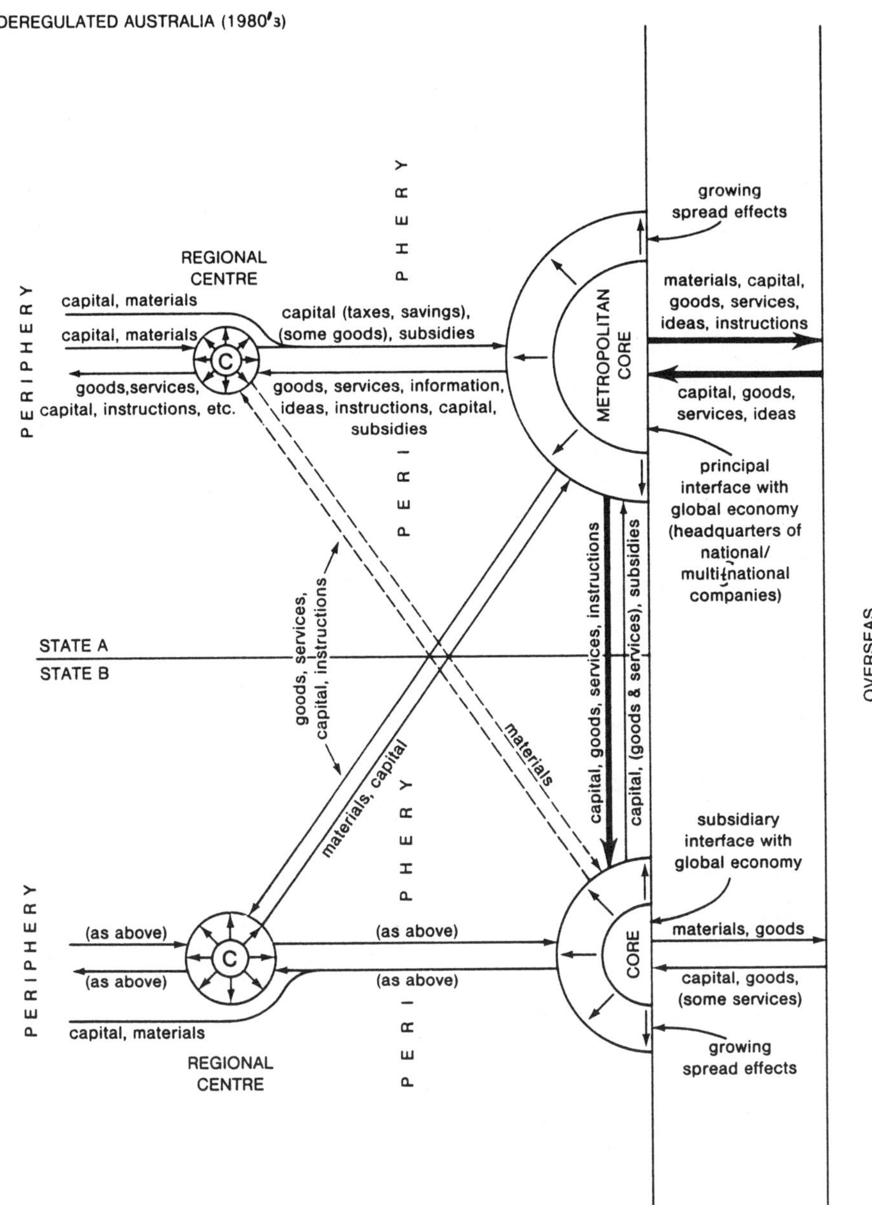

an efficient manner so that production is maximised and consumers are able to purchase goods and services as cheaply as possible. For markets to operate efficiently, they require large flows of information and geographical concentrations of traders who can interact with each other. Moreover international trade in capital and currencies is aided if there is one dominant financial centre within each country which serves to summarize the relevant information about national economic conditions. Thus there is a tendency for one major financial centre to emerge in each country — for example, London, New York and Tokyo — with a number of subsidiary markets possible if the size or structure of the country warrants it. In the USA, for example, there are commodity markets for farm produce in Chicago (in the centre of the corn belt) and another important financial market on the West Coast split between Los Angeles and San Francisco.

In Australia Sydney is the dominant national financial centre, as noted in Chapter 2. Melbourne's secondary role arises from its large population size relative to both Sydney and the country as a whole and from its being home to many large industrial companies. Both Sydney and Melbourne also gain from being the most important administrative, communications and production cores in the domestic economy and consequently the locations with the best overseas communications, especially for air travel. Thus they have become the commercial interface between Australia and the rest of the world, bringing accelerated economic development through the growth of employment in financial services. Sydney is also one of the main destinations for investment capital in the property sector, and this has fuelled further output through a boom in both the residential and commercial construction industries. We can expect Brisbane and south-east Queensland stretching from Noosa to Coolangatta to make inroads into the commercial dominance of both Sydney and Melbourne, especially Brisbane.

We also saw in Chapter 2 that certain other industry sectors have benefitted from Australia's economic malaise and the accompanying decline in the dollar's value. Among these are tourism, gold production, and some parts of manufacturing industry, including segments of the automobile industry exporting components such as engines or specialist vehicles. For the moment, these producers have to thank the opportunity provided by the emergence of a more competitive economy under pressure of international forces, as well as other favourable secular trends. Many industries with poor comparative advantage, especially in the manufacturing arena — the TCF group, metal fabrication and mainstream vehicle-building industries spring to mind — tend to suffer accelerated decline in a less protected environment. These industries are often concentrated geographically, and their prosperity (or lack of it) can consequently play a large role in the welfare of particular places. Moreover, the advent of an open economy may witness greater fluctuations in regional fortunes. Those parts of the economy and their respective regions which have been long exposed to world markets, especially those involved with primary production for export (including coal, wheat, and wool), are familiar with cyclical booms and busts. Perhaps urban Australia may become more accustomed to this experience.

Australian governments, especially state governments charged constitutionally with their territorial development, have long promoted regional development via formal or quasi-regional policies, including a battery of public infrastructure works targetted on particular localities. In the nineteenth century railway, port and road construction opened up much of the interior (Blainey, 1966). More recently, dams, irrigation works, electricity transmission lines, and domestic satellites have had a similar effect. Many of these works are difficult to justify on a benefit-cost basis (Davidson, 1969) and might never have been built in an era of fiscal conservatism imposed by an open economy. Where governments have to balance budgets, reduce taxes, and get value for public monies, infrastructure works like the Ord Dam are not an alluring prospect. Perhaps rural Australia has seen the last of this kind of big-ticket gift from the rest of the nation. A benefit-cost study was used by the Hawke government to escape the Fraser government's commitment to the Darwin–Alice Springs railway. However, political desperation borne of recession may lead to some large infrastructure projects in the early 1990s. A favourite is upgrading the trunk rail route from Brisbane to Adelaide via Sydney and Melbourne.

Other regional development strategies such as land grants and soldier settlement schemes gave way eventually in the post-war period to more formal regional policy aimed at promoting the economic growth of selected regions. Supposedly integrated packages of economic incentives to entice businesses to non-metropolitan locations were created by marrying grants, loans, subsidies, and fiscal incentives to such items as relocation assistance, training programs, and management advisory services. Decentralisation programs were most fully developed in NSW and Victoria during the 1960s and supplemented by the New Cities program of the Whitlam years (Harris and Dixon, 1978).

None of these specialist area development policies has altered Australia's economic geography in a significant way from what would have occurred in their absence. This outcome results mainly from under-funding, lack of long-term political commitment, inappropriate policy, and the overwhelming regional consequences of sectoral policy. It was inappropriate, for example, to base decentralisation policy on manufacturing industry at the very moment when that sector was commencing its long downward slide, or to try to conjure up growth centres without propulsive industries.

A respectable case can be made that, apart from the level of commodity prices and the general provision of public services, the principal determinants of rural welfare are the kinds of sectoral policies listed in Table 5.10. It has been argued, for example, that industry protection policy constitutes a multi-billion dollar per annum subsidy of metropolitan communities by rural dwellers (Hyde, 1985). If so, one year's income transfer far outweighs the total moneys ever spent by all federal and State governments on formal regional policy. Of course, there have been many sectoral subsidies in the

Table 5.10 Sectoral policies influencing rural welfare

A Federal government

Policy arenas with respect to:

- Trade (tariffs, quotas, bounties, trade promotion, bilateral and multilateral negotiations over trade barriers)
- Macro-economic management (fiscal and monetary policy, interest rates, capital inflow, currency value, budget deficits)
- Industry policy (research and development, depreciation of plant and equipment, investment allowances)
- Education and training
- Labour relations
- Communication and transport
- Health and welfare
- Foreign policy (e.g. trade embargoes)
- Immigration policy
- Mineral exploration and exploitation
- Farm production (industry rationalisation policy, marketing schemes)

Statutory authorities such as:

- Conciliation and Arbitration Commission
- Commonwealth Grants Commission
- Meat and Livestock Corporation
- Telecom
- Australia Post
- AUSSAT

B State government

Policies with respect to such matters as:

- siting of hospitals, schools, power stations, and other public facilities
- investment in roads, railways, ports, and power stations
- charging for public services such as water for irrigation, rail freight, electricity etc.
- afforestation, national parks and wilderness areas, the use of Crown lands, and soil conservation
- environmental planning (concerning in particular the development of hobby farms and rural retreats)
- production and marketing of farm output (mainly through industry boards) and mineral exploration/extraction

reverse direction: to the cost of transport and communications in remote areas; as tax relief to counter the higher cost of living; and to health and education. The system of State and federal awards set up by the Conciliation and Arbitration Commission may also militate significantly against job creation in rural areas by sustaining their wage levels above market clearing rates, though Clark (1991) has his doubts, and it almost goes without saying that the whole gamut of federal macro-economic and foreign policy can dramatically alter the prosperity of various parts of non-metropolitan Australia.

In Australia's nascent deregulated economy sectoral influences are becoming more powerful. Australia is increasingly in competition with others for the available pool of investment capital and associated production and material living standards. Policy-makers at the federal level are therefore fundamentally concerned with creating a favourable investment image. In this climate the nation's *aggregate* performance on the international league ladder becomes important. Regional issues are devalued, and investment tends to be welcomed no matter where it is located.

This philosophy emerged most acutely in Britain soon after Mrs. Thatcher's 1979 election victory. Her government perceived a lack of national growth as the principal problem and proceeded to scale down significantly what had hitherto been a politically bi-partisan regional development strategy. That cannot happen in Australia because top-down regional policy orchestrated by State and federal governments is now all but dead. The rise of the international economy also means that any *regional* policy is much less likely to succeed because it has to overcome the ever stronger locational forces of MNCs, commodity markets, currency levels and so on, requiring the diversion of large amounts of scarce public capital.

The third of the four principal mechanisms determining regional well-being (p. 277) arises from the second and involves shifting power relations between tiers of government. The federal government, as the tier responsible for macro-economic policy and for Australia's external relations, is gaining ascendancy over State governments in many business-related policy arenas. The operation of large domestic and international firms serving national rather than local markets is facilitated by uniform company management laws, uniform accounting, uniform production and distribution (packaging, advertising, transportation and storage) standards, and uniform stock market regulations with respect to capital raising, profit reporting etc. To the extent that these are introduced, State sovereignty is diminished. This was clearly the case at the start of the 1990s when national strategies for road and rail transport were unveiled and the Australian Securities Commission was approved by State governments. The federal government, as signatory to a number of international treaties on such matters as labour regulation (the International Labor Organisation) and environment protection (the World Heritage Organisation), is apparently able to over-ride State policy on those matters too (see Chapter 4). The management and regulation of new technologies also falls substantially in the federal domain, notably in the realm of data banks, telecommunications, satellites, and broadcasting. Furthermore the spread of corporate crime and trade in illegal narcotics across state and national frontiers necessitates an organisation such as the National Crime Authority to co-ordinate police investigations into such matters. In short, this raises the question as to whether the existing pattern of States and their constitutional responsibilities is appropriate for the corporate world of the 1990s.

State governments, it was noted earlier, are responsible for the development of their territories. But a competitive world imposes major constraints on what they can do towards that end. More than ever, governments are involved in a race to secure private investment for their States — hence the proliferation of State development strategies in NSW, Victoria and elsewhere, the creation of fast track mechanisms to steer investment proposals through the minefield of bureaucratic red tape, the negotiation of deals to provide necessary infrastructure works at public expense or the supply of cheap electricity from State grids, a procession of State Premiers travelling on overseas junkets to drum up investment in their bailiwicks, and increasingly 'responsible' budgets trying to create the impression of an attractive investment climate. Many of these features were apparent in the late 1970s as States competed for MNC investment in aluminium smelters. One consequence is that State governments are not too particular where development proceeds. Another is the potential for conflict between State and federal tiers over any action by the latter which might choke off development. Many examples exist where the federal government has used its powers for environmental conservation to quarantine State resources such as timber, minerals, and hydroelectric power in the supposed national interest. Among the 'causes célèbres' are logging in the Daintree and mining on Fraser Island, the prevention of dam construction on the Gordon River, the refusal to permit mining at Coronation Hill in Kakadu Stage III, and procrastination over approval for a paper mill at Wesley Vale in Tasmania.

As regional development has disappeared from national and State agendas, it has surfaced, as Jacobs (1986) suggests it should, at the local level. Many local governments have investigated the prospect of local employment initiatives and much has been written on the subject (see, for example, Blakely and Bowman (1985) and Kirwan (1987)). The irony of this train of events is that in some respects Australian local government is ill-equipped to operate as a development agency. It is not a sovereign tier of government but has a limited range of functions delegated by State Acts. It is poorly funded. And most significantly, if the federal government is losing sovereignty over national development, local government, which is at the bottom of the economic heap, will likewise have very little power over either the rate of local investment or the profitability of existing ventures.

When countries or States compete with each other they can at least vary significantly the cost inputs to industry or their fiscal regimes in a manner which may attract the investor's attention. Local governments have, in contrast, few economic weapons in their armoury. The ones they have include cut-rate holidays, low cost leases on business premises, advance construction of commercial premises or the possibility of joint ventures, but generally these are not of major significance in the business calculus, even for small firms. One must therefore remain at best ambivalent about the ability of local authorities to accelerate their area's economic growth in the absence of any clearly distinguishing and valuable asset such as an important tourist attraction.

Finally, the growth of the large company, made possible by modern communications technology and inevitable by commercial pressures, has proved a mixed blessing to the economic prospects of many rural settlements. This issue is treated in greater detail in the next Chapter. In effect service provision in rural areas has been enhanced by large national companies taking over independent local firms or by establishing branch outlets. On the positive side, this process gives rural dwellers access to many high quality price competitive services on a par with their metropolitan counterparts. This colonisation of the bush also yields some debits. There may be a decline in the level of local entrepreneurship as businesses are taken over or bankrupted by the superior competitive power of the large corporation. Furthermore, the colonisation process is locationally selective. It focuses more on major regional centres at the expense of smaller service centres. It is the former which have branches of Myer, K Mart, Big W and many lesser retail chains together with the higher level financial services offered by the trading banks.

In summary, this analysis of regional resource allocation has sought to show that the growth of the global economy and the large corporation have led to certain government policy responses and that, when these events are combined, they have several profoundly uncomfortable regional consequences. Regional development prospects appear to be becoming more capricious, and they are less in the hands of interested local communities whose welfare is increasingly decided in boardrooms located elsewhere. The commercial dominance of Sydney and Melbourne is growing, if anything, but with considerable spread effects to major regional centres. The latter are, however, offset by large backwash effects elsewhere in the non-metropolitan urban system. Regional development strategies have almost disappeared from the agendas of State and federal governments as they struggle to come to grips with a dominant market order over which they seem to have little control. In these circumstances regional development policy seems to have about as much chance of success as King Canute had in turning back the tide. Paradoxically, today's regional development strategies are now in the hands of local government, though it is singularly ill-equipped for the task. Yet economic growth, it seems, is still the touchstone of community success and a powerful incentive for local initiative, irrespective of economic reality.

Possibilities for the Future

Why study the future?

Throughout recorded history, and no doubt well before, humankind has sought to predict and control the future. In both primitive tribal society and early civilisation the immediate stimulus for prediction was the perceived need to avert, or at least ameliorate, such unpleasant, but all too frequent, catastrophic events as natural disaster, famine, disease, death and war. In contrast, the rhythms of daily life changed only gradually and provided little cause for alarm. The warning of, and response to, impending catastrophe was frequently metaphysical: a visit to the Oracle at Delphi or the Haruspex, or appeal to the deities. This is only to be expected in societies possessing little scientific knowledge and information, and consequently limited ability to control their own destinies.

How different things look from the perspective of late twentieth century western civilisation. Beginning with the Renaissance and reinforced by the industrial revolution, millenia of slowly changing technology have been replaced by an age of accelerating scientific discovery and invention. The sum total of human information of both a factual and scientific or explanatory kind is vast and growing rapidly. This has several important effects.

Fear of social and economic change has in large measure replaced fear of catastrophe (Toffler, 1971). At the same time science and reason combined have given society some means of anticipating and controlling events. For much of the last century or so, both have steadily encroached on God's domain in the management of human affairs, though often not with the degree of success expected (de Hoghton *et al.*, 1971). Finally, the relaxation of environmental, religious and, to a certain extent, economic constraints has fractured social consensus on many issues. The few broad socio-economic classes identified by Marx and many other writers seem to have dissolved into a clamour of competing, but shifting, interest groups which advocate various economic, social, moral, cultural, and lifestyle conditions and preferences. Each of us can identify with a uniquely personal and somewhat eclectic basket of interest groups. We are increasingly bound only loosely to broad social groupings through such diverse conditions as patriotism, allegiance to key political institutions, or shared economic circumstance.

Thus we live in an age of uncertainty, confronted by rapidly changing economic and social circumstances which are themselves heavily, though not totally, influenced by technological innovation. This rapid change is matched by growing speculation about the future for a variety of technical, practical and cultural reasons. Improvements in the techniques of forecasting have made predictions more reliable and useful. Growth in scientific knowledge permits the construction of more complex and realistic models of human or physical systems. Better models, when combined with improvements in statistical information, and computer technology, yield more accurate forecasts.

The social demand for accurate forecasts has also grown (Bell, 1974). Both governments and corporations are increasingly exposed to the need for heavy capital investment in projects with long lead times (see Chapters 2 and 5). The longer the interval before capital costs are recouped, the riskier the venture and the greater the prospect of resource misallocation. Worse still, the degree of risk probably increases exponentially with time. In such circumstances forecasts (especially in respect of supply and demand interactions for products, materials or services) play a vital role in project selection and timing. Forecasts can also aid the management of existing infrastructure, plant and equipment, production systems, and stocks of scarce resources by permitting those in control to anticipate and avoid bottlenecks, scarcities and other system malfunctions.

If we accept the view that human beings have a fair measure of control over the form and pace of technological change (Hawken *et al.*, 1982), it follows that the future is not predetermined. Rather, a range of outcomes is possible depending on choices which communities make now. Some studies of the future therefore identify certain possible courses of action and try to evaluate their possible consequences in, say, the medium term (perhaps 15-20 years).

In this way it might be possible for communities to select a preferred outcome and adopt the appropriate package of policies or controls to bring it about. The feasibility and desirability of such a strategy rests heavily on the reliability of the forecasts made.

Another practical consequence of studying the future is that people may become less apprehensive about the impacts of technologically induced change, and more willing to accommodate it. That was one of the aims of the Hawke government's Commission for the Future. It hoped that discussion of technological change promoted through various publications, workshops and seminars would help make Australians more flexible in their attitudes to work practices, new production methods, new forms of employment, retraining, different lifestyles and so on. One outcome of a greater future orientation is expected to be a more productive and wealthy nation. Gloom about the future, note Hawken *et al.* (1982), is apt to be self-fulfilling.

Finally, several cultural benefits can stem from studies of the future (Kahn and Weiner, 1967). People may become more forward looking and less wedded to long-established institutions or patterns of behaviour. Curiosity about the future train of events may be satisfied even if there is no intent to control, or adapt to, the events foreseen. Utopian dreaming, or the imagination of ideal societies, for example, is a way of conceiving the future which probably serves more to ennoble the human spirit than to have practical effect. Sometimes, though, humans have combined vision with action to give effect to their ideals, as did several philanthropic nineteenth century industrialists who constructed new towns or garden suburbs at places like New Lanark, Port Sunlight and Bourneville.

The aim of this Chapter is to sketch briefly the possible medium term futures for Australia. Particular attention will be paid to:

1 patterns of primary production and service distribution in rural areas and aspects of rural lifestyle;
2 the location of manufacturing industry;
3 the spatial structure of cities; and
4 patterns of regional development.

Such a geographical emphasis is important. The combination of technological development and socio-economic change, according to Crawford (1979), Jones (1982), and Fagan (1991) may have marked spatial effect. Yet in some respects the rigidity or durability of the physical environment and human-made infrastructure reduces or deflects the forces for change. Some estimation of the form and incidence of spatial change is therefore a necessary input into such activities as the provision of government services, environmental planning, and private land development. For the private individual, it may also satisfy or spur curiosity, help refine preferred choices, suggest behavioural adaptations, or signpost opportunity. Perhaps then there is some benefit to be gained from placing the geographical consequences of the forces for change more squarely on the agenda for debate.

In addition, the Chapter has two subsidiary aims:

- to demonstrate that the geographical form of economic and social development may vary considerably, according to a small number of critical social and economic choices the community may make in response to international pressures or the internal conflict of ideas.
- to examine briefly the art of conjecture and the merits of scenario construction as a means of forecasting.

The term 'forecasting', which implies conjectural estimates, is preferred to the word 'prediction', which implies a more precise declaration about events.

It is now an appropriate moment in Australia's history to consider the future. Despite a tendency for all writers to see their epoch as pivotal (Clarke, 1979; Drucker, 1969), there is considerable evidence to suggest that this country stands at a major watershed in its evolution. More than at any time since the mid-1940s, large changes are occurring to numerous facets of economy and society, often in an interrelated way. Table 6.1 lists some of the more important changes taking place.

Naturally, such turbulent conditions as those displayed in Table 6.1 make forecasting more hazardous. Simultaneously we confront more choices and those options we select may have a great effect in shaping the future. Yet paradoxically such turbulence may make our forecasts potentially more valuable, provided they are reasonably accurate.

Alternative approaches to the study of the future

None can tell the future precisely. Rather the aim of any study of the future must be to construct forecasts which are logically consistent, plausible and reasonably comprehensive in terms of content. A plausible future should have at least some possibility of occurrence, and preferably a high probability. The quality of forecasts deteriorates, however, with increasing time span such that projections beyond twenty years are generally too risky to be meaningful. This applies less to thinking about political and social institutions than to the commercial world where invention and innovation proceed rapidly. In such a country as Australia, not given to political revolution, its institutions evolve slowly. The present and the past therefore weigh heavily in future events. In contrast, the range, prices, and quantities of goods and services produced may change rapidly. How many people in the late 1960s predicted the enormous effect of the Organisation of Petroleum Exporting Countries (OPEC) on the development and wealth of nations, and the omnipresence of cheap powerful personal computers, widespread satellite communications or genetic engineering? In the realm of technology, in contrast to the political and social sphere, the past may have very little bearing on the future.

Table 6.1 Current major economic and social changes in Australia in the early 1990s

Change	*Proximate cause*
A Economic	
1 Declining commodity prices over the long term	Growth in global production (due to subsidies, improved technology—green revolution, new mineral discoveries etc.) coupled with relatively slower growth in demand (more efficient use of resources; and slow to moderate economic growth in major markets).
2 Low income for many primary producers (especially of grains, sugar, coal, iron-ore, nickel, etc.)	A.1, plus high levels of indebtedness from earlier expansionary phase and high real interest rates
3 Currency depreciation	A.1, plus surge in manufactured imports resulting from previously overvalued currency and reductions in domestic industry protection; and large overseas debt with associated repayments of principal and interest
4 Static standard of living	A.2, A.3, plus high real interest rates and low domestic rate of economic growth
5 Change from a high inflation to low inflation régime	Recession, exacerbated by A.2
6 High real interest rates	Premium required to attract capital inflow from overseas to prevent an even larger currency depreciation and keep overseas debt level in check; restricts blow-out in domestic consumption
7 Low economic growth perhaps risk of further A.3	A.2, plus investors wary of A.6 and
8 Maintenance of high unemployment (more than 10 per cent)	A.7
9 Reduced employment in high protection manufacturing industries (e.g. textiles, clothing, footwear (TCF), automotive, metal fabrication)	Government restructuring policy: ameliorated by A.3 (*de facto* protection)
10 Re-industrialisation in globally competitive medium-high technology industries—export orientation	A.3

B Social and political

1 A concomitant of major economic change and uncertainty appears to be a conservative and libertarian backlash against the creeping collectivism of the post-war period. In the 1980s emphasis was placed on the need for efficiency, entrepreneurship, increased productivity and individual responsibility for social welfare ahead of equity considerations and collective well-being. In part this was a precondition for accelerated economic development, but may also have reflected

attempts by some groups to preserve or improve their well-being in response to static living standards (A.4). The 1990s are likely to see a resurgence of equity and collective concerns, though not so far as to reduce efficiency's dominance.

2 Australia is growing in political maturity and independence as a response to an increasingly hostile international trading environment. Protectionism and trade wars may see a realignment of political ties somewhat away from traditional OECD links and towards regional political groupings (ASEAN, and APEC, for example) or lobby groups of middle-ranking resource producing nations.

3 Australia continues its transition to a post-industrial society, giving rise to growing tensions between citizens who are formally qualified to perform responsible, interesting and personally satisfying jobs and those who in increasing numbers are marginal to the workforce by virtue of inflexible or outdated skills and attitudes. Rapid economic change will exacerbate these problems as old industries are replaced by new ones requiring new skills at possibly new locations.

The sketching of alternative futures necessarily involves components susceptible to various rates of change. In many respects humans act out their lives on a slow-changing stage. Economic and social infrastructure have long life-expectancy and additions to the capital stock proceed slowly. For example, the pattern of railways in New South Wales has altered little in fifty years: a few closures here and there and some additions such as the Sandy Hollow line to the Ulan coalfield and the Eastern Suburbs line in Sydney. Nor can we readily circumvent constraints of the physical environment. The fertility of land, climatic conditions, and the locations of mineral deposits are generally fixed. Only water resource management policies, which have led to widespread irrigation farming, and, to a lesser extent, animal or plant breeding and land management practices, have substantially overcome environmental limitations in Australia. Finally, the complex apparatus of the State and its policies also impart an element of stability in the evolution of society.

Nevertheless, events can change rapidly within this framework, spurred on by resource discovery and development, new lifestyle preferences, migration, or commercial pressure to redevelop the existing built environment. Marked geographical change can occur where development is areally concentrated or where uses of existing infrastructure are re-arranged. The rapid growth of settlements on the New South Wales north coast — Port Macquarie and Coffs Harbour, for example — testifies to this. The gentrification of old inner city areas by young upwardly mobile professionals who replace the long-established elderly or working-class residents has occurred in all State capitals: Carlton in Melbourne and Paddington in Sydney spring to mind. And office towers have invaded the residential neighbourhoods of St. Kilda and North Sydney with little effective resistance, changing their entire character.

At a low level, forecasting is a common human activity. We all have poorly formed expectations based on hopes, fears, accepted rules-of-thumb (often culturally or class-based), personal values, personal information (albeit incomplete and misconceived), and the ideas of others. These expectations range from mere feelings of foreboding or portent to intendedly rational visions and idealisations. Such projections are unlikely to be accurate, though that is not impossible.

In order to study the future, we need to adopt a systematic, rational and comprehensive mode of analysis. The one chosen should partly reflect the purpose of the study. Some forecasts are, for example, concerned with rather narrow issues: company performance as measured by return on shareholder's funds; the future value of shares, currency or commodities; the output of industry sectors; population growth. Often the projections are short-term, the range of possible outcomes is narrow, sound quantitative data are available, and effective models exist to process that information. Other studies are more broadly based and concerned with the development of major themes: economic development; environmental limitations; the impact of particular technologies; the consequences of political ideologies; social relationships. Nevertheless, they all tend to be *partial* approaches to the future from the perspective of committed interest groups or idealogues and they often tend to ignore the important inter-linkages between themes. Elaborate, though frequently speculative and untested, theories or models are set up and used to project events on the basis of incomplete and risky data. Indeed, Caldwell (1985) feels that some of the 'limits to growth' literature (suggesting that population pressure may exhaust the earth's resources) sacrifices truth to moral fervour and rectitude. Frequently, too, the findings are proselytized with an almost religious fervour.

In an attempt to avoid these partial approaches, many researchers have turned to futurology, a holistic attempt to integrate a variety of economic, social, political, and possibly environmental themes on a broad canvas so as to arrive at a forecast of what the future might be like. The task is Herculean. Ideally the analyst requires a vast understanding of human affairs. Often, however, integration is purchased at the expense of depth of analysis, and imagination substitutes, to some extent, for factual substance. Nevertheless, futurologies such as those from Toffler, Gershuny, Hawken and many others have a wide audience and have been influential in shaping public opinion. This is because they combine elements of scientific prediction, social commentary, and scenario in a populist manner.

Scientific studies of the future proceed by constructing quantitative models of society or the environment. The models identify key variables involved in social or environmental processes and the cause–effect relationships between them. Such models can usually be tested by seeing how well present known conditions can be predicted by inserting past information into them. If a model produces reasonably accurate forecasts in this way it can be used, with suitable caution, to project events. Such models vary from the relatively simple (for example the cohort-survival model used in population projection) to complex models of national economies (such as the Treasury's ORANI model) or of the global environment (as used by the Club of Rome or developed by Forrester). Many of the models used by geographers and planners in the spatial analysis of industry, retail distribution, urban structure or regional development have, alas, weak predictive power. This stems mainly from their failure to include an adequate range of causal variables and the difficulties inherent in building space into analyses of economic and social processes.

In contrast, *social commentaries* on the future tend to penetrate below the surface appearances of society in an attempt to discover fundamental mechanisms at work. These mechanisms are frequently abstract and difficult to quantify. The ideas of class and class struggle, of centre–periphery relationships, of Kondratieff long-waves, of stages of growth or of inevitable historical progression toward communism fit this category. All have something important to say about the evolution of economy and society through time, but in a qualitative not quantitative sense. They cannot be ignored, but equally cannot provide any clear-cut projections over a specified time-period. Moreover, the reliance placed on this type of mechanism depends on the analyst's value-system and ideology. A socialist would set greater store by the mechanism of class conflict than a conservative or libertarian thinker, for example. And a neo-classical economist would value mathematical models more highly than sub-surface mechanisms.

One feature which distinguishes academic futurologies from the more populist ones is the extensive use of *scenarios*. A scenario presents a picture of whatever is under investigation — for example, the spatial distribution of manufacturing industry — at some future date. This we may term an end-state scenario. It may also outline the train of events leading to that end state (a process scenario). Given different assumptions about the future conditions of certain key variables responsible for determining the evolution of events, it is possible to create a set of alternative scenarios which define approximately the range of possible outcomes. This sort of exercise is not just a question of academic analysts hedging their bets; it has considerable practical importance.

In scenarios, we are reminded that the future is not preordained. Rather, the outcome depends on the decisions made by a wide range of actors: governments, companies, social groups or individuals. Some futures may be commonly judged as more desirable than others. In that case, policy-makers or decision-makers may come together and co-ordinate their activities to promote desirable outcomes and avoid those deemed inferior. The extent of co-ordination necessary depends on the probability of occurrence of the preferred option. Such probabilities can be gauged roughly, and those of a high order may come about with little effort at social engineering. Even if community consensus over preferred futures is impossible, or one particular outcome seems more or less inevitable whatever we do, as technological determinists would have us believe, scenario construction may at least alert us to future economic and social problems which may need remedial action.

Given its importance, scenario construction is the method of analysis chosen to realise this chapter's previously stated aims. The use of judgement and imagination to interpret a mass of social, economic, political and cultural information on which scenario construction relies, is particularly appropriate in an era of turbulent change such as Australia currently confronts. In these circumstances past performance and current trends are less of a guide to future events than would normally be the case, and creative thinking therefore assumes a larger role.

Towards scenario construction

Some preliminaries can be dispensed with quickly. First, as Australia faces an era of rapid change consequent upon the kinds of forces listed in Table 6.1, it would be unduly risky to make any projections beyond a relatively short period of 12–15 years (i.e. to the first decade of the next century). Even then, some major geographical changes may occur, as we shall see. Secondly, three principal process scenarios will be constructed, and other possible futures will be considered briefly. The three scenarios are: *muddling through; premature post-industrialism; and market economics*. We will describe the three scenarios and then examine their implications for the future geographical pattern of Australia's economy and society.

Scenario construction is an exercise in large-scale data gathering and analysis. One way to lighten the informational burden is to use the Delphi technique. This enables numerous experts in a given field to define the key factors and interrelationships of a target system and to comment on its likely evolution. Newton and Taylor (1987) adopted this approach in their study of future spatial structures for Sydney and Melbourne. Its drawback seems to be the likely dominance of conventional wisdom in the responses. This is an important defect because the most valuable component of scenario construction is probably the opportunity provided for imaginative lateral thinking based on a coherent set of values and ideology. As a result the Delphi technique has not been followed here. The scenarios constructed below represent the personal evaluations of the authors and, as such, reflect their personal knowledge and political ideology rather than some wider spectrum of expert opinion.

The kinds of conditions that need to be considered in any scenario of Australia's future include: public policies on a range of issues; institutional structures and power relationships within them; social attitudes and behaviours; the degree of conflict between interest groups and the viability of arrangements for conflict resolution; business corporate structures and their decision-making processes. A more extensive and detailed list is presented in Table 6.2. Though daunting at first sight, the large number of rather complex variables is closely interrelated. For example, relationships between the

Table 6.2 Major issues in the development of scenarios

A Economic

1 National macro-economic management with respect to:
Money supply, interest rates, credit availability
Budget deficit, balance of payments
Currency value
Industry policy: protection, export incentives, venture capital
Labour policy: wage rates, unemployment, training, work practices, union power, labour flexibility
Fiscal policy: tax levels, tax structure, corporation taxes, etc.
Market regulation: freedom of entry, monopolies, consumer protection, product standards, equal opportunity, etc.

2 Business structures and attitudes
Attitudes towards profit, entrepreneurship and innovation, risk, product quality, consumer satisfaction, research and development, labour relations, competition
Level of competition faced, efficiency in management (chain of command as short as possible), receptivity to new ideas from the workforce, use of cost-saving strategies (JIT, TQC, etc.), use of appropriate/modern technology to full capacity

3 Technological development

B Social

4 Social attitudes towards production:
Work ethic, productivity, entrepreneurship and business leadership, adoption of new technology, learning new skills/work practices

5 Attitudes towards consumption:
Thrift, self sufficiency/personal responsibility, living within means

6 Interpersonal relationships:
Attitudes towards justice, equity, fairness
Family ties, marital arrangements, care of elderly, etc.

C Social and political institutions

7 Size of government, scope of responsibilities, efficiency in service delivery, decentralisation of power, flexibility/adaptability of structure, existence of checks and balances, quality of advice.

D Other issues

8 Resource discovery and management

9 Demographic changes
In Australia the following are especially important:
Rate of immigration
Ageing of the population

economic variables are for the most part well-established through a large body of economic theory, though some differences in interpretation may result from cultural outlook and political philosophy. Furthermore, thinking about social processes and political institutions is often linked in a consistent way with economic preferences through the same cultural and political outlooks.

The three scenarios under study cover much of the ground examined by earlier writers such as Kasper and Parry (1978), Kasper *et al.* (1980) and Kahn and Pepper (1980). In some senses, then, the scenarios of muddling through, premature post-industrialism, and market economics draw on a range of antecedent scenarios devised by earlier writers. The main features of these antecedent scenarios are summarized in Table 6.3 (*see* pp. 298–99).

Muddling through

'Muddling through' is the most likely course of events in Australia, principally because governments face a short three-year electoral cycle. Consequently they are forever faced with the task of forging coalitions of consent from among numerous competing interest groups in order to win and retain office. Typical interest groups include the aged, families, the unemployed, the welfare lobby in general, defence interests, small businessmen, farmers, financiers, industrial corporations, unions, environmentalists, educationalists, feminists, health service providers and regional development lobbies. As Olson (1982) notes, the number and power of such groups appears to be growing in western democracies. Government's increased responsibilities may be partly a response to and partly the cause of this situation. We have therefore reached a position where much is demanded and expected of government, but where it is extremely difficult to reconcile competing claims.

Some claims are clearly opposed in the sense that attainment of one may injure another. For example, policies designed to protect the profitability of and employment in manufacturing industry are likely to reduce farm incomes; and an increase in the proportion of gross national product (GNP) claimed by labour can only be at the expense of returns to capital. Other claims are not quite so antithetical. Resource development may threaten the environment, though not invariably so. Education, health and other social services compete for the welfare dollar. Now that Australian society seems to be nearing the pain threshold of taxation where, as a result, there seems to be little scope for an increase in the proportion of GNP allocated to such services, we have what economists call a 'zero-sum' game. In short, increased expenditure on one social service can only be purchased at the expense of a commensurate decrease in the others. Thus, while Australia's welfare bill may change little, there is ample scope for conflict between competing welfare sectors. The competing sets of interests could be reconciled, but only by an unlikely increase in government welfare expenditure. One way round the problem is to remove as many people as possible, mainly middle to high income earners, from the welfare trough by forcing them to provide privately for their pensions through superannuation, for education through fees and for health care through medical insurance.

Some claims are particularly difficult to evaluate even though experience suggests that they are opposed. This is especially true of claims that balance future costs against present benefits. If present-day society increased its rate of savings at the expense of consumption, for example, that money could be invested in capital projects of an infrastructure or production kind which might increase the rate of economic growth for the benefit of future generations. Likewise we may conserve our known scarce resources for the enjoyment of our descendants. This is advocated by those who want to preserve a rainforest such as that at Daintree in North Queensland and wilderness areas like those of south-west Tasmania, or to conserve oil reserves by reducing consumption of petroleum products. The latter argument is complicated further by the possibility of discovering additional reserves or substitution by alternative energy sources, perhaps of a renewable kind (wind, solar, and water power or nuclear fusion). Should these options become viable, a conservation policy may represent a lost opportunity. These controversial matters have been the focus of quite different assessments by several recent Australian writers. Mercer (1991) and Birrell *et al.* (1982) advocate the conservation of scarce and fragile resources for the enjoyment of future generations. They adopt the rather conservative philosophy that where we cannot be sure of the future impact of present development we must assume the worst as a basis of policy. In contrast, many pro-development interest groups pursue short-term perspectives and seek immediate gratification. Governments are sandwiched somewhere in the middle. However, if they are doing their job properly, governments ought to emphasise their responsibility for the nation's long-term welfare. The problem lies in deciding what welfare goals to pursue and in holding the line against short-term predation.

In some respects the defence of future interests is a special case of a more general problem. Just as those interests are unable to articulate their position except, for example, through the altruism of present-day conservationists or the sacrifice of parents seeking the best for their children, there are many contemporary interests which are relatively powerless through lack of resources or organisation, but are nevertheless deserving of public support. Some segments of the unemployed, homeless families, battered wives, single-parent families and so on come into this category. Power does not equal merit in the struggle between interests. Governments have a moral duty to protect the weak.

With all these conflicting claims, the art of government in a plural society requires skills of reconciliation, arbitration, consensus-building, moral leadership, imagination, a vision of the future, and an ability to respond quickly to short-term crisis. Such is the complexity of this task, that muddling through, or what Lindblom (1959) aptly calls disjointed incrementalism, may be the only feasible strategy.

Table 6.3 The development of scenarios

		Antecedent scenarios		
Scenario	**Present title**	**Kasper and Parry (1978)**	**Kasper et al. (1980)**	**Kahn and Pepper (1980)**
A	**Muddling through:** (Reform with consensus) Includes most of the aspects adjacent with major exceptions marked*. Capital markets have been substantially freed and the mid-1980s economic crisis has encouraged more rapid structural change as anticipated by Kahn and Pepper.	**Canadian strategy** Slow structural reform punctuated with stop-gap protectionism*. Policy uncertainty and reversals create uncertain investment climate. Modest immigration (population growth averaging 1.5 per cent p.a.). [GNP growth at 2.5 per cent p.a./per capita]	**Mercantilist trend** Continued protection against import competition and changes implied by new technology*. Restrictions on capital markets*. Rigid wage structures Government as major provider of social services (education/health, etc.). Short-term electoral policies + extensive policy input by producer groups. Consumerism/environmentalism aided by bureaucratic regulation. [GNP growth 1.7 per cent p.a./ per capita]	**Business as usual + reformed protectionism** Production inefficient, uncompetitive (except in traditional export sectors - mainly primary materials). Some economic reforms as a consequence of marked deterioration in economic performance. Workforce unionised and strike-prone. Strong egalitarian ethic. Empty, urban, sports loving, rich(?). Some drive for excellence/ achievement: science, culture, sport, high tech industry.
B	**Premature post-industrialisation** See Kahn and Pepper. This rather compassionate, egalitarian and hedonistic post-industrialism is premature in the sense that productive capacity may not sustain it without national impoverishment or because economic growth (through scenario C) could lead to much better provision of services. An inferior form of post-industrialism.			**Premature post-industrialism** Emphasis on welfare and leisure substitutes for the work ethic. Continued growth of social and recreational services; shorter working week/life without commensurate growth of productivity, output and GNP.

	Market economics	German strategy	Libertarian alternative	Economic dynamism
C	As adjacent: the strategies are reasonably consistent and also supplement each other. Some attributes have already been realised (for example, much freer capital markets). Others have attracted government sympathy or some initiative (lower industry protection/ export-oriented manufacturing).	Consistent/long-term structural adjustment policies based on lower industry protection, leading to: Specialisation in internationally competitive production; Cost-competitive transport networks; Free capital markets; Promotion of capital investment in promising activities; Consistent manpower policies; Strong immigration. [GNP growth 4 to 4.5 per cent p.a./per capita]	Free international trade. Acceptance of structural changes implied by new technologies. Free capital markets. Anti-monopoly policies/ avoidance of restrictive trade practices. Less restricted labour markets. Reduced government role in many basic services. Resurgence of manufacturing in traditional locations; growth in resource-rich states. Greater availability of venture capital. Removal of double taxation of dividends. [GNP growth 3.8 per cent p.a./per capita]	Emphasis on achievement Manufacturing to become export oriented (specialised, technological, and/or capital intensive). It may contract in size. Concentration of economic growth on resource development and farming where Australia's comparative advantage lies. Loose labour market. Improved workforce skills through enhanced training programmes.

This situation is reinforced by the fact that governments are increasingly losing sovereignty over decision-making, as noted in Chapter 5. In effect, they are not entirely free to resolve conflicting claims as they see fit. Instead, there are international forces at work which may force certain courses of action rather than others. These forces include other perhaps more powerful governments; international agencies such as the United Nations, the European Commission in Brussels, the International Monetary Fund and OPEC; commodity markets dealing in grains (e.g. Chicago), metals (e.g. London), currency (London, New York, Tokyo); multinational companies whose annual turnovers may exceed the national products of middle-ranking European nations; and even private social organisations such as Amnesty International and Oxfam. Unfortunately, many of these forces, and more especially the economic ones, can be capricious.

For example, OPEC managed to quadruple the price of a barrel of oil in 1973, causing large-scale economic dislocation around the world. Between 1980 and 1986 the price of oil slumped from over US$30 a barrel to as little as US$9, largely because OPEC nations lost control of the market through a combination of their own excessive production and the expanding output of such non-OPEC nations as the UK. In 1970 gold fetched about A$30 per ounce but by 1986 this had risen to A$600, fuelling a boom in Australian gold production. Part of this price rise reflects a sharp decline in the international value of the Australian dollar against the United States dollar and other currencies. Thus from a position of parity in the early 1980s (US$l = A$1), the Australian currency was traded as low as US 57¢ in 1986.

Rapid changes like these can make the government's task of managing conflicting claims upon it more difficult. Thus powerful new claimants may emerge to upset existing coalitions and understandings because changes in the international economic order may engineer large-scale and unpredictable shifts in wealth between individuals and between regions. For example, the various devaluations of the Australian dollar in recent years have tended to benefit the country's tourist industry, certain manufacturing industries, gold-mining areas and cattle-raising rural regions. Several other regions or industry sectors have performed poorly because the benefits of currency devaluation have been swamped by low commodity prices and rising costs: grain and wool growers and coal miners can be included here. Conflicts between old and new interests are often attended by inflexible institutional structures which retard necessary system adjustments. The whole edifice of Australian labour relations, including the trade structure of unions, their attitudes to employers, the rituals and attitudes of the Australian Industrial Relations Commission, and the perceived role of unions in a 'corporate state' could constitute one such barrier to rapid change which governments must adapt to in responding to new circumstances.

In short, a turbulent decision-making environment means that government will find great difficulty in controlling affairs because of both heightened conflict and its own inability to respond quickly enough to needs and opportunities. Nor in such circumstances is it easy to frame a coherent vision of where society is proceeding or ought to proceed. Consequently, public administration tends to create the impression of adapting piecemeal to events.

In the muddling through scenario we can expect no rapid change from the current structure of economy and society. Table 6.4 sets out, in summary form, the principal attributes of a muddling through society. Such a society would tend toward the characteristics set out in the right hand column (though not necessarily precluding contrary elements included in the left hand column). In short, it would be a somewhat corporatist and centralized society in which important decisions tend to be made by, and sometimes to the benefit of, those major interest groups which by mutual agreement have access to the levers of government.

In the Australia of the 1980s those groups with access to government comprised three main types: large unions, major companies, and the bureaucracy (including major public infrastructure provision agencies). Each has

Table 6.4 The polarities of the 'market economics' and 'muddling through' scenarios

Market economics	*Muddling through*
A Business environment	
competitive	monopolistic
ease of entry	entry regulated
deregulated	regulated
unconventional	conventional
risk-taking	risk-adverse
investment/saving	consumption
development	conservation
future oriented	present oriented/backward looking
entrepreneurial	managerial
decentalised power	centralised power
individualist	corporatist
less certainty	greater certainty
greater adaptability	less adaptability
lower tax regime	higher tax regime
growth oriented	less store set by growth
B Social environment	
individual/family responsibility for social welfare	collective responsibility for social welfare
conformist social relations	non-conformist social relations
private social services	public social services
lower tax regime	higher tax regime
investment/saving (frugality)	consumption
equitarian/libertarian	egalitarian
emphasis on work ethic	lower work ethic, emphasis on rights

substantial power to control the well-being of other non-core economic and social groups with little fear of contradiction or reprisal. Yet each depends on the co-operation of the others for maintenance of its own power base, so that mutual (or corporate) decision-making becomes a valuable, if not always absolutely essential, exercise. A classic manifestation of the corporate state was the 'Accord' set up by the Hawke Labor Government in 1983 between unions and government. The scheme was also tacitly accepted by many larger businesses. Unions perceived a gain because wage increases were guaranteed to at least match monetary inflation without the need for extensive (and costly to the membership) industrial activity such as strikes. As a bonus, weaker unions would be protected to some extent from declining wages relative to more powerful unions because everyone's wages would rise by roughly the same proportion. Large corporations saw some advantage in the form of greater industrial harmony, lower demands for wage increases than would have occurred under 'collective bargaining', and the little restraint imposed on their ability to pass on cost increases in the form of higher prices. Finally, the government anticipated greater ability to predict its income and expenditure and manage the rate of inflation, and the benefit of greater national output.

It is doubtful that these aims were realised. The Liberal party has long argued that the Accord mechanism prevented rapid adjustment to the nation's boom–bust cycle of the late 1980s and early 1990s. It probably institutionalised the culture of high inflation longer than was necessary, but may have had the benefit of helping to buy union acceptance of reduced industry protection. Whatever the case, all three parties to the Accord saw, in effect, that mutual co-operation would erect a cocoon of security around them in the face of a largely hostile world.

Risk minimisation was the order of the day: indeed this is the hallmark of a corporate state. It can be reflected in many aspects of economic and social management. For instance, the exertions and uncertainties of competition may be eased by erecting barriers, with government connivance, to entry in many industries, trades or professions. Indeed government often protects most vehemently the quasi-monopoly power of its own physical infrastructure, health and educational services. Regulations can be used to prevent or retard, for example, the emergence of new types of education or medical service, new airlines or bus services, alternative sources of power, and innovative building designs, land tenure systems or patterns of land use. Examples of all these can be found in Australia. This kind of risk-aversion is not of course restricted to government administration and is equally applicable to many corporate activities: the whole apparatus of industry protection is one example.

Another form of risk avoidance is the centralisation of power in the hands of the large corporation or government department. Large organisations, it seems, are better able to hide their mistakes or financial losses and to tide themselves over adverse events. Sometimes, of course, it is only the large organisation which has the financial resources, market power, and will-power needed to launch new products and services. However, frequently such bodies are bastions of the conventional and the standardized, with innovative and entrepreneurial flair in inverse proportion to their lengthy hierarchical managerial structures. Their very size tends to make them less adaptable to changing circumstances. And, as Galbraith (1967) has noted, the emergence of technostructures (or technical–managerial elites) in large organisations, who are divorced from the real owners either private or public, serves to reinforce the preference for risk avoidance and for the personal financial or status benefits to be derived from increased organisational size. Organisational aggrandisement is, in short, a circular and cumulative temptation.

The interdependencies of corporatism are linked closely to collective responsibility. Those who pursue risk minimization in production are likely to be receptive to the idea of the welfare state whose role it is to reduce the risk of social misfortune among weaker, less able, or unlucky members of the community. What is more, the corporate imperative may result in large-scale, uniform, all-embracing and centralized welfare services. Indeed, many of these services are likely to be made available, perhaps compulsorily, to those who could, and would prefer to, make private arrangements. Such services will increase taxation, encourage consumption in general due to reduced need to save for a rainy day, increase consumption of those services which are unpriced and subsidized, and generally reduce the incentive to work hard. Ultimately the preference for consumption over thrift, for public welfare over private, and for tax over incentive will tend to retard the rate of economic growth. One of the paradoxes of the welfare state is that it tends to permit the emergence of non-conformist social relations. Governments typically provide a social safety net in the form of allowances (or transfer payments) to children, single parents, the aged, and persons who are incapacitated or unemployed (see Chapter 3). Such payments undoubtedly contribute to the breakdown of the traditional nuclear family and to the spawning of alternative lifestyles.

Contemporary Australia shares many of the attributes of a corporatist society. Moreover, this has been an enduring phenomenon. From the moment the First Fleet arrived, the fabric of society has been fashioned by power elites in which government has participated as the dominant partner in coalition with other interests. At various times these groups have included the squattocracy, farming communities in general, mining interests, developers, unions, conservationists, small business, and large corporations. The dominant role of government seems to be planted firmly in the national ethos (see Chapter 4). In part this probably reflects the public purpose and management of initial settlement, but it also testifies to the size and harshness of the new environment which made its effective development beyond the capabilities of thinly scattered private individuals. Initially government's role was mainly restricted to infrastructure development in order to facilitate the production of primary raw materials: railways, roads, ports, and, more recently, power, telecommunications and water storage. Later it extended to commodity marketing, education, health, industrial development, immigration, and, mainly through universities and the CSIRO, research and development. For much of this time the private sector was happily cosseted behind a wall of anti-competitive government regulation. This applies to both large and small business. The dominant imperative of all these programs is, in line with the corporatist ethic, production with commercial security. In a parallel way, the development of democratic institutions has necessitated the purchase of electoral support by means of strategies designed to increase consumption with social security.

Australian corporatism therefore has wide allegiance right across the political spectrum. Small businessmen and farmers are generally attached to regulated trading hours, licenses and marketing boards; miners like exploration and production subsidies; unions for the most part feel secure within the club-like Industrial Relations Commission with its conciliation and arbitration processes; and corporations are happy to run cap-in-hand to the government for subsidies and protection in adverse trading conditions. However, none of these separate groups is now able to dominate the others and corporate coalitions emerge. Federally, under the Hawke government, these coalitions tended to be the combination of large unions, major companies and the bureaucracy identified earlier. But they alone are an insufficient electoral coalition so that fringe groups have also to be attracted: perhaps pensioners, the welfare lobby, unemployed persons, conservationists and disaffected members of other interest groups. In the outer are those other interests (including small business owners and farmers) who are awaiting their turn in the corporate inner circle.

Interestingly, Australian economic and social conditions resulting from different coalitions seem to differ little. This is probably a consequence of the powerful role of government as a major partner in such coalitions, the reasonably frequent rearrangement of dominant coalitions, the need to humour fringe groups for electoral gain, and the fact that the major interest groups are rarely monolithic. Indeed, major interest groups are sufficiently large and diverse to make it difficult for them to frame clear-cut aims and to enforce membership adherence. This reduces their power despite apparently large financial assets, volume of production or membership. On the other hand, small groups, which may even be located outside the dominant corporate structure, can thwart the latter's intentions for, as Olson (1982) notes, they have disproportionately great organisational power for collective action. Larger groups may also act coherently, however, when facing dire circumstances.

In this way, therefore, Australia's pluralist tendencies temper its corporatist leanings to produce a relatively stable pattern of economic and social relationships. Corporatism is, nevertheless, intimately bound up with two characteristics of the national ethos: risk aversion and reliance upon government for risk insurance. It is likely on these grounds to be an impediment to change, reducing society's capacity to adopt new technology, and to revise institutional/administration structures or to reallocate resources to better uses in response to changing conditions. Corporate policy-making (or alternatively consensus politics) was seen at its worst in the tax-reform debate of 1985. The goods and services tax option (Option C) had the support of the then Treasurer, Keating, his department, many business interests and a large number of economists. It was rejected because key parties to the Tax Summit, especially welfare and union groups in the Labor party's own constituency, combined to protect their special interests as they saw them and the government was naturally unwilling to confront them.

Given this situation, are such corporate coalitions likely to continue in their present vein? The number of interest groups is growing. So is their access to, and skill in using, communications media. One risk here is that the clamour of demands may induce decision-making paralysis in government. That, too, could bring about sub-optimal resource allocation and reduced growth. Risk aversion and a preference for a corporate state are also likely to endure. These dysfunctional responses might be reduced by winding back the domain and power of the state so that there is less for interest groups to capture, though that is a difficult task. The one great exception to this in the 1980s — financial deregulation — was a commercial necessity given the global freedom of financial markets. Its potential use to discipline all sectors of the economy, government included, was also perceived. More typically, the reduction of industry-protection measures (tariffs, quotas and bounties) and the reform of such industries as the waterfront has been slow and tortuous.

Several conclusions emerge. The pluralist corporatist structure of Australian institutions, attitudes and decision-making is set to continue. Interest groups are finely balanced in terms of their power to influence the direction of policy towards their own ends. Whatever changes occur to this superstructure are likely to proceed slowly and incrementally. Per capita economic growth as measured by GNP will probably be moderate over the 15 or so years under discussion due to rigidities and inefficiencies inherent in the pluralist-corporatist state. Kasper and Parry (1978) and Kasper *et al.* (1980) estimate a per capita growth rate of between 1.7 and 2.5 per cent per annum for this kind of scenario, or close to the long-run post-war average.

It is possible that growth rates could be sustained at a higher average figure, say 3 to 3.5 per cent. This requires a fortunate conjunction of several beneficial mechanisms: running a slightly undervalued currency over the period in question; a steady recovery in commodity prices helped along by faster global economic growth; a sustained period of low inflation; redirection of domestic production to export markets to reduce debt levels and the high cost of servicing them — up to one quarter of export receipts. The first of these would increase returns to exporters of primary materials, manufactured goods or services or protect producers of products destined for local markets from imports. Low debt and inflation would undoubtedly encourage both foreign and domestic investment.

Japanese corporatism has proved highly successful at promoting sustained economic growth through similar policy setting to these, though that nation started with several immense advantages that Australia does not have. These include:

- a high level of personal savings (thrift),
- long-term business and investment horizons,
- strong mutual business support networks (*Keiretsu*),
- a willingness to accept new technology (to innovate), and
- a relatively homogeneous society compared with Australia's fractured pluralism.

Business is also much more competitive than in Australia, in line with Porter's (1990) prescriptions. Admittedly, there are many segments of Japanese economy and society that are rather traditional, risk adverse, and inefficient: rice growing and wholesale distribution spring to mind. In short, Japanese corporatism has a strange duality. It is simultaneously open and progressive and backward-regarding.

One concomitant of moderate economic growth is likely to be an equally modest rate of immigration. During the last twenty years or so the migrant intake has been a reasonable barometer of economic health (see Figure 6.1). The peak intakes occurred in the buoyant conditions of the late 1960s and following the resources boom of 1980/81. Troughs occurred in conjunction with the economic crises of 1961, the mid-1970s and 1982/83. Australia's population growth is crucially dependent on the rate of migration. The

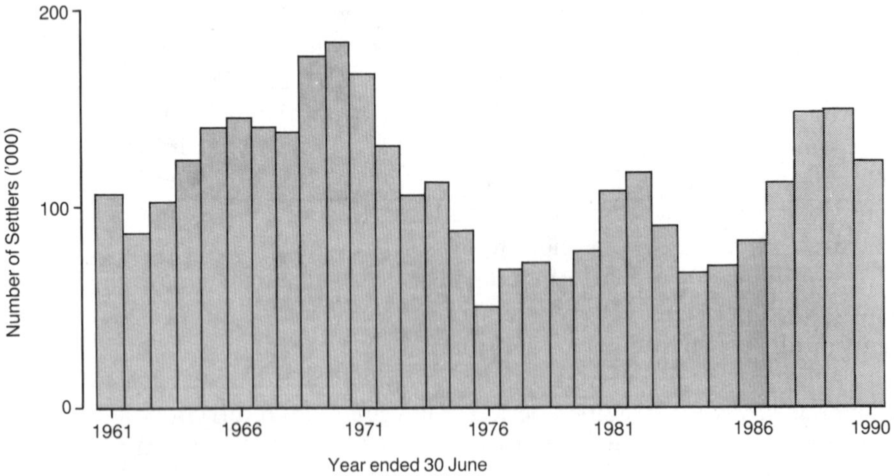

Fig. 6.1 Settler numbers

Department of Immigration and Ethnic Affairs (1986) estimated that average annual population growth in the period 1985–2020 would be 0.84 per cent with 75 000 immigrants a year, 1.11 per cent with 125 000, and 1.27 per cent with 155 000. If the level of about 90 000 migrants a year were maintained over the next 15 years, Australia's total population might reach between 18.5 and 19.0 million in the early years of the twenty-first century. This is an increase of between 2.5 to 3.0 million over the 1986 figure, and represents an annual growth rate of about 1.1 per cent averaged over the period.

Premature post-industrialism

The term 'post-industrialism' conjures up many different images. At its most basic it signifies a shift in employment away from the direct production of raw materials, and especially manufactured goods, towards services. This is a consequence of new scientific, production and management technologies which enable far fewer process workers to maintain or increase current output. Service employment takes many forms.

Some jobs are ancillary to production: in finance, the law, accountancy, insurance, real estate, vocational education and training, research and development in such institutions as universities and the CSIRO, advertising, data processing and analysis, some transport activities, repair and maintenance, and so on.

Others are concerned with enhancing individual quality of life. These include personal services (such as hair care and restaurants), recreation and entertainment services, jobs in recreational education and health, and also many of the business or maintenance services already mentioned.

Yet others are involved with community welfare: looking after the sick, weak, incapacitated and disadvantaged, administering to spiritual well-being; the policing of law and order; and the provision of public goods such as parks, libraries and environmental protection. We might also include what Gershuny (1978) calls the self-service economy: people providing a wide range of goods and services for themselves supported, perhaps, by transfer payments from the rest of the community. This is also referred to as the 'household economy' or 'prosuming' (Toffler 1983), or 'ownwork' (Robertson, 1985).

The concept of post-industrialism goes further, however, than the juggling of employment or occupational statistics. Some of these are suspect anyway. For example, many services are in fact an integral part of commodity production. In the past they were often provided in-house by primary or secondary establishments and counted as manufacturing employment. Increasingly they are contracted in from specialist suppliers and classified differently.

Toffler (1980) sees post-industrial society as offering more flexible working conditions in terms of location and the scheduling of hours worked. Individuals may increasingly work at home in the 'electronic cottage' at whatever times suit them. Furthermore, for those who form the technical elite, or 'cognitariat' (mind workers) as Toffler (1983) calls them, the quality of work will improve by becoming more resourceful, innovative and creative (see also Asimov, 1984). To some extent work conditions will improve across the board as jobs become less tied to the rhythm of machines, more responsible, more decentralized and less routine: Robertson (1985) calls this the end of the age of employment. In short, job quality will greatly improve.

Simultaneously the quantity of work required of everyone may decrease. To quote Robertson (1985), 'people in jobs will work fewer hours in the day, fewer days in the week, fewer weeks in the year, fewer years in a life-time than they do now'. Jones (1982; 1986) strongly agrees. The corollary of less work is more leisure. Many writers such as Dahrendorf (1975) and Miles (in Parker, 1983) welcome the prospect of increased leisure, seeing it as intrinsically satisfying, a route to enhanced personal development, and a contribution to greater work effort. One problem is that the concept of a 40 hour working week is now deeply ingrained in western society (in fact, the Swiss and the Japanese, two nations with highly successful economies, work closer to 44 hours). Those with jobs may often be reluctant to work less hours, with the consequence that the need for a reduced work effort may create a class of permanently unemployed, or underemployed people. For others part-time work may be the best option available. In this way there is a risk of two classes of worker emerging: a full-time cognitariat or technical elite (Bell, 1974) who will have access to self-fulfilling work and the levers of power, and 'shadow' workers involved in less satisfying, labour absorbing or 'shadow' work (Jones 1982; 1986).

Another major theme in the analysis of post-industrial futures is the end of mass production (Toffler, 1980; Hawken, 1983; Schumacher, 1973). This view seems to rest on the premise that creative thinking, research and development, innovative design and high quality (almost craft) production are best carried on in small enterprises.

Economies of scale in production are also becoming less important for everyday manufacturing or processing activities. Robotics and miniaturisation now enable the efficient production of customized goods with small runs at decentralized locations. Two small-scale examples familiar to everyone are hot bread shops and fast photo finishing. Mini-steelworks using scrap steel input are another more conventional example. Gershuny (1978) wisely advises against taking this theme too far and regards the continued production of cheap mass-produced tools and equipment as an essential pre-requisite for his self-service household economy. In practice, then, mass production is likely to remain important in post-industrial societies, but, being amenable to automation, is likely to employ relatively few people. Some automobile assembly lines are now almost completely automated, for example.

Several important consequences of 'de-massification' have been mooted. Small-scale enterprises are likely to avoid the pyramid-shaped managerial hierarchies of their corporate counterparts (Toffler, 1980; Gershuny, 1978; Klaus, 1984). High technology businesses frequently have virtually horizontal management relationships characterised by widespread consultation and participation in decision-making. Naisbitt (1984) calls this 'networking'. The rise of small-scale business anticipated by these and other writers should help to decentralize economic and political power and to decentralize employment in a geographical sense. Robertson (1985) envisages decentralized employment as a result of increasing self-employment in small business and the development of 'ownwork'.

These developments may lay the ground-work for local employment initiatives (LEIs) (see Blakely and Bowman 1985, 1986 and OECD 1985 for a discussion of what is involved) and community enterprises. The theme of de-massification can also be extended to welfare services where Naisbitt (1984) anticipates self-help and community support replacing large-scale institutional help. All of these trends should reduce economic and social alienation in the community, although both Bell (1967) and Galbraith (1967) see a similar trend in large corporations, too, as they move from an economising mode to a socialising mode. In other words, large corporations will become increasingly aware of their social welfare as well as profit-making responsibilities. Their social welfare function ranges from the quality of employment for individual workers through to the prosperity of those settlements whose economies they may dominate, and on to the well-being of entire nations.

There is little consensus on the precise nature of post-industrial society. The previous discussion gives some idea of the flavour of the debate by outlining many of the attributes frequently considered. These include:

- the rise of the service sector;
- the creation of intellectual elites (generally information workers) and the de-skilling of process workers;
- the increase of available leisure time;
- the demise of mass society and its replacement with small-scale enterprises producing quality customized products; and
- the possibility of geographical decentralisation in economic control and production.

Most writers agree that the high productivity of post-industrial society allows citizens to pursue self-fulfilment, one of the most elevated of Maslow's (1954) hierarchy of needs. Social welfare is also promoted. All these trends of course may be over-stated, but probably contain a kernel of truth. We can certainly assume that Australia's development over the medium term will at least partially mirror those trends.

Effective and sustained post-industrialism depends, however, on the occurrence of several critical and-interrelated events. The shift to a service economy — particularly those services concerned with welfare and final consumption

— requires high productivity from the primary, secondary and ancillary service sectors. This can come about via the substitution of capital for labour (automation) or through the development of high-technology industries whose high added value reflects well-developed workforce skills in design, imagination, research and development, and entrepreneurship. For both to occur, a society needs to value and reward innovation and to have flexible social institutions which permit changes to take place with a minimum of friction. Rapidly growing productivity can then be used to fund the comparative luxuries of short working hours, increased leisure activities and more personal or social services.

A society embarking on premature post-industrialism effectively puts the cart before the horse. It acquires the trappings of improved lifestyle and consumption, but omits to develop a highly productive raw materials, manufacturing and ancillary services base (Table 6.3). Ancillary services are the bastions of national wealth. Their output can be traded internationally for goods or services produced more efficiently elsewhere. The process by which nations specialize in those activities where they have comparative advantage and trade their output should theoretically add greatly to national income. Australia's comparative advantage has traditionally lain in mining and farming raw materials, but there is no reason why this should not be extended to knowledge-based industries. Once wealth has been created, a portion can be siphoned off for consumption, provided sufficient resources are left to reinvest in further wealth-creating activities.

Premature post-industrialism is inherently unstable as a basis on which society may develop. An emphasis on improved lifestyle and greater consumption reduces and may even halt investment in productive facilities. Consequently, the nation's capital stock may remain static or decline, after allowing for normal wear and tear and obsolescence. Alternatively, those often capital intensive industries on which future national prosperity depends may have difficulty raising the necessary finance.

Societies where consumption runs ahead of output tend to have low levels of savings and high interest rates, except where consumption can be financed by overseas borrowings. Borrowing overseas can be a recipe for national insolvency if taken to excess. Such societies present would-be entrepreneurs or investors in production facilities with other major problems. First, taxation needs to rise to improve services where there is little increase in the output of materials and goods. This acts as a disincentive to investment. Secondly, low growth societies may channel much effort into the debate over how to divide up the existing cake rather than expand it. The risk is that society may become conservative as existing entitlements are defended. Thirdly, workers are often desperate to hang on to existing jobs if few are being created in new enterprises. This can make it difficult for management to introduce labour-saving technology in existing industries.

The consequence of all these events is likely to be low economic growth which in turn aborts post-industrial tendencies. The full liberating potential of late twentieth century technology cannot then be realised. Social cleavages may be exacerbated between those who wish to see capital accumulation and investment and those who prefer consumption; between those who wish to maximize private consumption and the welfare lobby; between traditionalists and innovators; and, in Australia's case, between city and country and between advocates of increased and decreased immigration. The greater these cleavages, the lower the rate of economic growth. Argentina used to be testimony to this (Duncan and Fogarty, 1984) before she decided that efficient production was the way to salvation.

How prone is Australia to premature post-industrialism? The popular interpreters of Australian culture such as Horne (1964), McGregor (1968) and Conway (1971) paint a generally unflattering picture of a shallow, materialist and hedonist society. On the positive side there is an element of egalitarianism, tolerance, stoicism and ability to improvise. These were borne of hardships encountered by self-reliant pioneers who initially tamed the harsh continent. Talk of mateship and a fair go is a residual testament to this philosophy, though somewhat frayed at the edges over the last two decades. That was an era of heightened social competition for resources in the face of recurrent economic recession and income stagnation. The relatively egalitarian distribution of income and wealth across the country (see Chapter 3) stems from something other than philosophy, specifically the early unionisation of labour and its strength relative to capital in a rapidly growing frontier society. These same forces gave rise to early representative democracy in 1860 which, when coupled with considerable national wealth (Australia had the highest per capita GNP of any country by 1900), created an advanced network of social services (see Chapter 4). Social progress seemed to encounter few barriers and was accompanied by the easy-going somewhat laconic philosophy of 'she'll be right'. As Horne (1964, p. 20) notes, 'Australia is not a society of striving or emulation'.

Unfortunately the long post-war boom which ground to a halt in the early 1970s served to reinforce the worst traits of Australian society. Growth was easy: the growth of import-substituting industries behind high tariff walls; reasonable prices for farm output; a mining boom; large-scale immigration leading to strong demand in the construction and related industries. Wage increases and restrictive work practices were granted easily, consumption was strong, capital inflow remained high, leisure time increased, a hedonistic culture developed especially among the young, and alternative lifestyles multiplied. Perhaps the pace of these developments was most frantic immediately preceding the global economic crisis of the mid-1970s with which Australia was not well-equipped to cope. Those years closely resembled the description of early post-industrialism: a self-indulgent society busy expanding consumption of goods and services on a declining primary and secondary base.

The hangover lasted five years from 1975 to 1980, and during this period the nation adjusted little to the commercial opportunities opening up in the Asia-Pacific region, or to the dark clouds of competition approaching both primary and secondary sectors. Perhaps this, too, was a consequence of a self-indulgent smugness. Come the short-lived resources boom in the early 1980s, strategically placed segments of the workforce could not resist a slice of the action and diverted capital funds to consumption by way of large wage increases and sometimes successful claims for a shorter working week.

To summarize this argument, the Australian psyche is probably predisposed to the benefits of post-industrialism — the increased consumption and quality of life aspects — but maybe not to the effort and changes required to achieve them. Furthermore, two resources booms in the last twenty years (the first was in the late 1960s and laid the groundwork for the fling in the early 1970s) have seen the nation squander its endowment. If this diagnosis is true, any resurgence in national fortunes — perhaps in the 1990s — could give rein yet again to premature post-industrial urges, and abort recovery. Thus this scenario will at least see retarded economic growth periodically. Should Australians adopt a full-blooded form of premature post-industrialism as a way of life, and this cannot be regarded as very probable in the current political environment, it could be disastrous for national welfare. There is no place in the cut-throat commercial world of the 1990s for lazy, combative and self indulgent societies. We could easily follow the trail blazed so ignominiously by Peronist Argentina: declining, or at best static, living standards; decay of social institutions; unemployment and inflation; relative impoverishment of the countryside; uncompetitive industrial production; decaying physical infrastructure; and low population growth on account of immigration being unpopular.

Market economics

In many respects the market economics scenario is the antithesis of the two previous scenarios. In part, it constitutes the streamlining and diminution of the pluralist corporatist state by reducing the role of government and placing greater reliance on market mechanisms for the production of goods and services. Simply stated, if governments produce or regulate less, there is less for interest groups to fight over and less opportunity to thwart forces for change. In these conditions economy and society should become more adaptive and flexible, and more able to identify and seize opportunity. In part, also, this scenario represents discipline rather than self indulgence, thrift rather than consumption, work rather than pleasure.

A glance at Table 6.3 reveals similarities between Market Economics and the political platforms of the Liberal 'dries', the so-called 'new right', and even some right-wing members of the Labor Party. Political patronage may enable some progress towards market economics but, in line with earlier arguments about the corporate state, the institutional and attitudinal blockages to change may be so great that the thorough application of market ideas is unlikely to emerge triumphant over the medium term. The speed at which its ideas are assimilated could, however, make a considerable difference to the rate of improvement in Australia's well being and the geographical pattern of social and economic development.

The market economics scenario owes much to the libertarian tradition which runs from Adam Smith in the eighteenth century to Friedrich Hayek in the twentieth. This line of thought was very much alive in the Australia of the 1980s through the work of numerous 'think-tanks' such as the Centre for Independent Studies in Sydney and the Centre of Policy Studies, the Tasman Institute, and the Institute of Public Affairs in Melbourne. Table 6.4 defines in more detail some of the scenario's major characteristics. They tend towards the left-hand column. The business climate is open and competitive, entrepreneurial and risk-taking, innovative and adaptable, future oriented, geared towards savings and investment, and growth. All of this is encouraged by the incentive effects of low taxation and the uncertainty prompted by competition. The latter is certainly consistent with Porter's advocacy of integrated industrial nodes comprising large numbers of related and highly competitive businesses (Porter, 1990). Also conducive to business development, though not included in Table 6.4 because it may also be an attribute of the corporate state, is fiscal and monetary sobriety. This involves low budget deficits (government income approximately matches its expenditure), low inflation (only a slow decline in the value of money), an appropriate, perhaps slightly undervalued, exchange rate, and a rough balance of international trade, though erring towards surplus. Market supporters also point to the benefits of international trade, though not necessarily targeted specifically to the Asia-Pacific region as proposed by Garnaut (1989). One further impetus for rapid growth is identified by Hughes (1985). She advocates increasing the use rate of capital stock in many parts of the economy from a typical miserable 20% to the 50–60% prevalent in many of Australia's competitors or, hopefully, the 80% reached in parts of the Singapore economy. Moreover, the investment regime should favour the rapid depreciation of the capital stock so that plant and equipment represent the latest technology.

In theory these conditions should bring about rapid economic growth. The evidence from Table 6.5 is that theory matches practice. Those countries of East and South-east Asia which have competitive entrepreneurial business climates (including Taiwan, South Korea, Hong Kong, Singapore, Thailand and Malaysia) have all experienced rapid economic growth in the last two

Table 6.5 An international comparison of economic growth rates

Country	*Average annual real growth in GDP 1976/86*[1]
Japan	4.1
South Korea	7.1
Taiwan	7.6
Thailand	6.0
Hong Kong	7.8
Singapore	6.8
People's Republic of China	6.7
USA	2.6
OECD average	3.4
Australia	3.0

1 Per capita figures need to be discounted by approximately the percentage rate of population growth

Source: National Australia Bank, *Monthly Summary*, March 1987

decades. The same applied to Japan throughout most of the twenty years prior to the early 1970s. Now that country, like Australia, has to cope with structural change in a mature economy which has developed numerous interest groups and institutional blockages. Perhaps extremely rapid growth can only be sustained starting from a low level of economic well-being. Certainly all the major industrial (OECD) economies, including well-run nations such as Western Germany, Switzerland and Japan, are struggling to maintain even moderate economic development. This explains why Kasper and Parry (1978) and Kasper *et al.* (1980) only anticipate sustained Australian growth rates of about 4–5% per capita per annum under favourable conditions.

This rate may seem hardly better than the 2 per cent expected under the muddling through scenario. The apparently small difference is however misleading. Table 6.6 shows why. An economy growing at 2 per cent in real (inflation-adjusted) terms over 15 years will end up nearly 35 per cent better off than at the start. One growing at nearly 5 per cent will be twice as well off. The geographical consequences of such a difference would be profound, especially if large-scale immigration were encouraged (perhaps 180 000 to 200 000 per annum) by rapid development. This could lift the rate of growth from say 4.5 per cent in per capita terms to approximately 6 per cent in absolute terms. The size of the Australian economy could under these conditions grow 140 per cent in 15 years. Indeed the regional consequences of this scenario would be greater still since the essence of a dynamic economy is the widespread destruction of existing businesses or output and their replacement by others. Some places could therefore lose or gain markedly.

Market economics would also serve to demolish further many of the already somewhat frayed stereotypes of Australian society. As Table 6.3 suggests, the disciplines of the market-place would be accompanied necessarily by a strong work ethic and greater individual or family responsibility for

Table 6.6 Total percentage growth for various annual growth rates and time periods

Number of years	*Compound rate of growth per annum (%)*					
	1	*2*	*3*	*4*	*5*	*6*
5	5.1	10.4	15.9	21.7	27.6	33.8
10	10.5	21.9	34.4	48.0	62.9	79.1
15	16.1	34.6	55.8	80.1	108.0	140.0

social well-being. Many social services — especially in the area of health and education — may be privatized either in delivery or funding on the grounds of efficiency and lower taxes. Tax reduction would also flow from the means-testing of transfer payments (pensions, child allowances, spouse rebates) so that only those who need assistance get it. It is likely that greater individual responsibility would increase thrift and this, in turn, would make available more capital for business expansion. Unemployment benefits could be reduced to encourage job-seeking, or tied to skill improvement in some way so as to increase workforce utility and flexibility. Such processes may well have the effect of reinforcing the nuclear family and making experimentation with new social relationships less attractive. Another far-reaching implication of market economics might be the restoration of full employment. This could occur if labour markets were deregulated sufficiently to allow the demand for, and supply of, different types of labour skills to be equated through the price mechanism.

Lest these ideas be seen as a reversion to the kind of conflicting class relationships Marx detected in nineteenth century industrial Britain, it should be noted that nothing could be further from the truth. For one thing, a strong social safety net would be in place. More significantly, 'Ultimate sources of productivity advance...lie in social arrangements' (Blandy *et al.*, 1985, p. 5); new kinds of worker-management relationships would be necessary for Australia to overcome its 20–40% productivity lag behind Western Germany and the United States. In other words, the workforce, not capital spending or automation, is the primary source of productivity gains, and people should therefore be treated with respect and dignity and as partners. Nelson amplifies this view:

> ...How workers feel about their job, about fellow workers, about management, and about their organisation, may be more important in influencing productivity than is the particular way they are instructed to do their work, the formal organisational structure, or even financial incentives...(in Blandy *et al.*, 1985, p. 6)

Furthermore (p. ll), 'Organisations (and societies) with high dynamic capability are those with loose organisational structures, but a strong shared sense of purpose or mission'. Gone, in this view, is the language of alienation and class conflict.

The range of possible mechanisms is enormous for bringing about the changes above. It includes everything from worker representation on boards of directors, the formation of worker co-operatives, non-hierarchical management structures, the use of productivity bonuses and stock options, company training programmes, setting up work teams, quality control circles, to generous rewards for suggestions improving product design or construction and so on. These are more likely to take root and become widespread faster in the competitive hothouse of market economics than in the other scenarios. In such an environment even entrepreneurial functions could become decentralized down to the shop floor. However, Blandy *et al.*, (1985) wonder if the necessary changes in Australia's social arrangements are achievable given the massive effort required to overcome embedded interest groups, old-style class antagonisms, an outmoded restrictive union structure, and a lack of entrepreneurship. Perhaps, though, certain localities or States may be more amenable to altered social relationships than others. For example, it is not difficult to see the mining and heavy manufacturing industries lagging in innovative social relationships, whereas high technology manufacture already manifests them in large measure. Could the Trades Hall Councils of Newcastle, Wollongong and Geelong be the nemesis of those cities? On the other hand, Australia's competitive federalism might ensure that the successful application of market ideas in one state could spread rapidly to the rest.

If we assume that population growth under a high immigration regime averages 1.6 per cent per annum over the 15 years from 1986, Australia's population should rise from 16 million to 20.3 million. This is 1.3 to 1.8 million more than projected in the muddling through scenario and represents a 50 per cent faster growth rate.

Other scenarios

Numerous other scenarios can be envisaged, but none so likely as the three already discussed. Three of the more prominent alternatives are listed below, with special emphasis on their weaknesses.

A socialist Australia

So many versions of the 'socialist Australia' scenario could be possible that it is not easy to distil general features which cannot be labelled a caricature of individual positions. The outcome could be an accelerated version of premature post-industrialism, as consumption growth rapidly exceeds the production of basic goods and materials and labour productivity. No shortage of deserving causes for public expenditure might be found: welfare housing; increased pensions and benefits; the arts; work schemes for the unemployed; capital works of an infrastructure kind; investment in research and development; and expanded technical and higher education. The funding of these programs is problematic. Budget deficits tend to be inflationary, especially if sustained over a long period, and force up interest rates to levels that distort or stifle investment. Overseas borrowing has eventually to be repaid and this simply cannot be done if the money goes to consumption rather than production for export. Redirection of resources by means-testing benefits or reducing defence expenditure could help a little. Increased company taxes would work to lower investment. Higher income taxes on the wealthy might work if they were happy to have lower disposable incomes, but are normally assumed to reduce the incentive to produce goods and services. Those affected by increased taxes would almost certainly try to maintain their well-being with inflationary price rises or wage increases.

On the production side, inefficiency and slow growth are a probable outcome. Where existing jobs are threatened by overseas imports, economic recession or declining demand there could be a strong temptation to protect or feather-bed them at the consumers' expense and to the disadvantage of more competitive sectors. Some monopoly producers, for example BHP steel, may be nationalized though the benefit is unclear. The usual level of capital inflow from overseas investors which is needed to finance the deficit on current (trade) account could be restricted to prevent national assets falling in foreigner's hands. Such financial xenophobia can however only reduce national economic growth, especially if locally available investment funds are also used to buy-back-the-farm. A socialist government may also be lured into the almost impossible task of picking and supporting 'high-tech' winners. Not even the famed Ministry for International Trade and Industry in Japan (MITI) has been very good at it.

All of these factors, together with high tax and inflation, would probably create an unappetizing investment climate. The resulting stagnation would make it difficult to supply improved public services. In short, there are many negative aspects to the scenario. Moreover it is most unlikely to be realised for at least three reasons:

- It is against the tenor of the age, notably deregulation and small government.
- Given a choice between private or public self-indulgence, Australians would most assuredly choose the former.
- Socialism demonstrably failed in Eastern Europe.

An ascetic Australia (or abstinence with a touch of romanticism)

Some commentaries on the future express extreme optimism. Kahn *et al.* (1976), for example, see so few constraints on economic growth that gross world product can expand from $5.5 trillion in 1976 to $300 trillion in 2176 (at constant prices). At the opposite extreme are the pessimists. One school which developed in the early 1970s centred around the idea that resources are limited and will soon be exhausted at projected rates of usage (Forrester, 1971; Meadows *et al.* 1972; Mesarovic and Pestel, 1974). Schneider (1976) also points out that climatic catastrophe could limit economic growth and that idea has become enshrined in writings on the greenhouse effect (Henderson-Sellers and Blong, 1989; Pearman, 1988; Daly, 1989; and Falk and Brownlow, 1989). Acceptance of resource or environmental limitations similarly features prominently in the writings of many subsequent writers such as Johnson (1978), Heilbroner (1975, 1976), Schumacher (1973) and Trainer (1985). In general these writers respond to the problem by advocating the production of necessary goods and services at a local level using local resources and appropriate small-scale technology. Not only would this reduce the consumption of non-renewable resources but there would be other beneficial social consequences: a greater sense of community; less alienation, fuller development of human potential; greater spirituality, the development of self-reliance; democratic decision-making; maintenance of tradition; and reverence for the environment. Schumacher calls this 'Buddhist Economics' to denote the middle way between material heedlessness and traditional immobility. Heilbroner sees this type of society as the end result of the decline of capitalism, but a long time in the future. Here we label it an 'Ascetic Australia'.

This vision is heir to other traditions. One stance, as exemplified by the visions of Thomas Jefferson, William Cobbett and Henry David Thoreau, romanticizes bucolic lifestyles and disparages city living as a threat to human well-being and good social order. Others such as Georg Simmel and Louis Wirth accept that the crowding of large cities leads to psychic frustration and social friction (Smith, 1980), though they reject rural lifestyles as a distinct improvement. Even proponents of rapid growth and technological change seem to have reservations about the growth of large cities. Toffler (1971) laments transience of the kind associated most with urban living, notably the throw-away lifestyle, nomadic existence, transient social relationships, transient art and culture, love of novelty, and the flood of options confronting citizens. And Kahn *et al.* (1976), the high priests of development, mention the 'failures of success': the loss of uplifting ideals and the distinction between superior and inferior performance; the loss of tradition, patriotism, and faith — everything that cannot be justified by reason; and the absence of realisation of higher goals — God, honour and great projects. All these problems might be solved by Buddhist economics.

A second strand to ascetic thinking stems from anarchist writings. Peter Kropotkin, for example, developed his views of society as mutual aid after a critical visit to the watch-making Jura region of Switzerland where he saw a kind of Buddhist economics in action (Galois, 1977). Thirdly, there has been a long tradition of utopian rural settlement culminating in the practical success of the Israeli kibbutz movement (Sommerlad *et al.*, 1985). These somewhat austere communes evolved in the early days of Jewish settlement in Palestine as an effective means of land development, as a physical defence against hostile Palestinian communities, and as a way of preserving Jewish culture. They were often highly self-sufficient, providing manufactured goods and a range of social services in addition to agricultural output. Furthermore, kibbutzim are more a society than a federation of individual family units and thus tend to suppress individuality. To some extent, therefore, they reflect Kropotkin's ideals, though they are a long way from Buddhist economics.

Collectively these beliefs and ideals have had, and still have an important influence on western society. Australia has a well-developed commune (or alternative lifestyle) movement dedicated to Robertson's (1985) SHE society — Sane, Humane, Ecological. Many of these settlements are located in secluded valleys of the north coast region of NSW — around Lismore and near Bellingen in particular. Typically they emphasize or involve communal ownership of land, harmony with nature, organic agriculture, craft industry, self-help housing using local materials, abstinence from mass consumption, and some mutual support. In short, they are a step towards Buddhist economics. Several claims are made for the commune movement. The first is that it is quietly setting the trends for Australia's conventional future in the 1990s. Secondly, it may be used by government as a way of coping with the human overflow of technocratic society (the unemployed can be put to work cheaply). Thirdly, it is a hedge against change, a store of potential sociological novelties, a device to keep alive alternatives to dominant emphases, and a nursery for new cultural patterns. The second of these received the sanction of the former Prime Minister, Bob Hawke, when he suggested the creation of Australian kibbutzim.

Several studies have, however, demolished many of the romantic notions concerning communes (Johnson, 1978; Munro-Clark, 1986; Sommerlad *et al.* 1985). They are often dependent on the society which envelops them to sustain their usually low standard of living. Many would collapse without the dole cheque and other social security payments. They need tourists to buy crafts, public education and health services, paved roads, electricity and so on. They are no utopia, nor a long-term solution to unemployment.

Communes, therefore, are unlikely to be the dominant path to the future, certainly not in the next ten to fifteen years. However, they might survive as an adjunct to (post-) industrial society for a long time by providing sanctuaries for those who see possessions as emotionally crippling, or romance in poverty, or who seek spiritual liberation in perhaps temporary retreat from a competitive world.

Catastrophe

Numerous possibilities for disaster exist, though few are likely to reach the status of catastrophe and few have even a remote chance of occurrence. The major possibilities as far as Australia is concerned are set out in Table 6.7. For the most part, the disasters with the greatest potential magnitude and

Table 6.7 Types of disaster

Disaster	*Duration of effect*[1]	*Magnitude of effect*[2]	*Probability of occurrence*[3]
A Environmental			
Widespread drought	S	S	L
Large earthquake (major city)	S-M	S	S[4]
Rising sea-level	L	M-L	S
Widespread desertification	L	S	S-M
Widespread salination	L	S	S-M
Acid rain	L	S	S[5]
Major livestock/crop disease	M-L	M-L	S-M
B Economic/technological			
Widespread substitution of Australian resources by synthetics or alternative supplies	S-M	M	S[5]
Global depression	M	M-L	S
Dramatic rises in fuel prices	M	M-L	S-M
C Political disaster			
Australia invaded after conventional war	M	M-L	S[5]
War elsewhere (northern hemisphere) destroys Australian export markets	M-L	M-L	S[5]
Nuclear war followed by nuclear winter	L	L	S[5]

1 S, M, L = short, medium, or long-term.
2 In terms of the degree to which the long-term path of Australian development is diverted, S, M, L = small, moderate, large.
3 In the medium term (the next fifteen years), S, M, L = small, moderate, large.
4 Newcastle experienced a major earthquake in 1990.
5 All of these most unlikely to occur within the time frame set.

duration have a very low probability of occurrence, while widespread drought, which occurs frequently, often has little long-term effect. This is because drought is expected, and various coping strategies have been devised by farmers, government, financial and other business institutions, and infrastructure suppliers. Only two of the matters listed seem to have a high risk attached to them within the medium-term: livestock or plant disease and the price (or availability) of fuel. Australia has probably the world's toughest quarantine regulations in an attempt to prevent serious diseases, noxious plants and animals, or insect pests reaching these shores. In such cases as the rabbit, cane toad, Patterson's Curse and the European wasp, regulations came too late or were evaded, innocently or otherwise. Other pests have, with effort, been largely controlled — the prickly pear for example.

Fortunately, the potentially greatest threat to rural Australia, foot and mouth disease, has yet to arrive. In Europe, where livestock are closely supervised, the disease is quickly spotted and the affected animals killed. In Australia, the extensive nature of grazing would severely hamper control of the disease. For example, cattle on the great pastoral leases of northern Australia may come into human contact once in two or three years at best. If the disease should arrive here and spread quickly, the whole pastoral sector might be decimated and along with it a large slice of export earnings. Current regulations and their enforcement are, however, probably sufficient to control the problem. This applies, too, to plant diseases and pests. In this case biological control through genetic engineering or predation, and chemical control, are also possible. Our general opinion is that a major farming catastrophe sufficient in size to alter the direction of Australia's economic and social evolution is therefore an unlikely occurrence.

On the subject of fuel availability, we must acknowledge the great dependence of the Australian way of life on its use. The production and distribution of materials, goods and services, extensive suburbia, households and recreation are all energy intensive. All could be forced to adjust substantially to either large price rises or to shortages in supply or both combined. The two oil crises of the 1970s engineered by OPEC (in 1973 and 1979) saw the price of unrefined oil rise from about US$4 to nearly US$35 a barrel for some grades. This certainly had the effect of reducing profligacy in energy consumption: more energy efficient machines, appliances and vehicles emerged. This, coupled with the fact that Australia was to a certain extent an energy rich country with at least two thirds self-sufficiency in oil, led to little change in producer or consumer behaviour. Next time round, things may be different. Many of the easier technological improvements in fuel use efficiency may have been realised. Australia's oil self-sufficiency may decline rapidly in the 1990s in the quite likely event of no further large oil fields being discovered. This will expose the nation to the whims of producer nations and the oil companies, and to the blockage of sea lanes. Energy availability and price could therefore constitute an important problem, though principally in the short to medium-term until substitute fuels became available. These include hydrogen gas, oil distilled from coal and oil shale, and ethanol distilled from sugar cane. In practice, however, significant disruptive price changes or alterations in energy availability are unlikely, although some short-run changes will undoubtedly occur — as with the 1991 Gulf War.

It is our view, shared with Daly (1989) that the greenhouse effect will not lead to significant climatic change or sea-level rise in our forecast period. And despite calls from various quarters (Henderson-Sellers and Blong, 1989 and others) for plans to be made to obviate dangerous rises in sea-level, none have yet been put in place that are likely to alter Australia's economic and social geography to any marked degree. For example, there are several plans in place to open more coal mines and raise coal exports, despite its contribution to the expansion of carbon dioxide, one of the principal greenhouse gases.

The geographical impact of the scenarios

What implications do these scenarios have for the geographical pattern of social and economic development in Australia? The remainder of this chapter attempts to provide some answers to this question. The scenes depicted are best regarded as informed conjectures coloured with a touch of imagination. No claim is made for their accuracy. There are too many unknowns: large-scale shocks such as drought, famine, war, trade wars or global recession; synergisms (the chance meetings of different technologies giving rise to new technologies and products); and serendipities (important, but unintended, consequences of innovations or decisions). These unknowns may not matter greatly. The broad-brush pictures presented may indeed be most influenced by the quasi-ideological conditions of the three scenarios outlined above. Particular attention is paid to four issues: rural life; manufacturing industry; the structure of cities; and the pattern of regional development.

Rural life

This discussion of rural life is restricted to those localities whose dominant economic base is farming. It purposefully excludes such industrial cities as Newcastle and Geelong, coastal resorts, and company mining towns, although it is recognized that most of rural Australia also performs non-farming functions such as tourism and recreation, mining, and secondary industry. Many rural areas also serve a dormitory function for metropolitan cores.

Patterns of primary production

Rural Australia is in the throes of one of its periodic upheavals. Sometimes these are the consequence of cyclical downturn in a key industry, as in the wool industry in the early 1970s and again in the early 1990s and the wheat industry in 1991. Often, however, they result from more permanent events. These include the loss of export markets, domestic restructuring of markets as the regulations surrounding the production of milk, eggs, fruit and the like are swept away, from changing consumer demand, or from import penetration occasioned by lower cost, though not necessarily more efficient, producers entering the market place (as with foreign supplies of concentrated orange juice).

From the mid-1980s onwards serious structural problems emerged in sections of the rural economy, especially in the sugar, grain and wool industries. The issue was and is fundamentally one of low commodity prices and high costs (see Table 6.8).

Table 6.8 Indicators of the rural economy (1980–81 = 100)

	1979/80	*'81/82*	*'83/84*	*'85/86*	*'87/88*	*'89/90*	*'91/92*[1]
Volume of production							
Crops	119	125	154	141	130	138	119
Livestock production	103	102	106	116	126	141	116
Total	110	112	122	121	123	133	119
Prices received	94	99	109	112	142	155	132
Prices paid	88	111	134	152	172	200	203
Farmers' terms of trade	107	89	82	73	83	78	66
Real net value of farm production	167	77[2]	83	24	71	60	4
Gross value of production							
Crops	115	108	120	93	85	n.a.	n.a.
Livestock products	104	100	96	102	152	n.a.	n.a.
Total	112	100	101	90	100	101	74

1 Forecasts
2 The index for 1982/83 was 3

Sources: computed from Australian Bureau of Agricultural and Resource Economics (1989); *Agricultural and Resources Quarterly*, 3(4), 1991

Indeed, farmers' terms of trade have slipped between a quarter and one third over the last decade on average, and much more in some industries. Low prices stem from global over-production of many items brought about by more efficient production techniques — for example the green revolution — and subsidies of the kind made available to European Community (EC) farmers. This problem is likely to persist for the rest of this century as farm productivity improves, production subsidies prove difficult to reduce, and there is strong competition to remove surplus stocks. Indeed if Russia, the Ukraine, and the remaining CIS states — some of the world's major food importers — were to improve their disastrous farm productivity by even a moderate amount, commodity prices could fall much further, assuming the absence of production restraint elsewhere. To some extent Australian farmers were cushioned against declining prices in the 1980s by the depreciation of the Australian dollar against other currencies. This had the effect of increasing income received by producers because most internationally traded commodities are priced in US dollars. Unfortunately, currency depreciation also has the effect of raising costs. The prices of farm machinery, fertilizer, fuel, shipping charges and interest rates on borrowings have all risen sharply, doubling over the last decade (Table 6.8). Of course these cost increases affect the whole farm sector, but the sugar and grain sectors have been particularly hard hit because they are more capital intensive than many of the others, especially meat and wool. It is not surprising, therefore, that sugar and grain production have witnessed the greatest number of bankruptcies and forced departure of families from the land. Many of those that remain have exceedingly low farm-based incomes.

Bureau of Agricultural Economics projections for 1985/86 gave 53 per cent of wheat and crop family farms a negative income, and an average of –$7500 each (Table 6.9). The projection for sugar specialists was worse: –$16 600. This follows –$5984 and –$8120 for the previous two years. All these figures allow for depreciation, without which cash operating surpluses would have resulted. By 1988/89 incomes had rebounded in most sectors, beef being the major exception. In yet another swing of the pendulum the rural recession of 1991/92 saw incomes plummet in the grain and sheep sectors while the beef industry did well.

Table 6.9 illustrates well the extreme variability in farm income that can result from the interplay of climate (1991 saw a major drought in Queensland and northern NSW) and dramatically declining commodity prices. It also demonstrates both the low level of per capita farm incomes even in a good year (1988/89) once income is distributed across family members. Table 6.9 testifies, too, to the importance of off-farm income. This amounted to almost 70 per cent of farm income in the beef sector in 1988/89. The table does not reveal that within these parameters there were marked regional variations in well-being. Many producers in Victoria and southern NSW at least harvested excellent crops in 1991, even if they did receive low unit prices.

In some respects the financial stress of grain and sugar producers arises not from bad luck with depressed prices which should, perhaps, have been foreseen, but from imprudent investment decisions. Table 6.10 shows that many rural export sectors, and especially textile fibres, saw strong price increases in the period 1977–1989 that kept pace with inflation averaging 9 per cent per annum. Many farmers therefore borrowed heavily to expand the size of their properties and to purchase expensive machinery. Financing these debts constitutes a major problem, given subsequent adverse commodity price movements, the rapid decline in land values, the surge in farm costs, and domestic interest rates that reached 20 per cent or more in 1990. Table 6.11 gives the average debt for different types of family farm in relation to capital value. In both the years listed cropping sectors had a greater debt ratio than livestock industries, mainly on account of their heavier capital requirements. Note that the falling debt ratios apparent in Table 6.11 may be illusory to some extent. It seems that market value of rural holdings rose during the relatively prosperous years from 1987 to 1990. Land values have since slumped and markedly exacerbated debt ratios. Short-term volatility seems to be an endemic feature of rural industry.

In 1984/85 25 per cent of wheat/other crop and rice farms — two of the most indebted sectors — had debts of at least $150 000 compared with the average of about $123 000 and $104 000 respectively. The BAE (1986a)

Table 6.9 Average farm income, by type of farm—selected years

	Family farms						
	1986	*% change*	*1988/89*			*Broad acre farm cash income 1991/92*	*Change on previous year (%)*
	Farm income	*1984/85 to 1985/86*	*Farm income*	*Income per working year of family labour*	*Off farm income*		
Wheat						43 000	–10
Wheat & other crops	–7 500	–143	33 680	18 520	9 420		
Mixed livestock, crops	4 500	–76	53 150	27 470	8 410	29 000	7
Sheep	12 200	–51	54 540	30 170	12 070	2 000	–90
Beef	16 200	–22	17 960	8 460	12 390	39 000	22
Sheep, beef	14 100	–55	35 290	19 980	10 150	19 000	–34
Dairy	8 800	–42	40 850	21 610	6 050	n.a.	
Horticulture	6 200	–35	23 920	12 430	8 680	n.a.	
Total	6 700	–66	41 700	21 900	9 580	23 000	–18

n.a. Not available

Sources: Bureau of Agricultural Economics (1986a); Australian Bureau of Agricultural and Resource Economics (1991b); Tucker *et al.* (1990)

Table 6.10 Price indices for various export categories 1979/80 = 100

	1977/78	*'79/80*	*'81/82*	*'83/84*	*'85/86*	*'87/88*	*'89/90*	*'91/92*[1]
Rural								
Meat	54	100	88	105	119	131	147	140
Cereal	76	100	112	123	132	111	153	125
Textile fibres	77	100	110	123	136	240	223	143
Total Rural	67	100	94	115	136	189	200	158

Sources: Foster and Stewart (1991) for data up to 1989/90; Australian Bureau of Agricultural and Resource Economics (1991b), for 1991/92 data; Australian Bureau of Agricultural and Resource Economics (1989) for 'Total Rural'

believed that interest payments on farm debts as a proportion of total costs increased from 7.7 per cent in 1980/81 to 12 per cent in 1985/86. It estimated that perhaps 10 per cent of wheat/other crops farms were 'at risk' in 1985/86 (BAE, 1986b). However, the proportion of wheat and sugar farms would have been higher than this. Also the proportion of at risk farms in NSW (13 per cent) and Western Australia (20 per cent) considerably exceeded that elsewhere. Within the sugar industry alone there were some regional differences in the proportion of farms at risk. Cash operating surpluses were lowest in the central and southern producing regions (i.e. south of Bowen). ABARE figures for 1990/91 suggest that about 5 per cent of broadacre farms will face considerable short-term financial stress (Hall *et al.*, 1991). These were defined as farms with a negative farm cash operating surplus over the two financial years to 1990/91 and liquid assets less than debt in 1989/90 (Hall *et al.*, 1991). The types of property at risk in the early 1990s were mainly in wheat and other

Table 6.11 Average business debt and capital for family farms, 1984/85 & 88/89

	1984/85			*1988/89*		
Farm type	*Debt $000*	*Capital $000*	*Ratio (d:c)*	*Debt $000*	*Capital $000*	*Ratio (d:c)*
Wheat & other crops	124	784	0.16	117	734	0.16
Mixed livestock, crops	76	676	0.11	115	984	0.12
Sheep	56	533	0.10	73	994	0.07
Beef	32	650	0.05	73	1 196	0.06
Sheep, beef	73	803	0.09	81	1 087	0.07
Dairy	46	414	0.11	66	781	0.08
Horticulture	28	180	0.16	42	359	0.12
Rice	104	695	0.15	n.a.	n.a.	n.a.
All	67	607	0.11	85	946	0.09

n.a Not available

Source: Tucker *et al.* (1990)

cropping, wool, and perhaps sugar and especially those located in NSW, Western Australia and Queensland. Remember, though, that farm prosperity can change rapidly in both directions as indicated by the performance of the beef industry.

The short-term (the next five years) will continue to witness a continued shake-out of grain and livestock producers, irrespective of which scenario is the most accurate predictor of Australia's performance. It will take various forms. Some marginal grain producers located on the furthest inland edge of the wheat–sheep zone will leave the industry and switch to pastoral activities, especially as beef is presently among the more profitable rural activities and has relatively low debt/capital ratios (Table 6.11). Thus the boundary of the pastoral zone will move seawards. This might lead in turn to the abandonment of even more remote and marginal pastoral properties, a move that is likely to be environmentally beneficial if it protects fragile ecosystems from over-grazing. Farm consolidation will occur within the heart of the wheat–sheep zone as unviable producers leave voluntarily or are foreclosed by banks and other lending institutions. Industry survivors should be able to acquire low-priced land and second-hand machinery, thereby improving their own economic performance. Some properties will also shift in part to more profitable activities, especially cotton where possible or oil seeds. These possibilities are somewhat limited by the looming risk of over-production in those sectors that remain attractive (BAE 1986a, 1986b).

Structural adjustment in sugar-growing areas will be difficult. Some farm consolidation will occur, but switching to other activities is not so easy. Sugar monoculture, and the chemicals needed to support it can sterilize the soil for a number of years. Cane-growers must have access to a mill within their district, but once production falls below a certain threshold the mill becomes unviable. Should it close, even relatively prosperous cane farms could be forced out of the industry. The industry is also highly regulated and protected so that there is little incentive to reduce production or to shift it from less to more suitable (and profitable) localities. Nevertheless, some sugar regions are changing to other production. For example, farmers in the Bundaberg area, which has good access to metropolitan markets, have been developing horticultural output such as tomatoes. This diversification will continue despite some recovery of sugar prices in 1986/87 and subsequently, from the low point reached in 1985.

There are few bright spots anywhere in Australian farming. Most broadacre cropping suffers the same problems and responses as wheat or sugar, but to a lesser extent. The prospects for rice producers seem particularly poor due to rapidly increasing production in export markets causing a price slump at the same time as large increases in the cost of water for irrigation supplied by the NSW Water Resources Commission (BAE, 1986b). Thus the average farm cash operating surplus in the rice-growing areas of NSW fell an estimated 60 per cent from $32 262 in 1983/84 to $12 900 in 1985/86. Japan may succeed in preventing all but token rice imports into its highly protected market. Thus the rice industry also experiences the volatility in well-being typical of the farm sector and for much the same reasons.

Coarse grain and oilseed prices have gently declined for some time and are expected to continue in that vein (Australian Bureau of Agricultural and Resource Economics, 1991b). Horticultural products may be better off price-wise, but not greatly so. Milk production is flat and the price of manufacturing milk is declining slowly.The dairy industry also faces increased competition from New Zealand exports under the Closer Economic Relations (CER) agreement. This decline will mainly affect Victoria and Tasmania, the main sources of manufacturing milk.

The best prospects for profitable farming among traditional sectors over the short-term seem to lie in beef, cotton and viticulture. However, wheat prices had rebounded by the start of 1992 to their highest absolute level in ten years and the wool price indicator was close to 650¢ per kg clean, close to the 700¢ received before the abandonment of the floor price scheme. Tables 6.9 and 6.11 testify to the relatively good economic health of beef farms, due to reasonably strong United States, and Japanese and east Asian demand for beef. This picture is not, however, uniform. In the mid-1980s 19 per cent of Northern Territory and 8 per cent of Queensland beef producers were thought to be 'at risk' due to high operating costs, compared with 3 per cent nationally.

One of the few star performers has been the wine industry, reflecting strong export growth and maybe excessive vine destruction under a vine pull scheme promoted by the federal government in 1985. Exports have not surprisingly been fuelled by competitive pricing, research and development into better production systems, good quality control and strong capital investment in modern facilities.

Numerous other rural primary industries have been promoted as a means of economic salvation for hard-pressed farmers (Table 6.12). There are successful producers in each of the fields listed and some expansion is possible. Incomes can be high on account of the specialist markets served and the quality of the product. Risks are also great. Markets have to be sought,

Table 6.12 Alternative farm production

1 Fresh vegetables for Asian markets
2 Fish and crustaceans in farm dams or specially constructed fish farms
3 Special wools/fibres—mohair, cashmere, vicuna
4 Special meats—buffalo, venison, kangaroo, crocodile, rabbit, goat
5 Skin production—emu, ostrich, crocodile
6 Exotic fruits and nuts
7 Australian wildflowers
8 Industrial crops—for example, jojoba beans, aloe vera
9 Timber production—particularly specialist hardwoods

products promoted, and research and development carried out into such diverse issues as production, harvesting, storage, transport, and processing. In the short term these initiatives are too small-scale to represent the salvation of the rural sector, though some may become major additions to it in the course of time.

In the medium term the three scenarios outlined earlier assume some prominence in shaping the course of events. There are reasons to suspect that the market economics scenario would be altogether the most favourable for primary producers. It could lower producer debt burden by reducing inflation and interest rates; by preserving the gains of dollar devaluation; by restraining cost rises for labour, machinery, fertilisers and other inputs; and by creating and encouraging investment. The Bureau of Agricultural Economics (1986c) estimated that the removal of tariff protection in Australia would increase the revenue added by the rural sector by 17 per cent in the short run or about $1.5 billion. In this scenario, the Australian dollar would probably have a slightly lower value as high interest rates would not be used to prop up the currency and manufacturing industries would be more exposed to overseas competitors. Consequently, primary exporters would tend to receive higher prices for their output. In short, more farming sectors would be more profitable, given a set of global market conditions, than under the other two scenarios. One consequence would be to retard farm consolidation and rural depopulation, and to preserve the family farm as a viable unit. On the other hand, the deregulation of produce marketing arrangements, which is a logical component of a libertarian economic order, would forcibly rationalise several farm sectors and reduce both output and the number of producers. The dairy, egg, horticulture, and sugar industries are particularly prone to artificial marketing arrangements at the expense of consumers, reflecting their orientation towards the domestic market. This scenario also encourages research and development, innovation and entrepreneurship. All of these are needed to preserve the long-term technological lead of Australian producers and for the development of the kinds of produce cited in Table 6.12. The Bureau of Agricultural Economics (1986a, p. 75) believed that farmers were under-investing in research and development to their future detriment. Also under the market economics scenario, Australia's population would grow more rapidly, thereby creating a larger domestic market for some producers. To some extent this could counter the effects of market deregulation. In conclusion, then, market economics could help create a prosperous rural sector employing more people than now (perhaps an increase of 40 000 to 440 000), even though this would constitute a smaller fraction of a larger labour force.

In contrast, the premature post-industrial scenario is likely to work against primary producers by reducing their income, inhibiting investment and development, and preventing structural change in favour of new, more profitable products. This would be the consequence of diverting national wealth towards consumption and away from investment, particularly through high taxation and public expenditure on welfare services. It is not difficult to imagine that, in a highly regulated society, the interests of the rural primary sector (accounting for only 5 per cent of the workforce in 1990) would be swallowed by urban interests. And in a slow-growing society that could mean the protection of employment in various manufacturing industries at the expense of rural, and many other, consumers. The prevention of import competition would have the effect of improving Australia's trade balance slightly. This in turn would lead to currency appreciation and a reduction of farm export incomes. Where the rural sector enlists the aid of government it may be to protect existing interests by suppressing competition, raising consumer prices, or providing input subsidies. Possible mechanisms include many of the produce marketing boards or corporations, guaranteed price schemes, super-phosphate bounties and the like. Such schemes admittedly reduce producer risk and tend to even out the stream of income, but they also reduce their impetus for innovation and efficiency inherent in relatively free markets. Graphic evidence for the adverse consequences of industry regulation is contained in a critical report of the wool industry by the Centre for International Economics (1991). Far from being an efficient market oriented activity, as perceived by the wool growers themselves, the industry is painted as risk adverse, lacking in research and development and somewhat contemptuous of its market.

It was noted earlier that a lazy, consumption-oriented and risk-adverse society would tend to run large budget and trade deficits, suffer repeated currency devaluations, and experience high interest rates. The last-named would of course make life difficult for debt-ridden rural industries. One final straw to break the back of the rural sector would be a low growth in domestic demand due to low rates of immigration and low natural population growth. What would be the consequences of all this? Various possibilities can be suggested: rural impoverishment; the accelerated demise of the family farm and its replacement by various forms of agri-business whose size and diversity of interests protects it from financial mishap; rural depopulation; a contraction of farm output towards the coastal ecumene and away from marginal areas; and concentration on traditional items with some element of public subsidy. The number of people employed in agriculture, forestry, fishing and hunting declined from 412 000 (7.5 per cent of the workforce) in 1971 to 400 000 (6.2 per cent) in 1984 (ABS, 1987). Under the premature post-industrial scenario this number could well reach 360 000 by early next century.

The remaining and most probable scenario, muddling through, would yield intermediate results. Rural producers would be unable to contribute their full potential to Australian development because of a variety of financial, institutional and attitudinal constraints. The rural workforce might decline slowly to 380 000 in the medium term as a consequence of widespread financial stress which is likely to continue through the early 1990s. There is some reason to believe that in due course, however, some of the weakest producing sectors will struggle back to modest prosperity. High real interest rates will come down; production surpluses will be cut back in overseas countries (especially through cuts in subsidies under the EC's Common Agricultural Policy as a result of the GATT round); input price rises will be moderated, especially in the areas of transport, waterfront and labour costs through micro-economic reform; natural disasters such as drought, flood or intense cold may lower output and reduce stocks; and new seed varieties or husbandry techniques could increase yields. The major point is that under the muddling through scenario those matters over which Australia has substantial control would ameliorate only slowly and in a disjointed way. Thus the current rural recession might be deeper and more prolonged than for the market economics scenario.

Economic conditions may have considerable effect on the spatial pattern of rural production in the medium term, but there are also other important issues not considered by the scenarios. The kinds of catastrophe discussed previously (for example, foot and mouth disease) may be unlikely, but their impact could be great should they occur. Their geographical incidence is also virtually unpredictable. Less problematical are changes to the area under crops or horticulture. We have already noted a possible contraction of marginal cropping areas which could occur in all the mainland States under the premature post-industrial scenario. Output could also fall as the result of soil salination problems in irrigation areas, especially in the lower Murray/Murrumbidgee region. Conversely, there is limited scope for the expansion of irrigation farming from additional water storage schemes. The Burdekin dam completed in 1987 is almost certainly the last great storage scheme of the twentieth century aimed largely at increasing or opening up agricultural output. Its potential for increasing regional development in the lower Burdekin area around Ayr is clouded by poor prospects in the sugar and rice industries — two obvious users of the water.

More intensive livestock production is another possibility. The full potential of the Ord Dam is also still a long way off realisation, but this does not seem likely over the next 15 years. Another issue to consider is whether changing farmer attitudes towards their lifestyle might have geographical consequences. To what extent might harsh environment, lack of services, and remoteness contribute to the contraction of output in the pastoral zone (apart from difficult economic conditions or, in the case of parts of Northern Australia, matters like the Brucellosis Eradication Scheme for cattle)? Recent years have seen a decline in cattle production in the Northern Territory, Western Queensland and the Gulf Country in particular, but this trend may now have ended with a return of some prosperity to the industry. This suggests predominantly economic rather than behavioural causes behind the contraction.

It is difficult to assess the likely geographical consequences of technological changes in farming, though more so in cropping than livestock husbandry.

For the most part their form, consequences and extent of implementation can only be guessed. Some developments reduce the costs of production and marketing — for example, larger tractors, specialist implements, mechanical harvesting (of fruit, nuts, timber, etc.), more environmentally tolerant crops, faster growing species, crop rotations requiring less fertilizer, computer aided livestock marketing, larger genetically engineered animals conforming to market preferences for grades of meat, better irrigation farming methods, gantry farming and so on. Cost reductions improve profitability, assuming prices remain constant, and help to keep producers on the land. Unfortunately they often require heavy capital investment which discriminates against small producers in favour of large ones and against family units in favour of corporate holdings (which may have access to cheaper finance as larger, and — if broadly based — lower risk borrowers). Alas, new technology also tends to increase the quantity of output which will, if demand is fixed, lower prices. This reduces the profitability of non-adopters and places considerable pressure on them to invest in the new technology or get out of the industry. Hence there arises the inexorable tendency towards larger production units implied in Table 6.13. The table masks a growth in the number of small horticulture and viticulture enterprises, often in coastal locations, and market drop in the number of broadacre units in inland areas. Interestingly, BAE figures suggest that greater use of capital is not necessarily accompanied by greater intensity of production for any particular item. The greater use of capital has at least three geographical effects:

Table 6.13 The number of rural establishments, farm employees and the volume of rural production

	Establishments	*Farm employment '000*	*Rural production (by volume), 1979/80 = 100*
1950/51	203 350	474	
1960/61	202 800	448	Unavailable
1970/71	189 400	415	
1975/76[1]	180 400	379	94
1976/77	173 650	373	
1980/81	175 760	382	102
1981/82[2]	174 470	380	
1983/84[3]	174 030	383	111
1986/87	167 200	393	
1987/88[4]	126 543	391	112

1 exclusion of farms with production below $1 500 in 1976/77
2 exclusion of farms with production below $2 500 in 1981/82
3 exclusion of farms with production below $10 000 in 1983/84
4 exclusion of farms with production below $20 000 in 1987/88

Sources: Bureau of Agricultural Economics (1986c); Australian Bureau of Agriculture and Resource Economics (1989)

1 the volume of output in a given area may increase through farmers switching to more intensive crops;
2 the extension of environmental or economic limits to production; and
3 a reduction in the density of rural settlement as holdings are consolidated or family farms give way to other management structures.

The first and third options are likely to occur in the medium-term, albeit slowly and on a small scale, but it is difficult to see an expansion under most types of production given difficulties in selling present output at an economic price. The main exception may be cotton, as its prices remain buoyant.

Alternative uses for rural areas

The post-war years have witnessed a breakdown of the clear distinction between city and country in many parts of Australia. This has occurred adjacent to metropolitan cores and even around large regional centres as rural land uses have been replaced by urban-related uses. Examples include: the development of hobby farms or rural retreats where owners commute to work in the neighbouring metropolis; increased recreational use of the countryside in areas set aside for nature conservation (national parks and wilderness areas), participation in various activities like water sports, trail bikes, horse riding and hunting; and the development of such tourist attractions as health farms, dude ranches, museums, pioneer villages, and steam railways.

Such activities may often conflict with each other and with traditional primary production. To reduce potential conflict, most Australian governments have developed complex environmental planning policies and related administrative frameworks. These tend to protect existing rural interests. For example, prime agricultural land is conserved in NSW by directing hobby farms towards low quality land and through policies of minimum subdivision size (at least 40 ha in many places). Rural residential subdivisions are frequently restricted to certain localities to facilitate efficient service provision — sealed roads, electricity, water, for example. Further community cost savings can be realised by preventing subdivisions in flood- or fire-prone areas. Such considerations affect the development of multiple occupancy communes too, though in this instance planning mechanisms have also had to come to grips with new tenure systems and non-standard building methods. Communes may proclaim severance from urban society but in practice they are sustained by rejection of urban values (materialism, regimentation etc.), and are sometimes financially supported by transfer payments from urban dwellers. Thus they may be an adjunct of urban culture. The move for environmental conservation is also largely urban-based and has given rise to another regulatory system aimed at the rigid separation of farming activities and such conservation areas as national parks and nature reserves. Parks and Reserves serve as important tourist and recreation destinations for urban dwellers, especially when located close to metropolitan centres. Many farmers also have promoted farm holidays and recreational activities and pursued environmental conservation as profitable adjuncts to their conventional activities.

Much of the legislative system needed to control the externalities of urban encroachment on the countryside is already in place. Nor are major innovative uses of the countryside likely to emerge. The main questions concern the scale and location of encroachment. Some major differences could result from the three scenarios, especially differences between the premature post-industrial and market economics scenarios.

A more rapidly growing and wealthy population under the market economics scenario would exert considerable pressure on the countryside. The demand for rural residential accommodation would be particularly strong as telecommunications technology lessens the distinction between home and work-place. Many people will be able to work at home (several days a week) using a computer terminal and may only rarely need to travel to the 'employer' office or factory. For the self-employed in many occupations, home and work-place could well be the same thing. In both situations the temptation will be strong to live in congenial rural surroundings. This pressure would be greatest around the metropolitan and regional centres which will continue to absorb much of the population growth. In contrast, the commune movements could face a difficult future. Lower unemployment levels could reduce the flow of recruits, though to some extent disenchantment with the materialism and individualism of market economics, and inability to cope with its intellectual or skill demands, could reinforce the attractiveness of alternative lifestyles. However, low levels of welfare benefit and the strict policing of entitlement would exacerbate the financial problems of a movement whose second generation could find materialism an attractive alternative to genteel poverty. The pro-development ethos could result in few additions to the stock of national parks, nature reserves and wilderness areas and many might be managed privately to improve access and ensure the provision of public facilities. Some encroachment on those which currently exist can be expected: mineral exploration and extraction in such sensitive localities as the Kakadu National Park and the Barrier Reef Marine Park; selective logging of areas such as the Lemonthyme region of Tasmania; and resort development of the kind proposed in 1985 for Lindeman Island in the Whitsunday Group. Finally, the scenario's business oriented and deregulatory environment would lead to less rigid planning control of many types of rural development. Farmers, for example, should be able to obtain more easily planning approval for subdivision of part of their properties for rural residential purposes, the creation of tourist facilities, or the development of on-farm industries.

Premature post-industrialism could yield both different outcomes to the previous discussion or similar outcomes for different reasons. It would undoubtedly be more environment- and conservation-minded, leading to the creation of new parks and the careful management of existing ones. Similarly, planning regulations are likely to be strictly enforced over rural residential and recreational developments to preserve public amenity. The rate of development applications or proposals would also be rather lower in a stagnant economy, and possibly less concentrated in the vicinity of large cities. In contrast, greater levels of unemployment and generous welfare provision would make new commune development attractive in many environmentally desirable locations, especially throughout NSW and south-east Queensland.

If, as has been suggested, this scenario accentuates or prolongs rural recession and brings about the significant impoverishment of rural Australia, pressure will be brought to bear on governments to aid the rural economy by relaxing constraints on what land-owners can do with their properties. As with the previous scenario, this relaxation could include industrial or tourist developments. Some farms could become owned by several individuals or families who maintain output as before while running them as large-scale hobby farms. If most owners wanted to live on their property some subdivision would be necessary to provide individual home-sites using, perhaps, a kind of strata-title tenure system akin to blocks of apartments. Such an arrangement would have the benefit of keeping uneconomic farm units in production and maintaining rural population.

The more probable muddling through scenario will contain elements of both the others. In practice this means the continuation of existing trends under reasonably strict environmental planning controls. It is worth stressing that the benefits, if that is what they can be called, of urban encroachment into the countryside will be localised. The areas affected will include: the immediate hinterlands of metropolitan and regional cities; localities close to major tourist or recreational attractions or, in some instances, en route to them; and picturesque, climatically favourable locations suitable for commune development. Put another way, the great bulk of rural Australia west of the continental divide or outside the orbit of Adelaide and Perth is likely to miss out.

Country towns

According to the 1981 census there were approximately 1200 non-metropolitan settlements in Australia, with populations ranging between 200 and 100 000 (Sorensen and Weinand, 1985). Together they account for about 25 per cent of the nation's population. Another 11.5 per cent live in tiny hamlets or on the land. Most of those 1200 places act as service centres to the farm sector; for many it is their sole *raison d'être*. They provide goods and services both for final consumption by farm households (food, personal services, education, health care etc.) and for input into the production process (seed, fertilizer, sheep drench, fencing, irrigation equipment, tractors etc.). Consequently the economic health of many places is heavily dependent on the prosperity of the local farmers, at least in the short-term. Naturally, the people who supply these goods and services also purchase items for their own consumption so that money flows in a circular and cumulative way around the local economy. The magnitude of these secondary flows is itself dependent on the prosperity of primary producers. Figures 6.2 and 6.3 indicate the relationship between events in a settlement's hinterland and its own prosperity (Sorensen, 1991).

In the longer term, other issues affect the prosperity of non-metropolitan settlements: the changing patterns of consumer demand; advances in retail and service technology including new products or services; and the ability of individual communities to develop alternative economic bases. The first two issues are interrelated and multi-faceted. Simply stated, all consumers basically want high quality goods and services delivered at moderate prices with a maximum of choice and a minimum of delay and in pleasant surroundings. Events have conspired to favour major regional service centres in most, if not

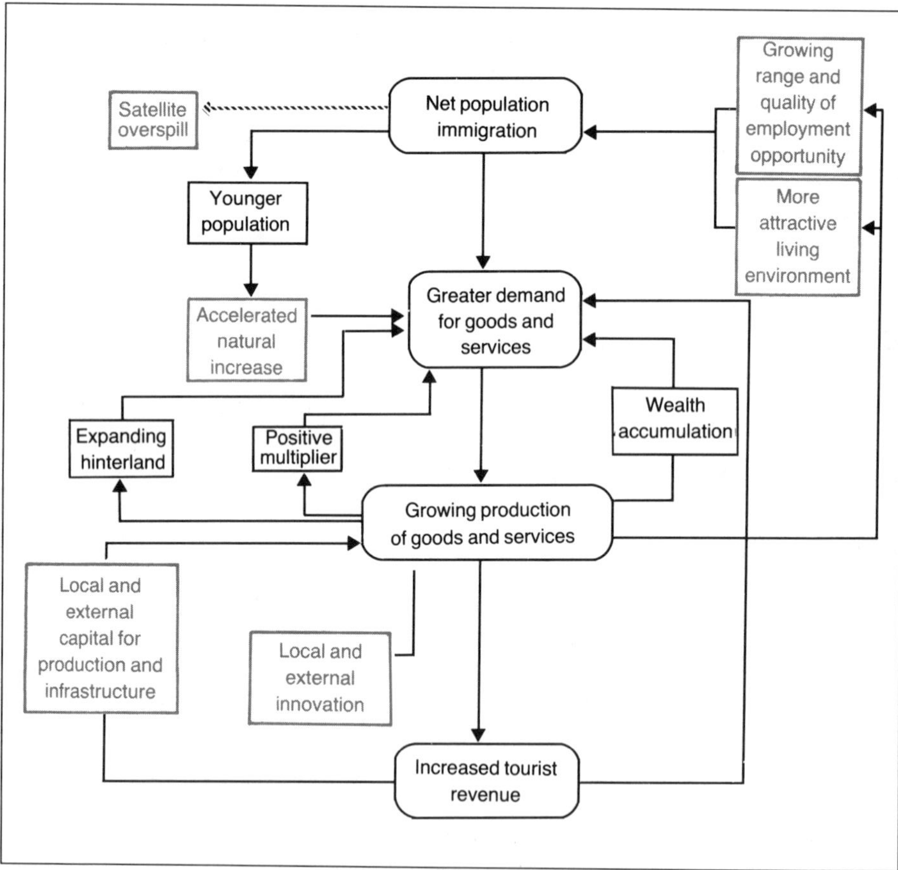

Fig. 6.2 Virtuous cycle of settlement growth

all, of these respects. For example, high-technology farming requires numerous specialist inputs such as high quality financial advice from banks and accountants, complex large-scale machinery, sub-contracted services (aerial crop spraying or top dressing, fencing, dam construction, irrigation works, soil preparation and so on) and scientific analyses (of disease, soil deficiency, crop yields, livestock performance). Many of these can only be delivered from major centres whose market areas contain populations in excess of substantial

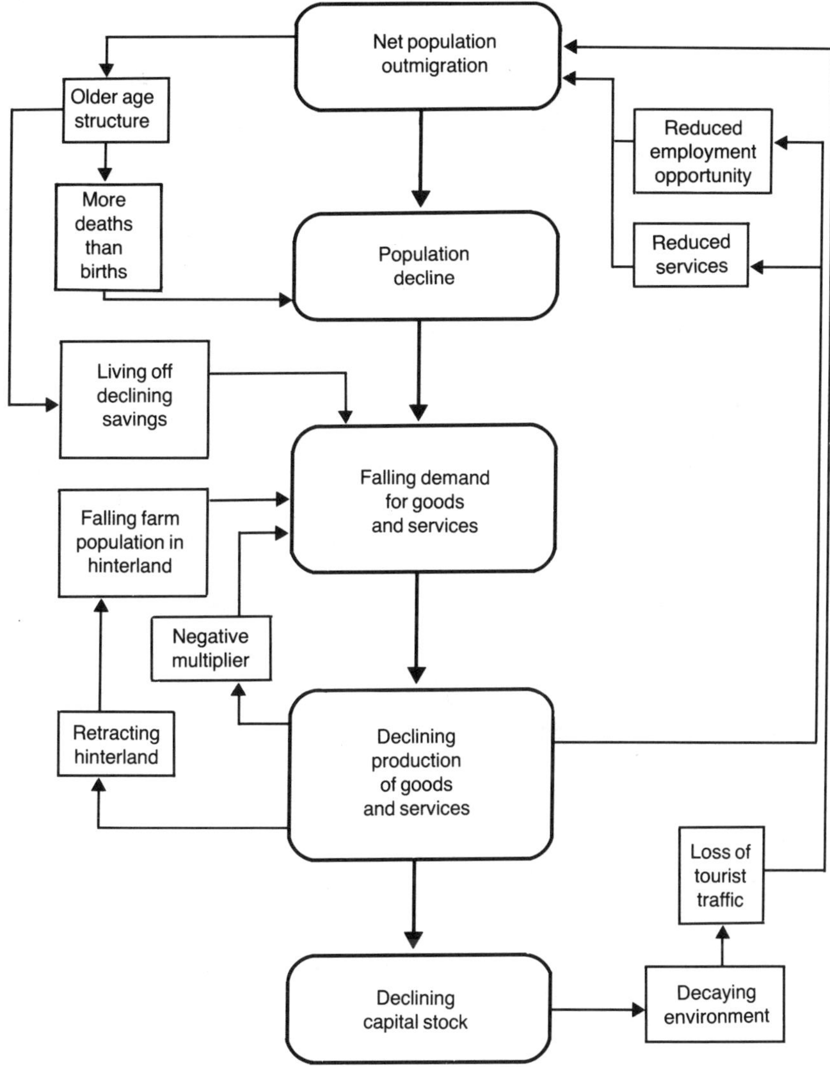

Fig. 6.3 Vicious cycle of settlement decline

supply thresholds. Large centres may also be able to sustain competing suppliers which should lead to higher quality service and some price competition. Once individual farms could be virtual self-sufficient production units, but modern technology is making this increasingly less so. In effect the on-farm population is moving into town, especially into high order service centres. Furthermore, as services become more specialized it is those high order centres which are best placed to deliver them.

The supply of goods and services for final consumption has witnessed similar trends. Many people no longer place their spare cash in savings bank accounts. Instead they play the stock market, dabble in gold futures, or invest in cash management trusts among a large range of alternatives. Once again it is the large regional centres which can help with this kind of investment and related advice. The same applies to clothing, furnishings, restaurants, health services, education, cultural services, legal advice ... indeed just about anything. Regional centres win out in other ways. They are the first to receive discount (mass)-retailing establishments like K Mart or Big W or branches of other state or national chains, all of whose purchasing power helps ensure competitive prices. Such large organisations are much more able to withstand rural recessions, droughts and other cyclical stresses than small independent and often under-financed local businesses. Regional centres receive much of the new investment in buildings, shop-fittings, pedestrian malls and other features which make shopping a pleasurable experience. Their range of services makes them attractive destinations for multi-purpose trips.

Most of these trends appear to be on-going and mutually reinforcing. There is, however, perhaps one wild card in the deck. The rise to dominance of regional centres has been aided by the increasing mobility of rural populations. During much of this century roads have been improved, making journeys more reliable and faster; car ownership has grown; and running costs have declined. In the admittedly unlikely event of fuel shortages and rapidly rising vehicle running costs some smaller settlements could regain trade presently leaked to larger places. The final nail in the coffin of many small settlements remains, nevertheless, a steadily declining on-farm population. The extent to which this can be retarded could be vital for their survival, but the prognosis must be gloomy in the current rural recession.

Many service centres have reduced their reliance for development and well-being on their rural hinterlands by generating alternative economic bases. Typical activities include manufacturing for national or global markets (e.g. Akubra hats at Kempsey), specialist education (the University of New England, Armidale or private schools at Charters Towers), tourism (Alice Springs), alternative lifestyles (Bellingen and Nimbin), retirement (Coffs Harbour), unemployment (Byron Bay), defence (Wagga Wagga, Seymour, Exmouth), recreational opportunities (skiing in the Australian Alps), and culture (country music at Tamworth). Such activities can either spread the economic risks faced by a community or magnify them.

Alternative bases with long-term stability are attractive. The university in Armidale, being publicly funded, effectively sustains that city through drought or rural recession. On the other hand private manufacturing or processing industry can destabilize a community should it close down (O'Neill, 1991; Winchester, 1991). For example, Tenterfield experienced the closure of two nearby abattoirs in the early 1980s and saw its unemployment rate rise to over 20 per cent. Those towns with a strong mining sector also have a risky existence. Broken Hill, Mt. Isa, Queenstown and Kalgoorlie have all faced some hard times and will continue to do so. The broader a community's base the more stable its economy will be. Not surprisingly, regional centres have easily the most diverse economic structures, a situation which is likely to be reinforced in future. This is because commercial development and the growth of alternative economic bases are also interrelated. One feeds the other to some extent, although some major developments depend on local resources or initiatives and could spring up in some unlikely places. It would not have been easy in 1930 to predict a university located in Armidale, for example.

The main forces that impact on country towns that were identified in Figures 6.2 and 6.3 are displayed spatially in Figures 6.4 and 6.5. They have existed for a long time and will continue in the medium term. Their geographical and historical incidence is not uniform, but is dependent to some extent on the state of regional and national economic health (Sorensen, 1990a). A rural crisis accelerates the departure of people from the land and the closure of small businesses, particularly in lower order service centres. A ratchet effect operates, as indicated in Figure 6.6. In prosperous times businesses in small towns survive the increasing leakage of trade to higher order centres, the encroachment on their trade areas, and a slowly dwindling farm population, by disinvestment (living off capital). In effect maintenance is reduced, there is a failure to invest in new fittings and equipment, and stock levels are run down: hence the dilapidated look of many small businesses. Owners may also feel obliged to keep going because no-one would purchase their business and they could not readily set up elsewhere due to lack of capital. Once a rural crisis comes along a rapid decline in trade will kill off weaker businesses, adversely affecting the viability of some of the remainder — though, as has sometimes been noted, others may gain because customers or clients cannot afford to travel to more distant places or because competition is reduced.

The effects of the three scenarios on rural settlement are difficult to gauge. Market economics may well, as we have seen, help re-establish a profitable primary sector and encourage alternative economic bases. At first sight this should anchor the existing settlement pattern and protect smaller places. In practice, its effects could be both large-scale and uneven. The next fifteen years should see the complete integration of regional centres with the national economy, and regional businesses based on the larger centres will continue to set up branches in smaller places to create integrated regional economies.

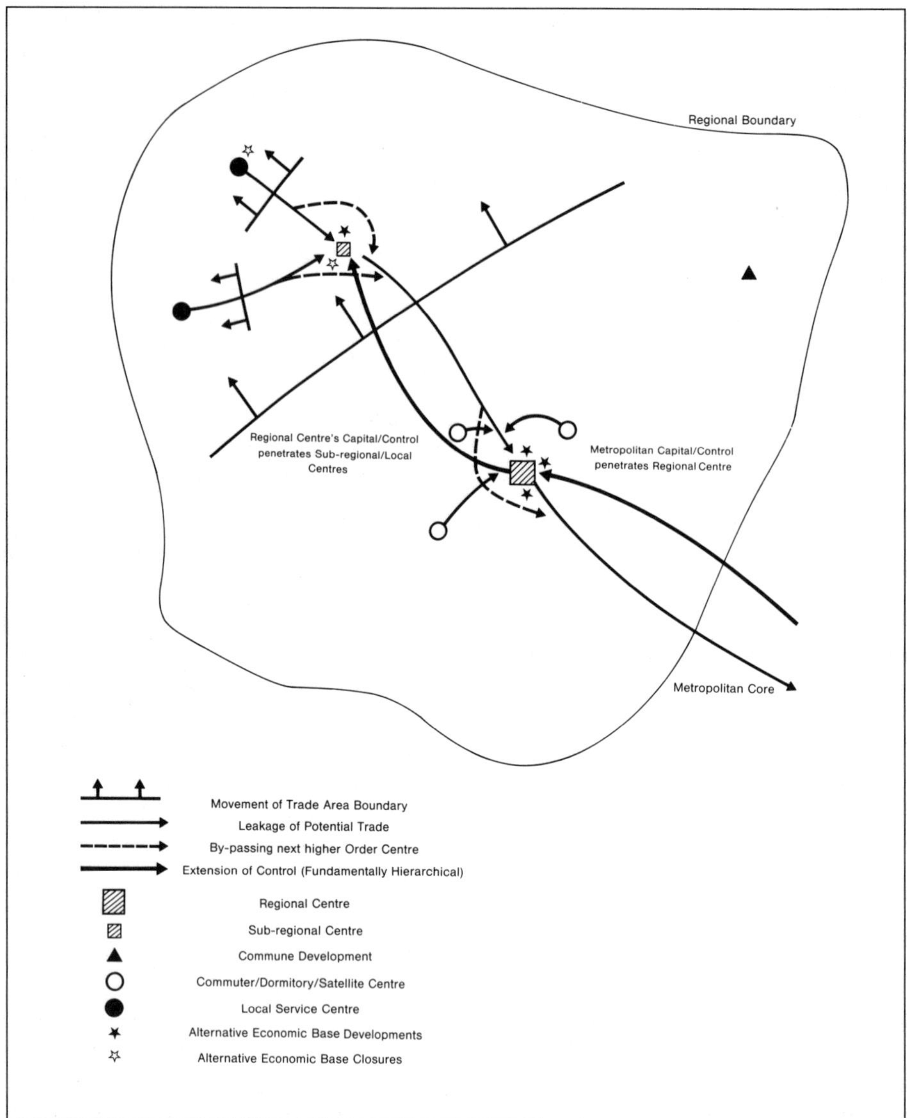

Fig. 6.4 Patterns of retail/service trade in a hypothetical rural region

These regional business networks could be in any line of commercial activity. Thus the commercial dominance of regional centres over their hinterlands will be reinforced, and their trade area boundaries will expand outwards at the expense of weaker centres.

In the New England region (Figure 6.7) both Tamworth and Armidale share this role, one dominating commercially and industrially and the other in education, culture and tourism. Armidale also has some prospect of

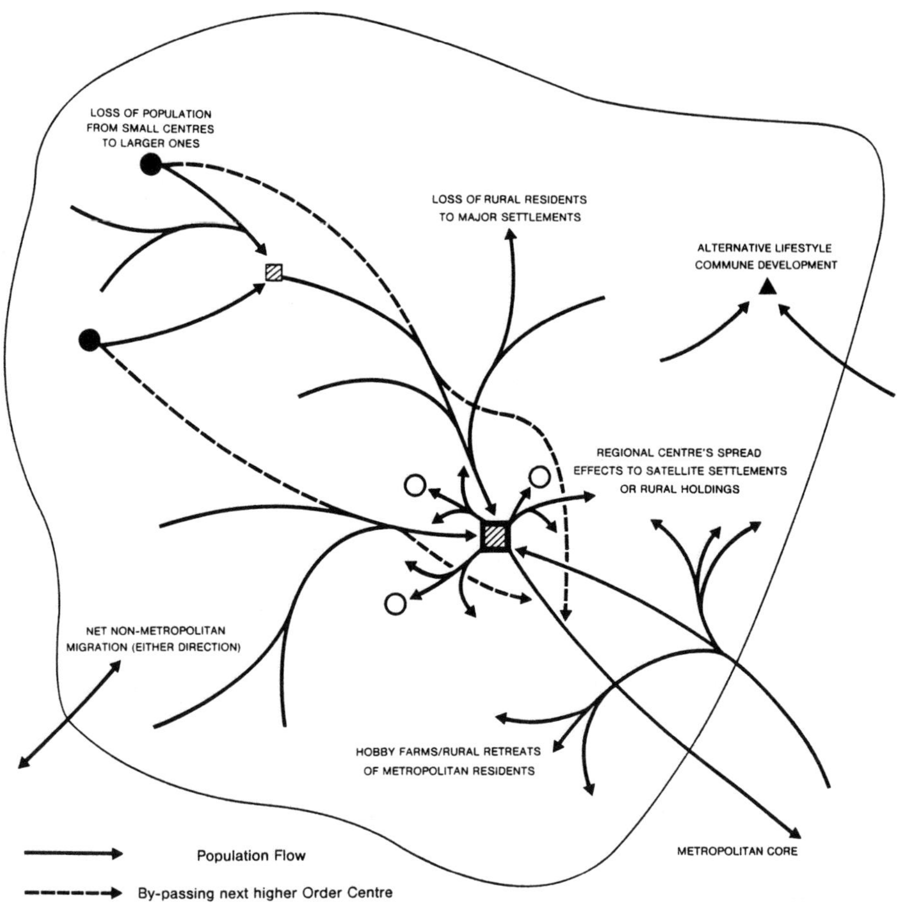

Fig. 6.5 Population flows in a hypothetical rural region

developing hi-tech industry and services in association with the university's technology park. Both will continue to expand at the expense of other localities. Both cities have already developed satellite centres and an extensive belt of rural residential subdivisions (Figure 6.7) which should continue to grow rapidly. The sub-regional centres' growth trajectory will heavily depend on their ability to attract alternative economic bases. For Gunnedah that might be coal-mining or electricity generation; for Narrabri, Moree and possibly, Manilla it could be an extension of irrigation farming involving new higher value-added crops and more intensive production coupled with first-stage processing industries. For other places, even under the most favourable growth conditions, life will be a struggle. Local employment initiatives promoted by dynamic councils or chambers of commerce in the new entrepreneurial climate could stem trade leakage to large centres, encourage retirement or commuter settlement, or develop recreational or tourist attractions,

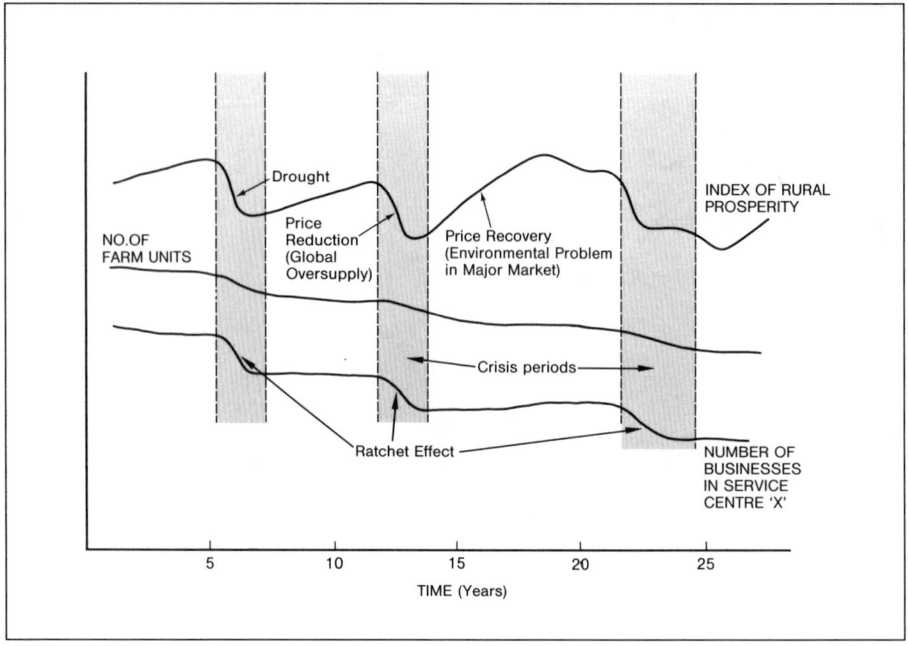

Fig. 6.6 The effect of rural prosperity on small business viability

according to local opportunities. Such developments are unlikely to assuage the chiliastic tendencies of most communities, but the outcome would be much preferable to that likely under the premature post-industrial scenario. One important caveat is necessary. Even the most optimistic circumstances will provide no avenue for salvation for some localities, especially those in geographically remote areas, where few development opportunities present themselves, where rural recession has bitten deepest, and where the adjustment to the settlement system has possibly lagged behind earlier imperatives for change.

Premature post-industrialism would be a disaster for the great bulk of rural settlement, the principal exceptions being regional service centres, coastal settlements with resort potential, and localities attractive for rural residential or commune development. Small communities would suffer in at least five ways: a low level of profitability in farming, rural depopulation, fewer opportunities for developing a broader economic base, reduced incentives for business investment and perhaps earlier business failure. Regional service centres could also experience many of these events, but are insulated from their worst effects because of the government or corporate nature of much of their employment. Muddling through would once again yield outcomes intermediate between the market economics and the premature post-industrial scenarios.

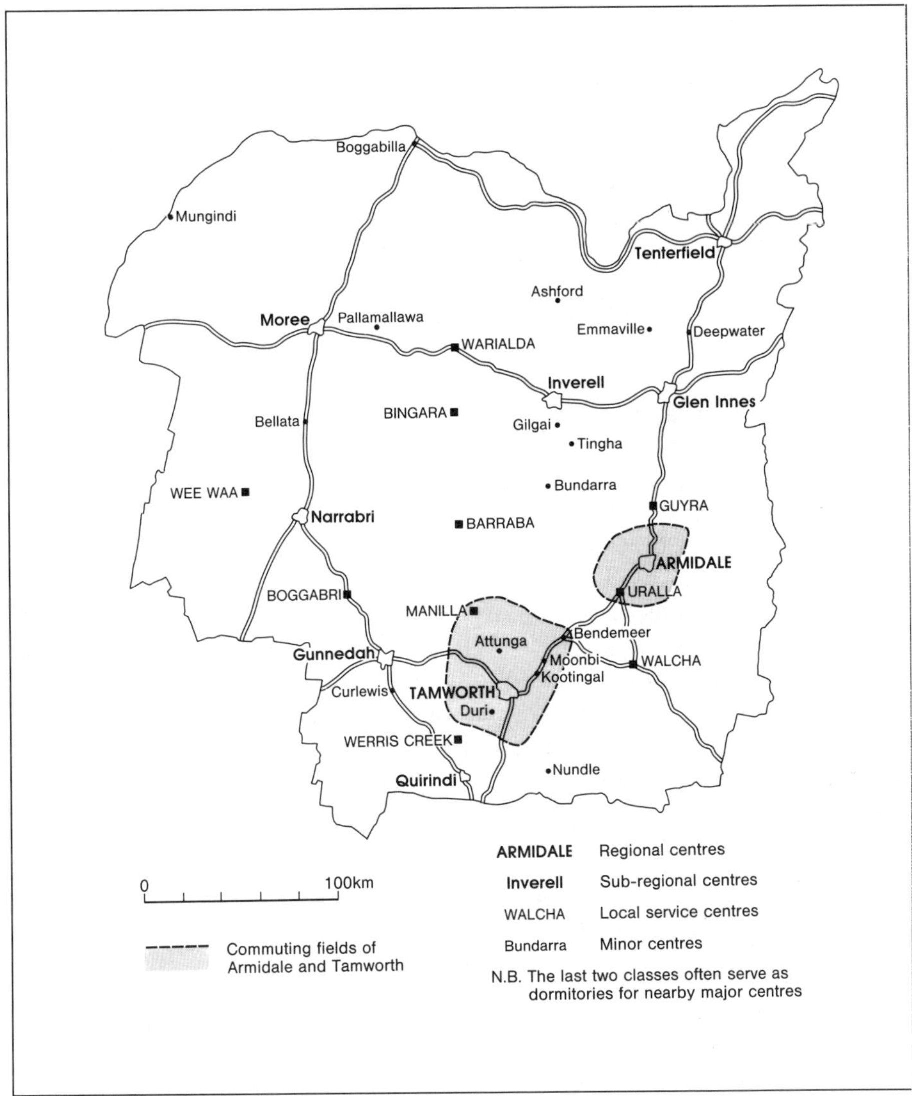

Fig. 6.7 Service centres in the New England region

Concluding remarks

Three interrelated components of rural life have been examined and it seems they all gain most from the market economics scenario. This emphasizes production rather than consumption and envisages a smaller role for government. Consumption can be encouraged by increasing the profitability of producing goods and related services. Rural Australia could gain disproportionately if, as we suspect, the production of traded goods and services constitutes a rather higher fraction of its gross product compared with the rest of the country. Smaller government is important in that urban dwellers, who are dominant in the political process, can appropriate fewer resources for their own benefit (for example the whole apparatus of industry protection), and there are fewer time-consuming and expensive regulations to comply with. The premature post-industrial scenario clearly works to the disadvantage of rural areas, and ultimately to the whole country, because rural areas account for a large proportion of exports. In 1984/85 raw materials and first-stage processing of mainly rural origin accounted for about $21 billion out of an export total of $30.7 billion (68%). Admittedly this declined slightly by 1990/91 to about 64 per cent of the $65 billion worth of exports. The industry protection inherent in this scenario would ultimately therefore serve to depress both rural and urban incomes. In practice a pluralist–corporatist Australia, which is central to the muddling through scenario, is likely to fall between the two extremes and fail to realise the country's full economic potential. Maybe that is the price of democratic government.

Little has been said in the foregoing discussion about the possible impact of major external shocks. They are easier to identify than to evaluate: commodity trade wars; large-scale military conflict in the northern hemisphere perhaps among members of the fragmenting CIS; rapidly increasing fuel prices; plant or livestock disease; and new technologies or discoveries which greatly increase the supply of raw materials. It is probable that none of these will be of sufficient magnitude in the medium term to distort our forecasts. It is worth noticing our earlier findings, however, that market economics are likely to cope better with external shocks than the other scenarios.

Manufacturing industry

This section is concerned with sketching some general impressions of the geographical organisation of Australia's manufacturing industry under the three main scenarios. Topics of interest include the changing site of the industrial workforce, the industry sectors likely to grow most rapidly in employment and output, and their regional patterns of growth and decline. No attempt is made to give precise predictions of the geographical structure of particular industries.

In 1990 the estimated percentage of the workforce employed in manufacturing establishments (as distinct from supplying services to the manufacturing sector) was about 15.3%. Between 1947 and the late 1960s the corresponding figure ranged between 25% and 28%, but since then there has been a precipitous decline. The present figure is low for the OECD group of countries, among which Western Germany has over 25 per cent of its workforce in manufacturing while Britain and Japan have over 20 per cent. The point of these comparisons is that, under the favourable business conditions that might accompany the market economics scenario, there is the prospect of manufacturing industry increasing its share of the workforce quite sharply rather than losing it as is generally assumed.

Let us estimate conservatively that under a pro-business economic climate the share could rebound to 18 per cent over the medium-term. A low valued dollar, effective investment strategies, greater product research and development, aggressive overseas marketing, efficient management, and more worker participation could possibly achieve that target. To reach it, a large number of new jobs would have to be created to make up for those lost in such declining sectors as the TCF group, and to employ the large increase in additional workers resulting from population growth to 20.3 millions and an increase in the already high participation rate from 62 per cent to, say, 65 per cent. Using these figures we may calculate a workforce of about 8.45 million in 2001 of whom 1.5 million (18 per cent) will be in manufacturing. The 1990 pre-recession figure was about 1.2 million, so we are estimating that the scenario could yield a 65 per cent increase in the manufacturing workforce. The increased participation rate to 65 per cent reflects several trends: a continued growth in female employment, the re-entry into the job market of discouraged job-seekers, strengthened immigration of young workers, a reversal of the recent sharp trend to earlier retirement, and lifting the female retirement age to 65. These should outweigh substantially a trend for those over 15 years of age to participate longer in full-time education.

In conditions of the premature post-industrial scenario, the present decline in manufacturing employment in both relative and absolute terms could well continue. By 2001 only 12 per cent of the workforce may be in secondary industry. If we assume that the rate of immigration slows to perhaps 30 000 per annum and the medium-term population reaches 17.5 millions with a workforce participation rate of 58 per cent, we can estimate the manufacturing workforce in 2001 at 780 000. This is a fall of over 35 per cent on current figures. As in previous analyses the most likely outcome lies between the extremes of these forecasts. Should participation rates remain at current levels, Australia's population reach 19 million, and the industrial workforce retain its current share of the total, employment in manufacturing industry could reach 1.4 million. This represents a moderate growth of 18 per cent. This figure may be conservative if manufacturing responds positively to the opportunities presented by the 1980s currency devaluations.

Which industries are likely to prosper or decline under the three scenarios and what could be the geographical consequences? The market economics scenario represents such a turn-around from the general trends of the last 15 years that the past performance of specific industry sectors may be no guide to the future, though the textile clothing and footwear industries (ASIC 23 and 24, also known as TCF) could be an exception. They performed particularly poorly in the thirteen-year period to 1987/88, losing over 17 per cent of their workforce and recording a real decline in their turnover, despite high rates of industry protection (tariffs and quotas on imported goods) (see Table 6.14). Some of the remaining 65 800 jobs in the sector (Table 6.15) must be at risk even in the most favourable investment circumstances. This is because of the current government-sponsored program to restructure the industry through phased tariff reductions following successive IAC and Industry Commission (IC) recommendations on the subject (IAC, 1986; Industry Commission, 1990). Indeed, progress towards a market economics scenario would probably lower tariffs still further than the proposed 112 per cent in 1995, forcing an even larger adjustment on the industry. This may mean turning towards high quality output to secure the industry's future. Note, too, the industry's low turnover and wages (Table 6.15). It is hardly the epitome of the clever country.

Table 6.14 suggests that Victoria may have to bear the brunt of the restructuring process, with its strong representation in industry. Conversely, the less industrialized states stand to lose less. The other sectors to perform poorly are ASIC 32 and 33 (transport equipment and other machinery), and, in employment terms only, ASIC 28 (non-metallic mineral products). The latter produces building and construction materials which have low value in relation to weight and are therefore effectively protected by Australia's geographical isolation (hence the low protection level of 3 per cent). This situation is likely to remain and the industry would benefit greatly from the fastest possible rates of population and output growth. Its spatial distribution across the States is, moreover, roughly proportional to their populations.

ASIC 32 and 33 comprise, along with 31 (fabricated metal products) and 34 (miscellaneous products), the potential high technology sectors. Their growth is the touchstone of national prosperity, and a likely adjunct of the market economics scenario. In other words we could see a major performance reversal for transport equipment and other machinery. Already the dollar devaluations and steadily reduced industry protection appear to have set events in motion. There are increased exports of cars and their components, and a growing offset industry for commercial aircraft and military equipment. The potential is enormous for niche products ranging from medical equipment, specialist computer chips and software, pharmaceuticals, ceramics, paint drying processes and plant genetics through to sporting goods, outdoor clothing, household appliances, solar heaters, agricultural machinery, construction equipment, specialist boats (including aluminium catamarans and many other items). Niche products are specialist items serving numerically small but discriminating markets. Economies of scale are relatively unimportant, which makes these items particularly suitable for local production where mass economies are difficult to achieve. Tasmania, the ACT and the Northern Territory currently have weak representation in ASIC 31–34 (Table 6.14) though that does not preclude their development of hi-tech products.

The remaining manufacturing sectors not so far mentioned should fare well in any dynamic business environment, with the possible exception of

Table 6.14 Manufacturing industry performance 1974–75 to 1987–88 and interstate concentration 1987–88[1]

	Percentage change 1974/75 to 1987/88				*State representation[3]*	
ASIC code	*Employment*	*Turnover (constant '74/75 values)[2]*	*Turnover per employee (constant terms)*	*Effective % rate of protection (1988/89)*	*Above average*	*Below average*
21	–11.2	12.8	27.1	3	Tas, Qld	
23	–18.6	16.6	43.3	79	Tas, Vic	Qld
24	–17.1	–0.7	19.7	170	Vic	WA, Tas, SA, Qld
25	0.5	23.0	22.4	17	Tas, ACT, WA, Qld	
26	4.9	53.0	45.9	12	ACT, Tas	
27	–16.1	50.2	78.9	12		SA, Qld
28	–21.7	23.2	57.3	3	WA, NT	
29	–24.5	12.8	49.3	9	NT, NSW	Vic
31	–7.5	22.4	32.3	20		
32	–24.7	10.2	46.3	39	SA	ACT, NT, Tas, WA
33	–32.0	–5.5	39.0	19		NT, Tas, ACT, Qld
34	–7.4	34.3	45.0	20		ACT, Tas, NT
Australia Total	–15.8	18.1	40.3	17		

1 Excluding single-plant enterprises with fewer than 4 employees
2 Using the CPI as a deflator
3 Above average—sector's share of State employment ≥ 1.4 expected level;
Below average—sector's share of State employment < 0.7 expected level; States are listed with most extreme cases first.

Sources: ABS, *Manufacturing Industry, Australia*, 1988/89; ABS, *Census of Manufacturing Establishments*, 1974/75.

Table 6.15 Manufacturing industry statistics 1989/90[1]

	Establishments	*Employment '000*	*Turnover $m*	*Wages & salaries $m*	*Employees per establishment*	*Turnover per employee $'000*	*Wages per employee $'000*	*Effective rate of protection (%)*
21 Food, etc.	4 177	171.7	33 256	4 206	41.1	193.7	24.5	3
23 Textiles	914	29.0	4 126	738	31.7	142.3	25.4	79
24 Clothing/footwear	2 683	65.8	5 052	1 283	24.5	76.8	19.5	170
25 Wood etc.	6 945	83.6	8 289	1 856	12.0	99.1	22.2	17
26 Paper/printing etc.	4 737	106.8	13 590	3 030	22.5	127.2	28.4	12
27 Chemical	1 141	51.7	18 883	1 720	45.3	365.2	33.3	12
28 Non-metallic, etc.	1 877	42.8	7 856	1 258	22.8	183.6	29.4	3
29 Basic metal products	820	67.1	20 578	2 326	81.8	306.7	34.7	9
31 Fabricated metal products	6 686	104.9	12 778	2 649	15.7	121.8	25.3	20
32 Transport equipment	2 125	106.0	16 677	2 932	49.9	157.3	27.7	39
33 Other machinery	5 716	134.6	15 902	3 606	23.5	118.1	26.8	19
34 Miscellaneous	3976	64.0	8 059	1 620	16.1	125.9	25.3	20
Total	41 797	1 028.0	165 045	27 220	24.6	160.5	26.5	17

1 end of June

Source: ABS, *Manufacturing Industry, Australia*, 1989/90, Preliminary.

ASIC 29 (basic metal products). The steel and aluminium industries have tended to perform poorly even in the most prosperous of industrial countries. In Australia they may fall prey to cheap exports from newly industrialising countries (NICs) in Asia and elsewhere. NSW appears to have a weakness in its industrial structure with above average representation of ASIC 29 (Table 6.14).

Several further issues need to be considered in forecasting the medium-term spatial pattern of manufacturing under the market economics scenario.

1 **Inter-state population growth**. Table 6.16 shows some positive correlation in recent years between industry performance on a number of variables and population growth, at least in the larger States. Queensland, Western Australia, the Northern Territory and the ACT all experienced above average population growth and strong growth in turnover, number of work-places and workforce. In both Queensland and the Northern Territory, turnover per work-place declined sharply over the decade to 1988/89 and the figures suggest the creation of a large number of very small enterprises. Indeed, throughout Australia, recent years have seen a marked trend towards smaller establishments in terms of numbers of employees, though turnover per work-place has increased everywhere but the Queensland and the Northern Territory.

The trend towards more rapid population growth across northern and western Australia should be maintained in the medium-term, given their low population base and under-utilized resources. The industry sectors which may prosper most in those states are resource processing and construction (ASIC 27–29). In addition, the entrepreneurial climates of south-east Queensland and Perth (less so), may inspire development of numerous small hi-tech firms in ASIC 31–34. The Multi-Function Polis planned for an Adelaide swamp is unlikely to reach fruition quickly, if at all, given expressions of doubt by potential Japanese investors. Without it, South Australia could struggle to develop a major technology base. Part of the problem concerns the location preferences of high-tech industry (see item 3 below), which seem to favour Sydney and Melbourne. Despite winding back the scale of public administration, Canberra's population should also continue to record good growth, though at a lower rate than previously. In part, the impetus should be the development of small innovative businesses in ASIC 31–34.

2 **Immigration**. High levels of immigration running at up to 180 000 or more per annum could increase the population growth of State capitals, and in particular the traditional destinations of Sydney and Melbourne. However, better international communications to and from the other State capitals should help them attract a higher share of immigration than in the past.

Table 6.16 Percentage change in manufacturing industry statistics, by State, 1978/79 to 1988/89

State	*Population share (Dec 1988) %*	*Establishments (at 30 Jun)*	*Employed persons (whole year)*	*Turnover*	*Employment per establishment*	*Turnover per establishment*
NSW	34.1	6.7	–16.5	148.2	–21.73	3.89
Vic	25.6	14.8	–5.8	186.4	–17.94	11.47
Qld	17.0	67.5	16.8	202.5	–30.24	–19.28
SA	8.4	19.0	–3.5	185.0	–18.89	7.06
WA	9.6	19.7	10.6	200.7	–7.65	12.25
Tas	2.7	22.1	3.6	176.8	–15.19	1.31
N T	0.9	86.0	66.7	207.9	–10.42	–26.05
ACT	1.7	17.1	27.0	252.9	8.49	34.70
Australia	100.0	18.7	–10.0	179.4	–20.82	3.39

1 Establishments with four or more employees;
2 Inflation adjusted

Sources: ABS: Australian Demographic Statistics; *Manufacturing Industry, Australia*, 1989/90, Preliminary (8201.0)

3 **Locational preferences of hi-tech industry**. Several overseas studies have demonstrated that hi-tech industries, which will be an important, though not dominant, component of Australia's industrial revival, prefer to locate close to military establishments, defence contractors, research institutes (private or public, including universities), other hi-tech industries and pleasant living environments (Hall, 1987; Gordon and Kimball, 1987; Hall and Markusen, 1985). In Australia, this set of conditions can only be met at present in Sydney and Melbourne and, less so, in the other State capitals.

However, national spending on research development is currently so paltry (EPAC, 1986c) and the defence industry so small that another Silicon Valley, Route 128 or M4 Corridor is unlikely to emerge in Australia. Rather, hi-tech districts may arise within our cities like those close to Macquarie University at North Ryde in Sydney (Hutchinson and Searle, 1987) or Monash University in Melbourne (Newton and O'Connor, 1987). Planners may also attempt, with varying degrees of success, to force hi-tech development by setting up 'technology parks'. Adelaide has a Technology Park located 13 km from the city centre on a 85 ha site, and the concept has performed well. Queensland mooted a much more grandiose Technopolis in the mid-1980s, and plans were under way at about that time for a park at Werribee between Melbourne and Geelong to focus on biotechnology (March, 1986).

4 **National integration of production and markets**. Recent advances in transportation technology and organisation mean that most of the Australian market for goods is now within about 36 hours by road or rail from either

Sydney or Melbourne. Producers seeking a national market, especially in ASIC 31–34 which are not tied so much to the processing of local raw materials as ASIC 21 and 25-29, will be strongly tempted to locate close to one of those centres and avoid the traditional rather inefficient duplication of plant and equipment in two or more cities. This situation is likely to be accelerated by the plan to upgrade and construct a standard gauge rail link between Brisbane and Adelaide via Sydney and Melbourne. This was announced in Prime Minister Keating's February 1992 economic statement.

5 **The bane of over-specialisation**. Even under the market economics scenario, the future of such industrial cities as Wollongong, Newcastle, Geelong, and Whyalla is unlikely to be dynamic. They are located too far from centres of innovation and have problems of image. Their workforces tend not to have the kinds of skills demanded by hi-tech industry. Nevertheless, rapid economic growth could lead to a resurgence of their traditional industries and ease the pain of structural adjustment.

6 **Non-metropolitan industry**. Rural areas will continue to experience difficulty in attracting any large-scale or innovative industrial development other than that which services the local economy or processes its output. No great expansion in local raw materials processing seems imminent or has a place in a high labour cost and, hopefully, 'clever' economy. Naturally, there will be exceptions, but a market economics scenario could see a moderate resumption of emigration by young people looking for work in capital cities.

7 **Tariff reduction**s of the magnitudes currently in place will advantage manufacturing output in Queensland and Western Australia and impact adversely on Victoria (EPAC, 1991a). The effects in the other states will tend to balance out.

If we put all these factors together the aggregate change in Australia's manufacturing employment under an market economics scenario might resemble Figure 6.10.

Premature post-industrialism creates quite a different picture (Figure 6.9). Some pockets of growth in industrial employment are feasible in regions such as Perth, Darwin and south-east Queensland where strong population growth will occur. Only a slight loss of manufacturing employment, if any, should occur throughout much of rural Australia due to the predominance of existing raw materials processing activities. These are often export oriented and insulated against poor domestic conditions. Both Melbourne and Sydney stand to lose manufacturing employment following the restructuring of existing industries and the absence of adequate replacements. The worst fate is reserved for the industrial cities named above. Their concentration of employment in smokestack and sometimes heavily protected industries,

Fig. 6.8 Medium-term trends in manufacturing employment: location map

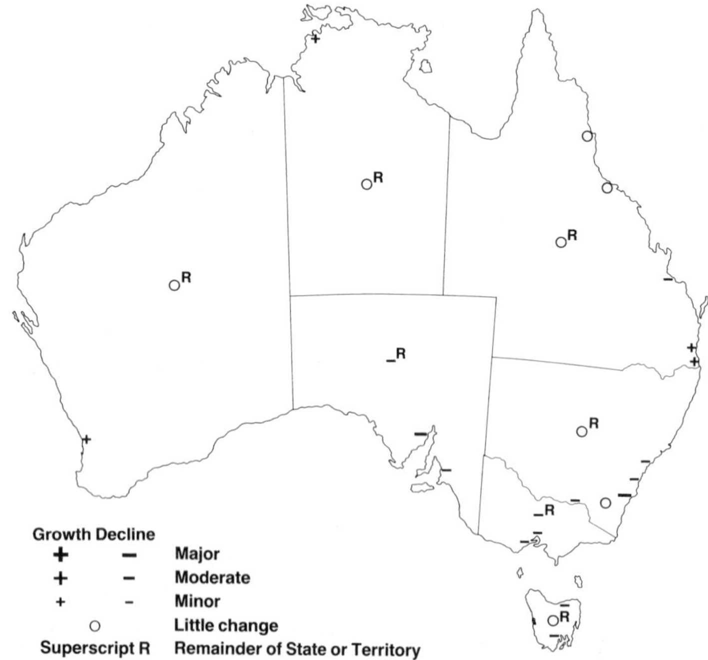

Fig. 6.9 Medium-term trends in manufacturing employment: premature post-industrialization

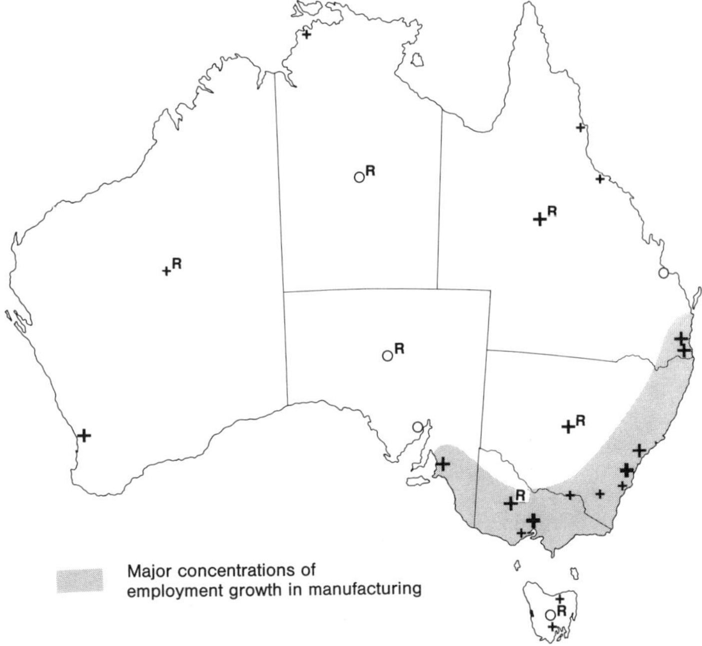

Fig. 6.10 Medium-term trends in manufacturing employment: market economics

together with narrow employment bases, especially in the case of Wollongong, do not augur for a bright future. In this scenario the traditional rural to city or near-city pattern of migration could also cease. Coupled with low overseas immigration, there is a risk of the populations of Sydney and Melbourne becoming static or even beginning to decline.

The structure of cities

Many scores of factors may determine the evolution of urban areas. Some of the more important ones as determined by a panel of experts are listed in Table 6.17. The problem is not only to list them, but to determine which are the most important and how they relate to each other. The list in Table 6.17 is understandably, but unfortunately, concerned primarily with technical matters. Such matters are important, but not so much as is conventionally thought.

Significantly, the list excludes many crucial behavioural variables: community attitudes, public decision-making processes, and organisational and institutional structures. These provide a kind of 'stage' on which technical processes are acted out, although we should not exclude the possibility of technical developments changing part of the scenery. In effect the three scenarios outlined earlier form the 'stage' and constitute a superior base for

Table 6.17 A content analysis of an exploratory futures survey

Rank	*Subject*	*Per cent of respondents identifying subject*
1	Real price of oil	46
2	Unemployment	28
3	Emphasis on environment and conservation of resources	25
4=	State of national economy	23
4=	Diversity in, and substitution of, transport modes (ranging from low technology modes such as walk/cycle, through individual and mass transit systems to high technology modes such as pipelines/ guideways)	23
6	Application of telecommunications technology (e.g. satellite communication) in productive processes and the organisation of industry	21
7=	Substitution of telecommunications for some forms of travel (e.g. shopping at a distance via videotex)	19
7=	Level of social disorganisation (e.g. crime, violence)	19
9=	Polarisation of the population, emergence of 'two nation syndrome', with a wealthy elite minority and an economically disadvantaged majority	18
9=	Application of computer technology (e.g. microprocessors) in productive processes and the organisation of industry	18
9=	Ageing of the population	18
12=	Size of households	16
12=	Shift to labour-displacing (rather than labour-complementing) technology	16
14	Leisure time available to workers	14
15=	Income differentials between skilled, semi-skilled and unskilled occupations	12
15=	Real value of wages and salaries	12
15=	Private vehicle ownership, availability and use	12
15=	Diversity of lifestyles	12
19=	Rate of household formation (net effect of divorce/separation rate, marriage-remarriage rate, youth leaving parental home)	11
19=	Real cost of housing and land	11
19=	Improved vehicle design (cost, safety, efficiency, emissions)	11
19=	Education level among the population	11
19=	Changes in structure and operation of firms and their human organisation	11
24=	Level of government spending on urban infrastructure (e.g. roads, utilities)	9
24=	Rate of population growth	9

Source: Newton and Taylor (1987)

forecasting than a mere catalogue of technical changes because they describe mechanisms by which different types of changes may be linked. Moreover, the strength of the links and the speed at which they take effect are dependent on the political–economic–social–cultural scenario in effect. For example, the real price of oil could affect private vehicle ownership much less in a prosperous open society than in the stagnant closed one indicated by premature post-industrialism. One would also expect land-use changes to proceed more rapidly in the former than the latter because of fewer behavioural and

Table 6.18 The development of urban form under the market economics scenario

1 Efficient use of capital
  1.1 The 24-hour city?
  1.2 Polycentric commercial development
  1.3 Flexible work arrangements

2 Reduced segregation of land uses
  2.1 Merging city and countryside
  2.2 Blurred distinction between:
    home and work
    industry and commerce
    wholesale and retailing

3 Increased functional distinction of commercial core

4 Increased variety of lifestyles and neighbourhood segregation

5 Intensification of land use

6 Strong interest in aesthetics/supply of public goods at a local level such as parks, theatres, sports facilities, libraries, health clinics.

structural blockages. Of course, these views are open to challenge. It could be argued, for example, that societal arrangements are just as rigid as the built environment and it is therefore the kinds of variables in Table 6.17 which change rapidly to determine future form.

This debate might be clarified by sketching the evolution of a hypothetical Australian city (called Sydbourne?) under both the market economics and premature post-industrial scenarios. These scenarios have the potential, in the short-term at least, to generate substantial differences in urban form. Table 6.18 sets out some of the likely features of the former. A few comments are briefly presented for each theme:

1 Much of the capacity of Australian cities, whether shops, offices, factories, roads or public transport is hopelessly under-utilised. The greater possible use of this capacity under market economics, even if it does not reach a 24-hour day, could greatly reduce the need for expenditure on facilities needed to service a growing population, and for land dedicated to them. Existing shopping centres could, for example, service a much larger population if they were open on weekends and later at night. Polycentric commercial development, in the form of regional centres, is currently under way in all state capitals, but can be taken much further, especially if circumferential routes interlinking the sub-centres are improved at the expense of radial routes. Commercial and employment decentralisation could also be aided by the (rather unlikely) market pricing of public transport. These events, and the growth of flexible work arrangements (working at home in the 'electronic cottage' or non-standard work hours) under the impetus of new telecommunications technology, should reduce pressure on routeways and the early need for their upgrading. Equally important, the costs of congestion and commuting could be reduced.

2 There will be much reduced separation of many land uses as a consequence of both commercial and individual location preferences. The blurring of city and countryside and home and work have already been noted. Various forms of exurbia, ranging from the quarter acre to the hobby farm, will be sought and permitted with two conditions: no serious loss of amenity for urban dwellers; and users pay the full cost of community services provided for their lifestyle preference. The entrepreneurial climate will make it easier to start businesses in residential neighbourhoods, including small-scale fabricating activities. Also mixed commercial zones will occur as the distinctions between fabrication, research and development, distribution and administration continue to break down. Small factories will find themselves located next to retail warehouses or computer software firms. These trends could be aided by the scenario's deregulatory ethic.

3 This locational freedom is likely to be accompanied by a greater variety of lifestyles. At one time, social class and perhaps ethnicity were the main determinants of neighbourhood character. Other factors now distinguish areas and help determine where one lives: type of work (routine/creative); atmosphere (bohemian, cosmopolitan, tranquil etc.); the presence of mutual support networks (important in ethnic, racial or sexual minority communities and among the elderly); stage in life-cycle and type of family structure; access to various kinds of recreational opportunity (culture, sporting, gastronomic); and financial assets and budgetary allocation of scarce resources.

Lifestyle diversification, and consequently a fragmentation of social areas within cities, is a strong possibility, though we noted earlier that extreme lifestyle experimentation is not encouraged by a somewhat sober market order. Gentrification will no longer be seen as a monolithic process of the invasion of run-down neighbourhoods by moneyed individuals. Increasingly such neighbourhoods will become identified with a unique set of social characteristics. In one sense, therefore, the social structure of cities may become more pronounced in contradiction to the economic structure. However, this process will be blurred by the speed of social change and related geographical adjustment possible in a deregulated entrepreneurial and innovative society. The social attributes of some neighbourhoods could become exceptionally fluid through the repeated invasion and succession of different interest groups.

4 Throughout these comings and goings, the commercial cores of large cities will evolve functionally in a more sober unidirectional way. Unlike suburban commercial centres which will increasingly be tied in with local or state-wide industry and public administration, city centres will become primarily the locus of national and especially international circuits of capital and culture. As Australia is increasingly integrated with the global economy, the city centre will physically expand both horizontally and vertically (through high-rise office and residential construction) to accommodate it. The city centre will also retain its public policy-making and ceremonial roles and will continue to embody the history and traditions of the community.

5 Rapid population growth will lead to acute housing problems which can only be solved by increasing residential densities in addition to continued fringe urban expansion. A more flexible urban planning system which accompanies the market economics scenario will permit, and indeed encourage, innovative high density design and new forms of property tenure. State government instrumentalities and private industry or commerce will both be encouraged to redevelop under-used inner urban sites for residential purposes. Increased residential densities should make the supply of public transport more efficient for users and more cost effective for the tax-payer.

6 Not surprisingly a more wealthy society and one which is living at higher densities will have a strongly developed sense of the aesthetic and appreciate greatly well maintained parks or other public open spaces. Indeed, it is quite likely that the quality of civic life will blossom under the market economics scenario and be reflected across a large range of social, cultural and recreational services. Wealth and civic pride have long gone hand in hand, whether it be Pericles' Athens, the Medici's Florence or de Tocqueville's small town America.

In conclusion, Australia's large cities could, under conditions of economic renaissance, become pleasant and exciting places in which to live for just about all. We might look forward to richly diverse living environments which enable most people to find a suitable niche capable of realising their human potential and to a golden age of civic achievement. Some clues have been presented as to how such cities may be organised spatially, and Figure 6.11 distils these schematically for a hypothetical city sector.

The premature post-industrial scenario's urban vision is substantially different. There would be some impetus to use capital more efficiently because of its scarcity and high cost. However, the more flexible use of facilities may not be the outcome, because union interests may be able to defend the existing patterns of working hours. Alternatively the little available capital can be stretched by delaying new investment and maintaining the existing urban fabric. This could also be an attractive option if low population growth reduces the demand for additional facilities. There is however the risk that, if economic growth ceased or was insufficient to meet consumer expectations, both private and public consumption could only be maintained in the

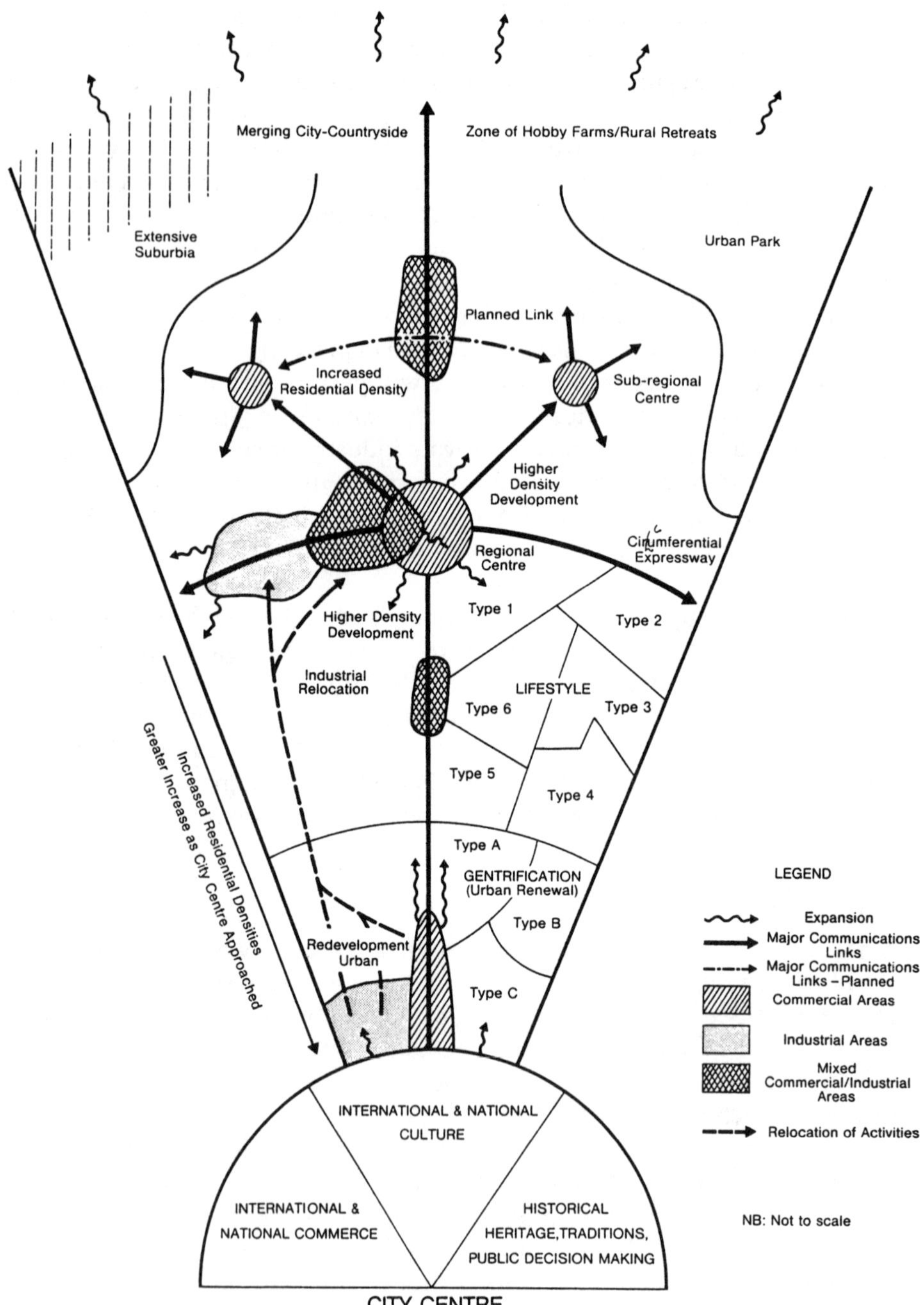

Fig. 6.11 Structural changes in a hypothetical city sector under the economic rationalism scenario

short-term by living off capital and avoiding maintenance of infrastructure and buildings. This strategy would accelerate the physical decay of the built environment, as has happened to parts of New York's infrastructure (e.g. bridges, roads, sewers and the subway system). Sydney, Melbourne and other places could rapidly go down the same path. Decay would likewise extend local civic services of the types listed in Table 6.18 (item 6).

Low levels of population growth and investment in the built environment do not necessarily betoken relatively unchanging patterns of land use. The extent of change is likely to vary according to the social and economic status of neighbourhoods. A feature of post-industrial societies noted earlier is the potential schism between the cognitariat (and possibly also administrative gatekeepers) who form a prosperous elite and the rest of the community who are poorly paid and leisured. In the premature post-industrial scenario neither group would be as well off financially as in a true post-industrial society, but the distinction probably remains valid. Indeed it could dominate the social–spatial patterning of cities, especially as the financial stringencies of this scenario will suppress the emergence of many new lifestyle preferences. The cognitariat's well-heeled neighbourhoods will maintain present environmental planning barriers to the infusion of extraneous commercial activities or social groups. In lower income neighbourhoods by way of contrast, the unemployed, part-time and financially constrained are likely to mix residential accommodation with a wide variety of industrial and commercial activities to make ends meet. Commercial centres will also reflect this dichotomy, but paradoxically in an inverse kind of way. In lower income regions of the city, the retention of existing industry structures behind protective tariff barriers, and the relative lack of investment in new commercial developments, should assist the survival of traditional patterns of land-use segregation. In the more prosperous parts, investment in new industrial, office, and commercial premises will be substantially interspersed. While the problem of urban decay would undoubtedly impinge on all residents it is likely to be much more severe in those poorer neighbourhoods where less investment occurs than in more wealthy localities. Finally, low population growth will greatly reduce the rate of fringe urban expansion and simultaneously reduce any impetus for more intensive land uses.

In summary, the premature post-industrial scenario could witness the emergence of the contemporary intra-urban equivalent of Disraeli's two nations: a small modern sector and a large, but relatively impoverished, traditional sector. Once again, the muddling through scenario would contain elements of each of the other two scenarios. Which combination emerges depends greatly on the membership of the corporate state and the kinds of trade-offs negotiated either between the members themselves or between the members and other coalitions of interest groups. Also influential in the outcome will be the level of national wealth and social outlook created as a result of these power plays.

Patterns of regional development

This section brings together the findings of the previous three, together with some additional relevant information, to sketch patterns of regional development as expressed by population growth. The projections are contained in Figure 6.12 and ignore particular spot developments, especially in farming, mining or tourism which are difficult to foresee. Common to all three scenarios is net migration of Australian residents from all States to Western Australia (Perth) and the Top End, and from the interior to the coast. In the case of the market economics scenario, prosperous farming areas located within the ecumene are likely to intercept some of that coastwards drift. A third general trend is the northwards movement of population from south-east Australia towards the NSW north coast region and south-east Queensland in the first instance and secondarily to northern Queensland. In our judgement the movement out of rural areas will be strongest under the premature post-industrial scenario and weakest under market economics, while the northwards population drift is the reverse. The patterns shown in Figure 6.10 are net movements which disguise smaller movements, in the opposite direction.

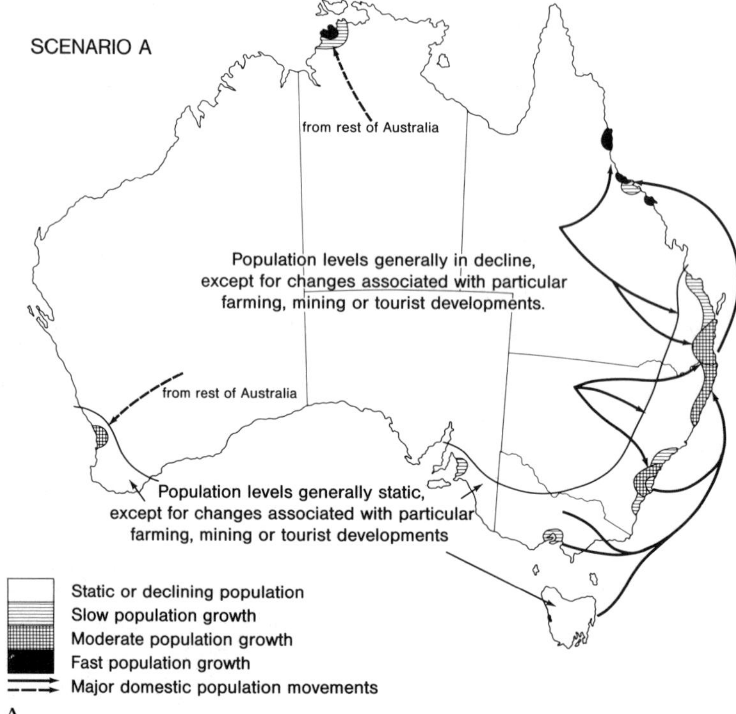

Fig. 6.12 Regional population change: medium-term projections under different scenarios

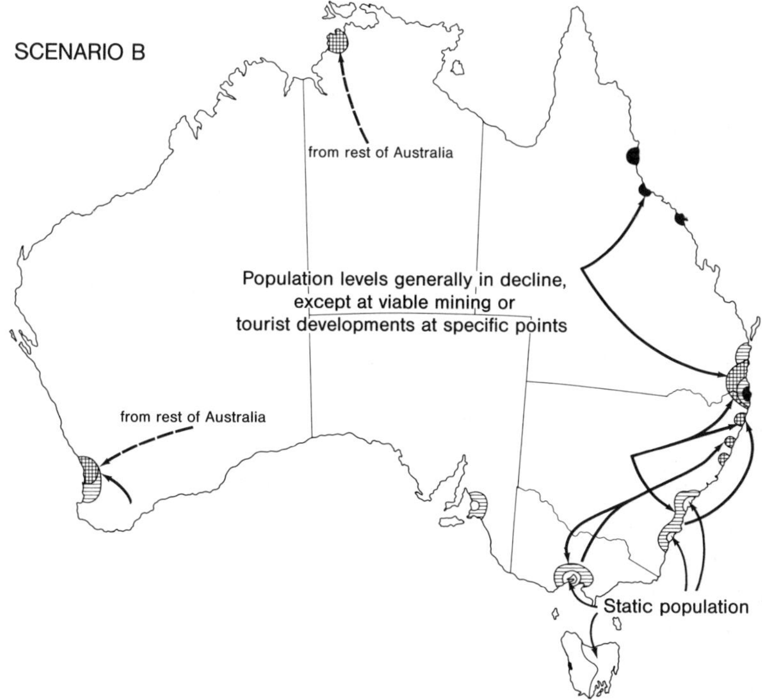
SCENARIO B
from rest of Australia
Population levels generally in decline, except at viable mining or tourist developments at specific points
from rest of Australia
Static population

B

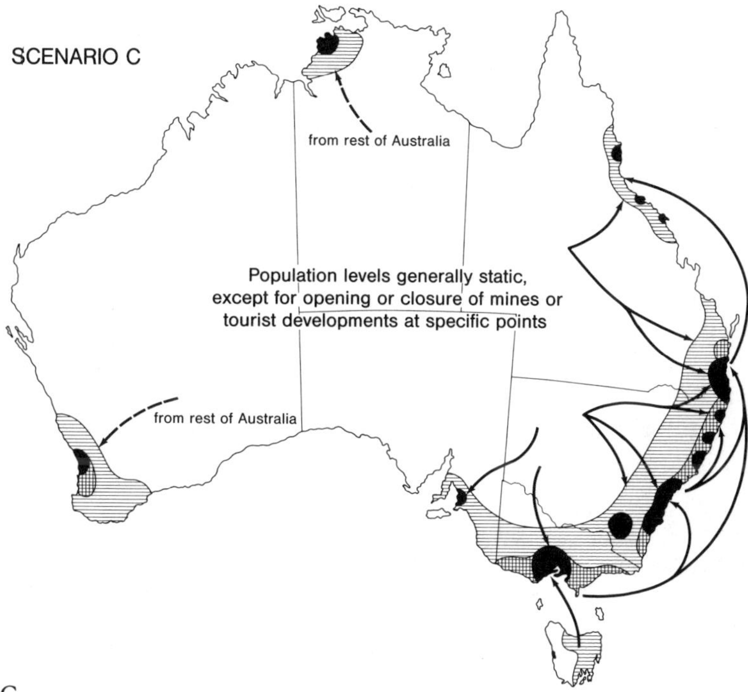
SCENARIO C
from rest of Australia
Population levels generally static, except for opening or closure of mines or tourist developments at specific points
from rest of Australia

C

Of these three trends, northward coastal migration is the strongest, especially in a wealthy society. This reflects four main factors. First, the number of elderly (aged 60+) is expected to grow by 50 per cent between 1981 and 2001 (from 2 million to 3 million) irrespective of the scenarios presented (Kendig and McCallum, 1986). [Note that the scenarios tend to affect population dynamics through overseas immigration, but few immigrants are elderly.] Thus there is going to be a large increase in people who would like to move either to pleasant living environments either in circum-metropolitan locations (such as the Blue Mountains and the Central Coast around Sydney) or on the NSW north coast or south-eastern Queensland. Both types of movements are dependent on the disposable incomes of potential migrants. This is expected to be highest under the market economics scenario.

The second factor is the increased footloose nature of manufacturing industry which enables entrepreneurs to seek out excellent living environments. Thirdly, international tourism to Australia seems set to increase for both the muddling through and market economics scenarios, and much of this, together with the employment it creates, will be channelled to tropical or sub-tropical coastal regions. Finally, even under premature post-industrialism, those areas will attract the young, unemployed and alternative lifestyle seekers.

A feature of Figure 6.12B is the low population growth of cities such as Melbourne, Sydney, Adelaide, Geelong, Newcastle and Wollongong surrounded by faster growth in their immediate hinterlands. Low economic growth should not reduce greatly the demand for rural residential lifestyles in the short-term: indeed it might be encouraged. In conditions of economic restraint the elderly are also likely not to retire such great distances.

To some extent the pattern of population growth will be determined by the development of infrastructure, especially water resources and transport. A few examples will suffice. The construction of the Very Fast Train (VFT) from Sydney to Melbourne via either Cooma and Bairnsdale or Albury would increase the commercial dominance of those cities and aid the growth of regions in between, including Canberra (Dale Budd and Associates Pty. Ltd., 1986). Indeed, anything designed to get people or goods quickly, cheaply and reliably from A to B should work to the benefit of A and B and places in between. National highway construction, airline deregulation, rail electrification (as for example between Newcastle and Wollongong), pipeline construction, and improved port efficiency all help. Dam construction for water storage and regulation has long had the effect, noted earlier, of intensifying and diversifying rural output. Such developments tend, however, to have geographically constrained effects.

Constraints

These need not detain us long. The scenarios which have been sketched are rather general and devoid of detail. It could hardly be otherwise, since the projections are for periods up to 15 years and are concerned with complex issues. Nor does it matter greatly whether or not the pictures presented are found convincing. The main purposes of the chapter have been to illustrate that quite different geographical patterns of social and economic development are possible given different scenarios. In this way it is hoped to get the reader thinking about the probability and desirability of particular outcomes and how those desired events might be put into effect. The chapter has also tried to point out that future geographical patterns are predominantly shaped by a basket of interrelated political, economic, social and behavioural conditions. We hope these goals have been achieved.

The scenarios may seem far-fetched. In one sense that is true because it is a little easier to sketch more extreme circumstances and compare the images created. In another sense it is not true. The evolution of Argentinian society over the last forty years was, until recently, uncomfortably close to the premature post-industrial scenario. Further, Australia's economic catharsis over the period 1985–87 and 1990–92 may indeed have set the scene for a thorough-going bout of market economics. Of course, even if one accepts the scenarios as being plausible, logical and possible, the reader might object that their geographical consequences are overstated, especially the impression that the market economics scenario will usher in a golden age of achievement and prosperity for many areas. That is the reader's prerogative. Each of the scenarios has an ideological flavour, and ideologies are personal constructs which cannot be proved in a conventional sense.

Conclusion

THE previous six chapters have discussed in some detail numerous aspects of contemporary Australia, including some current ideas on where the nation is headed in the next few years. We started with an examination of the nation's people. Particular attention was given to evolving patterns of immigration and their consequences for ethnic mix, to the fate of the Aboriginal people, to present demographic structures (including the ageing of the population), and to trends in internal migration. Since most of these issues can only be explained adequately by tracing the course of European settlement in the past two hundred years, this chapter also provided an excellent vehicle for a brief résumé of the country's history.

The next major issue concerned the types of economic activity in which the bulk of Australians are currently engaged and their location patterns. In order to explain these adequately, the analysis commenced with a brief introductory survey of the state of the economy and its recent evolution, and presented an *a priori* model of the factors which determine the location of productive activities. This was followed by a more detailed analysis of the performance and spatial organisation of selected industry sectors, including farming, mining and manufacturing. Some activities are obviously more prosperous than others and, since they are often tied to restricted locations, it follows that considerable variation in place prosperity can arise. This, in turn, is one element of the third issue considered: quality of life and community well-being. Problems of definition and measurement connected with these terms received considerable attention, prior to discussion of geographical equity in the provision or availability of health care, housing and employment. Subsequent discussion focussed on the role of the welfare state in correcting the observed spatial imbalances in well-being. At one level this involved detailing the kinds of program pursued by different tiers of government, but the explanation of why particular strategies were chosen necessitated some understanding of the role and structure of the state.

This understanding was provided by Chapter 4 which set out to elucidate the constitutional and delegated responsibilities of Australia's three tiers of government in theory and practice. This stressed both the growing dominance of the federal tier over the others through, among other things, its financial power and conduct of foreign affairs, and also the importance of intergovernmental financial relationships in determining the ability of different agencies to discharge their responsibilities. The energy with which governments pursue particular issues, and the form that the resultant policies take, were seen to be partly determined by ideology. They are also influenced by the electoral procedures in force. Explanation in geography is therefore inseparable from an understanding of the state in general and politics in particular. To some extent governments are losing sovereignty over policy-making areas which were previously their preserve. Nowhere is this more true than in the domain of macro-economic management. Chapter 5 set out to chronicle the emergence of the global economy, the forces which underlie it, and the restraints which private market mechanisms impose on the nation state. It was noted that Australia's economic and social geography will increasingly depend on the extent to which domestic outlooks and attitudes become congruent with, or diverge from, those elsewhere, but notably among peer group nations in the OECD. It also became apparent that Australia's wholehearted integration into the global economy would have particularly severe effects on the prospects for government sponsored regional development strategies.

The description and explanation of contemporary economy, society and polity provided by the first five chapters provided a necessary grounding for the final substantive chapter which probed the alternative paths to development confronting Australia in the medium term. Among the reasons advanced for considering the future was the idea that Australia stands at a crucial, somewhat pivotal, juncture in her history, and that current choices made between a range of possible courses of action by principally our political and business leadership could be instrumental in bringing about either great prosperity or social disaster. Three main scenarios were drawn and their implications assessed for several selected geographical issues, particularly rural Australia and the location of manufacturing industry. The value of this exercise also lay in the way in which it integrated, perhaps imperfectly, notions taken from several social science disciplines, notably economics, sociology and political science.

Indeed, one of the main unifying, though implicit, themes of the book is the indivisibility of the social sciences. It should be clear by now that not only are political, economic and social events or choices mutually interdependent, but that they, too, both influence and are influenced by geographical circumstances — and, for that matter, technology. For example, we have shown how the evolution of political structures (such as the pattern of States and their constitutional responsibilities, the role of the Commonwealth, political parties, electoral systems, and statutory authorities like the Commonwealth Grants Commission) reflects significantly both the struggle of small numbers of European settlers to come to grips with a large and environmentally harsh continent, and also the patterns of economic life imposed or constrained by those conditions. Conversely, political arrangements have at some times influenced greatly the geographical distribution of various industries, especially through policies designed to accelerate State or regional growth, or protect activities from domestic or overseas competition. We have also demonstrated that these processes are themselves interrelated with a host of social attitudes and community perceptions about such issues as nationhood, colonial dependency, defence strategy, environmental opportunity, equity and so on. All of these events are in turn dependent on a set of technological developments which tend to be autonomous in the sense that most tend to originate overseas and in the sense that, once invention occurs, the dynamics of market competition ensure implementation unhindered by attempts at social control (see Chapter 5).

The last point testifies also to a second major theme which emerges in the book. This concerns the large degree to which the explanation of Australia's contemporary geography depends on foreign ideas, decisions or events occurring over the last two hundred years. We have seen how the principal influences on the pattern of Australian development have varied from time to time and ranged from Britain's penal policies to competitive imperial expansion by European powers, the investment policies of foreign companies, war and its aftermath (especially the immigration of displaced persons), and the rise of the global economy. It is inevitable that the development path of a small open society will be heavily influenced by events elsewhere, though this problem seems to be particularly acute in Australia's case due to the origins of settlement and a colonial history. Only in recent years has Australia begun to shed her cultural cringe and exhibit a degree of cultural, political and economic maturity. This will not necessarily reduce the range and force of foreign influences, but should allow the nation to modify their form and influence, or adapt more rapidly and beneficially to changed circumstances. Moreover, both government and private companies or individuals are probably now in the best position they have even been to influence world affairs.

A third implicit theme is change and the tensions it engenders. Australia, as almost everywhere, is experiencing accelerating forces for change which collide with a variety of relatively rigid social, political and economic structures. These are often incapable of rapid adaptation, though that is not necessarily a bad thing as stable society requires familiar reference points and needs some mechanism to ensure that changes work to overall community benefit. We noted the conservatism of the political system — for example, the system of States, the Constitution and the monarchy; an enduring sense of justice (manifested occasionally in the tall poppy syndrome); long-standing feelings of strategic insecurity with respect to Asian nations and of interracial intolerance; and a predisposition towards doing just enough to pass muster, hedonism, and property ownership and development. Against these are ranged several major impetuses for change. Some, like new technology, growing social pluralism (or fragmentation), and the rising dominance of urban culture are all-pervasive. Others constitute discrete system shocks of varying orders of magnitude. Significant events among the latter, which we have noted, include the discovery of gold in the 1850s; the advent of nationhood in 1901; the Second World War; depressions in the 1890s, 1930s and, who knows, the 1990s; post-war immigration; the 1960s mineral boom; and financial deregulation in 1983. Conflict, it was noted, creates winners and losers and thereby social tensions. It has also had the effect of encouraging avoidance mechanisms. The corporate society, attempts to centralise political and economic power, log-rolling coalitions, and a preference for disjointed incremental decisions are four such consequences, all of which tend to lead to sub-optimal resource allocation in an economic sense. We also saw how this problem has traditionally been compounded by a lack of national vision and striving. This may be a consequence of complacency, easy wealth, and self-satisfaction, though it must surely arise in part from Australians' long-perceived inability to mould their own destiny.

Another issue to receive an airing was the extent to which the geographical environment has been an active or passive element in Australian development. To some extent it has acted as a passive stage on which events have unfolded. Physical features such as climate, drainage, slope, altitude, and soils are relatively fixed. So, too, for a long time have been many features of the human landscape: the pattern of roads and railways, of settlement, and many forms of economic activity. On the other hand, the nation's geography is under constant re-evaluation in the light of changing technology, social preferences, growing financial resources to spend on infrastructure works, and discovery of minerals, to name but four processes. Moreover, environment has frequently proved to be the mother of invention, especially in the realm of farm and mine technology, and in the delivery of community services to remote areas. It has also helped to mould several key aspects of the national psyche such as the fixation with irrigation works and the perceived need for a rapid expansion of population. In short, we have argued in several places that the unique character of the Australian environment has been a significant active determinant of human response, not just a general constraint on action.

Tensions arise not just from change, but also from a lack of congruence between image and reality or from social and economic inequality. All these have been explored to some extent. Initially the friction between image and reality arose from a misreading of the possibilities and constraints of the physical environment by early settlers, but, as we have learned to come to terms with it, the focus of misperception has shifted more to aspects of society. Thus Australia is increasingly divorced from the widespread image of a wealthy, resource-rich, egalitarian, caring, and educated society. In particular, we have demonstrated an apparent increase in the inequality of both income and wealth in recent years, though to date this has not translated into widespread social confrontation except for small-scale ethnic conflict. However, despite the generally perceived egalitarianism of much of the period from 1850 to 1970, social conflict was often not far from the surface: between, for example, the squatter and the small selector, the grazier and the dispossessed aborigine, the miner and the landowner, or the Chinese and Europeans. Social inequity has often had an ethnic base, leading to its being discounted by the dominant cultural group. In addition, there has been a long-running geographical inequity of significant proportions between the city and the bush. This has often been reflected in lower incomes, poorer services, lower activity rates, and a narrower range of jobs in rural areas. Economic tensions abound, many of which have been discussed. The interests of farmers, miners, and manufacturers substantially conflict. So do those of the old protected industries and small-scale, scientific, high technology firms. Small business frequently sits in a different camp from big business; likewise domestic producers and their multinational counterparts. Public providers of some goods and services sometimes resent competition from less shackled private companies or vice versa.

Political tensions are also endemic and serious in Australia. The problem with the greatest geographical expression is the unresolved struggle between forces for the centralisation of power both in Canberra and in State capitals. Local interests have increasingly been subordinated to these tiers of responsibility, often to the detriment of local interests. This, however, raises the unresolved and perhaps unanswerable question of the relative desert of respective local and national viewpoints where they are in conflict. Also important is the potential for conflict between individual and corporate interests discussed in Chapter 6, and between alternative would-be coalitions of interests.

Not all contrasts betoken conflict. Many add interest to day-to-day existence, enhance the quality of life, or distinguish Australia from the gamut of other countries. In a geographical sense, this is a large continent with few people, and most of those cling to the coastal strip, leaving the interior almost empty. Yet, paradoxically, the lifestyle of the interior is often romanticised as the epitome of the nation. Maybe this reflects those other paradoxes: the urban nation with a high degree of metropolitan primacy whose economic viability floats on a raft of rural exports; and, related to this, the somewhat embarrassing control of the productive periphery by a rather parasitic core. Culturally, too, there are some fascinating contrasts. As we revealed in Chapter 1, Aboriginal culture is one of the oldest in the world, yet it is juxtaposed to one of the newest and most brittle. We have long seen ourselves as an outpost of European civilization in an alien Asian corner of the world, though that is breaking down slowly to accentuate another contrast — an ethnic melting pot dominated by a British heritage particularly manifest in language, law and political institutions. There are also emerging many social contrasts, reflecting the increasingly plural nature of community interests, and rapidly changing economic circumstances. New wealth confronts old, environmentalists challenge the still strong development ethic, the elderly separate themselves from the young, families have different interests and outlooks from those of the yuppies and the dinkies, the lifestyles of the unskilled, under-employed, or unemployed increasingly seem to diverge from those of the cognitariat, and so on. Furthermore, these divergent interests have been seen increasingly to take on geographical expression. For example, the social patterning of cities and their immediate hinterlands is becoming more pronounced, and there is the rapid development of special purpose wilderness or national park areas.

Several of the contrasts we have discussed are primarily economic. Thus we have characterised Australia as an almost Third World resource-based economy with a superstructure of First World services and lifestyles. There is also the perhaps dangerous preference for consumption over investment and production, yet yearning for the fruits of post-industrial society which may rest largely on the nation's capacity to expand production. We cannot have both present consumption and a dynamic post-industrial future. Often, private affluence juxtaposes public poverty, though the reverse is not unknown where governments build monuments to themselves like the new parliament house in Canberra.

All these themes are interesting in their own right. Taken together, they provide a holistic (or integrated) picture of contemporary Australia. Description begs explanation, and we have sought not only to document as concisely as possible present circumstances, but also to identify clearly the mechanisms which underpin them. In the light of these findings we have felt able to gaze into our crystal ball and draw conclusions about possible future courses of events. You may not agree with them, but at least we have given you some ammunition to refute them and draw your own.

References

Abrams, M. 1973, 'Subjective social indicators', *Social Trends* 4, 35–50.

Adrian, C. (ed.) 1984a, *Urban Impacts of Foreign and Local Investment in Australia*, AIUS, Canberra.

Adrian, C. 1984b, 'Foreign investment in urban property', in C.Adrian (ed.), *Urban Impacts of Foreign and Local Investment in Australia*, AIUS, Canberra.

Adrian, C. 1984c, 'Institutional constraints on the post-war provision of fire services in Sydney', *Australian Geographer* 16, 38–50.

Alejandro, C.F.D. 1983, 'Open economy, closed polity', in D. Tussie (ed.), *Latin America in the World Economy: New Perspectives*, Gower, Aldershot.

Alexander, I. 1981, 'Post-war metropolitan planning: goals and realities', in P. N. Troy (ed.) *Equity in the City*, Allen and Unwin, Sydney.

Altman, J. 1988, *Aborigines, Tourism, and Development: The Northern Territory Experience*, NARU, Darwin.

Anderson, P. 1992, 'Learning to live with credit report cards',*Australian Financial Review* 12 February

Anon 1991a, 'Australians, government and the market', *Australian Financial Review* 13 August

Anon 1991b, 'Australia abroad: adapting to a global market', *Australian Financial Review* 14 August

Antcliff, S. 1988, 'Behind the rhetoric: a closer look at the New Right', *Australian Quarterly* 60, 63–9.

Asimov, I. 1984, 'Creativity will dominate our time after the concepts of work and fun have been blurred by technology', in American Society for Personnel Administration, *Work in the 21st Century,* Hippocrene Books Inc., New York.

Australian Bureau of Agricultural and Resource Economics 1989, *Commodity Statistical Bulletin*, AGPS, Canberra.

Australian Bureau of Agricultural and Resource Economics 1990, *Agriculture and Resources Quarterly* 2 (4).

Australian Bureau of Agricultural and Resource Economics 1991a, *Agriculture and Resources Quarterly* 3 (3).

Australian Bureau of Agricultural and Resource Economics 1991b, *Agriculture and Resources Quarterly* 3 (4).

Australian Bureau of Statistics 1984a, *Interstate Migration Australia*, ABS, Canberra.

Australian Bureau of Statistics 1984b, *Social Indicators No. 4*, AGPS, Canberra.

Australian Bureau of Statistics 1987, *Internal Migration Australia: 12 Months Ended 13 May 1986*, AGPS, Canberra.

Australian Bureau of Statistics 1989, *State and Local Government Finance 1987/88*, AGPS, Canberra.

Australian Bureau of Statistics 1990, *Commonwealth Government Finance, Australia 1987/88*, AGPS, Canberra.

Australian Bureau of Statistics 1991, *1989–90 National Health Survey: Summary of Results Australia*, ABS, Canberra.

Australian Bureau of Statistics 1992, *International Investment Position, Australia*, ABS, Canberra.

Australian Ethnic Affairs Council 1978, *Australia as a Multicultural Society*, AGPS, Canberra.

Australian Institute of Urban Studies 1971, *First Report of the Task Force on 'New Cities for Australia'*, AIUS, Canberra.

Australian Manufacturing Council 1990, *The Global Challenge: Australian Manufacturing in the 1990s*, Australian Manufacturing Council, Melbourne.

Australian Population and Immigration Council 1977, *Immigration Policies and Australia's Population*, AGPS, Canberra.

Australian Population and Immigration Council/Australian Ethnic Affairs Council 1979, *Multiculturalism and its Implications for Immigration Policy*, AGPS, Canberra.

Badcock, B.A. 1977, 'Educational achievement and participation rates in Sydney', *Australian Geographer* 13, 325–31.

Badcock, B. 1984, *Unfairly Structured Cities*, Basil Blackwell, Oxford.

Badcock, B. 1991, 'Where have financial deregulation and structural reform got the housing sector in Australia?', *Australian Geographer* 22, 129–3.

Bauer, R.A. 1966, 'Detection and anticipation of impact: the nature of the task', in R.A. Bauer (ed.), *Social Indicators*, MIT Press, Cambridge, Mass.

Bell, D. 1974, *The Coming of Post-Industrial Society*, Heinemann, London.

Bennett, R.J. 1980, *The Geography of Public Finance*, Methuen, London.

Berger, P.L. 1986, *The Capitalist Revolution*, Basic Books, New York.

Betts, K., I. Burnley, B. Birrell & J.W. Smith 1991, 'Forum: the immigration debate', *Urban Policy and Research* 9, 57–66.

Birdsell, J.B. 1975, *Human Evolution*, Rand McNally, New York (2nd edition).

Birrell, R. & K. Betts 1988, 'The FitzGerald Report on immigration policy: origins and implications', *Australian Quarterly* 60, 261–74.

Birrell, R. & D. Hill 1979, 'Population policy and the natural environment', in R. Birrell *et al.* (eds), *Refugees,Resources, Reunion: Australia's Immigration Dilemmas*, VCTA Publishing, Melbourne.

Birrell, R., D. Hill & J. Stanley (eds) 1982, *Quarry Australia: Social and Environmental Perspectives on Managing the Nation's Resources*, Oxford University Press, Melbourne.

Blainey, G. 1966, *The Tyranny of Distance*, Sun Books, Melbourne.

Blainey, G. 1982, *The Blainey View*, ABC/Macmillan, Sydney.

Blainey, G. 1984, *All For Australia*, Methuen Hayes, Sydney.

Blakely, E.J. & K. Bowman 1985, *Taking Local Development Initiatives: The Local Development Planning Process*, AIUS, Canberra.

Blakely, E.J. & K. Bowman 1986, *Taking Local Development Initiatives: A Guide to Economic and Employment Development for Local Government Authorities*, AIUS, Canberra.

Blandy, R., P. Dawkins, K. Cannicott, P. Kain, W. Kasper & R. Kriegler 1985, *Structured Chaos: The Process of Productivity Advance*, OUP, Melbourne.

Bloomfield, G.T. 1981, 'The changing spatial organisation of multinational corporations in the world automotive industry', in F.E.I. Hamilton and G.J.R. Linge (eds), *Spatial Analysis, Industry and the Industrial Environment, Vol. II: International Industrial Systems*, Wiley, Chichester.

Booker, M. 1978, *Last Quarter*, Melbourne University Press, Melbourne.

Bottomley, G. 1988, 'Ethnicity, race and nationalism in Australia: some critical perspectives', *Australian Journal of Social Issues* 23, 168–83.

Bradshaw, J. 1972, The concept of social need, *New Society* 19 (496), 640–3.

Breheny, M.J. & R.W. McQuaid 1985, *The M4 Corridor: Patterns and Causes of Growth in High Technology Industries*, Department of Geography Uni-versity of Reading, Reading.

Brennan, T. 1973, *New Community: Problems and Policies*, Angus and Robertson, Sydney.

Brennan, T. 1978, 'Urban social policy', in P. Scott (ed.), *Australian Cities and Public Policy*, Georgian House, Melbourne.

Broom, D.H. (ed.) 1984, *Unfinished Business: Social Justice for Women in Australia*, Allen and Unwin, Sydney.

Browett, J. & R. Leaver 1989, 'Shifts in the capitalist economy and the national economic domain', *Australian Geographical Studies* 27, 31–46.

Brunton, R. 1992, 'Environmentalism and sorcery', *Environmental Backgrounder* No. 8, 31 January.

Bryson, L. & F. Thompson 1972, *An Australian Newtown*, Penguin, Ringwood.

Buchanan, M.E. 1976, *Attitudes Towards Immigrants in Australia*, AGPS, Canberra.

Bullivant, B.M. 1989, 'The pluralist crisis facing Australia', *Australian Quarterly* 61, 212–8.

Bureau of Agricultural Economics 1982, *The Australian Forestry Sector: Its Size and Characteristics*, AGPS, Canberra.

Bureau of Agricultural Economics 1986a, *Quarterly Review of the Rural Economy 8(1)*, AGPS, Canberra.

Bureau of Agricultural Economics 1986b, *Farm Surveys Report*, AGPS, Canberra.

Bureau of Agricultural Economics 1986c, *Quarterly Review of the Rural Economy 8(2)*, AGPS, Canberra.

Bureau of Agricultural Economics 1987a, *Quarterly Review of the Rural Economy 9*, AGPS, Canberra.

Bureau of Agricultural Economics 1987b, *Farm Surveys Report*, AGPS, Canberra.

Bureau of Immigration Research 1991, *Australia's Population Trends and Prospects 1990*, AGPS, Canberra.

Bureau of Industry Economics 1983, *Job Losses in Small Country Towns: A Case Study of Adjustment to Abattoir Closures in Tenterfield*, NSW, AGPS, Canberra.

Bureau of Industry Economics 1984, *Tourist Expenditure in Australia*, AGPS, Canberra.

Bureau of Industry Economics 1987, *Review of Venture Capital in Australia and the MIC Program*, AGPS, Canberra.

Bureau of Industry Economics 1989, *The 150% Tax Concession for Research and Development Expenditure: Interim Report*, AGPS, Canberra.

Bureau of Mineral Resources 1987, *Australian Mineral Industry Review for 1984*, AGPS, Canberra.

Burke, B. 1984, 'Federation after the Franklin', *Australian Quarterly* 56, 4–10.

Burnett, R. & A. Burnett (eds) 1981, *Australia–New Zealand Economic Relations: Issues for the 1980s*, Australian National University Press, Canberra.

Burnley, I.H. 1976, *The Social Environment*, McGraw-Hill, Sydney.

Burnley, I.H. 1977, 'Resettlement of immigrant communities in urban Australia', in M.J. Bowen (ed.), *Australia 2000: The Ethnic Impact*, University of New England Publishing Unit. Armidale.

Burnley, I.H. 1980, *The Australian Urban System*, Longman Cheshire, Sydney.

Burnley, I.H. 1988, 'Population turnaround and the peopling of the countryside: migration from Sydney to country districts of New South Wales', *Australian Geographer* 19, 268–83.

Burnley, I.H. 1989a, 'Population and Sydney', in: J.V. Langdale, D.C. Rich, & R.V. Cardew (eds), *Why Cities Change Updated*, Geographical Society of New South Wales, Sydney.

Burnley, I.H. 1989b, 'Settlement dimensions of the Vietnam-born population in metropolitan Sydney', *Australian Geographical Studies* 27, 129–54.

Butlin, M.W. 1977, *A Preliminary Annual Data Base 1900/1 to 1973/4*, Reserve Bank of Australia, Sydney.

Byrnes, M. 1987, 'Australian business makes itself at home offshore', *Australian Financial Review* 28 September 1987.

Caldwell, J.C. 1985 'Man and his futures', in R.B. McKern and G.C. Lowenthal (eds), *Limits to Prediction*, Australian Professional Publications, Sydney.

Cameron, J.M.R. 1974, 'Information distortion in colonial promotion: the case of Swan River colony', *Australian Geographical Studies* 12, 57–76.

Campbell, J.K. 1981, *The Australian Financial System: Final Report of the Committee of Inquiry*, AGPS, Canberra.

Carroll, J. 1991, 'Forget the level playing field, it's protect or perish', *The Weekend Australian* 26 October.

Carson, E., P. Fitzgerald & A. Jordan 1989, '*Discouraged Workers: A Study of Long- Term Unemployment and Sickness Beneficiaries Aged 45–54*, Department of Social Security, Canberra.

Cass, B. 1985, 'Why women must screen tax changes', *Australian Society* 4(5), 20–3.

Cass, B. 1988, *Income Support for the Unemployed in Australia*, AGPS, Canberra.

Cassie, I. 1987, 'Australian taxes low by OECD standards', *Australian Financial Review* 21 September 1987.
Caves, R.E. & L.B. Krause (eds) 1984, *The Australian Economy: A View from the North*, Allen and Unwin, Sydney.
Centre for International Economics 1991, *Wool into the 21st Century: Structuring the Industry for Success and Implications for the Stockpile*, Centre for International Economics, Canberra.
Chapman, R.J.K. & M. Wood 1984, *Australian Local Government: The Federal Dimension*, Allen and Unwin, Sydney.
Chisholm, A. & T. Anderson 1991, 'Woods, wildlife and wilderness: managing Australia's native timber forests', in A. Moran, A. Chisholm, & M. Porter *Markets, Resources and the Environment*, Allen & Unwin, Sydney.
Clark, D. 1987, 'A target zone would just cause more problems in setting exchange rates', *Australian Financial Review* 21 September 1987.
Clark, D. 1991, 'Becoming more economics: student economic brief', *Australian Financial Review* 5 June.
Clark, G.L. 1991, 'Dimensions of global economic restructuring and the idea of decentralising labour relations in Australia', *Australian Geographical Studies* 29, 226–45.
Clark, G.L. & M. Dear 1984, *State Apparatus*, Allen and Unwin, Boston.
Clarke, H., A. Chisholm, G. Edwards, & J. Kennedy 1990, *Immigration, Population Growth and The Environment*, AGPS, Canberra.
Clarke, I.E. 1979, *The Pattern of Expectation 1644–2001*, Jonathan Cape, London.
Clayton, S. 1983, 'Social need revisited', *Journal of Social Policy* 12, 215–34.
Coates, B.E., R.J. Johnston & P.L. Knox 1977, *Geography and inequality*, OUP, Oxford.
Cockburn, C. 1977, *The Local State: Management of Cities and People*, Pluto Press, London.
Collie, M.J.S. 1990, 'The case for urban consolidation', *Australian Planner* 28, 26–33.
Collingbridge, G. 1982, *The First Discovery of Australia and New Guinea*, Pan Books, Sydney.
Commission of Inquiry into Poverty 1975, *First Main Report*, AGPS, Canberra.
Commonwealth Grants Commission 1981, *Report on State Tax- Sharing Entitlements 1981*, AGPS, Canberra.
Commonwealth of Australia 1973, *Year Book Australia No. 59*, AGPS, Canberra.
Commonwealth of Australia 1978, *Year Book Australia No. 63*, AGPS, Canberra.
Commonwealth of Australia 1979, *Year Book of Australia no. 64*, AGPS, Canberra.
Commonwealth of Australia 1981, *Year Book Australia No. 65*, AGPS, Canberra.
Commonwealth of Australia 1983, *Year Book Australia No. 67*, AGPS, Canberra.
Commonwealth of Australia 1984, *Year Book Australia No. 68*, AGPS, Canberra.
Commonwealth of Australia 1985, *Year Book Australia No. 69*, AGPS, Canberra.
Commonwealth of Australia 1986, *Year Book Australia No. 70*, AGPS, Canberra.
Commonwealth of Australia 1988a, *Towards A Fairer Australia*, AGPS, Canberra.
Commonwealth of Australia 1988b, *Final Report of the Constitutional Commission*, AGPS, Canberra.

Commonwealth of Australia 1989, *New Choices in Housing: Guidelines for Cost-Effective Residential Land Development*, AGPS, Canberra.

Commonwealth of Australia 1990, *Year Book Australia No. 73*, AGPS, Canberra.

Commonwealth of Australia 1991a, *Labour Force Australia 1989*, AGPS, Canberra.

Commonwealth of Australia 1991b, *Year Book Australia No. 74*, AGPS, Canberra.

Conway, R. 1971, *The Great Australian Stupor*, Sun Books, Melbourne.

Cook, L.H. & M.G. Porter (eds) 1984, *The Minerals Sector and the Australian Economy*, Allen and Unwin, Sydney.

Cook, L.H. & E. Sieper 1984, 'Minerals sector growth and structural change', in L.H. Cook & M.G. Porter (eds), *The Minerals Sector and the Australian Economy*, Allen and Unwin, Sydney.

Cooper, M. 1982, 'The state of the rural sector', in W. Hanley and M. Cooper (eds), *Man and the Australian Environment*, McGraw-Hill, Sydney.

Crawford, J.G. 1979, *Report of the Study Group on Structural Adjustment, Volume 1, Chapter 14*, AGPS, Canberra.

Crisp, L.F. 1965, *Australian National Government*, Longman, Melbourne.

Crough, G. & E. Wheelwright 1982, *Australia: A Client State*, Penguin, Ringwood.

Crough, G., T. Wheelwright & T. Wilshire 1980, Introduction, in G. Crough *et al.* (eds), *Australia and World Capitalism*, Penguin, Ringwood.

Cunningham, C.J. 1992, 'Landscape and legend: the noble toils of Francis Barrallier', *Proceedings of the Joint IAG/NZGS Conference*, Auckland, 1992.

Dahrendorf, R. 1975, *The New Liberty: Survival and Justice in a Changing World*, Stanford University Press, Stanford.

Dale Budd & Associates Pty Ltd 1986, *Sydney to Melbourne in Three Hours by VFT*, CSIRO, Canberra.

Daly, J.L. 1989, *The Greenhouse Trap: Why The Greenhouse Effect Will Not End Life On Earth*, Bantam Books, Sydney.

Daly, M.T. 1982a, 'Finance, the capital market and Sydney's development', in R.V. Cardew *et al.* (eds), *Why Cities Change*, Allen and Unwin, Sydney.

Daly, M.T. 1982b, *Sydney Boom Sydney Bust*, Allen and Unwin, Sydney.

Daly, M.T. 1987, 'Capital cities', in D.N. Jeans (ed.), *Australia: A Geography, Vol. 2: Space and Society*, Sydney University Press, Sydney.

Daly, M.T. 1988, 'Australian cities: the challenge of the 1980s', *Australian Geographer* 19, 149–61.

Davidson, B. 1969, *Australia Wet or Dry? The Physical and Economic Limits to the Expansion of Irrigation*, Melbourne University Press, Melbourne.

Day, L.H. & D.T. Rowlands (eds) 1988, *How Many More Australians? The Resource and Environmental Conflicts*, Longman Cheshire, Melbourne.

Day, M.F. (ed.) 1981, *Australia's Forests: Their Role in Our Future*, Australian Academy of Sciences, Canberra.

Day, R.A. & D.J. Walmsley 1978, 'Trendies and workers — inner suburban attitudes', *Royal Australian Planning Institute Journal* 16, 72.

Day, R.A. & D.J. Walmsley 1981, 'Residential preferences in Sydney's inner suburbs: a study in diversity', *Applied Geography* 1, 185–97.

Dear, M. 1981, 'A theory of the local state', in A.D. Burnett and P.J. Taylor (eds), *Political Studies from Spatial Perspectives*, Wiley, New York.

de Hoghton, C., W. Page & G. Streatfield 1971, *...And Now the Future*, Political and Economic Planning, London.

Department of Aboriginal Affairs 1986, *Aboriginal Statistics 1985*, AGPS, Canberra.

Department of Environment and Planning 1985, *Internal Migration: An Exploration of NSW Trends Since 1970*, DEP, Sydney.

Department of Home Affairs and Environment 1983, *Australian Urban Environmental Indicators*, AGPS, Canberra.

Department of Immigration and Ethnic Affairs 1978, *1788–1988: Australia and Immigration*, AGPS, Canberra.

Department of Immigration and Ethnic Affairs 1984, *Australia: Statement Prepared for the International Conference on Population*, Mexico City, August 1984, AGPS, Canberra.

Department of Immigration and Ethnic Affairs 1985, *Australia's Population Trends and Prospects 1984*, AGPS, Canberra.

Department of Immigration and Ethnic Affairs 1986, *Australia's Population Trends and Prospects 1986*, AGPS, Canberra.

Department of Immigration, Local Government and Ethnic Affairs 1988, *Immigration: A Commitment to Australia*, AGPS, Canberra.

Department of Industry, Technology and Commerce 1990, *Australian Model Code for Residential Development*, AGPS, Canberra.

Department of Mineral Resources 1984ff, *Metal and Mineral Prices: Monthly Reports*, DMR, Sydney.

Department of National Development 1965, *Atlas of Australian Resources (2nd Series): Fish and Fisheries*, Department of National Development, Canberra.

Department of National Mapping 1982, *Atlas of Australian Resources (3rd Series): Agriculture*, Department of National Mapping, Canberra.

Department of Sport, Recreation and Tourism 1985, *Australian Tourism Trends: An Overview*, AGPS, Canberra.

Department of Trade 1983, *Australia New Zealand Closer Economic Relations Trade Agreement*, AGPS, Canberra.

Department of Trade 1986, *Survey of Major Western Pacific Economies (4th edition)*, AGPS, Canberra.

Dickey, B. 1980, *No Charity There: A Short History of Social Welfare in Australia*, Nelson, Melbourne.

Dilnot, A. 1990, 'From most to least: new figures on wealth distribution', *Australian Society* 9 (7), 14–7.

Donald, O. 1981, 'Medical services', in P.N. Troy (ed.), *Equity in the City*, Allen and Unwin, Sydney.

Doran, C.R. 1984, 'An historical perspective on mining and economic change', in L.H. Cook & M.G. Porter (eds), *The Minerals Sector and the Australian Economy*, Allen and Unwin, Sydney.

Dornbusch, R. & S. Fischer 1984, 'The Australian macroeconomy', in R.E. Caves & L.B. Krause (eds), *The Australian Economy: A View from the North*, Allen and Unwin, Sydney.
Douglas, D. 1982, *The Economics of Australian Immigration*, Department of Adult Education University of Sydney, Sydney.
Drucker, P.F. 1969, *The Age of Discontinuity*, Heinemann, London.
Drucker, P.F. 1986, 'The changed world economy', *Foreign Affairs* 64 (4), 768–91.
Duncan, T. & J. Fogarty 1984, *Australia and Argentina: On Parallel Paths*, Melbourne University Press, Melbourne.
Economic Planning and Advisory Council 1986a, *Business Investment and Capital Stock*, Office of EPAC, Canberra.
Economic Planning and Advisory Council 1986b, *Human Capital and Productivity Growth*, Office of EPAC, Canberra.
Economic Planning and Advisory Council 1986c, *Technology and Innovation*, Office of EPAC, Canberra.
Economic Planning and Advisory Council 1986d, *Regional Impact of Industry Assistance*, Office of EPAC, Canberra.
Economic Planning and Advisory Council 1991a, *Urban and Regional Trends and Issues*, Office of EPAC, Canberra.
Economic Planning and Advisory Council 1991b, *Competitiveness: The Policy Environment*, Office of EPAC, Canberra.
Economic Planning and Advisory Council 1991c, *Improving Australia's Inflation Performance*, Office of EPAC, Canberra.
Economist 1984, 'The World in Figures', *Economist*, London.
Edmunds, M. 1988, 'Challenges for the treaty', *Australian Society* 7 (7), 27–9.
Edwards, M., T. Harper, & M. Harrison 1985, 'Child support: public or private duty?', *Australian Society* 4 (4), 18–22.
Else-Mitchell, R. 1980, 'The Australian federal grants system and its impact on fiscal relations of the federal government with state and local governments', *Australian Law Journal* 54, 480–8.
Emery, F.E. & E.L. Trist 1973, *Towards a Social Ecology*, Plenum, London.
Eyles, J. 1985, 'From equalisation to rationalisation: public health care provision in NSW', *Australian Geographical Studies* 23, 243–68.
Fagan, R.H. 1987, 'Australia on the periphery', in D.N. Jeans (ed.), *Australia: A Geography, Vol. 2: Space and Society*, Sydney University Press, Sydney.
Fagan, R.H. 1991, 'Industry policy and the macro-economic environment', *Australian Geographer* 22, 102–5.
Falk, J. & A. Brownlow 1989, *The Greenhouse Challenge: What Is To Be Done?*, Penguin, Ringwood.
Faulkner, H.W. 1981, 'Journey pattern adjustments on Sydney's metropolitan fringe: an exploratory study', *Australian Geographer* 15, 17–26.
Ferrer, A. 1983, 'Towards a theory of independence', in D. Tussie (ed.), *Latin America in the World Economy: New Perspectives*, Gower, Aldershot.

Fiedler, M.R.G. 1983, *A Wealth Tax: A Study of its Economic Aspects with Special Reference to Australia*, Australian Tax Research Foundation, Sydney.
Fincher, R. 1991, 'Locational disadvantage: an appropriate policy response to urban inequities', *Australian Geographer* 22, 132–5.
Foreign Investment Review Board 1985, *Annual Report 1983/4*, AGPS, Canberra.
Foreign Investment Review Board 1986a, *Annual Report 1984/5*, AGPS, Canberra.
Foreign Investment Review Board 1986b, *Annual Report 1985/6*, AGPS, Canberra.
Foreign Investment Review Board 1990, *Annual Report for 1989/90*, AGPS, Canberra.
Foreign Investment Review Board 1991, *Annual Report for 1990/1*, AGPS, Canberra.
Forrester, J.W. 1971, *World Dynamics*, MIT Press, Cambridge, Mass..
Forsyth, P.J. 1984, 'Transport infrastructure and mining industry development', in P.J. Lloyd (ed.), *Mineral Economics in Australia*, Allen and Unwin, Sydney.
Foster, L. & A. Seitz 1990, 'The OMA survey on issues in multicultural Australia', *Australian Quarterly* 62, 277-92.
Foster, L. & D. Stockley 1988, 'The rise and decline of Australian multiculturalism: 1973-1988', *Politics* 23, 1-10.
Foster, R.A. & S.E. Stewart 1991, *Australian Economic Statistics 1949/50 to 1989/90*, Reserve Bank of Australia Occasional Paper No. 8, Sydney.
Frank, A.G. 1967, *Capitalism and Underdevelopment: Historical Studies of Chile and Brazil*, Monthly Review Press, New York.
Freestone, R. 1977, 'Provision of child care facilities in Sydney', *Australian Geographer* 13, 318-25.
Galbraith, J.K. 1967, *The New Industrial State*, Penguin, Harmondsworth.
Gale, F. 1977, 'A social geography of Aboriginal Australia', in D.N. Jeans (ed.), *Australia: A Geography, Vol. 2: Space and Society*, Sydney University Press, Sydney.
Galligan, B. 1980, 'The founders' design and intention regarding responsible government', in P. Weller and D. Jaensch (eds), *Responsible Government in Australia*, Australasian Political Studies Association, Melbourne.
Galligan, B. 1982, 'Federalism and resource development in Australia and Canada', *Australian Quarterly* 54, 236–51.
Galois, R. 1977, 'Ideology and the idea of nature: the case of Peter Kropotkin', in R. Peet (ed.), *Radical Geography*, Methuen, Chicago.
Garnaut, R. 1989, *Australia and the Northeast Asian Ascendancy*, AGPS, Canberra.
Gart, M.J. 1986, 'The British company that found a way out', *Fortune* 74 (2), 104–6 and 179–85.
Gershuny, J. 1978, *After Industrial Society*, Macmillan, London.
Gill, F. 1989, 'Labour market flexibility — to what end?', *Australian Quarterly* 61, 456–67.
Gordon, R. & L. Kimball 1987, 'The impact of industrial structure on global high technology location', in J. Brotchie *et al.* (eds), *Technological Change and Urban Form*, Croom Helm, Beckenham.

Graycar, A. (ed.), 1978, *Perspectives in Australian Social Policy*, Macmillan, Melbourne.

Graycar, A. 1979, *Welfare Politics in Australia*, Macmillan, Melbourne.

Graycar, A. 1983, 'Retreat from the welfare state', in A. Graycar (ed.), *Retreat from the Welfare State*, Allen and Unwin, Sydney.

Gregory, R.G. 1984, 'Some implications of the growth of the mineral sector', in P.J. Lloyd (ed.), *Mineral Economics in Australia*, Allen and Unwin, Sydney.

Gunnersen, T.H. 1981, 'Economic considerations of Australian forestry', in M.F. Day (ed.), *Australia's Forests: Their Role in Our Future*, Australian Academy of Sciences, Canberra.

Haigh, R. and Rieder, L. 1989, 'Report on the economic impacts of tourism in New South Wales and Australia: input-output analysis', in NSW Tourism Commission, *The Economic Impacts of Tourism*, NSW Tourism Commission, Sydney.

Hall, N., J. Harris, N. Wallace, S. Dunne & J. Tucker 1991, 'Outlook for Australian farm incomes', in Australian Bureau of Agricultural and Resource Economics, *Farm Surveys Report*, AGPS, Canberra.

Hall, P. 1987, 'The geography of high technology: an Anglo- American comparison', in J. Brotchie *et al.* (eds), *Technological Change and Urban Form*, Croom Helm, Beckenham.

Hall, P. & A. Markusen (eds) 1985, *Silicon Landscapes*, Allen and Unwin, London.

Halligan, J. & C. Paris 1984, 'The politics of local government', in J. Halligan and C. Paris (eds), *Australian Urban Politics*, Longman Cheshire, Melbourne.

Hamilton, F.E.I. & G.J.R. Linge (eds) 1981, *Spatial Analysis, Industry and the Industrial Environment, Volume 2: International Industrial Systems*, Wiley, Chichester.

Hanley, W. & M. Cooper (eds) 1982, *Man and the Australian Environment*, McGraw-Hill, Sydney.

Harding, A. 1984, *Who Benefits? The Australian Welfare State and Redistribution*, Social Welfare Research Centre UNSW, Sydney.

Harris, C.P. 1974, 'Commentary on local and regional government', in R.L. Mathews (ed.), *Fiscal Federalism: Retrospect and Prospect*, Centre for Research on Federal Financial Relations ANU, Canberra.

Harris, C.P. & K.E. Dixon 1978, *Regional Planning in NSW and Victoria since 1944 with Special Reference to the Albury–Wodonga Growth Centre*, Centre for Research on Federal Financial Relations ANU, Canberra.

Hartley, P.R. 1984, 'Foreign ownership and the Australian mining industry', in L.H. Cook & M.G. Porter (eds), *The Minerals Sector and the Australian Economy*, Allen and Unwin, Sydney.

Harvey, M.E. 1976, *The Impact of the Wool Crisis on the Bourke Economy Between 1968/9 and 1970/1: A Regional Input–Output Study*, Department of Agricultural Economics and Business Management UNE, Armidale.

Hawke, R.J.L. 1989, *Rural and Regional Australia*, Department of the Prime Minister, Canberra.

Hawken, P. 1983, *The Next Economy*, Holt, Rinehart, and Winston, New York.

Hawken, P., J. Ogilvy & P. Schwartz 1982, *Seven Tomorrows*, Bantam Books, New York.

Head, B.W. 1984, 'Australian resource development and the national fragmentation thesis', *Australian New Zealand Journal of Sociology* 20, 306–31.

Head, B. 1988, 'The Labor government and 'economic rationalism'', *Australian Quarterly* 60, 466–77.

Heathcote, R.L. 1972, 'The visions of Australia, 1770–1970', in A. Rapoport (ed.), *Australia as Human Setting*, Angus and Robertson, Sydney.

Heathcote, R.L. 1977, *'Pastoral Australia'*, in D.N. Jeans (ed.), *Australia: A Geography*, Sydney University Press, Sydney.

Heilbroner, R.L. 1975, *An Enquiry into the Human Prospect*, Norton & Co., New York.

Heilbroner, R.L. 1976, *Business Civilisation in Decline*, Norton & Co., New York.

Helliwell, J. & P. Boxall 1978, 'Private sector wealth: quarterly estimates for use in an aggregate model', *Economic Record* 54, 45–64.

Henderson, R.F. (ed.) 1981, *The Welfare Stakes: Strategies for Australian Social Policy*, IAESR, Melbourne.

Henderson, R. & D. Hough 1984, 'Sydney's poor get squeezed', *Australian Society* 3 (11), 6–8.

Henderson-Sellers, A. & R. Blong 1989, *The Greenhouse Effect: Living In A Warmer Australia*, University of New South Wales Press, Sydney.

Higgott, R. 1984, 'Export-oriented industrialisation, the new international division of labour and the corporate state', *Australian Geographical Studies* 22, 58–71.

Hill, S. & R. Johnston (eds) 1983, *Future Tense? Technology in Australia*, University of Queensland Press, Brisbane.

Holmes, J.H. 1973, 'Population concentration and dispersion in Australian States: a macrogeographic analysis', *Australian Geographical Studies* 11, 150–70.

Holmes, J.H. 1977, 'Population', in D.N. Jeans (ed.), *Australia: A Geography, Vol. 2: Space and Society*, Sydney University Press, Sydney.

Holmes, J.H. 1987, 'Locational disadvantage and inverse health care in Queensland: a response', *Australian Geographical Studies* 25, 110–20.

Holmes, J.H. 1988, 'Remote settlements', in R.L. Heathcote (ed.), *The Australian Experience*, Longman Cheshire, Melbourne.

Homel, R. & A. Burns 1985, 'Through a child's eyes: quality of neighbourhood and quality of life', in I. Burnley and J. Forrest (eds), *Living in Cities*, Allen and Unwin, Sydney.

Hore-Lacey, I. 1982, 'Mining in Australia', in W. Hanley and M. Cooper (eds), *Man and the Australian Environment*, McGraw- Hill, Sydney.

Horne, D. 1964, *The Lucky Country: Australia in the Sixties*, Penguin, Ringwood.

Horne, D. 1970, *The Next Australia*, Angus and Robertson, Sydney.

Horne, D. 1976, *Money Made Us*, Penguin, Ringwood.

Hosomi, T. & A. Okumura 1982, 'Japanese industrial policy', in J. Pinder (ed.), *National Industrial Strategies and the World Economy*, Allenhead, Osmun & Co., New Jersey.

Howard, C. 1983, 'External affairs power of the Commonwealth', *Current Affairs Bulletin* 60 (4), 16–24.

Howitt, R. 1989, 'Resource development and Aborigines: the case of Roebourne 1960–1980', *Australian Geographical Studies* 27, 155–69.

Hudson, P. 1989, 'Change and adaptation in four rural communities in New England, NSW', *Australian Geographer* 20, 54–64.

Hughes, C.A. 1977, 'Malapportionment and gerrymandering in Australia', in R.J. Johnston (ed.), *People, Places, and Votes: Essays on the Electoral Geography of Australia and New Zealand*, Department of Geography UNE, Armidale.

Hughes, H. 1985, *Australia in a Developing World*, ABC, Sydney.

Hughes, S. 1987, 'Futures traders deal in present tension', *Australian Financial Review* 15 October 1987.

Hugo, G. 1986, *Australia's Changing Population: Trends and Implications*, OUP, Melbourne.

Hugo, G. 1988, 'Mobile or moribund? Population dynamics', in R.L. Heathcote (ed.), *The Australian Experience*, Longman Cheshire, Melbourne.

Hugo, G. 1990a, *Atlas of the Australian People: South Australia*, AGPS, Canberra.

Hugo, G. 1990b, *Atlas of the Australian People: Tasmania*, AGPS, Canberra.

Humphreys, J.S. 1985, 'A political economy approach to the allocation of health care resources: the case of remote areas of Queensland', *Australian Geographical Studies* 23, 222–42.

Humphreys, J.S. 1988, 'Planning for remote settlements — people, place and prosperity', in T.B. Brealey *et al.* (eds), *Resource Communities*, CSIRO, Melbourne.

Humphreys, J.S. 1990, 'Super clinics or a country practice? Contrasts in rural life and health service provision in northern New South Wales', in D.J. Walmsley (ed.), *Change and Adjustment in Northern New South Wales*, Department of Geography and Planning, University of New England, Armidale.

Humphreys, J.S. & H.C. Weinand 1991, 'Evaluating consumer preferences for health care services in rural Australia', *Australian Geographer* 22, 44–56.

Hutchinson, B. & G. Searle 1987, 'High technology industry location and planning policy in the Sydney region', in J. Brotchie *et al.* (eds), *Technological Change and Urban Form*, Croom Helm, Beckenham.

Hyde, J. 1985, 'Fear of favour', *Inside Australia* 1 (3), 4–6.

INDECS 1986, *State of Play 4*, Allen and Unwin, Sydney.

Industries Assistance Commission 1986, *The Textile, Clothing and Footwear Industries*, AGPS, Canberra.

Industry Commission 1990, *Annual Report for 1989/90*, AGPS, Canberra.

International Institute for Management Development 1991, *1990 World Competitiveness Report*, IIMD, Lausanne.

Jackson, J.T. 1985, 'Community health care in Victoria', *Australian Geographical Studies* 23, 312–32.

Jacobs, J. 1986, *Cities and the Wealth of Nations*, Penguin, Harmondsworth.

Jacobs, J.M. 1988, 'Politics and the cultural landscape: the case of Aboriginal Land Rights', *Australian Geographical Studies* 26, 249–63.

Jamrozik, A. 1983, 'Universality and selectivity: social welfare in a market economy', in A. Graycar (ed.), *Retreat from the Welfare State*, Allen and Unwin, Sydney.

Jayasuriya, L. 1990, 'Rethinking Australian multiculturalism: towards a new paradigm', *Australian Quarterly* 62, 50–63.

Jeans, D.N. (ed.) 1987, *Australia: A Geography, Vol. 2: Space and Society*, Sydney University Press, Sydney.

Johnson, W. 1978, *Muddling Towards Frugality*, Sierra Club Books, San Francisco.

Johnston, R.J. & P.J. Taylor 1986, *A World in Crisis? Geographical Perspectives*, Basil Blackwell, Oxford.

Jones, B. 1982, *Sleepers, Wake!*, OUP, Melbourne.

Jones, B. 1986, 'Work, income and leisure trends in Australia', in R. Castle *et al.* (eds), *Work, Leisure and Technology*, Longman Cheshire, Melbourne.

Jones, M.A. 1980, *The Australian Welfare State*, Allen and Unwin, Sydney.

Jones, M.A. 1981, *Local Government and the People*, Hargreen, Melbourne.

Kahn, H. 1970, *The Emerging Japanese Superstate*, Penguin, Harmondsworth.

Kahn, H. & T. Pepper 1980, *Will She be Right? The Future of Australia*, University of Queensland Press, Brisbane.

Kahn, H. & A.J. Weiner 1967, *The Year 2000*, Macmillan, New York.

Kahn, H. *et al.* 1976, *The Next 200 Years*, William Morrow & Co., New York.

Kasper, W. & T.G. Parry (eds) 1978, *Growth, Trade and Structural Change in an Open Australian Economy*, Centre for Applied Economic Research, UNSW, Sydney.

Kasper, W., R. Blandy, J. Freebairn, D. Hocking, & R. O'Neill 1980, *Australia at the Crossroads*, Harcourt, Brace Jovanovich, Sydney.

Kemeny, J. 1983, *The Great Australian Nightmare*, Georgian House, Melbourne.

Kendig, H. 1979, *New Life for Old Suburbs*, Allen and Unwin, Sydney.

Kendig, H.L. & J. McCallum 1986, *Greying Australia: Future Impacts of Population Ageing*, AGPS, Canberra.

Kirk, M. 1986, *A Change of Ownership: Aboriginal Land Rights*, Jacaranda Press, Sydney.

Kirwan, R. 1987, 'Local economic growth and comparative advantage', in J. Conroy (ed.), *Australian Regional Developments, Volume 6*, AGPS, Canberra.

Klaus, G. 1984, 'Corporate pyramids will tumble when horizontal organizations become the new global standard', in American Society for Personnel Administration, *Work in the 21st Century*, Hippocrene Books, New York.

Krause, L.B. 1984, 'Australia's comparative advantage in international trade', in R.E. Caves & L.B. Krause (eds), *The Australian Economy: A View from the North*, Allen and Unwin, Sydney.

Krause, L.B. & S. Sekiguchi (eds) 1980, *Economic Interaction in the Pacific Basin*, Brookings Institution, Washington.

Langmore, J. & D. Peetz (eds) 1983, *Wealth, Poverty and Survival: Australia in the World*, Allen and Unwin, Sydney.

Lee, G. 1978, *Inflation, Personal Income Taxation and the Distribution of Income*, CEDA, Sydney.

Lindblom, C.E. 1959, 'The science of 'muddling through'', *Public Administration Review* 19, 79–88.

Lindblom, C.E. 1968, *The Policy Making Process*, Prentice-Hall, Englewood Cliffs.

Linge, G.J.R. 1987, 'Manufacturing', in D.N. Jeans (ed.), *Australia: A Geography, Vol. 2: Space and Society*, Sydney University Press, Sydney.

Linge, G.J.R. 1991, 'If we are to prosper, the economy must become more productive', *Australian Geographer* 22, 105–8.

Lloyd, P.J. (ed.) 1984, *Mineral Economics in Australia*, Allen and Unwin, Sydney.

Logan, M.I., C.A. Maher, J. McKay & J.S. Humphreys 1975, *Urban and Regional Australia*, Sorrett, Melbourne.

Mackellar, M. 1979, 'The 1978 immigration decisions — a reply', *Australian Quarterly* 51, 93–103.

Maddox, G. 1982, 'The federal environment of Australian politics', in W. Hanley & M. Cooper (eds), *Man and the Australian Environment*, McGraw-Hill, Sydney.

Maddox, G. 1985, *Australian Democracy in Theory and Practice*, Longman Cheshire, Melbourne.

Maher, C.A. 1984, *Residential Mobility Within Australian Cities*, AGPS, Canberra.

Maher, C. 1985, 'The changing character of Australian urban growth', *Built Environment* 11 (2), 69–82.

Maher, C. 1988, 'Process and response in contemporary urban development: Melbourne in the 1980s', *Australian Geographer* 19, 162–81.

Management and Investment Companies Licensing Board 1985, *Annual Report 1983/4*, AGPS, Canberra.

Manne, R. 1991, 'The future of conservatism', *Quadrant* 36, 49–55.

Manning, I. 1976, 'The geographic distribution of poverty in Australia', *Australian Geographical Studies* 14, 133–47.

March, D. 1986, 'Werribee as a focus for biotechnology industry', *Australian Urban Studies* 14 (3), 1–3.

Marshall, A. 1991, 'Immigration, unemployment and the 1991 recession', *BIR Bulletin* 4, p. 19.

Marshall, T.H. 1963, *Social Policy*, Hutchinson, London.

Maslow, A.H. 1954, *Motivation and Personality*, Harper and Row, New York.

Mathews, R.L. 1975, 'Fiscal equalization in Australia: the methodology of the Grants Commission', *Finanzarchiv* 34, 66–85.

Mathews, R.L. 1976, *The Changing Patterns of Australian Federalism*, Centre for Research on Federal Financial Relations, ANU, Canberra.

Mathews, R.L. 1977, *Philosophical, Political and Economic Conflicts in Australian Federalism*, Centre for Research on Federal Financial Relations, ANU, Canberra.

Mathews, R. 1980, 'The structure of taxation', in J. Wilkes (ed.), *The Politics of Taxation*, Hodder and Stoughton, Sydney.

Mathews, R.L. & W.R.C. Jay 1972, *Federal Finance: Intergovernment Financial Relations in Australia since Federation*, Nelson, Sydney.

McColl, F.D. 1984, 'Foreign investment in Australian mining', in P.J. Lloyd (ed.), *Mineral Economics in Australia*, Allen and Unwin, Sydney.

McGregor, C. 1968, *Profile of Australia*, Penguin, Ringwood.

McKiggan, I. 1977, 'The Portuguese expedition to Bass Strait in AD 1522', *Journal of Australian Studies* 1 (1), 2–32.
McLachan, I. 1985, 'Turning the tide of regulation', *Inside Australia* 1 (2), 27–8.
McPhail, I. 1978 'Local government', in: P.N. Troy (ed.) *Federal Power in Australia's Cities*, Hale & Iremonger, Sydney.
McPhail, I.R. & D.J. Walmsley 1975, 'Commentary on GOVERNMENT mapsheet', in *Atlas of Australian Resources* (2nd series), Department of Minerals and Energy, Canberra.
Meadows, D.H., D.L. Meadows, J. Randers & W.W. Behrens 1972, *The Limits to Growth*, Pan Books, Sydney.
Meinig, D.W. 1970, *On the Margins of the Good Earth: The South Australian Wheat Frontier, 1869–84*, Seal Books, Chicago.
Mendelsohn, R. 1979, *The Condition of the People: Social Welfare in Australia 1900–1975*, Allen and Unwin, Sydney.
Mendelsohn, R. 1982, *Fair Go: Welfare Issues in Australia*, Penguin, Ringwood.
Mercer, D. 1991, *A Question of Balance: Natural Resources Conflict Issues in Australia*, The Federation Press, Sydney.
Mesarovic, M. & E. Pestel 1974, *Mankind at the Turning Point*, Hutchinson, London.
Moore, D. 1989, 'Why Australia has a current account problem', *Policy* 5 (3), 5–7.
Morris, J. 1981, 'Urban public transport', in P.N. Troy (ed.), *Equity in the City*, Allen and Unwin, Sydney.
Morrison, P.S. 1990, 'Migrants, manufacturing and metropolitan labour markets in Australia', *Australian Geographer* 21, 151–63.
Moseley, M.J. 1979, *Accessibility: The Rural Challenge*, Methuen, London.
Mowbray, M. 1985, 'Social unrest sparks the welfare response — Mt Druitt 1981', *Australian Quarterly* 57, 85–94.
Mulvaney, D.J. 1969, *The Prehistory of Australia*, Thames- Hudson, London.
Mulvaney, D.J. & J.P. White (eds) 1987, *Australians to 1788*, Fairfax, Syme and Weldon Associates, Sydney.
Munro-Clark, M. 1986, *Communes in Rural Australia*, Hale and Iremonger, Sydney.
Murphy, P.A. & D. Roman 1989, 'Regional development policy in New South Wales: contemporary needs and options', *Australian Quarterly* 61, 262–75.
Murphy, P.A. & R.B. Zehner 1988, 'Satisfaction with sunbelt migration', *Australian Geographical Studies* 26, 320–34.
Murphy, P.A., I.H. Burnley, H.R. Harding, D. Weisner & V. Young 1990, *Impact of Immigration on Urban Development*, AGPS, Canberra.
Musgrave, R.A. & P.B. Musgrave 1980, *Public Finance in Theory and Practice*, McGraw-Hill, New York.
Myrdal, G. 1957, *Economic Theory and Underdeveloped Regions*, Methuen, London.
Naisbitt, J. 1984, *Megatrends*, Futura, London.
National Inquiry into Local Government Finance 1985, *Report*, AGPS, Canberra.
National Population Inquiry 1975, *Population and Australia: Volumes 1 &2*, AGPS, Canberra.

Neutze, M. 1977, *Urban Development in Australia*, Allen and Unwin, Sydney.

Neutze, M. 1978, *Australian Urban Policy*, Allen and Unwin, Sydney.

Neutze, M. 1981, 'Housing', in P.N. Troy (ed.), *Equity in the City*, Allen and Unwin, Sydney.

Nevile, J. 1990, *The Effect of Immigration on Australian Living Standards*, AGPS, Canberra.

Ncvilc, J.W. & N.A. Warren 1984, 'How much do we know about wealth distribution in Australia?', *Australian Economic Review* 68, 23–34.

Newton, P. & O'Connor 1987, 'The location of high technology industry: an Australian perspective', in J. Brotchie, P. Newton, P. Hall & P. Nijkamp (eds), *Technological Change and Urban Form*, Croom Helm, Beckenham.

Newton, P. & M. Taylor 1987, 'Probable urban futures', in J. Brotchie *et al.* (eds), *Technological Change and Urban Form*, Croom Helm, Beckenham.

Norman, N.R. & F. Meikle 1985, *The Economic Effects of Immigration on Australia*, CEDA, Sydney.

O'Connor, K. & D. Edgington 1984, 'Tertiary industry and urban develop-ment: competition between Sydney and Melbourne', in C. Adrian (ed.), *Urban Impacts of Foreign and Local Investment in Australia*, AIUS, Canberra.

O'Connor, P. (1990), 'Privatisation and welfare services', *Australian Journal of Social Issues* 25, 27–39.

O'Faircheallaigh, C. 1988, 'Land rights and mineral exploration: the Northern Territory experience', *Australian Quarterly* 60, 70–84.

Office of Local Government 1984, *Digest of Local Government Statistics 1983*, AGPS, Canberra.

Office of Local Government 1989, *The Australian Local Government Handbook*, AGPS, Canberra.

O'Leary, J. & R. Sharp (eds) 1991, *Inequality in Australia: Slicing the Cake*, Heinemann, Melbourne.

Olson, M. 1982, *The Rise and Decline of Nations*, Yale University Press, New Haven.

O'Neill, P.M. 1991, 'Plants on stand-by: the textile and clothing industry in non-metropolitan areas of New South Wales and Victoria', *Australian Geographer* 22, 108–12.

Organisation for Economic Co-operation and Development 1973, *List of Social Concerns Common to Most OECD Countries*, OECD, Paris.

Organisation for Economic Co-operation and Development 1982, *Revenue Statistics of OECD Member Countries 1965–81*, OECD, Paris.

Organisation for Economic Co-operation and Development 1985, *Creating Jobs at the Local Level*, OECD, Paris.

Organisation for Economic Co-operation and Development 1986, *Living Conditions in OECD Countries*, OECD, Paris.

Painter, M. 1988, 'Australian federalism and the policy process: politics with extra vitamins', *Politics* 23, 57–66.

Papadakis, E. 1990, 'Conjectures about public opinion and the Australian welfare state', *Australian and New Zealand Journal of Sociology* 26, 209–34.

Paris, C. 1984, 'Private rental housing in Australia', *Environment and Planning* 16A, 1079–98.

Paris, C. 1985, 'Housing issues and policies in Australia', *Built Environment* 11, 97–116.

Paris, C. *et al.* 1985, 'From public housing to welfare housing', *Australian Journal of Social Issues* 20, 105–17.

Parker, S. 1983 *Leisure and Work*, Allen & Unwin, Sydney.

Pearman, C.I. (ed.) 1988, *Greenhouse: Planning For Climatic Change*, CSIRO, Canberra.

Peterson, D., S. Dunne, P. Morris & P. Knopke 1991, 'Developments in debt for broadacre agriculture', *Agriculture and Resources Quarterly* 3, 349–60.

Piggott, J. 1984, 'The distribution of wealth in Australia — a survey', *Economic Record* 60, 252–65.

Pinch, S. 1991, 'The impact of centralisation upon geographical variations in the provision of aged care services: a comparison of outcomes in Melbourne and Adelaide', *Australian Geographical Studies* 29, 26–41.

Pinder, J. (ed.) 1982, *National Industrial Strategies and the World Economy*, Allenhead, Osmun & Co., New Jersey.

Pitchford, J. 1989, 'The current account: still a secondary issue', *Policy* 5 (3), 8–11.

Planning and Environment Commission 1978, *Social Indicators*, PEC, Sydney.

Podder, N. 1972, 'Distribution of household income in Australia', *Economic Record* 48, 181–200.

Podder, N. & N.C. Kakwani 1976, 'Distribution of wealth in Australia', *The Review of Income and Wealth* 22, 75–92.

Porter, M.G. 1984, 'Mining and the economy — some key issues', in L.H. Cook & M.G. Porter (eds), *The Minerals Sector and the Australian Economy*, Allen and Unwin, Sydney.

Porter, M. 1990, *The Competitive Advantage of Nations*, Free Press, New York

Powell, J.M. 1976, *Environmental Management in Australia, 1788–1914*, OUP, Melbourne.

Powell, J.M. 1978, *Mirrors of the New World*, ANU Press, Canberra.

Powell, J.M. 1988, *An Historical Geography of Modern Australia*, Cambridge University Press, Cambridge.

Power, J.M. & R.L. Wettenhall 1976, 'Regional government versus regional programs', *Australian Journal of Public Administration* 35, 114–29.

Power, J., R. Wettenhall & J. Halligan 1981, 'Overview of local government in Australia', in J. Power *et al.* (eds), *Local Government Systems of Australia*, AGPS, Canberra.

Prest, W. & R.L. Mathews (eds), *The Development of Australian Fiscal Federalism: Selected Readings*, ANU Press, Canberra.

Preston, N. 1991, 'Land laws without the rights', *Australian Society* 10 (7), 5–7.

Pronk, J.P. 1983, 'The new international economic order: a second look', in J. Langmore & D. Peetz (eds), *Wealth, Poverty and Survival: Australia in the World*, Allen and Unwin, Sydney.

Pusey, M. 1991, *Economic Rationalism in Canberra: A Nation- Building State Changes Its Mind*, Cambridge University Press, Cambridge.

Raskall, P.L. 1977, *The Distribution of Wealth in Australia, 1966–72*, Planning Research Centre, University of Sydney, Sydney.

Raskall, P. 1986, 'Who's got it? Who needs it?', *Australian Society* 5 (3), 12–5.

Raskall, P. 1987, 'Wealth: who's got it? who needs it?', *Australian Society* 6 (5), 21–4.

Rich, D.C. 1987, *The Industrial Geography of Australia*, Methuen, Sydney.

Rich, D.C., R.V. Cardew & J.V. Langdale 1982, 'Themes in urban development and economic change', in R.V. Cardew, R.V. Cardew, J.V. Langdale and D.C. Rich (eds), *Why Cities Change*, Allen and Unwin, Sydney.

Rimmer, P.J. & D.K. Forbes 1982, 'Underdevelopment theory: a geographical review', *Australian Geographer* 15, 197–211.

Roberti, P. 1974, 'Income distribution: a time-series and a cross-section study', *Economic Journal* 84, 629–38.

Robertson, J. 1985, *Future Work: Jobs, Self-Employment and Leisure After the Industrial Age*, Universe Books, New York.

Romanyshyn, J.M. 1971, *Social Welfare: Charity to Justice*, Random House, New York.

Rowland, D.T. 1979, *Internal Migration in Australia*, AGPS, Canberra.

Rowley, C.D. 1972, *The Destruction of Aboriginal Society*, Penguin, Ringwood.

Rowse, T. 1990, 'The revolution in Aboriginal affairs', *Australian Society* 9 (3), 15–8.

Rugman, A.M. (ed.) 1982, *New Theories of the Multinational Enterprise*, St Martin's Press, New York.

Rydon, J. 1973, 'The electoral system', in H. Mayer and H. Nelson (eds), *Australian Politics*, Cheshire, Sydney.

Sandercock, L. 1975, *Cities For Sale*, Melbourne University Press, Melbourne.

Sandercock, L. & M. Berry 1983, *Urban Political Economy: The Australian Case*, Allen and Unwin, Sydney.

Sanders, W. 1988, 'The CDEP Scheme: bureaucratic politics, remote community politics and the development of an Aboriginal 'workforce' program in times of rising unemployment', *Politics* 23, 32–47.

Sarkissian, W. & T. Doherty 1984, Living in Public Housing, NSW Housing Commission, Sydney.

Saunders, P. & B. Bradbury 1989, 'Galluping poverty', *Australian Society* 8 (9), p. 27.

Sawer, G. 1969, *Modern Federalism*, Watts, London.

Schneider, S.H. 1976, *The Genesis Strategy: Climate and Global Survival*, Plenum Press, New York.

Schumacher, E.F. 1973, *Small is Beautiful*, Bland and Briggs, London.

Schumpeter, J. 1954, *Capitalism, Socialism and Democracy*, Allen and Unwin, London.

Scott, R. 1980, 'Conclusions: interest groups and the Australian political process', in R. Scott (ed.), *Interest Groups and Public Policy*, Macmillan, Melbourne.

Senate Standing Committee on Trade and Commerce 1982, *The Development of the Australian Fishing Industry: Report*, AGPS, Canberra.

Sharman, C. 1977, *The Premiers' Conference: An Essay on Federal State Interaction*, Department of Political Science ANU, Canberra.

Shaw, A.G.L. 1966, *Convicts and the Colonies*, Faber and Faber, London.

Sheehan, P. 1980, *Crisis in Abundance*, Penguin, Ringwood.

Shergold, P.R. 1984, 'Immigration today: fact and fiction', in F. Milne & P. Shergold (eds), *The Great Immigration Debate*, Federation of Ethnic Community Councils of Australia, Sydney.

Sloan, J. & R. Kriegler 1984, 'Technological change and migrant employment', *Australian Quarterly* 56, 216–26.

Smith, M.P. 1980, *The City and Social Theory*, Basil Blackwell, Oxford.

Social welfare Policy Secretariat 1981, *Report on Poverty Measurement*, AGPS, Canberra.

Sommerlad, E.A., P.L. Dawson & J.C. Altman 1985, *Rural Land Sharing Communities: An Alternative Economic Model?*, AGPS, Canberra.

Sorensen, A.D. 1990a, 'Virtuous cycles of growth and vicious cycles of decline: regional economic change in northern New South Wales', in D.J. Walmsley (ed.), *Change and Adjustment in Northern New South Wales*, Department of Geography and Planning, University of New England, Armidale.

Sorensen, A.D. 1990b, *Ideas for Metropolitan Transit: Improving Sydney's Public Transport System*, Report to the Ministry of Transport, Sydney.

Sorensen, A.D. 1991, 'Multi-function polis: the definition of a concept', *Regional Science Review* 18, 1–19.

Sorensen, A.D. & H.C. Weinand 1985, 'Settlement types', in R. Powell (ed.), *Rural Labour Markets in Australia*, AGPS, Canberra.

Sorensen, A.D. & H.C. Weinand 1991, 'Regional well-being in Australia revisited', *Australian Geographer* 29, 42–70.

South, P.M. 1981, 'World view and Australian perspective', in M.F. Day (ed.), *Australia's Forests: Their Role in Our Future*, Australian Academy of Science, Canberra.

Spann, R.N. 1979, *Government Administration in Australia*, Allen and Unwin, Sydney.

Spear, A. 1989, *The New South Wales Competitiveness Study*, NSW Tourism Commission, Sydney.

Stilwell, F.J.B. 1974, *Australian Urban and Regional Development*, ANZ Book Company, Sydney.

Stilwell, F. 1981, 'Unemployment and socio-economic structure', in B. Cass (ed.), *Unemployment: Causes, Consequences, and Policy Implications*, Social Welfare Research Centre, UNSW, Sydney.

Stimson, R.J. 1982, *The Australian City: A Welfare Geography*, Longman Cheshire, Melbourne.

Storer, D. 1980, 'Migrants and unemployment', in G. Crough *et al.* (eds), *Australia and World Capitalism*, Penguin, Ringwood.

Tait, D. *et al.* 1989, 'Understanding ethnic small business: a case study of Marrickville', *Australian Journal of Social Issues* 24, 183–98.

Task Force on Co-ordination in Welfare and Health 1977, *First Report: Prospects for Change in the Administration and Delivery of Programs and Services*, AGPS, Canberra.

Taylor, J. 1989a, 'Public policy and Aboriginal population mobility: insights from the Katherine Region, Northern Territory', *Australian geographer* 20, 47–53.

Taylor, J. 1989b, 'Migration and population change in Northern Territory', *Australian Geographical Studies* 27, 182–98.

Taylor, M.J. & N.J. Thrift 1984, 'The regional consequences of a dualistic industrial structure: the case of Australia', *Australian Geographical Studies* 22, 72–87.

Teese, R. 1987, 'Regional differences in high and technical school demand in Melbourne, 1951–1985', *Australian Geographical Studies* 25, 84–101.

Thorne, A.G. 1971, 'Mungo and Kow Swamp: morphological variation in Pleistocene Australians', *Mankind* 8, 85–9.

Thrift, N. 1986, 'The geography of international economic disorder', in R.J. Johnston & P.J. Taylor (eds), *A World in Crisis?: Geographical Perspectives*, Basil Blackwell, Oxford.

Titmuss, R.M. 1968, *Commitment to Welfare*, Allen and Unwin, London.

Toffler, A. 1971, *Future Shock*, Pan Books, London.

Toffler, A. 1980, *The Third Wave*, William Morrow & Co., New York.

Toffler, A. 1983, *Previews and Premises*, William Morrow & Co., New York.

Trainer, F.F. 1985, *Abandon Affluence!*, Zed Books, London.

Troy, P.N. 1981, 'Introduction', in P.N. Troy (ed.), *Equity in the City*, Allen and Unwin, Sydney.

Tucker, J. *et al.* 1990, 'Financial performance of Australian farms', in Australian Bureau of Agricultural and Resource Economics, *Farm Surveys Report*, AGPS, Canberra.

Tullock, G. 1981, *Rhetoric and Reality in Income Redistribution*, Centre for Independent Studies, Sydney.

Tussie, D. (ed.) 1983, *Latin America in the World Economy: New Perspectives*, Gower, London.

United Nations 1986, *National Accounts Statistics: Main Aggregates and Detailed Tables, 1983*, United Nations, New York.

United Nations 1990, *National Accounts Statistics: Main Aggregates and Detailed Tables, 1988*, United Nations, New York.

Valuer-General's Department 1985, *New South Wales Real Estate Market*, Valuer-General's Department, Sydney.

Valuer-General's Department 1990, *New South Wales Real Estate Market*, Valuer-General's Department, Sydney.

Van Dugteren, T. (ed.) 1976, *Who Gets What? The Distribution of Wealth and Power in Australia*, Hodder and Stoughton, Sydney.

Vipond, J. 1985, 'Unemployment — a current issue in intra-urban inequalities', in I. Burnley & J. Forrest (eds), *Living in Cities*, Allen and Unwin, Sydney.

Vipond, J. 1986, 'The changing face of poverty', *Australian Society* 5 (2), 19–21.

Wade, P.B. 1974, 'Recent developments in fiscal federalism in Australia, with special reference to revenue sharing and fiscal equalisation', in R.L. Mathews (ed.), *Fiscal Federalism: Retrospect and Prospect*, Centre for Research on Federal Financial Relations, ANU, Canberra.

Wadley, D. & D. Rich 1983, *The Australian Industrial System 1950–81: Review and Classified Bibliography*, Department of Geography, University of Tasmania, Hobart.

Wajcman, J. & S. Rosewarne 1986, 'The 'feminisation' of work', *Australian Society* 5 (9), 15–7.

Walmsley, D.J. 1978, 'The influence of distance on hospital usage in rural New South Wales', *Australian Journal of Social Issues* 13, 72–81.

Walmsley, D.J. 1980a, *Social Justice and Australian Federalism*, Department of Geography, University of New England, Armidale.

Walmsley, D.J. 1980b, 'Welfare delivery in post-industrial society', *Geografiska Annaler Series B* 62, 91–7.

Walmsley, D.J. 1984a, 'Fiscal equalisation and Australian federalism, 1971–1981', *Environment and Planning C* 2, 93–106.

Walmsley, D.J. 1984b, 'Australian local government in the 1970s', *Australian Geographical Studies* 22, 88–99.

Walmsley, D.J. 1985, 'The High Court and the Constitution', *Australian Geographical Studies* 23, 129–33.

Walmsley, D.J. 1988a, *Urban Living: The Individual in the City*, Longman, London.

Walmsley, D.J. 1988b, 'Space and government', in R.L. Heathcote (ed.), *The Australian Experience*, Longman Cheshire, Melbourne.

Walmsley, D.J. 1990, 'Adaptation to change and uncertainty: the social implications for Australia', in R. Hayter and P. Wilde (eds), *Industrial Transformation and Challenge in Australia and Canada*, Carleton University Press, Ottawa.

Walmsley, D.J. & G.J. Lewis 1984, *Human Geography: Behavioural Approaches*, Longman, London.

Walmsley, D.J., T.F. Saarinen & C.L. MacCabe 1990, 'Down under or centre stage? The world images of Australian students', *Australian Geographer* 21, 164–73.

Walmsley, D.J. & H.C. Weinand 1991, 'Changing retail structure in southern Sydney', *Australian Geographer* 22, 57–66.

Walsh, M. 1979, *Poor Little Rich Country*, Penguin, Ringwood.

Ward, R. 1958, *The Australian Legend*, OUP, Melbourne.

Ward, R. 1982, *Australia Since the Coming of Man*, Lansdowne Press, Sydney.

Watson, A. 1990, *Unravelling Intervention in the Wool Industry*, Centre for Independent Studies, Sydney.

Watson, S. 1988, *Accommodating Inequality*, Allen & Unwin, Sydney.

Weinand, H. 1985, 'The rural workforce', in R. Powell (ed.), *Rural Labour Markets in Australia*, AGPS, Canberra.

West, K. 1983, 'Federalism and resources development: the politics of State inequality', in A. Patience and A. Scott (eds), *Australian Federalism: Future Tense*, OUP, Melbourne.

West, K. 1984, *The Revolution in Australian Politics*, Penguin, Ringwood.

Wettenhall, G. 1989, 'No, prime minister', *Australian Society* 8 (3), 29-32.

Wettenhall, R.L. 1983, 'Quangos, quagos and the problems of non-ministerial organisation', in G.R. Curnow and C.A. Saunders (eds), *Quangos: The Australian Experience*, Hale and Iremonger, Sydney.

Wheelwright, E. 1984, 'The political economy of foreign domination', in P.J. Lloyd (ed.), *Mineral Economics in Australia*, Allen and Unwin, Sydney.

White, J.P. & J.F. O'Connell 1982, *A Prehistory of Australia, New Guinea and Sahul*, Academic Press, Sydney.

Whitelaw, J.S. & J.S. Humphreys 1980, 'Migrant response to an unfamiliar residential environment', in I.H. Burnley *et al.* (eds), *Mobility and Community Change in Australia*, University of Queensland Press, Brisbane.

Whitlam, E.G. 1972, *ALP Policy Speech*, ALP, Canberra.

Wildman, P. *et al.* 1990, 'Push from the bush: revitalization strategies for smaller rural towns', *Urban Policy and Research* 8, 51–9.

Wilensky, H.L. & C.N. Lebeaux 1965, *Industrial Society and Social Welfare*, Free Press, New York.

Williams, P. 1984, 'Economic processes and urban change: an analysis of contemporary patterns of residential restructuring', *Australian Geographical Studies* 22, 39-57.

Williams, R.N. 1983, 'Ownership of dwellings and personal wealth in Australia', *Australian Economic Review* 62, 55–62.

Wilson, M.G.A. 1990, 'The end of an affair? Geography and fertility in late post-transitional societies', *Australian Geographer* 21, 53–66.

Wilson, P. 1986, *International Economics: Theory, Evidence and Practice*, Wheatsheaf Books, Brighton.

Wilson, W. 1990, 'Residential relocation and settlement adjustment of Vietnamese refugees in Sydney', *Australian Geographical Studies* 28, 155–77.

Winchester, H.P. 1991, 'Recession, restructuring and workplace reform: unemployment and the underclass in Australia in the 1990s', *Australian Geographer* 22, 112–6.

Windschuttle, K. 1979, *Unemployment*, Penguin, Ringwood.

Windschuttle, K. 1984, 'High tech and jobs', *Australian Society* 3 (11), 11–3.

World Bank 1990, *World Development Report — 1990*, Oxford University Press, Oxford.

Yates, I. & A. Graycar 1983, 'Non-government welfare: issues and perspec-tives', in A. Graycar (ed.), *Retreat From the Welfare State*, Allen and Unwin, Sydney.

Young, C. 1988, 'Towards a population policy: myths and misconceptions concerning the demographic effects of immigration', *Australian Quarterly* 60, 220–9.

Young, C. 1990, *Australia's Ageing Population:Population Policy Options*, AGPS, Canberra.

Young, E.A. 1988, 'Aborigines and land in northern Australian development', *Australian Geographer* 19, 105–16.

Zubrzycki, J. 1977, 'Towards a multicultural society in Australia', in M.J. Bowen (ed.) *Australia 2000: The Ethnic Impact*, University of New England Publishing Unit, Armidale.

INDEX